DIARY OF
GIDEON WELLES

IN THREE VOLUMES
VOLUME II

Abraham Lincoln

DIARY OF
GIDEON WELLES

SECRETARY OF THE NAVY UNDER
LINCOLN AND JOHNSON

WITH AN INTRODUCTION BY JOHN T. MORSE, JR.
AND
WITH ILLUSTRATIONS

VOLUME II

APRIL 1, 1864 — DECEMBER 31, 1866

BOSTON AND NEW YORK
HOUGHTON MIFFLIN COMPANY
The Riverside Press Cambridge
1911

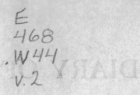
Published October 1911

CONTENTS

XVIII

APRIL, 1864

XIX

MAY, 1864

XX

JUNE, 1864

XXI

JULY, 1864

XXII

AUGUST, 1864

CONTENTS

XXIII

SEPTEMBER, 1864

XXIV

OCTOBER AND NOVEMBER, 1864

CONTENTS

XXVIII

MARCH, 1865

XXIX

APRIL, 1865

XXX

MAY AND JUNE, 1865

CONTENTS

XXXI

JULY, 1865

XXXII

AUGUST, 1865

XXXIII

SEPTEMBER — DECEMBER, 1865

XXXIV

JANUARY, 1866

XXXV

FEBRUARY, 1866

CONTENTS

XLI

AUGUST, 1866

XLII

SEPTEMBER, 1866

XLIII

OCTOBER AND NOVEMBER, 1866

XLIV

DECEMBER, 1866

ILLUSTRATIONS

ILLUSTRATIONS

DIARY OF GIDEON WELLES

VOLUME II

APRIL 1, 1864—DECEMBER 31, 1866

DIARY OF GIDEON WELLES

APRIL 1, 1864 — DECEMBER 31, 1866

XVIII

Seward and the Case of the Sir William Peel, captured in Mexican Waters —
John M. Forbes's Opinions on the National Convention — The Sey-
mours of Connecticut — The Wilkes Court Martial adjourned — Du
Pont's Intrigues against the Department — Death of John C. Rives —
The Debate on the Resolution to expel Representative Long from the
House — The Matter of the French Tobacco at Richmond — Cabinet
Discussion of the Financial Situation — The Gold Panic abated —
Chase's Financiering — Able Naval Officers sustain the Secretary's
Course in Relation to Du Pont — Sumner on the Currency Question —
An Estimate of General Banks — Halleck's Opinion of Banks — Pro-
posed Demonstration up the James River — The Feud between Chase
and the Blairs — Charges of Improprieties in the Treasury Depart-
ment — Wilkes found Guilty.

April 1, 1864, *Friday.* The *Chronicle* of this morning
contains my letter, with some errors, to the Senate in response to a call relating to transfers. It makes some commotion among the Members of Congress, and will cause
some in the War Department, I presume.

There was nothing of special interest to-day in the Cabinet. Stanton was not present, nor was Blair. Chase calls
for largely additional taxes, which I have no doubt are
necessary. There should have been heavier taxes the last
two years, — at least double what have been collected.
Undoubtedly demagogues will try to prevent this necessary
measure for party ends, but I believe the good sense and
intelligence of the people will prevail over the debasing
abuse of party. I apprehend that Chase is not making the
most of his position, and think he has committed some
errors. No one could have altogether avoided them.

Seward spoke to me concerning the case of the Sir William Peel, captured at the mouth of the Rio Grande. She had carried contraband ostensibly to Matamoras, but portions had gone direct to Brownsville, and cotton had been brought direct from that place in return. It is claimed, however, that she was captured in Mexican waters, though near the United States, and therefore Seward says she must be given up. I asked him to whom. If captured in Mexican waters, no power but Mexico could make the claim. This he undertook to deny, provided the government of Mexico was enfeebled by revolution and not able to sustain itself. But I told him if able to assert and maintain neutrality, then Mexico, and she alone, could intervene; if not able to maintain her claim of neutrality, no other one could make a claim of Mexican jurisdiction.

I am fearful he will make a misfire on this question. He has never looked into maritime law, and will make any sacrifice of national or individual rights to keep in with England.

April 2, Saturday. John M. Forbes called. After talking on one or two subjects he spoke of the National Convention and his regret that the call was so early, and asked me as one of the committee to reconsider the subject. Told him I would hear and consider anything from him, but that my mind was deliberately made up, and I thought the sooner the nomination was made, the better united we should be. He went over the usual ground, — if the summer campaign was unfortunate, etc., etc., how could we change our candidates? I answered we did not intend to be unfortunate, but if we were, I could not see how any different candidate would help the Union cause. Reverses might strengthen the Copperheads.

He then talked of the President, — his want of energy, decision, promptness, in consequence of which the country suffered. It was evident from what I gathered that Mr. Forbes wanted another candidate than Abraham Lincoln, and hence he desired delay. Forbes means well. His heart is right. He is shrewd and sagacious, but men betray their feelings and partialities unavoidably. I have no doubt he desires to have Mr. Chase a candidate, though he speaks of only Ben Butler, whom he dislikes.

Cautioned Fox to beware of yielding to the suggestions and opinions of detective Olcott, unless fully satisfied by facts in his possession. Mr. Wilson, the counsel, must advise in these matters, and nothing be done in the way of seizure and arrest but by Mr. Wilson's direction.

April 4, Monday. Heard an excellent discourse yesterday from Bishop Whipple.

Called on Stanton, respecting the letters of General Gillmore from June 12 to July 6, 1863.

Had a call from J. P. Hale respecting appointments. This man, so long a Senator, has no comprehensive or statesmanlike views. Would set aside legislative action and law because he thinks it operates hard on a lieutenant whom he knows.

April 5, Tuesday. The returns of the Connecticut election come in favorably. Buckingham is reëlected by a largely increased majority, and the Unionists have two thirds at least of the Legislature. This disposes of another of the Seymours. O. S. Seymour, the defeated Democratic candidate, has respectable abilities and industry. In the latter respect he is very different from T. H. Seymour, the last year's candidate. The latter was marked by indolence for his own from boyhood. Always lazy, proud, and opinionated, but with genius and a fair share of talents if put to any use. He is excessively fond of adulation, and seeks the caresses of the young and the ignorant. Origen S. is a trimmer in politics, more pliable than Tom, though each has a trait of insincerity. Eaton, who has been rather the leader of the anti-War faction, was a candidate for Representative in Hartford and defeated. It is an evidence of returning sense among some of the community. Last year he was chosen by a majority of some three hundred. Now he is defeated.

April 6, Wednesday. Little of importance. Some movements by the army in contemplation, yet nothing has been communicated to the Navy Department, except an intimation that ironclads may be wanted on the James River. This intimation, or obscure request, comes indirectly from General Grant; nothing from the War Department proper.

April 7, Thursday. Adjourned the Wilkes court martial to-day until Monday, the 18th inst. The testimony is all in, and the case will go to judgment as soon as the arguments are delivered. Defense wanted eight to ten days, and the members of the Court desired to go home for a few days. Every effort has been made to evade the issues in this case and to get up false ones. All of Wilkes's long letters have been introduced, etc., etc.

April 8, Friday. Answered a letter from J. P. Hale, Chairman of Naval Committee, on the question of increasing the Marine Corps. In answering the inquiries of Mr. Hale, it is important to so word my communication as to leave the honorable gentleman some discretion, for he makes it a rule to oppose any measure which the Department strongly recommends. Mr. Rice, Chairman of the Naval Committee of the House, informs me of a conversation he had with Hale a few days since, when he lectured Hale severely for his course. Told him that, while professing to be a friend of the Administration, he exerted himself to see if he could not in some way find fault with it, as though he could gain popularity to himself personally while denouncing the Administration and especially that branch of it with which he was more particularly identified. Hale replied that he had the most implicit confidence in the integrity and fidelity of Gideon Welles, but that he had no confidence in Mr. Fox or Admiral Smith, etc., etc.

But little at the Cabinet. Neither Chase nor Blair attended. Seward says our friends in the British Ministry are to be defeated. Told him I regretted it, but that it was not an unmitigated evil. I had not the apprehensions from it which he seemed to entertain. I certainly felt disinclined to make concessions to retain them.

Called this evening on Admiral Dahlgren, who is inconsolable for the loss of his son. Advised him to get abroad and mingle in the world, and not yield to a blow that was irremediable.

Wise, who is Chief *ad interim* of the Ordnance Bureau, is almost insane for the appointment of Chief, and, like too many, supposes the way to promotion is by denouncing those who stand in his way, or whom he supposes stand in his way. Mr. Everett writes to old Mr. Blair against Dahlgren. Admiral Stringham and Worden called on me yesterday in behalf of Wise and both opposed D. They were sent by Wise.

April 9, Saturday. Senator Wilson to-day and Mr. Rice yesterday called in relation to the investigations which Olcott is prosecuting in Boston. They both were moved to call by Smith brothers, who are beginning to feel uneasy. Their attacks on others, if not their wrong acts, have provoked inquiries concerning themselves. I remarked to each of the gentlemen that the Smiths had nothing to apprehend if they had done no wrong.

Finished draft of letter in reply to three resolutions — one of the Senate and two of the House — inquiring concerning the ironclads, Du Pont's attack last April, etc. The documents to be sent are voluminous. Du Pont instigated the inquiry, and will be very likely to regret it, not having seen my report and accompanying papers. He evidently thought I would not publish the detailed reports, which he had secured and prepared for a purpose, but I had communicated them with my report. Spaulding, one of the Naval Committee, allowed himself to be used in the intrigue, and, to his discredit, called for the documents which I had sent in with report and which had been printed before his resolution was offered, though he avers I had not presented them. Few of the Members of Congress do their work thoroughly, or give matters examination, and hence, like Spaulding, are often victimized. But Du Pont and his friend Winter Davis, like all intriguers, overrode themselves in some of their movements. For two years Du Pont was the petted man of the Department. He has abilities and had courted and brought into his clique many of the best officers of the Navy. These always were lauding him. Those who were not of his circle were silent, and I had to form my opinions and conclusions from what I saw and heard. Fox was very devoted to him and could never do too much for him. To no man has he ever evinced more partiality. As a general thing, I have thought Fox, considering his associations and prejudices formed in the service, has been fair and just towards the officers, but Du Pont asked for nothing that Fox was not willing and urgent to have me grant, yet eventually D. turned upon him.

April 11, *Monday.* John C. Rives, it is stated, died yesterday. He was a marked character, guileless, shrewd, simple-hearted, and sagacious, without pretension and without fear, generous and sincere, with a warm heart but no exterior graces. I first met him in the winter of 1829 in the office of Duff Green, where he was bookkeeper. In the winter of 1831, I think, we met at Georgetown at the house of Colonel Corcoran. F. P. Blair, whom I met on the same evening for the first time, had been out with Rives to try their rifles. They had first met a few days previous. Rives was then a clerk in the Fourth Auditor's office, — Amos Kendall. The latter passed the evening with us. Years later Rives and myself became well acquainted. He was first bookkeeper and then partner of Blair and made the fortunes of both.

In the House of Representatives a sharp and unpleasant

discussion has been carried on, on a resolution introduced
by the Speaker, Colfax, to expel Long, a Representative
from Ohio, for some discreditable partisan remarks, made
in a speech last Friday. There being an evening session,
I went to the Capitol for the first time this session. Heard
Orth, Kenyon, Winter Davis, and one or two others. The
latter was declamatory, eloquent, but the debate did not
please me, nor the subject. Long I despise for his declarations, but Colfax is not judicious in his movement. Long
went beyond the line of his party, and Colfax cannot make
them responsible for Long's folly.

April 12, *Tuesday.* To-day have a letter from Admiral
Lee respecting the exportation of French tobacco from
Richmond. This is an arrangement of Mr. Seward to
which I have always objected, but to which the President
was persuaded to yield his assent some months ago. The
subject has lingered until now. Admiral Lee says the
French naval vessels and transports are at the Roads and
about to proceed up the James River, and inquires if he
shall keep an account of their export.

I took the dispatch to the Cabinet-meeting to ascertain
from Mr. Seward what his arrangements were, but he was
not present. When the little business on hand was disposed of, I introduced the subject to the President, who
told me he had seen the dispatch to me and also one to Mr.
Stanton from General Butler. He saw them both at the
telegraph office, and after he got home he had sent for
Fred Seward and Mr. Stanton. They appear neither of
them to think the subject of much consequence, but after
Stanton had returned to the War Department and read
Butler's dispatch, he sent the President word that Mr.
Seward ought to give the subject attention. The President
had therefore told Fred Seward to telegraph his father,
who is in New York, to return.

It is curious that the President, who saw Admiral Lee's
dispatch to me, should have consulted the Secretary of

War and Assistant Secretary of State without advising
me, or consulting me on the subject. He was annoyed, I
saw, when I introduced the topic. The reason for all this
I well understood. He knew full well my opposition to this
whole proceeding, which I had fought off two or three
times, until he finally gave in to Seward. When, therefore,
some of the difficulties which I had suggested began to arise,
the President preferred not to see me. It will not surprise
me if this is but the beginning of the trouble we shall experience.

At the Cabinet-meeting, Chase, after presenting his
weekly exhibit, showing our national debt to be over sixteen hundred millions, said he should have to request the
Navy Department and also that of the Interior to make no
farther calls on the Treasury for coin. I told him he must
provide for foreign bills which stood different from any
others, and if he had paid the Interior or any other Department than the State and Navy, which had foreign bills,
and possibly the War Department some foreign purchases,
I thought it not right; that I had experienced great difficulty in making California payments, but had met them,
because I supposed all domestic bills were treated alike.

Chase did not meet the point squarely, but talked on
other subjects, and answered some questions of the President's about the daily custom receipts, and explained
the operations of his gold dollar certificates, etc. I brought
him back to the Navy matter by asking him how our paymasters and agents were to draw abroad, — by what standard of value. He said the legal-tender standard. "What is
that standard," I inquired, "in Nassau, in Rio, in China,
or London?"

He made me no other answer than that he was anxious
to reduce the price of gold, and that something must be
done to effect it. Talked of taxing bank circulation and
driving it out of existence. I told him that might be a step
in the right direction, perhaps, provided he did not increase his paper issues, but that if he issued irredeemable

Treasury paper instead to an unlimited amount, there would be no relief; that by reducing the amount of paper and making it payable in specie on demand he would bring his legal tenders and gold nearer to equality. The President remarked that something must be done towards taxing the bank paper; said he did not fully comprehend the financial questions in all their bearings; made some sensible inquiries of Mr. Chase concerning his issues, which were bought for custom-house purposes.

Mr. Usher made some inquiries and suggestions about bringing down the price of gold and compelling banks and others to disgorge that were worthy an old Whig of thirty years gone by. His ideas were crude, absurd, and ridiculous. He evidently has never given the subject attention.

Mr. Grimes and Mr. Hale had a round in the Senate yesterday. The former had the best of the debate, but still did not do himself, the Department, and the service full justice.

April 13, *Wednesday.* Matters press on the Department. Have been very busy. Some talk with Rice about Annapolis and the Naval School, League Island and the navy yard. Suggested that New England must not monopolize and that we should avoid even the appearance of sectionalism.

Consulted Mr. Eames yesterday and again to-day in relation to the investigations into the frauds of naval contractors and others. Told him he must go to Boston to supervise Olcott, who is fierce in diving into matters and often, I apprehend, without judgment.

April 14, *Thursday.* The *Baltimore American* of this morning contains my report in relation to the ironclads and Du Pont. A synopsis, very brief, has been sent out by the agent of the newspapers, but the press only to a limited extent publishes even that meagre abstract. I believe the *New York Tribune* does not publish it or take any notice of

it. Du Pont and his satellites have been busy, and Greeley
and others take such a partisan, personal view of all questions that no honest or fair treatment can be expected of
them in a case like this. Without ever looking at facts,
Greeley has always vigorously indorsed Du Pont and had
his flings at the Navy Department.

Gold is reported at 190 to-day; that is, it requires one
hundred and ninety dollars of Treasury notes, Chase's
standard, to buy one hundred dollars in gold, paper has so
depreciated.

April 15, *Friday.* Chase and Blair were neither of them
at the Cabinet-meeting to-day, nor was Stanton. Seward
takes upon himself the French tobacco question. He
wishes me to procure some one to investigate and report
on the facts of the case of the Sir William Peel. I told him
I thought Charles Eames as good a counsellor on prize
matters as any lawyer whom I knew, and if referred to
me I should give the case to Eames.

The gold panic has subsided, or rather abated. Chase is
in New York. It is curious to see the speculator's conjectures and remarks on the expedients and subterfuges that
are resorted to. Gold is truth. Its paper substitute is a
fiction, sustained by public confidence in part because
there is a belief that it will ultimately bring gold, but it has
no intrinsic value and the great increase in quantity is
undermining confidence.

The House passed a resolution of censure on Long for
his weak and reprehensible speech. It is a pity the subject
was taken up at all. No good has come of it, but I hope no
harm. Lurking treason may feel a little strengthened by
the failure to expel.

April 16, *Saturday.* Had a long telegram at midnight
from Cairo, respecting Rebel movements in western Kentucky, — at Paducah, Columbus, Fort Pillow, etc. Strange
that an army of 6000 Rebels should be moving unmolested

within our lines. But for the gunboats, they would re-
possess themselves of the defenses, yet General Halleck
wants the magnanimity and justice to acknowledge or
even mention the service.

There is still much excitement and uneasy feeling on the
gold and currency question. Not a day but that I am
spoken to on the subject. It is unpleasant, because my
views are wholly dissimilar from the policy of the Treasury
Department, and Chase is sensitive and tender — touchy,
I may say — if others do not agree with him and adopt his
expedients. Mr. Chase is now in New York. He has directed the payment of the May interest, anticipating that
throwing out so much gold will affect the market favorably.
It will be likely to have that effect for a few days but is no
cure for the evil. The volume of irredeemable paper must
be reduced before there can be permanent relief. He attributes to speculators the rise in gold! As well charge the
manufacturers with affecting the depth of water in the rivers, because they erect dams across the tributaries! Yet
one cannot reason with our great financier on the subject. He will consider it a reflection on himself personally
and claims he cannot get along successfully if opposed.

I remarked to Senator Trumbull, whom I met when taking my evening walk last Thursday, and was inquired of,
that I could hardly answer or discuss his inquiry in regard
to the gold excitement, because in a conversation which we
had a year or two since, when one of the bills was pending,—
the first, I believe, — I had said to him I was a hard-
money man and could indorse no standards but gold and
silver as the measure of value and regretted and distrusted
the scheme of legal paper tenders. Chase heard of that conversation and claims I was embarrassing the Treasury.

This sensitiveness indicates what I fear and have said,
viz. Chase has no system on which he relies, but is seeking
expedients which tumble down more rapidly than he can
construct them. He cannot stop what he and others call
"the rise of gold," but which is really the depreciation of

paper, by the contrivances he is throwing out. The gold dollar, the customs certificates, the interest-bearing Treasury notes, etc., etc., are all failures and harmful and will prove so. The Secretary of the Treasury found a great and rich country filled with enthusiasm in a noble cause and full of wealth, with which they responded to his call, but *their* recourses and sacrifices were no evidence of financial talent on the part of the Secretary who used them.

The Secretary is not always bold, and has not enforced taxation; he is not wise beyond others, and has not maintained the true measure of value; he resorts to expedients instead of abiding by fixed principles. By multiplying irredeemable paper and general inflation, his "ten forty" five-per-cents may be taken, but at what cost to the country! He is in New York and may negotiate a loan; but if he does, it will be with the banks and, I presume, at six per cent. If so, the banks will not be able to help the speculators, and they, being cramped, will suffer, and perhaps fail. The fancy stocks will be likely to fall under this operation, and the surplus money may seek government securities, but under the inflation how expensive to the country!

April 18, *Monday*. The steamer Chenango exploded her boilers in New York Harbor, and I feared there might have been mischief, such as [an] incendiary shell in the coal, but the reports indicate that such was not the case.

I am gratified to find so many sagacious and able naval officers sustaining me and my course in relation to Du Pont. There is no man in the service who is so skillful and successful at intrigue as S. F. Du Pont. He has his cliques and has laid his plans adroitly, and may, for a time, be successful in deceiving the public by artful means, but it cannot last. Truth is mighty and will prevail.

Stocks have had a heavy fall to-day in New York, and there are reported failures. It is a temporary check, I apprehend, a reaction or pause resulting from some action of Mr. Chase in New York. He has doubtless effected a loan with the banks, and they have closed on some of their customers. Money, or investments, are tending to government securities, rather than railroad and other like investments, for the moment.

April 19, *Tuesday.* The President did not make his appearance to-day in Cabinet. He was in Baltimore last evening at the opening of the fair, and is reported to have made a speech. He has a fondness for attending these shows only surpassed by Seward. Neither Seward, nor Blair, nor Chase was present with us to-day. Blair was with the President at Baltimore. Being a Marylander, there was propriety in his attendance.

April 20, *Wednesday.* The last public evening reception of the season took place last evening at the Executive Mansion. It was a jam, not creditable in its arrangements to the authorities. The multitude were not misbehaved, farther than crowding together in disorder and confusion may be so regarded. Had there been a small guard, or even a few police officers, present, there might have been regulations which would have been readily acquiesced in and observed. There has always been a want of order and proper management at these levees or receptions, which I hope may soon be corrected.

April 21, *Thursday.* There was a pleasant party at our house last evening, with an attendance of about three hundred. All passed off pleasantly, and all who expressed themselves seemed much gratified, as we were. It is spoken of as one of the most agreeable parties of the season.

Olcott and Wilson were here on Tuesday. The former is very full of frauds in Boston and is rabid to be at the books of certain parties. The man has an insatiate appetite to get on the track of suspected parties. He shows not only keen scent but much sagacity. Mr. Wilson has his

charges and specifications against the parties in New York
prepared and in the hands of the copyists.

April 22, Friday. Neither Seward nor Chase nor Stanton was at the Cabinet-meeting to-day. For some time
Chase has been disinclined to be present and evidently for
a purpose. When sometimes with him, he takes occasion to
allude to the Administration as departmental, — as not
having council, not acting in concert. There is much truth
in it, and his example and conduct contribute to it.
Seward is more responsible than any one, however, although he is generally present. Stanton does not care
usually to come, for the President is much of his time at the
War Department, and what is said or done is communicated by the President, who is fond of telling as well as of
hearing what is new. Three or four times daily the President goes to the War Department and into the telegraph
office to look over communications.

Congress is laboring on the tax bill. The Members fear
to do their duty because taxation is unpopular. An old
infirmity. Chase has not pressed for it heretofore for the
same reason.

April 23, Saturday. We have met with some disaster in
North Carolina. Am apprehensive the army has been a
little delinquent.

General Butler has telegraphed to Fox, who is an old
boyhood associate and acquaintance, to come down to
Hampton Roads. Wants help. Asks F. to induce the President to go down, but he declines, — wisely, I think.
Troops are getting in at Fortress Monroe, and the indications in this vicinity warn us that the strength is being
gathered for a conflict.

Sumner called on me to-day. Had just come from
Chase; spoke of the finances and currency. I told him I
was a hard-money man and could not unlearn old ideas,
and had no time to study new theories. He laughed and

said that things in these days must conflict with my old opinions. It is evident that our statesmen do not realize the importance nor condition of the money and currency question.

April 25, Monday. Reverses in North Carolina are bad at this time. The death of Flusser is most unfortunate. I presume the blame of the disasters will be attributed to the Navy, which, in fact, is merely auxiliary to the army. Letter-writers and partisan editors who are courted and petted by the military find no favor with naval men, and as a consequence the Navy suffers detraction.

Burnside's army corps passed through Washington to-day, whites, blacks, and Indians numbering about 30,000. All the indications foreshadow a mighty conflict and battle in Virginia at an early day.

Fox and Edgar have gone to Fortress Monroe. Calls for naval aid and assistance come up from that quarter.

April 26, Tuesday. Sent a letter to Naval Committee in favor of an iron navy yard, transmitting former communications. Action is required and should have been taken by Congress long since.

Neither Chase nor Blair were at the Cabinet to-day, nor was Stanton. The course of these men is reprehensible, and yet the President, I am sorry to say, does not reprove but rather encourages it by bringing forward no important measure connected with either. As regards Chase, it is evident he presumes on his position and the condition of the finances to press a point, hoping it may favor his aspirations.

Stanton has a cabinet and is a power in his own Department. He deceives the President and Seward, makes confidants of certain leading men, and is content to have matters move on without being compelled to show his exact position. He is not on good terms with Blair, nor is Chase, which is partly attributable to that want of concert which

2

frequent assemblages and mutual counselling on public measures would secure. At such a time the country should have the combined wisdom of all.

Rear-Admiral Porter has sent me a long, confidential letter in relation to affairs on Red River and the fights that have taken place at Mansfield, Pleasant Hill, etc. The whole affair is unfortunate. Great sacrifice of life and property has been made in consequence of an incompetent general in command. It is plain from Admiral Porter's account that Banks is no general, has no military capacity, is wholly unfit for the position assigned him. He has never exhibited military capacity, and I regret the President should adhere to him. It is to be attributed in a great degree to Seward, who caused Butler to be superseded by Banks, and naturally desires he should not prove a failure, and therefore hopes and strives against facts. Banks has much of the demagogue, is superficially smart, has volubility and a smack of party management, which is often successful. The President thinks he has Presidential pretensions and friends to back him, but it is a great mistake. Banks is not only no general, but he is not much of a statesman. He is something of a politician, and a party man of his own stamp, and for his own advancement, but is not true and reliable.

There is an attempt to convert this reverse into a victory, but the truth will disclose itself. The President should, if Porter's statements are reliable, dismiss Banks, or deprive him of military command.

I asked Halleck, who called on me to-day, what the army opinion was of the recent conflicts on Red River. He said we undoubtedly had the worst of it, and that Banks had no military talent or education. While I do not place a high estimate on Halleck himself, his expressed opinion of Banks corresponds with my own. Whether he will recommend the withdrawal of Banks from the army remains to be seen.

April 27, *Wednesday.* The Wilkes court martial has closed its labors. The proceedings have not been reported, but, as the members are anxious to get home, I have adjourned the court for ten days, unless sooner convened or dissolved.

George Bliss, Jr., counsel for Scofield, who is under arrest as a fraudulent contractor, writes a tart letter respecting his client. I have referred him to Wilson, Judge Advocate. He says by telegraph Wilson has not reached New York. I am sorry for this delay. Fox and Edgar returned this evening from Hampton Roads, — absent two days.

April 28, *Thursday.* Admiral Lee sends me a confidential dispatch and also a communication to him from General Butler. On the latter Fox has made a proper indorsement. On the 26th inst. General B. calls on the Admiral for naval coöperation. Wants ironclads and gunboats to proceed to Richmond; is going to move on the 30th inst.; the expedition or movement is to be secret; they are to pass above City Point, etc., etc. Only four days to improvise a navy, and they are to proceed up a river whose channel is not buoyed out. The scheme is not practical, yet it has the sanction of General Grant. It must, however, be a blind, intended to deceive the enemy, and to do this effectually he must first deceive our own people. A somewhat formidable force has been gathered in General Butler's department, and there is no doubt but that General B. himself fully believes he is to make a demonstration up James River. It may be that this is General Grant's intention also, but if it is, I shall be likely to have my faith in him impaired. Certainly there have been no sufficient preparations for such a demonstration and the call upon the Navy is unreasonable.

April 28, *Thursday.* The opinion in regard to General Banks is very unanimous. None speak favorably of him as a military man, and his civil administration is much censured. Whether the President will continue to sustain him is to be seen.

General Frank Blair has resigned his seat in the House, and the President has revoked the acceptance of his military resignation. This is a stretch of power and construction that I do not like. Much censure will fall on the President for this act, and it will have additional edge from the violent and injudicious speech of General Blair denouncing in unmeasured terms Mr. Chase. He also assails the appointees of Chase, and his general policy touching agent's permits in the valley of the Mississippi as vicious and corrupt. I have an unfavorable opinion of the Treasury management there and on the coast, and there are some things in the conduct of Chase himself that I disapprove.

The Blairs are pugnacious, but their general views, especially those of Montgomery Blair, have seemed to me sound and judicious in the main. A forged requisition of General Blair has been much used against him. A committee of Congress has pronounced the document a forgery, having been altered so as to cover instead of $150 worth of stores some $8000 or $10,000. He charges the wrong on the Treasury agents, and Chase's friends, who certainly have actively used it. Whether Chase has given encouragement to the scandal is much to be doubted. I do not believe he would be implicated in it, though he has probably not discouraged, or discountenanced it. Chase is deficient in magnanimity and generosity. The Blairs have both, but they have strong resentments. Warfare with them is open, bold, and unsparing. With Chase it is silent, persistent, but regulated with discretion. Blairs make no false professions. Chase avows no enmities.

April 29, *Friday.* Usher relates to me to-day some damaging stories concerning the Treasury. I cannot but think them exaggerations. I know, from some reliable and unmistakable sources, that there have been improprieties

among the subordinates of a licentious character, and that
Chase is cognizant of the facts. It has surprised me that,
knowing the facts, he should have permitted the person
most implicated to retain a position of great trust. Only
great weakness, or implication in error would give a solution. I do not for a moment entertain the latter, and the
former is not a trait in his character.

These matters cannot be suppressed. Blair says Chase
will not assent to a committee. He cannot avoid it, and
since Frank Blair has left, I think he will not attempt it.
Colfax, the Speaker, will give him pretty much such a
committee as he wishes. The majority will be friends of
Chase, as they should be, and none probably will be unfair
opponents.

The President to-day related to two or three of us the
circumstances connected with his giving a pass to the half-
sister of his wife, Mrs. White. He gave the details with
frankness, and without disguise. I will not go into them
all, though they do him credit on a subject of scandal and
abuse. The papers have assailed him for giving a pass to
Mrs. White to carry merchandise. Briefly, Mrs. W. called
at the White House and sent in her card to Mrs. Lincoln,
her sister, who declined to receive or see her. Mrs. W. two
or three times repeated these applications to Mrs. L. and
the President, with the same result. The President sent a
pass, such as in some cases he has given, for her to proceed
South. She sent it back with a request that she might take
trunks without being examined. The President refused.
She then showed her pass and talked "secesh" at the
hotel, and made application through Mallory first and
then Brutus Clay. The President refused the former and
told Brutus that if Mrs. W. did not leave forthwith she
might expect to find herself within twenty-four hours in
the Old Capitol Prison.

April 30, *Saturday.* The Wilkes court martial found
him guilty on all charges and sentenced him to three years'

suspension and a reprimand. It is a light punishment for the conviction.

Army movements indicate an early and great battle, but when and where to be fought is unknown in Washington.

Congress to-day has ordered a committee on the Treasury. It is made up as only Colfax could do it. Some able friends of Chase are on it, and Brooks . . . is associated with them.

Thirty years ago I was accustomed to meet Brooks, then a resident of Portland, Maine. He was at that time a zealous Whig partisan, with no settled principles. Judging from the *New York Express*, his paper, I think he has changed very little, though now elected by, and acting with, those who call themselves Democrats and have a Democratic organization.

XIX

Investigating the Massacre at Fort Pillow — Cabinet Discussion of the Massacre — Rumors of the Battle of the Wilderness — Admiral Porter's Report of Banks's Mismanagement of the Red River Expedition — The President's Disappointment in Banks — News of the Loss of General Wadsworth and General Sedgwick — McClellan and Politics— Secretary Chase declines to pay Bills abroad in Coin — Joy over the Victory at Spottsylvania — A Visit to the Confederate Prisoners at Belle Plain — Talk with Governor Morgan on Abuses in Cotton Speculations — Trouble at the Charlestown Navy Yard — Publication of a Forged Proclamation — Arrest of a Spaniard charged with Participating in the Slave Trade — Chase on the Cotton Speculations — The Seizure of two New York Newspapers for publishing the Forgery.

May 2, Monday. Rumors thick and unpleasant in regard to the clerks and women employed at the Treasury. Much is doubtless exaggeration, but there are some disagreeable truths.

May 3, Tuesday. At the Cabinet-meeting the President requested each member to give him an opinion as to what course the Government should pursue in relation to the recent massacre at Fort Pillow. The committee from Congress who have visited the scene returned yesterday and will soon report. All the reported horrors are said to be verified. The President wishes to be prepared to act as soon as the subject is brought to his notice officially, and hence Cabinet advice in advance.

The subject is one of great responsibility and great embarrassment, especially before we are in possession of the facts and evidence of the committee. There must be something in these terrible reports, but I distrust Congressional committees. They exaggerate.

Mrs. W. and Edgar left to-day for New York. She is to spend a few days at Irvington; Edgar to complete his college course.

Tom is filled with unrestrained zeal to go to the army. It is much of it youthful fervor but none the less earnest.

May 4, Wednesday. Our forces are gathering in considerable strength at Hampton Roads. Besides the naval vessels there are in the Roads over two hundred army transports. Whether the movement is to be up James River exclusively or a portion up the York and Pamunkey is not known.

May 5, Thursday. I have written a letter to the President in relation to the Fort Pillow massacre, but it is not satisfactory to me, nor can I make it so without the evidence of what was done, nor am I certain that even then I could come to a conclusion on so grave and important a question. The idea of retaliation, — killing man for man, — which is the popular noisy demand, is barbarous, and I cannot assent to or advise it. The leading officers should be held accountable and punished, but how? The policy of killing negro soldiers after they have surrendered must not be permitted, and the Rebel leaders should be called upon to avow or disavow it. But how is this to be done? Shall we go to Jeff Davis and his government, or apply to General Lee? If they will give us no answer, or declare they will kill the negroes, or justify Forrest, shall we take innocent Rebel officers as hostages? The whole subject is beset with difficulties. I cannot yield to any inhuman scheme of retaliation. Must wait the publication of the testimony.

May 6, Friday. At the Cabinet-meeting each of the members read his opinion. There had, I think, been some concert between Seward and Stanton and probably Chase; that is, they had talked on the subject, although there was not coincidence of views on all respects. Although I was dissatisfied with my own, it was as well as most others.

Between Mr. Bates and Mr. Blair a suggestion came out that met my views better than anything that had previously been offered. It is that the President should by proclamation declare the officers who had command at the massacre outlaws, and require any of our officers who may capture them, to detain them in custody and not exchange them, but hold them to punishment. The thought was not very distinctly enunciated. In a conversation that followed the reading of our papers, I expressed myself favorable to this new suggestion, which relieved the subject of much of the difficulty. It avoids communication with the Rebel authorities. Takes the matter in our own hands. We get rid of the barbarity of retaliation.

Stanton fell in with my suggestion, so far as to propose that, should Forrest, or Chalmers, or any officer conspicuous in this butchery be captured, he should be turned over for trial for the murders at Fort Pillow. I sat beside Chase and mentioned to him some of the advantages of this course, and he said it made a favorable impression. I urged him to say so, for it appeared to me that the President and Seward did not appreciate it.

We get no tidings from the front. There is an impression that we are on the eve of a great battle and that it may already have commenced.

May 7, Saturday. Some fragmentary intelligence comes to us of a conflict of the two great armies. A two days' fight is said to have taken place. The President came into my room about 1 P.M., and told me he had slept none last night. He lay down for a short time on the sofa in my room and detailed all the news he had gathered.

Mr. Wing, a correspondent of the *New York Tribune*, called upon me this evening. He brings the first news we have had, but this is not full and conclusive.

May 9, Monday. We had yesterday great feelings, deep interest, but little news, — little in the way of detail, though great in importance. Nothing came from General Grant, who is no braggart and does not mean to have tidings precipitated in advance. A dispatch from General Ingalls to Quartermaster-General Meigs calls for forage, which indicates an onward movement. Other incidental information is to the same effect. At least this is my inference and others' also.

To-day's news confirms the impression, yet we have nothing specific. All our conclusions, however, are one way, and there can be no doubt the Rebels have fallen back and our forces have advanced.

Mr. Heap, clerk to Rear-Admiral Porter, arrived yesterday from Alexandria on the Red River. He brings a deplorable account of affairs in a confidential dispatch from Admiral Porter and more fully detailed by himself. The misfortunes are attributed entirely and exclusively to the incapacity of General Banks. Neither Admiral Porter nor Mr. Heap admit any mitigating circumstances, but impute to his imbecility the loss of the expedition and the probable sacrifice of the fleet and the army. They accuse him of equivocating, of electioneering, of speculating in cotton and general malfeasance and mismanagement.

I took Heap with me to the President and had him tell his own story. It was less full and denunciatory than to me, but it seemed to convince the President, who I have thought was over-partial to Banks, and I have thought that Seward contributed to that feeling. The President, after hearing Heap, said he had rather cousined up to Banks, but for some time past had begun to think he was erring in so doing. He repeated two verses from Moore, commencing

"Oh, ever thus, from childhood's hour,
 I've seen my fondest hopes decay," etc.

It would not do to retain him in military command at such obvious sacrifice of the public interest.

I am not one of the admirers of Banks. He has a certain degree of offhand smartness, very good elocution and command of language, with perfect self-possession, but is not profound. He is a pretender, not a statesman, a politician of a certain description; has great ambition but little fixed principle. It was Seward's doings that sent him to New Orleans.

Who got up the Red River expedition I know not, otherwise than by Admiral Porter, who writes me he has seen the orders from Halleck. I know that I called on Stanton in company with Seward last summer with a view of getting up an expedition to capture Mobile; that Stanton sent for General Halleck; that the latter, when he came, was not prepared to adopt our views, wanted to hear from General Banks, was thinking of operations west of the Mississippi, etc. Seward surrendered without a word of remonstrance. Halleck was to let us know as soon as he heard from Banks, and I have never had a word from him since.

May 10, *Tuesday*, At the Cabinet, the President read dispatches from General Grant, General Butler, General Sherman, and some others. I had previously seen some of these dispatches. They were all in good and encouraging tone. There have been some conflicting doubts in regard to General Wadsworth, who is undoubtedly slain, and his body is, I think, in the hands of the Rebels. Few nobler spirits have fallen in this war. He should, by good right and fair-dealing, have been at this moment Governor of New York, but the perfidy of Thurlow Weed and others defeated him. I have always believed that Seward was, if not implicated, a sympathizer in that business. No purer or more single-minded patriot than Wadsworth has shown himself in this war. He left home and comforts and wealth to fight the battles of the Union.

A scout came in this P.M. with dispatches from General Grant. He brings information that General Sedgwick was killed yesterday by a sharpshooter. He was among the good and brave generals, though not of the class of dashing officers, and was ever reliable and persistent. The death of no general officer during the war could be more depress-

ing, I apprehend, than this, and his loss at this juncture
will be felt by the army and country.

May 11, *Wednesday*. A craving, uneasy feeling per-
vaded the community through the day. No intelligence
from any quarter received, yet a conviction pervades
everywhere that much is being done. I was at the War
Department at 9 P.M. The President and Stanton were
anxiously waiting intelligence.

I met Blair as I came from the Department, who wished
me to go to his house. A letter from Governor Morgan
asking me to name the month to which I would postpone
the Union National Convention, if I desired a postponement, was received and answered by me this evening. It
was a singular document and surprised me. I spoke of it to
Blair, who said he had seen the circular last week. This
gave me even greater surprise, for Morgan has frequently
consulted and interchanged views with me, both of us
concurring against postponement. It was discussed by us
at our last interview.

Blair, as well as myself, was puzzled, but we both were
willing to believe that no mischief was intended. The
course of Thurlow Weed and some New York politicians
has been singular. Blair took from his pocket a letter from
Barlow of New York, a Copperhead leader, with whom, he
informs me, he has corresponded for some weeks past.
Barlow is thick with General McClellan, and Blair, who
has clung also to McC., not giving him up until his Wood-
ward letter betrayed his weakness and his ambition, still
thought he might have military service, provided he gave
up his political aspirations. It was this feeling that had
led to the correspondence.

I do not admire the idea of corresponding with such a
man as Barlow, who is an intense partisan, and Blair himself would distrust almost any one who should be in political communication with him. Blair had written Barlow
that he would try to get McC. an appointment to the army,

giving up party politics. Barlow replied that no party can give up their principles, and quotes a letter which he says was written by a distinguished member of Mr. Lincoln's Cabinet last September, urging the organization of a conservative party on the basis of the Crittenden compromise. This extract shocks Blair. He says it must have been written by Seward. I incline to the same opinion, though Usher crossed my mind, and I so remarked to Blair. Last September U.'s position was more equivocal than Seward's, and he might have written such a letter without black perfidy. Seward could not.

May 12, *Thursday.* Late last night, Mr. Byington, a newspaper correspondent, called at my house. He left General Grant's headquarters at 8 A.M. yesterday. Reports hard fighting on Tuesday, but represents our troops to have had the best of it. General Robinson, severely wounded, arrived in Washington.

Secretary Chase sends me a letter that the Treasury is unwilling to pay bills drawn abroad in coin, and wishes the Department to buy coin and pay the bills independent of the Treasury. In other words, the Treasury Department declines to meet government obligations as heretofore. It is incapable of discharging its fiscal duties, is no longer to be a fiscal but a brokerage establishment for borrowing money and issuing a baseless, fictitious paper currency. These are the inglorious results of the schemes and speculations of our financier, and the end is not yet. There will be a general breakdown under this management.

May 13, *Friday.* The army news is interesting and as well received as the great loss of life will permit. Hancock has made a successful onset and captured Edward Johnson and two other generals, with about fifty other officers and four thousand prisoners, thirty pieces of cannon, etc. General Sheridan, with his cavalry, has got in rear of Lee and destroyed about ten miles of railroad, captured two

trains, and destroyed the depot of Rebel supplies at Beaver
Dam. Our troops are in good heart and everything looks
auspicious for the republic. Many valuable lives have
been offered up for the Union, and many a Rebel has
fallen. I dwell not on particulars. The public press and
documents will give them. The tidings have caused joy to
the patriotic everywhere, but among the intense partisans,
known as Copperheads, it is obvious there is no gratification in the success of the Union arms. It is painful to witness this factious and traitorous spirit, but it plainly shows
itself.

I saw Governor Morgan yesterday respecting his circular. He says he sent it out in self-defense; that, while he
knew I would stand by him in resisting a postponement of
the convention, he was not certain that others would,
should things by any possibility be adverse. He says the
answers are all one way, except that of Spooner of Ohio,
who is for a postponement. This is indicative of the Chase
influence.

To-night Governor Morgan informs me that the hall
in which the convention is to meet has been hired by the
malcontents, through the treachery and connivance of H.
Winter Davis, in whom he confided. He called on me to
advise as to the course to be pursued. Says he can get the
theatre, can build a temporary structure, or he can alter
the call to Philadelphia. Advised to try the theatre for the
present.

Admiral Shubrick says Admiral Du Pont is writing a
book in vindication of himself; that he (Shubrick) and
other friends of Du Pont have counselled him against such
a course, but without effect; that he is under the control
of H. Winter Davis, etc., etc. The subject gives me no
concern or disquietude. If Du Pont desires to vindicate or
explain his acts, or to assail mine or me personally, I shall
not regret his proceeding. His great mistake is in overes-
timating his own personal consequence and undervaluing
his country. Vanity and the love of intrigue are his ruin.

Mr. Representative Gooch of the Charlestown, Massachusetts, district, has undertaken, with a few other interested spirits, to discuss the management of the navy yard, and has had much to say of the rights of the citizens and of the naval gentlemen. Wants the civilians to control the yard. In all matters of conflict between the government and the mischievous element of the yard, Mr. Gooch sides against the government. This morning he called on me to protest against Admiral Smith and the naval management of the yard. After hearing his complaints I remarked that the difficulties at that yard were traced mainly to Mr. Merriam, and antagonisms got up between civilians and naval officers had their origin with him and his associates. He wished me to order a restoration of all appointments in certain departments to Merriam, which I declined, but told him I would select two masters instead of leaving the employment of workmen with the Chief Engineer.

May 14, *Saturday.* Attended the funeral of Colonel Harris. His death gives embarrassment as to a successor. The higher class of marine officers are not the men who can elevate or give efficiency to the corps. To supersede them will cause much dissatisfaction. Every man who is over-slaughed and all his friends will be offended with me for what will be deemed an insult. But there is a duty to perform.

May 16, *Monday.* I yesterday took a steamer with a small company, consisting among others of Postmaster-General Blair, Senators Doolittle and Grimes, Messrs. Rice and Griswold of the Naval Committee, Count Rosen of the Swedish Navy, Mr. Hale (the newly selected Consul-General to Egypt), G. W. Blunt and Assistant Secretary Fox, Commander Wise, Dr. Horwitz, and two or three others, and went down the Potomac to Belle Plain. The day was pleasant and the sail charming. We reached Belle Plain about two P.M. and left a little past five. Is a

rough place with no dwelling, — an extemporized plank-
way from the shore some twenty or thirty rods in the rear.
Some forty or fifty steamers and barges, most of them
crowded with persons, were there. Recruits going forward
to reinforce Grant's army, or the wounded and maimed
returning from battle. Rows of stretchers, on each of
which was a maimed or wounded Union soldier, were wend-
ing towards the steamers which were to bear them to Washington, while from the newly arrived boats were emerging
the fresh soldiers going forward to the field. Working our
way along the new and rough-made road, through teams
of mules and horses, we arrived at the base of a hill some
two or three hundred feet in height, and went up a narrow
broken footpath to the summit, on which were the headquarters of General Abercrombie and staff. The ascent
was steep and laborious. We had expected to find the
prisoners here, but were told they were beyond, about one
and a half miles. The majority were disposed to proceed
thither, and, though tired and reluctant, I acquiesced.
The prisoners, said to be about 7000 in number, were en-
camped in a valley surrounded by steep hills, the circum-
ference of the basin being some two or three miles. Returning, we passed through the centre of this valley or
basin. The prisoners were rough, sturdy-looking men,
good and effective soldiers, I should judge. Most of them
were quiet and well-behaved, but some few of them were
boisterous and inclined to be insolent.

One of the prisoners, a young man of some twenty-five,
joined me and inquired if I resided in the neighborhood.
I told him at a little distance. He wished to exchange
some money, Rebel for greenbacks. When I told him that
his was worthless, he claimed it was better than greenbacks though not current here. I asked him if they had
not enough of fighting, opposing the Union and lawful
authority. He said no, there was much more fighting yet to
be done. Claimed that Lee would be in Fredericksburg
before the Union army could get to Richmond. Would not

believe that J. E. B. Stuart was killed, news of which I
received just as I came on board the boat this morning.
He was earnest, though uninformed, and said he was from
western North Carolina. Returning, we reached Washington at 9 P.M.

To-day I have been busy in preparing two or three
letters and matters for Congress.

Governor Morgan called on me relative to abuses in
cotton speculations, and malconduct of Treasury agents
and others. Some of the malpractices which are demoralizing the army and the officials and disgusting the whole
people in the lower Mississippi are becoming known, and
will, I trust, lead to legislative correction. As Morgan
introduced the subject and thought proper to consult me,
I freely gave him facts and my views, which conflict with
Chase and the Treasury management. A bill which Morgan showed me is crudely drawn but introduces, or makes,
an entire change. It is not, in some of its features, what I
should have proposed, but it will improve on the present
system.

May 17, Tuesday. A painful suspense in military operations. It is a necessary suspense, but the intense anxiety is
oppressive, and almost unfits the mind for mental activity.
We know it cannot be long before one or more bloody battles will take place in which not only many dear friends
will be slaughtered but probably the Civil War will be decided as to its continuance, or termination. My faith is
firm in Union success, but I shall be glad when faith is *past*.

There was nothing special to-day at the Cabinet. No
information received from the Army of the Potomac.
Sherman had had hard fighting in northern Georgia at
Resaca, and the Rebels under Johnston have retreated.

The President informs me that four of the Massachusetts delegation have waited upon him in relation to the
condition of affairs at the Charlestown Navy Yard. They
fear the Navy has too much control, and charge Admiral

2

Smith with opposition to the Administration. I stated briefly to the President some of the difficulties, and that Mr. Gooch was not a free agent when there was a conflict or difference between the Government and the Navy Yard, that G. could not do otherwise than go with the men in the yard, and that Merriam was a cunning fellow who stirred up a citizen's feeling for selfish purposes.

Things are getting in such condition that I see no alternative but to dismiss the man Merriam. Admiral Stringham writes me that M. has got up a paper or memorial to the Massachusetts Senators and Representatives which he has hired a man to circulate for signatures, remonstrating against the naval management of the yard and getting up a hostile feeling. It is this, I presume, which led to the call on the President.

Met Governor Morrill this evening, who at once spoke of the misconduct of the Treasury agents. We frankly discussed the subject. He is on the Committee of Commerce and has a right to know the facts, which I gave him. The whole proceeding is a disgrace and wickedness. I agree with Governor M. that the Secretary of the Treasury has enough to do to attend to the finances without going into the cotton trade. But Chase is very ambitious and very fond of power. He has, moreover, the fault of most of our politicians, who believe that the patronage of office, or bestowment of public favors, is a source of popularity. It is the reverse, as he will learn.

May 18, *Wednesday*. Selected the Visitors to the Naval Academy, although we have not yet the appropriation bill, but we can no longer delay, if there are to be Visitors. Congress is very dilatory in necessary business, and yet impatient of delay in others.

Mr. Seward called on me this afternoon at a late hour in reference to alleged misconduct of the Marigold, which is charged with firing a gun at a blockade-runner within six hundred yards of Morro Castle. As Temple, Fleet Captain of the East Gulf Squadron, had left me but a few moments previously, I sent for him, there having been no report of the case. While waiting for Temple, Mr. S. informed me that a forged proclamation had been published by sundry papers in New York, among others by the *World* and *Journal of Commerce*, imposing a fast on account of the failures of Grant and calling for a draft of 300,000 men. Seward said he at once sent on contradicting it and had ordered the English steamer to be delayed. He then had called on Stanton to know whether such a document had passed over the regular telegraph. Stanton said there had not. He (S.) then ordered that the other line should be at once seized, which was done. Seward then asked if the *World* and *Journal of Commerce* had been shut up. Stanton said he knew of their course only a minute before. Seward said the papers had been published a minute too long; and Stanton said if he and the President directed, they should be suspended. Seward thought there should be no delay.

Gold, under the excitement, has gone up ten per cent, and the cotton loan will advance on the arrival of the steamer at Liverpool with the tidings. It seems to have been a cunningly devised scheme, — probably by the Rebels and the gold speculators, as they are called, who are in sympathy with them.

May 19, *Thursday.* The bogus proclamation has been the principal topic to-day. The knowledge that it is a forgery has not quieted the public mind.

There seems to be fighting both in front and on the James River, but nothing decisive is accomplished. I feel solicitous in regard to Butler, who, though a man of ability, has not the military knowledge and experience for so large and responsible a command.

May 20, *Friday.* The Secretary of State is becoming very anxious in view of our relations with France. Wants the ironclad Dictator should be sent over soon as possible.

I told him she was yet in the hands of the contractor, and was likely to be for some time, and when we had her I was not certain that it would be best to send her across the Atlantic. But he was nervous; said it was the only way to stop the Rebel ironclads from coming out, unless Grant should happen to get a victory.

The recent arrest of a Spaniard (Arguellis) who was in New York, and who was abducted, it is said, by certain officials under instructions or by direction of the Secretary of State is exciting inquiry. Arguellis is accused of having, in some way, participated in the slave trade. But if the assertion be true, we have no extradition treaty with Spain, and I am therefore surprised at the proceeding. There is such hostility to the slave trade that a great wrong may perhaps be perpetrated with impunity and without scrutiny, but I hope not. Nothing has ever been said in Cabinet on the subject, nor do I know anything in regard to it, except what I see in the papers.

Mr. Seward sometimes does strange things, and I am inclined to believe he has committed one of those freaks which make me constantly apprehensive of his acts. He knows that slavery is odious and all concerned in slave traffic are distrusted, and has, it seems, improved the occasion to exercise arbitrary power, expecting probably to win popular applause by doing an illegal act. Constitutional limitations are to him unnecessary restraints.

Should there be an investigation instituted and mere denunciation of the act, the President will be called upon to assume the responsibility, yet I am persuaded he has nothing to do in this affair beyond acquiescing without knowledge in what has been done. Could the abduction by any possibility be popular, Mr. S. expects it to inure to his credit.

May 21, *Saturday.* Last night I was at a party at Mr. Chase's, or his daughter Mrs. Sprague's, and late in the evening he spoke to me of the great abuses in cotton speculations. It was a new and singular theme for him, and I said it could not be otherwise than demoralizing. He said, "Yes, your whole fleet out West is infected; Porter devotes his attention to getting cotton and has a boat to himself, with a piano and his pipe, on these cotton raids." I replied this could not be so. The naval men could capture and retain nothing, which the courts do not adjudge to be good prize. We were interrupted at this point. I conclude the Committee on Commerce have notified Chase that they disapprove of his "Trade Regulations," and this outburst on the Navy is to turn off attention from his officials. But we shall see.

Lieutenant-Commander S. L. Phelps has been with me this evening and given me many interesting details concerning the Red River expedition and the incompetency of General Banks. Among other matters he relates some facts in regard to cotton speculations by persons connected with General Banks — some of his staff — that are exceedingly discreditable. Among others whom he specially mentions is one Clark from Auburn, New York, who appears to be managing director of the cotton operations.

Our gunboats are detained above the falls at Alexandria and we may lose them, though it is possible there yet may be a rise before June. The expedition has many bad features, of which we shall be better informed hereafter.

May 23, Monday. A late dispatch on Saturday night from Cairo informs me that a dam at Alexandria has been constructed and our fleet is passing the falls. Lieutenant-Commander Phelps had left my house only about an hour before the dispatch was received. We had passed most of the evening in discussing Red River affairs. The news of the passage of the whole fleet is since confirmed. It is most gratifying intelligence.

The author of the forged proclamation has been detected. His name is Howard, and he has been long connected with the New York press, but especially with the

Times. If I am not mistaken, he has been one of my assailants and a defamer of the Department. He is of a pestiferous class of reckless sensation-writers for an unscrupulous set of journalists who misinform the public mind. Scarcely one of them has regard for truth, and nearly all make use of their positions to subserve selfish, mercenary ends. This forger and falsifier Howard is a specimen of the miserable tribe.

The seizure of the office of the *World* and *Journal of Commerce* for publishing this forgery was hasty, rash, inconsiderate, and wrong, and cannot be defended. They are mischievous and pernicious, working assiduously against the Union and the Government and giving countenance and encouragement to the Rebellion, but were in this instance the dupes, perhaps the willing dupes, of a knave and wretch. The act of suspending these journals, and the whole arbitrary and oppressive proceedings, had its origin with the Secretary of State. Stanton, I have no doubt, was willing to act on Seward's promptings, and the President, in deference to Seward, yielded to it.

These things are to be regretted. They weaken the Administration and strengthen its enemies. Yet the Administration ought not to be condemned for the misdeeds of one, or at most two, of its members. They would not be if the President was less influenced by them.

May 24, Tuesday. Nothing especial at the Cabinet. The condition and position of the armies canvassed. Chase was not present. He seldom attends of late.

Seward urges the departure of the Niagara. I have no doubt that Sanford, our Minister at Belgium, one of Seward's pets, who is now here, has been instrumental in urging this matter. He wants a public vessel to carry him abroad, and has cajoled Seward . . . to effect this object. I do not like to be bamboozled, as Colonel Benton says, by such fellows as Sanford.

There are, however, some reasons to influence action.

Seward sent to my house on Saturday evening a bundle of dispatches from Mr. Dayton, and also from Mr. Bigelow, our consul at Paris, relative to the conduct and feelings of the French Government. That breaking through the blockade for tobacco looks mischievous, and one or more vessels ought doubtless to appear in European waters.

Bigelow, in his confidential dispatch, tells Seward that it was not judicious to have explained to the French Government in regard to the resolution of our House of Representatives that they would maintain the Monroe Doctrine.

May 30, *Monday.* My constant application has left me no time for several days to jot down occurrences and make remarks.

Mr. Sanford was very pertinacious and determined in his scheme of going out in the Niagara, and represented that Mr. Seward favored it. I am inclined to think Seward fell into the arrangement without much thought. This is the best view for Seward. Sanford is . . . fond of notoriety; delights to be busy and fussy, to show pomp and power; and to have a vessel like the Niagara bear him out to his mission would have filled him with delight, but would not have elevated the country, for Sanford's true character is known abroad and wherever he is known, which is one of obtrusive intermeddlings, — not that he is mischievously inclined, but he seeks to be consequential, wants to figure and to do.

The consul at Bermuda having written us that the Florida was there on the 14th inst., I wrote Mr. Seward that the Niagara would be directed to cruise and get across in about thirty days, consequently Mr. Sanford had better leave by packet steamer. Mr. Seward writes me today that he concurs with me fully.

The army movements have been interesting for the last few days, though not sensational. Grant has not obtained a victory but performed another remarkably successful flank movement. Sherman is progressing in Georgia.

May 31, *Tuesday.* No special matters in Cabinet. Mr. Seward sent me on Saturday a correspondence between himself and Lord Lyons and the Treasury Department relative to a large amount of cotton which was purchased a few months since in Georgia by one John Mulholland, an Englishman, who desires to bring it out, or, if he could not do that, to have it protected. The Secretary of State wrote the Secretary of the Treasury for views. The Treasury thought the proposition to bring it out inadmissible, but when our military lines were so extended as to include this cotton the agents of the Treasury would give it the same care as the property of loyal citizens; thinks it would be well to advise the Navy and War Departments to instruct their officers. Hence the communication to me.

I decline giving any such instructions, and so have written Mr. Seward, considering it illegal as well as inexpedient, telling him it would be a precedent for transferring all the products of the South into foreign hands to pay for munitions of war which we should be bound to protect. None but Englishmen would have the presumption to make such a request. It is entitled to no respect or consideration. Not unlikely it is cotton of the Rebel government covered up.

XX

June 1, *Wednesday.* Called on the President relative to the appointment of midshipmen. After looking over the list with some care, he finally designated two sons of officers [and] one apprentice, and desired me to complete the nominations.

When I called on the President, Major-General Schenck was with him, and, as I went in, was giving the President a list of names of persons to be selected to fill the board about to be appointed on the question of retired officers, his brother, Commodore Schenck, being one. It was a cool proposition, but characteristic of General Schenck, and I think of the Schencks generally.

We have to-day the results of a meeting of strange odds and ends of parties, and factions, and disappointed and aspiring individuals at Cleveland. Frémont is nominated as their candidate for President and John Cochrane for Vice-President. The gathering had the nomination of Frémont in view, though other objects were professed.

I very earnestly supported Frémont in 1856. He was

then put forward as the representative of the principles for which we were contending, and I have no reason to give that he was not faithful to the cause. He was, however, as soon as nominated, surrounded, to a great extent, by bad men, in whom no good man had confidence. His bearing was very well so far as he appeared before the public. I saw that he was anxious to be elected but not offensively so; he was not obtrusive, but, on the contrary, reserved and retiring. In nothing did he show extraordinary ability or character, but my conclusions were that his real traits were undeveloped. He did not grow upon me as reserved men usually do. Colonel Benton had in former years extolled him, though opposed to his candidacy. Governor Marcy, no friend of Benton, and not partial to Frémont, had, when Secretary of War, given him name and fame by a most remarkable indorsement in his able report in (I think) 1848.

I have since learned that that part of Marcy's report was written by Colonel Benton himself, and that President Polk compelled Marcy to incorporate it in the annual report of the War Department. The affair seems incredible almost to me, who knew the several parties, but I learn it in a way that leaves no doubt of its truth. Marcy had ability but was timid and subservient. Frémont has gained no reputation during the War. In power his surroundings have been awful. Reckless, improvident, wasteful, pompous, purposeless, vain, and incompetent. In his explorations, however, he showed perseverance and endurance, and he had the reputation of attaching his men to him. His journals were readable, but I have been told they were prepared and mostly written by Colonel Benton. On all occasions he puts on airs, is ambitious, and would not serve under men of superior military capacity and experience. Frémont first and country after. For a long time he has been in foolish intrigues for the Presidency, and the Cleveland meeting is a Frémont meeting, though others have been concerned.

I am surprised that General Cochrane should have embarked in the scheme. But he has been wayward and erratic. A Democrat, a Barnburner, a conservative, an Abolitionist, an Anti-abolitionist, a Democratic Republican, and now a radical Republican. He has some, but not eminent, ability; can never make a mark as a statesman. It will not surprise me if he should change his position before the close of the political campaign, and support the nominees of the Baltimore Convention. There is not a coincidence of views and policy between him and Frémont, and the convention which has nominated them is a heterogeneous mixture of weak and wicked men. They would jeopard and hazard the Republican and Union cause, and many of them would defeat it and give success to the Copperheads to gratify their causeless spite against the President. He is blamed for not being more energetic and because he is despotic in the same breath. He is censured for being too mild and gentle towards the Rebels and for being tyrannical and intolerant. There is no doubt he has a difficult part to perform in order to satisfy all and do right.

This war is extraordinary in all its aspects and phases, and no man was prepared to meet them. It is much easier for the censorious and factious to complain than to do right. I have often thought that greater severity might well be exercised, and yet it would tend to barbarism.

No traitor has been hung. I doubt if there will be, but an example should be made of some of the leaders, for present and for future good. They may, if taken, be imprisoned or driven into exile, but neither would be lasting. Parties would form for their relief, and ultimately succeed in restoring the worst of them to their homes and the privileges they originally enjoyed. Death is the proper penalty and atonement, and will be enduringly beneficent in its influence.

There was, moreover, an aristocratic purpose in this Rebellion. An aristocracy of blood and wealth was to have been established. Consequently a contrary effect would work benignantly. Were a few of the leaders to be stripped of their possessions, and their property confiscated, their families impoverished, the result would be salutary in the future. But I apprehend there will be very gentle measures in closing up the Rebellion. The authors of the enormous evils that have been inflicted will go unpunished, or will be but slightly punished.

June 2, Thursday. There is intense anxiety in relation to the Army of the Potomac. Great confidence is felt in Grant, but the immense slaughter of our brave men chills and sickens us all. The hospitals are crowded with the thousands of mutilated and dying heroes who have poured out their blood for the Union cause. Lee has returned to the vicinity of Richmond, overpowered by numbers, beaten but hardly defeated.

June 3, Friday. For several days the delegates to the National Convention have been coming in. Had a call from several. Met a number at the President's. All favor the President. There is a spirit of discontent among the Members of Congress, stirred up, I think, by the Treasury Department. Chase has his flings and insinuations against the President's policy, or want of policy. Nothing suits him.

There seems some difference among the delegates about the Vice-Presidency, but they will be likely to renominate Hamlin, though he has not much personal strength and has not the mind and temperament to build up a party for the country. There is an impression here that he has great strength in New England, but that is not my opinion. He has party cunning and management but not breadth and strength and is but little cared for there; is not offensive or obnoxious, but there is no zeal for him. As the President is a Western man and will be renominated, the Convention will very likely feel inclined to go East and to renominate the Vice-President also. Should New York be united on

Dix or Dickinson, the nomination would be conceded to
the Empire State, but there can be no union in that State
upon either of those men or any other.

June 4, Saturday. Many delegates to Convention in
town. Some attempts made by Members of Congress to
influence them. The friends of Chase improve the opportunity to exclaim against Blair.

There has been continued fighting, though represented
as not very important. Still there is heavy loss, but we
are becoming accustomed to the sacrifice. Grant has not
great regard for human life.

June 6, Monday. Am urged to go to Baltimore but do
not deem it advisable. Some talk with Blair respecting
Chase and Seward, who, though not assimilating and unlike in many respects, continue to get along. Each has a
policy which seems to me unsound, and Blair coincides
with me, but is so intent on other matters, personal to the
Blairs and the vindictive war upon them, that he is compelled to defer the differences on grave questions to what
so nearly concerns him.

I am uncomfortable about the extradition, or rather the
abduction, of Arguellis, the Spaniard. The act shocks me,
and the Administration will justly be held accountable.
Some of us who know nothing on the subject will have to
share the responsibility. I knew nothing of the subject, nor
that there was such a man, until after the wrong had been
committed and the man was on his way to Cuba. Marshal
Murray then informed me, and said he was here to escape
the grand jury. A few days after the subject was alluded
to in the Cabinet. Seward introduced it incidentally, partly
as a feeler and partly to affirm hereafter that the subject
had been mentioned. A few words passed between him
and the President. As no one said a word by way of comment, I inquired if there was not a law in New York against
abduction? Seward claimed there was no law prohibiting

the extradition, — that we might do it or not. It was an act of comity merely; Spain could not demand it, etc., etc. It was in answer to these remarks that I put the inquiry. I saw it grated, and when I further remarked if there was no treaty or law for it, I should doubt the propriety of acting, I saw I was making discord, and the subject dropped. The arrest is an arbitrary and unauthorized exercise of power by the Secretary of State.

June 7, Tuesday. The Convention to-day is the absorbing theme but there is something from the army relative to the late fights that disturbs me. We have had severe slaughter. Brave men have been killed and maimed most fearfully, but Grant persists.

June 8, Wednesday. The President was renominated to-day at Baltimore. A contest took place in regard to Missouri, and the wrong delegates were admitted by an almost unanimous vote. A strange perversion. There was neither sense nor reason nor justice in the decision. Rogues, fanatics, hypocrites, and untruthful men secured and triumphed over good and true men. Prejudice overcame truth and reason. The Convention exhibited great stupidity and actually stultified itself in this matter.

When the vote of the Convention was taken on the nomination for President, it was found the Missouri delegation who had been admitted were not in harmony with the Convention. They would not vote for Mr. Lincoln. He had all the rest of the votes. There was much intrigue and much misconception in this thing.

On the question of Vice-President there was greater diversity of opinion at the beginning, but ultimately and soon all united on Andrew Johnson. Personally I did not regret this result, although I took no part in its accomplishment. The delegates and papers of my State generally have disapproved of Hamlin's course towards me, and I have no doubt it contributed to their casting a united vote at the start for Johnson. Hamlin and his friends will give me credit for influence which I do not possess, and ascribe to me revenge for malevolence I have never felt. Without cause and because I would not extend undue favor to one of his friends by official abuse, he has treated me coldly, discourteously, and with bad temper, — so much so as to attract attention and inquiry, and lead to opposition to his renomination.

June 9, *Thursday.* There seems to be general satisfaction with the nominations made at Baltimore, and with the resolutions adopted. Except the nomination for Vice-President, the whole proceedings were a matter of course. It was the wish of Seward that Hamlin should again be the Vice, and the President himself was inclined to the same policy, though personally his choice is Johnson. This, I think, was the current Administration opinion, though with no particular zeal or feeling. Blair inclined to the policy of taking Hamlin, though partial to Johnson. I took no part and could not well take any. Yet to-day from several quarters it is said to me that Connecticut overthrew Hamlin, and that it was my doings which led to it. While this is not correct, I am nowise disposed to be dissatisfied with the change that has been made.

Concluded to retire the marine officers who are past the legal age, and to bring in Zeilin as Commandant of the Corps. There seems no alternative. . . .

June 10, *Friday.* The caucus of the New Hampshire members of the legislature friendly to the Administration has resulted in the substitution of Cragin for John P. Hale. This will be a sore and sad disappointment to Hale, who had until recently thought himself invincible in New Hampshire. Although I have no doubt he would make terms with the Copperheads if he could, they would not with him, and it therefore seems scarcely possible that it can be otherwise than he will be fully and finally defeated.

[1] Four pages omitted on account of a duplication in the manuscript.

I rejoice at it, for he is worthless, a profligate politician, a poor Senator, an indifferent statesman, not without talents, though destitute of industry, and I question his integrity. He has some humor, is fond of scandal, delights in defaming, loves to oppose, and is reckless of truth in his assaults. The country will sustain no loss from his retirement. As chairman of the Naval Committee and the organ of communication between the Navy Department and the Senate, he has rendered no service, but has been a constant embarrassment and obstruction. During the whole of this civil war, when all our energies and efforts were exerted in the cause of the Union and the country, no assistance, no word of encouragement even, has ever come to the Department from John P. Hale; but constant assaults, insinuations, and pronounced, if not wilful and deliberate, misrepresentations have emanated from him. Of course, I shall not regret his defeat, for though his term does not expire till the close of this Administration, and my connection with the Government may terminate at the same time, I am glad that his factious conduct is not indorsed by his State, and that the buffoon and vilifier will not be in a position to do further injury. He has been less offensive this session than heretofore, whether because he had become aware that his conduct did not meet the approval of the people and the election was at hand, I care not to judge.

A letter from Admiral Gregory, inclosing a report from himself and Chief Engineer King on the Chimo, one of the light-draught monitors, gives a bad account. There have been mistakes and miscalculations in this class of vessels of a serious character. Stimers and Fox have had them in charge, and each has assured me that my apprehensions were groundless. Fox has been persistent in this matter, and assumed that the objections were wholly groundless. Admiral Gregory has also given me strong assurances that all was right. The Chimo, the first, would, he said, be a little deep, but this would be obviated in all the others, and not very bad in her case. I am not satisfied with Stimers's management, yet Fox has in this matter urged what has been done. The report indicates unfitness on the part of Stimers, who miscalculated or made no calculation for displacement, has become vain, and feared to acknowledge his error.

June 11, *Saturday.* There is very little from the army that is decisive or satisfactory. Constant fighting is going on, killing without any battle. The bodies of our brave men, slain or mutilated, are brought daily to Washington by hundreds. Some repulse we have had beyond what is spoken of, I have no doubt. But our army holds on with firmness, and persistency, and courage, — being constantly reinforced.

June 20, *Monday.* A very busy and eventful week has passed without my having time to jot down incidents, much less observations and reflections. Among other matters, on representations made by attorneys, detectives, and others, I directed the arrest of Smith Brothers, in Boston. It is stated they have attempted to defraud the government in the delivery of the articles under contract. Mr. Wilson, Mr. Goodman, Mr. Eames, Mr. Watkins, Mr. Fox, Mr. Faxon, Admiral Smith, all concur in opinion as to the criminality of the Smiths. Yet they stand high in Boston as pious, sharp men, who profess great honesty and much religion. The arrest will bring down abuse and hostility upon me from many. But duty demanded action, however unpleasant.

Mr. Rice called on me early Saturday morning with a telegram received at midnight from Mrs. Smith, concerning the arrest of her husband. She is in great distress and has the earnest sympathy of Mr. Rice, who believes the Smiths innocent. He says the arrest has ruined forever the families, whether innocent or guilty. Mr. Gooch soon came in with a similar telegram, received at midnight, and went over the same story more briefly. Gooch felt bad and had slept but little. I told Mr. Rice that the parties should have the benefit of bail, or rather that I had written Mr. Wilson, authorizing bail. Colonel Olcott writes Fox, to whom these matters are specially committed, opposing bail; wants them confined in Fort Warren, where they have been sent, until he has examined their papers. He is a cormorant, searching papers, utterly reckless. I told Fox that I wished a firm but mild man; that I would not be oppressive. But Fox is violent against these men, who, he believes, are hypocrites and rascals. While I may not differ with him in that respect, they have rights in common with us all that must be respected and not rudely violated.

Preliminary measures for the arrest and trial of Henderson, Navy Agent at New York, have been taken. From the statements of Savage, Stover, and others he has been guilty of malfeasance, although standing high in the community as a man of piety and purity. It has been with reluctance that I have come to the conclusion that it was my duty to ask his removal and take measures against him. But I am left no alternative. That he, like all the Navy Agents, was getting rich at the public expense I have not doubted, — that there were wrong proceedings in this matter I fully believed, — and yet to break with old friends was and is unpleasant. My own impression is that Henderson has kept more accurate accounts than his predecessors, and I expect his books will square up faithfully, — accurate in dollars and cents, — but the wrong has been in another way. His representative, and friend, and fellow church-member Odell has looked into the subject, and says he has committed great frauds.

The gold bill, as it is called, has been finally enacted and we shall soon ascertain whether it effects any good. Chase and his school have the absurd follies of the Whigs and John Law in regard to money and finance. I have no confidence in his financial wisdom or intelligence on those subjects.

We get no good army news from Petersburg. Our troops

have suffered much and accomplished but little, so far as I
can learn. But there is disinclination to communicate
army intelligence, as usual. Were the news favorable, it
would be otherwise.

The President in his intense anxiety has made up his
mind to visit General Grant at his headquarters, and left
this P.M. at five. Mr. Fox has gone with him, and not unlikely favored and encouraged the President in this step,
which I do not approve. It has been my policy to discour-
age these Presidential excursions. Some of the Cabinet
favored them. Stanton and Chase, I think, have given them
countenance heretofore.

He can do no good. It can hardly be otherwise than
harmful, even if no accident befalls him. Better for him and
the country that he should remain at his post here. It
would be advantageous if he remained away from the War
Department and required his Cabinet to come to him.

June 21, *Tuesday.* The President being absent, there
was no Cabinet-meeting to-day. Massachusetts Representatives are sensitive and sore concerning the arrest of the
Smiths. I wrote Mr. Wilson not to be severe and to take
bail.

June 22, *Wednesday.* Much sensational news concerning
delay of army movements. I am inclined to think our people have learned caution from dear experience, — dear in
the best blood of the country.

Gold had gone up to-day to 230. Legislation does not
keep down the price or regulate values. In other and
plainer terms, paper is constantly depreciating and the
tinkering has produced the contrary effect from that intended by our financiers.

June 23, *Thursday.* A call in force this A.M. from a large
portion of the Massachusetts delegation in behalf of the
Smith brothers, now in Fort Warren, wanting them to be

bailed, but at the same time admitting a bail bond to be useless or valueless. They proposed, however, the whole Massachusetts delegation should unite in a bond, guaranteeing the appearance of the Smiths for trial. Told them I thought this not a proper proceeding, that it was perhaps doubtful whether bail could properly be taken, that I had written to Mr. Wilson that I wished, if it could be done, that there should be bail, etc., etc. The interview was long; Senator Wilson, Mr. Rice, Mr. Dawes were the principal speakers.

In the afternoon Mr. Rice called at my house with a telegram to the effect that Mr. Wilson would be willing to take bail, but that Assistant Secretary Fox, who has the matter in special charge, had written him not to do so without the consent of Colonel Olcott, etc. I told Mr. Rice, I thought there must be some misapprehension, that I thought Mr. Wilson would act discreetly and properly, that we should probably hear from him by to-morrow morning's mail. He was earnest, sensitive, and expressed great distrust, or want of confidence in Mr. Fox. I told him, while Mr. Fox was very earnest and persevering, I thought it an error to impute to him personal enmity against the Smiths and others.

Admiral Lee sends me some papers relative to a permit issued by General Butler to one Lane, of the steamer Philadelphia, to trade in Chowan River, North Carolina. It was a little, dirty, speculating intrigue, initiated as early as last March, in a letter from General Butler addressed to the President, proposing to send in ploughs, harrows, and farming utensils to loyal farmers in North Carolina, in exchange for cotton and products of the country, — plausible and taking rascality. The President indorsed that he approved the object. On this General Butler granted a permit. Captain Smith, senior officer in the Sounds, declined to recognize it, but detained the boat and sent the papers to Admiral Lee. The latter failed — called the paper many names, said President's permit must be respected.

I showed the papers to Seward and Blair, and was disposed to telegraph and detain the vessel. B. was inclined, though doubtingly, to favor my views, S. advised waiting the arrival of the President, but both condemned the proceedings as wholly improper.

Some warm discussion took place, Rice tells me, in the House on the currency and financial questions, showing serious differences in the Ways and Means Committee and between them and the Secretary of the Treasury. It will not surprise me should radical differences be developed. The whole system is one of error, ruinous error to the country.

June 24, *Friday.* Telegraphed to Wilson directly on reaching Department (and finding no letter from Wilson), directing him to bail the Smiths in sums of $20,000 each.

Have given some examination of the Scofield trial, which is very voluminous, and had Watkins investigate, review, and report. I conclude to approve the finding, though there may be some irregularities and mistakes adverse to the Government. Mr. Bliss, counsel for S., filed a document, excepting to some legal points, yesterday. To-day, after learning my conclusion and looking at the finding, he takes stronger exceptions and declares the finding not conformable to facts and evidence. He wishes me to submit the legal questions to the Attorney-General or some one else. Alluded to Mr. Eames. Wishes Mr. Watkins to examine the evidence. To Eames he says that it is the intention of Scofield and his counsel to prosecute the members of the court individually for false imprisonment. To Watkins, he further says that it is their intention to hold me accountable, and to have me arrested when I am in New York. All this does not induce me to change my conclusion of approving the verdict of the court martial, but I think it may be proper to advise the court that it is in error on the subject of jurisdiction, — that they can take cognizance of open-market purchases as well as others, and though, had they done so, the punishment might have been greater, yet I will still approve the finding. Let him have the benefit of the mistake the court has made.

Fox is much dissatisfied with the verdict. Thinks it inadequate; should have been imprisoned five years and fined one hundred thousand dollars. He wishes me to return the papers for revision, and to state the punishment is inadequate. But this is not advisable, even were it strictly correct and allowable. The ends desired will be accomplished by this punishment. A more severe one, such as he suggests, will endanger a reaction.

The President was in very good spirits at the Cabinet. His journey has done him good, physically, and strengthened him mentally and inspired confidence in the General and army. Chase was not at the Cabinet-meeting. I know not if he is at home, but he latterly makes it a point not to attend. No one was more prompt and punctual than himself until about a year since. As the Presidential contest approached he has ceased in a great measure to come to the meetings. Stanton is but little better. If he comes, it is to whisper to the President, or take the dispatches or the papers from his pocket and go into a corner with the President. When he has no specialty of his own, he withdraws after some five or ten minutes.

Mr. Seward generally attends the Cabinet-meetings, but the questions and matters of his Department he seldom brings forward. These he discusses with the President alone. Some of them he communicates to me, because it is indispensable that I should be informed, but the other members are generally excluded.

June 25, Saturday. There are some blunders in the finding of the court in Scofield's case that I do not like. I telegraphed to Wilson, Judge-Advocate, to come here for consultation and explanation, but a telegram just received says he is unable from indisposition.

The Treasury management is terrible, ruinous. Navy

requisitions are wantonly withheld for weeks, to the ruin of the contractor. In the end the government will suffer greatly, for persons will not under these ruinous delays deal with the government at ordinary current rates. The pay of the sailors and workmen is delayed until they are almost mutinous and riotous. There is no justifiable excuse for this neglect. But Mr. Chase, having committed blunders in his issues, is now desirous of retiring certain paper, and avails himself of funds of creditors on naval account to accomplish this. It is most unjust. The money honestly due to government creditors should not be withheld for Treasury schemes, or to retrieve its mistakes.

I am daily more dissatisfied with the Treasury management. Everything is growing worse. Chase, though a man of mark, has not the sagacity, knowledge, taste, or ability of a financier. Has expedients, and will break down the government. There is no one to check him. The President has surrendered the finances to his management entirely. Other members of the Cabinet are not consulted. Any dissent from, or doubts even, of his measures is considered as a declaration of hostility and an embarrassment of his administration. I believe I am the only one who has expressed opinions that questioned his policy, and that expression was mild and kindly uttered. Blair said about as much and both [he and I] were lectured by Chase. But he knew not then, nor does he know now, the elementary principles of finance and currency. Congress surrenders to his capricious and superficial qualities as pliantly as the President and the Cabinet. If they do not legalize his projects, the Treasury is to be closed, and under a threat, or something approaching a threat, his schemes are sanctioned, and laws are made to carry them into effect ; but woe awaits the country in consequence.

June 27, *Monday.* I sent Mr. Eames to New York last evening to consult with Mr. Wilson in the New York and Boston cases, giving my views in each. Henderson will struggle hard to get clear, and no effort must be spared to elicit the truth. Scofield's case must be straightened, or rather court must be straightened in his case. In the case of the Smiths at Boston, I fear there has been unnecessary harshness. Olcott has made an ostentatious display of authority and been, I apprehend, tyrannical and oppressive. He is a harsh, rough instrument, and I shall be glad when he shall have done service with me. Yet in saying this I admit from what I have seen he has some good qualities as a detective. I have seen nothing to doubt his honesty; he is industrious and indefatigable, but vain, reckless, regardless of private rights, and all his qualities have been exercised in the case of the Smiths, who are shrewd, piously honest, self-righteous, and wary as well as sharp. It will not surprise me if they prove an overmatch for him and the lawyers.

I have a very earnest letter to-day from William C. Bryant in behalf of his partner and publisher, Henderson. It was handed to me by Mr. Odell, Representative from Brooklyn, and inclosed was also an open letter to the President, which he wished me to deliver. Mr. O. is, like H., a prominent member of the Methodist Church. They are of opposite politics. Of course Mr. H. stimulated Mr. B. to write these letters, and, having got them, sends them through his religious associate. Mr. B. evidently believes H. innocent and injured. This is natural. Odell knows he is not. Morgan believes that both Bryant and Godwin are participants in the plunder of Henderson. I have doubts as regards B., who is feeling very badly, and thinks there is a conspiracy in which Seward and Thurlow Weed are chiefs. I am supposed to be an instrument in their hands, and so is the President. But it so happens that neither of them knew any of the facts until the arrest of Henderson and his removal were ordered.

It grieves me that the *Evening Post* and Mr. Bryant should suffer by reason of the malfeasance of Henderson. As regards Godwin, I cannot say that my faith in him is much greater than in Henderson, and yet I know but little of him. The *Evening Post* does not sustain the character which it had under Bigelow and Leggett. Bryant is a good general editor in many respects, but the political character of the paper has been derived in a great degree from others. Of late there have been some bad surroundings. Opdyke, J. G. C. Gray, D. D. Field, and others of like complexion have been the regents and advisers of Godwin, until the paper is losing some of its former character, — perhaps more than any of us are aware.

I dined to-day with Attorney-General Bates, and after my return this evening wrote a reply to Bryant's letter, disabusing his mind of some of its errors, provided his convictions are open to the truth.

Mrs. Franklin J. Smith of Boston sends me through Senator Sumner a touching and affecting letter in behalf of her husband. I gave Mr. Bryant's letter to the President, who read it aloud to me and said he would reply.

June 28, *Tuesday.* We have bad news from Sherman to-day. Neither Seward, Chase, nor Stanton was at the Cabinet-meeting. The President, like myself, slightly indisposed.

Mrs. General Hunter was at our house this evening and has tidings of a favorable character from her husband, who is in the western part of Virginia. Has done great mischief to the Rebels, and got off safely and well. This small bit of good news is a relief, as we are getting nothing good from the great armies.

Gold has gone up to 240. Paper, which our financiers make the money standard, is settling down out of sight. This is the result of the gold bill and similar measures, yet Chase learns no wisdom. We are hurrying onward into a financial abyss. There is no vigorous mind in Congress to check the current, and the prospect is dark for the country under the present financial management. It cannot be sustained.

June 29, *Wednesday*. Nothing from the army. We hear that the pirate Alabama is at Cherbourg. Is she to remain there to be repaired? Seward tells me he knows one of the French armed vessels recently sold is for Sweden, and he has little doubt both are; that the French government is not deceitful in this matter.

Congress is getting restive and discontented with the financial management. The papers speak of the appointment of Field, Assistant Secretary, to be Assistant Treasurer at New York, in the place of Cisco. I doubt if any one but Chase would think of him for the place, and Chase, as usual, does not know the reason. But Field has talents, and Chase takes him from association. Morgan prefers Hillhouse, and Seward wants Blatchford.

The closing hours of Congress are crowded, as usual, but I believe matters are about as square as usual. Our naval bills have mostly been disposed of.

June 30, *Thursday*. All were surprised to-day with the resignation of Secretary Chase and the nomination of Governor David Tod as his successor. I knew nothing of it till the fact was told me by Senator Doolittle, who came to see and advise with me, supposing I knew something of the circumstances. But I was wholly ignorant. Chase had not thought proper to consult me as to his resignation, nor had the President as to his action upon it, or the selection. My first impression was that he had consulted Seward and perhaps Blair. I learn, however, he advised with none of his Cabinet, but acted from his own impulses. I have doubts of Tod's ability for this position, though he has good common sense and was trained in the right school, being a hard-money man. Not having seen the President since this movement took place, I do not comprehend his policy. It can hardly be his intention to reverse the action of Chase entirely without consulting those who are associated with him in the Government. And yet the selection of Tod indicates that, if there be any system in the movement. The

SALMON P. CHASE

President has given but little attention to finance and the currency, but yet he can hardly be ignorant of the fact that Chase and Tod are opposites. The selection of Tod is a move in the right direction if he has made the subject a sufficient study to wield the vast machine. On this point I have my doubts. His nomination will disturb the "Bubbles," — the paper-money men, — and the question was not acted upon but referred to the Finance Committee, who have been with the Senate. I have no doubt their astonishment at the obtrusion of a hard-money man upon them was made manifest.

Blair and Bates both called at my house this evening and gave me to understand they were as much taken by surprise as myself. Mr. Bates says he knows nothing of T. Blair expresses more apprehensions even than myself, who have my doubts.

The retirement of Chase, so far as I hear opinions expressed, — and they are generally freely given, — appears to give relief rather than otherwise, which surprises me. I had thought it might create a shock for a brief period, though I did not fear that it would be lasting. I look upon it as a blessing. The country could not go on a great while longer under his management, which has been one of expedients and of no fixed principles, or profound and correct financial knowledge.

It is given out that a disagreement between himself and the President in relation to the appointment of Assistant Treasurer at New York was the cause of his leaving. I think likely that was the occasion of his tendering his resignation, and I have little doubt he was greatly surprised that it was accepted. He may not admit this, but it is none the less true, I apprehend. Yet there were some circumstances to favor his going, — there is a financial gulf ahead.

XXI

July 1, *Friday.* This day is the anniversary of my birth. I am sixty-two years of age. Life is brief. Should I survive another year, I shall then have attained my grand climacteric. Yet it is but the journey of a day, and of those who set out with me in the morning of life how few remain! Each year thins out the ranks of those who went with me to the old district school in my childhood.

Governor Tod has declined the position of Secretary of the Treasury. It does not surprise me. Senator Fessenden has been appointed, who will, it is said, accept, which does surprise me. I doubt if his health will permit him to bear the burden. He has abilities; is of the same school as Chase. Has been Chairman of the Committee of Finance during Chase's administration of the Treasury, and, I have supposed, a supporter of his policy. Yet I have had an impression that Fessenden is an improvement upon Chase, and I trust he is.

But the President's course is a riddle. Tod is a hard-money man; Fessenden has pressed through Congress the paper system of Chase. One day Tod is selected; on his refusal, Fessenden is brought forward. This can in no other way be reconciled than in the President's want of knowledge of the subject. His attention never has been given to the finances. He seems not aware that within twenty-four hours he has swung to opposite extremes.

Seward can hardly have been consulted, for Fessenden has been his sharp and avowed opponent of late, and unless he has changed, or shall change, will prove a troublesome man for him in the Cabinet.

The President has great regard for Chase's abilities but is glad to be relieved of him, for C. has been a load of late, — is a little disappointed and dissatisfied, has been captious, and uncertain, favored the faultfinders, and, in a way, encouraged opposition to the President.

July 2, Saturday. The last business day of the session, and many of the Members have gone home already. Much is done and omitted to be done during the last hours of Congress. Members do wrong in abandoning their post at these important periods, and no one who does it should be trusted. I am told by the members of our naval committees that all naval matters are rightly done up in the two houses, but I discredit it. Some matters will be lost, and hurried legislation is always attended with errors.

July 5, Tuesday. On the morning of Sunday the 3rd, went with Postmaster-General Blair and family and my own family, also Mr. Fox, Mr. Faxon, Dr. Horwitz, Commander Aulick on an excursion down the Potomac and Bay to the Capes, to Norfolk, and Fortress Monroe, returning to Washington this A.M. at five o'clock. National salutes were fired from the American, English, and French frigates and also from the Fortress at meridian on the 4th. The jaunt was very pleasant.

Telegrams this A.M. inform us that the pirate Alabama was sunk on the 19th of June off Cherbourg by the steamer Kearsarge, Commodore Winslow, after a fight of one hour

2

and a half. Informed the President and Cabinet of the tidings, which was a matter of general congratulation and rejoicing.

Mr. Fessenden appeared at Cabinet-meeting as the successor of Mr. Chase. Although the regular day of meeting, all were specially notified, and all promptly attended. The President appeared more constrained and formal than usual. When Mr. Stanton came in, he was accompanied by a clerk, whom he seated at the President's table. The subject of trade and especially trade in cotton with the Rebels, was the subject of general interest which the President desired to lay before us. He appeared to have no fixed purpose in his own mind. Alluded to a Mr. Atkinson who had called on him. Said that Mr. A. had impressed him with some very striking facts. The most prominent was, that although the Rebels sold less cotton they received about as much for it in consequence of high price as when they had more of the article. The President thought it might be well to take measures to secure the cotton, but was opposed to letting the Rebels have gold.

Seward was voluble but not clear and pointed. Fessenden had seen Atkinson, had interview with him, thought him intelligent. On the subject of trade with the Rebels was not posted. Stanton made extended, and in the main sensible and correct, remarks, being wholly opposed to fighting and trading at the same time with the Rebels, ground which I have uniformly taken, but have not always been supported. Blair made a few sensible remarks, as did Mr. Bates. Usher, thinking it apparently a duty to say something, talked without much point or force, on a subject he did not understand, nor to which he had given much attention. Mr. Bates made a legal suggestion. As Stanton had pretty clearly expressed my views, I did not care to multiply words farther than to say so, and to regret that a bill had passed the last moment of the session depriving the Mississippi Squadron of prize.

This was done, I understand, at the instigation of Chase,

who could not have been aware of the effect of what he urged. The incidental remarks of some of the gentlemen on the subject of trade, and especially of restrictions on gold, struck me as the wretched remnants of error which I hope will go out with Mr. Chase. I also trust we shall get rid of his trade regulations, trading agents, and other mischievous machinery.

The subject of the arrest and trial of General Dix in New York for suspending the publication of the *World* and *Journal of Commerce* was brought forward. There was a little squeamishness with some on the subject. The President very frankly avowed the act to be his, and he thought the government should protect Dix. Seward was positive and bold on that.

I expressed no opinion, nor did Blair or Bates. While I regret that the papers should have been suppressed or meddled with, I would not, I think, permit a general officer to be arrested and tried by a State judge for obeying an order of the President. If there is a disposition to try the question before the United States tribunals, it would be well to permit it. This was my hasty conclusion.

July 6, *Wednesday*. Admiral Porter called on me to-day direct from his command. Had a long interview on his affairs.

Received dispatches to-day from Captain Winslow of the Kearsarge relative to sinking the Alabama. Wrote congratulatory letter. There is great rejoicing throughout the country over this success, which is universally and justly conceded a triumph over England as well as over the Rebels. In my first draft, I made a point or two, rather too strong perhaps, against England and the mercenary, piratical spirit of Semmes, who had accumulated chronometers.

While our people generally award me more credit than I deserve in this matter, a malevolent partisan spirit exhibits itself in some, which would find fault with me because this battle did not sooner take place. These assaults disturb me less, perhaps, than they ought; they give me very little uneasiness because I know them to be groundless. Violent attacks have been made upon the Department and myself for the reason that our naval vessels were not efficient, had no speed; but in the account of the battle, the Kearsarge is said, by way of lessening the calamity, to have had greater steaming power than the Alabama, and to have controlled the movement. Our large smooth-bore guns, the Dahlgrens, have been ridiculed and denounced by the enemies of the Navy Department, but the swift destruction of the Alabama is now imputed to the great guns which tore her in pieces.

A summer raid down the valley of the Shenandoah by the Rebels and the capture of Harper's Ferry are exciting matters, and yet the War Department is disinclined to communicate the facts. Of course, I will not ask. A few words from Stanton about "cursed mistakes of our generals," loss of stores that had been sent forward, bode disaster. General Sigel is beaten and not the man for the command given him, I apprehend. He is always overwhelmed and put on the run. It is represented that the Rebel army is in large force, 30,000 strong, under Ewell. We always have big scares from that quarter and sometimes pretty serious realities. I can hardly suppose Ewell there with such a command without the knowledge of Grant, and I should suppose we would hear of the movement of such a body from other sources. But the military authorities seem not to know of them.

I have sometimes thought that Lee might make a sudden dash in the direction of Washington or above, and inflict great injury before our troops could interfere, or Grant move a column to protect the city. But likely Grant has thought and is prepared for this; yet he displays little strategy or invention.

July 7, Thursday. I am apprehensive of trouble in making future contracts. Old contractors have been attacked and called to account, and will be shy. But the great damage is from the neglect or delay of the Treasury, which does not pay. Honest contracts are not fairly treated by the Treasury. Men are kept out of their money after due, wrongfully. I had the material, and began the preparation, for a pretty strong statement to Mr. Chase at the time he resigned.

Very mischievous efforts are being made in some quarters to injure the President and assist Chase by reason of his going out. I know nothing of the particulars from either of them, but I feel a conviction that the country is benefited by Mr. Chase's retirement. His longer continuance in the Treasury would have been a calamity. It would have been better could he have left earlier.

July 8, *Friday.* The War Department keeps very close as to matters at Harper's Ferry and vicinity. There is either little knowledge of what is doing, or a very great reluctance to communicate. Mr. Felton, President of the Philadelphia, Wilmington & Baltimore R. R. sends me a letter by private hands, stating that while he was not alarmed, he desired a gunboat at Gunpowder Creek, etc., to protect railroad property. Sent Fox to inquire of General Halleck as to the necessity. General H. thinks it unnecessary; but will advise us in season if wanted. Beyond this nothing is communicated.

Stanton tells me that he has no idea the Rebels are in any force above, and should not give them a serious thought, but that Grant says he thinks they are in force, without, however, giving his reasons or any facts. The President has been a good deal incredulous about a very large army on the upper Potomac, yet he begins to manifest anxiety. But he is under constraint, I perceive, such as I know is sometimes imposed by the dunderheads at the War Office, when they are in a fog, or scare, and know not what to say or do. It is not natural or the way of the President to withhold information, or speculation at such times, and I can always tell how things are with Halleck and Stanton when there are important movements going on. The President is now enjoined to silence, while Halleck is in a perfect maze, bewildered, without intelligent decision or self-reliance, and Stanton is wisely ignorant. I am inclined to believe, however, that at this time profound ignorance reigns at the War Department concerning the Rebel raid in the Shenandoah Valley; that they absolutely know nothing of it, — its numbers, where it is, or its destination. It has to me appeared more mischievous than to others. I think we are in no way prepared for it, and a fierce onset could not well be resisted. It is doubtful, however, whether the onset will be made, for it is the nature of man to lose his opportunities. The true course of the Rebels is to strike at once at this point.

July 9, *Saturday.* The Rebel invasion of Maryland, if not so large or formidable as last year and year before, looks to me very annoying, the more so because I learn nothing satisfactory or reliable from the War Office, and am persuaded there is both neglect and ignorance there. It is evident there have not been sufficient preparations, but they are beginning to move. Yet they hardly have any accurate information. Stanton seems stupid, Halleck always does. I am not, I believe, an alarmist, and, as I have more than once said, I do not deem this raid formidable if rightly and promptly met, but it may, from inattention and neglect, become so. It is a scheme of Lee's strategy, but where is Grant's?

The Blairs have left, strangely, it appears to me, at this time, on a fishing excursion among the mountain streams of interior Pennsylvania, and the ladies have hastily run off from Silver Spring to Cape May, leaving their premises at a critical moment.

Our Alabama news comes in opportunely to encourage and sustain the nation's heart. It does them as well as me good to dwell upon the subject and the discomfiture of the

British and Rebels. The perfidy of the former is as infamous as the treason of the latter. Both were whipped by the Kearsarge, a Yankee ship with a Yankee commander and a Yankee crew.

July 10, *Sunday.* When at the Department, Sunday morning, the 10th, examining my mail, one of the clerks came in and stated that the Rebel pickets were on the outskirts of Georgetown, within the District lines. There had been no information to warn us of this near approach of the enemy, but my informant was so positive — and soon confirmed by another — that I sent to the War Department to ascertain the facts. They were ignorant — had heard street rumors, but they were unworthy of notice — and ridiculed my inquiry.

Later I learned that young King, son of my neighbor Z. P. K., was captured by the Rebel pickets within the District lines and is a prisoner.

July 11, *Monday.* The Rebels are upon us. Having visited upper Maryland, they are turning their attention hitherward. General Wallace has been defeated, and it was yesterday current that General Tyler and Colonel Seward were prisoners, the latter wounded. But it seems only the last is true of the latter.

There is now a call from the War Department for gunboats at Havre de Grace, Gunpowder and Bush Rivers. Have ordered off three, but was afraid they would not arrive in season, for the call was not made and its necessity was scouted at Headquarters until the Rebels had cut the York and Baltimore Road. We have word by telegram this P.M. that the bridge over Gunpowder has been burned but a gunboat was on hand. Have no particulars.

Tom G. Welles was this day appointed to the staff of General McCook. I regret his passion for the service and his recklessness and youth.

The Rebel pickets appear in strength in front of Forts

Stevens and DeRussy on the borders and within the District lines. Went to Stanton, but got from him nothing at all. He exhibits none of the alarm and fright I have seen in him on former occasions. It is evident he considers the force not large, or such that cannot be controlled, and yet he cannot tell their number nor where they are.

I rode out this evening to Fort Stevens, latterly called Fort Massachusetts. Found General Wright and General McCook with what I am assured is an ample force for its defense. Passed and met as we returned three or four thousand, perhaps more, volunteers under General Meigs, going to the front. Could see the line of pickets of both armies in the valley, extending a mile or more. There was continual firing, without many casualties so far as I could observe, or hear. Two houses in the vicinity were in flames, set on fire by our own people, because they obstructed the range of our guns and gave shelter to Rebel sharpshooters. Other houses and buildings had also been destroyed. A pretty grove nearly opposite the fort was being cut down. War would not spare the tree, if the woodman had.

I inquired where the Rebel force was, and the officers said over the hills, pointing in the direction of Silver Spring. Are they near Gunpowder or Baltimore? Where are they? Oh! within a short distance, a mile or two only. I asked why their whereabouts was not ascertained, and their strength known. The reply was that we had no fresh cavalry.

The truth is the forts around Washington have been vacated and the troops sent to General Grant, who was promised reinforcements to take Richmond. But he has been in its vicinity more than a month, resting, apparently, after his bloody march, but has effected nothing since his arrival on the James, nor displayed any strategy, while Lee has sent a force threatening the National Capital, and we are without force for its defense. Citizens are volunteering, and the employees in the navy yard are required to man the fortifications left destitute. Stanton and Halleck, who scouted Fenton's application and bluffed my inquiries, are now the most alarmed men in Washington.

I am sorry to see so little reliable intelligence. It strikes me that the whole demonstration is weak in numbers but strong in conception that the Rebels have but a small force. I am satisfied no attack is now to be apprehended on the city; the Rebels have lost a remarkable opportunity. But on our part there is neglect, ignorance, folly, imbecility, in the last degree. The Rebels are making a show of fight while they are stealing horses, cattle, etc., through Maryland. They might easily have captured Washington. Stanton, Halleck, and Grant are asleep or dumb.

The waste of war is terrible; the waste from imbecility and mismanagement is more terrible and more trying than from the ravages of the soldiers. It is impossible for the country to bear up under these monstrous errors and wrongs.

July 12, *Tuesday*. The Rebels captured a train of cars on the Philadelphia and Baltimore Road, and have burnt the bridges over Gunpowder and Bush Rivers. It is said there were 1500 of these raiders.

Governor Bradford's house, a short distance out of Baltimore, was burnt by a small party. General demoralization seems to have taken place among the troops, and there is as little intelligence among them at the War Office in regard to the Rebels. General Wallace and his force were defeated, and panic and folly have prevailed.

Admiral Goldsborough and some of our naval officers tendered their services, if required. It seemed to me unnecessary, for I do not believe the Rebels have a large concentrated force in this vicinity, or that they design to make an attack on the city, but for the Navy to hold back when all are being called out would appear bad. I therefore requested Fox to see General Halleck, who much wanted aid, and Goldsborough and the men were therefore ordered and have gone to Fort Lincoln. It would be much better to keep them at work.

We have no mails, and the telegraph lines have been cut; so that we are without news or information from the outer world.

Went to the President's at 12, being day of regular Cabinet-meeting. Messrs. Bates and Usher were there. The President was signing a batch of commissions. Fessenden is absent in New York. Blair informs me he had been early at the council chamber and the President told him no matters were to be brought forward. The condition of affairs connected with the Rebels on the outskirts was discussed. The President said he and Seward had visited several of the fortifications. I asked where the Rebels were in force. He said he did not know with certainty, but he thought the main body at Silver Spring.

I expressed a doubt whether there was any large force at any one point, but that they were in squads of from 500 to perhaps 1500 scattered along from the Gunpowder to the falls of the Potomac, who kept up an alarm on the outer rim while the marauders were driving off horses and cattle. The President did not respond farther than to again remark he thought there must be a pretty large force in the neighborhood of Silver Spring.

I am sorry there should be so little accurate knowledge of the Rebels, sorry that at such a time there is not a full Cabinet, and especially sorry that the Secretary of War is not present. In the interviews which I have had with him, I can obtain no facts, no opinions. He seems dull and stupefied. Others tell me the same.

It was said yesterday that the mansions of the Blairs were burned, but it is to-day contradicted.

Rode out this P.M. to Fort Stevens. Went up to the summit of the road on the right of the fort. There were many collected. Looking out over the valley below, where the continual popping of the pickets was still going on, though less brisk than yesterday, I saw a line of our men lying close near the bottom of the valley. Senator Wade came up beside me. Our views corresponded that the

Rebels were few in front, and that our men greatly ex-
ceeded them in numbers. We went together into the fort,
where we found the President, who was sitting in the shade,
his back against the parapet towards the enemy.

Generals Wright and McCook informed us they were
about to open battery and shell the Rebel pickets, and
after three discharges an assault was to be made by two
regiments who were lying in wait in the valley.

The firing from the battery was accurate. The shells
that were sent into a fine mansion occupied by the Rebel
sharpshooters soon set it on fire. As the firing from the fort
ceased, our men ran to the charge and the Rebels fled. We
could see them running across the fields, seeking the woods
on the brow of the opposite hills. It was an interesting and
exciting spectacle. But below we could see here and there
some of our own men bearing away their wounded com-
rades. I should judge the distance to be something over
three hundred yards. Occasionally a bullet from some long-
range rifle passed above our heads. One man had been shot
in the fort a few minutes before we entered.

As we came out of the fort, four or five of the wounded
men were carried by on stretchers. It was nearly dark as
we left. Driving in, as was the case when driving out, we
passed fields as well as roads full of soldiers, horses, teams,
mules. Camp-fires lighted up the woods, which seemed to
be more eagerly sought than the open fields.

The day has been exceedingly warm, and the stragglers
by the wayside were many. Some were doubtless sick,
some were drunk, some weary and exhausted. Then men
on horseback, on mules, in wagons as well as on foot, batteries of artillery, caissons, an innumerable throng. It was
exciting and wild. Much of life and much of sadness.
Strange that in this age and country there is this strife and
struggle, under one of the most beneficent governments
which ever blessed mankind and all in sight of the Capitol.

In times gone by I had passed over these roads little

anticipating scenes like this, and a few years hence they will scarcely be believed to have occurred.

July 13, *Wednesday.* It is no doubt true that the Rebels have left. I called on General Halleck on a matter of business, and while there, about 11, he had a telegram saying the Rebels passed through Rockville to the northwest about 3 this A.M. They are making, I remarked, for Edwards Ferry and will get off with their plunder if we have no force there to prevent. He said it was by no means certain they would cross at Edwards Ferry. We looked over the map together, and he, like myself, thought it probable they had taken that course. I remarked that they appeared not to have concentrated their force at any one place. Halleck asked by what authority I said that. There was harshness and spite in his tone. I coolly said by my own judgment and the observation of almost any one who had any intelligence on the subject. He said he did not think I had heard so from any military man who knew anything about it. I said no military man or any other had been able to tell me where they were concentrated to the amount of five thousand. Nor have I found any except Halleck, Hitchcock, and a few around the Department express an opinion that there was a large number, or that they were concentrated. They were defiant and insolent, our men were resolute and brave, but the Bureau generals were alarmed and ignorant, and have made themselves and the Administration appear contemptible.

The Rebels, before leaving, burnt the house of Judge Blair, Postmaster-General. This they claimed to have done in retaliation for the destruction of the house of Governor Letcher, — a disgraceful act and a disgraceful precedent. I have no idea that General Hunter or any officer authorized the burning of Letcher's house. It was doubtless done by some miscreants, hangers-on, stragglers, who ought to be punished. But men in authority appear to have had direction in burning Blair's house.

July 14, *Thursday*. Communication is again opened with the North. It is evident there was never any force sufficient to have interrupted it, had there been ordinary ability and sagacity on the part of the military. The *Chronicle* and the army papers are striving to make it appear there was a large Rebel force and that there had been serious danger, — that we have had a great deliverance.

July 15, *Friday*. We had some talk at Cabinet-meeting to-day on the Rebel invasion. The President wants to believe there was a large force, and yet evidently his private convictions are otherwise. But the military leaders, the War Office, have insisted there was a large force. We have done nothing, and it is more gratifying to our self-pride to believe there were many of them, especially as we are likely to let them off with considerable plunder scot-free.

The *National Intelligencer* comments with a good deal of truth and ability on our national humiliation, as exemplified in this late affair. There is no getting away from the statements and facts presented.

Seward and Stanton seem disturbed. There is something which does not suit them. Seward followed Stanton out, and had a talk in the anteroom. I met Solicitor Whiting as I left the White House, who was very anxious to talk. Deplored the miserable military management. Imputes the whole folly and scare to General Halleck. Says Stanton has disapproved his policy, but [that] the President clings to Halleck, who is damaging him and the Administration greatly; that Halleck and Blair are both injuring the President. "Why," said I, "you do not mean to identify Blair with this pitiful business." "Oh no," said he, "but Blair is so perverse on the slavery question that he is getting all the radical element of the country against the Administration." As I did not care to enter into controversy on that topic, and it was late, I left him. But the conversation indicates that Stanton intends to throw off responsibility on to Halleck.

Grant and the Army of the Potomac are reposing in immense force near Richmond. Our troops have been sent from here and drawn from all quarters to reinforce the great army, which has suffered immense losses in its march, without accomplishing anything except to reach the ground from which McClellan was withdrawn. While daily reinforced, Grant could push on to a given point, but he seems destitute of strategy or skill, while Lee exhibits tact. This raid, which might have taken Washington and which has for several days cut off our communications with the North, was devised by Lee while beleaguered at Richmond, and, though failing to do as much as might have been accomplished, has effected a good deal.

The deportment of Stanton has been wholly different during this raid from any former one. He has been quiet, subdued, and apparently oppressed with some matter that gave him disquiet. On former occasions he has been active, earnest, violent, alarmed, apprehensive of danger from every quarter. It may be that he and Halleck have disagreed. Neither of them has done himself credit at this time.

The arrest of Henderson, Navy Agent, and his removal from office have seriously disturbed the editors of the *Evening Post*, who seem to make his cause their own. This subject coming up to-day, I told the President of the conduct of his District Attorney, Delafield Smith, who, when the case was laid before him by Mr. Wilson, attorney for the Department, remarked that it was not worth while to prosecute, that the same thing was done by others, at Washington as well as New York, and no notice was taken of it. Wilson asked him if he, the prosecuting law officer of the Government, meant to be understood as saying it was not worth while to notice embezzlement, etc. I related this to the President, who thereupon brought out a correspondence that had taken place between himself and W. C. Bryant. The latter averred that H. was innocent, and denounced Savage, the principal witness against him, because arrested and under bonds. To this the President replied that the character of Savage before his arrest was as good as Henderson's before he was arrested. He stated that he knew nothing of H.'s alleged malfeasance until brought to his notice by me, in a letter, already written, for his removal; that he inquired of me if I was satisfied he was guilty; that I said I was; and that he then directed, or said to me, "Go ahead, let him be removed."

These are substantially the facts. I said to him that the attorneys who had investigated the subject expressed a full conviction of his guilt; that I had come to the same conclusion, and did not see how a prosecution and summary proceedings could be avoided.

The *Evening Post* manifests a belligerent spirit, and evidently intends to make war upon the Navy Department because I will not connive at the malfeasance of its publisher. In a cautious and timid manner they have supported the policy of the Navy Department hitherto, though fearful of being taunted for so doing. Because their publisher was Navy Agent they have done this gently. But they now, since Henderson's arrest and trial, assail the monitors and the monitor system, which they have hitherto supported, and insidiously and unfairly misrepresent them and the Department.

I am surprised at the want of judgment manifested in hastening to make this assault. It would have been more politic, certainly, to have delayed, for the motive which leads them to make this abrupt turn cannot be misunderstood. They know it is painful for me to prosecute one of their firm, that it pains me to believe him guilty, but that when the facts are presented, they should know me well enough to be aware that I would not cover or conceal the rascality even to oblige them. I claim no merit, but I deserve no censure for this plain and straightforward discharge of my duty.

I hear it said to-day that there has been disagreement between Stanton and Grant; that the latter had ordered

General Hinks to Point Lookout and Stanton countermanded the order for General Barnes.

July 16, Saturday. Mr. Faxon, Chief Clerk, is ill and
leaves for New York in the Tacoma. Shall greatly miss
him. No one can fill his place. Thomas G. Welles is with
his general, McCook, relieved from duty at Fort Stevens.
I observe and have for some time past that the *Gazette* at
Cincinnati, a paper in the interest of Mr. Chase, has been
violent and reckless in its assaults on the Navy Department. With some smattering information of matters generally, there is much palpable ignorance in regard to our
monitors, ordnance, etc.

July 18, Monday. I yesterday went with my sons and
Dr. Horwitz to Silver Spring, passing over the ground
of the late fight. The chimneys of the burnt houses, the
still barricaded road, the trampled fields, and other evidences bear testimony to what had occurred. The Blairs
were absent from Silver Spring, but we turned down the
lane which leads to it and went to the walls of Montgomery
Blair's house, situated pleasantly on a little wooded em-
inence. But all was silent. Waste and war. Judge B. tells
me the house and furniture cost him just about $20,000.
The Rebels have done him this injury, and yet some whom
they have never personally harmed denounce him as not
earnest in the cause, as favoring the Rebels and their views.
We went through the grounds to the mansion of the elder
Mr. Blair. The place was less injured than I had supposed,
and there must have been extra pains taken for the preserv-
ation of the shrubbery and the growing crops. Fields of
the best corn I have seen this year were untouched. What
depredation or plunder had been committed in the house
I could not tell, for it was closed. My son, who led our
pickets, was the first to enter it after the Rebels left. He
found some papers scattered over the floor, which he gathered up. There had been crowds of persons there filling

the house, sleeping on the floors, prying into the family privacy, but not more rudely, perhaps, than our own soldiers would have done, had the place been in their power.

July 19, *Tuesday.* At the Cabinet-meeting to-day, the President brought forward specially the riot in Coles County, Illinois, and the controversy between Governor Pierpont and General Butler, with especial reference in the latter case to affairs at Norfolk, where the military authorities have submitted a vote to the inhabitants whether they will be governed by martial law. Of course the friends of civil administration, who denied the validity of the whole proceeding, would not vote, and the military had it all as they pleased. This exhibition of popular sovereignty destroying itself pleases Butler. He claims to have found large quantities of whiskey, which he seized and sold. But all the whiskey in Norfolk is there under permits issued by himself. While Butler has talents and capacity, he is not to be trusted. The more I see of him, the greater is my distrust of his integrity. All whiskey carried to Norfolk is in violation of the blockade.

Mr. Ericsson and the newspapers are discussing the monitors. He is honest and intelligent, though too enthusiastic, and claiming too much for his invention, but the newspapers are dishonest and ignorant in their statements, and their whole purpose is to assail the Department. But the system will vindicate itself. There have been errors and mistakes in the light-class monitors. I trusted too much to Fox and Stimers, and am therefore not blameless. But I was deceived, without its being intended perhaps, supposing that Ericsson and Lenthall had a supervision of them until considerable progress had been made towards their completion. I confided in Fox, who was giving these vessels special attention, and he confided in Stimers without my being aware that he was giving him the exclusive management of them. Fox and Lenthall were daily together, and I had not a doubt that much of the consultation was

2

in regard to them, until, becoming concerned from what I heard, I questioned Lenthall direct, when he disclaimed all responsibility and almost all knowledge of them. I then inquired clearly and earnestly of Fox, who placed the whole blame on Stimers. The latter, I heard, had quarrelled with Ericsson and had been carrying forward the construction of these vessels, reporting and consulting with no one but Fox and Admiral Gregory.

July 20, *Wednesday.* My son, Thomas G. Welles, left to-day for the Army of the Potomac, having received orders from the War Department to report to General Grant. To part with him has been painful to me beyond what I can describe. Were he older and with more settled principles and habits, some of the anxieties which oppress me would be relieved. But he is yet a mere youth and has gone to the camp with boyish pride and enthusiasm, and will be in danger of being misled when beyond a parent's control. He is just eighteen and goes alone on his mission. I have tried to dissuade him so far as I could with propriety, but there was a point beyond which I could not well go. In the condition of the country and when others were periling their lives and the lives of their children, how could I refrain, and resist the earnest appeals of my son, whose heart was set upon going? To have positively prohibited him would have led to bad results, and perhaps not have accomplished the end desired. Yet it has been hard to part with him, and as he left me, I felt that it was uncertain whether we should ever meet again, and if we do he may be mutilated, and a ruined man. I have attended closely to my duties, but am sad, and unfit for any labor.

July 21, *Thursday.* Edgar and John left this morning for Connecticut.

Wrote a letter to Attorney-General Bates, transmitting copy of the report of Mr. Wilson inculpating Attorney Delafield Smith of New York in the management of the prosecution of the Navy Agent for embezzlement, suggesting that it be laid before the President for such action as he may order. I have already mentioned the course of Smith to him. I am apprehensive that Smith himself may be liable to be called to account for malconduct in other respects. But he is a pet of Seward, who sometimes closes his eyes to the obliquities of his friends.

It will not surprise me if Seward, Weed, and Smith make friends with Henderson and the *Evening Post* concern, with whom they have hitherto quarrelled, and try to screen or exculpate Henderson. In so doing a common war will be made on me. The *Post* has broken ground already in a remote way but sufficient to indicate malice and revenge, and their determination to defend Henderson's guilt.

July 22, *Friday.* At the Cabinet-meeting the President read his correspondence with Horace Greeley on the subject of peace propositions from George Saunders and others at Niagara Falls. The President has acquitted himself very well, — if he was to engage in the matter at all, — but I am sorry that he permits himself, in this irregular way, to be induced to engage in correspondence with irresponsible parties like Saunders and Clay or scheming busybodies like Greeley. There is no doubt that the President and the whole Administration are misrepresented and misunderstood on the subject of peace, and Greeley is one of those who has done and is doing great harm and injustice in this matter. In this instance he was evidently anxious to thrust himself forward as an actor, and yet when once engaged he began to be alarmed; he failed to honestly and frankly communicate the President's first letters, as was his duty, but sent a letter of his own, which was not true and correct, and found himself involved in the meshes of his own frail net.

Colonel Jaquess is another specimen of inconsiderate and unwise, meddlesome interference. The President assented to his measure and gave him a card, or passport, to go beyond our lines. There is no doubt that the Colonel was sincere, but he found himself unequal to the task he had undertaken. Instead of persuading Jeff Davis to change his course, Davis succeeded in persuading poor Jaquess that the true course to be pursued was to let Davis & Co. do as they pleased. The result was that Jaquess and his friend Gilmore (alias Kirke), who went to Richmond to shear, came back shorn.

In these peace movements, the President has pursued his usual singular course. Seward was his only confidant and adviser, as usual in matters of the greatest importance. He says that Mr. Fessenden accidentally came in on other business while he was showing Seward the Greeley correspondence, and he was let into a knowledge of what was going on, but no one else. John Hay was subsequently told, before going off, and now, to-day, the Cabinet are made acquainted with what has been done. The President, instead of holding himself open to receive propositions, has imposed conditions and restrictions that will embarrass the parties.

July 25, Monday. There has been a little ferment in military circles, as newspaper correspondents write. Blair told me a few days since that Cutts came on his steps to sympathize and express his regret that the vandals should have burnt his (Blair's) house. Blair said that nothing better could be expected while poltroons and cowards had the management of military affairs. Cutts left abruptly. I now hear it stated that General Halleck reported the remark to Stanton, and Stanton forwarded Halleck's letter to the President, who remarked that men would speak their minds freely in this country. I have no idea that either Halleck or Stanton will press the subject farther. It would please Blair, I think, if they would.

Mr. Solicitor Whiting spent an hour at my house last evening. The principal topic of discussion was that of Reconstruction. He maintains that the States which have

seceded have no rights, — that they cannot resume position
in the Union without consent, and the formation of a new
constitution in each which excludes slavery. I denied the
right of Congress to impose that condition on a State, like
North Carolina for instance, and insisted that the States
must be equal in political rights, — that if Massachusetts
or any of the old States reserved and retained that power,
it belonged as well to North Carolina. An amendment of
the Constitution would be necessary abolishing slavery in
all. Without meeting that point, he expressed a disbelief
in the reserved right of Massachusetts on that subject. He
denied that a majority, or the whole people, of North Carolina could establish or reëstablish a government and continue to be or to become a member of the Union after having been in rebellion, except by consent or permission.
"Then," said I, "you recognize the right and the fact of
secession." This he was unwilling to admit, but dwelt on
international law, belligerent attitudes, and matters outside of the Constitution to punish States inside. I asked
what he would do with loyal citizens in Rebel States, —
those who had never borne arms or done any act to forfeit
their allegiance, men like John Minor Botts or Andrew
Johnson, for instance. He maintained that being in States
that rebelled they were to be treated like the Rebels.

Solicitor Whiting is self-sufficient but superficial, with
many words, some reading, but no very sound or well-
founded political views. Yet he considers himself a *pater
conscriptus*, a teacher learned in the law and wise on the
subject of government. Seward consults him, and Stanton
uses him. He writes letters and opinions to order, gets up
pamphlets; is serving without pay, and is careful to tell
that fact. One of these years, sooner or later, let no one be
surprised to find all his services fully compensated. Men
who profess to serve the government gratuitously are
usually better paid than others.

Met General Emory at Blair's. Has just come in from
pursuit of the raiders, without overtaking them. Had quite

a talk concerning matters on the Red River and our disaster there. He gives an interesting detail. Tells the old story of a multitude of fussy men who accompanied Banks with little carpet-bags filled with greenbacks, etc.

Donald McKay publishes a letter defending the Navy Department from newspaper attacks on the subject of the monitors. It is very well done and unexpected. The *Evening Post* publishes it, and so does the *Times* copy it, but not yet the *Tribune*.

Blair is sore and vexed because the President frequently makes a confidant and adviser of Seward, without consulting the rest of the Cabinet. I told him this had been the course from the beginning; Seward and Chase had each striven for the position of Special Executive Counsel; that it had apparently been divided between them, but Seward had outgeneraled or outintrigued Chase. The latter was often consulted when others were not, but often he was not aware of things which were intrusted to Seward (who was superserviceable) and managed by him.

July 26, *Tuesday.* Fessenden has got out an advertisement for a new loan and an address to the people in its behalf. Am not certain that the latter is judicious. Capitalists will not as a general thing loan or invest for patriotism, but for good returns. The advertisement gives high interest, but accompanied by the appeal will excite doubt, rather than inspire confidence among the money-lenders. I am inclined to think he will get funds, for his plan is sensible and much wiser than anything of his predecessor. The idea with Chase seemed to be to pay low interest in money but high prices in irredeemable paper, a scheme that might have temporary success in getting friends and popularity with speculators but is ruinous to the country. The errors of Chase in this respect Mr. Fessenden seems inclined to correct, but other measures are wanted and I trust we shall have them.

Only Bates, Usher, and myself were at the Cabinet to-day. Stanton sent over to inquire if his attendance was necessary.

There are rumors that the retreating Rebels have turned upon our troops in the valley, and that our forces, badly weakened by the withdrawal of the Sixth Army Corps, are retreating towards Harper's Ferry. This is not improbable. They may have been strengthened as our forces were weakened.

Rode out this evening, accompanied by Mrs. Welles, and spent an hour with the President and Mrs. Lincoln at the Soldiers' Home.

The papers contain a letter from Governor Letcher stating that General Hunter gave the order for burning his (L.'s) house. I shall wish to hear from H. before believing that he could give such an order, and yet I confess I am not without apprehensions, for Hunter is not always possessed of so much prudence as one should have who holds so responsible a position. The burning of the Institute at the same place and time was not creditable to the army, and if there is any justification or ameliorating circumstances, they should be made to appear. The crude and indefensible notions of some of our people, however, are not general. Indiscriminate warfare on all in the insurrectionary region is not general, and few would destroy private property wantonly.

The New York papers are engaged in a covert and systematic attack on the Navy Department, — covert so far as the Republican or Administration press is concerned. Greeley of the *Tribune* is secretly hostile to the President and assails him indirectly in this way; so of the *Evening Post*, a paper hitherto friendly but whose publisher is under bail for embezzlement and fraud which the Navy Department would not conceal. The *Times* is a profligate Seward and Weed organ, wholly unreliable and in these matters regardless of truth or principle. It supports the President because it is the present policy of Seward. The principal editor, Raymond, is an unscrupulous soldier of fortune, yet recently appointed Chairman of the Republican National Executive Committee. He and some of his colleagues are not to be trusted, yet these political vagabonds are the managers of the party organization. His paper, as well as others, are in a combination with Norman Wiard and pretenders like him against the monitors. Let the poor devils work at that question. The people will not be duped or misled to any great extent by them.

There are demonstrations for a new raid into Maryland and Pennsylvania. I told the President I trusted there would be some energy and decision in getting behind them, cutting them off, and not permitting them to go back, instead of a scare and getting forces to drive them back with their plunder. He said those were precisely his views and he had just been to see and say as much to Halleck. I inquired how H. responded to the suggestion. The President said he was considering it, and was now wanting to ascertain where they had crossed the Potomac and the direction they had taken.

I apprehend it is not a large force, but a cavalry raid, which will move rapidly and create alarm. Likely they will go into the Cumberland Valley and then west, for they will scarcely take the old route to return. But these are crude speculations of mine. I get nothing from Halleck, and I doubt if he has any plan, purpose, or suggestion. Before he will come to a conclusion the raiders will have passed beyond his reach.

XXII

The Fiasco at Petersburg — Welles's Lack of Confidence in Grant — Attorney-General Bates's Opinion of the Cabinet and of General Halleck — Assault of Wade and Winter Davis upon the President for omitting to sign a Reconstruction Bill — Sheridan supersedes Hunter on the Upper Potomac — Party Assessments in the Brooklyn Navy Yard — Publication of the Niagara Peace Proceedings — Farragut passes Forts Morgan and Gaines — Count Gurowski and his Published Diary — The New York Press — Depredations by the Tallahassee — Outburst of Seward in the Cabinet — Unsuccessful Peace Proposals at Richmond — The President's Opinion of Greeley — How Farragut was discovered — Du Pont's Intriguing — The Character of Chase — Politics in the Brooklyn Navy Yard — Pressure from Massachusetts in Behalf of the Smith Brothers — Proposed Movement against Wilmington, N. C. — The Navy benefited by the Army Draft — McClellan nominated for President by the Democratic Convention.

August 1, *Monday.* We yesterday had word that our forces had mined and blown up a fortification in front of Petersburg. All sorts of stories were current, some of them absurdly wild and ridiculous. Petersburg was said to be in flames. Our army were reported to have undermined a large portion of the city. Men of sense gave credit to the absurdity. I went over to the War Department, and Stanton showed me a telegram from Grant, stating the mine had been sprung, but the result is inconclusive, and evidently, I think, a disappointment. Stanton seemed uncertain and confused.

Exciting and silly stories prevailed about the raid into Pennsylvania. Street rumors put the Rebels at 40,000, and the press states that number, but reports are contradictory. Am still of the opinion that the force is small and the scare great. Governor Curtin and all Harrisburg are doubtless in a ferment. Was told the bells in Harrisburg were all ringing an alarm. I asked if it included the dinner-bell of Governor Curtin, for he would be frantic to stir up the people, and never disbelieved the largest fib that was sent abroad.

Had a letter from Tom this A.M., dated at Headquarters
of the 18th Army Corps, at midnight of the 29th, stating
an assault was to be made in the morning. Could not give
details. There would be a sharp conflict, and he would do
his duty. Bidding good-bye and sending love to all. This
evening we hear from him after the fight, that he was well
but tired and exhausted.

The President went yesterday to Fortress Monroe to
meet General Grant, by prior arrangement, which made
me distrust final operations at Petersburg, for if such were
the fact, he could not well be absent. The President tells
me the movement was well planned and well executed up
to the closing struggle, when our men failed to do their
duty. There must, I apprehend, have been fault in the
officers also, — not Grant, who originates nothing, is dull
and heavy, but persistent.

August 2, Tuesday. Judge Thomas and Mr. Train, counsel for Smith Brothers of Boston, had an interview of nearly
two hours with me on Saturday, wishing the trial postponed,
a different court, and that the trial should take place in
Boston. They called and were with me half an hour yesterday. Finally arranged that the trial should be postponed four weeks, until Tuesday the 30th, although their
friends had urged a speedy trial, but declined other
changes. Two hours later the President sent for me and
also for Mr. Fox. On going to the Executive Mansion, I
found Messrs. Thomas and Train with the President,
where they had gone over the whole subject that they had
previously discussed with me. The President heard them
kindly and then said he could not act without consulting
me. I remarked that I had given the subject a hearing and
examination, and supposed it was disposed of. The President said he could not interfere, but should be glad if it
could be arranged so as to give them time and also a trial
at Boston.

I wrote a letter to Pickering, Winslow & Co., who, with

certain Bostonians, wish to do something to assist the
blockade. They hardly know what or how.

At the Cabinet, Messrs. Blair, Bates, and myself were
present. Fessenden and Usher are absent. Seward and
Stanton had been there in advance. There is design in all
this. Went over proceedings of the armies at Atlanta and
Petersburg. Stanton dislikes to meet Blair in council,
knowing that B. dislikes and distrusts him. Seward and
Stanton move together in all matters, yet Seward fears a
quarrel with Blair, and he tries to keep in with him and at
the same time preserve his intimacy with Stanton. Both
mouse about the President, who, in his intense interest and
inquisitiveness, spends much of his time at the War Department, watching the telegraph. Of course, opportunities
like these are not lost by Stanton, and, General Halleck
being placed here indorsed by General Scott as the military adviser of the President, he has equal or greater advantages to play the sycophant, and does so.

The explosion and assault at Petersburg on Saturday
last appears to have been badly managed. The results were
bad and the effect has been disheartening in the extreme.
There must have been some defect or weakness on the
part of some one or more. I have been waiting to get the
facts, but do not yet get them to my satisfaction. It is
stated in some of the letters written that lots were cast as
to which corps and which officers should lead in the assault.
I fear there may be truth in the report, but if so, and Grant
was in it or cognizant of it, my confidence in him — never
very great — would be impaired. I should not be surprised to learn that Meade committed such an act, for I do
not consider him adequate to his high position, and yet I
may do him injustice. My personal acquaintance with him
is slight, but he has in no way impressed me as a man of
breadth and strength or capabilities, and instead of selecting and designating the officer for such a duty, it would be
in accordance with my conceptions of him to say, Let any
one, Cast lots, etc., but I shall be reluctant to believe this

of Grant, who is reticent and, I fear, less able than he is credited. He may have given the matter over to Meade, who has done this. Admiral Porter has always said there was something wanting in Grant, which Sherman could always supply, and *vice versa*, as regards Sherman, but that the two together made a very perfect general officer and they ought never to be separated. If Grant is confiding in Meade, — relying on him, as he did on Sherman, — Grant will make a failure, I fear, for Meade is not Sherman, nor the equal of Sherman. Grant relies on others, but does not know men, — can't discriminate. I feel quite unhappy over this Petersburg matter, — less, however, from the result, bad as it is, than from an awakening apprehension that Grant is not equal to the position assigned him. God grant that I may be mistaken, for the slaughtered thousands of my countrymen who have poured out their rich blood for three months on the soil of Virginia from the Wilderness to Petersburg under his generalship can never be atoned in this world or the next if he without Sherman prove a failure. A blight and sadness comes over me like a dark shadow when I dwell on the subject, a melancholy feeling of the past, a foreboding of the future. A nation's destiny almost has been committed to this man, and if it is an improper committal, where are we?

The consequence of the Petersburg failure, and the late successful raid of the Rebels, will embolden them to our injury. They will take courage, keep fewer troops to man their batteries at Richmond, and send more to harass our frontiers, perhaps to strengthen Hood in opposing Thomas and Sherman.

In the mean time, where is Halleck and what is he doing? I hear nothing of him, do not see him. The President goes to advise with him, but I do not think he is ever wiser or better for these interviews.

Seward and Stanton make themselves the special confidants of the President, and they also consult with Halleck, so that the country is in a great degree in the hands of this triumvirate, who, while they have little confidence in each other, can yet combine to control or influence the President, who is honest.

Attorney-General Bates, who spent last evening with me, opened his heart freely as regards the Cabinet. Of Blair he thought pretty well, but said he felt no intimacy with, or really friendly feelings for, any one but me; that I had his confidence and respect, and had from our first meeting. Mr. Seward had been constantly sinking in his estimation; that he had much cunning but little wisdom, was no lawyer and no statesman. Chase, he assures me, is not well versed in law principles even, — is not sound nor of good judgment. General Halleck he had deliberately charged with intentional falsehood and put it in writing, that there should be no mistake or claim to have misapprehended him. He regretted that the President should have such a fellow near him.

August 4, Thursday. This day is set apart for fasting, humiliation, and prayer. There is much wretchedness and great humiliation in the land, and need of earnest prayer.

General Hooker has arrived from Atlanta, having left in a pet because General Howard was given McPherson's position. He is vain, has some good and fighting qualities and thinks highly and too much of himself.

August 5, Friday. Only four of us with the President today. Mr. Fessenden has gone to Maine. Seward and Stanton were absent when the rest were there.

I was with the President on Wednesday when Governor Morgan was there, and the President produced the correspondence that had passed between himself and Chase at the time C. resigned. It was throughout characteristic. I do not think the event was wholly unexpected to either, and yet both were a little surprised. The President fully understands Chase and had made up his mind that he would not be again overridden in his own appointments.

Chase, a good deal ambitious and somewhat presuming, felt he must enforce his determinations, which he had always successfully carried out. In coming to the conclusion that a separation must take place, the President was prompted by some, and sustained by all, his Cabinet without an exception. Chase's retirement has offended nobody, and has gratified almost everybody.

I told Blair as we left the Executive Mansion to-day that I felt depressed in consequence of the result at Petersburg, beyond what I ought from the fight itself, in consequence of impaired confidence in Grant. He tried to encourage me and partially succeeded. I do not distrust or depreciate General G.; but, if he has ability, I think he needs a better second in command, a more competent executive officer than General Meade, and he should have known that fact earlier. The knowledge of the worth of our generals is often purchased at too great a cost of blood and treasure. It is dear tuition.

August 6, *Saturday.* I had a telegram from Tom this morning, stating that Colonel Stedman was mortally wounded and would probably not survive the night, that General Ord desired his promotion without delay, that it might be received before his death, and wishing me to call at once on the President. I did so, who responded readily to the recommendation, and I then, at his request, saw Secretary Stanton, who met me in the right spirit.

While at the President's Blair came in, and the President informed us he had a telegram from Greeley, desiring the publication of the whole peace correspondence. Both Blair and myself advised it, but the President said he had telegraphed Greeley to come on, for he desired him to erase some of the lamentations in his longest letter. I told him while I regretted it was there, the whole had better be published. Blair said it would have to come to that ultimately. But the President thought it better that that part should be omitted.

I remarked that I had seen the Wade and Winter Davis protest. He said, Well, let them wriggle, but it was strange that Greeley, whom they made their organ in publishing the protest, approved his course and therein differed from the protestants. The protest is violent and abusive of the President, who is denounced with malignity for what I deem the prudent and wise omission to sign a law prescribing how and in what way the Union shall be reconstructed. There are many offensive features in the law, which is, in itself, a usurpation and abuse of authority. How or in what way or ways the several States are to put themselves right — retrieve their position — is in the future and cannot well be specified. There must be latitude given, and not a stiff and too stringent policy pursued in this respect by either the Executive or Congress. We have a Constitution, and there is still something in popular government.

In getting up this law it was as much an object of Mr. Winter Davis and some others to pull down the Administration as to reconstruct the Union. I think they had the former more directly in view than the latter. Davis's conduct is not surprising, but I should not have expected that Wade, who has a good deal of patriotic feeling, common sense, and a strong, though coarse and vulgar, mind, would have lent himself to such a despicable assault on the President.

There is, however, an infinity of party and personal intrigue just at this time. A Presidential election is approaching, and there are many aspirants, not only for Presidential but other honors or positions. H. Winter Davis has a good deal of talent but is rash and uncertain. There is scarcely a more ambitious man, and no one that cannot be more safely trusted. He is impulsive and mad and has been acute and contriving in this whole measure and has drawn Wade, who is ardent, and others into it. Sumner, I perceived, was bitten before he left Washington. Whether he has improved I am not informed. Sumner is not a constitutionalist, but more of a centralist than the generality of our people, and would be likely to sanction what seem to me some of the more offensive features of this bill. Consolidating makes it more a government of the people than of the States.

The assaults of these men on the Administration may break it down. They are, in their earnest zeal on the part of some, and ambition and malignity on the part of others, doing an injury that they cannot repair. I do not think Winter Davis is troubled in that respect, or like to be, but I cannot believe otherwise of Wade and others; yet the conduct of Wade for some time past, commencing with the organization of the present Congress in December last, has, after the amnesty proclamation and conciliatory policy of reconstruction, been in some respects strange and difficult to be accounted for, except as an aspiring factionist. I am inclined to believe that he has been bitten with the Presidential fever, is disappointed, and, in his disappointment, with a vague, indefinite hope that he may be successful, prompted and stimulated not only by Davis but Colfax, he has been flattered to do a foolish act.

August 8, Monday. Going into the War Department yesterday morning to inquire if any tidings had been received concerning Colonel Stedman of the 11th Connecticut Infantry, who was wounded, probably mortally, on Friday, I found the President with General Grant, Stanton, and General Halleck in the Secretary's room. I proposed leaving on making the single inquiry, provided they were in secret council, but the President and General Grant declared they were not, for me. Learning that poor Stedman was dead, and that some little intelligence had been received from Mobile, I soon left, for there was, it appeared to me, a little stiffness as if I had interrupted proceedings. General Grant has been to Frederick and placed Sheridan in command of the forces on the upper Potomac instead of Hunter, which is a good change, for H., though violently earnest, is not exactly the man for that command. I think him honest and patriotic, which are virtues in these days, but he has not that discretion and forbearance sufficient to comprehend rightly the position that was given him.

Mr. Seward sent me to-day some strange documents from Raymond, Chairman of the National Executive Committee. I met R. some days since at the President's, with whom he was closeted. At first I did not recognize Raymond, who was sitting near the President conversing in a low tone of voice. Indeed, I did not look at him, supposing he was some ordinary visitor, until the President remarked, "Here he is; it is as good a time as any to bring up the question." I was sitting on the sofa but then went forward and saw it was Raymond. He said there were complaints in relation to the Brooklyn Navy Yard; that we were having, and to have, a hard political battle the approaching fall, and that the fate of two districts and that of King's County also depended upon the Navy Yard. It was, he said, the desire of our friends that the masters in the yard should have the exclusive selection and dismissal of hands, instead of having them subject to revision by the Commandant of the yard. The Commandant himself they wished to have removed. I told him such changes could not well be made and ought not to be made. The present organization of the yard was in a right way, and if there were any abuses I would have them corrected.

He then told me that in attempting to collect a party assessment at the yard, the Naval Constructor had objected, and on appealing to the Commandant, he had expressly forbidden the collection. This had given great dissatisfaction to our party friends, for these assessments had always been made and collected under preceding administrations. I told him I doubted if it had been done, — certainly not in such an offensive and public manner; that I thought it very wrong for a party committee to go into the yard on pay-day and levy a tax on each man as he received his wages for party purposes; that I was aware parties did strange things in New York, but there was no

2

law or justice in it, and the proceeding was, in my view, inexcusable and indefensible; that I could make no record enforcing such assessment; that the matter could not stand investigation. He admitted that the course pursued was not a politic one, but he repeated former administrations had practiced it. I questioned it still, and insisted that it was not right in itself. He said it doubtless might be done in a more quiet manner. I told him if obnoxious men, open and offensive opponents of the Administration, were there, they could be dismissed. If the Commandant interposed to sustain such men, as he suggested might be the case, there was an appeal to the Department; whatever was reasonable and right I was disposed to do. We parted, and I expected to see him again, but, instead of calling himself, he has written Mr. Seward, who sent his son with the papers to me. In these papers a party committee propose to take the organization of the navy yard into their keeping, to name the Commandant, to remove the Naval Constructor, to change the regulations, and make the yard a party machine for the benefit of party, and to employ men to elect candidates instead of building ships. I am amazed that Raymond could debase himself so far as to submit such a proposition, and more that he expects me to enforce it.

The President, in a conversation with Blair and myself on the Wade and Davis protest, remarked that he had not, and probably should not read it. From what was said of it he had no desire to, could himself take no part in such a controversy as they seemed to wish to provoke. Perhaps he is right, provided he has some judicious friend to state to him what there is really substantial in the protest entitled to consideration without the vituperative asperity.

The whole subject of what is called reconstruction is beset with difficulty, and while the executive has indicated one course and Congress another, a better and different one than either may be ultimately pursued. I think the President would have done well to advise with his whole Cabinet in the measures he has adopted, not only as to reconstruction or reëstablishing the Union, but as to this particular bill and the proclamation he has issued in regard to it.

When the Rebellion shall have been effectually suppressed, the Union government will be itself again, — reunion will speedily follow in the natural course of events, — but there are those who do not wish or intend reunion on the principle of political equality of the States. Unless they can furnish the mode and terms, and for fear they may not be successful, various schemes are projected.

The issuing of the proclamation with reasons for not signing the bill, and yet expressing his acquiescence in the policy if any of the States adopt it, is denounced as anomalous; so is the condition of the country, and so will be reunion, whenever and however it may take place. I have never asked who was the adviser and counsellor of the President in issuing the proclamation. It is sufficient that I was not. There is one who was, and how many more is not material. There may have been one, possibly two, but the project is wholly the President's.

August 9, Tuesday. At the Cabinet to-day there was no special business. Seward and Stanton were not present. Mr. Fessenden is absent in Maine. Governor Hahn of Louisiana was present a short time.

Alluding to the Niagara peace proceedings, the President expressed a willingness that all should be published. Greeley had asked it, and when I went into the President's room Defrees[1] was reading the proof of the correspondence. I have advised its entire publication from the first moment I had knowledge of it. Whether it was wise or expedient for the President to have assented to Greeley's appeal, or given his assent to any such irregular proceedings, is another thing, not necessary to discuss. Mr. Seward was consulted in this matter, and no other one was called in that I am aware. Mr. Fessenden says he happened, accidentally

[1] John D. Defrees, the government printer.

and uninvited, tô come in and was knowing to it. No other member of the Cabinet was consulted, or advised with, until after the meeting took place at Niagara.

Fox left this P.M. for his annual vacation in New Hampshire. Faxon returned last Wednesday. The absence of either of them makes my duties more arduous.

General Averill is reported to have thrashed the raiders on the upper Potomac.

News of Farragut's having passed Forts Morgan and Gaines was received last night, and sent a thrill of joy through all true hearts. It is not, however, appreciated as it should be by the military. The President, I was sorry, spoke of it as important because it would tend to relieve Sherman. This is the narrow view of General Halleck, whom I tried to induce to make a joint demonstration against Mobile one year ago. He has done nothing new and only speaks of the naval achievement as a step for the army. While I regard the acts and opinions of Halleck as of little worth, I regret that from constant daily intercourse he should be able to imbue the President at times with false and erroneous notions. Halleck never awarded honest credit to the Navy; the President never knowingly deprived them of any merit. Yet I have mentioned the result.

Passing from the Executive Mansion to the Navy Department, I met the Count Gurowski, a Polish exile and a very singular man of most unhappy manners and temper. He has made himself obnoxious to almost everybody by constant and everlasting faultfinding and denunciation of almost everybody. Yet he has a strong but fragmentary mind with quite a retentive memory. Violent, self-opinionated, acrimonious, dissatisfied, he nevertheless has had great experience and often expresses opinions on questions that have passed and been disposed of that are sound and striking. They are, however, rather reminiscences of the opinions of others, reflections of their views, than original thoughts on his part. At least, such have been my conclusions of him. So far as I can judge, he has no proper discriminating powers, no just perceptions of character, is a creature of violent impulses and hatreds. Easily flattered, and as easily offended. A rough, uncouth bear, with no nice sense of honor, and when his prejudices are enlisted, has not a very great regard for truth, I fear.

He has just put out two volumes of a diary, in horrid style and bad English, commenting with great freedom on men and things, abusing in clumsy language almost all public characters. It so happens that I am one of the few that have escaped his assaults, without ever having courted favor, or, it seems, offended him. But shortly after the appearance of the last volume, a party was given by me to the Cabinet and to Congress. All my associates except Stanton he had coarsely abused and very many of the members. I did not think proper to invite the Count to meet these men, and he has exhibited unmistakable rage and disgust at the supposed slight. Of course, no cause of offense having been given, there is no way of appeasing this Polish bear. I have, therefore, not attempted it nor noticed his indignation. Meeting him to-day, as I have stated, he saw and recognized me, seemed to be embarrassed and to hesitate, then dropped his head and, turning off when within about fifty feet, he went far around, with his head bent over, shame and passion in his countenance. Poor Gurowski!

August 10, *Wednesday*. The tidings this evening from Mobile, derived from the Rebels, are satisfactory. It is stated that the Tecumseh was sunk by Fort Morgan's guns. I discredit this. She may have grounded or she may have encountered a torpedo; but most likely it was one of the river boats, though they, being of light draft, would be less likely to keep the channel and encounter the obstructions and torpedoes. If the guns of Fort Morgan sunk an ironclad, it was doubtless one of the river monitors.

August 11, *Thursday.* The papers speak of a violent altercation between Blair and Stanton on Tuesday in Cabinet. It so happened that Stanton was not present with Blair. I do not believe that the two have interchanged words for weeks. There never was cordiality between them. It is also stated that three or four members of the Cabinet have resigned. Stanton, it is said with some earnestness, and reasserted, has tendered his resignation. There is no truth in any of these rumors, — not a shadow to build upon. If Stanton ever, at any time or under any circumstances, has spoken in whisper to the President of resigning, he did not mean it, for he would be, I think, one of the very last to quit, and never except on compulsion. I have little doubt that Blair would leave to-morrow, provided he could carry Stanton out with him and he could be got out in no other way.

August 12, *Friday.* This has been one of the warmest and most uncomfortable days of the season. For several days the weather has been extremely warm. A telegram from New York to-day said that ice could not be procured so rapidly as was wanted for the steamer to proceed to the squadron at Mobile to relieve the wounded and sick. I directed them to seize if necessary. Delay is not admissible at such a time.

Have news this evening that a new pirate craft, the Tallahassee, has appeared off New York, burning vessels. Steamers ordered off in pursuit.

Stanton not at the Cabinet. Had undoubtedly seen the President and Seward in advance, done his errand, and got away before Blair arrived. Fessenden has not yet returned.

August 13, *Saturday.* Had some talk with Senator Lot Morrill, who is a good deal excited, not to say alarmed. The slow progress of our armies, the mismanagement of military affairs exemplified in the recent raids, the factious and discontented spirit manifested by Wade, Winter

Davis, and others, have generated a feeling of despondency in which he participates. Others express to me similar feelings.

There is no doubt a wide discouragement prevails, from the causes adverted to, and others which have contributed. A want of homogeneity exists among the old Whigs, who are distrustful and complaining. It is much more natural for them to denounce than to approve, — to pull down than to build up. Their leaders and their followers, to a considerable extent, have little confidence in themselves or their cause, and hence it is a ceaseless labor with them to assail the Administration of which they are professed supporters.

The worst specimens of these wretched politicians are in New York City and State, though they are to be found everywhere. There is not an honest, fair-dealing Administration journal in New York City. A majority of them profess to be Administration, and yet it is without sincerity. The *New York Herald* with a deservedly bad name, gives tone and direction to the New York press, particularly those of Whig antecedents and which profess to support the Administration. It is not, of course, acknowledged by them, nor are they conscious of the leadership, but it is nevertheless obvious and clear. When the *Herald* has in view to defame or put a mark upon a man, it commences and persists in its course against him. He may be the friend of the *Tribune* and *Times*. Of course, they do not at first assent to what is said by the *Herald*. Sometimes they will make a defense, — perhaps an earnest and strong one, — but the *Herald* does not regard it and goes on attacking, ridiculing, abusing, and defaming. Gradually one of the journals gives way, echoes slightly the slanders of the *Herald*, and having once commenced, it follows up the work. The other journals, when things have proceeded to that length, also acquiesce. This is a truthful statement of the standing and course and conduct of the papers I have named.

The *Times* is a stipendiary sheet; its principal editor, Raymond, mercenary, possessing talent but a subservient follower of Weed and Seward. At present, the paper being in the hands of Thurlow Weed and *sic*, it will not for the campaign openly attack the President, who is the candidate. But it will, under the lead of the *Herald*, attack any and every member of the Cabinet but Seward, unless Seward through Weed restrains him.

The *Tribune* is owned by a company which really desired to give a fair support to the Administration, but Greeley, the editor, is erratic, unreliable, without stability, an enemy of the Administration because he hates Seward, a creature of sentiment or impulse, not of reason nor professed principle. Having gone to extremes in the measures that fermented and brought on this war, he would now go to extremes to quell it. I am prepared to see him acquiesce in a division of the Union, or the continuance of slavery, to accomplish his personal party schemes. There are no men or measures to which he will adhere faithfully. He is ambitious, talented, but not considerate, persistent, or profound.

The *Evening Post* is a journal of a different description and still retains some of its former character for ability and sense. Bryant, I am inclined to believe, means well, and of himself would do well. But he is getting on in years, and his son-in-law Godwin attempts to wield the political bludgeon. In him the mercenary and unscrupulous partisan is apparent. I was compelled to expose Henderson, the publisher, for malfeasance, and the commission before whom he was arraigned held him to bail for embezzlement. The *Post* blackguarded the witness, and Godwin said that if the Navy Department could afford to do without the *Evening Post*, the *Evening Post* could afford to do without the Navy Department. This Colonel Olcott tells me Godwin said to Wilson, the attorney for the Department.

These are the Administration journals in the city of New

York. Thurlow Weed has control of the *Evening Journal* of Albany and to a considerable extent of the press of the State of Whig antecedents. He is sagacious, unscrupulous, has ability and great courage, with little honest principle, is fertile in resources, a keen party tactician, but cannot win respect and confidence, for he does not deserve them. For some time past he has been ingratiating himself with the Copperhead journals and leaders, and by his skill has made fools of their editors, but I apprehend has not fooled their leading managers. He evidently believes, not without reason, he is using them; they know they are using him; to some extent each may deceive the other. There is a feigned difference between him and Seward, or there has been, but no one is misled by it. Weed is indispensable to Seward and the master mind of the two. This is as well known to the Copperhead leaders as to any persons. Recently Weed has been here and has had interviews with the President, to what purpose, whether of his own volition or by invitation, I have never inquired. I have noticed that Seward endeavors to impress on the President the value of Weed's opinion, especially in party matters.

August 15, *Monday*. Depredations by the piratical Rebel Tallahassee continue. We have sixteen vessels in pursuit, and yet I feel no confidence in their capturing her. It is so easy to elude the pursuit of the most vigilant — and many in command are not vigilant — that it will not surprise me if she escapes. Should that be the case, the Navy Department will alone be held responsible. I am already censured in some of the papers for not having vessels, two or three, cruising at the time she appeared. Had that been the case we could not have communicated with them when we received intelligence, but, being in port, several were at once dispatched in pursuit. I find I have become very indifferent to the senseless complaints of the few loud grumblers.

From Mobile Bay the news continues favorable. Had

Farragut's preliminary dispatch of the 5th to-day. Have just written a congratulatory letter to him. These letters are difficult to pen. They must be brief and comprehensive, satisfactory to the Navy, the Government, and country, and not discreditable to the Department.

August 16, *Tuesday.* Have been compelled to advise the Treasury that their management and delay is destroying the public credit. Men will not contract with the government if in violation of good faith they are kept out of their pay for months after it is due. Mr. Fessenden has not yet returned.

At the Cabinet-meeting to-day Mr. Seward inquired of me in relation to some captured cotton claimed by the French. I told him I had no recollection of it, but, if a naval capture, it had been sent to the courts for adjudication. This, he said, would not answer his purpose. If they had no business to capture it, the French would not be satisfied. I remarked that neither would the courts, who, and not the State or Navy Departments, had exclusive jurisdiction and control of the matter; it was for the judiciary to decide whether the capture was good prize, and whether, if not good prize, there was probable cause, and to award damages if there had been a flagrant wrong committed.

As Mr. Seward has no knowledge of admiralty or maritime law or of prize proceedings, I was not displeased that Mr. Bates took up the matter and inquired by what authority he or the Executive Department of the government attempted to interfere with a matter that was in court. Seward attempted to reply, but the Attorney-General was so clearly right, and Seward was so conscious of his inability to controvert the law officer, that he flew into a violent rage and traversed the room, said the Attorney-General had better undertake to administer the State Department, that he wanted to keep off a war, he had kept off wars, but he could not do it if he was to be thwarted and denied informa-

tion. I told him he would have all the information we had
on the subject, but it was no less clear that until the judicial remedies were exhausted there should be no Executive
interference, no resort to diplomacy or negotiations.

It was to me a painful exhibition of want of common intelligence as to his duties. He evidently supposes that his
position is one of unlimited and unrestrained power, that
he can override the courts and control and direct their action, that a case of prize he can interfere with and withdraw if he pleases. All his conversation exhibited such
utter ignorance of his own duties and those of the court in
these matters that one could scarcely credit it as possible.
But it has been so through his whole administration of the
State Department.

My impression was, on witnessing his outbreak and
hearing his remarks, that, having the senatorship in view,
he was proposing to leave the Cabinet, and I am by no
means certain that he has not some thoughts of such a
step, — men aspiring for office often have strange fancies,
— and, in his wild fancy and confidence in the ability and
management of his friend Weed, thinks that he can indorse him into the Chicago Convention a fortnight hence.
This last I do not suppose, and yet there is design in what
took place. "There were," said he, "twenty-eight Senators
who undertook to expel me from the Cabinet, but they did
not succeed. I have been here to keep the peace and I have
done it so far. You," turning to the Attorney-General,
"may get another and have war," etc., etc., etc.

August 17, *Wednesday.* I wrote a letter to the Secretary
of State, softly pointing out the proper course of proceeding
in this French claim for captured cotton, for I should be
sorry to have him let down himself and the Government.
But I know not how, having taken charge of this claim, he
will receive it. I think, however, he will show his shrewdness and tact and take the hint, if he has not committed
himself, as he often does, without being aware of the effect.

Had quite a talk to-day with Mr. Lenthall, Naval Constructor, on the subject of the light-draft monitors and
his duties generally. He claims to know but little about
them. I told him this would not answer, that I should hold
him responsible for what pertained to his bureau; that it
was his duty to criticize, and let me know what, in his
opinion was wrong; that it was his duty to know, and he
must not plead ignorance to me; that on important matters
I did not want his views second-handed, but he must come
to me direct. From what I could learn in relation to the
light-draft vessels, I had come to the conclusion that,
while I had trusted to him, he had mere superficial conversations with Mr. Fox, without seeing or advising with me,
and I apprehended Fox and Stimers had been going on
without consulting others, with confident belief they would
give us very superior vessels, until they awoke to the fact
that they were not Naval Constructors or the men to do
this work, except under the advice and direction of experts.
I had supposed until last spring that Lenthall and Ericsson
were giving the light ironclads their attention, but I found
they were not, and I had not been advised of the fact. My
plain talk seemed to astonish, and yet not altogether dis-
please Lenthall. He said he had no doubt Mr. Fox and Mr.
Stimers had committed the great mistake I alluded to.
They thought after submitting their plans to him, without,
however, procuring from him any computations, but an
expression, that struck him more favorably than Ericsson
that they could show off something for themselves that
would give them a name.

Fred Seward called on me with a letter from Raymond
to his father inquiring whether anything had been effected
at the navy yard and custom-house, stating the elections
were approaching, means were wanted, Indiana was just
now calling most urgently for pecuniary aid. I told Seward
that I knew not what the navy yard had to do with all
this, except that there had been an attempt to levy an assessment on all workmen, as I understood, when receiving

their monthly pay of the paymaster, by a party committee who stationed themselves near his desk in the yard and attempted the exaction; that I was informed Commodore Paulding forbade the practice, and I certainly had no censure to bestow on him for the interdiction. If men choose to contribute at their homes, or out of the yards, I had no idea that he would object, but if he did and I could know the fact, I would see such interference promptly corrected; but I could not consent to forced party contributions. Seward seemed to consider this view correct and left.

I am sadly oppressed with the aspect of things. Have just read the account of the interview at Richmond between Jaquess and Gilmore on one side and Jeff Davis and Benjamin on the other.[1] What business had these fellows with such a subject? Davis asserts an ultimatum that is inadmissible, and the President in his note, which appears to me not as considerate and well-advised as it should have been, interposes barriers that were unnecessary. Why should we impose conditions, and conditions which would provoke strife from the very nature of things, for they conflict with constitutional reserved rights? If the Rebellion is suppressed in Tennessee or North Carolina, and the States and people desire to resume their original constitutional rights, shall the President prevent them? Yet the letters to Greeley have that bearing, and I think them unfortunate in this respect.

They place the President, moreover, at disadvantage in the coming election. He is committed, it will be claimed, against peace, except on terms that are inadmissible. What necessity was there for this, and, really, what right had the President to assume this unfortunate attitude without consulting his Cabinet, at least, or others? He did, he says, advise with Seward, and Fessenden, who came in

[1] An account of the interview of Colonel James F. Jaquess and Mr. James R. Gilmore with the President of the Confederacy and his Secretary of State, written by Mr. Gilmore, appeared in the *Atlantic Monthly* for September, 1864.

accidentally, also gave it his sanction. Now Seward is a trickster more than a statesman. He has wanted to get an advantage over Horace Greeley, and when the President said to Greeley, therefore, that no terms which did not include the abolition of slavery as one of the conditions [would be admissible], a string in Greeley's harp was broken. But how it was to affect the Union and the great ends of peace seems not to have been considered. The Cabinet were not consulted, except the two men as named, one, if not both, uninvited, nor as regarded Jaquess and Gilmore in their expedition. It will be said that the President does not refuse other conditions, and that he only said "to whom it may concern" he would make peace with those conditions, but that he does not refuse different and modified conditions to others. (It was undoubtedly an adroit party movement on the part of the President that rebuked and embarrassed Greeley and defeated a wily intrigue.) But, after all, I should, even with this interpretation, wish the President not to be mixed up with such a set, and not to have this ambiguity, to say the least. Most of the world will receive it as a distinct ultimatum.

August 18, *Thursday.* Mr. Seward brought me this A.M. a dispatch from Consul Jackson at Halifax, saying the pirate Rebel Tallahassee had arrived at that port. I had on Sunday morning last, the 14th, sent orders to Commodore Paulding to immediately dispatch the San Jacinto, then just arrived at New York and in quarantine, to proceed to Halifax, anticipating that the pirate craft would go thither for coal. The Commodore on the same day sent me a dispatch that orders had been given the San Jacinto to proceed to sea, and a second telegram, received that evening, said she would pass through the Sound. When, therefore, I to-day got word that the Tallahassee was in Halifax, I thought the San Jacinto should be there. I immediately inquired at what time she had sailed, that I might calculate with some certainty. This evening I have a telegram from Captain Case, Executive Officer, Brooklyn Yard, that the San Jacinto has not yet sailed but was coaled and ready and would proceed in the morning. I know not when I have been more disappointed and astonished, and I have just written for an explanation. It cannot have been otherwise than there was inattention and neglect, for there could have been no purpose or design to defeat my orders. But the sin — which is great, and almost inexcusable — of this neglect will fall on me, and not on the guilty parties. They have defeated my plans and expectations, and I shall be assailed and abused by villainous partisans for it.

I trust some of the officers who have been sent in pursuit will have the perseverance and zeal to push on to Halifax, yet I have my apprehensions. They lack persistency. Not one of them is a Farragut, or Foote, or Porter, I fear. But we will see.

I have ordered the Pontoosuc, which is at Bangor, to proceed immediately to Halifax, and trust she will get there. The Merrimac is somewhere on the Banks and may fall in with the Tallahassee. Budd, who commands the Merrimac, will prove an ugly customer for the pirate, if he falls in with him.

August 19, *Friday*. Much pressed with duties. A pleasant hour at the Cabinet, but no special subject. Fessenden still absent. Stanton did not attend. Blair inquired about the Niagara peace correspondence. The President went over the particulars. Had sent the whole correspondence to Greeley for publication, excepting one or two passages in Greeley's letters which spoke of a bankrupted country and awful calamities. But Greeley replied he would not consent to any suppression of his letters or any part of them; and the President remarked that, though G. had put him (the President) in a false attitude, he thought it better he should bear it, than that the country should be distressed by such a howl, from such a person, on such an occasion. Concerning Greeley, to whom the President has

clung too long and confidingly, he said to-day that Greeley
is an old shoe, — good for nothing now, whatever he has
been. "In early life, and with few mechanics and but little
means in the West, we used," said he, "to make our shoes
last a great while with much mending, and sometimes, when
far gone, we found the leather so rotten the stitches would
not hold. Greeley is so rotten that nothing can be done
with him. He is not truthful; the stitches all tear out."

Both Blair and myself concurred in regret that the President should consult only Seward in so important a matter, and that he should dabble with Greeley, Saunders, and
company. But Blair expresses to me confidence that the
President is approaching the period when he will cast off
Seward as he has done Chase. I doubt it. That he may
relieve himself of Stanton is possible, though I see as yet
no evidence of it. To me it is clear that the two S.'s have an
understanding, and yet I think each is wary of the other
while there is a common purpose to influence the President.
The President listens and often defers to Seward, who is
ever present and companionable. Stanton makes himself
convenient, and is not only tolerated but, it appears to me,
is really liked as a convenience.

Seward said to-day that Mr. Raymond, Chairman of
the National Executive Committee, had spoken to him
concerning the Treasury, the War, the Navy, and the
Post-Office Departments connected with the approaching
election; that he had said to Mr. Raymond that he had
better reduce his ideas to writing, and he had sent him
certain papers; but that he, Seward, had told him it
would be better, or that he thought it would be better, to
call in some other person, and he had therefore sent for
Governor Morgan, who would be here, he presumed, on
Monday. All which means an assessment is to be laid on
certain officials and employees of the government for party
purposes. Likely the scheme will not be as successful as
anticipated, for the depreciation of money has been such
that neither can afford to contribute. Good clerks are

somewhat indifferent about remaining, and so with mechanics. I cannot, for one, consent to be an instrument in this business, and I think they must go elsewhere for funds. To a great extent the money so raised is misused, misapplied, and perverted and prostituted. A set of harpies and adventurers pocket a large portion of the money extorted. It is wanted now for Indiana, a State which has hosts of corrupt and mischievous political partisans who take to themselves large pay for professed party services without contributing anything themselves.

August 20, *Saturday.* My sons Edgar and John got home this morning from a visit to Connecticut. Have word that the Pontoosuc arrived at Halifax about four hours after the Tallahassee had sailed, — having been ordered off by the authorities. This warning was not, however, until she had got more than half the coal she wanted, and, I am suspicious, after a knowledge of the fact that the Pontoosuc was on its way to Halifax, for the order of the Department to the Pontoosuc was sent to Bangor by open telegraph, not in cipher.

I yesterday wrote a rebuke to Paulding in relation to the neglect in sending forward the San Jacinto, also for omitting to send me a copy of instructions, and also for not advising me of the return of the Grand Gulf and the Eolus, by telegraph. All was lazily sent by mail. On sending to him to at once send out the Grand Gulf again, I am informed her engines are taken to pieces and it will require two days to get her ready. Among the commanders there has been, as I apprehended, an indifference that is discreditable. Several of them were on the track of the pirate, fell in with the wrecks and floating cargoes of his victims, and, with an eye to salvage, then turned about and returned. These fellows will never wear an admiral's flag on the active list, or command a squadron in time of war.

As I expected, the papers — particularly the Administration papers in New York — are very abusive of me be-

2

cause the Tallahassee is not captured. The blame is thrown entirely on the Department, no censure on the officers who were negligent in obeying orders. On the other hand, not one word of commendation is given by these journals to the Department for the success at Mobile. Such is the justice and intelligence of miserable partisans and an unscrupulous partisan press.

August 22, *Monday.* Mr. Fessenden returned yesterday, — a long absence for such a period as this. The course pursued at the Treasury Department in withholding money from the naval contractors for months after it is due is reprehensible and injurious in the highest degree to the public credit. Mr. F. is not responsible for this wrong. It was the work of Chase, who, in order to retire his interest-bearing notes, seized the money which legitimately belonged to the naval contractors to the amount of $12,000,000. As a consequence we shall lose some of our best contractors, who feel there is bad faith and no dependence on the government.

Some of the contractors for light-draft monitors are writing pressing letters. If disposed to act fairly, they should be promptly met; but if attempting to take advantage of our necessities, we must see that the public suffers no detriment.

Olcott, the detective, sends me a curious letter of E. Delafield Smith, with a not less curious indorsement by Olcott. Smith thinks the transactions of his office have been scrutinized and asks Olcott. O. inquires of me how he shall answer.

August 23, *Tuesday.* Received dispatches to-day from Admiral Farragut confirming intelligence received several days since through Rebel sources. The official account confirms my own previous impressions in regard to operations. Secretary Stanton in one of his bulletins represented that Fort Gaines had surrendered to General Granger and the army. It is shown that the proposition of Colonel Anderson, who commanded the fort, was to surrender to the fleet after the monitors had made an assault, that Admiral Farragut consulted with General Granger, that the terms were dictated from the squadron, that Colonel Anderson and Major Brown went on board the Admiral's vessel when the arrangement was consummated, etc.

Why should the Secretary of War try to deprive an officer like Farragut and the naval force of what is honestly their due? It is only one of many like occurrences during the War. I do not recollect a single instance of generous award to the Navy by Stanton or Halleck. Some will doubtless get in error by it, but I think the country mainly rightly appreciates it, and history may put all right. Not the history of this day and period; a generation at least must pass away before the errors, prejudices, and perversion of partisans will be dissipated, and the true facts be developed. I have had but brief opportunities to look into the so-called histories of the great events now passing, but the cursory examination which I have given let me see mountains of error, and much of it, I am sorry to say, was not unintentional on the part of the writers. Facts were made or worked to suit the partialities or prejudices of the person who professed to record them. Many in this day who read and hear of the capture of New Orleans believe it · was taken by General Butler and the army, who were a hundred miles distant when the city surrendered, and it is obviously the purpose of the Secretary of War to so spread such an impression in regard to the capture of Fort Gaines, so that the Navy shall not have the credit.

It does not surprise nor grieve me that another and different class — the intense partisan — should wholly ignore the Navy Department in all naval victories. No word of credit is awarded us by them for the late achievement, yet I know the people are not wholly ignorant on the subject. Some of the more thoughtful will appreciate the labor and responsibility devolving on those who prepared the work,

and furnished the means for the work in hand. Some credit
is due for the selection of Farragut in the first instance.
Mervine had been first assigned to command the blockade
in the Gulf. I found when organizing the squadron at the
commencement of the Rebellion that there was pressure
and claim of usage for the senior officers. Many who were
counted best had seceded and proved traitors. My thoughts
turned to Gregory for that command, but Paulding, who
was then the detailing officer, persuaded me to take Mervine. It was a mistake. Gregory is infinitely the better
man. A few months satisfied me that Mervine, a worthy
man doubtless, was good for nothing as an officer for such
duties as the times required, and he was detached. He and
his friends were greatly miffed and wanted a court of inquiry. Anxious to secure an efficient man for his successor,
I consulted many and scrutinized carefully. The choice
was eventually narrowed down to two, McKean and C. H.
Bell. Foote, whom I consulted with others, after much
hesitation inclined me to McKean, of whom I thought well
from his promptness and patriotism immediately on his return from Japan in the Niagara. He was certainly an improvement on Mervine, but yet not the man, I was soon
convinced, — partly from ill health, — for the work that
was wanted.

When the expedition to New Orleans was determined
upon, the question as to who should have command of the
naval forces became a subject of grave and paramount importance. I had heard that Farragut resided in Norfolk at
the beginning of the troubles, but that he abandoned the
place when Virginia seceded and had taken up his residence
in the city of New York. The fact interested me. I had known
something of him in Polk's administration, and his early
connection with Commodore Porter was in his favor. All
that I heard of him was to his credit as a capable, energetic,
and determined officer, of undoubted loyalty. Admirals
Joe Smith and Shubrick spoke well of him. The present
Admiral D. D. Porter, who, with others, was consulted,

DAVID GLASGOW FARRAGUT

expressed confidence in him, and as Porter himself was to take a conspicuous part in the expedition, it had an important influence. But among naval officers there was not a united opinion. Most of them, I think, while speaking well of Farragut, doubted if he was equal to the position, — certainly not so well appointed a man as others, — but yet no one would name the man for a great and active campaign against Mobile or some other point. They knew not of New Orleans. After the question was decided, and, I believe, after Fox and D. D. Porter both wrote Farragut unofficially of his probable selection to command the new Gulf Squadron, I was cautioned in regard to the step I was taking. Senator Hale, when he learned the fact, asked me if I was certain of my man, — Southern born, a Southern resident, with a Southern wife, etc. Several Members of Congress questioned me closely; few knew Farragut, who had not then carved out a great name, and there was, I became conscious, a general impression or doubt whether I had not made a mistake. I will not follow the subject here. His works speak for themselves, and I am satisfied the selection was a proper one, probably the very best that could be made.

At that time Du Pont was in favor, almost a favorite. He had sought to be, or his friends had sought to have him, transferred to Washington to take the place of Paulding. Seward proposed it, and thought Paulding might be otherwise provided for, suggesting the navy yard at Philadelphia or Brooklyn, or a squadron. I did not assent to the arrangement, and the President, who saw I had some feeling on the subject, concurred with me emphatically. Seward said the subject had been brought to him by Winter Davis, — in other words, Du Pont.

I did not then, as I do now, know thoroughly either Davis or Du Pont. It was a skillful intrigue, yet it did not succeed. But the blockade, requiring a close and minute hydrographical knowledge of the coast, brought me in contact with Mr. Bache of the Coast Survey. Mr. Bache sought to make our acquaintance personal and intimate, and but for my unremitting and ceaseless devotion to pressing current duties I should have fully responded. But I had not time. I think he saw and appreciated it, and he intimated, not exactly proposed, a board to take up the subject of our Southern coast, its channels, approaches, inlets, and defenses in detail, and report to me. It struck me favorably, and Du Pont was put upon that board with him, was brought to Washington, and commenced forming a clique while reporting on the surveys of the coast. He moved with great skill, and I, being unsuspicious, was, I can perceive, to some extent deceived. But I think the ill success of the intrigue of H. Winter Davis and himself through Seward led Du Pont to the conclusion that he would not be likely to make head against me during this administration. He therefore changed his tactics, became greatly friendly and profoundly respectful, designing, if he could, to use me. To some extent he did so. Old Admiral Shubrick was his relative and patron. Mr. Fox was devoted to him, and I listened much to Fox as well as to Shubrick. Admiral Paulding, then here, was kindly disposed, as detailing officer, to second Du Pont, and Admiral Davis was his shadow. Of course with such surroundings, and with Du Pont himself, who became friendly, I think truly friendly, and almost deferential, I yielded much to his wishes and recommendations. It was early arranged that he should have a squadron to effect a lodgment at some port on the South Atlantic. Fernandina was much thought of, but Port Royal and Bull's Bay were mentioned. A division of the Atlantic Squadron, then commanded by Admiral Stringham, became indispensable, and Stringham himself, having taken offense, unwisely, at some order issued in my absence, proposed to resign just as the subject of dividing the squadron was taken up, which made the way clear for Du Pont. He took the Navy Register and made to a great extent his selection of officers. It was a Du Pont squadron emphatically. Poor Mercer, who had been his devoted friend, was detached from the Wabash, which was made Du Pont's flag-ship, and died of a broken heart. But neither Farragut nor David D. Porter were within the charmed circle. Du Pont had some jealousy, I saw, of Porter, but none of Farragut. I do not remember to have ever heard a complimentary remark of F. from Du Pont, but he evidently considered him a fair fighting officer, of ordinary standing, — not one of the élite, not of the Du Pont Navy. Of Porter he entertained a higher opinion, but he was no favorite, and, without any charge against him, I was given to understand that he was a troublesome fellow. . . .

August 24, *Wednesday*. A comparatively quiet day. The consul at Halifax is telegraphing me that Rebel armed vessels are soon to be off the coast. He does not give me his authority nor any facts. Such apprehensions are constantly being expressed by the Northern Governors and municipal authorities every season. I shall not be surprised if there is some foundation for this. At all events, have sent orders to be prepared.

August 25, *Thursday*. Most of the vessels sent out in pursuit of the Tallahassee have returned, and with scarcely an exception the commanders have proved themselves feeble and inefficient. Imputations of drunkenness and of disloyalty or of Rebel sympathy are made against some of them. As usual, there may be exaggerations, but there is some truth in some of the reports.

Calling on the President near eleven o'clock, I went in as usual unannounced, the waiter throwing open the door as I approached. I found Messrs. Seward, Fessenden, and Stanton with Raymond, Chairman of the Executive National Committee, in consultation with the President. The President was making some statement as to a document of his, and said he supposed his style was peculiar and had its earmarks, so that it could not be mistaken. He kept on talking as if there had been no addition to the company, and as if I had been expected and belonged there. But the topic was not pursued by the others when the President ceased. Some inquiry was put to me in regard to intelligence from the fleet at Mobile and the pursuit of the Tallahassee. Mr. Fessenden rose and, putting his mouth to the ear of the President, began to whisper, and as soon as I could answer the brief inquiries, I left the room.

It was easy to perceive that Seward, Stanton, and Raymond were disconcerted by my appearance. Except the whispering by Fessenden I saw nothing particular on his part. It appeared to me he was being trained into a process. Stanton, with whom he seems to have a sort of sympathy, is evidently used as an intermediate by Seward to make them (Seward and Fessenden) friends, and this gathering I could easily read and understand, although it may be difficult to describe the manner, etc., which made it clear to me.

The Democrats hold a party nominating convention next Monday at Chicago, which is naturally attracting a good deal of attention. There is a palpable effort to give éclat, and spread abroad a factitious power for this assemblage in advance. To this the Administration journals, and particularly those of New York, have conduced. I do not think that anything serious is to be apprehended from that convention, if Seward can keep quiet; but his management, which is mismanagement, and his shrewdness, which is frequently untowardness, will ever endanger a cause.

I hear little of Chase, though I doubt not that his aspirations are unextinguished. That he is disappointed because his retirement made so little sensation and has been so readily acquiesced in, I have no doubt. I have heard that he had written a friend here to the effect that it was expedient, under the circumstances, to support Lincoln, although he had many dislikes to the man and his policy. But I am assured he has an expectation, sometimes amounting to confidence, that Frémont will ultimately be withdrawn and that there will then be union and harmony. I

can believe most of this. Chase has a good deal of intellect,
knows the path where duty points, and in his calmer moments, resolves to pursue it. But, with a mind of considerable resources, he has great weaknesses in craving aspiration which constantly impair his strength. He has inordinate ambition, intense selfishness for official distinction
and power to do for the country, and considerable vanity.
These traits impair his moral courage; they make him a
sycophant with the truly great, and sometimes arrogant
towards the humble. The society of the former he courts,
for he has mental culture and appreciation, but his political
surroundings are the mean, the abject, the adulators and
cormorants who pander to his weaknesses. That he is irresolute and wavering, his instinctive sagacity prompting
him rightly, but his selfish and vain ambition turning him
to error, is unquestionably true. I have little doubt, however, that he will, eventually, when satisfied that his own
personal aspirations are not to be gratified, support the re-
election of the President. Am not certain it is not already
so arranged.

August 26, *Friday.* Am harassed by the pressure on the
enlistment question. A desire to enter the Navy to avoid
the draft is extensive, and the local authorities encourage
it, so that our recruiting rendezvous are, for the time being,
overrun. The Governors and others are applying for more
rendezvous in order to facilitate this operation. The draft
for five hundred thousand men is wholly an army conscrip-
tion. Incidentally it aids the Navy, and to that extent
lessens the number of the army. I have been willing to avail
ourselves of the opportunity for naval recruiting, but the
local authorities are for going beyond this and making our
enlistments a primary object of the draft. Because I cannot
consent to this perversion I am subjected to much captious
criticism, even by those who should know better.

Neither Stanton, Blair, nor Bates were to-day at the
Cabinet-meeting. Judge Johnson of Ohio informs me that

Wade is universally denounced for uniting with Winter Davis in his protest, and that he has been stricken from the list of speakers in the present political campaign in that State.

August 27, Saturday. Much party machinery is just at this time in motion. No small portion of it is a prostitution and abuse. The Whig element is venal and corrupt, to a great extent. I speak of the leaders of that party now associated with Republicans. They seem to have very little political principle; they have no belief in public virtue or popular intelligence; they have no self-reliance, no confidence in the strength of a righteous cause, little regard for constitutional restraint and limitations. Their politics and their ideas of government consist of expedients, and cunning management with the intelligent, and coercion and subornation of the less informed.

Mr. Wakeman, the postmaster at New York, with whom I am on very good terms, — for he is affable, insinuating, and pleasant, though not profound nor reliable, — a New York politician, has called upon me several times in relation to the Brooklyn Navy Yard. He is sent by Raymond, by Humphrey, by Campbell and others, and I presume Seward and Weed have also been cognizant of and advising in the matter. Raymond is shy of me. He evidently is convinced that we should not harmonize. Wakeman believes that all is fair and proper in party operations which can secure by any means certain success, and supposes that every one else is the same. Raymond knows that there are men of a different opinion, but considers them slow, incumbrances, stubborn and stupid, who cannot understand and will not be managed by the really ready and sharp fellows like himself who have resources to accomplish almost anything. Wakeman has been prompted and put forward to deal with me. He says we must have the whole power and influence of the government this coming fall, and if each Department will put forth its whole strength and energy in our

favor we shall be successful. He had just called on Mr.
Stanton at the request of our friends, and all was satisfactorily arranged with him. Had seen Mr. Fessenden and
was to have another interview, and things were working
well at the Treasury. Now, the Navy Department was
quite as important as either, and he, a Connecticut man,
had been requested to see me. There were things in the
Navy Yard to be corrected, or our friends would not be
satisfied, and the election in New York and the country
might by remissness be endangered. This must be prevented, and he knew I would use all the means at my disposal to prevent it. He then read from a paper what he
wanted should be done. It was a transcript of a document
that had been sent me by Seward as coming from Raymond, for the management of the yard, and he complained
of some proceedings that had given offense. Mr. Halleck,
one of the masters, had gathered two or three hundred
workmen together, and was organizing them with a view to
raise funds and get them on the right track, but Admiral
Paulding had interfered, broken up the meetings, and prohibited them from assembling in the Navy Yard in future.

I told him I approved of Paulding's course; that there
ought to be no gathering of workmen in working hours and
while under government pay for party schemes; and there
must be no such gatherings within the limits of the yard at
any time. That I would not do an act myself that I would
condemn in an opponent. That such gatherings in the
government yard were not right, and what was not right I
could not do.

He was a little staggered by my words or manner, or
both; insisted we could not succeed without doing these
things, that other parties had done them, and we must;
but he had full confidence I would do right and should tell
them so when he returned.

Neither Wakeman nor those who sent him are aware that
the course which he would pursue would and ought to destroy any party. No administration could justify and sus-

tain itself that would misuse power and the public means
as they propose. Such action would sooner or later destroy
the government. Their measures would not stand the test
of investigation, and would be condemned by the public
judgment, if healthy. They are not republican but imperial.

August 29, Monday. We have word through Rebel
channels that the Union forces have possession of Fort Morgan. This will give us entire control of the Bay of Mobile.

The President sent me a bundle of papers, embracing a
petition drawn up with great ability and skill, signed by
most of the Massachusetts delegation in Congress and a
large number of the prominent merchants in Boston, asking
special favors in behalf of Smith Brothers, who are under
arrest for fraudulent deliveries under contract, requesting
that the trial may be held in Boston and that it may be
withdrawn from the military and transferred to the civil
tribunals. Senator Sumner and Representative Rice wrote
special letters to favor the Smiths. The whole scheme had
been well studied and laboriously got up, and a special
delegation have come on to press the subject upon the
President.

He urged me to relieve him from the annoying and tremendous pressure that had been brought to bear upon him
in this case by religious or sectarian and municipal influence. I went briefly over the main points; told him the
whole subject ought to be referred to and left with the
Navy Department in this stage of the proceedings, that I
desired him to relieve himself of all care and trouble by
throwing the whole responsibility and odium, if there was
odium, on the Navy Department, that we could not pursue a different course in this case from the others, — it
could not be made an exception. He then asked why not
let the trial take place in Boston and thus concede something. I told him this might be done, but it seemed to me
inexpedient; but he was so solicitous—political and party
considerations had been artfully introduced, against which

little could be urged, when Solicitor Whiting and others averred that three Congressional districts would be sacrificed if I persisted — that the point was waived and the President greatly relieved. The President evinced shrewdness in influencing, or directing me, but was sadly imposed upon by the cunning Bostonians.

A Mr. Buel, formerly of Connecticut, who has recently taken up his residence in Bermuda, called on me a day or two since with a letter from Collins Brothers, of Hartford, who presented him as a worthy, truthful, and reliable man, brought up by themselves, — had lived with them from 1854 to 1862, etc., — representing that he had matters of moment to communicate, etc. Buel wanted permission to export four horses to Bermuda, where he was engaged largely in agriculture, with a view of supplying New York and New England with early vegetables. In this matter I declined to interfere farther than to indorse the respectability of the Messrs. Collins. But Buel had a public matter to communicate. When at Bermuda, Consul Allen had introduced him to a Mr. Bailor, who claimed to be a commissioner duly authorized by the authorities of the State of Georgia to negotiate for peace. His credentials he had given into the hands of Consul Allen, from whom they were stolen when going from Hamilton to St. George's, at a house where he stopped with a lady who had come with him that distance. Not only were Bailor's credentials stolen, but his own dispatches to our government. As he deemed the subject of great importance, and as Bermuda was filled with Rebels and their sympathizers, Consul Allen hastened to St. George's, where the packet was about to sail, and, having no time to write an explanatory letter, had merely penned a line, and opened his heart to Mr. Buel, to whom he communicated the above facts, which Buel narrated to me. Bailor had come on from Bermuda to New York with Buel, and is now in Washington or on his way hither from New York.

Buel, besides the indorsement of the Messrs. Collins,

had the appearance of an honest man, but the story appeared to me so absurd and incredible in many and most respects, that I gave it little weight, and felt inclined to believe that both he and Allen were imposed upon. So believing, I soon dismissed Mr. Buel, referring him in the matter of his horses to the Secretary of the Treasury, or War, or both.

To-day, when leaving the President, Buel met me in the outer hall, where he was in waiting, and again introduced the subject of his horses and Bailor. The latter, he said, was in Washington, had had interviews with the President and Mr. Seward, had dined with the Secretary of State on Saturday, etc., and suggested that it might be well for the President to see him (Buel) on the matter of Bailor's credentials; and he wanted also a definite answer about the horses. The latter, I perceived, was the most interesting and absorbing topic with him, and I was therefore for passing on, when it occurred to me that if Bailor was really here, having interviews with the President and Secretary of State, whether empowered or not, — an intriguing busybody or mischief-maker, — I ought perhaps to inform the President in regard to Buel and mention my own impressions. I therefore returned to the President, briefly stated the facts, and asked if he would see Bailor. He was evidently a little surprised at my knowledge of Bailor, said he had been here and got in with Seward, who had become sick of him, he thought, and the President himself believed Bailor a "shyster." I introduced Buel, who did not remove the impression that Bailor was a "shyster," and most of the conversation was on the condition of Bermuda and Buel's private affairs.

The Rebel leaders understand Seward very well. He is fond of intrigue, of mystery, of sly, cunning management, and is easily led off on a wild chase by subtle fellows who can without difficulty excite his curiosity and flatter his vanity. Detectives, secret agents, fortune-tellers are his delight: and the stupid statements of Bailor, especially when corroborated by Allen, who is evidently a victim, imposed upon him.

August 30, *Tuesday.* Not much of interest at the Cabinet. Seward, Blair, and Bates absent from Washington. The capture of Fort Morgan is confirmed by accounts from Sherman.

Am trying to arrange for changes in command of our squadrons and of our navy yards. Something must be done to close the entrance to Cape Fear River and port of Wilmington. I give no credit to the newspaper gossip of connivance on the part of our naval officers with blockade-runners which many good men believe; but there is a want of effective action. Admiral Lee is true and loyal, careful, and circumspect almost to a fault, but, while vigilant, he has not dash and impetuous daring, and there seems some defect in the blockade which makes Wilmington appear an almost open port. It is true that blockade-running has become systematized into a business, and the ingenuity and skill of Englishmen and the resources of English capital are used without stint in assisting the Rebels.

I have been urging a conjoint attack upon Wilmington for months. Could we seize the forts at the entrance of Cape Fear and close the illicit traffic, it would be almost as important as the capture of Richmond on the fate of the Rebels, and an important step in that direction. But the War Department hangs fire, and the President, whilst agreeing with me, dislikes to press matters when the military leaders are reluctant to move.

Fox urges the immediate recall of Farragut and giving him the North Atlantic Squadron. But to withdraw Farragut from Mobile suddenly will give cause for censure. The country is expecting the capture of the city of Mobile. I do not think it an important object at this moment. We have the bay and have closed all communication from abroad. To capture the city will be difficult, very difficult if the army does not take the principal work in hand. If

Farragut is recalled, the failure or omission to take the city will be imputed to the Navy Department. Besides, to withdraw Farragut and place him in the North Atlantic Squadron will be to advertise our object, and cause the Rebels to prepare for the work of defense. These and other considerations have weight, and prevent me from acting. It is important, however, that the port of Wilmington should be closed, and no effort should be spared to secure that object. Stanton expressed himself willing in our last conversation but doubted if General Grant could be brought into the movement just now, and was, I saw, disinclined himself to advise or recommend the measure. Have had some talk with Fox and sent him to urge Halleck and Stanton. He had an errand to perform with the President and proposed to open the subject to him also. As I had done so several times, and always found the President willing, and on the last two or three occasions solicitous, yet, like Stanton, deferring to Grant, I thought well of the proposition. It was suggested that Gillmore was at leisure or would be a good officer to command in such an expedition. I have a good opinion of Gillmore as a second officer and as an engineer or artillery officer, but his skill and strength in other respects and particularly in organizing and controlling men and planning and carrying out details of an important movement as chief are questionable, and therefore, I should, unless satisfied by competent men who know him better than I do, hesitate in regard to his selection. This is pretty plain and direct work, and he may succeed. Stanton has agreed to send for Gillmore and get his views. In some proposed changes of our squadron commands I find embarrassments. This one of taking Farragut from the West Gulf and transferring him to the North Atlantic is one. It will be a right and proper measure at the right time. But who shall succeed him? Dahlgren has asked to be relieved of his present command, which he earnestly sought, but I am doubtful about giving him the Western Gulf. Though I do not question his courage, which, however, is artificial, he evades responsibility, is craving in his demands, and profuse in expenditure. Fox has advised his transfer to the Mississippi, and that Porter should take Dahlgren's command. But this change does not suit me nor would it gratify either of those admirals. A second suggestion from Fox is that Porter should have command of a flying squadron for the defense of the coast and the West Indies which it is proposed to raise. This strikes me more favorably, provided he is to leave the Mississippi.

August 31, *Wednesday*. The complaints in regard to recruiting are severe and prolonged. They come in numbers. It seems to be taken for granted that we can open a rendezvous in every county. I have no doubt that the rendezvous are overcrowded and that abuses are practiced in consequence. The impending draft for the army indirectly benefits the Navy, or induces persons to enter it. Their doing so relieves them and their localities from the draft. Hence the crowd and competition. Then come in the enormous bounties from the State and municipal authorities over which naval officers have no control, and which lead to bounty-jumping and corruption.

Admiral Porter came by order. Says he prefers remaining in his present command. In a long interview our interchange of opinion concerning men and naval matters was on the whole satisfactory.

General McClellan was to-day nominated as the candidate of the so-called Democratic party. It has for some days been evident that it was a foregone conclusion and the best and only nomination the opposition could make. The preliminary arrangements have been made with tact and skill, and there will probably be liberality, judgment, and sense exhibited in launching and supporting the nominee, which it would become the Union men to imitate. That factious, narrow, faultfinding illiberality of radicals in Congress which has disgraced the press ostensibly of the

2

Administration party, particularly the press of New York City, has given strength to their opponents. McClellan will be supported by War Democrats and Peace Democrats, by men of every shade and opinion; all discordant elements will be made to harmonize, and all differences will be suppressed. Whether certain Republican leaders in Congress, who have been assailing and deceiving the Administration, and the faultfinding journals of New York have, or will, become conscious of their folly, we shall soon know. They have done all that was in their power to destroy confidence in the President and injure those with whom they were associated. If, therefore, the reëlection of Mr. Lincoln is not defeated, it will not be owing to them.

In some respects I think the President, though usually shrewd and sensible, has mismanaged. His mistakes, I think, are attributable to Mr. Seward almost exclusively. It has been a misfortune to retain Stanton and Halleck. He might have brought McClellan into the place of the latter, and Blair had once effected the arrangement, but Seward defeated it. As I have not been in the close confidence of the President in his party personal selections and movements, I am left to judge of many things, as are all the Cabinet except Mr. Seward and to some extent Mr. Stanton, who is in the Seward interest. It has seemed to me a great misfortune that the President should have been so much under the influence of these men, but New York State is a power and Seward makes the most of it. I have regretted that the President should have yielded so much to Greeley in many things and treated him with so much consideration. Chase and Wade, though not in accord, have by their ambition and disappointments done harm, and, in a less degree, the same may be said of Mr. Sumner. Others of less note might be named. Most of them will now cease grumbling, go to work to retrieve their folly so far as they can. Possibly the New York editors may be perverse a few weeks longer, sufficiently so to give that city overwhelmingly to the opposition, and perhaps lose the State.

Seward will, unintentionally, help them by over-refined intrigues and assumptions and blunders. It has sometimes seemed to me that he was almost in complicity with his enemies, and that they were using him. I am not certain that the latter is not true.

It is an infirmity of the President that he permits the little newsmongers to come around him and be intimate, and in this he is encouraged by Seward, who does the same, and even courts the corrupt and the vicious, which the President does not. He has great inquisitiveness. Likes to hear all the political gossip as much as Seward. But the President is honest, sincere, and confiding, — traits which are not so prominent in some by whom he is surrounded.

XXIII

September 1, *Thursday.* Great is the professed enthusiasm of the Democrats over the doings at Chicago, as if it
were not a matter of course. Guns are fired, public meetings held, speeches made with dramatic effect, but I doubt
if the actors succeed even in deceiving themselves. Notwithstanding the factious and petty intrigues of some
professed friends, a species of treachery which has lurked
in others who are disappointed, and much mismanagement
and much feeble management, I think the President will
be reëlected, and I shall be surprised if he does not have a
large majority.

At Chicago there were extreme partisans of every hue,
— Whigs, Democrats, Know-Nothings, Conservatives, War
men and Peace men, with a crowd of Secessionists and
traitors to stimulate action, — all uniting as partisans,
few as patriots. Among those present, there were very
few influential names, or persons who had public confid-

ence, but scoundrels, secret and open traitors of every color.

General Gillmore and Fox went yesterday to the front to see General Grant and try to induce him to permit a force to attack and close the port of Wilmington. It is, undoubtedly, the most important and effective demonstration that can be made. If of less prestige than the capture of Richmond, it would be as damaging to the Rebels.

September 2, Friday. Admiral Farragut's dispatch relative to the capture of Fort Morgan and the infamous conduct of General Page in spiking his guns after his surrender is received. It was most disgraceful and would justify severe treatment.

Some of the Administration presses and leaders have undertaken to censure me for slighting Du Pont. Not one of them awards me any credit for selecting Farragut. Yet it was a great responsibility, for which I was severely criticized, and until he had proved himself worthy of my choice, I felt it.

The contrast between Farragut and Du Pont is marked. No one can now hesitate to say which is the real hero; yet three years ago it would have been different. Farragut is earnest, unselfish, devoted to the country and the service. He sees to every movement, forms his line of battle with care and skill, puts himself at the head, carries out his plan, if there is difficulty leads the way, regards no danger to himself, dashes by forts and overcomes obstructions. Du Pont, as we saw at Sumter, puts himself in the most formidable vessel, has no order of battle, leads the way only until he gets within cannon-shot range, then stops, says his ship would not steer well, declines, however, to go in any other, but signals to them to go forward without order or any plan of battle, does not enjoin upon them to dash by the forts; they are stopped under the guns of Sumter and Moultrie, and are battered for an hour, a sufficient length of time to have gone to Charleston wharves, and then they are signalled to turn about and come back to the Admiral out of harm's way.

When I appointed Du Pont to command a squadron, I met the public expectation. All but a few naval officers, most of whom were under a cloud, approved and applauded so judicious a selection. But no cheering response was made to the appointment of Farragut. Some naval officers said he was a daring, dashing fellow, but they doubted his discretion and ability to command a squadron judiciously. Members of Congress inquired who he was, and some of them remonstrated, and questioned whether I was not making a mistake, for he was a Southern man and had a Southern wife. Neither the President nor any member of the Cabinet knew him, or knew of him except, perhaps, Seward, but he was not consulted and knew nothing of the selection until after it was made. When told of the appointment, he inquired if Farragut was equal to it, and asked if it would not have been better to have transferred Du Pont to that command.

Farragut became a marked man in my mind when I was informed of the circumstances under which he left Norfolk. At the time the Virginia convention voted to secede he denounced the act, and at once abandoned the State, leaving his home and property the day following, avowing openly and boldly, in the face and hearing of the Rebels by whom he was surrounded, his determination to live and die owing allegiance to no flag but that of the Union under which he had served. This firm and resolute stand caused me not only to admire the act, but led me to inquire concerning the man. I had known of him slightly during Polk's administration, when I had charge of a naval bureau, remembered his proposition to take San Juan d'Ulloa at Vera Cruz, and all I heard of him was well, but he was generally spoken of as were other good officers. Fox, Foote, and Dahlgren gave him a good name. Admiral D. D. Porter was emphatic in his favor, and his knowledge and estimate of men were generally pretty correct. Admiral Smith considered him a bold, impetuous man, of a great deal of courage, and energy, but his capabilities and power to command a squadron was a subject to be determined only by trial.

Had any other man than myself been Secretary of the Navy, it is not probable that either Farragut or Foote would have had a squadron. At the beginning of the Rebellion, neither of them stood prominent beyond others. Their qualities had not been developed; they had not possessed opportunities. Foote and myself were youthful companions at school. And I have stated the circumstances under which Farragut was brought to my notice. Neither had the showy name, the scholastic attainments, the wealth, the courtly talent, of Du Pont. But both were heroes. Du Pont is a polished naval officer, selfish, heartless, calculating, scheming, but not a hero by nature, though too proud to be a coward.

September 3, *Saturday*. New York City is shouting for McClellan, and there is a forced effort elsewhere to get a favorable response to the almost traitorous proceeding at Chicago. As usual, some timid Union men are alarmed, and there are some, like Raymond, Chairman of the National Committee, who have no fixed and reliable principles to inspire confidence, who falter, and another set, like Greeley, who have an uneasy, lingering hope that they can yet have an opportunity to make a new candidate. But this will soon be over. The Chicago platform is unpatriotic, almost treasonable to the Union. The issue is made up. It is whether a war shall be made against Lincoln to get peace with Jeff Davis. Those who met at Chicago prefer hostility to Lincoln rather than to Davis. Such is extreme partisanism.

We have to-day word that Atlanta is in our possession, but we have yet no particulars. It has been a hard, long struggle, continued through weary months. This intelligence will not be gratifying to the zealous partisans who have just committed the mistake of sending out a peace platform, and declared the war a failure. It is a melancholy and sorrowful reflection that there are among us so many who so give way to party as not to rejoice in the success of the Union arms. They feel a conscious guilt, and affect not to be dejected, but discomfort is in their countenances, deportment, and tone. While the true Unionists are cheerful and joyous, greeting all whom they meet over the recent news, the Rebel sympathizers shun company and are dolorous. This is the demon of party, — the days of its worst form, — a terrible spirit, which in its excess leads men to rejoice in the calamities of their country and to mourn its triumphs. Strange, and wayward, and unaccountable are men. While the facts are as I have stated, I cannot think these men are destitute of love of country; but they permit party prejudices and party antagonisms to absorb their better natures. The leaders want power. All men crave it. Few, comparatively, expect to attain high position, but each hopes to be benefited within a certain circle which limits, perhaps, his present ambition. There is fatuity in nominating a general and warrior in time of war on a peace platform.

September 5, Monday. Mr. Blair returned this morning from Concord. He had, I have little doubt, been sent for, partly to see and influence me. I am not sufficiently ductile for Mr. Raymond, Chairman of the National Executive Committee, who desires to make each navy yard a party machine. The party politicians of King's County wish to make the Brooklyn Navy Yard control their county and State elections, and this not by argument, persuasion, conviction, personal effort on their part, but by the arbitrary and despotic exercise of power on the part of the Secretary of the Navy. I told Blair I could not be instrumental in any such abuse, and read to him Admiral Paulding's letter. I should have read it to Raymond, had he possessed the manliness to call on me. But he says I am unapproachable, a wall that he cannot penetrate or get over. E. B. Washburne is in this business; so are Usher and others. They want me to do a mean thing, and think it would benefit the party,—a most egregious error, were I so weak as to listen to them. The wrong which they would perpetrate would never make a single convert, control a single vote, but it would create enmities, intensify hatred, increase opposition. They would remove any man who is not openly with us and of our party organization, would employ no doubtful or lukewarm men in the yard, whatever may be their qualifications or ability in their trade. But removing them would not get us their vote, and instead of being lukewarm or doubtful they would be active electioneers against us, exciting sympathy for themselves and hatred towards the Administration for its persecution of mechanics and laborers for independent opinions.

Blair like a man of sense, has a right appreciation of things, as Paulding's letter satisfied him. Whether it will Raymond and Washburne is another question, about which I care not two straws; only for their importuning the President, would not give the old Whig Party a moment's attention. His good sense and sagacity are against such exercise or abuse of power and patronage, as I heard him once remark. It is an extreme of partyism such as is practiced in New York.

Blair informed me that Simeon Draper is appointed Collector of New York, and the evening papers confirm the fact. I also learn from Blair that Chase opposed the appointment of Preston King, saying he was not possessed of sufficient ability for the place. Gracious heaven! A man who, if in a legal point of view not the equal, is the superior of Chase in administrative ability, better qualified in some respects to fill any administrative position in the government than Mr. Chase! And in saying this I do not mean to deny intellectual talents and attainments to the Secretary of the Treasury. Mr. Fessenden also excepted to King, but not for the reasons assigned by Mr. Chase. It is because

Mr. King is too obstinate! He is, indeed, immovable in maintaining what he believes to be right, but open always to argument and conviction. If the opposition of Fessenden is not dictated by Chase, he has fallen greatly in my estimation, and I am in any event prepared to see the Treasury Department fall away under such management. The selection of Sim Draper with his vicious party antecedents is abominable. I am told, however, that prominent merchants advised it. This shows how little attention should be paid in such matters to those who traffic. I have no confidence in Draper. I look upon him as corrupt, and his appointment will beget distrust in the Administration. I so expressed myself to Mr. Blair, although he had acquiesced in the selection, — not from choice, but to prevent the place from being conferred upon another.

September 6, Tuesday. A disagreeable, rainy day. Only a light Cabinet-meeting. As usual the dignitaries were absent, but Seward is not in Washington. Fessenden and Stanton were not with us, and Usher has gone to Indiana. Mr. F. W. Seward is always punctually present when his father is away, and remained to the last. Governor Koerner sent his name in before we left and was introduced. He is recently from Spain. Says Semmes was taunted into fighting the Kearsarge by French and other European officers.

September 9, Friday. At the Cabinet council Fessenden introduced some trade regulations prepared with the intention of carrying out the last enactment of Congress, and designed to supersede all former regulations. This last law is, so far as he could make it so, a creation of Mr. Chase, and I am surprised that Senators Morrill and Morgan should have yielded to him. The regulations of Mr. Fessenden are tainted with Chase's schemes and errors, and belong to the same school of monopoly permits and favoritism. They met with little favor, however. The President

objected at the threshold to that part of the plan which
threw upon him the odium, and labor, and responsibility
of selecting the agents who were to proceed within the
Rebel lines. Both he and Mr. Fessenden, however, started
with the assumption, and as a settled fact, that the cotton
within the Rebel lines must be sought for and brought out,
— trading on the part of the government with the enemy.
The only difference between them was whether it should
be by a few selected agents specially permitted, or whether
it should be open to all who wished to trade with the
Rebels. Mr. Fessenden's plan was the first, the President's
was the last. All gave a preference to the President's plan,
or view of opening the traffic to all if to any. Mr. Stanton
stated some of the objections to traffic beyond our lines,
and thought, if it were to be done, it should be in concurrence with the generals in the Departments. Mr. Blair
questioned the whole policy of trading with the enemy, or
having dealings with them while in a state of war. The
principles of absolute non-intercourse with those in arms
which I have always maintained no one undertook now to
controvert when suggested by Mr. Blair. The President
explained his views were that extensive regions lay open
where neither army was in possession, where there was an
abundance of cotton which the parties or owners (non-bel-
ligerents) would bring forward, but the moment the cotton
appeared, approaching a market, it was immediately
seized and appropriated by our own soldiers and others.
It was plunder. He desired to correct this, and wished Mr.
Fessenden to so modify and so shape his regulations as to
effect it.

The position of Mr. Blair I deem eminently correct as
between people of different nations. But this is not our
case; ours is not an ordinary war, and our great primary
fundamental purpose is a restoration of the Union. Commercial intercourse is not one of the means of attaining that
end. A large portion of the people in the Rebel region are
not enemies of the Union; they sincerely desire its restora-

tion and the benefits that would flow from it. Give them, whenever amicable, the opportunity. Promote friendly intercourse. Let the people in such portions of the country as are not strictly in military occupation come forward with their cotton and begin to feel that they are of us and we of them. Tennessee and Kentucky, northern Georgia and Alabama, the entire country bordering on the Mississippi, etc., etc., can thus, under skillful and right treatment be soon reclaimed. We want no frontiers.

The success of Sherman at Atlanta, following on that of Farragut at Mobile, has very much discomposed the opposition. They had planned for a great and onward demonstration for their candidate and platform, but our naval and army successes have embarrassed them exceedingly. General McClellan, in his letter of acceptance, has sent out a different and much more creditable and patriotic set of principles than the convention which nominated him; but the two are wholly irreconcilable. It will be impossible for Vallandigham, Wood, Tom Seymour, Long, Brooks, and men of that stripe to support McClellan without an utter abandonment of all pretensions to consistency or principle. Yet some of that class will be likely to adhere to him, while those who are sincere will not. But the letter will be likely to secure him more friends than he will lose by it.

September 10, *Saturday.* Seward made a speech at Auburn, intended by him, I have no doubt, as the keynote of the campaign. For a man of not very compact thought, and who, plausible and serious, is often loose in his expressions, the speech is very well. In one or two respects it is not judicious and will likely be assailed.

Chase, who has been expressing his discontent, not in public speeches but in social intercourse down East, is beginning to realize that the issue is made up, — no new leaders are to be brought forward, — and he will now support Lincoln in order to defeat McClellan. So with others. After doing what they could to weaken the President and impair confidence in him, they now turn in and feel the necessity of counteracting their own unwise and mistaken policy.

Mr. Fessenden assures me that the payment of Navy requisitions commences forthwith, and will be prosecuted earnestly. It certainly is time. There are over thirteen millions of suspended requisitions in the Treasury, every dollar of which is due the parties. Many of them should have been paid three and four months ago. Chase commenced this system of deferring payments for value received. I have explained matters to Mr. Fessenden, who, however, does not yet, I apprehend, fully realize the consequences and the great wrong. The credit of the Department and of the government is seriously impaired, and the Navy Department is by these delays compelled to pay an extra price for everything it purchases, because the Treasury does not promptly pay the requisitions drawn on it. My administration of the Department is injured by these delays, and made to appear extravagant in its expenditures, when it is in fact the only one, except the Post-Office, that struggles for economy.

September 12, *Monday.* No news of special importance to-day. The election in Maine is eliciting comments. The opposition are expecting to make large gains, while the friends of the Administration are pretty confident they will maintain their majority of last year. Both parties evidently consider the result as indicative of the great result in the fall, and for this reason more than usual interest is manifested.

September 13, *Tuesday.* Had an interesting half-hour talk with J. M. Forbes, a sensible man and true patriot. He wishes the President to make the issue before the country distinctly perceptible to all as democratic and aristocratic. The whole object and purpose of the leaders in the Rebellion is the establishment of an aristocracy, although

not distinctly avowed. Were it avowed, they would have
few followers. Mr. Forbes wishes me to urge this subject
upon the President. It is not in my nature to obtrude my
opinions upon others. Perhaps I err in the other extreme.
In the course of the conversation he related a violent and
strange assault that was made upon him by Mr. Seward
some time since, in the railroad cars or on the platform at a
stopping-place, denouncing him for trying to postpone the
nominating convention. Mr. Blair, in walking over with
me, took the opportunity of stating his conviction that
there was a deep intrigue going forward on the part of the
"little villain" — using Greeley's epithet to Raymond —
to effect a change of Cabinet next March. The grumbling
and the complaint about the employés in the Navy Yards
meant more than was expressed. It is to gradually work
upon the President and get him, if possible, dissatisfied
with me and with the administration of the Navy Department. I doubt if this is so and yet should not be at all
surprised to find Blair to be right in his conjectures. I
know that the managers are very much dissatisfied because
I do not make the yards bitterly partisan, and permit levies
for money to be made on the workmen for party purposes.
This is particularly the case at the Brooklyn yard. Raymond has in party matters neither honesty nor principle
himself, and believes that no one else has. He would compel men to vote, and would buy up leaders. Money and
office, not argument and reason, are the means which he
would use. This fellow, trained in the vicious New York
school of politics, is Chairman of the Republican National
Committee; is spending much of his time in Washington,
working upon the President secretly, trying to poison his
mind and induce him to take steps that would forever
injure him. Weed, worse than Seward, is Raymond's
prompter, and the debaucher of New York politics.

September 14, *Wednesday*. I had a formal call to-day
from a committee consisting of Mr. Cook of Illinois, a
member of the National Committee, Mr. Humphrey, an

ex-Member of Congress from Brooklyn, and two or three
other gentlemen. Mr. Cook opened the subject by presenting me a resolution, adopted unanimously by the National
Committee, complaining in general terms that the employés of the Brooklyn Navy Yard were, a majority of
them, opposed to the Administration. He also presented a
paper which the President had given him from certain
persons in Massachusetts and New Hampshire, complaining in a similar manner of the condition of affairs in the
Charlestown and Kittery navy yards. Our interview was
long, and matters were pretty fully gone into. After reading the papers, I stated that these were charges in general
terms, and asked if they had any specific facts, anything
tangible for us to inquire into. Was there any case within
their knowledge, or the knowledge of any one to whom
they could refer, of wrong, of disloyalty, of offensive political bearing? They were evidently unprepared to answer. Mr. Cook said he had understood there were some
warrant officers who ought to be removed. I explained
there were naval officers and there were civilians in the
Navy Yards. The former were detailed to duty, the latter
are appointees of the Department. The masters are appointed by the Department and they employ all the workmen, subject to the approval of the chiefs of their respective departments. I had appointed and retained all the
masters in Brooklyn by the advice of Mr. Humphrey and
his associates. If there were any improper persons employed there, it was by the masters thus selected on Mr.
Humphrey's recommendation. Mr. Cook said he had not
fully understood this matter. Mr. Humphrey said there
were a good many disloyal men in the yard. I requested
him to point them out, to give me their names, to specify
one. He was not prepared, nor were either of the men with
him. Mr. Humphrey said that a majority of the men in the
yard were Copperheads, opposed to the Administration. I
asked him how he knew that to be the case, for I could not
credit it. He said he had been told so, and appealed to the

master joiner, who was present, — a little deaf. The master joiner thought that four sevenths were opposed to the Administration. I inquired on what data he made that statement. He said he had no data but he could tell pretty well by going round the yard and mingling with the men. I told him that besides introducing partyism into the yard, which was wrong, his figure was mere conjecture, and asked if their ward committees in the city outside the yard did their duty, — if they canvassed their wards, knew how many navy yard men were in each ward, and how they stood relatively with parties. They were aware of no such canvass, had no facts, had done nothing outside.

But the burden of their complaint was against Mr. Davidson, the Assistant Naval Constructor, who would not dismiss, or give his approval to dismiss, any man of the opposition. Again I asked for facts. "Why, if there is this wrong, has not a case been brought to my knowledge? You must, certainly, among you all, know of a single case if there is such a grievance as you represent." Mr. Humphrey appealed to the master joiner, who related the circumstance of a difference that had grown up between a workman and a quarterman, an appeal was made to Mr. Hallock, the master, Hallock wrote his dismissal for insubordination, and Mr. Davidson had not approved it; no action had yet been taken.

This was the only case they could recollect. This, I told them, was not a case of disloyalty, or objectionable party opinion, but one of discipline. If as stated, the facts should have been reported to me, and I would have given them attention. But nothing, they were confident, could be done with Mr. Davidson to favor the Republican Party. I asked Mr. H. if he knew Mr. Davidson's political opinion. Told him Mr. D. had been recommended by every Republican Member of Congress from Philadelphia. Mr. H. did not know what his opinions were, but he had no sympathy with us. I told him my impressions were that D. was a friend and supporter of the President, but he had gone a stranger to Brooklyn, and been treated with neglect and now was much misrepresented; that I was satisfied and confirmed that my impressions were correct, that there was no proper party organization in Brooklyn, that they had no proper canvass, that they did not labor and exert themselves properly, but sat down leisurely and called on the President and Secretary of the Navy to do their party work and organization for them; that in this way they could never make themselves formidable. They must mingle with the people, be with them and of them, convince them by intercourse that the Republicans were right. That they should invite the employees to their meetings, furnish them with arguments, get them interested, and they would, in that way, have their willing efforts and votes.

They thought, they said, they had a pretty good organization, but if allowed to go into the yard they could better organize, it would help them much. I told them I thought such a proceeding would be wrong; it was a maxim with me not to do that which I condemned in another. They said if they could go near the paymaster when he was paying the men off, and get the assessment off each man, it would greatly aid them. I told them it would help them to no votes. The man who was compelled to pay a party tax could not love the party who taxed him. His contribution must, like his vote, come voluntarily, and they must persuade and convince him to make him earnest and effective.

I promised to write instructing Delano, the constructor, to pass on the selections and dismissals of men, and not to depute this duty to his assistant. This, they thought, would afford them relief, and though I perceived there was disappointment in the matter of money-getting, which is obviously the great object in view, they went off apparently satisfied with the victory for Delano.

September 15, Thursday. Admiral Farragut writes that his health is giving way under the great labor imposed and long-continued service in the Gulf and the Caribbean Sea. Says he must have rest and shore exercise. The Department had ordered him North to command the North Atlantic Blockading Squadron and capture Wilmington. These orders he had not received when his dispatch was written, and I am exceedingly embarrassed how to proceed. Fox tells me that Grant, with whom he has conversed, would not be satisfied with Lee. Grant had so said or intimated to him when Fox was sent with Gillmore to consult with Grant in regard to operations at Wilmington. My own convictions are that Lee is not the man for that. That kind of work is not in him, except under the immediate orders of another. He is true and loyal, prudent and cautious. Farragut would take the place three times while Lee was preparing, and hesitating, and looking behind for more aid. It pains me to distress him and the Blairs by detaching him and ordering another to the work, but individual feelings, partialities, and friendships must not be in the way of public welfare.

The importance of closing Wilmington and cutting off Rebel communication is paramount to all other questions, — more important, practically, than the capture of Richmond. It has been impossible to get the War Department and military authorities to enter into the spirit of this work. They did not appreciate it. But they and Grant have now engaged in it, and Grant is persistent. Just at this crisis Farragut unfortunately fails. It is unavoidable, a necessity. He would not ask relief if not compelled to, and may try to obey the orders, though I think not; and if he offers to, I shall not, under the present aspect of affairs, accept the service from him. But who shall take his place? Lee is not the man, whatever his worth in other respects. Admiral Porter is probably the best man for the service, but his selection will cut Lee to the quick. Porter is young, and his rapid promotion has placed him in rank beyond those who were his seniors, some of whom it might be well to have in this expedition. But again personal considerations must yield to the public necessities. I think Porter must perform this duty. Neither Goldsborough nor Du Pont are men for such service. Nor is Davis. Dahlgren has some good qualities, but lacks great essentials and cannot be thought of for this command. His promotion is not and never will be popular with the Navy. Men as well as officers participate in this feeling. I regret it. I strove to have him suppress his aspirations as premature and not earned afloat. But it is difficult to reason with vain ambition. Dahlgren is not for such a duty the equal of Porter, even were he popular with the service and the country. I see no alternative but Porter, and, unprejudiced and unembarrassed, I should select him. The movement is secret, and I have no one to confer with but Fox, who is over-partial to Porter and whose opinion is foregone, and known already before asking.

Now, how to dispose of Lee? I think we must send him for the present to the West Gulf, and yet that is not strictly right, perhaps, to others. His harvest of prize money, I think, is greater than that of any other officer, and the West Gulf, should Wilmington be closed, will be likely, if the war continues, to be the theatre of blockade-running. I think, however, Lee must, for a time at least, have the position.

September 16, *Friday*. At the Cabinet nothing of interest. Seward and Fessenden were early there and left. Judge Otto,[1] who was present in the place of Usher, presented a paper for the removal of Charles L. Lines, a land officer in Kansas, stating he was a troublesome man and an opponent of the Administration. It is not usual for me to volunteer remarks touching the appointments of another Department, but I could not forbear saying this statement if correct was extraordinary, — that Lines was an old Whig, — we had been old opponents in Connecticut, — that he, in earnest zeal, went early to Kansas, had made sacrifices of

[1] William T. Otto, Assistant Secretary of the Interior.

domestic comfort, had lost one or two sons there, and I should be surprised if he was not a friend of the President. Otto said he knew nothing on the subject. It was a question in which Senator Jim Lane took an interest and had been submitted by Mr. Edmunds.[1] The President said he was sorry Lane had come here just at this time, for he would want him (the President) to adopt all his personal quarrels. For the present, and until he knew more, he declined to interfere.

Acting Admiral Bailey has come here, and dislikes, I presume, his orders to the Portsmouth Navy Yard, — would have preferred his command of the East Gulf Squadron. I had supposed he desired and would be gratified with the change. But prize money is a great stimulant.

September 17, *Saturday.* Talked over the subject of Wilmington, examined its localities, and considered the position of things fully with Porter and Fox. I had intended Blair should have been present, for the meeting was at his house, but he was compelled to leave for Baltimore.

Porter has preferred retaining the Mississippi Squadron, but repeated what he has heretofore said, — that he had been treated kindly by the Department, and if I ordered him to go over Niagara Falls in an iron pot he should obey the order. In other words, he and every naval officer must submit and give up their own wishes to the orders of the Department without a murmur of dissent.

There was a special Cabinet-meeting to-day on the subject of the abandoned plantations. A person of the name of Wright wishes the President to put him in possession of what he claims to be his plantation, now in the occupancy of Mr. Flanders, the Treasury agent. It seems that F. has fifty-two of these plantations, — or had some time since, perhaps he has more now.

The President said serious questions were rising in regard to this description of property; appeals were made to

[1] James M. Edmunds, Commissioner of the General Land Office.

him, and he could not undertake to investigate and adjust them. Quite a discussion took place in which the President, Mr. Bates, and Mr. Stanton took the principal part. It was not made distinctly to appear how these plantations came into the hands of Mr. Flanders, the Treasury agent. All who were present, except Mr. Bates and myself, seemed to take it for granted that it was legitimate and proper. They said the law had prescribed how abandoned plantations became forfeit. Mr. Stanton said he had given the subject great attention and most thorough investigation, and he made a somewhat emphatic and labored argument, telling the President (very properly I think) he could not, and ought not to, take upon himself the details of these embarrassing questions; that when Admiral Farragut and General Butler took possession of New Orleans, many of the inhabitants fled, leaving their plantations, and kept themselves within the Rebel lines; thousands of negroes were left unprovided for. It became necessary for the government to provide for them; the military authorities had taken up their deserted plantations and seized others, and let them out for the negroes to work. When Mr. Chase got his Treasury agents at work, it was thought best to turn these plantations over to him. After a little time, Chase became sick of his bargain, and desired the War Department to retake possession and responsibility but he (S.) had, declined.

Mr. Bates wanted a definition of "abandoned." Was it "abandonment" for a man to leave his home with his family and go for a few months to the North, or to Cuba, or to Richmond? etc. Mr. Stanton said the statute made that clear, but Mr. Bates thought Congress, though they made law, did not make dictionaries. I put the question if a man had two plantations, one in Alabama and one in Louisiana, at the time of the capture of New Orleans, and he, being in Alabama, remained there, within the Rebel lines, attending to his private domestic affairs, whether that would be an abandonment of his Louisiana plantation so that Mr. Flanders could take and hold it. I also asked if there was not a preliminary question to all this, — would it not be necessary to ascertain by proper, legal inquiry whether the owner was a Rebel and traitor.

There is too much of a disposition to jump to a conclusion — to take for granted — on many occasions. The owner by legal title-deeds and records is entitled to his land unless he has forfeited it. If a Rebel and traitor, he may have forfeited it, but who is to decide that he is a traitor? Not the military commander or quartermaster, and yet no other officer or tribunal has passed over them.

Some difference appeared between Fessenden and Stanton as to which should have the custody of the plantations. F. thought the agent should report to S. and *vice versa*. If seized or taken possession of from military necessity, I have never been able to see why the Treasury agent should have them. If not a military necessity, how can he have possession, except under some legal decision? It is not sufficient that the law says the land of a traitor shall be forfeited. Who shall expound and carry the law into effect, transferring title? Not the Treasury agent, certainly.

The President said he wished some means devised to relieve him from these questions. He could not undertake to investigate them. Stanton said that was true, but that, having given the subject great consideration, he was prepared to say what in his opinion was best, — that was that the whole of the matters pertaining to abandoned plantations should be turned over to the War Department and he would organize a bureau or tribunal to make rightful disposition of each case presented.

September 19. *Monday.* Grant has gone up to the Shenandoah to see Sheridan. I had advised Porter and Fox to visit Grant on James River, but this prevented, and yesterday it was said at the War Department he would be here to-day. We now learn he has already returned to the Army of the Potomac, so P. and F. left this P.M. to visit

him and arrange particulars. Grant has not yet decided
or made known what general he shall select for this service.

September 20, *Tuesday*. Intelligence reaches us this
morning that Sheridan has achieved a great victory over
Early in the valley of the Shenandoah, after much hard
fighting. This will do much to encourage and stimulate all
Union-loving men, and will be ominous to Lee.

At Cabinet-meeting. Met Fessenden on my way, who
said he had called in but the President told him there was
"no business." This is the announcement three out of four
days of meeting. Sometimes matters are brought forward
notwithstanding. I found the Postmaster-General and the
Attorney-General with the President. In a few minutes
Fessenden returned, and shortly after Stanton came in.
It was easy to perceive that the latter was full, — that he
had something on the brain, — and I concluded he had
additional tidings from Sheridan. But, the President
being called out just as he entered, Stanton went and
seated himself by Fessenden and conversed in an under-
tone. He had remarked as he came in that he had sent for
Mr. Seward. When Seward arrived, Stanton unfolded and
read a telegram, stating two steamers had been captured
on Lake Erie by Rebels from Canada. This he said was a
matter that immediately concerned the State and Navy
Departments. He inquired what naval force we had there.
I told him I apprehended more than we were authorized to
have by treaty stipulations. He inquired what the treaty
was; said he knew nothing about that. Seward explained.
Stanton wanted to know where the Michigan was. I told
him she had lain at Johnson's Island most of the summer
to aid the army and guard prisoners and my impression was
that she was still there. As usual, he was excited, and,
as usual, a little annoyed that I viewed the matter coolly.
He soon left, and Seward also, each agreeing to let me
know as soon as they had farther information. On my re-

turn to the Department I telegraphed to Commodore Rodgers in New York to hold himself in readiness to obey any orders, and also to Admiral Paulding to have one hundred picked men and officers ready to proceed on immediate service if required. I then called on Stanton, who agreed to furnish transportation for these men and four guns to Buffalo, if the occasion needed them, — and he was confident it would, — thought they had better be sent at all events, officers, men, and guns. I thought it premature but that we would be prepared. Just before leaving the Department for the day, Stanton sent me a dispatch just received, that some Rebel refugees had come on board the packet-boat Parsons at Malden, the boat being on her way from Detroit to Sandusky; had risen on the officers and crew and seized the boat, had subsequently seized and sunk the Queen of the West, then run their own boat into a Canada port and disabled and then deserted her. I called on Stanton at the War Department on my way home and remarked the flurry was pretty well over, and the fuss ended. He did not, he said, consider it so by any means. One vessel was destroyed, and one was rushing over the lake and all our vast shipping on the Lakes was at its mercy. I requested him to reread the dispatch he had sent me. He did so, and was a little nonplussed; but said the pirate was there and would do the same thing over again. I thought not immediately. He thought they would at once, and we should be prepared by having two more naval vessels. The army had two, he said, which they would turn over to us. I remarked that we had best keep within the terms of the treaty, and call on the British authorities to do their duty. I remarked this was a piece of robbery and could not be considered in any other light; that the robbers had come from Canada and risen upon the vessel upon which they had embarked, and had fled into Canada with the stolen property. The State Department had, or should have, the question now in hand. This, I perceived, was letting off the affair in too quiet a way to suit the Secretary

of War, and I left him. He is always in an excited panic, a
sensational condition, at such times.

There was some conversation after the others left, between the President, Blair, and myself — chiefly by them
— in regard to men and things in Maryland. In the early
days of the Administration, H. Winter Davis and his crew
had been more regarded than they deserved.

Some matters in Dakota were also alluded to. Todd,
who succeeded in obtaining the seat of delegate over Dr.
Jayne, brother-in-law of Trumbull, had undertaken to be
exacting, and the President had told him so. I well remember that early in the Administration Trumbull had pressed
the appointment of his brother-in-law to that Territory,
against the wishes and convictions of the President. It
appeared to me that Trumbull was unreasonable, but he
then succeeded. His brother-in-law had just previously
been elected to the Illinois Senate by seven votes in a district that was usually Democratic; his appointment compelled him to resign and a candidate of opposite politics
was elected. The control of the legislature went into other
hands; Richardson, an opponent of the Administration, was
elected;[1] a quarrel then broke out in Nebraska between the
two — Jayne and Todd — from Springfield, etc., etc.

September 21, *Wednesday.* The victory of Sheridan has a
party-political influence. It is not gratifying to the opponents of the Administration. Some who want to rejoice
in it feel it difficult to do so, because they are conscious
that it strengthens the Administration, to which they are
opposed. The partisan feeling begins to show itself strongly
among men of whom it was not expected. In New York
there has been more of this than elsewhere. Robert C.
Winthrop, once potent and powerful in Massachusetts, a
man of position and of talent, not a great man, but a
scholar of taste and pretension, a gentleman and statesman, made his appearance in New York, with Fernando

---

[1] To the United States Senate, — William A. Richardson.

and Ben Wood, Rynders,[1] and others, whom in other days he detested. Winthrop is a disappointed man. He had high aspirations and high expectations, and not without reason. Had he pursued a faithful, conscientious course, he would have won high official distinction and influence. But, confident of his strong position in New England and with the Whigs, he courted their enemies, repelled the Republicans and fell. As he swerved from the track, Sumner and others, who did not, perhaps, regret his error, stepped forward, and poor Winthrop in a very short time found that instead of gaining new friends he had lost old ones. For several years he felt very uncomfortable, and has now committed another great mistake. The *National Intelligencer*, which has endeavored to hold a position of dignified neutrality during this Administration, has finally given way and become strongly partisan. This I regret, for the editor has ability, and has made his paper respectable. His discussions of current and important questions have been highly creditable and often instructive, and I cannot but think it unfortunate that he should take an attitude which will injure him and his paper and do good to no one.

Some attempt is made by the Richmond papers to help the cause of McClellan by an affectation of dread of his superior military attainments and abilities and his greater zeal for the Union. The effort is so bald, so manifestly intended for their sympathizing friends, that no one can be deceived by it. There was a time when such stuff had a market in the North, but that time has gone by.

September 22, Thursday. Senator Harris called on me. He is jubilant over Sheridan's success, but much disturbed by the miserable intrigues of Weed and Seward in the city of New York. Says he has told the President frankly of his error, that he has only given a little vitality to Weed, whose influence has dwindled to nothing, and would have entirely perished but for the help which the President has given

[1] Isaiah Rynders, a local politician of New York.

him. This he is aware has been effected through Seward, who is a part of Weed. The removal of Andrews as Naval Officer, the appointment of Wakeman to his place, causing Wakeman to leave the post-office, into which they have thrust Kelly, an old fiddler for Seward in other years, is a Weed operation. Seward carried it out.

Blair tells me that Weed is manœuvring for a change of Cabinet, and Morgan so writes me. He has for that reason, B. says, set his curs and hounds barking at my heels and is trying to prejudice the President against me. Not unlikely, but I can go into no counter-intrigues. If the President were to surrender himself into such hands, — which I do not believe, — he would be unworthy his position. He has yielded more than his own good sense would have prompted him already. For several months there has been a pretended difference between Seward and Weed; for a much longer period there has been an ostensible hostility between Weed and Sim Draper. I have never for a moment believed in the reality of these differences; but I am apprehensive the President is in a measure, or to some extent, deceived by them. He gives himself — too much, I sometimes think — into the keeping of Seward, who is not always truthful, not sensitively scrupulous, but a schemer, while Weed, his second part, and of vastly more vigor of mind, is reckless and direct, persistent and tortuous, avaricious of late, and always corrupt. We have never been intimate. I do not respect him, and he well knows it. Yet I have never treated him with disrespect, nor given him cause of enmity, except by avoiding intimacy and by declining to yield to improper schemes of himself and his friends. On one occasion, at an early period of the Administration, Mr. Seward volunteered to say that he always acted in concert with Weed, — that "Seward's Weed and Weed's Seward." If, as Blair supposes, Weed is operating against me, Seward probably is also, and yet I have seen no evidence of it, — certainly none recently.

September 23, Friday. No business of importance brought before the Cabinet to-day. Some newspaper rumors of peace, and of letters from Jeff Davis and others, all wholly groundless. Seward and Fessenden left early. Mr. Bates and myself came out of the Executive Mansion together and were holding a moment's conversation, when Blair joined us, remarking as he did so, "I suppose you are both aware that my head is decapitated, — that I am no longer a member of the Cabinet." It was necessary he should repeat before I could comprehend what I heard. I inquired what it meant, and how long he had had the subject submitted or suggested to him. He said never until to-day; that he came in this morning from Silver Spring and found this letter from the President for him. He took the letter from his pocket and read the contents, — couched in friendly terms, — reminding him that he had frequently stated he was ready to leave the Cabinet when the President thought it best, etc., etc., and informing him the time had arrived. The remark that he was willing to leave I have heard both him and Mr. Bates make more than once. It seemed to me unnecessary, for when the President desires the retirement of any one of his advisers, he would undoubtedly carry his wishes into effect. There is no Cabinet officer who would be willing to remain against the wishes or purposes of the President, whether right or wrong.

I asked Blair what led to this step, for there must be a reason for it. He said he had no doubt he was a peace-offering to Frémont and his friends. They wanted an offering, and he was the victim whose sacrifice would propitiate them. The resignation of Frémont and Cochrane was received yesterday, and the President, commenting on it, said F. had stated "the Administration was a failure, politically, militarily, and financially," that this included the Secretaries of State, Treasury, War, and Postmaster-General, and he thought the Interior, but not the Navy or the Attorney-General. As Blair and myself walked away together toward the western gate, I told him the suggestion

MONTGOMERY BLAIR

of pacifying the partisans of Frémont might have been brought into consideration, but it was not the moving cause; that the President would never have yielded to that, except under the pressing advisement, or deceptive appeals and representations of some one to whom he had given his confidence. "Oh," said Blair, "there is no doubt Seward was accessory to this, instigated and stimulated by Weed." This was the view that presented itself to my mind, the moment he informed me he was to leave, but on reflection I am not certain that Chase has not been more influential than Seward in this matter. In parting with Blair the President parts with a true friend, and he leaves no adviser so able, bold, sagacious. Honest, truthful, and sincere, he has been wise, discriminating, and correct. Governor Dennison, who is to succeed him, is, I think, a good man, and I know of no better one to have selected.

Blair has just left me. I was writing and just closing the preceding page as he called. He says he has written his resignation and sent it in or rather handed it to the President. The letter from the President which he received this morning was to him entirely unexpected. But, though a surprise, he thinks it right and will eventuate well. That Seward has advised it he does not doubt, though the President does not intimate it. But the President tells him that Washburne recommended it. Strange if the President is influenced by so untruthful, unreliable, and mean a man as Washburne. But Washburne thinks it will help the President among the Germans. The President thinks it is necessary to conciliate Weed (he might have said Chase also) who, with his friends, defeated Wadsworth for Governor two years ago. Such are Blair's conclusions and, I may add, my own. Yet I cannot but think there must be something ulterior, for it is unlike the President to dismiss an acknowledged and true friend, a public officer who has, he says, discharged his duties well and against whom there is no complaint. Why, then, is he dismissed or asked to resign, when there is no cause? My impression is that the

President does not intend to part with Blair, and I shall be disappointed if he is not recalled, perhaps to some other position in the Cabinet, perhaps to act in an important capacity for the restoration of the Union. But this is all speculative.[1]

September 24, Saturday. Sheridan follows up his work, and bids fair to disperse and annihilate Early's entire army. The effect of his successive victories has been a great fall in the price of gold, or an appreciation of paper currency. We are, I think, approaching the latter days of the Rebellion. The discomfiture of Early is likely to make Lee's continuance in Richmond uncomfortable, yet where can he go to make a more effectual stand? Some indications of a desire on the part of the authorities of Georgia to effect a restoration, are more than intimated, and a prevalent feeling of despondency is manifest throughout the Rebel region. An effective blow by Grant at Richmond or the retreat of the Rebel army will be the falling in of the crater.

September 26, Monday. The consuls in London, Liver-

---

[1] At a subsequent period the President informed me that Mr. Chase had many friends who felt wounded that he should have left the Cabinet, and left alone. The Blairs had been his assailants, but they remained and were a part of the Administration. This Mr. C. and his friends thought invidious, and the public would consider it a condemnation of himself and an approval of the Blairs. If Montgomery Blair left the Cabinet, Chase and his friends would be satisfied, and this he (the President) thought would reconcile all parties, and rid the Administration of irritating bickerings. He considered both of them his friends, and thought it was well, as Chase had left, that Blair should go also. They were both in his confidence still, and he had great regard for each of them.

The relations of Stanton with Blair were such that it was difficult for the two to remain and preserve the unity and freedom necessary for good administration and social intercourse. It was not Seward's policy to advise the dismissal of Blair, but he would strenuously urge that Stanton, between whom and Blair there was hostility, should be retained. At this time the President was greatly embarrassed by contentions among his friends, by nominal Republicans, by intense radicals, and the strong front of the Democrats. — G. W.

pool, etc., report a probable change of tactics by the Rebels in fitting out fast-sailing privateers to depredate on our commerce. It is a policy that has been a constant source of apprehension to me from the time it was determined to have a blockade — an international process — instead of closing the ports, which is a domestic question. The Rebels failed to push the privateering scheme, as I have always believed under secret admonitions from England and France. Those governments have not conformed to the extent expected to Rebel views, and not unlikely a demonstration may be made on our commerce, perhaps on some one of our light-armed blockaders by a combination of two or three of their purchased cruisers.

September 27, *Tuesday*. Received mail from Admiral Farragut. Among his dispatches one confidential, inclosing a letter from General Canby, who had received a singular order signed by the President, directing that one A. J. Hamilton should be permitted to export cotton from Sabine Pass, Galveston, etc., himself, and that Hamilton's written order should be a permit for others to export. As General Canby, to whom this document was directed, has no control over the squadron, he had inclosed the President's order to Admiral Farragut. The Admiral had transmitted it to the senior officer off Galveston, and communicated copies of the whole correspondence to me, remarking that it would lead to immense swindling.

I submitted this extraordinary document to the President, and remarked as I did so, that in the discussions that had taken place on this subject on two or three occasions within the last six weeks, and since this order (dated, I think, the 9th of August) was issued, no allusion had been made to it, that it conflicted with the blockade which the Department was obliged to enforce, and that I was surprised on receiving the information. The President seemed embarrassed but said he believed it was all right. "How right?" I inquired. He said it was one of Seward's arrangements, that he guessed would come out well enough; but evidently did not himself know, or, if he knew, was unwilling or unable to explain.

This is another specimen of the maladministration and improper interference of the Secretary of State. Commencing with the first expedition sent out to supply Sumter, which he took measures to defeat, there has been on his part a constant succession of wrong acts, impertinent intrigues in the affairs of other Departments, blunders and worse than blunders, that disgrace the Administration. There is unmistakable rascality in this cotton order. Thurlow Weed was here about the time it was issued, and it will not surprise me if he has an interest in it.

Seward thinks to keep his own name out of the transaction. The President has been made to believe that the order was essential; the Secretary of State has so presented the subject to him that he probably thought it a duty. There are times when I can hardly persuade myself that the President's natural sagacity has been so duped, but his confidence in Seward is great, although he must know him to be, I will not say a trickster, because of his position and our association, but over-cunning to be strictly honest. And when I say this, I do not apply to him dishonesty in money transactions when dealing with men, or the government perhaps, but political cheating, deceiving, wrong administration. He knows this scheme to bring out cotton was a fraud, and hence, instead of coming directly to me, who have charge of the blockade, or bringing the question before the Cabinet in a frank and honorable manner, there is this secret, roundabout proceeding, so characteristic of the Secretary of State.

He insisted on a blockade at the beginning. Would not listen to closing the ports. Would make it an international, not permit it to be a domestic, question. Now, in violation of international law and of fair and honorable blockade, he and his friends are secretly bringing out cotton from Texas. This is not in good faith, but is prostituting the government and its action. I regret that Farragut did not disregard the order until it came to him legitimately through the proper channel.

Had a call from my old friend the elder Blair. It was not unexpected. Detaching Lee from the North Atlantic Squadron I supposed would cause dissatisfaction to Lee, who would, through his wife, stimulate her father to make an effort in his behalf. The old man got word to-day that Lee was detached and hastened to me. He thought himself hard used in the blows that fell upon his children. Frank had been smitten for exposing Frémont and Chase. Montgomery had been dismissed from the Cabinet, and simultaneously Lee had been detached from his command after two years' faithful service. I told him the case appeared a hard one as he presented it; that I felt the removal of Montgomery from our counsels as the greatest misfortune that had befallen the Cabinet, but my consolation was that it would only be temporary and he would certainly soon have as honorable a position; that Frank had done and was doing great service, which the country would, if it did not already, appreciate; that Lee was not degraded in being assigned to another command. I knew him to be cautious and vigilant, but not, perhaps, the man for an immediate demonstration, an assault requiring prompt action. He had labored well, and in a pecuniary point of view been better paid than any man in the Navy.

The old man wanted me to recommend him for promotion to a full commission as rear-admiral, but that, I told him, followed deserving action. It must be earned.

Acting Admiral Lee has acquitted himself very well, — has discharged his duties intelligently and firmly. But he can never be a great commander. While he has administered the affairs of his squadron safely, he has failed to devise and execute any important act. The same opportunities in the hands of Porter, or Foote, or Farragut, and, I think, of John Rodgers, would have shown vastly more important results. His caution runs into timidity. He is

2

avaricious and ambitious, I fear ungenerous and illiberal; is destitute of heroic daring.

September 28, *Wednesday.* I called to-day on Secretary Fessenden with Farragut's dispatch and the order of the President permitting A. J. Hamilton of Texas to bring out cotton, to the Treasury agent. He disclaims all knowledge of the transaction and says he will not recognize it. Looks upon it as an outrageous swindle, violating the blockade, and imposing upon the country. "Why," he pertinently inquires, "was not this question, so important, not submitted to the whole Cabinet." He was very earnest and wished me to again inquire of the President in regard to it.

Had an interview with Attorney-General Bates respecting some questions submitted to him for opinion. The old gentleman is very honest and right-minded; delights to be thought a little — or a good deal — obstinate, if satisfied he is right.

The finding of a court martial in the case of Commander Downes of the R. R. Cuyler, which ran short of fuel, and he, instead of using his sails and striving to get into port, proceeded to dismantle his vessel, burning his spars, guncarriages, caissons, etc., bought lumber from on board a merchant vessel on its way to Cuba; and for all this sends in a dispatch complaining of his engineer and preferring charges against him, without any seeming consciousness that he was responsible himself, or blamable. But the court condemns Downes and dismisses him from the service. The sentence is severe but correct, though the punishment may be mitigated. It is necessary, however, to correct a rising error among a certain class of officers who are inclined to relieve the commander of a ship of responsibility, — a pernicious error that would, if acquiesced in, demoralize the service. That his engineer was in fault is doubtless true, but the commander must make himself acquainted with the condition of his vessel and its equipment. Downes has proved himself an officer of merit in some respects, and it must be remembered to his credit at a time when a great failing has put him in jeopardy.

September 29, *Thursday.* The appointments to the Naval Academy are a great annoyance and often a great embarrassment. Of course the Secretary is much blamed for every disappointment, although he has none but contingent appointments. Persons often apply to the President, who is restricted in his appointments, but who gives a favorable indorsement to almost all. Each considers this abundant to secure him a place, and denounces me if he does not succeed.

I again spoke to the President in relation to his order to A. J. Hamilton, and remarked to him that it was in conflict with the blockade. He was disturbed, and said Seward had fixed that up, and he presumed it was right. "Suppose you see Seward yourself," said he. This I must do, but to little purpose, I apprehend.

The great fall in gold within a few days begins to effect prices. In other words, commodities are getting nearer their actual value by the true money standard. Recent victories have largely contributed to this, but there are other causes, and I think Fessenden may be a more correct financier than Chase, but neither is exactly fitted for the place.

September 30, *Friday.* At the Cabinet-meeting Seward produced a telegram from Governor Nye of the Nevada Territory, stating that the new constitution had been adopted by the people, and desired the President to issue a proclamation announcing the fact pursuant to law. The telegram stated the vote, which was very decisive, and Seward thought sufficient was done by the Governor in sending this word to authorize the President to act; but the latter queried whether he ought not first to see the constitution, and know what were its provisions, and whether a more formal communication than a telegraphic dispatch ought not to be received. Seward, however, was, in his loose way of treating the most important questions, ready to act, said almost everything was done nowadays by telegraph. He received and sent the most important communications in that way, and presumed the other Departments did also, and turned to Fessenden as if to have him verify the fact. Fessenden said, however, with some sharpness, the President would do as he pleased, but that he, Fessenden, would not put his name to a proclamation under such circumstances, but would have, in a proper form, the fact.

The President, differing with Seward, yet unwilling to give dissatisfaction, told him he might prepare a proclamation, and in the mean time he would examine the laws and consider the subject. No reasons were given for the extreme haste exhibited. Seward said the Governor was very anxious about it, and Nye, a Democrat of former years, is one of his pets and somewhat thick of late with both him and Weed. I suggested that if the people had framed and adopted their constitution, and it was not inconsistent with the Federal Constitution, it was and would be their form of government, whether the President enunciated the fact a few days earlier or not, that being a mere ministerial act. But, supposing there was some objectionable feature, — that they had extended or altered the prescribed boundaries, or inserted some improper provisions, — the President might feel himself greatly embarrassed if he acted without knowledge.

This, however, is a specimen of the manner in which the Secretary of State administers affairs. He would have urged on the President to this unwise proceeding to gratify one of his favorites. It is a trait in his character.

XXIV

Seward and the Texas Cotton Matter — Arranging for an Exchange of
Naval Prisoners — Fessenden on the Naval Officers — Relations of
Fessenden, Stanton, and Seward — The Bounty to enlisting Marines —
Death of Judge Taney — A Call from General Banks — Getting the
Election Returns — Cabinet Discussion of the President's Message,
especially as to Reconstruction — The Discovery of Gold in the Territories and the Treasury's Fiscal Policy — Discussion of the Chief-Jus-
ticeship of the Supreme Court — Resignation of Attorney-General
Bates — Solicitor Whiting's Aspirations — Judge Taney's Compliment to the Navy Department — The Case of the Captured Confederate Cruiser Florida — The Attitude of the *New York Evening Post*
towards the Navy Department — Political Tour of Governors Morgan
and Morrill before the Election — The Labor of preparing an Annual
Report — Proposal that the Navy Department take a Ship building in
the United States for Japan.

October 1, *Saturday*. The President yesterday made inquiry of me as to the disposition made of Farragut. Informed me that General Canby wanted him to remain at
Mobile, and that F. preferred doing so to coming to Wilmington. I told him Farragut was relieved of the latter
duty, and he could remain as long as he pleased in the Gulf.
This morning the President called at the Navy Department
and made further inquiry. Said that Halleck and Sherman
had some movements on hand, and the War Department
also, and would like to know if F. could remain. I told him
he could.

Shortly after he left, two dispatches from Admiral Farragut came on to my table, received by this morning's
mail, in which he expressed decided aversion to taking
command at Wilmington.

These dispatches inform me that General Canby has an
expedition on foot for the capture of Mobile, that he is
getting troops for this purpose, etc., all of which has been
studiously kept from the Navy Department, and now

when ready to move, they are embarrassed. I immediately went over to the War Department and the President was there. He was, I soon saw, but slightly informed of the proposed army movement, but Stanton and Halleck, finding they had refined too much, had communicated hastily with him, in order that he should see me.

All this is bad administration. There will be want of unity and concert under such management. It is not because the President has any want of confidence in his Cabinet, but Seward and Stanton both endeavor to avoid Cabinet consultations on questions of their own Departments. It has been so from the beginning on the part of the Secretary of State, who spends more or less of every day with the President and worms from him all the information he possesses and can be induced to impart. A disposition to constantly intermeddle with other Departments, to pry into them and often to control and sometimes counteract them, has manifested itself throughout, often involving himself and others in difficulty. Chase for some time was annoyed that things were so but at length went into competition for the President's ear and company. He did not succeed, however, as against Seward, though adopting his policy of constant attendance. Stanton has been for the departmental system always. Pressing, assuming, violent, and impatient, intriguing, harsh, and arbitrary, he is often exceedingly offensive in his manners, deportment, and many of his acts.

A majority of the friends of the Administration in the last Congress was opposed to the President, but his opponents were the cronies and intimates of Stanton, or Chase, who, however, were not cordial towards one another or in anything but in their hostility to the President. Stanton kept on more intimate terms with the President, while his friends were the most violent in their enmity. Wade, Winter Davis, and men of that description were Stanton's particular favorites and in constant consultation with him.

October 3, *Monday*. Had an interview with Seward, agreeable to the wishes of the President, concerning the order to A. J. Hamilton for bringing out cotton. I perceived that S. was prepared for me, and had expected an earlier call. He said that the scheme was one by which certain important persons in the Rebel cause were to be converted. Had himself not much faith that it would amount to anything, and yet it might. The President believed there would be results; but had been very confidential and secret in all that was done. He (S.) had drawn up the order carefully by special request of the President, but had never communicated to any one but Stanton what had been done. Some time since Stanton had got some inkling of the subject and had directly applied to him for information, and when this was done he did not feel at liberty to withhold from a colleague intelligence sought. But he at once informed the President that he had told Stanton. Nothing had yet been done, and nothing farther said, until I had brought up the subject. I remarked that the subject was of a character which seemed to deserve general consultation in the Cabinet, for three of the members besides himself were concerned in its executions; that I was especially so, it being my special duty to prevent intercourse with the Rebels and enforce the blockade. But this order conflicted with that duty, was not in good faith, I apprehended, with others of our people, or with foreign powers. I told him I had made inquiries of Fessenden, for the order expressly referred to the Treasury agents, and they would of course report to him. Seward said there was no interference with the blockade. He had prepared the order with great care and sent one copy to General Canby, and one to Admiral Farragut, and proposed to send and get it for my perusal, give me a copy if I wished. I told him I already had a copy, which seemed to surprise him. He appeared not to be aware that it was the duty of a naval officer to communicate his official acts to the Navy Department; that all the three Departments must come into possession of this confidential circular, and not unlikely it would go into the courts. He is not yet dispossessed of his early error that the government can be carried on by executive order regardless of Department or laws.

October 4, *Tuesday*. But little at the Cabinet of special importance. Governor Dennison, the new Postmaster-General, for the first time took his seat.

Late in the afternoon the President called upon me to inquire respecting arrangements for a proposed exchange of naval prisoners which was making some disturbance at the War Department and with General Butler. For some fifteen months our naval officers and men who had been captured remained in Rebel prisons. Their number was not large, but the omission to exchange, whether from neglect or design, was justly causing dissatisfaction. For more than a year I had, at various times, made inquiry of the Secretary of War and at the War Department, generally oral, but sometimes by letter, and received evasive answers, — of difficulties on account of remoteness, of unusual prisoners, of refusal by the Rebels to exchange negroes, — but with assurances that matters would be soon adjusted. Some of our men we had learned were in irons and in close confinement, with slight prospect of relief. I gave the President briefly the facts, — that there had been no exchange of naval prisoners for fourteen or fifteen months, that in the exchanges going on no naval prisoners were embraced, that appeals earnest and touching had been made to me by our prisoners and by theirs, but I had been able to afford no relief.

An informal correspondence after months of unavailing effort through the War Department channel had sprung up between Mr. Fox and Webb, who commanded the Atlanta, and was a prisoner in Fort Warren, they having been some years ago shipmates. Fox had written Webb in reply to an application for release that we were willing to exchange but the Rebel authorities would not. This had led the Rebel prisoners in Fort Warren to write most earnestly to Richmond. A few weeks since Lieutenant-Commander Williams had been released at Charleston, and sent to our fleet under flag of truce with thirty days' leave to effect an exchange, and brought me a letter from Mallory, "Secretary Confederate Navy," stating he had not received letters which had been sent, but accepting a proposition to exchange naval officers, and proposing himself to exchange *all* naval prisoners. This had been assented to by us, and we now sent orders for the Circassian to proceed with a hundred or two prisoners to Port Royal and bring home our men. But after instructions had been sent to Boston for them to go by the Circassian, we had received by telegram from Ould[1] word that the yellow fever prevailed at Charleston, with a suggestion that the proper exchange could take place on the James River. When this suggestion was made, I objected to it from an impression that it would come within the army cartel and cause difficulty, but after discussing the subject with Mr. Fox, who dwelt on the infection, getting yellow fever in the squadron and at Port Royal, and some conversation with General Hitchcock, I reluctantly yielded assent. Word had been sent to our senior officer, Melancthon Smith, on the James, who had communicated with Butler, and hence the difficulty.

October 5, Wednesday. The President came to see me pretty early this morning in relation to the exchange of prisoners. It had troubled him through the night. I was at no loss to perceive that behind the subject of exchange there were matters undisclosed to me. He read again this morning the closing remarks of a long telegram from Butler. I have no question there were improper remarks in that dispatch which they at the War Department were unwilling either Mr. Fox or myself should see, for I called Fox in to have all the facts disclosed. He and Webb had, by their correspondence, led to the late movement, which

[1] Acting for the Confederate government.

was, however, humane and right. The President said he wanted the subject to be got along with harmoniously, that they were greatly ruffled at the War Department, and if I had no objection he would go and see Seward, tell him the facts, get him to come over, and bring the Secretary of War and all in interest to a consultation. I told him I had no objection, nor any feeling, as it affected myself, on the subject. All I wanted was our imprisoned men.

In less than an hour the President returned with Seward. We went briefly over the question and read to him Mallory's letter. After discussing the subject, went, by request of the President, with him to the War Department. General Hitchcock and General Halleck came in soon. Stanton was ill-mannered, as usual, where things did not please him, and on one or two occasions a little offensive. Did not know why there should be different exchanges; the Rebels would not recognize negroes. I told him that, while general cartel was neglected, the army were making exchanges here, and by Butler on the James, Sherman at Atlanta, Canby at New Orleans, and Foster at Hilton Head. I thought it proper and felt it my duty to see that the naval men were not entirely neglected. That no question as regards color had ever come up in regard to naval exchange; that colored men in our service were not a distinct organization, etc., etc. It was, he said, our duty to prevent Rebel masters from reclaiming slaves who had been in our service. He thought I ought not to write the Confederate Secretary of the Navy, recognizing him as Secretary. That the slave-owners would insist on retaining and reclaiming their slaves wherever and whenever they could, I had no doubt. It was a question of property, and of local and legal right with them which we could not prevent. It was a complicated and embarrassing question, but he must not suppose, nor would the country permit our countrymen to suffer in captivity on such a question. To absolutely stop exchanges because owners held on to their slaves when they got them was an atrocious wrong, one that I would not be a party to.

As regarded Mallory, I told him I had carefully avoided giving him a title, — that I had written to the Hon. Mr. Mallory in answer to a communication I had received.

The President said that the correspondence was a past transaction, — that we need not disturb that matter; the Navy arrangement must go forward, and the Navy have its men. He wrote and read a brief letter to General Grant proposing to turn over the prisoners we had sent to him. After reading it he asked for comments and opinions. General Hitchcock, a man of warm sympathies but little moral courage, began a speech, sycophantic to Stanton, intimating that the War Department should have exclusive control of the cartel, etc. I told him I was perfectly willing and desired it, if they would not obstruct the exchange but get back our men. All assented to the President's letter. Stanton and Seward preferred it should be addressed to General Butler instead of General Grant, but the President preferred addressing the General-in-Chief and I commended his preference. We telegraphed Capt. Melancthon Smith, to turn the prisoners over to General Grant to be disposed of.

In the course of the conversation, Stanton, who began to feel that his position might not stand, said he had known nothing about these exchanges. I told him we had written him requesting that the Rebel prisoners at different points might be sent to Fort Warren in order to be exchanged. General Hitchcock, his commissioner, had been consulted in the matter, and had communicated with Mr. Fox, to whom had been given the charge of details for the Navy, as General Hitchcock had them for the War Department. General Hitchcock himself had proposed that we should take some one or two army men on board the Circassian as a special favor. After this matter was disposed of, and before leaving the room, Seward spoke aside to the President and also to the Secretary of War, stating he had appointed a meeting between them and Weed and Raymond, who were in the building, he had no doubt. As I came out of the

Secretary's apartment, Weed was in the opposite room, and evidently saw me, for he immediately stepped aside so as not to be seen. It was not an accidental move, but hastily and awkwardly done. They waited half behind the door until we passed out.

October 6, Thursday. Admiral Porter has arrived from Cairo and proceeds to-morrow to Hampton Roads to take command of the North Atlantic Squadron. It is with reluctance that he comes into this transfer, but yet he breathes not an objection. I should not have mentioned the circumstance but for the fact that many put a false construction upon it. He will have a difficult task to perform and not the thanks he will deserve, I fear, if successful, but curses if he fails.

October 7, Friday. The President was not at his house to-day. Mr. Bates had said to me that the President told him there was no special business. Nevertheless, I preferred soon after twelve to walk over, having some little business of my own. Fessenden, Usher, and myself arrived about the same moment, and we had half an hour's friendly talk. In the course of it, Fessenden took an occasion to pass an opinion upon certain naval officers, showing the prejudiced partisan rather than the enlightened minister and statesman. Farragut, he said, was the only naval officer who has exhibited any skill and ability; there were undoubtedly other officers, but they had not been brought out. I inquired what he thought of Foote. "Well, I allude more particularly to the living," said he, "but what is Lee, that you have kept him in? Is there any reason except his relationship to the Blairs and to Fox?" — he knew of no other reason. I inquired when Lee had been remiss, and asked him if he knew that Montgomery Blair and Lee were not on speaking terms and had not been for years. He seemed surprised and said he was not. I told him such was the case; that he had never expressed a wish in Lee's behalf to me, or manifested any gratification at that selection, but on the contrary, I knew Blair had thought, with him, that it was an appointment not judicious. I did not tell F. of the narrow animosity of Lee towards Fox. But all this spleen came, I knew, from the War Department and certain influences connected with it. Dahlgren he also denounced, yet when I inquired if he had ever investigated the subject, if he was aware that Dahlgren had maintained an efficient blockade, while Du Pont, whom he half complimented, had not [sic]. "Then," said I, "what do you say of Porter?" He admitted that he had thought pretty well of Porter until he begun to gather in cotton, and run a race with Banks to get it instead of doing his duty. I told him this was ungenerous and, I apprehended, a sad mistake on his part. The whole tenor of the conversation left no doubt on my mind that Stanton, Winter Davis, Wade, Chase, the thieving Treasury agents and speculators had imposed on Fessenden.

. . . Fessenden is, in some personal matters, very much of a partisan, and his partisan feelings have made him the victim of a very cunning intrigue. He dislikes Seward, and yet is, through other instrumentalities, the creature to some extent of Seward.

Stanton, having been brought into the Cabinet by Seward, started out as a radical. Chase and others were deceived by his pretensions at the beginning, but some time before leaving the Cabinet, Chase found a part of his mistake. Fessenden and others have not yet. They suppose Stanton is with them; Seward knows better. I have no doubt but Stanton when with Fessenden, Wade, and others acquiesces and participates in their expressed views against Seward. Hating Blair, it has grieved Stanton that Lee, the brother-in-law of Blair, should have command, and Fessenden has been impressed accordingly. Himself inclined to radicalism on the slavery issue, though in other respects conservative, Fessenden, who is in full accord with Chase, has a dislike to Blair, an old Democrat but who is represented as the friend of Seward. Yet Blair has no more confidence in, or regard for, Seward than Fessenden has, and I have been surprised that he should acquiesce in the erroneous impression that is abroad. It is easy to perceive why Seward should favor the impression alluded to. Blair was ready to accept the denunciatory resolution of the Baltimore convention as aimed at him, whereas it was intended more particularly for Seward. The Missouri radicals are some who were deceived by the impression that Seward and Blair were a unit. In the convention there was a determination to get rid of Mr. Seward, but the managers, under the contrivance of Raymond, who has shrewdness, so shaped the resolution as to leave it pointless, or as not more direct against Seward than against Blair, or by others against Chase and Stanton.

October 10, *Monday.* Advised with the President in regard to a proceeding of the late Colonel Harris, who offered a bounty, or directed the recruiting officer to promise a bounty, of $100 to each marine who should enlist. It came to my knowledge in July, 1863, and I prohibited it, because it would create dissatisfaction with the sailors. The legal point I did not examine, but I was opposed to it as impolitic and inexpedient. In reply to my inquiries as to when he commenced giving this bounty, he said in June, and I supposed it was the preceding June and therefore covered but one month, the bounty to be paid after two years service. But I now learn it commenced in June, 1862, and consequently covers thirteen, instead of one month, and that there are over eleven hundred so enlisted. I decided they must be discharged or paid the bounty, and as there was a question as to the legality of the bounty, I thought it best, so long as I supposed there was only one month's enlistment, to discharge, but when I ascertained it was for more than a year and embraced over eleven hundred, I thought best to reëxamine the whole subject with the President. He concurs with me and decides it is best to pay the bounty.

October 11, *Tuesday*. The President and Seward called on me this forenoon relative to New York voters in the Navy. Wanted one of our boats to be placed at the disposal of the New York commission to gather votes in the Mississippi Squadron. A Mr. Jones was referred to, who subsequently came to me with a line from the President, and wanted also to send to the blockading squadrons. Gave permission to go by the Circassian, and directed commanders to extend facilities to all voters.

Much is said and done in regard to the soldier's vote, and many of the States not only have passed laws but altered their constitutions to permit it. The subject is one that has not struck me favorably. I have not, perhaps, given it the consideration that I ought, — certainly not enough to advocate it, — and yet it seems ungracious to oppose it. Were I to vote on this question at all, I should, with my present impressions. vote against it.

October 12, *Wednesday*. Returns of the elections from Pennsylvania, Ohio, and Indiana come in to-day. They look very well, particularly the two latter. Pennsylvania does not quite come up to my expectations. The city of Philadelphia has done very well, but in too many of the counties there are Democratic gains, — not such, perhaps, as to overcome the Union majorities, but will much reduce them.

October 13, *Thursday*. The President is greatly importuned and pressed by cunning intrigues just at this time. Thurlow Weed and Raymond are abusing his confidence and good nature badly. Hay says they are annoying the President sadly. This he tells Mr. Fox, who informs me. They want, Hay says, to control the Navy Yard but dislike to come to me, for I give them no favorable response. They claim that every mechanic or laborer who does not support the Administration should be turned out of employment. Hay's representations alarmed Fox, who made it a point to call on the President. F. reports that the President was feeling very well over the election returns, and, on the subject of the Navy Yard votes, expressed his intention of not further interfering but will turn the whole matter over to me whenever the politicians call upon him. I have no doubt he thinks so, but when Weed and Raymond, backed by Seward, insist that action must be taken, he will hardly know how to act. His convictions and good sense will place him with me, but they will alarm him with forebodings of disaster if he is not vindictive. Among other things an appeal has been made to him in behalf of Scofield, a convicted fraudulent contractor, who is now in prison to serve out his sentence. Without consulting me, the President has referred the subject to Judge-Advocate-General Holt, to review and report to him. Holt knows nothing of the case, and, with his other duties, cannot examine this matter thoroughly. Why should the President require him, an officer of another Department, wholly unacquainted with the subject, to report upon it? There are probably two thousand pages of manuscript. The New York party jobbers are in this thing. They will . . . try to procure [Scofield's] release and pardon for a consideration.

October 14, *Friday.* Seward was quite exultant over the elections; feels strong and self-gratified. Says this Administration is wise, energetic, faithful, and able beyond any of its predecessors; that it has gone through trials which none of them has ever known, and carried on, under extraordinary circumstances and against combinations such as the world has never known, a war unparalleled in the annals of the world. The death of Judge Taney was alluded to. His funeral takes place to-morrow. The body will pass from his residence at 7 A.M. to the depot; and be carried to Frederick, Maryland. Seward thought it his duty to attend the funeral in this city but not farther, and advised that the President should also. The Attorney-General deemed it his duty and a proper courtesy to go with the remains to F. The President inquired my views. I thought the suggestions in regard to himself and Messrs. Seward and Bates very well, and it would be best not to take official action but to let each member of the Cabinet act his pleasure. For my own part, I felt little inclined to participate. I have never called upon him living, and while his position and office were to be respected, I had no honors for the deceased beyond those that were public. That he had many good qualities and possessed ability, I do not doubt; that he rendered service in Jackson's administration is true, and during most of his judicial life he was upright and just. But the course pursued in the Dred Scott case and all the attending circumstances forfeited respect for him as a man or a judge.

October 15, *Saturday*. The speeches of Jeff Davis betoken the close of the War. The rebellion is becoming exhausted, and I hope ere many months will be entirely suppressed. Not that there may not be lingering banditti to rob and murder for a while longer, the offspring of a demoralized state of society, but the organized rebellion cannot long endure.

One of the assistants from the office of Judge-Advocate Holt came from that office to make some inquiries as to the views of the Department in Scofield's case. He says that Thurlow Weed and Raymond are very urgent in the matter, and that some one named Williamson is active and pressing. I have no doubt a heavy fee lies behind a pardon in this case, which is pressed upon the President as if it were all-essential that it should be granted before the election. It pains me that the President should listen to such fellows in such a matter, or allow himself to be tampered with at all. The very fact that he avoids communicating with me on the subject is complimentary to me; at the same time it is evident that he has some conception of the unworthy purpose of the intriguers I mention.

General Banks called on me yesterday formally before

2

leaving Washington. I have not previously seen him since he returned, though I hear he has called on part of the Cabinet. We had some conversation respecting his command and administration in Louisiana. The new constitution, the climate, etc., were discussed. Before leaving, he alluded to the accusations that had been made against him, and desired to know if there was anything specific. I told him there had been complaints about cotton and errors committed; that these were always numerous when there were reverses. That, he said, was very true, but he had been informed Admiral Porter had gone beyond that, and was his accuser. I remarked that several naval officers had expressed themselves dissatisfied, — some of them stronger than Admiral Porter, — that others besides naval officers had also complained.

The *Republican* of this evening has an article evidently originating with General Banks, containing some unworthy flings at both Lee and Porter. Banks did not write the paragraph nor perhaps request it to be written, but the writer is his willing tool and was imbued with General Banks's feelings. He is doubtless Hanscom, a fellow without conscience when his interest is concerned, an intimate and, I believe, a relative, of Banks.

November 25. For some weeks I have been unable to note down occurrences daily. On the evening of the election, the 8th, I went to the War Department about nine o'clock by invitation of the President. Took Fox with me, who was a little reluctant to go lest he should meet Stanton, who had for some days been ill. The Department was locked, but we were guided to the south door. The President was already there, and some returns from different quarters had been received. He detailed particulars of each telegram which had been received. Hay soon joined us and, after a little time, General Eaton. Mr. Eckert, the operator, had a fine supper prepared, of which we partook soon after 10. It was evident shortly after that the election had gone pretty much one way. Some doubts about New Jersey and Delaware. We remained until past one in the morning and left. All was well.

The President on two or three occasions in Cabinet-meeting alluded to his message. It seemed to dwell heavy on his mind, — more than I have witnessed on any former occasion. On Friday, the 25th, he read to us what he had prepared. There was nothing very striking, and he evidently labors in getting it up. The subject of Reconstruction and how it should be effected is the most important theme. He says he cannot treat with Jeff Davis and the Jeff Davis government, which is all very well, but whom will he treat with, or how commence the work? All expressed themselves very much gratified with the document and his views. I suggested whether it would not be well to invite back not only the people but the States to their obligations and duties. We are one country. I would not recognize what is called the Confederate government, for that is a usurpation, but the States are entities and may be recognized and treated with. Stanton, who was present for the first time for six weeks, after each had expressed his views, and, indeed, after some other topic had been taken up and disposed of, made some very pertinent and in the main proper and well-timed remarks, advising the President to make no new demonstration or offer, to bring forward his former policy and maintain it, to hold open the doors of conciliation and invite the people to return to their duty. He would appeal to them to do so, and ask them whether it would not have been better for them and for all, had they a year since accepted his offer.

Each of the members of the Cabinet were requested to prepare a brief statement of the affairs of their respective Departments. Seward had already handed in much of his. I told the President I would hand him my brief the next day.

At this meeting on the 25th, Mr. Usher made some allusion to the gold that was forthcoming in the Territories.

The President interrupted him, saying he had been giving that matter a good deal of attention and he was opposed to any excitement on the subject. He proposed that the gold should remain in the mountains until the War was over, for it would now only add to the currency and we had already too much currency. It would be better to stop than to increase it.

Mr. Fessenden said something must be done, for he could not any longer negotiate on the basis of paying interest in coin. We cannot, he says, get the specie and must stop paying it out. I was amused. Neither of them appeared to have even the rudiments of finance and currency. Gold is no longer a currency with us. It is merchandise, and all that may be got from Idaho, Nevada, Arizona, and California will not swell the volume of currency. Our banking and irredeemable paper issues are legal tenders and made currency not based on specie, and of course it is an inferior currency.

Our Secretary of the Treasury must learn that if he does not demand and pay out gold he will have none. If he will reduce the volume of paper currency, so as to create a demand for gold, he will get it, but he will never have it if he slights it. He has schemes for getting out cotton to relieve him and the Treasury in making payments, and the blockade is to be indirectly violated in order to get cotton from the Rebels with which to purchase gold. Of course we shall have to pay the Rebels if not in gold, in its equivalent, for all the cotton we get of them, and shall thus furnish them with the sinews of war.

It cannot be otherwise than that the country will become impoverished with such ideas pervading the government. There will be devastation and ruin, if not corrected, before us. Fessenden is of the old Whig school of folly on finance and currency; is resorting to flimsy expedients, instead of honest, hard truth. Gold is truth; irredeemable paper and flimsy expedients are not.

[*November* 26, *Saturday.*] I called on the President Saturday, the 26th, as I had promised him I would the day before, with my abstract for the message, intending to have a full, free talk with him on the subjects that were under review the day previous. But Mr. Bates was there with his resignation, and evidently anxious to have a private interview with the President.

The question of Chief Justice has excited much remark and caused quite a movement with many. Mr. Chase is expecting it, and he has many strong friends who are urging him. But I have not much idea that the President will appoint him, nor is it advisable he should. I had called on the President on the 23d, and had some conversation, after dispatching a little business, in regard to this appointment of Chief Justice. He said there was a great pressure and a good many talked of, but that he had not prepared his message and did not intend to take up the subject of judge before the session commenced.

"There is," said he, "a tremendous pressure just now for Evarts of New York, who, I suppose, is a good lawyer?" This he put inquiringly. I stated that he stood among the foremost at the New York bar; perhaps no one was more prominent as a lawyer. "But that," I remarked, "is not all. Our Chief Justice must have a judicial mind, be upright, of strict integrity, not too pliant; should be a statesman and a politician." By politician I did not mean a partisan. [I said] that it appeared to me the occasion should be improved to place at the head of the court a man, not a partisan, but one who was impressed with the principles and doctrines which had brought this Administration into power; that it would conduce to the public welfare and his own comfort to have harmony between himself and the judicial department, and that it was all-important that he should have a judge who would be a correct and faithful expositor of the principles of his administration and policy after his administration shall have closed. I stated that among the candidates who had been named, Mr. Montgomery Blair, it appeared to me, best conformed to these requirements; that the President knew the man, his ability, his truthfulness, honesty, and courage.

The President at different points expressed his concurrence in my views, and spoke kindly and complimentarily of Mr. Blair, but did not in any way commit himself, nor did I expect or suppose he would.

I have since seen and had a full conversation with Blair. We had previously exchanged a few words on the subject. I then stated to him that, while it would gratify me to see him on the bench, I preferred that he should continue in active political life, and that I had especially desired he should go into the War Department. This point was alluded to in our present interview, and he confessed the War Department was more congenial to his feelings, but Seward wanted a tool there, and if he had influence, it would be exerted against him (Blair) for that place. Yet in a conversation which he had with Seward about a week since, Seward had given him (Blair) to understand that he was his (Seward's) candidate for Chief Justice. I told him that he could hardly be sincere in this, for Evarts would not consent to be a candidate nor think of it if Seward was not for him. Blair seemed a little shocked with this view of facts, and remarked that if Seward was not for him he was an infernal hypocrite.

Blair says he is singularly placed at this juncture, for the Marylanders are disposed to put him in the Senate at this time, while this judicial appointment is pending. I told him that personally I should be as much pleased to see him in the Senate as in the Court.

Governor Dennison, Postmaster-General, called at my house this evening to have some conversation on the subject of judge. He says he is and was at the last session committed for his fellow townsman Judge Swayne, who was at the time recommended by all on the bench; that he had called on the President at that time in behalf of Swayne, and the President then remarked that that seemed a set-

EDWARD BATES

tled question in which all were agreed. Governor D. is now a little embarrassed, for he feels particularly friendly to Blair.

As regards Mr. Chase, Governor D., like myself, thinks it impossible that he should receive the appointment, — that it is one which the President cannot properly make. Says they could not assimilate, and that, were Chase in that position, — a life tenure, — he would exhibit his resentments against the President, who he thinks has prevented his upward official career. He then told me that he labored to get Chase into the Treasury, and how sadly he had been disappointed over his failure as a financier. One of the strong traits of Chase, he says, is the memory of differences, and that he never forgets or forgives those who have once thwarted him. He may suppress his revenge, but it is abiding.

The resignation of Attorney-General Bates has initiated more intrigues. A host of candidates are thrust forward, or are thrusting themselves forward. Evarts, Holt, Cushing, Whiting, and the Lord knows who, are all candidates. Under the circumstances it appears to me the appointment must go to one of the Border States, and hence I have thought Holt would most probably be the candidate of the President. He is, moreover, of Democratic antecedents; still I have no information on the subject.

Fox tells me that Whiting sought him yesterday and introduced the subject of the Navy Department, and inquired of Fox if he would remain were I to leave. To this F. says he replied he thought not, for we had got along so well together that he did not believe he could be reconciled to another. Whiting told him that would have great influence in the matter; that it was thought Senator Grimes might be offered the appointment if there was a change. All of this means that Whiting wants to be Attorney-General, but New England cannot have more appointments, and the little fellow is intriguing for a remote chance. Could the Secretary of the Navy come from Iowa, the Attorney-General, he thinks, might be selected from New England. The game is very easily read. Little Whiting's intrigues are not equal to his egotism, and yet he is a convenient instrument for others. He writes for Stanton, for Seward, and for the President, and intrigues generally. But he overestimates himself. He will never go into the Cabinet.

R. H. Gillett, formerly Solicitor of the Treasury, now a practicing lawyer, chiefly in the Supreme Court, stopped me a few mornings since to relate his last interview with Judge Taney. They were discussing governmental affairs. The Chief Justice was, he says, communicative and instructive. He said the Navy Department made less noise than some of the others, but no Department of the government was so well managed or better performed its duty.

This was, and is, high praise from a quarter that makes it appreciated. The Chief Justice could, as well as any man, form a correct opinion, and in giving it he must have been disinterested. Twenty-five and thirty years ago we were slightly acquainted, but I do not remember that I have exchanged a word with him since the days of Van Buren, — perhaps I did in Polk's administration. The proceedings in the Dred Scott case alienated my feelings entirely. I have never called on him, as I perhaps ought in courtesy to have done, but it was not in me, for I have looked on him and his court as having contributed, unintentionally perhaps, but largely, to the calamities of our afflicted country. They probably did not mean treason but thought their wisdom and official position would give national sanction to a great wrong. Whether Judge T. retained any recollection of me, or our former slight acquaintance, I probably shall never know, but his compliment I highly value.

The case of the Florida has from time to time and in various ways been up. She was taken by Collins in the Wachusett at Bahia and brought to Hampton Roads. Having been captured in neutral waters, a great outcry has

gone up from the English press and people, and some of our
own have manifested a morbid sentiment with those English who have nothing to do with the subject. The Secretary of State has not known what to say, and, I think, not
what to do. In our first or second conversation he expressed a hope that we should not be compelled to give up
the Florida, and this he repeated in each of our subsequent
interviews. I told him the idea ought not to be seriously
thought of for a moment, and said that I knew of no instance where a belligerent armed vessel had been restored.
That he owed a respectful apology to Brazil, I not only
admitted but asserted. We have disturbed her peace, been
guilty of discourtesy, etc., etc. Yet Brazil herself has in the
first instance done wrong. She has given refuge and aid to
the robbers whom she does not recognize as a government.
She has, while holding amicable relations with us, seen these
pirates seize and burn our merchant vessels, and permitted
these plundering marauders to get supplies and to refit in
her ports, and almost make her harbors the base of operations. What Brazil will demand or require I know not.
Although she has done wrong to us in giving comfort and
assistance to these robbers, I would make amends for her
offended sovereignty by any proper acknowledgments. I do
not believe she will have the impudence to ask restitution.
If she did, it would be under British prompting and I would
not give it. The case is not as if the war was between two
nations. Yet some of our politicians and editors are treating it as such. Among others the *New York Evening Post*. I
am inclined to think there is something personal towards
me in this pertness of the *Evening Post*. The papers have
alluded to differences between Seward and myself. There
has been no such controversy or difference as the *Post* represents on this subject. All our talk has been amicable,
he doubtful and hesitating, I decided and firm on certain
points which, if he does not assent to, he does not controvert. But the publisher of the *Evening Post* is held in bail
for malfeasance at the instance of the Navy Department.

Great efforts have been made to let him off, to which I could not yield, and his case is to come off before the grand jury now in session. Under these circumstances the editors of the *Post* are very willing to differ with me on a public question, and yet they would never admit that they were actuated by personal considerations or a design to influence and bias the jury. It is, they think, their nice sense of honor, which would have us, as a nation, humble ourselves to Brazil for having taken a pirate by the throat within her jurisdiction, and that same sense of honor would screen a malefactor from exposure and punishment.

Brazil, and other governments who have given shelter, comfort, and aid to the piratical vessels that have plundered our commerce under a pretended flag which neither Brazil nor any other nation recognizes, committed the first great wrong. The government of Brazil is aware that the Rebel pirates have no admiralty court, that they have never sent in a vessel captured for condemnation; therefore Brazil herself, by permitting and acquiescing in the outrages on a friendly nation, is the first aggressor, and she should be held to it. If we have injured Brazil, let us make reparation, full and ample. If she has injured us, let her do her duty also, in this respect. So far as her majesty is disturbed by our taking a sneaking thief, whom she was entertaining, by the throat, — an outlaw with some of his robberies upon him, — let all proper atonement be made.

I suggested to Mr. Seward that proceedings should be commenced against the prisoners captured on the Florida as pirates, but he shrank from it, although it would have relieved him of many difficulties. It would not have been wrong to have gone to extremes with them, but the prosecution would bring out the true points and stop noise.

Governor Morgan detailed his journey with Governor Morrill through the different States, visiting the different governors and our political friends prior to the election, under an appointment, it seems, from the Secretary of War, ostensibly to attend to the draft. It was when polit-

ical affairs looked darkest. He thinks that he and M. under
this appointment and visit did much to dissipate the gloom.
The intrigues of the radicals were totally defeated, and,
after opposing and abusing the President, all of them
finally came in, as I had no doubt they would. Morgan
says the malcontents held their final secret meeting at the
house of one of the editors of the *Evening Post.*

Chase was, Morgan says, open and sharp in his opposition to the President, — they heard of him at various
places, — but, finding he could accomplish nothing, he
eventually came in, called on the President, procured the
sacrifice of Blair as a pretext for his wounded and bruised
feelings and those of his friends. This is Morgan's representation.

There was probably something in this, and also, I think,
in the intrigues of Thurlow Weed. Strange antagonisms
seem to have been harnessed up together in some party-
political personal operations. Morgan thinks Chase will be
appointed Chief Justice, but I do not yet arrive at that
conclusion. The President sometimes does strange things,
but this would be a singular mistake, in my opinion, for
one who is so shrewd and honest, — an appointment that
he would soon regret. In this M. agrees with me, and also
that Blair is the man.

The place of Attorney-General has been tendered to
Holt, who declines it, preferring his present position. This
I think an error; that is, no man should decline a place of
such responsibility in times like these when the country is
so unanimous in his favor. Whiting, Solicitor of the War
Department and patent lawyer, is sorely disappointed.

November 30, *Wednesday.* Have just finished and sent
my report to the printer. It is long and has been a wearisome and laborious business. To weigh conflicting claims
and opinions, to make needed suggestions of reform and
improvement, without exciting hostility or committing
error, to do justice to merit, to avoid the commission or

omission of acts which provoke controversy, to speak of
one's own acts without egotism and yet without want of
manly self-respect, to condense much in little space, to
narrate briefly the deeds of our naval men, to encourage
and stimulate them in well-doing, with a multitude of
detail, make the preparing of an annual report in a time
like this very laborious. The reports of the Chiefs of Bureaus and of naval officers are to be scanned with care; the
various briefs and suggestions submitted have to be canvassed and weighed, and the views, whether adopted or
rejected, to be criticized. To get this off my hands is a
great relief. What censures and complaints and criticisms,
just and unjust, may follow for the next few days and weeks
do not trouble me. I am only now glad that the labor is off
my hands, and I dismiss it from my mind. If its suggestions and recommendations shall elicit investigation, inquiry, or action, I, conscious of right intentions, shall try
to be prepared in the premises.

There are some singular movements in regard to our relations with Japan and certain transactions connected with
that people that cause me annoyance. Some two years ago,
or more, our Minister or Commissioner to Japan notified
the State Department or the Secretary of State that the
Japanese government wanted two or three of our vessels,
and had placed in his hands, or would place in the hands
of such persons as he, the Minister, might select, $600,000
for the purpose. Mr. Pruyn, the Minister, accepted the
trust and appointed his brother-in-law, Lansing, and Thurlow Weed to execute it. Mr. Seward addressed a note to
me on the subject, submitting the letter. I advised that
the government in no way should become involved in the
affair, and gave offense to Weed, who, not friendly before,
has intrigued against me ever since. My advice would have
been the same, had any other person than Weed been
named. Without regarding my suggestions, the work went
on. One of the vessels is finished. I know not whether
more than one has been commenced. A difference has

grown up between Japan and the European powers, and, under the direction of Mr. Pruyn, our Minister, we have joined in the fight, become involved in an English and French war with Japan, although the Japanese have no quarrel with us. Now comes an inquiry to me from persons sent here by Weed, to know if the Navy Department will not examine, approve, and take this vessel, which has been built and been paid for. I am not pleased with the management or proposed arrangement. This whole proceeding on the American side had appeared to me a fraud and swindle to enrich Weed & Co. It is wicked to prostitute the government to such a private purpose, and to impose upon the Japanese, who have trusted us. I am opposed to having the Navy Department mixed up in any manner with this scheme, and have let the President know what I think of it and Seward also. Weed does not approach me on the subject. He has not been able to use the Navy Department as he wishes, and, like John P. Hale, is at enmity with me because I will not consent to be used in swindling operations. New York party politics are always more or less personal. Party organizations are considered convincing contrivances to be used by leading managers for their benefit.

XXV

December 3, Saturday. The President read his message at a special Cabinet-meeting to-day and general criticism took place. His own portion has been much improved. The briefs submitted by the several members were incorporated pretty much in their own words. One paragraph proposing an Amendment to the Constitution recognizing the Deity in that instrument met with no favorable response from any one member of the Cabinet. The President, before reading it, expressed his own doubts in regard to it, but it had been urged by certain religionists.

I should have been glad, and so stated, had there been a more earnest appeal to the Southern people and to the States respectively to return to duty. I would have said to the people that their States are part of the Union; that they were not to be considered, not to be treated, as outlaws; that, by returning to their allegiance, their persons and property should be respected; and I would have invited State action.

Mr. Seward spoke to me before the message was taken

up, respecting the Japanese vessel. He said it was desirable we should take it. I inquired if it would not involve us in difficulty with Japan, and whether we were really acting in good faith. "Oh," he said, "the money should be returned to them whenever they made a demand, but if they got such a vessel they would begin to play the pirate and raise the devil."

The President seemed disinclined to interest himself in the matter, indicating, I thought, that Seward had settled the question with him, and that my objections would not be likely to prevail. Fessenden made one inquiry, and Dennison another, each of a general character but indicating a concurrence with me, and Seward made haste to turn off and introduce another topic.

Thurlow Weed and Lansing, the brother-in-law of Pruyn, are awaiting the action of the government. They have, and for two years have had, $800,000 in gold belonging to the Japanese in their hands, and it is an important question to them.

December 5, *Monday.* Congress convened. A quorum present in each house, but the President did not send in his message. I had calls from many Members. All in good spirits and hopeful.

Mr. Seward sent for my perusal a draught of an executive order forbidding the Japanese vessel from leaving, and authorizing the Navy Department to purchase. I dislike this thing in every aspect, and am not disposed to be mixed up with it. Some weeks since application was made for a survey and appraisal of this vessel. This was ordered, as is usual in all cases, and without any connection with the government or the Japanese. The Board valued her at $392,000, and at this price we, under direction of the President at the solicitation of Seward, agreed to take her. These late government movements make it embarrassing. I declined to give any opinion or make any suggestion in regard to the executive order, but said orally to the clerk that our offer was still considered as good, irrespective of other matters. Two hundred thousand dollars in gold would purchase this vessel; in paper currency she is appraised at $392,000. It is easy to perceive that Mr. Weed and Mr. Pruyn will realize a clever sum for their labors. They have had for one or two years the use of $800,000 in gold. This vessel has not cost them over $200,000 in gold. The government takes it at $392,000 and must pay that sum in gold to Japan. Who pockets the $192,000? It cannot be otherwise than that this subject will be inquired into. It ought to be.

December 6, Tuesday. Nothing of moment at the Cabinet. Neither Seward nor Fessenden was present. The new Attorney-General declines to be sworn in until confirmed.

Shortly after leaving the Cabinet I heard that Chase had been nominated to, and confirmed by, the Senate as Chief Justice. Not a word was interchanged in the Cabinet respecting it. Stanton, who came in late and just as we were leaving, professed to have come over merely to learn if the message had been received, and how. It is possible he was in the secret, but no other one who was present, and his knowledge is perhaps doubtful. The President had said to us before Stanton came in that he had sent up yesterday the nominations of Dennison and Speed, but mentioned no others. I am sorry he should have withheld the fact, which we all knew in less than one hour, that he had to-day sent in Chase for Chief Justice. Dennison informs me that he went to the theatre with the President last evening and parted with him after 11 o'clock, and not a word was said to him on the subject.

I hope the selection may prove a good one. I would not have advised it, because I have apprehensions on that subject. Chase has mental power and resources, but he is politically ambitious and restless, prone to, but not very skillful in, intrigue and subtle management. If he applies himself strictly and faithfully to his duties, he may succeed on the bench, although his mind, I fear, is not so much judicial as ministerial. He will be likely to use the place for political advancement and thereby endanger confidence in the court. He, though selfishly stubborn sometimes, wants moral courage and frankness, is fond of adulation, and with official superiors is a sycophant. I hope the President may have no occasion to regret his selection.

December 8, Thursday. The Senate have since commencement of the session labored over the question of continuing or displacing Hale from the position of Chairman of the Naval Committee. He has been, without cause or reason, a constant and vindictive opponent of the Department, at times annoying and almost embarrassing its action. I have forborne any controversy with him, and, in my acts and recommendations, have generally been sustained by Congress and the country. One year ago, at the commencement of this Congress, it appeared to me that the Senate owed to itself, not less than the Department and the country, the duty of substituting another for this factious and unworthy man. As they did not do it then, I scarcely expected they would do it now. He then appealed to them feelingly, and implored them to help him because his election was pending. Some of them thought the lesson had been instructive and would prove useful, as they assured me, and therefore voted for him. His conduct disappointed them but did not me.

This year he is not present, but went to Halifax the week before the session commenced, and from there writes a beseeching letter, begging to serve out the few weeks that remain of his Senatorial life on the Naval Committee. Sumner, who too often permits his personal sympathies to overrule public duty in matters of this kind, labored hard, I am told, for Hale. Action was postponed from day to day to gather strength, but a last attempt to retain him was made this morning and he received but seven votes. I have avoided, properly, introducing the subject

2

to any Senator while the question was pending, and to three or four who have spoken to me, I have been cool and reserved. Yet, not unlikely, Hale will be violent and abusive towards me. Perhaps not; he is uncertain and unreliable. I feel indifferent. His career is about closed. It has never been useful or wholesome. He has no constructive ability; can attack and try to pull down, but is unable to successfully defend and build up.

The Members of Congress and the press, with scarcely an exception, are complimentary to my report. Even the *New York Times* and *Herald* commend it. But the *Times* of to-day has a captious, faultfinding article. It is dissatisfied, because, in stating facts, I mention that the Navy has been always ready to coöperate with the army at Wilmington, was ready and waited at Mobile, Texas, etc., etc. This the *Times* denounces as attacking the War Department or army. If to tell the truth is so construed, I cannot help it. For a long time the *Times* has been profuse in its censures of the Navy Department in regard to Wilmington. Mr. Seward, knowingly, was guilty of the same injustice in his speech delivered to the crowd from his parlor window the week of the election. These men do not wish the truth disclosed. They cannot romance and falsify me as they have done in this respect.

December 9, Friday. At the Cabinet little as usual was done. Fessenden and Stanton were not present. Seward came late. No measure of any importance was introduced. Seward, Usher, and myself came out together, the other two a little in advance of me. Seward took Usher aside in the large hall just as they were coming out, and he spoke and beckoned to me also after the others had turned off to come with them. He said, as I came up, that he was remarking to Usher that Congress and the country were full of speculations about appointments; that he did not care a damn about himself, — if the President wanted him he would remain, and would go if he did not. He was going to take no part against any other member of the Cabinet, but should stand by them. Usher said it was important that he should know, for he had to depend on his salary or income for his support, and probably Mr. S. could let him know what were the President's intentions. The subject seemed to be one on which the two had been previously conversing, and U. was evidently in some suspense or anxiety. I did not see nor apprehend the pertinency or occasion for the conversation, except that U. may have heard, or learned, something which has disturbed him, and sought information from S., who chose to have me hear him utter nonsense to Usher.

I remarked that I gave no thought to the rumors, manufactured by correspondents and quidnuncs; that if Members of Congress or committees attempted to dictate to the President, he would know how to appreciate them. The conversation did not exceed five minutes, perhaps not more than three. We then came out, but Usher seemed disturbed and clung to and walked off with Seward, although his carriage was waiting in the opposite direction.

December 10, *Saturday*. Blair called on me in somewhat of a disturbed state of mind and wanted my advice. He had had one interview with the President since I last saw him, in which the President said he disliked to remove Hoffman from the collectorship of Baltimore, but that the Spanish mission would be vacant, and he would place that at Blair's disposal to arrange with Senator Hicks and Hoffman, as he pleased. Blair replied that he could go into no such arrangement; that he had no confidence in Hoffman, who is wholly unreliable, had deserted everybody and ought to be discarded. The appointment of Chase has brought the Maryland malcontents into position, and the trimmers, including Hicks and his friend Governor Swann, were looking to what they thought the rising power. Blair fears the President is flinching and will succumb, and thought it advisable that he, or some one, should have an explicit conversation with the President, and wanted my advice. I told him that it seemed to me very important that such a conversation should take place, but no one could do this so well as himself. As regarded myself, it was a weakness with me not to obtrude advice; it was with reluctance I gave the President unasked my opinion on any subject, and on the several matters connected with his plans he himself could best discuss them with the President. Blair agreed with me and said he would see the President, and would boldly and frankly express himself. Blair's present view is to go into the Senate, in place of Governor Hicks, who wishes to be made collector of Baltimore. Of course Hoffman, the present collector, must be removed as the initiatory step to this end.

December 15, Thursday. The Members of Congress have hardly commenced work as yet. They are feeling about. The malcontents are not in better mood than before the election. Chase's appointment gives satisfaction to Senator Sumner and a few others; but there is general disappointment. Public sentiment had settled down under the conviction that he could not have the position. Sumner helped to secure it for him. The President told Chandler of New Hampshire, who remonstrated against such selections, that he would rather have swallowed his buckhorn chair than to have nominated Chase.

Sumner declares to me that Chase will retire from the field of politics and not be a candidate for the Presidency. I questioned it, but S. said with emphasis it was so. He had assured the President that Chase would retire from party politics. I have no doubt Sumner believes it. What foundations he has for the belief I know not, though he speaks positively and as if he had assurance. My own convictions are that, if he lives, Chase will be a candidate and his restless and ambitious mind is already at work. It is his nature.

In his interview with me to-day, it being the first time

we have met since he reached Washington, Sumner commenced by praising my report, which he complimented as a model paper, — the best report he had read from a Department, etc., etc. As he is a scholar and critic, a statesman and politician capable of forming an opinion, has culture, discrimination, and good judgment, I could not but feel gratified with his praise. He says he read every word of it. Very many Members have given me similar complimentary assurances, but no one has gratified me so much as Sumner.

December 16, *Friday*. Met Attorney-General Speed to-day at Cabinet-meeting and was introduced by the President. Mr. Seward read the correspondence with the Brazilian representative in relation to the capture of the Florida. It is quite diplomatic, but Seward has the best of it thus far, for the Brazilian commenced too strong and has overshot the mark. What ground Seward will ultimately occupy is uncertain. He does not know himself, I apprehend; indeed, he has more than once said as much to me. I desire him to maintain our rights while doing justice to Brazil. Why has she given shelter and refuge and aid and supplies to Rebel pirates who are depredating on the commerce of a nation with which she is on terms of amity? Put her on the defensive.

Preston King dined with me to-day. Had a couple of hours' very agreeable conversation with him. He is a man of wonderful sagacity; has an excellent mind and judgment. Our views correspond on most questions. On the suppression of the Rebellion, on the rights of the States, on the reestablishment of the Union, on the extinguishment of slavery, there was entire concurrence of opinion. I did not doubt our agreement on these points before we met. I had touched on them with some others and found great bewilderment. There is, I think, no man in the Cabinet but Dennison who agrees with me on the subject of State rights. Seward on two or three occasions has had flings against what he calls "the damned doctrine"; but how he can have a Union without the distinctive States he has never intimated or explained. He has, I think, no sound views, substantial principles, perceptions, or settled convictions on the subject of national or State rights. Trained in the school of expedients, his tendencies are those of a large majority of Congress as to centralism. Conservatives and radicals each move in that direction, whatever disagreements they may have in other respects. Chase as much as Seward disregards the rights of the State on certain matters affecting personal rights where he has a theory of his own. Hence my chief regret that he should have received his present appointment. His one idea is the extinguishment of slavery, and to accomplish that end he would not be restrained by any reserved rights of the States.

We have intelligence of the release of the robbers and murderers who fled into Canada after their work at St. Albans. The Governor-General and the Canadian authorities denounce and disavow the act of the judge, which is an outrage that cannot be acquiesced in, or submitted to for a moment, yet I fear Seward will hesitate.

Senator Wade called on me yesterday, and was, as he always has been with me, very pleasant and affable. I think, however, the old man is a little acrimonious towards the President. He is Chairman of the Committee on the Conduct of the War, with Chandler, Gooch, etc. It is a convenient machine to cover up what the War Department wishes to have covered up, and it can be directed against those that the War Department would assail. It is a child of Stanton's.

H. Winter Davis made an attack on Seward in the House and got defeated, which evidently disturbed him. He and Thad Stevens and others had an opportunity to ventilate their feelings, They do not like Seward and are running their heads and putting their hands into all sorts of mischief and indiscretion to relieve their hostility. Both Stevens and Davis have talents but lack wisdom.

Had a call yesterday and to-day from Spencer of New York, who wishes to have Scofield, the imprisoned contractor, released. Scofield was convicted and is now in Fort Lafayette. Has been confined about six months since he was sentenced. Was to be imprisoned for one year and pay a fine of $20,000. Is ready to pay the fine, claims to have been imprisoned three months before sentence. Wants remission of the rest of his term. Spencer says Mr. H. J. Raymond, Mr. Darling, and others, good Administration men, desire S. released and have petitioned to that effect. Spencer says that he has taken a very active part, presided at the Cooper Institute meetings, never before asked a favor.

I inquired of him whether he was here as a friend of Scofield, as a politician and friend of the Administration, or professionally for his client. He admitted it was the latter, did not know Scofield. I inquired why he then spoke of it as a favor, a favor to himself. He appeared a little discomposed for a moment, but said it was to him a favor in this way: if he was successful in this case, it would be of some pecuniary benefit and lead to additional business. "Favors from the government," said I.

I informed him, both yesterday and to-day, that I could not favor any remission; that I considered Scofield a bad man, of loose and demoralizing motives, whose association with yard employees was pernicious; that his punishment was light. Our conversation was full and long. He said yesterday he wished to present the case to the President, but did not desire to do this without first informing me. To-day he told me that he had been waiting six hours with Judge Anthon of New York for an interview, but, desiring to get off this evening, he called again on me while Judge A. was waiting.

About half an hour after he left me, the President sent for Fox, and I have no doubt it is to get his views and opinions in regard to Scofield. Thinks I am prejudiced, or it is so represented, Spencer having seen me. Not infrequently, when parties fail with me, they go to the President, and of course state their ill success, but, claiming to have a case, press him to act, and he, knowing from them my decision, sends for Fox to get the facts. It is not a very satisfactory way, but is the President's peculiarity. He sometimes has excused himself on the ground that he did not wish to disturb me to come over when he only wished to make a simple inquiry, etc., — supposed Fox might know the facts. Weed and his set have Scofield in hand; want his money for electioneering purposes. Thinks he would succeed if I were away or not consulted.

.   .   .   .

Stanton came in this morning to tell me he had just got a telegram from General Thomas, announcing the defeat and annihilation of Hood's army. Present indications are an early closing of the Rebellion. If we have tolerable success the next ten days, they will have no formidable army but Lee's at Richmond.

December 17, Saturday. Admiral Dahlgren writes me that Sherman is with him in his cabin (14th inst.).

Mr. Chandler,[1] employed by the Department to attend to alleged frauds in the Philadelphia Navy Yard, arrived here this morning. Discloses great rascalities, of which we shall have more hereafter. Among others he mentions the facts connected with young Clandaniels, who was seduced by Scofield. Living on a salary of $750, pinched for subsistence, the serpent Scofield approached him, gave him in friendly kindness $50. He made further gratuities, then proposed to him, he being clerk of the storekeeper, to pass short weights and measure. To receipt for 70,000 pounds when there were but 50,000. His share in these villainies, C. says, is about $5000. He restores $3600 and his gold watch.

I directed Fox to go and request the President to be pre-

---

[1] William E. Chandler, subsequently Secretary of the Navy under President Arthur and Senator from New Hampshire.

sent in order that he might hear Chandler's statement, for, as I anticipated, the President had sent for Fox yesterday to inquire respecting Scofield. The President came, and on hearing Chandler's statement, seemed glad to know the facts. Says Thurlow Weed first came to him in behalf of Scofield; that he was disposed to act from representations then made, two or three months ago (it was before election); that he had communicated with me at that time, and sent the papers to Governor Morgan, who had given them over to Anthon, Judge-Advocate-General, to make a summary; that Anthon had done so and said Scofield was rightly convicted. Yesterday Mr. Spencer and others had pressed him very hard to release Scofield on his paying the fine, but he remarked he had some other matters pending. He therefore had sent for Fox to know how matters were.

I hardly think they will get Scofield released, after to-day's interview. But the President does not rightly appreciate Weed & Co., who are concerned in this business. He says Weed, on seeing Judge Anthon's report, said he had nothing further to say. Nor has he. But Raymond and Darling and others have been pushed forward, Raymond willingly, and doubtless under the expectation of high fees, for Scofield and others bid high.

This is one of the cases that has caused the malevolent intrigues of Raymond, Weed, and others against me. I have been in the way of their greed and intrigues. They could not use me but they have secretly slandered me, — had their insinuations, flings, and contrivances through the press and social circles to injure me in public estimation. The work has been very adroitly done, but the President, while standing firmly by me, is not aware, I think, of the real motives that move them.

December 19, *Monday*. The contractors for the Puritan and Dictator are in trouble and embarrassed. Congress has extended to them relief, contingent on my action. If I do not so interpret the resolution as to render immediate assistance, I shall be censured for delay. If I take the responsibility of acting promptly and before reports are made the censure will be no less severe. That the contractors can fulfill all the stipulations, every one knows to be improbable, — I may say impossible. If I rigidly require them, the men will be ruined and the country not benefited. If I waive the impossible, and accept what is practicable, I shall give the censorious and malicious opportunities to assail and denounce me. I covet no such discretionary power.

Commodore Rodgers writes that the Dictator has arrived safely at Hampton Roads and performed satisfactorily, but fails to give details.

Captain Winslow called on me to-day. He is looking well and feels happy. Luck was with him in the fight with the Alabama.

The House of Representatives to-day passes a resolution of H. Winter Davis, aimed at the Secretary of State for his management of foreign affairs, and asserting the authority of the House in these matters. There is a disposition to make the legislative, fortunately the representative branch, the controlling power of the government. The whole was conceived in a bad spirit and is discreditable to the getters-up and those who passed the resolutions. Davis has never been, and never will be, a useful Member of Congress. Although possessing talents, he is factious, uneasy, and unprincipled. He is just now connected with a clique of malcontents, most of whom were gathering a few months [ago] around our present Chief Justice. An embryo party is forming and we shall see what comes of it and whether the ermine is soiled.

Wise of the Ordnance Bureau writes me a long letter in answer to a dispatch from Dahlgren in regard to casting solid and hollow guns, etc. It is a controversy in which I do not care to become embroiled. D. is sensitive and proud; W. has been meddlesome and perhaps unjust. D. feels hurt; W. feels rebuked.

December 20, *Tuesday*. Only three of us at the Cabinet-meeting. Speed is attending the Court. The others absent, as usual, without cause, and the course pursued sustains them in this neglect. Seward is at the President's every day when there is no Cabinet-meeting and at a different hour on Cabinet days. As Stanton does not go to the President, the President goes to Stanton. Not unfrequently he hurries at the close to go to the War Department. Fessenden frets because there are no Cabinet consultations and yet stays away himself.

Old Tom Ewing of Ohio was hanging around the door of the Executive Mansion as I went in. I stopped for a moment to exchange civilities. Usher, who followed me, informed the President that the old man was waiting for an interview and thought of leaving, but U. advised him to remain now that he had got there. The President expressed his regret at Usher's advice and, turning to me, said, "You know his object?" I said it was probably Wilkes' case. The President said it was, and, notwithstanding Wilkes had abused both him and me, he was inclined to remit his sentence, — looking inquiringly at me as he spoke. I told him that I should not advise it; that at the proper time and in the proper way something might be done, perhaps, without injury, though Wilkes had no claim, and this hiring old Mr. Ewing, who is selling his personal influence, is all bad. Usher took strong and emphatic ground against any favor to Wilkes, who is heartless and insubordinate.

It is a misfortune that the President gives his ear to a class of old party hacks like Ewing and Tom Corwin, men of ability and power in their day, for whom he has high regard but who are paid to come here and persuade the President to do wrong. Ewing would not, of himself, do or advise another to do what he beseeches of the President, except for money. All this the President has the sagacity to see, but hardly the will to resist. I shall not be surprised if he yields, as he intimated he was ready to do before any remark from me.

The Senate and House to-day passed an act in conformity with my recommendation, indorsed by the President, creating the office of Vice-Admiral, to correspond with the army grade of Lieutenant-General.

Mr. Usher relates a conversation he had with General Heintzelman at Steubenville in regard to General McClellan, in which General H. says he has been reading and reviewing the events and incidents of the Peninsular Campaign, and he is fully convinced that McClellan intended to betray the army. General H. tells how he was left and the guard at a bridge over which it was necessary he should pass was withdrawn, without notice to him, although he had sent three times to McClellan for instructions and received none. Other singular and unaccounted-for facts are mentioned.

I have heard these intimations from others who had similar suspicions and convictions, but I have never yet been willing to believe he was a traitor, though men of standing call him such. His conduct was strange and difficult to be reconciled with an intelligent and patriotic discharge of the duties of his position. I long ago, and early indeed, was satisfied his heart was not earnest in the cause. He wanted to be victorious in any conflict as he would in a game of chess. Massachusetts and South Carolina were equally at fault in his estimation, and he so declared to me at Cumberland on the Pamunkey in May, 1862.[1] The disasters before Richmond followed soon after, and these were succeeded by his inexcusable conduct and that of his subordinate generals in failing to reinforce and sustain Pope and our army at the Second Battle of Bull Run.

But while I have never had time to review the acts of that period, I still incline to the opinion that his conduct was the result of cool and selfish indifference rather than of treachery and positive guilt. General Heintzelman and others are not only prejudiced against him but positively inimical.

[1] See vol. i, p. 107.

December 21, *Wednesday*. Wrote Gilpin, District Attorney at Philadelphia, in answer to his private letter as to prosecution for frauds in Philadelphia Navy Yard.

The papers are publishing the details of the expedition to Wilmington, and disclosing some confidential circumstances which ought not to be made public. One of the Philadelphia editors says the facts were ascertained and given to the press by Osborn of New York, a prowling mercenary correspondent of the newspapers who buys blackmail where he can, and sells intelligence surreptitiously obtained. I wrote to the Secretary of War, giving him the facts for such action as he may be disposed to take. He informed Fox that he would arrest and try by court martial.

Intelligence of the death of Mr. Dayton, our Minister to France, creates some commotion among public men. The event was sudden and his loss will be felt. . . . I had a light and pleasant acquaintance with him when in the Senate some fifteen or eighteen years ago, and we had some correspondence and one or two interviews in the Frémont campaign in 1856, when he was pleased to compliment me, on comparing Connecticut and New Jersey, with having done much to place my own State in a right position. We met again in the spring of 1861. He was a dignified and gentlemanly representative, not a trained diplomat, and unfortunately not acquainted with the language of the French Court. A numerous progeny has arisen at once to succeed him. John Bigelow, consul at Paris, has been appointed Chargé, and I doubt if any other person will be selected who is more fit. Raymond of the *Times* wants it, but Bigelow is infinitely his superior.

December 22, *Thursday*. The Secretary of War returns my letter concerning the disclosures made of the Wilmington expedition with an indorsement of Assistant-Secretary Dana stating the Secretary desires to know what action I wish to have taken.

I have noticed that our energetic and prompt Secretary

of War always desires a strong backer. He does rash and violent things, but he always wants some one to bear the brunt, or one on whom he can, if trouble ensues, throw the responsibility. The Judge-Advocate-General is attached to the War Department, there is a Solicitor of the War Department, the provost marshals are appointments of that Department. I sent the Secretary the facts in Osborn's case, giving names, and he now wishes me to specify his course of action, while I have none of the machinery or officers which Congress has assigned to him in abundance.

I indorsed on the letter that as the expedition was joint, — Army and Navy, — I had supposed it sufficient to advise him of the facts in order to have the offenders punished, that I thought the offense ought not to pass unnoticed, and that I recommended the person who had given the subject for publication should be arrested and tried by military court martial. This I know will not be satisfactory, but it is as much as I, clothed with no power, ought to do.

December 23, Friday. Being a little late at Cabinet, found the President, Seward, and Stanton with my letter before them in relation to Osborn. Stanton was evidently not satisfied with my presentation of the case, and yet was not prepared to specify his objections. He spoke of the publishers as equally deserving arrest, which I did not controvert, but expressed an opinion that all implicated should be attended to. I furnished proof as to the complicity of Osborn. On this further proceedings might be had. Seward was interested in a late singular decision of Judge Wylie of the District Court against Baker, for false arrest and imprisonment at the instigation of the late Secretary of the Treasury, the present Chief Justice Chase. Under this decision, he said, no Cabinet officer was safe. Stanton said he would be imprisoned a thousand years at least.

This proceeding of the court had evidently caused Stanton to hesitate in the matter of Osborn, and hence he wanted me to make special request for the arrest, not only of O. but the different editors, who, he thought, should be punished. I did not incline to that view. O. had surreptitiously obtained information and sold to editors. The President remarked that he thought an example of Osborn might answer without a squabble with the editors. Both he and Stanton dwelt on the disinclination of General Dix to have a fight with newspapers.

An investigation as to the true condition of matters with Judge Wylie in the Baker and Gwin case was directed. The President suggested a difference in this and arrests under the military department.

I have had much difficulty in regard to the Dictator and the Puritan. The large balance due falls heavily on the contractors, who claim they are losing interest at the rate of about two hundred and fifty dollars per day. It is very hard that they should thus suffer, but the law for their relief is very bungling in its phraseology. I have delayed action, and consulted with several. Admiral Smith, Fox, and Faxon advise payment. Lenthall objects. I requested Senator Grimes to examine the papers and the law yesterday, and had intended to associate Mr. Rice with him, so as to have an opinion from the Chairman of each naval committee; but Rice had gone to Boston. Grimes advised payment, so I ordered half a million to be paid towards the Puritan, but none to the Dictator until we had a more satisfactory and full report.

December 24, Saturday. Called on the President to commute the punishment of a person condemned to be hung. He at once assented. Is always disposed to mitigate punishment, and to grant favors. Sometimes this is a weakness. As a matter of duty and friendship I mentioned to him the case of Laura Jones, a young lady who was residing in Richmond and there engaged to be married but came up three years ago to attend her sick mother and had been unable to pass through the lines and return. I briefly stated her case and handed a letter from her to Mrs. Welles that he might read. It was a touching appeal from the poor girl, who says truly the years of her youth are passing away. I knew if the President read the letter, Laura would get the pass. I therefore only mentioned some of the general facts. He at once said he would give her a pass. I told him her sympathies were with the Secessionists, and it would be better he should read her own statement. But he declined and said he would let her go; the war had depopulated the country and prevented marriages enough, and if he could do a kindness of this sort he was disposed to, unless I advised otherwise. He wrote a pass and handed me.

The numerous frauds at the Philadelphia Navy Yard are surprising. But it is well to have an exposure, hit where and whom it may.

In the trial of Thurlow Weed at New York for libel on Opdyke, Stover, contractor, convicted of fraud, was a witness and gave strange testimony. Plaintiff's counsel sued for exemplified copy of his conviction. If it comes properly from the court, must grant it, but am not disposed to be mixed up with the parties.

Osborn writes, or telegraphs, denying explicitly and unequivocally any knowledge of the publication of the contraband news respecting the attack on Fort Fisher, and wishes me to communicate to Secretary Stanton. Sent Stanton a copy of the dispatch.

December 25, Sunday. Have intelligence this evening of the capture of Savannah. Hardee fled with his forces.

The Rebellion is drawing to a close. These operations in the heart of the Rebel region are destroying their self-confidence, and there are symptoms of extreme dissatisfaction among them.

Mr. Eads and Miss Eads of St. Louis, Mr. Faxon, and Sam Welles and L. F. Whitin dined with us.

December 26, *Monday.* Received a letter from Osborn denying that he furnished information concerning operations against Fort Fisher. At the same time Mr. Faxon tells me that Hart, a correspondent of the *Rochester Democrat*, says that paper was informed a fortnight previous.

Mr. Fox presses for further and more earnest application to Stanton for the punishment of O. Says Stanton thinks and asserts that I am not very anxious on the subject. In other words he desires me to importune him to harsh and general measures against O. and others. As O. is doubtless already arrested, I wrote Stanton transmitting his denial, also the letter of the *Philadelphia Press*, stating besides the assertion of Hart, and recommended a speedy trial.

Three hundred guns were fired by order of the Secretary of War on Vermont Avenue on account of the capture of Savannah. I felt as joyful as any one, perhaps, over Sherman's success, but I should have dispensed with over two hundred and sixty of those guns, had I made the order.

We have nothing definite or satisfactory from the Wilmington expedition. The weather has not been favorable, and there has been almost too imposing a force to furnish us as good success as we have sometimes had.

I have no faith in General Butler's scheme of knocking down Fort Fisher by blowing up a vessel filled with powder. Herein I differ with military men. The ordnance officers of the Navy and army advised the scheme, and are, as is also Fox, quite confident of its success. (Butler's influence.) I hope it may be so, and that the powder vessel may get near Fort Fisher, and be left by the crew before the explosion. Could we get Wilmington now along with Savannah, the Rebellion would run low.

December 27, *Tuesday.* Mr. Seward sends me a letter from the British Chargé, stating her Majesty's desire to confer the Order of the Bath on Lieutenant Pearson [1] and

---

[1] Lieut. Frederick Pearson, who commanded the United States ship in the fight of Sept. 5–8, 1864, with the Japanese.

2

desiring my opinions. I am opposed to the whole thing, and regret that our Minister should have pressed our naval officers to take any part in the fight with the Japanese. It appears to me to have been unnecessary to say the least, and this English compliment is designed to fasten us more closely with the allies against a people who have manifested more friendly feelings towards us than any Christian power. Mr. Thurlow Weed and Mr. Pruyn may be benefited. They have the money of the Japanese in their pockets.

At Cabinet to-day Seward, Fessenden, and Stanton were absent, the three most important of all who should be present at these meetings. The President was very pleasant over a bit of news in the Richmond papers, stating the fleet appeared off Fort Fisher, one gunboat got aground and was blown up. He thinks it is the powder vessel which has made a sensation. It will not surprise me if this is the fact. I have at no time had confidence in the expedient. But though the powder-boat may fail, I hope the expedition will not. It is to be regretted that Butler went with the expedition, for though possessed of ability as a civilian he has shown no very great military capacity for work like this. But he has Weitzel and if he will rely on him all may be well. I am apprehensive from what I have heard that too large a portion of the troops are black or colored, but fear there are too few of either kind, and no first-rate military officers to command and direct them. The Navy will, I think, do well. It is a new field for Porter, who has been amply supplied with men and boats.

December 28, *Wednesday*. I received a dispatch last evening about midnight, from Lieutenant-Commander Preston on board the Santiago de Cuba at Fortress Monroe, having been sent off from Wilmington by Admiral Porter. The information is not altogether satisfactory. The powder-boat was blown up about three hundred yards from Fort Fisher. No mention is made of results. I apprehend nothing serious. Have had no faith in this experiment at any time. I fear Porter relied too much upon it, and should not be surprised if the expedition would have done better without than with it. The troops are said to have disembarked above Fort Fisher, to have taken some earthworks and prisoners, and then to have reëmbarked. This reads of and like Butler. I will not prejudge the men or movements.

Mr. Seward sent me to-day a line from Thurlow Weed, who wanted the pardon or release of Stover. I sent Mr. Seward word how I had disposed of a similar application from the opposite party, *viz.* declining to furnish copies to outside parties who were in controversy. Mandates from the court must be respected. He made a second application with similar result, and directly after the second call I received an application from Mr. Brown, agent for the opposite parties, stating the court had granted a commission which would be here to-morrow with interrogatories to examine me and the Assistant Secretary. Calling on Mr. Seward in the afternoon, I showed him Brown's letter. He advised me not to testify nor to give any copies of any record. I told him there might be some difficulty or complaint. He said no, he always refused; told of their sending an officer on one occasion to arrest him, [and that] he applied to and got from the War Department a guard. It was all under the authority of the President, who would refuse to give copies of the record and restrain the heads of Department from acting as witnesses in such cases. I told him I had received no such authority from the President and should prefer to have it in writing from the President himself. I added that if he knew what was the President's order or position, he could put it in writing on the back of the paper of Brown, and I would stop and get the President's signature. He took up a pen, but dropped it and said it had better not be in his handwriting.

After being out a little time, he returned, followed soon after by Mr. Hunter with a paper a little longer than seemed to me necessary, and with an unfinished sentence.

I remarked that the President might say if he thought proper the public interest required this testimony should be withheld. But this did not suit S., who directed how the paper should be finished.

Returning, I called on the President, who had a large crowd in attendance, chiefly females. I stated briefly the case and handed him the paper, which he carefully read, but said he should want to think of the subject some before putting his name to the paper. I told him I was glad of it, and would leave the paper with him and would call at ten to-morrow for an answer, provided he should then be ready to give one. This met his approval.

December 29, *Thursday.* I called at the Executive Mansion at precisely ten this A.M. The President was not in. Mr. Attorney-General Speed came in soon after, and, while waiting for the President I stated to him the case. He said he had heard something from Mr. Seward concerning it last evening. On the question of giving exemplified copies of public records and trial by court martial he was partly decided that copies should be furnished. The President came in while we were discussing the subject, and said he had not fully determined, but his opinion from the consideration he had given it coincided with that of Mr. Speed, but he proposed to send for Mr. Seward, who shortly came. On hearing that the President had hesitated in signing the paper prepared by him and doubted its correctness, he was very much surprised, not to say chagrined; but when Speed joined in those doubts, Seward was annoyed, indeed quite angry. He denied that the public papers of any Department were to be subjected to private examination, and most emphatically denounced any idea of furnishing copies on the claim or demand of any State court or any court in a private suit. If it was conceded in a single instance, it must be in all. "And," said he, pointing to the private shelves of the President, which he keeps locked, "they will demand those papers." "But those," said the President,

"are private and confidential, a very different affair."
"Call them," said Seward, "what you please, you cannot
retain them from Congress or the court if you concede the
principle in this case. You cannot discriminate on their
call; they will not admit the rectitude of your judgment
and discrimination, if you give up to them the right of the
demand now made on the Secretary of the Navy. He
must not furnish them copies nor must he testify."

Without being convinced, the President was an attentive
listener, and I think his faith was somewhat shaken. "We
will look at this matter fully and carefully," said he. "If
the Secretary of State is right, we shall all of us be of his
opinion, for this is a big thing, and this question must have
been up and passed upon before this day."

He then decided he would have a legal opinion from the
Attorney-General, and framed questions for him to answer.
Some modifications were suggested, and the matter closed
for the present by the President instructing me not to give
my evidence or copies till this question was decided.

Lieutenant[-Commander] Preston arrived this P.M. with
dispatches from Rear-Admiral Porter off Wilmington. The
expedition has proved a failure. The powder-ship was a
mere puff of smoke, doing no damage so far as is known.
In this I am not disappointed. The Navy silenced the batteries and did, so far as I can learn, all that we had a right
to expect. From Lieutenant[-Commander] Preston's oral
account, as well as from the dispatches, the troops appear
to have behaved well. It was a mistake that General Butler, a civilian without military knowledge or experience in
matters of this kind, should have been selected for this
command. He is not an engineer, or an artillerist. He
did not land. General Weitzel is wholly under his influence, and the two did nothing. Had the military been
well commanded the results would, in some respects, have
been different, and, I think, a success. General Butler has
won laurels under the smoke and fire and fight of the Navy,
— as at Hatteras or at New Orleans, — and he flattered

himself that he should in like manner be favored at Wilmington.

General Grant ought never to have given him this command. It is unfortunate that Butler is associated with Grant, for he has great mental power which gives him undue ascendancy over his official superior. Certainly General Grant must have known that Butler was not the proper officer for such an expedition. Why did he give B. this command?

Fox says Grant occasionally gets drunk. I have never mentioned the fact to any one, not even to my wife, who can be trusted with a secret. There were such rumors of him when in the West. . . .

Went with Fox to the President with Admiral Porter's dispatches. He read them carefully through, and after a very brief conversation I asked what was now to be done. The President said he must refer me to General Grant so far as the military part was concerned. He did not know that we wanted any advice on naval matters.

I said we had a large squadron there which we could not retain on that station unless something was to be effected, for it was wasting our naval strength. He said he hoped we had at this time enough vessels to close the ports to blockade-runners, and again said, "I must refer you to General Grant."

We left the President about 3.30 P.M. I had then much of my mail to get off. Did not leave the Department until ten. After dinner, took my usual walk. Fox called at my house, and a dispatch was framed to Grant as the President had directed. I said to Fox that it ought to go through Stanton, or that he should see it. When he was leaving and after he had got the door open, Fox said Stanton might not be at the Department, and would be likely to oppose if he was, and he doubted if it was best to say anything to him. Inconsiderately I assented, or rather did not dissent.

December 30, *Friday.* At Cabinet various speculations.

Fessenden and Stanton, as usual, absent. President says Stanton readily gives up Butler, but makes a point whether Porter is any better. I do not admit this to be just to Porter, who is an energetic officer, though naval-wise not a lucky one, nor has he some of the qualities which give an easy time to those who administer the Department and would wish to economize in expenditures. There may be with some of those who coöperate with him cause to complain that he is not always observant of their rights, yet I do not remember to have heard that complaint from Sherman, Grant, or any trained military man. I do not suppose he has great respect for Butler, as a general or as the commander of the military of this expedition. But I have not yet heard of anything derelict on his part, or any act of commission or omission towards the military commander.

December 31, *Saturday.* Mr. Stanton sent, informing me he had a private telegram from General Grant which he would submit. I had last night word from General G. informing me of the fact.

Stanton I found in a very pleasant mood, not at all disposed to defend or justify Butler, whose course he commented on and disapproved. In doing this, however, he censured Porter as being indiscreet and at fault; but when I dissented and asked wherein he was to blame, Stanton made no attempt to specify, but spoke of him as blatant, boisterous, bragging, etc. The dispatch of General Grant stated he had received my telegram, that he should immediately organize another expedition secretly, which he hoped to get off by Monday, would give sealed orders not to be opened until outside, and that no one but himself, the quartermaster, and telegraphic operator in cipher should have the contents. Stanton said no one but himself and the telegraph-operator knew the contents. I told him I should inform Fox, for I must have some one to assist and with whom alone I would consult.

Commodore Rodgers came up from the fleet and entered just after I returned from the War Department. He is very indignant that the military part of the expedition should have been such a total failure, and is indignant towards Butler, who, he says, has defeated the whole expedition, which, with a military commander of courage and skill, would have been a success. I went with the Commodore to the President, who read Admiral Porter's dispatch and listened calmly to the statements of Rodgers denouncing Butler and his failures, at Petersburg, at Richmond, and now at Wilmington.

Sent Fox to Stanton to detain the steamboat at Baltimore until a special messenger, Lieutenant-Commander Preston, could arrive and proceed in her to Hampton Roads and there take a boat for Wilmington. Telegraphed to Norfolk to have a boat ready for Preston to go immediately on board. The Newbern was ready, Barry telegraphs this evening. Preston bore dispatch to Porter to hold his own, for Grant promises to send a military force by Monday or at farthest by Tuesday.

Butler has a well-prepared article in the *Norfolk Régime*, written by Clark, the editor, a creature of his but a man of some ability. The general himself undoubtedly assisted in its concoction. But military as well as naval men, without a single exception that has come to my knowledge, censure the general and commend the admiral. My own convictions are decidedly with the Navy, and I believe I can judge impartially, notwithstanding my connection with the Navy. I do not think Grant entirely exempt from blame in having permitted such a man as Butler to have command of such an expedition. I so told Stanton this morning, and recommended to him that they should be dissociated, — that Butler should be sent to some distant position, where he might exercise his peculiar and extraordinary talent as a police officer or military governor, but not to trust him with any important military command. I am not certain we should have been able to engage the army in this expedition but for Butler, and we could not have enlisted Butler had we not assented to the powder-boat. That was not regular military, and had it been a success, the civilian General would have had a triumph.

XXVI

XXVI

The Peace Mission of the Blairs — Sherman's Captured Cotton — The Wilmington Expedition — Discussion of what to do with the Negroes — General Butler's Dismissal from Command of the Army of the James — An Estimate of his Character — Death of Edward Everett — His Support of the Navy Department — Rejoicings over the Capture of Fort Fisher — Attitude of *Evening Post* and Mr. Bryant towards the Navy Department — Stanton's Visit to Savannah — Southern Pride — Efforts on behalf of the Smith Brothers after their Conviction — Prospects of Peace — The Qualities of Assistant Secretary Fox — The Constitutional Amendment abolishing Slavery passes the House.

January 1, 1865, *Sunday.* The date admonishes me of passing time and accumulating years. Our country is still in the great struggle for national unity and national life; but progress has been made during the year that has just terminated, and it seems to me the Rebellion is not far from its close. The years that I have been here have been oppressive, wearisome, and exhaustive, but I have labored willingly, if sometimes sadly, in the cause of my country and of mankind.

What mischief has the press performed and is still doing in the Rebel States by stimulating the people to crime by appeals to their manhood, to their courage, to all that they hold dear, to prosecute the war against the most benignant government that a people ever had! Violent misrepresentation and abuse, such as first led them to rebel, are still continued. The suppression for a period of the Rebel press in Richmond, Charleston, and one or two other points would do more than armies in putting an end to this unnatural war.

Mr. Solicitor Chandler, who has charge of the cases of fraud at the Philadelphia Navy Yard, made a report and spent some time with me this morning.

Had some talk with Mr. Merritt,[1] Fox, and Faxon concerning Osborn, the reporter for Sunday newspapers of naval matters. Merritt thinks he is misapprehended in regard to late publications. Fox thinks not, and claims he has facts showing Osborn to be an unmitigated rascal. I am inclined to think him a bad fellow, but am not altogether satisfied with the course pursued in his arrest.

January 2, Monday. This is the day for official interchange, yesterday being Sunday. Was at the Executive Mansion precisely at twelve, as requested, with Mrs. Welles, the first Cabinet officer to arrive, I believe, although the others were there within ten minutes. Many of the foreign ministers and their suites were there, probably all. Some of them came in advance. Remained over half an hour and returned home. Received until 4 P.M. The day is one which the people seem to enjoy, and one which they want. A little more system at the President's would improve matters.

January 3, Tuesday. Much engaged. The two days have brought an amount of business which it is difficult to dispose of in a single day. But three of us at the Cabinet-meeting. Various little matters talked up.

Old Mr. Blair was lingering in an adjoining room during the latter part of our sitting. Rumor has said that he and his son Montgomery had gone on a peace mission, and that Davis had invited them to Richmond. Nothing has been said to me on the subject, yet I am inclined to believe there has been a demonstration sufficient for the rumor. They have, for some purpose, been to the front, their absence has been longer than was contemplated, but I am not confident that any results have been obtained.

Simeon Draper, Collector of Customs at New York, called on me a few days since, stating that he had been appointed cotton agent by the Secretary of the Treasury, to

[1] M. F. Merritt of Connecticut, a personal friend of Secretary Welles.

proceed to Savannah and dispose of the captured cotton recently taken by Sherman. Draper called to get from me a letter of introduction to Rear-Admiral Dahlgren, as he would be likely to be thrown in Dahlgren's company. Of course, I could not refuse. But the idea of sending such a man on such a mission, when he has more than any one honest man can do to discharge his duties as a collector faithfully, sickened me. Fessenden certainly knows as little of men as Chase. This mission of Draper will be a swindle, I can scarcely doubt. A ring will be formed for the purchase of the cotton, regardless of public or private rights.

January 4, Wednesday. Called on the President to consult as to the selection of counsel in the Henderson case, since the death of William Curtis Noyes. Told him I thought we should have the best lawyer we could obtain, for the defense had secured Evarts and Pierrepont, and suggested the name of O'Conor provided we could secure his services. He is of the opposite party in politics, but in a matter of this kind the public interest should not be permitted to suffer from that cause. It may be difficult to secure him, for I understand he has relinquished his practice. The President heartily concurred in my views and earnestly advised that O'Conor should be employed.

The President does not yet decide whether exemplified copies shall be furnished in the Stover case, but Mr. Speed informs me that there can be no question that they should be furnished. This will, I presume, be the result; but, inquiring to-day for the record, it is found to be missing from the Department. Some months since the President called for it, and it was, I understood, committed to the custody of Mr. Browning, counsel for Stover.

A special messenger from Admiral Porter brings word that the fleet is at Beaufort. Rode home with Stanton, who tells me the troops are embarking at Hampton Roads to-day for Wilmington.

January 5, Thursday. Congress reassembled to-day. Many Members absent. Some talk with Montgomery Blair relative to the visitation of himself and father with a view of reaching Richmond. He says they got no answer from Jeff Davis until since their return to Washington. His father will go down again in a few days. Sent for Commander Parker to come here with the Don to convey [him] as likely to attract less attention.

The papers comment on his mission. A corps of correspondents always on the watch will form often very shrewd and sometimes very correct opinions as to the object and purpose of movements. In this instance, the first intimation which I had or saw was in the *National Intelligencer*, which has recently changed hands, and which heretofore has not had the reputation of giving first news.

January 6, Friday. Special messenger from Admiral Porter arrived this morning with dispatches. Left the Admiral and the fleet in Beaufort, coaling, refitting, taking in supplies, etc. He is not for giving up, but is determined to have Wilmington. We shall undoubtedly get the place, but I hardly know when. In the mean time he holds a large part of our naval force locked up. Admirals, like generals, do not like to part with any portion of their commands. As things are, I cannot well weaken him by withdrawing his vessels, yet justice to others requires it. Admiral Porter wrote to General Sherman in his distress, and he sent me Sherman's reply. It shows great confidence on the part of General 'Sherman in the Admiral, and this confidence is mutual. Instead of sending Porter troops he writes him that he proposes to march through the Carolinas to Wilmington and in that way capture the place. He does not propose to stop and trouble himself with Charleston. Says he shall leave on the 10th inst. if he can get his supplies, and names two or three places on the seaboard to receive supplies; mentions Bull's Bay, Georgetown, and Masonborough. His arrangement and plan strike me favorably; but it will be four or five weeks before he can reach Wilmington, and we cannot keep our vessels there locked up so long. Besides, General Grant has sent forward a military force from Hampton Roads to coöperate with the fleet, a fact unknown to Sherman when his letter was written. Whether this will interfere with or disarrange Sherman's plan is a question. I am told General Terry is detailed to command the military. He is a good man and good officer yet not the one I should have selected unless attended by a well-trained and experienced artillery or engineer officer.

I am apprehensive that General Grant has not discriminating powers as regards men and fails in measuring their true character and adaptability to particular service. He has some weak and improper surroundings; does not appreciate the strong and particular points of character, but thinks what one man can do another can also achieve.

The papers are discussing the Wilmington expedition. Generally they take a correct view. The *New York Tribune*, in its devotion to Butler, closes its eyes to all facts. Butler is their latest idol, and his faults and errors they will not admit, but would sacrifice worth and truth, good men and the country, for their parasite.

At the Cabinet-meeting no very important matter was taken up. There was a discussion opened by Attorney-General Speed, as to the existing difficulties in regard to the government of the negro population. They are not organized nor is any pains taken to organize them and teach them to take care of themselves or to assist the government in caring for them. He suggests that the Rebel leaders will bring them into their ranks, and blend and amalgamate them as fighting men, — will give them commissions and make them officers. The President said when they had reached that stage the cause of war would cease and hostilities cease with it. The evil would cure itself. Speed is prompted by Stanton, who wants power.

January 14, *Saturday*. The week has been one of interesting incidents, incessant occupation. Admiral Farragut came a week since and called on me. After half an hour or more of conversation on affairs connected with his command, the capture of Mobile, and matters generally, I went with him to the President. In the evening, he, with Mrs. F. and Captain Drayton, spent the evening with us.

Much speculation has been had concerning the dismissal of General Butler. It was anticipated that, being a favorite with the extremists, his dismissal would create a great excitement, but it has passed off without irritation, almost without sensation. The quidnuncs and, indeed, most of the public impute his dismissal from the Army of the James to the Wilmington failure; but it will soon be known that General Grant desired to get rid of him. Butler's greater intellect overshadowed Grant, and annoyed and embarrassed the General-in-Chief.

General Butler's farewell to his army is in many respects skillful and adroit, but in some respects will prove a failure. He does not conceal his chagrin but has hardly discovered whom to strike.

The *New York Tribune* has striven to warp and torture facts to help Butler, regardless of others and of stern truth. But the *Tribune* is unsupported. Of course the Rebels and Copperheads will be gratified, and do not conceal their joy. They have some cause for their hate, for he has been a severe, perhaps in some cases an oppressive, governor.

I cannot forget, while glad he is withdrawn from the Fort Fisher command, which he was unfitted to fill, the service which he rendered at Baltimore and in Maryland early in the War, nor his administrative ability at New Orleans, with some infirmities it is true, but which was in many respects valuable to the country. Not a merit which he has should be obscured. I am not his admirer, and should lament to see him in any responsible position without a superior. He has inordinate and irrepressible ambition, and would scruple at nothing to gratify it and his avarice.

The Committee on the Conduct of the War have summoned him to Washington. There was mischief in this. He had been ordered by the President to Lowell. The President yielded. It was well, perhaps, for Butler was off duty. But in Washington he will help the mischiefmakers make trouble and stimulate intrigue and faction. Allied with Wade and Chandler and H. Winter Davis, he will not only aid but breed mischief. This is intended.

Seward fears him. There is no love between them, and yet S. would prefer to avoid a conflict. Butler has the reckless audacity attributed to the worst revolutionists of France, in the worst of times, but is deficient in personal courage. He is a suitable idol for Greeley, a profound philanthropist, being the opposite of G. in almost everything except love of notoriety.

The discoveries and disclosures in the Philadelphia Navy Yard are astounding. Some twenty or more arrests have been made, and many of the parties confess their criminality. Some of the worst have not, but the proof against them is strong.

As these men, with scarcely an exception, are friends of the Pennsylvania delegation and appointees of the Administration, extraordinary efforts will be made in their behalf. The Representatives in Congress have, however, thus far behaved pretty well. Kelley protests that he will stand by no culprit, yet several he pronounces to be among the honestest men in Philadelphia, — wants them released and restored.

In Boston the trial of Smith Brothers is brought to a close. It has been on hand some three months. This P.M. (Saturday) Senator Sumner and Representative Hooper called on me with a telegram from the counsel of Smith objecting to the court for the next trial. F. W. Smith's trial is ended; Ben is assigned for next week. The counsel request Sumner to call upon me, and, if I will not grant their request, to go to the President. I told them I was not disposed to consider the subject, and Sumner said he was not inclined to call on the President.

Contentions and rivalries in the Washington Navy Yard give annoyance. Twenty per cent of the workmen are dismissed by order of the Department, and the Senators and Representatives from Maryland object that any Marylander should be of the number dismissed. These strifes among the men and the combinations among the rogues and their friends in the different cities are exciting and drawing out attacks and intrigues against me. The interference of Members of Congress is injurious.

January 16, *Monday.* Mr. Eames has returned and brings me word that O'Conor decides he will not break over his rule of trying no more jury cases. He therefore declines to undertake the case of Henderson. Advises that I should take Caleb Cushing. This does not exactly comport with my views, and yet after looking over the whole ground it appears to me that the best thing I can do will be to give him the cases of the Navy agencies. The President, with whom I have consulted, approves this course.

Edward Everett died suddenly yesterday morning, the 15th. It seems a national loss, although he has reached a ripe age. His last four years have been useful and displayed more manly vigor and wholesome, intellectual, energetic action than he has ever before exhibited. Heretofore, with high mental culture and great scholastic attainments, his policy has been artificial and conventional, but latterly his course has been natural. At no moment of his life did he stand better with his countrymen than when stricken down. I am indebted to him for many encouraging words and kind support in my administration of the Navy Department. Our party associations ran in different channels until the advent of Lincoln, but from the commencement of the War he frankly, earnestly, and ef-

2

ficiently aided me in many ways. He has written much, and with success, for the Navy in this great struggle.

General Butler called on me this P.M. He has come to testify before the Committee on the Conduct of the War, — called probably on his own suggestion, — greatly preferring Washington, for the present at least, to Lowell. I am sorry he has come here. It is for no good or patriotic purpose, I apprehend. As for the "Committee on the Conduct of the War," who have brought him here, they are most of them narrow and prejudiced partisans, mischievous busybodies, and a discredit to Congress. Mean and contemptible partisanship colors all their acts. Secretly opposed to the President, they hope to make something of Butler, who has ability and is a good deal indignant. I am not disposed to do injustice to Butler, nor do I wish to forget the good service he has rendered, but I cannot be his partisan, nor do I think the part he acted in the Wilmington expedition justifiable. He does not state clearly what his expectations and intentions were, but is clear and unequivocal in his opinion that Fort Fisher could not be taken except by siege, for which he had no preparation. General Grant could not have been of that opinion or a siege train would have been sent. In a half-hour's conversation he made no satisfactory explanation, although ingenious and always ready with an answer.

January 17, Tuesday. The glorious news of the capture of Fort Fisher came this morning. We had two or three telegrams from Porter and officers of the Navy and Generals Terry and Comstock of the army. Fort Fisher was taken Sunday evening by assault, after five hours' hard fighting. The sailors and marines participated in the assault. We lose Preston and Porter, two of the very best young officers of our navy. Have not yet particulars.

This will be severe for Butler, who insisted that the place could not be taken but by a siege, since his powder-boat failed.

Wrote Admiral Porter a hasty private note, while the messenger was waiting, congratulating him. It is a great triumph for Porter, — greater since the first failure and the difference with Butler.

At the Cabinet-meeting there was a very pleasant feeling. Seward thought there was little now for the Navy to to do. Dennison thought he would like a few fast steamers for mail service. The President was happy. Says he is amused with the manners and views of some who address him, who tell him that he is now reëlected and can do just as he has a mind to, which means that he can do some unworthy thing that the person who addresses him has a mind to. There is very much of this.

Had an interview with Caleb Cushing, who called at my house, on the subject of retaining him in the cases of the Navy agencies. Mr. Eames, who came with him, had opened the subject, and agreed as to the compensation on terms which I had previously stipulated.

January 18, *Wednesday.* The congratulations over the capture of Fort Fisher are hearty and earnest. Some few whom I have met are a little out of humor. General Butler does not appear gladsome, and it is not in human nature that he should. H. Winter Davis, who for some cause avoids me, is not satisfied. I do not doubt that he is glad we have succeeded, but he does not like it that any credit should even remotely come to me. There are three or four like unto him.

Contractors are here innumerable for relief. Demagogues assail me on one hand for expenditures, while contractors complain that their bargains with the Department are so losing that they must have relief.

January 21, *Saturday.* The congratulations and hearty cheer of the people over the victory at Fort Fisher are most gratifying. It is a comfort, too, to see, with scarcely an exception, that there is a rightful appreciation of the true merits of those who engaged in the contest, as well as of those who planned and persistently carried out this work.

But there is a contemptible spirit in one or two partisan journals that indicates the dark side of party and personal malice. The *Evening Post* in the capture of Fort Fisher makes no mention of the Navy. In some comments the succeeding day, the ill feeling again displays itself. The army is extolled, the Navy is ignored in the capture, and turned off and told to go forward and take Wilmington, which the editor says Admiral Porter can do if as eager as he has been for cotton bales. This gross and slanderous injustice called out a rebuke from G. W. Blunt which the editor felt bound to publish, but accompanied it with churlish, ill-natured, virulent, and ill-concealed malevolence. All this acrimony proceeds from the fact that the publisher of the *Post* is arrested and under indictment for fraud and malfeasance, and the Navy Department has declined to listen to the appeals of the editors to forbear prosecuting him. Henderson's guilt is known to them, yet I am sorry to perceive that even Mr. Bryant wishes to rescue H. from exposure and punishment, and, worse than that, is vindictive and maliciously revengeful, because I will not condone crime. No word of kindness or friendship has come to me or been uttered for me in the columns of the *Post* since Henderson's arrest, and the Navy is defamed and its officers abused and belied on this account. In this business I try to persuade myself that Godwin and Henderson are the chief actors; but Mr. Bryant himself is not wholly ignorant of what is done.

At the Cabinet-meeting yesterday Stanton gave an interesting detail of his trip to Savannah and the condition of things in that city. His statements were not so full and comprehensive as I wished, nor did I get at the real object of his going, except that it was for his health, which seems improved. There is, he says, little or no loyalty in Savannah and the women are frenzied, senseless partisans. He says much of the cotton was claimed as British property, they asserting it had the British mark upon it. Sherman told them in reply he had found the British mark on every battle-field. The muskets, cartridges, caps, projectiles were all British, and had the British mark upon them. I am glad he takes this ground and refuses to surrender up property purchased or pretended to be purchased during the War, but which belongs in fact to the Confederate government. Mr. Seward has taken a different and more submissive view, to my great annoyance on more than one occasion, though his concessions were more generally to French claimants.

I am apprehensive, from the statement of Stanton, and of others also, that the Rebels are not yet prepared to return to duty and become good citizens. They have not, it would seem, been humbled enough, but must be reduced to further submission. Their pride, self-conceit, and arrogance must be brought down. They have assumed superiority, and boasted and blustered, until the wretched boasters had brought themselves to believe they really were a superior class, better than the rest of their countrymen, or the world. Generally these vain fellows were destitute of any honest and fair claim to higher lineage or family, but are adventurers, or the sons of adventurers, who went South as mechanics or slave-overseers. The old stock have been gentlemanly aristocrats, to some extent, but lack that common-sense energy which derives its strength from toil. The Yankee and Irish upstarts or their immediate descendants have been more violent and extreme than the real Southerners, but working together they have wrought their own destruction. How soon they will possess the sense and judgment to seek and have peace is a problem. Perhaps there must be a more thorough breakdown of the whole framework of society, a greater degradation, and a more effectual wiping out of family and sectional pride in order to eradicate the aristocratic folly which has brought the present calamities upon themselves and the country. If the fall of Savannah and

Wilmington will not bring them to conciliatory measures and friendly relations, the capture of Richmond and Charleston will not effect it. They may submit to what they cannot help, but their enmity will remain. A few weeks will enlighten us.

January 23, Monday. There was a smart brush in the House to-day between Brooks and Stevens, the cause of controversy General Butler, or rather a letter which Brooks had received and construed into a challenge. It will serve for a day or two to divert attention from the Wilmington affair, which must annoy Butler, who is still here under the order of the summons of the Committee on the Conduct of the War.

January 24, Tuesday. President sent for me this evening. Found Stanton with him, having a dispatch from General Grant desiring him to request me to remove Commander Parker, the senior officer on the upper James. After some conversation, informing them that we had two gunboats above, and that the Atlanta and Ironsides had been ordered thither, I mentioned that Farragut was here, and the President sent for him. On hearing how matters stood, he at once volunteered to visit the force. The President was pleased with it, and measures were at once taken.

I rode down to Willard's after parting at the Executive Mansion and had a few additional words with Admiral Farragut and invited Mrs. F. to stop at our house during the Admiral's absence.

January 28, Saturday. Have been busy, with no time to write in this book, — Congress calling for information, bills preparing, and a mass of investigations at the navy yards, all to be attended to in addition to current business. Mr. Fox has gone with General Grant to Fort Fisher. Strange efforts are being made by some of our Massachusetts men for Smith Brothers, who have been tried for frauds and convicted. This is but one of many cases, and to relieve them because they are wealthy, and have position, ecclesiastical and political, must prevent the punishment of others. The President wrote me that he desired to see the case before it was disposed of. I told him I certainly intended he should do so after witnessing the pressure that was brought to bear. He said he had never doubted it, but "There was no way to get rid of the crowd that was upon me," said he, "but by sending you a note."

The Philadelphia cases of fraud are very annoying and aggravating. Our own party friends are interceding for some of the accused. They have not yet, like the Massachusetts gents, besieged the President, but they will do so. Their wives and relatives are already appealing to me.

To-day J. P. Hale had a tirade on the Department, denouncing it for prosecuting the Smiths. Was malicious towards both the Assistant Secretary and myself, and strove, as he has formerly done, to sow dissension, and stir up bad feeling. The poor fellow is having his last rant and raving against the Navy Department.

January 30. Great talk and many rumors from all quarters of peace. The journeys of the elder Blair to Richmond have contributed to these rumors, both here and at Richmond. I am not certain that early measures may not be taken, yet I do not expect immediate results. There were, however, many singular things in the early days of these troubles, and there may be as singular things in its close. There is difficulty in negotiating, or treating, with the Rebels. At the commencement Mr. Seward consulted and diplomatized with the organs of the Rebels, and supposed he could shape and direct their movements. I should not be surprised were he to fall into the same train of conduct at the close, — perhaps with more success now than at the beginning. The President, with much shrewdness and much good sense, has often strange and incomprehensible whims; takes sometimes singular and unaccountable freaks. It would hardly surprise me were he to undertake to arrange terms of peace without consulting any one. I have no doubt that the senior Blair has made his visits in concert with the President. Seward may have been in the movement. He has queer fancies for a statesman. He told me last week that he had looked in no book on international law or admiralty law since he entered on the duties of his present office. His thoughts, he says, come to the same conclusions as the writers and students. This he has said to me more than once. In administrating the government he seems to have little idea of constitutional and legal restraints, but acts as if the ruler was omnipotent. Hence he has involved himself in constant difficulties.

Admiral Farragut returned from James River Saturday night and came directly to my house, and spent yesterday with me. The condition of things on the upper James was much as I supposed. Commander Parker seems not to have been equal to his position, but I must have his own account before forming a decided opinion.

I subsequently learned that Fox, who was present at the close of the interview at the President's on the evening of the 24th, and by whom I sent telegrams to General Grant and Commodore Parker, had, on reaching the telegraph office, substituted his own name for mine to the communications. Farragut, who was present and knew the facts and what took place at the President's, learned what Fox had done when he arrived at Grant's quarters, for he saw the telegrams. The proceeding was certainly an improper one, and it is not surprising that Farragut was indignant.

I have, on one or two occasions, detected something similar in Fox in regard to important orders, — where he had been intrusive or obtrusive, evidently to get his name in the history of these times, and perhaps to carry the

GUSTAVUS V. FOX

impression that he was at least a coadjutor with the Secretary in naval operations.

Farragut assures me he has observed and detected this disposition and some objectionable acts in Fox, as in this instance, which he thinks should be reproved and corrected, but while I regret these faults I have deemed them venial.

I perceive that Admiral Farragut, like many of the officers, is dissatisfied with Mr. Fox, who, he says, assumes too much and presumes too much. There is truth in this, but yet it is excusable perhaps. I wish it were otherwise. He is very serviceable and, to me, considerate, deferring and acquiescing in my decision when fixed, readily and more cheerfully than most others; but he is, I apprehend, often rough with persons who have business at the Department. In many respects, in matters that are non-essentials, I yield to him and others, and it annoys many by reason of his manner and language. His position is a hard one to fill. The second person in any organization, especially if he is true and faithful to his principal, incurs the censure and ill-will of the multitude. For these things allowance must be made. Fox commits some mistakes which cause me trouble, and it is one of his infirmities to shun a fair and honest responsibility for his own errors. This is perhaps human nature, and therefore excusable. With the Naval officers he desires to be considered all-powerful, and herein is another weakness. But he is familiar with the service and has his heart in its success.

Admiral Farragut favors a Board of Admiralty. It is a favorite theme with others to give naval ascendancy in court sessions. I can perceive arguments in its favor which would relieve the Secretary of labor, provided rightly constituted and properly regulated. There would, however, be jealousies in the service of such a board, as there are of the Assistant Secretary. It would be claimed that it dictated to the Secretary and abused his confidence. It would not be beneficial to the government and country.

January 31, *Tuesday.* I made a short stay at Cabinet to-day. The President was about to admit a delegation from New York to an interview which I did not care to attend. The vote was taken to-day in the House on the Constitutional Amendment abolishing slavery, which was carried 119 to 56. It is a step towards the reëstablishment of the Union in its integrity, yet it will be a shock to the framework of Southern society. But that has already been sadly shattered by their own inconsiderate and calamitous course. When, however, the cause, or assignable cause for the Rebellion is utterly extinguished, the States can and will resume their original position, acting each for itself. How soon the people in those States will arrive at right conclusions on this subject cannot now be determined.

John P. Hale is giving his last venomous rants against the Navy Department. He has introduced a resolution calling for certain information, the adoption of which was opposed by Conness, the small-pattern Senator from California. I should have been glad to have it slightly amended and adopted, although it might give me some labor, at a time when my hands are full, to respond.

XXVII

February 1, *Wednesday.* The board of which Admiral Farragut is President is in session. Their duties to advise on the subject of promotion for meritorious conduct in battle. I am not disposed to act under this law without consultation with and advice from earnest men in the service. There is a disposition to place Porter in advance by Fox, to which I cannot assent unless it comports with the views and opinions of senior men, who are entitled to speak on a question that so nearly concerns them. Admiral Porter is a man of courage and resources, but has already been greatly advanced, and has some defects and weaknesses.

February 2. The President and Mr. Seward have gone to Hampton Roads to have an interview with the Rebel commissioners, — Stephens, Hunter, and Campbell. None of the Cabinet were advised of this move, and without exception, I think, it struck them unfavorably that the Chief Magistrate should have gone on such a mission.

February 4, *Saturday.* There was yesterday no meeting of the Cabinet. This morning the members were notified to meet at twelve meridian. All were punctually on hand. The President with Mr. Seward got home this morning.

Both speak of the interview with the Rebel commissioners as having been pleasant and without acrimony. Seward did not meet or have interview with them until the President arrived. No results were obtained, but the discussion will be likely to tend to peace. In going the President acted from honest sincerity and without pretension. Perhaps this may have a good effect, and perhaps otherwise. He thinks he better than any agent can negotiate and arrange. Seward wants to do this.

For a day or two, the naval appropriation bill has been under consideration in the House. A combination, of which H. Winter Davis is the leader, made it the occasion for an onset on the Department and the Administration. The move was sneaking and disingenuous, very much in character with Davis, who is unsurpassed for intrigue and has great talents for it. He moved an amendment, having for its object a Board of Admiralty, which should control the administration of the Department. The grounds of this argument were that the Department had committed errors and he wanted a board of naval officers to prevent it. He presents the British system for our guidance and of course has full scope to assail and misrepresent whatever has been done. But, unfortunately for Davis, the English are at this time considering the question of abandoning their system.

Mr. Rice, Chairman of the Naval Committee, a Boston merchant, is reported to have made a full and ample and most successful reply to Davis, who was voted down. I have not doubted the result, but there was a more formidable effort made than was at first apparent. The Speaker, who is not a fair and ingenuous man, although he professes to be so, and also to be personally friendly to me, is strictly factious and in concert with the extremists. In preparation for this contest he had called General Schenck to the chair. Schenck is one of the Winter Davis clique, and so far as he dare permit it to be seen, and more distinctly than he supposes, has the sympathy of Colfax. Stevens, Chair-

man of the Ways and Means, is of the same stripe. It is
a combination of the radicals prompted and assisted by
Du Pont and Wilkes. Hitherto hating each other, and in-
vidiously drawing in others, the miserable wretched combinations of malcontents and intriguers, political and
naval, had flattered themselves they should succeed. But
they were voted down. I am told, however, that under
the rulings and management of the hypocritically sancti-
monious Speaker the subject is to be reopened.

February 6, Monday. There was a Cabinet-meeting
last evening. The President had matured a scheme which
he hoped would be successful in promoting peace. It was
a proposition for paying the expenses of the war for two
hundred days, or four hundred millions, to the Rebel
States, to be for the extinguishment of slavery, or for such
purpose as the States were disposed. This in few words
was the scheme. It did not meet with favor, but was
dropped. The earnest desire of the President to conciliate
and effect peace was manifest, but there may be such a
thing as so overdoing as to cause a distrust or adverse
feeling. In the present temper of Congress the proposed
measure, if a wise one, could not be carried through successfully.

I do not think the scheme could accomplish any good
results. The Rebels would misconstrue it if the offer was
made. If attempted and defeated it would do harm.

The vote of to-day in the House on the renewed effort
of Winter Davis to put the Navy Department in commission was decided against him. He and his associates had
intrigued skillfully. They relied on the Democrats going
with them in any measure against the Administration,
and, having succeeded in rebuking Seward for his conduct of our foreign affairs in not conforming to their views,
Davis and his friends now felt confident that they could
indirectly admonish me. But a portion of the Democrats
became aware of the intrigue, and declined to be made the

instruments of the faction. It seems to have been a sore disappointment.

February 7, Tuesday. Very little before the Cabinet. The President, when I entered the room, was reading with much enjoyment certain portions of Petroleum V. Nasby to Dennison and Speed. The book is a broad burlesque on modern Democratic party men. Fessenden, who came in just after me, evidently thought it hardly a proper subject for the occasion, and the President hastily dropped it.

Great efforts continue to be made to get the release of Smith brothers. Quite a number of persons are here in their interest, and Members of Congress are enlisted for them.

Efforts are being made to aid a set of bad men who have been cheating and stealing from the government in Philadelphia. Strange how men in prominent positions will, for mere party, stoop to help the erring and the guilty. It is a species of moral treason.

J. P. Hale is, as usual, loud-mouthed and insolent in the Senate, — belying, perverting, misstating, and misrepresenting the Navy Department. The poor fellow has but few more days in the Senate, and is making the most of them for his hate.

February 10, Friday. On Wednesday evening Mrs. W. held a levee, which always disarranges. The season has thus far been one of gaiety. Parties have been numerous. Late hours I do not like, but I have a greater dislike to late dinners. The dinner parties of Washington are to be deprecated always by those who regard health.

The President has communicated his movements tending to peace. Jeff Davis has published the letter of Stephens, Hunter, and Campbell. They do not materially differ. The prospect of peace does not seem nearer than before the interview took place, yet I trust we are approximating the much desired result. There are ultras among us who do not favor the cessation of hostilities except on terms and conditions which make that event remote. A few leading radicals are inimical to the Administration, and oppose all measures of the Administration which are likely to effect an immediate peace. They are determined that the States in rebellion shall not resume their position in the Union except on new terms and conditions independent of those in the proposed Constitutional Amendment. Wade in the Senate and Winter Davis in the House are leading spirits in this disturbing movement. It is the positive element, violent without much regard to Constitutional or State rights, — or any other rights indeed, except such as they may themselves define or dictate.

Not much was done to-day at the Cabinet. Some discussion of general matters. Speed suggested what if one of the States, Michigan for instance, should decline to send Senators or Representatives to Congress, or take any action of themselves in the conduct of the federal government; or supposing Michigan were to take such action or non-action, and the western peninsula of that State, being a minority, should non-concur with the State but persist in being represented in Congress. In the course of the remarks, I inquired what would be said or done provided any State should choose to adopt a different organization from any that we now have, — for instance, combine the executive, legislative, and judicial powers in the same hands, elect perhaps ten men and have one go out yearly. The subjects were novel. The President thought there were implied obligations on the part of each State to perform its duties to the general government which they could not neglect or refuse.

We get as yet no Secretary of the Treasury. Fessenden is *locum tenens*, reluctantly, I apprehend. The place is one which he does not like and cannot fill, and he is aware of it. Nor is he a very useful man to devise measures in council. He has ability as a critic and adviser but is querulous and angular. Some allowance must be made for infirm health, which has sharpened a sometimes unhappy temper. On two or three occasions he has manifested a passionate and almost vindictive ferocity towards Preston King which surprised me. His ability is acute rather than comprehensive. My intercourse with him has been pleasant, but not very intimate. We must soon know his successor. Of all the men named, Morgan is probably the best, and my impression is that he will finally be appointed. Some will object because Seward is from the same State, but that is a frivolous objection. I am not certain who the radicals are pressing for the place. They will not be pleased with Morgan if S. remains, but who their favorite is I do not learn.

February 11, *Saturday.* The local municipal authorities of New York City are taking high-handed ground in regard to naval enlistments in that city, — such as cannot be permitted. They forbid the recruiting of any in the city unless they are accredited to that locality.

A letter from the Secretary of the Treasury on the subject of trade regulations was got up by one who did not understand what he was writing about, or else intended no one else should understand. There is great swindling and rascality in carrying out these regulations.

February 21, *Tuesday.* Have had no time the last ten eventful days to open this book; and am now in haste.

In the Senate as well as in the House, there has been a deliberate and mendacious assault on the Navy Department, but with even less success than the first. Senator Wade moved to adopt the Winter Davis proposition for a Board of Admiralty. It obtained, I am told, but two votes. A proposition which, under proper direction and duly prepared was not destitute of merit as a naval measure, provided the government is to have a more military and central character, has been put down, probably for years, perhaps forever.

The scheme in this instance was concocted by a few party aspirants in Congress and a few old and discomfited naval officers, with some quiddical lawyer inventors, schemers, and contractors. They did not feel inclined to make an open assault on me; they therefore sought to do it by indirection. Much of the spite was against the Assistant Secretary, who may have sometimes been rough and who has his errors as well as his good qualities, but who has well performed his duties, — sometimes, perhaps, has overdone, — has his favorites and decided prejudices.

Senator Hale, while he does not love me, has now particular hatred of Fox, and in striving to gratify his grudge is really benefiting the man whom he detests. He and others in the House have spoken of F. as the actual Secretary instead of the Assistant, striving thereby to hold him to a certain degree of accountability, and also hoping to sow dissension between him and me. For three years Hale made it his chief business to misrepresent and defame me, and he had with him at the beginning some who have become ashamed of him. In the mean time he has obtained other recruits. Blaine of Maine dislikes Fox, and in his dislike denounces the Navy Department, which he says, in general terms, without mentioning particulars, is mismanaged.

But I have no reason to complain when I look at results and the vindication of able champions. They have done me more than justice. Others could have done better, perhaps, than I have done, and yet, reviewing hastily the past, I see very little to regret in my administration of the Navy. In the matter of the light-draft monitors and the double-enders I trusted too much to Fox and Stimers. In the multiplicity of my engagements, and supposing those vessels were being built on an improved model, under the approval and supervision of Lenthall and the advice of Ericsson, I was surprised to learn when they were approaching completion, that neither Lenthall nor Erics-

2

son had participated, but that Fox and Stimers had taken
the whole into their hands. Of course, I could not attempt
to justify what would be considered my own neglect. I
had been too confiding and was compelled, justly perhaps,
to pay the penalty in this searching denunciation of my
whole administration. Neither of the men who brought me
to this difficulty take the responsibility.

We have made great progress in the Rebel War within
a brief period. Charleston and Columbia have come into
our possession without any hard fighting. The brag and
bluster, the threats and defiance which have been for
thirty years the mental aliment of South Carolina prove
impotent and ridiculous. They have displayed a talking
courage, a manufactured bravery, but no more, and I
think not so much inherent heroism as others. Their ful-
minations that their cities would be Saragossas were
mere gasconade, — their Pinckneys and McGrawths and
others were blatant political partisans.

General Sherman is proving himself a great general, and
his movements from Chattanooga to the present demon-
strate his ability as an officer. He has, undoubtedly,
greater resources, a more prolific mind, than Grant, and
perhaps as much tenacity if less cunning and selfishness.

In Congress there is a wild, radical element in regard to
the rebellious States and people. They are to be treated
by a radical Congress as no longer States, but Territories without rights, and must have a new birth or creation by permission of Congress. These are the mistaken
theories and schemes of Chase, — perhaps in conjunction
with others.

I found the President and Attorney-General Speed in
consultation over an apprehended decision of Chief Justice Chase, whenever he could reach the question of the
suspension of the writ of *habeas corpus*. Some intimation
comes through Stanton, that His Honor the Chief Justice
intends to make himself felt by the Administration when
he can reach them. I shall not be surprised, for he is am-

bitious and able. Yet on that subject he is as much implicated as others.

The death of Governor Hicks a few days since has
brought on a crisis of parties in Maryland. Blair is a candidate for the position of Senator, and the President wishes
him elected, but Stanton and the Chase influence, including
the Treasury, do not, and hence the whole influence of
those Departments is against him. Blair thinks the President does not aid him as much as he had reason to suppose
he would, and finds it difficult to get an interview with him.
I think he has hardly been treated as he deserves, or as the
President really wishes, yet the vindictiveness of the Chief
Justice and Stanton deter him, control him against his
will.

The senior Blair is extremely anxious for the promotion
of his son-in-law, Lee, and has spoken to me several times
on the subject. He called again to-day. I told him of the
difficulties, and the great dissatisfaction it would give the
naval officers. Pressed as the old man is by not only Lee
but Lee's wife, and influenced by his own willing partiality, he cannot see this subject as I and others see it.

A few days since the President sent into the Senate
the nomination of Senator E. D. Morgan for the Treasury.
It was without consultation with M., who immediately
called on the President and declined the position.

Seward, whom I saw on that evening, stated facts to
me which give me some uneasiness. He called, he says,
on the President at twelve to read to him a dispatch, and
a gentleman was present, whom he would not name, but
S. told the gentleman if he would wait a few moments he
would be brief, but the dispatch must be got off for Europe.
The gentleman declined waiting, but as he left, the President said, "I will not send the paper in to-day but will
hold on until to-morrow." Seward says he has no doubt the
conversation related to M.'s nomination, but that, the
paper being made out, his private secretary took it up
with the other nominations, and the President, when aware

of the fact, sent an express to recall it, in order to keep faith with the gentleman mentioned. This gentleman was, no doubt, Fessenden.

I called on Governor Morgan on Sunday evening and had over an hour's conversation with him, expressing my wish and earnest desire that he should accept the place, more on the country's account than his own. He gave me no favorable response. Said that Thurlow Weed had spent several hours with him that morning to the same effect as myself and trying to persuade him to change his mind, but he would give Weed no assurance; on the contrary had persisted in his refusal. He, Morgan, was frank and communicative, as he has generally been with me on important questions, and reviewed the ground, State-wise and national-wise. "What," he inquired, "is Seward's object? He never in such matters acts without a motive, and Weed would not have been called here except to gain an end."

Seward, he says, wants to be President. What does he intend to do? Will he remain in the Cabinet, or will he leave it? Will he go abroad, or remain at home? These, and a multitude of questions which he put me, showed that Morgan had given the subject much thought, and especially as it affected himself and Seward. Morgan has his own aspirations and is not prepared to be used by Weed or Seward in this case.

My own impressions are that Morgan has committed a great mistake as regards himself. Seward may be jealous of him, as M. is suspicious he is, but I doubt if that was the controlling motive with S. I think he preferred Morgan, as I do, for the Treasury, to any tool of Chase. The selection, I think, was the President's, not Seward's, though the latter readily fell in with it. Blair had advised it. Fessenden was probably informed on the morning when Seward met him at the President's and desired to have the nomination postponed.

I am told Thurlow Weed expressed great dissatisfaction that Morgan did not accept the position. That Weed and

Seward may have selfish schemes in this is not unlikely, but whether they have or not, it was no less the duty of Morgan to serve his country when he could.

February 22. The late news combines with the anniversary to make this an interesting day. While the heavy salutes at meridian were firing, young Cushing came in with the intelligence of the capture of Fort Anderson. I went with him to the President. While there General Joe Hooker came in; and Seward, for whom the President had sent, brought a dispatch from Bigelow at Paris of a favorable character. General H. thinks it the brightest day in four years.

The President was cheerful and laughed heartily over Cushing's account of the dumb monitor which he sent past Fort Anderson, causing the Rebels to evacuate without stopping to even spike their guns.

The belief seems general that McCulloch will receive the appointment of Secretary of the Treasury. If I do not mistake, the rival opponents of the President desire this and have been active in getting up an opinion for the case. So far as I know the President has not consulted the Cabinet. Some of them, I know, are as unenlightened as myself. I know but little of McC.; am not sufficiently acquainted with him to object, or even to criticize the appointment. The fact that Fessenden and Chase are reputed to be in his favor, and that he has been connected with them and is identified with their policy gives me doubtful forebodings.

Governor Morgan called upon me and expresses a pretty decided conviction that McCulloch is not the candidate of Chase and Fessenden, does not indorse Chase's schemes and will put himself on the true basis. This gives me some confidence.

Met Speed at the President's a day or two since. He is apprehensive Chase will fail the Administration on the question of *habeas corpus* and State arrests. The President expresses, and feels, astonishment. Calls up the committals of Chase on these measures. Yet I think an adroit intriguer can, if he chooses, escape these committals. I remember that, on one occasion when I was with him, Chase made a fling which he meant should hit Seward on these matters, and as Seward is, he imagines, a rival for high position, the ambition of Chase will not permit the opportunity to pass, when it occurs, of striking his competitor. There is no man with more fierce aspirations than Chase, and the bench will be used to promote his personal ends.

Speed and myself called on Seward on Monday, after the foregoing interview with the President. Seward thinks Chase, if badly disposed, cannot carry the court, but this is mere random conjecture. He has, so far as I can ascertain, no facts. In the course of his remarks, Seward, who was very much disturbed, broke out strongly against Chase, who had, he said, been a disturber from the beginning and ought never to have gone into the Cabinet. He had objected to it, and but from a conviction that he (Seward) could better serve the country than any other man in the State Department, he would not have taken office with Chase for an associate. The Cabinet, with the single exception of Chase, had been harmonious and united. He spoke of the early trouble of the blockade, which he said Chase opposed, and then tried to make difficulty. It is not the first time when I have detected an infirmity of memory and of statement on this point. I at once corrected Seward, and told him I was the man who made the strong stand against him on the question of blockade, and that Chase failed to sustain me. I have no doubt that Seward in those early days imputed my course on that question to Chase's influence, whereas nothing was farther from the truth. I had not even the assistance I expected and was promised from Chase. Mr. Blair and Mr. Bates stood by me; Chase promised to, but did not. This conversation confirms an impression I have had of Seward, who imputed to others views derived from his rival antagonist. If I differed from him, he fully believed it was the intrigue of Chase that caused it, — a very great error, for I followed my own convictions.

Rumors and speculations of Cabinet changes have been thick for the last half of this month. Much has been said and done to effect a change in the Navy Department. Not that there is very great animosity towards me personally, or my course and policy, but then aspirants for Cabinet positions and changes multiply chances. There are three or four old naval officers who are dissatisfied with me and with almost everybody else, and who would be satisfied with no one. They fellowship with certain intriguers in Congress and out, and have exhausted themselves in attacking, abusing, and misrepresenting me.

This violence is just now strongest against Fox, who, as second or executive officer, is courted and hated. Finding that he sustains me, they detest him, and as is not uncommon are more vindictive towards him than towards the principal. He is sometimes rough and sailor-like in manner, which gives offense, but stands true to his chief.

There is a little clique of self-constituted and opinionated but not very wise radicals who assume to dictate to the Administration as regards men and measures, but who have really little influence and deserve none. Hale in the Senate and H. Winter Davis in the House may be considered the leaders. The latter is the centre of his few associates and has far greater ability than either. Generals Schenck and Garfield and a few others gather round him. The same men with a larger circle are hostile to Seward, against whom the strongest secret war is waged. Stanton is on terms with these men, and to some extent gives them countenance, even in their war upon the President, to whom they are confessedly opposed. Seward thinks to propitiate these men by means of Stanton, and perhaps he does in some measure, but the proceeding gives him no substantial strength. Stanton is faithful to none, not even to him.

In preparing a reply to Hale it has been necessary to append a reply also from Fox, who is drawn into the resolution. He (F.) and Blair have been preparing this with some circumspection and care. I do not think it a judicious paper in some respects. It is a tolerable statement of facts and proceedings in regard to the attempt to relieve Fort Sumter in 1861. Fox is the hero of his own story, which is always unpleasant. There is an extra effort to introduce and associate with him great names, which will be seized by his enemies. I am not sorry that certain facts come out, but I should be glad to have the whole story told of that expedition and others connected with it. No allusion is made to Commander Ward, who volunteered for this service and persisted in it until General Scott and Commodore Stringham finally dissuaded him.

Blair, in talking over the events of that period, gives me always some new facts, or revises old ones. He reminds me that he was determined at the time when the relief of Sumter was discussed, in case it was not done or attempted, to resign his seat in the Cabinet, and had his resignation prepared. But his father remonstrated and followed him to the Cabinet-meeting, and sent in a note to him from Nicolay's room. After the meeting adjourned and the members left, the elder Blair had an interview with the President and told him it would be treason to surrender Sumter. General Scott, General Totten, Admiral Stringham, and finally Ward had given it up as impossible to be relieved. Blair maintains that Seward was all that time secretly intriguing with the Rebel leaders, — that he was pledged to inform them of any attempt to relieve that fortress.

It was Seward, Blair says, who informed Harvey and had him telegraph to Charleston that a secret expedition was fitting out against Sumter. This betrayal by Harvey did not interfere with his mission to Lisbon. Why? Because he had Seward in his power. There are facts which go to confirm this. I have a confidential letter from the President of April 1, 1861, which reads more strangely now, if possible, than then, though I was astonished at that time and prepared for strange action if necessary.

XXVIII

March 1, *Wednesday.* Judge J. T. Hale called on me
to say he had had a conversation with the President and
had learned from him that I had his confidence and that he
intended no change in the Navy Department. He said a
great pressure had been made upon him to change. I have
no doubt of it, and I have at no time believed he would
be controlled by it. At no time have I given the subject
serious thought.

Mr. Eads and Mr. Blow inform me that Brandagee in
his speech, while expressing opposition to me for not favoring New London for a navy yard, vindicated my honesty
and obstinacy, which Blaine or some one impugned.
Blaine is a speculating Member of Congress, connected,
I am told, with Simon Cameron in some of his projects,
and is specially spiteful towards the Navy Department.
I do not know him, even by sight, though he has once or
twice called on me. Some one has told me he had a difficulty with Fox. If so, the latter never informed me, and
when I questioned him he could not recollect it.

March 2, *Thursday.* Had a houseful of visitors to witness the inauguration. Speaker Colfax is grouty because

Mrs. Welles has not called on his mother, — a piece of etiquette which Seward says is proper. I doubt it, but Seward jumps to strange conclusions.

Hale, as I expected he would, made an assault on Fox's appendix to my reply, and denounces it as egotistical autobiography, and is determined it shall not be printed. The poor fellow seems not aware that he is advertising and drawing attention to what he would suppress.

March 3, *Friday*. The city quite full of people. General Halleck has apprehensions that there may be mischief. Thinks precautions should be taken. Advises that the navy yard should be closed. I do not participate in these fears, and yet I will not say it is not prudent to guard against contingencies.

At the Cabinet-meeting to-day, the President gave formal notice that he proposed inviting McCulloch to the Treasury early next week. He said that doing this rendered a change necessary or essential in the Interior, concerning which he already had had conversation with Mr. Usher, and should have more to say; that in regard to the other gentlemen of the Cabinet, he wished none of them to resign, at least for the present, for he contemplated no changes.

March 4, *Saturday*. Was at the Capitol last night until twelve. All the Cabinet were present with the President. As usual, the time passed very pleasantly. Chief Justice Chase came in and spent half an hour. Later in the night I saw him in the Senate. Speed says Chase leaves the Court daily to visit the Senate, and is full of aspirations. I rode from the Capitol home at midnight with Seward. He expressed himself more unreservedly and warmly against Chase than I have ever heard him before.

The inauguration took place to-day. There was great want of arrangement and completeness in the ceremonies. All was confusion and without order, — a jumble.

The Vice-President elect made a rambling and strange harangue, which was listened to with pain and mortification by all his friends. My impressions were that he was under the influence of stimulants, yet I know not that he drinks. He has been sick and is feeble; perhaps he may have taken medicine, or stimulants, or his brain from sickness may have been overactive in these new responsibilities. Whatever the cause, it was all in very bad taste.

The delivery of the inaugural address, the administering of the oath, and the whole deportment of the President were well done, and the retiring Vice-President appeared to advantage when contrasted with his successor, who has humiliated his friends. Speed, who sat at my left, whispered me that "all this is in wretched bad taste"; and very soon he said, "The man is certainly deranged." I said to Stanton, who was on my right, "Johnson is either drunk or crazy." Stanton replied, "There is evidently something wrong." Seward says it was emotion on returning and revisiting the Senate; that he can appreciate Johnson's feelings, who was much overcome. I hope Seward is right, but don't entirely concur with him. There is, as Stanton says, something wrong. I hope it is sickness.

The reception at the President's this evening was a crowded affair, — not brilliant, as the papers say it was. In some respects the arrangement was better than heretofore for the Cabinet gentlemen and their families, but there is room for much improvement. Such was the crowd that many were two hours before obtaining entrance after passing through the gates. When I left, a little before eleven, the crowd was still going in.

The day has been fatiguing and trying. The morning was rainy. Soon after noon the clouds disappeared and the day was beautiful; the streets dreadful.

March 6, Monday. The weather continues to be fine. Thousands have left the city, which is still crowded. The inauguration ball of this evening is a great attraction,

HUGH McCULLOCH

particularly to the young. Seward has sent to me a request to attend, and Dennison desires it. I have no desire to go, but my family have, as well as my associates.

Current business at Department has accumulated, and the day has been one of unceasing application. Did not leave Department until after five o'clock. McCulloch's name was sent in to-day for the Treasury. I fear he wants political knowledge and experience, though as a financier he may not be unequal to the position; but will not prejudge him. He has been a successful banker, and that seems to have furnished the argument for his appointment. It by no means follows, however, that a successful banker, good at business details and accumulating interest, is able to strike out and establish the policy of the nation in regard to its currency and finance. He may have these essential financial qualities, but I do not think they entered into the considerations which led to his selection.

March 7, Tuesday. The meeting at the Cabinet was interesting, the topics miscellaneous. Vice-President Johnson's infirmity was mentioned. Seward's tone and opinions were much changed since Saturday. He seems to have given up Johnson now, but no one appears to have been aware of any failing. I trust and am inclined to believe it a temporary ailment, which may, if rightly treated, be overcome.

Chief Justice Chase spent an hour with the President last evening, and is urging upon him to exempt sundry counties in eastern Virginia from the insurrectionary proclamation. He did not make his object explicit to the President, but most of the Cabinet came, I think, to the conclusion that there was an ulterior purpose not fully disclosed.

It is obvious that Chase has his aspirations stimulated. This movement he considers adroit. By withdrawing military authority and restoring civil jurisdiction he accomplishes sundry purposes. It will strike a blow at State

individuality and break down Virginia, already by his aid
dismembered and divided. It will be a large stride in the
direction of the theory of the radicals, who are for reducing old States to a Territorial condition. It is centralizing,
to which he has become a convert; [it] will give the Chief
Justice an opportunity to exercise his authority on questions of *habeas corpus*, military arrests, etc.

The Chief Justice had also certain views on the present
condition of the blockade, and took occasion to inform the
President that his original opinion, which corresponded
with mine, had undergone quite a modification; that he is
now satisfied that closing the ports by a public or international blockade was better than to have closed them
by legislative enactment or executive order, in effect a
municipal regulation. Artful dodger. Unstable and unreliable. When Speed made some inquiry on these matters,
the President stated "it related to one of the early and most
unpleasant differences we had ever had in Cabinet." It
was one of the subjects that made me distrust and doubt
Chase, who, while fully assenting to my opinions in our
private conversations, did not vigorously sustain me in a
Cabinet discussion.

The Spanish mission being vacant, it was asked if any
of the number wished it. Whether it was intended as a
polite tender to Usher I know not, or to any other, but I
think not to any one but Usher, and perhaps not to him.
This mission is a sort of plaything in the hands of Seward.
The truth is, there is little utility in these legations near
the governments of foreign potentates, but they are convenient places for favorites or troublesome fellows who
are to be sent away.

March 10, *Friday*. At the Cabinet to-day Seward could
not suppress his delight over intelligence, just received,
that the Danish-French ironclad sold to the Rebels was
stopped at Corunna. We have had multitudinous and
various pieces of intelligence respecting this vessel, none

of them reliable. The next arrival may bring statements in direct opposition to those we now have.

Each of the Departments finished up their matters with the Senate, which will doubtless adjourn to-morrow.

March 11, *Saturday.* Mr. Eames tells me the Court has decided adversely in the matter of cotton captured by the Navy on the Red River. I perceive that the Court is adjudicating on the Treasury regulations and policy of the Chief Justice.

John P. Hale has been nominated and confirmed as Minister to Spain, a position for which he is eminently unfit. This is Seward's doings, the President assenting. But others are also in fault. I am told by Seward, who is conscious it is an improper appointment, that a majority of the Union Senators recommended him for the French mission, for which they know he has no qualifications, address, nor proper sense to fill. Some of the Senators protested against his receiving the mission to France, but Seward says they acquiesced in his going to Spain. I am satisfied that Seward is playing a game with this old hack. Hale has been getting pay from the War Department for various jobs, and S. thinks he is an abolition leader.

March 13, *Monday.* Rear-Admiral Porter spent the evening at my house. Among other things he detailed what he saw and knew of Jeff Davis and others in the early days of the Rebellion. He was, he admits, and as I was aware, on intimate terms with Davis and Mrs. Davis, and had been so for some years. On the evening after reception of the news that South Carolina passed the secession ordinance he called at Davis's house. A number of Secession leaders, he says, were there. It was a rainy, disagreeable evening, but Mrs. Davis came down stairs bonneted and prepared to go out. She caught him and congratulated him on the glorious news. South Carolina had declared herself out of the Union, which was to be broken up. She was going to see the President, Buchanan, and congratulate him. Wanted to be the first to communicate the intelligence to him. Porter told her the weather and roads were such she could not walk, and, one of the Members of Congress having come in a hack, he, Porter, took it and accompanied her. On the way he inquired why she should feel so much elated. She said she wanted to get rid of the old government; that they would have a monarchy South, and gentlemen to fill official positions. This, he found, was the most earnest sentiment, not only of herself but others. Returning in the carriage to Davis's house, he found that the crowd of gentlemen was just preparing to follow Mrs. D. to call on the President and interchange congratulations. They all spoke of Buchanan, he says, as being with them in sentiment, and Porter believes him to have been one of the most guilty in that nefarious business; that he encouraged the active conspirators in his intercourse with them, if he did not openly approve them before the world.

Governor Canby of Maine called on me a week ago and spoke of having a naval vessel on the eastern coast for recruiting purposes and for protection. After a little discussion of the subject, he said there was a committee in Washington who had procured themselves to be appointed to come on and make formal application; that they desired to attend the inauguration, and had got up this excuse; would make probably a little display and hoped they might be gratified with a few words of recognition, etc., etc. Two or three hours later, the committee, Mr. Poor and his two associates, came in with Mr. Pike, who introduced them. Mr. Poor was the chairman and presented me a paper containing sundry resolutions indorsed by the President, to the effect that he wished them to have vessels if they could be spared. Mr. Poor was verbose and pompous; let me know his official importance; wanted their application should be granted. I told them their proposition for steamers to patrol the Maine coast was inadmissible, but such protection as could be extended and the occasion required would be regarded. My remarks were not such as suited the pragmatical chairman. The other gentlemen exhibited more sense.

Two or three days after, I had a communication from the committee, who wanted to know if their application in behalf of the State of Maine could be granted. Remembering Governor Canby's remarks, I wrote them at some length the views I had expressed orally at our interview.

Soft words and a superfluity of them only added fuel to Chairman Poor's vanity, and he replied by a supercilious and silly letter which indicated a disposition to cut a figu and I replied by a brief but courteous line, tersely co.. taining the same opinions I had given.

March 14, *Tuesday.* The President was some indisposed and in bed, but not seriously ill. The members met in his bedroom. Seward had a paper for excluding blockade-runners and persons in complicity with the Rebels from the country.

John P. Hale's appointment to Spain was brought up. Seward tried to gloss it over. Wanted Hale to call and see me and make friends with Fox. Hale promised he would, and Seward thought he might get a passage out in a government vessel.

The capture and destruction of a large amount of tobacco at Fredericksburg has created quite a commotion. It was a matter in which many were implicated. Several have called on me to get permission to pass the blockade or have a gunboat to convoy them. One or more have brought a qualified pass from the President. Colonel Segar, the last of them, was very importunate. I told him, as I have all others, that I should not yield in this matter; that I was opposed on principle to the whole scheme of special permits to trade and had been from the time that Chase commenced it; that I was no believer in the policy of trading with public enemies, carrying on war and peace

2

at the same time. Chase was the first to broach and introduce this corrupting and demoralizing scheme, and I have no doubt he expected to make political capital by it. His course in this matter does much to impair my confidence in him. It was one of many not over scrupulous intrigues. Fessenden followed in the footsteps of Chase, not from any corrupt motives, nor for any political or personal aspirations, but in order to help him in financial matters. He had a superficial idea that cotton would help him get gold, — that he must get cotton to promote trade and equalize exchange.

March 15, *Wednesday.* A rumor is prevalent and very generally believed that the French mission has been offered Bennett of the *New York Herald.* I discredit it. On one or two occasions this mission has been alluded to in Cabinet, but the name of B. was never mentioned or alluded to. There are sometimes strange and unaccountable appointments made. . . .

March 16, *Thursday.* Mr. Blair wishes a young friend paroled, and requests me to see the President. I am disinclined to press these individual cases on the President. Mrs. Tatnall, wife of the Rebel commodore, desires to come North to her friends in Connecticut. Mrs. Welles, wife of Albert Welles, wants a permit to go to Mobile to join her husband. Miss Laura Jones, an old family acquaintance, wishes to go to Richmond to meet and marry her betrothed. These are specimen cases.

Blair believes the President has offered the French mission to Bennett. Says it is the President and not Seward, and gives the reasons which lead him to that conclusion. He says he met Bartlett, the [runner] of Bennett, here last August or September; that Bartlett sought him, said they had abused him, B., in the *Herald* but thought much of him, considered him the man of most power in the Cabinet, but were dissatisfied because he had not controlled the Navy Department early in the Administration and brought it into their (the *Herald's*) interest. Blair replied that the *Herald* folks had never yet learned or understood the Secretary of the Navy; that he was a hard-headed and very decided man in his opinions. He says Bartlett then went on to tell him that he was here watching movements and that they did not mean this time to be cheated. . . .

I am sorry to hear Blair speak approvingly of the appointment of Bennett, — . . . an editor without character for such an appointment, whose whims are often wickedly and atrociously leveled against the best men and the best causes, regardless of honor or right.

As for Bartlett, he is a mercenary . . . who sought to use the Navy Department and have himself made the agent to purchase the vessels for the Navy. Because I would not prostitute my office and favor his brokerage, he threatened me with unceasing hostility and assaults, not only from the *Herald* but from nearly every press in New York. He said he could control them all. I was incredulous as to his influence over other journals, and at all events shook him off, determined to have nothing to do with him. In a very short time I found the papers slashing and attacking me, editorially and through correspondents. Washburne, Van Wyck, D——, J. P. Hale, and others coöperated with them, perhaps intentionally; most certainly they were, intentionally or otherwise, the instruments of the combination of correspondents led on by this Bartlett, who boasted of his work and taunted me through others.

But the New York press was unable to form a public sentiment hostile to the administration of the Navy Department. There were a few, very few, journals in other parts of the country that were led astray by them, and some of the frivolous and surface scum of idle loungers echoed the senseless and generally witless efforts to depreciate my labors, but the people and a large portion of the papers proved friendly. The *New York Tribune* was, while professing friendship, the most malicious and mean; the *Times* and the *Herald* were about alike; the *Evening Post* gave me a halting support; the *Express* was, as usual, balderdash; the *Journal of Commerce* in more manly opposition; the *Commercial Advertiser* alone was at that time fair and honestly friendly. Most of the weeklies were vehicles of blackguardism against me by the combined writers. Although somewhat annoyed by these concerted proceedings in New York and Washington, formed for mischief, I was too much occupied to give much heed to the villainous and wicked course pursued against me.

March 18, *Saturday.* The President this day returned the abstract made by Eames in the case of F. Smith of Boston with an indorsement in his own handwriting, disapproving the verdict and annulling the proceedings. It is, I regret to say, a discreditable indorsement, and would, if made public, be likely to injure the President. He has, I know, been much importuned in this matter, as I have, and very skillful and persistent efforts have been pursued for months to procure this result. Senators and Representatives have interposed their influence to defeat the ends of justice, and shielded guilty men from punishment, and they have accomplished it. They have made the President the partisan of persons convicted and pronounced guilty of fraud upon the government. Of course, rascality will flourish. I regret all this on the President's account, as well as that of the ends of justice. I had in my letter to the President invited a conference after he had examined the case, and on Tuesday last, when he was not well and was in bed, I had, among other things, mentioned Smith's case. He said he had gone through with Mr. Eames' summing-up, an opinion which seemed to him to be able and impartial; that he had handed the paper to Sumner to read, etc., and he would see me in relation to it when Sumner returned the document.

Having got excited, he may have forgotten my request and his promise, and I have no doubt was reluctant to see me before the question was disposed of, knowing I should be unwilling to bring it up after such disposition. But this is unavoidable, for I must consult him as to Ben Smith and other cases hinged in with this.

The news from the army continues favorable, and it seems impossible for the Rebel leaders to continue much longer to hold out. Everything is giving way to the Union forces. The currency is getting into better shape, but there will be still tremendous struggles and revulsions before its sound restoration can be accomplished.

March 20, *Monday.* Seward sends me a half-scary letter from Sanford, who is in Paris, that Page intends coming out of Ferrol and fighting the Niagara. I do not believe it, though, were Page a desperate and fighting man, it would be probable. But Page wants power. Not unlikely his associates have come to the conclusion that there is no alternative, and that he must make up his mind to fight. Under this stimulant he may do so, but I have my doubts.

Craven is a good officer, though a little timid and inert by nature. The occasion is a great one for him and will rouse his energies. I wish he had smooth-bores instead of rifles on his vessel, provided they have a conflict; wish he was more of a rifle himself.

I apprehend Seward has been cheated and humbugged in regard to this vessel by the Rebels and the French, and I am not satisfied with the part Denmark has played. Our Minister does not appear to have been efficient in the matter, or if so, it has not been disclosed. The State Department is mum, troubled.

March 21, *Tuesday.* Called on the President this morning concerning the Smith case. Asked if the same course should be pursued with Ben as with Frank. He said yes

if there was no more evidence. I asked what I was to do
with the employees who had been in complicity with Smith
and passed his articles. We then had a little conversation
as regards the master machinist, Merriam, and one or two
others. The President said if they had been remiss, Smith's
pardon ought not to cover them.

I stated the case of —— of Philadelphia, a young contractor who had been detected like Smith, and under the
stern commands of his father-in-law had made a full confession, and the latter had made full restitution to the
amount of more than $14,800. That the President said
was a large amount, greatly exceeding Smith's. I told him
Smith had not been taken in hand by his father-in-law,
had made no confession, no restitution. Now the question
was whether I should prosecute ——, and have him fined
and imprisoned after doing all in his power to make the
government good, while Smith, an older and, I feared, a
much greater offender, who made no confession, no restitution, went unpunished.

The President was annoyed. I told him there were a
number of persons under bonds, who had confessed and
made restitution of smaller amounts. Were their offenses
to be overlooked or excused?

After some little talk, he wished me to get our solicitor
to look into these cases, and call again. He has evidently
acted without due consideration, on the suggestion and
advice of Sumner, who is emotional, and under the pressure of Massachusetts politicians, who have been active
to screen these parties regardless of their guilt.

When at the Cabinet to-day, the President and McCulloch wished to know if I would be willing to take Arnold
of Chicago for Solicitor of the Navy, and release Chandler
for a Treasury appointment. While I think Arnold a
worthy and an estimable man, I told the President and
Secretary of the Treasury I preferred that Chandler
should go forward with his duties. McCulloch was a little
pressing; the President, however, did not urge the matter.

March 22, *Wednesday.* Mr. Eames brings me the opinion of the Court in the cotton case of prize — Alexander — Red River cotton. I think Chief Justice Chase has got himself in a fix, and will have to back down. He must divest himself of personal aspiration and partisan feeling to be a successful judge. The Court will not be subservient to him if he commits such grave mistakes.

Olcott, the detective, or commissioner, writes Fox a strange letter about the conclusions in Smith's case. He has seen Sumner's argument, or a part of it, and is alarmed. Sumner says the Smiths should have some redress. Olcott intimates that if they propose to arrest him he will flee the country. The fellow has no moral courage. So long as the responsibility was with me, he was very courageous. He feared I would not fearlessly meet questions, was inclined to encourage me; but as soon as a cloud shadows his path — an ounce of responsibility comes upon him — the valiant commissioner wilts and is abject. I had on Monday told Chandler that in my opinion these traits belonged to Olcott; that he was rash, reckless, and arbitrary in the exercise of power but would cringe himself. C. reminds me of this estimate.

March 23, *Thursday.* An extra of the *Boston Journal* contains Senator Sumner's review, or argument, of the case of Smith Brothers. It is not a creditable document for Mr. Sumner in any aspect, and he will probably regret that he ever sent out such a document. A letter from Hooper accompanies the paper, quite as discreditable.

J. M. Forbes tells me he went into Sumner's room and found Hooper and Gooch there. The three were in high glee, and Sumner was detailing his success in getting the executive pardon. Forbes told them it was proper they should understand his position. He believed it was an executive error, but a greater error for Massachusetts Representatives to interfere and stop legal proceedings through their political influence. Sumner spoke of the smallness of the amount involved. Forbes replied that if one of his servants was detected, and convicted of having stolen a silver spoon, though only a teaspoon, he would kick him out of the house and not trust him farther. Nor would he be persuaded to excuse and take the thief into favor because he had been trusted with all his silver and only stolen, or been detected in having stolen, one small spoon.

The President has gone to the front, partly to get rid of the throng that is pressing upon him, though there are speculations of a different character. He makes his office much more laborious than he should. Does not generalize and takes upon himself questions that properly belong to the Departments, often causing derangement and irregularity. The more he yields, the greater the pressure upon him. It has now become such that he is compelled to flee. There is no doubt he is much worn down; besides he wishes the War terminated, and, to this end, that severe terms shall not be exacted of the Rebels.

March 24, Friday. Attorney-General Speed calls upon me in some trouble. The Secretary of the Treasury has asked his opinion whether appropriations for the next fiscal year which have been covered into the Treasury can be now drawn upon. This has been the practice during the War, but the First Comptroller objects to passing requisitions and questions its legality. In this ruling the Comptroller is probably strictly legally correct, but to attempt to rigidly enforce the law would be disastrous. The fault originates in the Treasury; the usage has been theirs; not only this, it has been their delinquency which makes the present difficulty. Paymasters do not settle their accounts promptly. The Fourth Auditor's office is two years behind, and their requisitions cannot be adjusted and carried to the proper appropriation until their accounts are settled at the Auditor's office. The Attorney-General thinks he shall legally be compelled to go with the Comptroller if required to give an opinion, and he thinks McCulloch inclined to exact it. In that event both Navy and Army must come to a standstill, the credit of the Treasury will be injured, loans cannot be negotiated, and the government will be involved in financial embarrassments.

A paymaster, for instance, especially a new one, commits errors in his drafts. He makes a requisition, perhaps for $100,000, and, in uncertainty from what appropriation the money should come, he draws the whole amount from "Pay of the Navy"; but $12,000 should have been from "Equipment," for coal, etc., $10,000 from "Provisions and Clothing," $10,000 from "Construction," and $12,000 is to pay prize; so that only $56,000 should have been taken from "Pay of the Navy." But this cannot be corrected and carried to the proper heads until the paymaster's account is settled, which will not be sooner than 1867. In the mean time the appropriation of "Pay of the Navy" is exhausted, through ignorance of the new paymasters and the carelessness of the old ones.

Wrote a letter to Olcott, the detective, as Stanton calls him, or, as he calls himself and wishes to be called, Commissioner, in answer to a strange letter from him proposing to make a report for Congress, to prevent the repeal of the law which subjects contractors to military arrest and trial by court martial. I gave him to understand that I had no hand in originating the law and could not, nor did I feel disposed to, interpose to prevent its repeal when Congress thought proper. Notified him that he would hereafter correspond with the Solicitor instead of Assistant Secretary, enjoined economy, etc., etc. It will not do to let this man go on unchecked. He is zealous, in a certain sense I think honest, but is rash, reckless, at times regardless of the rights of others, assumes authority, but I am inclined to believe acts with good intentions; and he is wild in his expenditures. Of course he will be dissatisfied and not unlikely abusive of me for checking and correcting his errors.

March 25, Saturday. Called on Secretary McCulloch to-day in relation to payment of our requisitions which the Comptroller, under the impression he is the government, has rejected. He sees the difficulty and the necessity of doing away with the objections interposed by the Comptroller, but yet knows not how to do it.

Senator Sumner called on me in relation to the case of the Smiths, or rather he introduced that subject among others in his visit. He usually calls on me for half an hour or an hour's conversation Saturday afternoon. He read me two or three letters from Boston correspondents, lauding his course and censuring the prosecution. They had touched his weak point. He was feeling well and was ready now to "do something for these men, who had been greatly, deeply wronged." I asked him if he was satisfied the government had not been injured by their transactions. He said the government could have been injured to but a small amount in very extensive transactions, and the injury, if there was any, only a single article, on which the government was under a strange misapprehension. Mr. Hooper was cited as authority in the matter of Banca and [Straits?] tin, which he claimed was identical. I told him the last *Prices Current* showed a difference of eight cents a pound. But I asked him what he had to say of the transaction of the Smiths in regard to anchors, an article in which they did not deal, but for which they had by some means and for some purpose got the contract; had them by collusion paid for in May; they were arrested on the 17th of June, when the articles, though paid for, were not all delivered. They had underlet the contract to Burns, who made the deliveries, and the anchors were many of them worthless, would not pass inspection; and the arrest before full and final delivery was plead as the excuse, although requisition had been issued in May. What of the files, machine-cut, instead of hand-cut as contracted? What of the combination with Henshaw not to bid, whereby they got a contract for a number of hundred tons of iron at $62.50, when other parties sold at the same time for $53? Sumner had not looked into these matters. He could not answer me. I showed him the correspondence of the Smiths with the Trenton Iron Company, expressly stipulating for inferior iron to be delivered to the navy yard, if it would pass inspection. After reading, he said he did not like the transaction. Evidently knew not the case in which he had interfered. I stated to him ——'s case, and asked his advice how to proceed, when —— had confessed and made full restitution, while the Smiths had done neither, and were pardoned.

March 27, Monday. Immediately after the capture of Charleston, it was suggested at one of the Cabinet-meetings, by Dennison and Speed, that we should go thither on the anniversary of the fall of Sumter and raise again the old flag. I declined to be a party in such a movement, as Sumter was already taken and the flag had been raised on its ruins. But others, I see, have taken a different view, and Stanton with a party is to go to Charleston for the purpose indicated. Without having heard a word from Seward, I shall expect him to work into the party. He likes fuss and parade; is already preparing his speech.

Ordered to-day the Wyoming to the East Indies. Had dispatches on Saturday from Craven, who is on the Niagara watching the Rebel ironclad Stonewall at Corunna. He says he is "in an unenviable and embarrassing position." There are many of our best naval officers who think he has an enviable position, and they would make sacrifices to obtain it. Perhaps Craven will fight well, though his language is not bold and defiant, nor his sentiments such as will stimulate his crew. It is an infirmity. Craven is intelligent, and disciplines his ship well, I am told, but his constant doubts and misgivings impair his usefulness.

March 28, Tuesday. Edgar, Fox, and others left to-day for a trip on the Santiago de Cuba, to Havana, Charleston, etc., etc. They were to return by the 15th *prox.*, but will hardly get back before the 17th.

The President being absent on a visit to the army near Richmond, there was to-day no Cabinet-meeting.

Comptroller Taylor declines to pass requisitions, and refuses to obey the Secretary of the Treasury; will act on the order of the President. I see not the distinction. If illegal, the order of the President does not legalize it.

The strict letter of the law is doubtless with the Comptroller in this matter of drawing money before the commencement of the fiscal year. But, unfortunately for him, he has acted otherwise and the usage of himself and predecessor, Comptroller Whittlesey, under Mr. Secretary, now Chief Justice, Chase, have been wholly different. Mr. Taylor said yesterday that he did not pass requisitions last year, that the appropriation bill did not pass until after the commencement of the fiscal year. But he is mistaken. The appropriation was covered into the Treasury in May, and we had drawn, and he had passed, over four millions before the 1st of July. He has this year paid over one million before he accidentally discovered that his action conflicted with the law. The Secretary of the Treasury sent to notify me that a draft for ten thousand dollars on "Pay of the Navy" was presented by Riggs & Co., and desired to know if I would not pay from some other appropriation. I declined to do the illegal act and complicate and embarrass accounts.

March 29, Wednesday. The Secretary of State has written me, requesting that J. P. Hale, recently appointed Minister to Spain, should be sent out in a public ship. I have written him in reply that it cannot be done without much inconvenience and expense; that it would be better to send out a purchased steamer with cabin room than to attempt to crowd him and suite on board a man-of-war. The whole scheme is petty foolishness, an attempt on the part of Seward to ingratiate himself with the Abolitionists, whom he privately denounces and ridicules. It is one of those small meannesses which aspiring and not over-scrupulous men sometimes resort to. A shameful prostitution, waste, and wrong.

March 30, *Thursday.* The President still remains with the army. Seward yesterday left to join him. It was after I saw him, for he was then expecting the President would return last evening or this morning. Stanton, who was present, remarked that it was quite as pleasant to have the President away, that he (Stanton) was much less annoyed. Neither Seward nor myself responded. As Seward left within less than three hours after this interview, I think the President must have telegraphed for him, and, if so, I come to the conclusion that efforts are again being made for peace.

I am by no means certain that this irregular proceeding and importunity by the Executive is the wisest course. Yet the President has much shrewdness and sagacity. He has been apprehensive that the military men are not very solicitous to close hostilities, — fears our generals will exact severe terms.

Mr. Faxon left this P.M. for Connecticut. His absence and that of Mr. Fox and Edgar will make my labors exceedingly arduous for the next fortnight, for Faxon will not return until week after next, and the others the week following.

March 31, *Friday.* I had a call to-day from Wylly Woodbridge of Savannah. We were fellow students and fellow boarders at good Parson Cornwall's at Cheshire Academy forty-four years ago. He much younger than myself. Time has ploughed his furrows deep since then, and of our companions much the larger portion have passed from earth.

General Butler called on me while we were conversing and had a pleasant interview. In speaking of his brief administration at Baltimore, General B. said if he had not

been summarily displaced and called to Washington, he
would within forty-eight hours have had Winans hung in
Union Square. Had that been done, he is confident it
would have checked the Rebellion. To have executed a
man of Winans' wealth and position would have struck
terror, — showed we were in earnest.

XXIX

April 1, *Saturday.* The President yet remains with the army, and the indications are that a great and perhaps final battle is near. Tom writes me, dating his letter "Headquarters Army of the James, near Hatcher's Run," saying he had scarcely slept for forty-eight hours, the army having commenced moving on the evening of the 27th, and his letter was dated the evening of the 29th. General Ord must, therefore, have moved his army from before Richmond, crossed the James, and got below Petersburg. I infer, therefore, that the demonstration will be on that plan, and I trust defeat and capture of Lee and his army.

Greeley's letter of last summer to the President, urging peace for our "bleeding, bankrupt, ruined country" has been published in England. This was the letter which led to the Niagara conference. I advised its publication and the whole correspondence at the time, but the President was unwilling just then, unless Greeley would consent to omit the passage concerning our ruined country, but to this Greeley would not consent, and in that exhibited weakness, for it was the most offensive and objectionable part of his letter.

How it comes now to be published in England I do not understand. I should have preferred its appearance at home in the first instance. Poor Greeley is nearly played out. He has a morbid appetite for notoriety. Wishes to be noted and forward in all shows. Four years ago was zealous — or willing — to let the States secede if they wished. Six months later was vociferating, "On to Richmond." Has been scolding and urging forward hostile operations. Suddenly is for peace, and ready to pay the Rebels four hundred millions or more to get it, he being allowed to figure in it. He craves public attention. Does not exhibit a high regard for principle. I doubt his honesty about as much as his consistency. It is put on for effect. He is a greedy office-hunter.

April 2, Sunday. A telegram from the President this morning to the War Department states that a furious fight is going on. Sheridan has got west of Petersburg on the South Side Railroad, creeping from the west, at the same time Grant has ordered an advance of our lines. Wright and Parke are said to have broken through the Rebel lines. General Ord is fighting, but results unknown. General Halleck states that Lee has undoubtedly sent out his force to protect the railroad and preserve his communications, that this has left Richmond weak, and Ord is pressing on the city. I inquired if Ord was not below Petersburg at Hatcher's Run. He said no, that was newspaper talk. Told him I had supposed otherwise.

On going to the War Department a few hours later to make further inquiries, I carried with me Tom's letter, but Halleck was not there. Stanton, however, maintained the same ground until I read Tom's letter, when he yielded.

April 3, Monday. Intelligence of the evacuation of Petersburg and the capture of Richmond was received this A.M., and the city has been in an uproar through the day.

Most of the clerks and others left the Departments, and there were immense gatherings in the streets. Joy and gladness lightened every countenance. Secessionists and their sympathizers must have retired, and yet it seemed as if the entire population, the male portion of it, was abroad in the streets. Flags were flying from every house and store that had them. Many of the stores were closed, and Washington appeared patriotic beyond anything ever before witnessed. The absence of the Assistant, Chief Clerk, and Solicitor compelled my attendance until after 3 P.M. close of mail.

Attorney-General Speed and myself met by agreement at Stanton's room last night at nine, to learn the condition of affairs with the armies. We had previously been two or three times there during the day. It was about eleven before a dispatch was received and deciphered. The conversation between us three was free, and, turning on events connected with the Rebellion, our thoughts and talk naturally traveled back to the early days of the insurrection and the incipient treason in Buchanan's cabinet. Stanton became quite communicative. He was invited, as I have previously understood, through the influence of Black. Says Buchanan was a miserable coward, so alarmed and enfeebled by the gathering storm as to be mentally and physically prostrated, and he was apprehensive the President would not survive until the fourth of March. The discussion in regard to the course to be pursued towards Anderson and the little garrison at Sumter, became excited and violent in December, 1860. On the 27th or 29th of that month there were three sessions of the Cabinet in council. Sitting late at night, Buchanan, wrapped in an old dressing-gown or cloak, crouched in a corner near the fire, trembled like an aspen leaf. He asked what he should do. Declared that Stanton said he ought to be hung and that others of the Cabinet concurred with him. This, Stanton said, grew out of his remarks that if they yielded up Sumter to the conspirators it was treason,

2

and no more to be defended than Arnold's. In the discussion Holt was very emphatic and decided in his loyalty, Toucey the most abject and mean. When called upon by the President for his opinion, Toucey said he was for ordering Anderson to return immediately to Fort Moultrie. He was asked if he was aware that Moultrie was dismantled, and replied that would make no difference, Anderson had gone to Sumter without orders, and against orders of Floyd, and he would order him back forthwith. Stanton says he inquired of Toucey if he ever expected to go back to Connecticut after taking that position, and Toucey said he did, but asked Stanton why he put the question. Stanton replied that he had inquired in good faith, that he might know the character of the people in Connecticut or Toucey's estimate of them, for were he, S., to take that position and it were known to the people of Pennsylvania, he should expect they would stone him the moment he set foot in the State, stone him through the State, and tie a stone around his neck and throw him in the river when he reached Pittsburg. Stanton gives Toucey the most despicable character in the Buchanan cabinet, not excepting Floyd or Thompson.

April 4, Tuesday. Very little intelligence received from the armies to-day. The President still at City Point, or its vicinity, holding interviews with the generals and having an eye to the close, which is near. In the mean time the Treasury is likely to suffer. The First Comptroller will not pass bill or requisition for pay. A draft for ten thousand dollars was presented to the Treasury which matured to-day, and the holder, Riggs, was referred to me to see if I could not make arrangement to pay under some other appropriation. I declined to move in the matter. The Kearsarge, destined for Europe, the Wyoming for Brazil, and other vessels are detained, and trouble wells up on every side.

April 5, Wednesday. We get no particulars of the surrender of Richmond, of the losses and casualties, of the time and circumstances of the evacuation. On Sunday afternoon Lee sent word to Davis that they were doomed, and advised his immediate departure. With heavy hearts and light luggage the leaders left at once.

Mr. Seward read to Mr. McCulloch and myself a proclamation which he had prepared for the President to sign, closing the ports to foreign powers, in the Rebel States. He and myself have had several conversations for the last two or three months on this subject. The time had arrived when it seemed to him proper to issue it, and unless the President returned forthwith it was, he thought, advisable that he, Mr. Seward, should go to Richmond and see him. He could also communicate with the President on the subject of payment of requisitions of the Navy and War Departments. Accordingly, a telegram was prepared and sent to the President, and Seward, anticipating that the President would remain a few days longer, made preparations to leave by procuring the promise of a revenue cutter to convey him. He is filled with anxiety to see the President, and these schemes are his apology.

Within half an hour after parting from Mr. Seward, his horses ran away with the carriage in which he was taking a ride, he jumped from the vehicle, was taken up badly injured, with his arm and jaw broken, and his head and face badly bruised.

April 6, Thursday. Commander Collins of the Wachusett, who captured the Florida, arrived to-day for trial, ordered by request of the State Department to satisfy the wounded honor of Brazil.

A telegram from Dr. E. W. Hale states J. T. Hale, late Member of Congress, is dying. He was a Representative in the three last Congresses, Chairman of the Committee of Claims, and one of the most sensible, useful, yet unpretending Members of the House. Too few men of that description are sent to Congress. Noisy, blatant, superficial declaimers and mere party intriguers are favorites.

April 7, Friday. We have word that Sheridan has had a battle with a part of Lee's army, has captured six Rebel generals and several thousand prisoners. His dispatch intimates the almost certain capture of Lee.

In the closing up of this Rebellion, General Grant has proved himself a man of military talent. Those who have doubted and hesitated must concede him some capacity as a general. Though slow and utterly destitute of genius, his final demonstrations and movements have been masterly. The persistency which he has exhibited is as much to be admired as any quality in his character. He is, however, too regardless of the lives of his men.

It is desirable that Lee should be captured. He, more than any one else, has the confidence of the Rebels, and can, if he escapes, and is weak enough to try and continue hostilities, rally for a time a brigand force in the interior. I can hardly suppose he would do this, but he has shown weakness, and his infidelity to the country which educated, and employed, and paid him shows gross ingratitude. His true course would be to desert the country he has betrayed, and never return.

Memo. This Rebellion which has convulsed the nation for four years, threatened the Union, and caused such sacrifice of blood and treasure may be traced in a great degree to the diseased imagination of certain South Carolina gentlemen, who some thirty and forty years since studied Scott's novels, and fancied themselves cavaliers, imbued with chivalry, a superior class, not born to labor but to command, brave beyond mankind generally, more intellectual, more generous, more hospitable, more liberal than others. Such of their countrymen as did not own slaves, and who labored with their own hands, who depended on their own exertions for a livelihood, who were mechanics, traders, and tillers of the soil, were, in their estimate, inferiors who would not fight, were religious and would not gamble, moral and would not countenance duelling, were serious and minded their own business, economical and thrifty, which was denounced as mean and miserly. Hence the chivalrous Carolinian affected to, and actually did finally, hold the Yankee in contempt. The women caught the infection. They were to be patriotic, Revolutionary matrons and maidens. They admired the bold, dashing, swaggering, licentious, boasting, chivalrous slave-master who told them he wanted to fight the Yankee but could not kick and insult him into a quarrel. And they disdained and despised the pious, peddling, plodding, persevering Yankee who would not drink, and swear, and fight duels.

The speeches and letters of James Hamilton and his associates from 1825 forward will be found impregnated with the romance and poetry of Scott, and they came ultimately to believe themselves a superior and better race, knights of blood and spirit.

Only a war could wipe out this arrogance and folly, which had by party and sectional instrumentalities been disseminated through a large portion of the South. Face to face in battle and in field with these slandered Yankees, they learned their own weakness and misconception of the Yankee character. Without self-assumption of superiority, the Yankee was proved to be as brave, as generous, as humane, as chivalric as the vaunting and superficial Carolinian to say the least. Their ideal, however, in Scott's pages of "Marmion," "Ivanhoe," etc., no more belonged to the Sunny South than to other sections less arrogant and presuming but more industrious and frugal.

On the other hand, the Yankees, and the North generally, underestimated the energy and enduring qualities of the Southern people who were slave-owners. It was believed they were effeminate idlers, living on the toil and labor of others, who themselves could endure no hardship such as is indispensable to soldiers in the field. It was also believed that a civil war would, inevitably, lead to servile insurrection, and that the slave-owners would have their hands full to keep the slaves in subjection after hostilities commenced. Experience has corrected these misconceptions in each section.

April 10, *Monday.* At day-dawn a salute of several guns was fired. The first discharge proclaimed, as well as words could have done, the capture of Lee and his army. The morning papers detailed the particulars. The event took place yesterday, and the circumstances will be narrated in full elsewhere.

The tidings were spread over the country during the night, and the nation seems delirious with joy. Guns are firing, bells ringing, flags flying, men laughing, children cheering; all, all are jubilant. This surrender of the great Rebel captain and the most formidable and reliable army of the Secessionists virtually terminates the Rebellion. There may be some marauding, and robbing and murder by desperadoes, but no great battle, no conflict of armies, after the news of yesterday reaches the different sections. Possibly there may be some stand in Texas or at remote points beyond the Mississippi.

Called on the President, who returned last evening, looking well and feeling well. Signed the proclamation closing the Southern ports. Seemed gratified that Seward and myself were united in the measure, remembering, I think, without mentioning, the old difference.

April 11, *Tuesday.* The cotton question was the chief topic at the Cabinet. Secretary McCulloch is embarrassed how to dispose of the Savannah capture. I am afraid of replevin and other troubles. Told him I thought it an error that the Rebel cotton had not been brought forward and sold in parcels instead of accumulating public and private in such quantity as to attract the vultures.

April 12, *Wednesday.* The President to-day issued a proclamation excluding after a reasonable time the naval vessels of those powers which deny hospitality to our ships, — in other words applying the principle of reciprocity. This rule I have long since urged upon the Secretary of State, but he has halted, put it off, and left us to put up with the insolence of the petty officials of John Bull. But we shall now assert our rights and, I hope, maintain them.

The President addressed a multitude who called upon him last evening in a prepared speech disclosing his views on the subject of resumption of friendly national relations.

April 13, *Thursday.* Gave the President the case of Stiners, court-martialed and condemned for fraud as a contractor, — similar in principle to the case of the Smiths in Boston.

Some conversation with him yesterday and to-day in regard to his speech Tuesday night and the general question of reëstablishing the authority of the government in the Rebel States and movements at Richmond.

The President asked me what views I took of Weitzel's calling the Virginia legislature together. Said Stanton and others were dissatisfied. Told him I doubted the policy of convening a Rebel legislature. It was a recognition of them, and, once convened, they would, with their hostile feelings, be inclined, perhaps, to conspire against us. He said he had no fear of that. They were too badly beaten, too much exhausted. His idea was, that the members of the legislature, comprising the prominent and influential men of their respective counties, had better come together and undo their own work. He felt assured they would do this, and the movement he believed a good one. Civil government must be reëstablished, he said, as soon as possible; there must be courts, and law, and order, or society would be broken up, the disbanded armies would turn into robber bands and guerrillas, which we must strive to prevent. These were the reasons why he wished

prominent Virginians who had the confidence of the
people to come together and turn themselves and their
neighbors into good Union men. But as we all had taken
a different view, he had perhaps made a mistake, and was
ready to correct it if he had.

I remarked, in the course of conversation, that if the
so-called legislature came together, they would be likely
to propose terms which might seem reasonable, but which
we could not accept; that I had not great faith in negotiating with large bodies of men, — each would encourage
the other in asking and doing what no one of them would
do alone; that he could make a better arrangement with
any one — the worst of them — than with all; that he
might be embarrassed by recognizing and treating with
them, when we were now in a condition to prescribe what
should be done.

April 14, *Friday.* Last night there was a general illum-
ination in Washington, fireworks, etc. To-day is the anniversary of the surrender of Sumter, and the flag is to be
raised by General Anderson.

General Grant was present at the meeting of the Cabinet to-day, and remained during the session. The subject
was the relations of the Rebels, the communications, the
trade, etc. Stanton proposed that intercourse should be
opened by *his* issuing an order, that the Treasury would
give permits to all who wished them to trade, excluding
contraband, and he, Stanton, would order the vessels to
be received into any port. I suggested that it would be
better that the President should issue a proclamation
stating and enjoining the course to be pursued by the
several Departments.

McCulloch expressed a willingness to be relieved of the
Treasury agents. General Grant expressed himself very
decidedly against them; thought them demoralizing, etc.
The President said we, *i. e.* the Secretaries of Treasury,
War, and Navy, had given the subject more attention than

he had and he would be satisfied with any conclusion we would unite upon. I proposed to open the whole coast to any one who wished to trade, and who had a regular clearance and manifest, and was entitled to a coast license. Stanton thought it should not extend beyond the military lines. General Grant thought they might embrace all this side of the Mississippi.

Secretary Stanton requested the Cabinet to hear some remarks which he desired to make, and to listen to a proposition or ordinance which he had prepared with much care and after a great deal of reflection, for reconstruction in the Rebel States. The plan or ordinance embraced two distinct heads, one for asserting the Federal authority in Virginia, the other for reëstablishing a State government. The first struck me favorably, with some slight emendations; the second seemed to me objectionable in several essentials, and especially as in conflict with the principles of self-government which I deem essential. There was little said on the subject, for the understanding was that we should each be furnished with a copy for criticism and suggestion, and in the mean time we were requested by the President to deliberate and carefully consider the proposition. He remarked that this was the great question now before us, and we must soon begin to act. Was glad Congress was not in session.

I objected that Virginia occupied a different position from that of any other State in rebellion; that while regular State governments were to be established in other States, whose Secession governments were nullities and would not be recognized, Virginia had a skeleton organization which she had maintained through the War, which government we had recognized and still recognized; that we to-day acknowledged Pierpont as the legitimate Governor of Virginia. He had been elected by only a few border counties, it was true; had never been able to enforce his authority over but a small portion of the territory or population; nevertheless we had recognized and sustained him.

The President said the point was well taken. Governor Dennison said he thought we should experience little difficulty from Pierpont. Stanton said none whatever.

I remarked the fact was not to be controverted that we had treated with the existing government and could not ignore our own acts. The President and a portion of the Cabinet had, in establishing the new State of West Virginia, recognized the validity of the government of Virginia and of Pierpont's administration, which had given its assent to that division. Without that consent no division could legally have taken place. I had differed with others in that matter, but consistency and the validity of our own act required us to continue to acknowledge the existing government. It was proper we should enforce the Federal authority, and it was proper we should aid Governor Pierpont, whose government was recognized and established. In North Carolina a legal government was now to be organized and the State reëstablished in her proper relations to the Union.

Inquiry had been made as to army news on the first meeting of the Cabinet, and especially if any information had been received from Sherman. None of the members had heard anything, and Stanton, who makes it a point to be late, and who has the telegraph in his Department, had not arrived. General Grant, who was present, said he was hourly expecting word. The President remarked it would, he had no doubt, come soon, and come favorable, for he had last night the usual dream which he had preceding nearly every great and important event of the War. Generally the news had been favorable which succeeded this dream, and the dream itself was always the same. I inquired what this remarkable dream could be. He said it related to your (my) element, the water; that he seemed to be in some singular, indescribable vessel, and that he was moving with great rapidity towards an indefinite shore; that he had this dream preceding Sumter, Bull Run, Antietam, Gettysburg, Stone River, Vicksburg,

Wilmington, etc. General Grant said Stone River was certainly no victory, and he knew of no great results which followed from it. The President said however that might be, his dream preceded that fight.[1]

"I had," the President remarked, "this strange dream again last night, and we shall, judging from the past, have great news very soon. I think it must be from Sherman. My thoughts are in that direction, as are most of yours."

I write this conversation three days after it occurred, in consequence of what took place Friday night, and but for which the mention of this dream would probably have never been noted. Great events did, indeed, follow, for within a few hours the good and gentle, as well as truly great, man who narrated his dream closed forever his earthly career.

I had retired to bed about half past-ten on the evening of the 14th of April, and was just getting asleep when Mrs. Welles, my wife, said some one was at our door. Sitting up in bed, I heard a voice twice call to John, my son, whose sleeping-room was on the second floor directly over the front entrance. I arose at once and raised a window, when my messenger, James Smith, called to me that Mr. Lincoln, the President, had been shot, and said Secretary Seward and his son, Assistant Secretary Frederick Seward, were assassinated. James was much alarmed and excited. I told him his story was very incoherent and improbable, that he was associating men who were not together and liable to attack at the same time. "Where," I inquired, "was the President when shot?" James said

[1] General Grant interrupted to say Stone River was no victory, — that a few such fights would have ruined us. The President looked at Grant curiously and inquiringly; said they might differ on that point, and at all events his dream preceded it. This was the first occasion I had to notice Grant's jealous nature. In turning it over in my mind at a later period, I remembered that Rawlins had been sent to Washington to procure action against General McClernand at Vicksburg. Later there was jealousy manifested towards General Thomas and others who were not satellites. — G. W.

he was at Ford's Theatre on 10th Street. "Well," said I, "Secretary Seward is an invalid in bed in his house yonder on 15th Street." James said he had been there, stopped in at the house to make inquiry before alarming me.

I immediately dressed myself, and, against the earnest remonstrance and appeals of my wife, went directly to Mr. Seward's, whose residence was on the east side of the square, mine being on the north. James accompanied me. As we were crossing 15th Street, I saw four or five men in earnest consultation, standing under the lamp on the corner by St. John's Church. Before I had got half across the street, the lamp was suddenly extinguished and the knot of persons rapidly dispersed. For a moment and but a moment I was disconcerted to find myself in darkness, but, recollecting that it was late and about time for the moon to rise, I proceeded on, not having lost five steps, merely making a pause without stopping. Hurrying forward into 15th Street, I found it pretty full of people, especially so near the residence of Secretary Seward, where there were many soldiers as well as citizens already gathered.

Entering the house, I found the lower hall and office full of persons, and among them most of the foreign legations, all anxiously inquiring what truth there was in the horrible rumors afloat. I replied that my object was to ascertain the facts. Proceeding through the hall to the stairs, I found one, and I think two, of the servants there holding the crowd in check. The servants were frightened and appeared relieved to see me. I hastily asked what truth there was in the story that an assassin or assassins had entered the house and assaulted the Secretary. They said it was true, and that Mr. Frederick was also badly injured. They wished me to go up, but no others. At the head of the first stairs I met the elder Mrs. Seward, who was scarcely able to speak but desired me to proceed up to Mr. Seward's room. I met Mrs. Frederick Seward on the third story, who, although in extreme distress, was, under the circumstances, exceedingly composed. I asked for the Secretary's room, which she pointed out, — the southwest room. As I entered, I met Miss Fanny Seward, with whom I exchanged a single word, and proceeded to the foot of the bed. Dr. Verdi and, I think, two others were there. The bed was saturated with blood. The Secretary was lying on his back, the upper part of his head covered by a cloth, which extended down over his eyes. His mouth was open, the lower jaw dropping down. I exchanged a few whispered words with Dr. V. Secretary Stanton, who came after but almost simultaneously with me, made inquiries in a louder tone till admonished by a word from one of the physicians. We almost immediately withdrew and went into the adjoining front room, where lay Frederick Seward. His eyes were open but he did not move them, nor a limb, nor did he speak. Doctor White, who was in attendance, told me he was unconscious and more dangerously injured than his father.

As we descended the stairs, I asked Stanton what he had heard in regard to the President that was reliable. He said the President was shot at Ford's Theatre, that he had seen a man who was present and witnessed the occurrence. I said I would go immediately to the White House. Stanton told me the President was not there but was at the theatre. "Then," said I, "let us go immediately there." He said that was his intention, and asked me, if I had not a carriage, to go with him. In the lower hall we met General Meigs,[1] whom he requested to take charge of the house, and to clear out all who did not belong there. General Meigs begged Stanton not to go down to 10th Street; others also remonstrated against our going. Stanton, I thought, hesitated. Hurrying forward, I remarked that I should go immediately, and I thought it his duty also. He said he should certainly go, but the remonstrants increased and gathered round him. I said we were wasting time, and, pressing through the crowd, entered the car-

---

[1] Montgomery C. Meigs, Quartermaster-General.

riage and urged Stanton, who was detained by others after he had placed his foot on the step. I was impatient. Stanton, as soon as he had seated himself, turned round, rose partly, and said the carriage was not his. I said that was no objection. He invited Meigs to go with us, and Judge Cartter of the Supreme Court [1] mounted with the driver. At this moment Major Eckert [2] rode up on horseback beside the carriage and protested vehemently against Stanton's going to 10th Street; said he had just come from there, that there were thousands of people of all sorts there, and he considered it very unsafe for the Secretary of War to expose himself. I replied that I knew not where he would be more safe, and that the duty of both of us was to attend the President immediately. Stanton concurred. Meigs called to some soldiers to go with us, and there was one on each side of the carriage. The streets were full of people. Not only the sidewalk but the carriage-way was to some extent occupied, all or nearly all hurrying towards 10th Street. When we entered that street we found it pretty closely packed.

The President had been carried across the street from the theatre, to the house of a Mr. Peterson. We entered by ascending a flight of steps above the basement and passing through a long hall to the rear, where the President lay extended on a bed, breathing heavily. Several surgeons were present, at least six, I should think more. Among them I was glad to observe Dr. Hall, who, however, soon left. I inquired of Dr. H., as I entered, the true condition of the President. He replied the President was dead to all intents, although he might live three hours or perhaps longer.

The giant sufferer lay extended diagonally across the bed, which was not long enough for him. He had been stripped of his clothes. His large arms, which were occasionally exposed, were of a size which one would scarce have expected from his spare appearance. His slow, full

[1] That is, of the Supreme Court of the District of Columbia.
[2] Maj. T. T. Eckert, Assistant Superintendent of the Military Telegraph.

respiration lifted the clothes with 'each breath that he took. His features were calm and striking. I had never seen them appear to better advantage than for the first hour, perhaps, that I was there. After that, his right eye began to swell and that part of his face became discolored.

Senator Sumner was there, I think, when I entered. If not he came in soon after, as did Speaker Colfax, Mr. Secretary McCulloch, and the other members of the Cabinet, with the exception of Mr. Seward. A double guard was stationed at the door and on the sidewalk, to repress the crowd, which was of course highly excited and anxious. The room was small and overcrowded. The surgeons and members of the Cabinet were as many as should have been in the room, but there were many more, and the hall and other rooms in the front or main house were full. One of these rooms was occupied by Mrs. Lincoln and her attendants, with Miss Harris. Mrs. Dixon and Mrs. Kinney came to her about twelve o'clock. About once an hour Mrs. Lincoln would repair to the bedside of her dying husband and with lamentation and tears remain until overcome by emotion.

[*April* 15.] A door which opened upon a porch or gallery, and also the windows, were kept open for fresh air. The night was dark, cloudy, and damp, and about six it began to rain. I remained in the room until then without sitting or leaving it, when, there being a vacant chair which some one left at the foot of the bed, I occupied it for nearly two hours, listening to the heavy groans, and witnessing the wasting life of the good and great man who was expiring before me.

About 6 A.M. I experienced a feeling of faintness and for the first time after entering the room, a little past eleven, I left it and the house, and took a short walk in the open air. It was a dark and gloomy morning, and rain set in before I returned to the house, some fifteen minutes [later]. Large groups of people were gathered every few rods, all anxious and solicitous. Some one or more from each group stepped forward as I passed, to inquire into the condition of the President, and to ask if there was no hope. Intense grief was on every countenance when I replied that the President could survive but a short time. The colored people especially — and there were at this time more of them, perhaps, than of whites — were overwhelmed with grief.

Returning to the house, I seated myself in the back parlor, where the Attorney-General and others had been engaged in taking evidence concerning the assassination. Stanton, and Speed, and Usher were there, the latter asleep on the bed. There were three or four others also in the room. While I did not feel inclined to sleep, as many did, I was somewhat indisposed. I had been so for several days. The excitement and bad atmosphere from the crowded rooms oppressed me physically.

A little before seven, I went into the room where the dying President was rapidly drawing near the closing moments. His wife soon after made her last visit to him. The death-struggle had begun. Robert, his son, stood with several others at the head of the bed. He bore himself well, but on two occasions gave way to overpowering grief and sobbed aloud, turning his head and leaning on the shoulder of Senator Sumner. The respiration of the President became suspended at intervals, and at last entirely ceased at twenty-two minutes past seven.

A prayer followed from Dr. Gurley; and the Cabinet, with the exception of Mr. Seward and Mr. McCulloch, immediately thereafter assembled in the back parlor, from which all other persons were excluded, and there signed a letter which was prepared by Attorney-General Speed to the Vice-President, informing him of the event, and that the government devolved upon him.

Mr. Stanton proposed that Mr. Speed, as the law officer, should communicate the letter to Mr. Johnson with some other member of the Cabinet. Mr. Dennison named me. I saw that, though all assented, it disconcerted Stanton, who had expected and intended to be the man and to have

Speed associated with him. I was disinclined personally to disturb an obvious arrangement, and therefore named Mr. McCulloch as the first in order after the Secretary of State.

I arranged with Speed, with whom I rode home, for a Cabinet-meeting at twelve meridian at the room of the Secretary of the Treasury, in order that the government should experience no detriment, and that prompt and necessary action might be taken to assist the new Chief Magistrate in preserving and promoting the public tranquillity. We accordingly met at noon. Mr. Speed reported that the President had taken the oath, which was administered by the Chief Justice, and had expressed a desire that the affairs of the government should proceed without interruption. Some discussion took place as to the propriety of an inaugural address, but the general impression was that it would be inexpedient. I was most decidedly of that opinion.

President Johnson, who was invited to be present, deported himself admirably, and on the subject of an inaugural said his acts would best disclose his policy. In all essentials it would, he said, be the same as that of the late President. He desired the members of the Cabinet to go forward with their duties without any change. Mr. Hunter, Chief Clerk of the State Department, was designated to act *ad interim* as Secretary of State. I suggested Mr. Speed, but I saw it was not acceptable in certain quarters. Stanton especially expressed a hope that Hunter should be assigned to the duty.

A room for the President as an office was proposed until he could occupy the Executive Mansion, and Mr. McCulloch offered the room adjoining his own in the Treasury Building. I named the State Department as appropriate and proper, at least until the Secretary of State recovered, or so long as the President wished, but objections arose at once. The papers of Mr. Seward would, Stanton said, be disturbed; it would be better he should be here, etc., etc. Stanton, I saw, had a purpose; among

2

other things, feared papers would fall under Mr. Johnson's
eye which he did not wish to be seen.

On returning to my house this morning, Saturday, I
found Mrs. Welles, who had been ill and confined to the
house from indisposition for a week, had been twice sent
for by Mrs. Lincoln to come to her at Peterson's. The
housekeeper, knowing the state of Mrs. W.'s health, had
without consultation turned away the messenger, Major
French, but Mrs. Welles, on learning the facts when he
came the second time, had yielded, and imprudently gone,
although the weather was inclement. She remained at the
Executive Mansion through the day. For myself, wearied,
shocked, exhausted, but not inclined to sleep, the day,
when not actually and officially engaged, passed off
strangely.

I went after breakfast to the Executive Mansion. There
was a cheerless cold rain and everything seemed gloomy.
On the Avenue in front of the White House were several
hundred colored people, mostly women and children,
weeping and wailing their loss. This crowd did not appear
to diminish through the whole of that cold, wet day; they
seemed not to know what was to be their fate since their
great benefactor was dead, and their hopeless grief affected
me more than almost anything else, though strong and
brave men wept when I met them.

At the White House all was silent and sad. Mrs. W. was
with Mrs. L. and came to meet me in the library. Speed
came in, and we soon left together. As we were descending
the stairs, "Tad," who was looking from the window at
the foot, turned and, seeing us, cried aloud in his tears,
"Oh, Mr. Welles, who killed my father?" Neither Speed
nor myself could restrain our tears, nor give the poor boy
any satisfactory answer.

[*April* 16.] Sunday, the 16th, the President and Cabinet
met by agreement at 10 A.M. at the Treasury. The President
was half an hour behind time. Stanton was more than
an hour late. He brought with him papers, and had many

suggestions relative to the measure before the Cabinet at our last meeting with President Lincoln. The general policy of the treatment of the Rebels and the Rebel States was discussed. President Johnson is not disposed to treat treason lightly, and the chief Rebels he would punish with exemplary severity.

Stanton has divided his original plan and made the reestablishing of State government applicable to North Carolina, leaving Virginia, which has a loyal government and governor, to arrange that matter of election to which I had excepted, but elaborating it for North Carolina and the other States.

Being at the War Department Sunday evening, I was detained conversing with Stanton. Finally Senator Sumner came in. He was soon followed by Gooch and Dawes of Massachusetts and some two or three others. One or more general officers also came in. Stanton took from his table, in answer to an inquiry from Sumner, his document which had been submitted to the Cabinet and which was still a Cabinet measure.

It was evident the gentlemen were there by appointment, and I considered myself an intruder or out of place. If so, Stanton did not know how to get rid of me, and it seemed awkward for me to leave. The others doubtless supposed I was there by arrangement; perhaps I was, but I felt embarrassed and was very glad, after he had read to them his first programme for Virginia, and had got about half through with the other, when Sumner demanded to know what provision was made for the colored man to vote. A line was brought me at this time by the messenger, which gave me an opportunity to leave.

[*April* 17.] On Monday, the 17th, I was actively engaged in bringing forward business which had been interrupted and suspended, issuing orders, and in arranging for the funeral solemnities of President Lincoln. Secretary Seward and his son continue in a low condition, and Mr. Fred Seward's life is precarious.

April 18, *Tuesday*. Details in regard to the funeral, which takes place on the 19th, occupied general attention and little else than preliminary arrangements and conversation was done at the Cabinet-meeting. From every part of the country comes lamentation. Every house, almost, has some drapery, especially the homes of the poor. Profuse exhibition is displayed on the public buildings and the dwellings of the wealthy, but the little black ribbon or strip of black cloth from the hovel of the poor negro or the impoverished white is more touching.

I have tried to write something consecutively since the horrid transactions of Friday night, but I have no heart for it, and the jottings down are mere mementos of a period, which I will try to fill up when more composed, and I have leisure or time for the task.

Sad and painful, wearied and irksome, the few preceding incoherent pages have been written for future use, for the incidents are fresh in my mind and may pass away with me but cannot ever be by me forgotten.

[*April* 19.] The funeral on Wednesday, the 19th, was imposing, sad, and sorrowful. All felt the solemnity, and sorrowed as if they had lost one of their own household. By voluntary action business was everywhere suspended, and the people crowded the streets.

The Cabinet met by arrangement in the room occupied by the President at the Treasury. We left a few minutes before meridian so as to be in the East Room at precisely twelve o'clock, being the last to enter. Others will give the details.

I rode with Stanton in the procession to the Capitol. The attendance was immense. The front of the procession reached the Capitol, it was said, before we started, and there were as many, or more, who followed us. A brief prayer was made by Mr. Gurley in the rotunda, where we left the remains of the good and great man we loved so well. Returning, I left Stanton, who was nervous and full of orders, and took in my carriage President Johnson and

ABRAHAM LINCOLN
From a portrait by Matthew Wilson, painted for Secretary Welles

Preston King, their carriage having been crowded out of place. Coming down Pennsylvania Avenue after this long detention, we met the marching procession in broad platoons all the way to the Kirkwood House on Twelfth Street.

There were no truer mourners, when all were sad, than the poor colored people who crowded the streets, joined the procession, and exhibited their woe, bewailing the loss of him whom they regarded as a benefactor and father. Women as well as men, with their little children, thronged the streets, sorrow, trouble, and distress depicted on their countenances and in their bearing. The vacant holiday expression had given way to real grief. Seward, I am told, sat up in bed and viewed the procession and hearse of the President, and I know his emotion. Stanton, who rode with me, was uneasy and left the carriage four or five times.

[*April* 21.] On the morning of Friday, the 21st, I went by appointment or agreement to the Capitol at 6 A.M. Stanton had agreed to call for me before six and take me in his carriage, the object being to have but few present when the remains were taken from the rotunda, where they had lain in state through Thursday, and were visited and seen by many thousands. As I knew Stanton to be uncertain and in some respects unreliable, I ordered my own carriage to be ready at an early hour. I wished also to take my sons with me to the obsequies, the last opportunity they or I would have to see the remains and to manifest our respect and regard for the man who had been the steady and abiding friend of their father. Stanton, as I expected, was late, and then informed me he had not, as he agreed he would, informed Governor Dennison of our purpose. He said he had to go for another friend, and wished me to take up Governor D. Not until I had got to Dennison's house was I aware of Stanton's neglect. It was then about six. Governor D., who had not yet risen, sent me word he would be ready in three minutes. I think he was not five. Stanton,

I perceived, did not tell me the truth about another visitor. He moved in great haste himself, being escorted by the cavalry corps which had usually attended the President.

We hurried on, reached the Capitol, and entered the rotunda just as Mr. Gurley was commencing an earnest and impressive prayer. When it was concluded, the remains were removed and taken to the depot, where, in waiting, were a car and train prepared for the commencement of the long and circuitous journey of the illustrious dead to his last earthly resting-place in Springfield, in the great prairies of the West. We were, as we had intended, an hour in advance of the time, and thus avoided the crowd, which before the train departed thronged the roads and depot.

The meeting of the Cabinet was not protracted. Stanton did not bring forward his reconstruction or reëstablishing scheme. He seemed desirous of evading or avoiding the subject. I alluded to but did not care to press it, if no one seconded me. We discussed the measure of amnesty, and the Attorney-General expressed his views as to the construction which he would put upon the proclamation and declarations of the late President. Stanton and he, I perceived, were acting in concert, and one if not two others had been spoken to in advance.

Stanton called at my house about 6 P.M. and invited me to a hasty Cabinet convention at 8 P.M. on important matters requiring immediate action. When we had assembled, General Grant and Preston King were also present. Stanton briefly mentioned that General Grant had important communications from General Sherman, and requested that he would read them, which he did. It stated he had made a peace, if satisfactory, with the Rebels, etc., etc. This and everything relating to it will be spread before the world. Among the Cabinet and all present there was but one mind on this subject. The plan was rejected, and Sherman's arrangement disapproved. Stanton and Speed were emphatic in their condemnation, though the latter expressed personal friendship for Sherman. General Grant, I was pleased to see, while disapproving what Sherman had done, and decidedly opposed to it, was tender to sensitiveness of his brother officer and abstained from censure. Stanton came charged with specified objections, four in number, counting them off on his fingers. Some of his argument was apt and well, some of it not in good taste nor precisely pertinent.

It was decided that General Grant should immediately inform General Sherman that his course was disapproved, and that generals in the field must not take upon themselves to decide on political and civil questions, which belonged to the executive and civil service. The military commanders would press on and capture and crush out the Rebels.

[*April* 22.] On Saturday, the 22d, I learned that General Grant left in person to go to General Sherman instead of sending written orders. This was sensible, and will insure the work to be well and satisfactorily done. Senator Sumner called on me with inquiries which he heard in the street relative to General Sherman. As he came direct from the War Department, I was satisfied that Stanton, as usual, after enjoining strict secrecy upon others, was himself communicating the facts in confidence to certain parties. One or two others spoke to me in the course of the afternoon on the same subject.

[*April* 23.] Sunday morning, the papers contained the whole story of Sherman's treaty and our proceedings, with additions, under Stanton's signature. I was not sorry to see the facts disclosed, although the manner and some of Stanton's matter was not particularly commendable, judicious, or correct. But the whole was characteristic, and will be likely to cause difficulty, or aggravate it, with Sherman, who has behaved hastily, but I hope not, as has been insinuated, wickedly. He has shown himself a better general than diplomatist, negotiator, or politician, and we must not forget the good he has done, if he has only committed an error, and I trust and believe it is but an error, — a grave one, it may be. But this error, if it be one, had its origin, I apprehend, with President Lincoln, who was for prompt and easy terms with the Rebels. Sherman's terms were based on a liberal construction of President Lincoln's benevolent wishes and the order to Weitzel concerning the Virginia legislature, the revocation of which S. had not heard.

Speed, prompted by Stanton, who seemed frantic but with whom he sympathized, expressed his fears that Sherman at the head of his victorious legions had designs upon the government. Dennison, while disapproving what Sherman had done, scouted the idea that he had any unworthy aspirations. I remarked that his armies were composed of citizens like ourselves, who had homes and wives and children as well as a government that they loved.[1]

April 25, Tuesday. I find myself unable to get Stanton and McCulloch to the sticking-point on the subject of opening our ports to coast trade. This and Reconstruction were the last subjects before President Lincoln at the Cabinet-meeting on the day before his death.

The course and position were discussed to-day in Cabinet with some earnestness. Speed came strongly charged, and had little doubt that Sherman was designing to put himself at the head of the army. Thought he had been seduced by Breckinridge, and was flattering himself that he would

[1] In reading and reconsidering this whole subject after the excitement and apprehensions stimulated by the impulsive zeal, if nothing more, of Stanton, I am satisfied that Sherman was less censurable than under the excitement at the time appeared, that he was in fact substantially carrying out the benignant policy of President Lincoln to which Stanton was opposed. No one, except perhaps Speed, fully sympathized with Stanton, yet all were in a degree influenced by him. At the time we had been made to believe, by the representations of Stanton, that he and Judge-Advocate-General Holt had positive evidence that Jeff Davis, Clay, Thompson, and others had conspired to assassinate Mr. Lincoln, Mr. Johnson, and most of the Cabinet. Strange stories were told us and it was under these representations, to which we then gave credit, that we were less inclined to justify Sherman. — G. W.

be able to control and direct public affairs. Governor Dennison, while censuring Sherman, would not condemn him unheard; he may have some reasons that we know not of, may have been short of ammunition or supplies.

I suggested that it might be vanity, eccentricity, an error of judgment, — the man may have thought himself to be what he is not, — that I had no fears of his misleading the army or seducing them to promote any personal schemes of ambition, if he had such. Every regiment, and probably every company, in that army had intelligent men, fit to be legislators; they were of us and a part of us, would no more tolerate usurpation on the part of Sherman than we would.

"Suppose," said Speed, "he should arrest Grant when Grant arrived at Raleigh," etc., etc. Men will have strange phantoms. I was surprised at Speed, but he has, evidently, conversed on this subject before with some one or more, who has similar opinions. This apprehension which I have sometimes heard intimated has never made a serious impression on me, for I have confidence in our people, and so I have in Sherman, who believed himself to be carrying out the wishes of Mr. Lincoln and the policy of the Administration. It is the result of the conference at City Point, and intended to be in furtherance of the proclamation of Weitzel, the revocation of which he has not seen.

In reflecting on this subject, I think we have permitted ourselves amid great excitement and stirring events to be hurried into unjust and ungenerous suspicions by the erroneous statements of the Secretary of War. Speed adopts and echoes the jealousies and wild vagaries of Stanton, who seems to have a mortal fear of the generals and the armies, although courting and flattering them. He went to Savannah to pay court to Sherman when that officer was the favored general and supposed to have eclipsed Grant, but, the latter having gained the ascendant by the fall of Richmond and the capture of Lee, Stanton would now reinstate himself with Grant by prostrating Sherman.

Had conversation with President Johnson in regard to a proclamation that we would no longer forbear proceeding against those who might be taken plundering our commerce as pirates. He concurred with me most fully, after discussing the question, and desired me to bring him the form of proclamation or have it prepared for the next Cabinet day. As the subject of preparing these papers belonged properly to the State Department, I felt it would be improper to slight Mr. Hunter, who is Acting Secretary. I therefore called upon him, and fortunately met Senator Sumner, Chairman of the Committee on Foreign Relations, who entered heartily into the measure and said he had some days since alluded to it as a step that should be taken.

When brought before the Cabinet, Stanton objected to it because the declaration had been made April 19, 1861, and though we had forborne for four years, no new enunciation should be made, but every man we now had or whom we should hereafter capture, should be hung. Speed took much the same ground, though more narrow and technical. President Johnson was very explicit in expressing his opinions, but as the subject was new and there were these differences of opinion it was postponed for consideration.

April 29, Saturday. Mellen, the Treasury agent, called on me to-day with a crude mess in relation to Treasury agents and trade regulations. I told him they were not what we wanted and I did not like them, that I thought the whole fabric which had been constructed at the Treasury should be swept away. He claims it cannot be done by the Executive under the law, and it is true Chase and his men have tied up matters by legislation, literally placing the government in the hands of the Treasury.

XXX

May 1, 1865.   .   .   .   .

May 2. A very protracted session of the Cabinet. The chief subject was the Treasury regulations. There was unanimity, except McCulloch, who clings to the schemes of Chase and Fessenden. The latter can, however, hardly be said to have schemes of his own. But the policy of Chase and his tools, which F. adopted, is adhered to by McCulloch, who is new in place and fears to strike out a policy of his own. He fears to pursue any other course than the one which has been prescribed.

McCulloch is a correct man in business routine but is not an experienced politician or educated statesman. He wants experience in those respects, and needs grasp and power to extricate himself from among a rotten and corrupt swarm of leeches who have been planted in the Treasury. Some legal points being raised, the subject was referred to Attorney-General Speed to examine and report.

Stanton produced a paper from Judge-Advocate-General Holt, to the effect that Jeff Davis, Jacob Thompson, Sanders,[1] and others were implicated in the conspiracy to

---

[1] George N. Sanders, a Confederate agent in Canada.

assassinate President Lincoln and others. A proclamation duly prepared was submitted by Stanton with this paper of Holt, which he fully indorses, offering rewards for their apprehension. McCulloch and Hunter, whose opinions were asked, went with Stanton without a question. I, on being asked, remarked if there was proof of the complicity of those men, as stated there was, they certainly ought to be arrested, and that reward was proper, but I had no facts.

May. The calls upon the President by associations claiming to represent States and municipalities are becoming less. To some extent they may have been useful in the peculiar condition of public affairs by inspiring confidence, and in giving the President an opportunity to enunciate his opinions in the absence of any inaugural, but they have been annoying at times, obstructions to business, and were becoming irksome. The President was not displeased with these manifestations and has borne himself well through a period which has been trying and arduous, and is gathering to himself the good wishes of the country.

I called up the subject of free communication through the coast to all vessels having regular clearance, but was told the President and Secretary of the Treasury were endeavoring to make a satisfactory arrangement which should be in conformity with the act of July 2, 1864. It is obvious that the intention of that act was to place the Treasury above, or independent of, the President, — one of Chase's demonstrations, and his hand is in this movement.

A proclamation, or order, that those who were taken plundering our commerce should be punished, and that forbearance to put in execution the proclamation of the 19th of April, 1861, would not longer be exercised, was opposed by Stanton and Speed. Others failed to sustain me, except McCulloch, who gave me partial support. Stanton considers it his special province to guard Seward's policy as it has been, not being aware that Seward has changed.

The subject of reëstablishing the Federal authority, and of a reorganization of the State governments in the insurrectionary region was discussed. The Secretary of War was requested to send copies of the modified plan to each head of Department, and a special Cabinet-meeting was ordered on Monday, the 8th, to consider the subject.

At the Cabinet-meeting the plan of asserting the Federal authority and of establishing the State government in Virginia was fully considered. Stanton's project with several radical amendments presented by me was adopted. I was surprised and gratified with the alacrity and cheerfulness he exhibited, and the readiness with which he adopted and assented to most of my amendments. In one instance he became a little pugnacious, Speed and Dennison having dissented. Two of my recommendations were not adopted, and as no other one presented amendments, I cared not to appear fastidious, but am nevertheless satisfied I was right. The session was long, over four hours.

May 9, *Tuesday.* A proclamation of amnesty proposed by Speed was considered and, with some changes, agreed to.

The condition of North Carolina was taken up, and a general plan of organization intended for all the Rebel States was submitted and debated. No great difference of opinion was expressed except on the matter of suffrage. Stanton, Dennison, and Speed were for negro suffrage; McCulloch, Usher, and myself were opposed. It was agreed, on request of Stanton, we would not discuss the question, but each express his opinion without preliminary debate. After our opinions had been given, I stated I was for adhering to the rule prescribed in President Lincoln's proclamation, which had been fully considered and matured, and besides, in all these matters, I am for no further subversion of the laws, institutions, and usages of the States respectively, nor for Federal intermeddling in local matters, than is absolutely necessary, in order to rid them of the radical error which has caused our national trouble.

All laws, not inconsistent with those of the conquerors, remain until changed to the conquered, is an old rule.

This question of negro suffrage is beset with difficulties growing out of the conflict through which we have passed and the current of sympathy for the colored race. The demagogues will make use of it, regardless of what is best for the country, and without regard for the organic law, the rights of the State, or the troubles of our government. There is a fanaticism on the subject with some, who persuade themselves that the cause of liberty and the Union is with the negro and not the white man. White men, and especially Southern white men, are tyrants. Senator Sumner is riding this one idea at top speed. There are others, less sincere than Sumner, who are pressing the question for party purposes. On the other hand, there may be unjust prejudices against permitting colored persons to enjoy the elective franchise, under any circumstances; but this is not, and should not be, a Federal question. No one can claim that the blacks, in the Slave States especially, can exercise the elective franchise intelligently. In most of the Free States they are not permitted to vote. Is it politic, and wise, or right even, when trying to restore peace and reconcile differences, to make so radical a change, — provided we have the authority, which I deny, — to elevate the ignorant negro, who has been enslaved mentally as well as physically, to the discharge of the highest duties of citizenship, especially when our Free States will not permit the few free negroes to vote?

The Federal government has no right and has not attempted to dictate on the matter of suffrage to any State, and I apprehend it will not conduce to harmony to arrogate and exercise arbitrary power over the States which have been in rebellion. It was never intended by the founders of the Union that the Federal government should prescribe suffrage to the States. We shall get rid of slavery by constitutional means. But conferring on the black civil rights is another matter. I know not the authority. The

President in the exercise of the pardoning power may limit or make conditions, and, while granting life and liberty to traitors, deny them the right of holding office or of voting. While, however, he can exclude traitors, can he legitimately confer on the blacks of North Carolina the right to vote? I do not yet see how this can be done by him or by Congress.

This whole question of suffrage is much abused. The negro can take upon himself the duty about as intelligently and as well for the public interest as a considerable portion of the foreign element which comes amongst us. Each will be the tool of demagogues. If the negro is to vote and exercise the duties of a citizen, let him be educated to it. The measure should not, even if the government were empowered to act, be precipitated when he is stolidly ignorant and wholly unprepared. It is proposed to do it against what have been and still are the constitutions, laws, usages, and practices of the States which we wish to restore to fellowship.

Stanton has changed his position, has been converted, is now for negro suffrage. These were not his views a short time since. But aspiring politicians will, as the current now sets, generally take that road.

The trial of the assassins is not so promptly carried into effect as Stanton declared it should be. He said it was his intention the criminals should be tried and executed before President Lincoln was buried. But the President was buried last Thursday, the 4th, and the trial has not, I believe, commenced.

I regret they are not tried by the civil court, and so expressed myself, as did McCulloch; but Stanton, who says the proof is clear and positive, was emphatic, and Speed advised a military commission, though at first, I thought, otherwise inclined. It is now rumored the trial is to be secret, which is another objectionable feature, and will be likely to meet condemnation after the event and excitement have passed off.

The rash, impulsive, and arbitrary measures of Stanton are exceedingly repugnant to my notions, and I am pained to witness the acquiescence they receive. He carries others with him, sometimes against their convictions as expressed to me.

The President and Cabinet called on Mr. Seward at his house after the close of the council. He came down to meet us in his parlor. I was glad to see him so well and animated, yet a few weeks have done the work of years, apparently, with his system. Perhaps, when his wounds have healed, and the fractured jaw is restored, he may recover in some degree his former looks, but I apprehend not. His head was covered with a close-fitting cap, and the appliances to his jaw entered his mouth and prevented him from articulating clearly. Still he was disposed to talk, and we to listen. Once or twice, allusions to the night of the great calamity affected him more deeply than I have ever seen him.

May 10, Wednesday. Senator Sumner called on me. We had a long conversation on matters pertaining to the affairs of Fort Sumter. He has been selected to deliver an oration on Mr. Lincoln's death to the citizens of Boston, and desired to post himself in some respects. I told him the influence of the Blairs, and especially of the elder, had done much to strengthen Mr. Lincoln in that matter, while Seward and General Scott had opposed.

Sumner assures me Chase has gone into Rebeldom to promote negro suffrage. I have no doubt that Chase has that and other schemes for Presidential preferment in hand in this voyage. S. says that President Johnson is aware of his (Chase's) object in behalf of the negroes, and favors the idea of their voting. On this point I am skeptical. He would not oppose any such movement, were any State to make it. I so expressed myself to Sumner, and he assented but intended to say the negroes were the people.

May 11. The papers, and especially those of New York, are complaining of the court which is to try the assassins, and their assault is the more severe because it is alleged that the session is to be secret. This subject is pretty much given over to the management of the War Department, since Attorney-General Speed and Judge-Advocate-General Holt affirm that to be legal, and a military court the only real method of eliciting the whole truth. It would be impolitic, and, I think, unwise and injudicious, to shut off all spectators and make a "Council of Ten" of this Commission. The press will greatly aggravate the objections, and do already.

May 12, *Friday*. The President does not yet sufficiently generalize, but goes too much into unimportant details, and personal appeals. He will, however, correct this with a little experience, I have no doubt.

I inquired of the Secretary of War if there is any foundation for the assertion that the trial of the assassins is to be in secret. He says it will not be secret, although the doors will not be open to the whole public immediately. Full and minute reports of all the testimony and proceedings will be taken and in due time published; and trusty and reliable persons, in limited numbers, will have permission to attend. This will relieve the proceeding of some of its objectionable features.

Stanton has undertaken to get the projected amnesty proclamation (as last altered, amended, corrected, and improved) printed, also the form of government for North Carolina as last shaped, and as far as anything decisive had taken place. Dennison inquired when he might have copies, and he promises to send immediately. The truth is, it is still in the hands of the President, who will shape it right. King has been of service in this matter.

May 13 *and* 14. The piratical ram Stonewall has reached Nassau and is anchored in the outer harbor, from which

2

our vessels are excluded. The State Department promise decisive measures with Sir Frederick Bruce and the British authorities.

Extraordinary efforts are made, in every quarter where it is supposed influence can be felt, to embarrass the Navy Department and procure favor for Henderson, Navy Agent, whose trial is near. G. W. Blunt has come on from New York for the express purpose of getting the case postponed, by inducing the Department to interfere. Told Blunt the case had gone to the courts and I could not undertake to interfere and direct the courts in the matter. The attorneys had the case in hand. Blunt requested me not to give a positive refusal till Monday. In the mean time Preston King called on me on Sunday, as I ascertained at the request of Blunt. King had, on two previous occasions, conversed with me on the subject, and then and now fully concurred in the propriety and correctness of my course. Mr. Lowrey, brother-in-law of Fox, has written the latter entreating him to favor Henderson, saying I would yield, if Fox would only take ground for H. Morgan has written me begging I will not incur the resentment of the editors of the *Post* by insisting on the prosecution. I am urged to do wrong in order to let a wrongdoer escape.

Intelligence was received this morning of the capture of Jefferson Davis in southern Georgia. I met Stanton this Sunday P.M. at Seward's, who says Davis was taken disguised in women's clothes. A tame and ignoble letting-down of the traitor.

May 15. Sir Frederick Bruce has not yet returned. Had an interview with Seward on the subject of the Stonewall. He is confident the English will deny her hospitality, but Hunter tells me they let her have enough coal to reach Havana. They dared not refuse! Will send two ironclads to encounter her, provided they can meet her.

May 16, *Tuesday*. Great questions not taken up at the

Cabinet. Several minor matters considered. Mr. Harlan, successor of Mr. Usher in the Department of the Interior, was with us to-day. Remarked to President Johnson that Governor Dennison and myself proposed leaving on Saturday next for Charleston, and if the subject of reconstruction and amnesty was to be taken up before we left, there might be haste. He said the whole matter would be satisfactorily disposed of, he presumed, before Saturday; is expecting some North Carolina Union men.

May 17, *Wednesday*. The Stonewall has gone to Havana. Seward promises to have Tassara posted. Is confident the Spaniards will exclude her from their ports; but thinks it would be well to have our ironclads sent out.

Seward is getting better, but is seriously injured and will be long in getting well. Fred lingers in a low state.

May 18, *Thursday*. Notice is given to-day of a grand parade of the armies of the Potomac, of the Tennessee, and Georgia, etc., etc., to take place on Tuesday and Wednesday next. This interferes with our proposed trip, which has so often been deferred. But there is no alternative. It will not do to be absent on such an historic occasion.

May 19, *Friday*. Preston King tells me he has a letter from Senator Dixon, speaking of me in very complimentary terms and expressing a wish that I may continue in the Cabinet, assuring K. that this is the sentiment of all parties in Connecticut. The President is not yet prepared to complete the Amnesty Proclamation, nor to issue the order for the reëstablishment of the authority of the local State governments. Our North Carolina friends have not arrived. Seward was to-day in the State Department, and the President with the rest of us went to his room. I noticed that his old crony and counterpart, Thurlow Weed, was with him as we entered. Seward was gratified and evidently felt complimented that we called. Was very decisive and emphatic on the subject of a proclamation declaring the Rebel vessels pirates and also a proclamation for opening the ports. Both these measures I had pressed rather earnestly; but Stanton, and Speed under Stanton's prompting, had opposed, for some assumed technical reason[?], the first, *i. e.* declaring the Rebel vessels pirates, and McCulloch the last, opening the ports. I was, therefore, pleased when Seward, unprompted, brought them both forward. I suggested that the proclamation already issued appeared to me to be sufficient, but I was glad to have his opinions on account of the opposition of Speed.

Received a telegram this P.M. from Commander Frailey and one from Acting-Rear-Admiral Radford, stating that the former, in command of the Tuscarora, had convoyed to Hampton Roads the William Clyde, having on board Jeff Davis, Stephens, etc.

This dispatch, addressed to me, Stanton had in his hand when I entered his room, whither he had sent for me. The telegraph goes to the Department of War, where it has an office, and I before have had reason to believe that some abuse — a sort of an espionage — existed. Half apologizing for an obvious impropriety, he said the custody of these prisoners devolved on him a great responsibility, and until he had made disposition of them, or determined where they should be sent, he wished their arrival to be kept a secret. He was unwilling, he said, to trust Fox, and specially desired me to withhold the information from him, for he was under the Blairs and would be used by them, and the Blairs would improve the opportunity to embarrass him.

I by no means concur in his censures or his views. Fox, like Stanton, will sometimes confide secrets which he had better retain, but not, I think, when enjoined. The Blairs have no love for Stanton, but I do not think he has any cause of apprehension from them in this matter.

He wished me to order the Tuscarora to still convoy and guard the Clyde, and allow no communication with the

prisoners except by order of General Halleck or the War
Department, — General Halleck, Stanton has ordered
down from Richmond to attend to this business, — and
again earnestly requested and enjoined that none but we
three — himself, General Grant, and myself — should
know of the arrival and disposition of these prisoners. I
told him the papers would have the arrivals announced in
their next issue.

Stanton said no word could get abroad. He had the telegraph in his own hands and could suppress everything.
Not a word should pass. I remarked he could not stop the
mails, nor passenger-boats, and twenty-four hours would
carry the information to Baltimore and abroad in that way.
Twenty-four hours, he said, would relieve him.

Stanton is mercurial, — arbitrary and apprehensive,
violent and fearful, rough and impulsive, — yet possessed
of ability and energy. I, of course, under his request, shall
make no mention of or allusion to the prisoners, for the
present. In framing his dispatch, he said, with some emphasis, the women and children must be sent off. We did
not want them. "They must go South," and he framed
his dispatch accordingly. When he read it I remarked,
"The South is very indefinite, and you permit them to
select the place. Mrs. Davis may designate Norfolk, or
Richmond." "True," said Grant with a laugh. Stanton
was annoyed, but, I think, altered his telegram.

May 20, *Saturday*. Stanton informed me this P.M. that
Halleck had gone from Richmond to Fortress Monroe and
he wished certain persons, whom he named, should be sent
in a naval vessel to Fort Warren, certain others to Fort
Delaware, others to Fort McHenry. He still urged secrecy,
but in less than an hour our regular dispatches by mail
stated the facts. Others also had them.

General Sherman is here. I have not yet met him, but I
understand he is a little irate towards Stanton and very
mad with Halleck. This is not surprising, and yet some

allowance is to be made for them. Sherman's motives cannot be questioned, although his acts may be. Stanton was unduly harsh and severe, and his bulletin to General Dix and specifications were Stantonian. Whether the President authorized, or sanctioned, that publication I never knew, but I and most of the members of the Cabinet were not consulted in regard to the publication, which was not in all respects correct. General Grant, who as unequivocally disapproved of Sherman's armistice as any member of the Administration, was nevertheless tender of General Sherman, and did not give in to the severe remarks of Stanton at the time.[1]

[May 22 and 23.] On the 22d and 23d, the great review of the returning armies of the Potomac, the Tennessee, and Georgia took place in Washington. I delayed my proposed Southern trip in order to witness this magnificent and imposing spectacle. I shall not attempt at this time and here to speak of those gallant men and their distinguished leaders. It was computed that about 150,000 passed in review, and it seemed as if there were as many spectators. For several days the railroads and all communications were overcrowded with the incoming people who wished to see and welcome the victorious soldiers of the Union. The public offices were closed for two days. On the spacious stand in front of the Executive Mansion the President, Cabinet, generals, and high naval officers, with hundreds of our first citizens and statesmen, and ladies, were assembled. But Abraham Lincoln was not there. All felt this.

May 24. I went with Postmaster-General Dennison and a portion of our families and a few friends on board the Santiago de Cuba, one of our fast vessels of about fourteen

[1] At a later period President Johnson assured me that Stanton's publication was wholly unauthorized by him, that he knew nothing of it until he saw it in the papers. We were all imposed upon by Stanton, who had a purpose. He and the Radicals were opposed to the mild policy of President Lincoln, on which Sherman had acted, and which Stanton opposed and was determined to defeat. — G. W.

hundred tons, on a trip to Savannah. The late President had suggested to me some weeks before his death that he would be pleased to go on such an excursion to Charleston, and visit Dahlgren, who was, with him, a favorite. Subsequent events and his protracted visit to the upper waters of the James and Richmond altered this plan, and might have defeated it, even had his life been prolonged.

His death postponed and seemed at times likely to defeat it altogether, but after repeated delays we on this day embarked and went down the Potomac. Of the voyage and its incidents I make here brief mention, for what is written is penned after our return, and from memory chiefly.

[*May 25 and 26.*] The day was fine and our sail down the river exceedingly pleasant. When I arose on the following morning, the 25th, we had passed Cape Henry and were at sea. The wind was strong from the southeast and the sea rough, with one or two smart storms of rain. Most of the passengers and some others were sick this and the following day, when we passed Cape Hatteras and Frying-Pan Shoals. Unexpectedly to myself, I was not seasick.

On the morning of Sunday, the 27th [*sic*],[1] we were off Charleston Bar, waiting the tide and a pilot. Admiral Dahlgren came down in a tug and brought the fleet pilot, who took us in. Fort Sumter, whose ruins were prominent, we passed, and Morris and Sullivan's Islands, with their batteries, and anchored the Santiago near the town.

May 27 [*sic*]. Mrs. Welles, who had not left her bed after retiring on the 24th on the lower Potomac, was brought upon deck and had a bed under the awning. The day was delicious, the air balmy, and she, as did all of us, enjoyed the scene. Our whole company, with the exception of Mrs. Welles and Mrs. Howard, went on shore and dispersed in squads over the city. With Dahlgren and a few others, I went to the Rebel navy yard and thence to the citadel and various parts of the city. Late in the afternoon we

---

[1] Sunday was the 28th.

took carriages which were politely furnished by General Hatch, and rode through the principal streets and into the suburbs, visiting the cemeteries, etc.

[*May* 29.] On Monday we took a morning ride, Mrs. Welles being able to go with us, and drove about the place. Returning to the wharf, we took a tug, visited the Pawnee, and then went to Sumter, Moultrie, Fort Johnston, etc. The day was beautiful and all enjoyed it.

There was both sadness and gratification in witnessing the devastation of the city and the deplorable condition of this seat of the Rebellion. No place has suffered more or deserved to have suffered more. Here was the seat of Southern aristocracy. The better blood — the superior class, as they considered themselves — here held sway and dictated the policy, not only of Charleston but of South Carolina, and ultimately of the whole South. The power of association and of exclusiveness has here been exemplified and the consequences that follow from the beginning of evil. Not that the aristocracy had more vigorous intellects, greater ability, for they had not, yet their wealth, their ancestry, the usage of the community gave them control.

Mr. Calhoun, the leading genius and master mind of the State, was not one of the élite, the first families, but was used, nursed, and favored by them, and they by him. He acknowledged their supremacy and deferred to them; they recognized his talents and gave him position. He pandered to their pride; they fostered his ambition.

Rhett, one of the proudest of the nobility, had the ambition of Calhoun without his ability, yet he was not destitute of a certain degree of smartness, which stimulated his aspirations. More than any one else, perhaps, has he contributed to precipitating this Rebellion and brought these terrible calamities on his State and country. The gentlemanly, elegant, but brilliantly feeble intellects of his class had the vanity to believe they could rule, or establish a Southern empire. Their young men had read Scott's novels, and considered themselves to be knights and barons bold, sons of chivalry and romance, born to fight and to rule. Cotton they knew to be king, and slavery created cotton. They used these to combine other weak minds at the South, and had weak and willing tools to pander to them in certain partisans at the North.

The results of their theory and the fruits of their labors are to be seen in this ruined city and this distressed people. Luxury, refinement, happiness have fled from Charleston; poverty is enthroned there. Having sown error, she has reaped sorrow. She has been, and is, punished. I rejoice that it is so.

On Monday evening we left for Savannah, but, a storm coming on, the Santiago put into Port Royal, having lost sight of our consort. It had been our intention to stop at this place on our return, but, being here, we concluded to finish our work, and accordingly went up to Beaufort. Returning, we visited Hilton Head and Fort Welles on invitation from General Gillmore.

[*May* 30.] Tuesday we proceeded up the Savannah River, and, on reaching the city, were provided with carriages to examine it and the environs. Savannah has suffered less from war than Charleston, and, though stricken, has the appearance of vitality if not of vigor.

We drove out to Bonaventura, the former possession of Tatnall, which has been converted into a cemetery. The place has an indescribable beauty, I may say grandeur, impressing me beyond any rural place I have visited. Long rows of venerable live oaks, the splendid and valuable tree of the South, festooned with moss, opened up beautiful vistas and drives. The place I can never forget.

I called on General Grover, in company with Admiral Dahlgren, and had half an hour's interesting conversation on the condition of affairs in Georgia and the South generally. General Birge of Connecticut called on us at the boat, where we also met Samuel Cooley of Hartford, an old and familiar acquaintance.

Mrs. Jefferson Davis was at the Pulaski House. She had accompanied her husband to Fortress Monroe, and been ordered South when he was committed to the Fortress. The vessel in which she came had been in sight of ours a considerable portion of the day before we reached Charleston, and was in that harbor when we arrived there, but left and arrived here before us.

We took our departure on the afternoon of Tuesday and passed down Thunderbolt Inlet to Wassaw Sound, going over the ground where the Weehawken captured the Atlanta. This Southern coast is a singular network of interior navigable waters interlacing each other, of which we knew very little before this Civil War. The naval men seemed to be better informed as regards the coast of Europe than their own country.

The sun had set when we reached Savannah River, and it was dark when we left. Most of the company were importunate to visit Havana, but I thought it not best, and the steamer therefore turned homeward.

[*May 31–June 7.*] We had calm and delightful weather. Were amused as persons on shipboard usually are. Off the entrance to Cape Fear we had some fishing. Saw and signalled a steamer on the inside near Fort Caswell, which came out to us. Two or three Treasury agents were on board, and Judge Casey of the Court of Claims, who is here, I surmise, like many others, for speculation.

During the night we were serenaded by a fine band, which had come off in a steamer. We ascertained in the morning that it was General Hawley and staff in an army boat, they having come down from Wilmington to meet us. By invitation we went on board with them and proceeded up the Cape Fear to Wilmington. The Santiago was directed to proceed around Smith's Island opposite to Fort Fisher and await us. The beach for some distance was strewn with wrecks of blockade-runners, — or, more modestly and correctly speaking, several were beached. Our jaunt to Wilmington was pleasant, and our ride through various streets exceedingly warm. We returned early in order to visit Fort Fisher by daylight. These formidable defenses, which we finally captured, have given me exceeding annoyance for several years. The War Department and military, so long as Halleck controlled, had no comprehension of the importance of capturing this place, and by so doing cutting off Rebel supplies.

We stopped a few hours at Fortress Monroe and walked round on the ramparts. Jeff Davis was a prisoner in one of the casemates, but I did not see him.

June 8. The Santiago arrived at the Navy Yard, Washington, this day, shortly after meridian. My two sons, Edgar and Tom, were awaiting our arrival and came off in the boat to receive us. All were well.

Governor Dennison and myself called immediately on the President and reported our return. We found him with a delegation headed by Judge Sharkey from Mississippi, concerning the subject of reorganizing that State. The President was glad to receive us, and invited us, after introduction, to participate in the discussion. Subsequently, after the delegation had withdrawn, we briefly reported the results of our observation as to the condition and sentiments of the people of North and South Carolina and Georgia.

Found matters at the Department had proceeded satisfactorily. Some matters which might have been disposed of awaited my action.

June 9, *Friday*. Attended Cabinet-meeting. Mr. Seward was present. We met in the Blue Room for his accommodation. Affairs of Texas were discussed. Hamilton, who was appointed military governor by Mr. Lincoln, is here pressing himself for a continuance in that position. There seemed a general disposition to acquiesce in that arrangement. I remarked that I was not personally familiar with ·Hamilton, but I supposed him loyal. He had been a profuse talker, but his profoundness and capability, and, I may add, his sincerity had sometimes appeared to me questionable. I mentioned Governor Pease as a loyal and reliable man of sound judgment, and undoubted ability and rightmindedness.

June 10, *Saturday*. Absorbed in bringing forward matters which had accumulated and disposing of them. The instructions to Rear-Admiral Goldsborough essentially as understood. Paymaster Cunningham says he has been told there will be expenditures to officers to travel and visit navy yards, and desires an authorization to pay bills. Declined to give it.

June 12, *Monday*. Sat an hour to Simmons for medallion. The President asked me if it would not be best under the circumstances, and as we had no word from Governor Pease, to continue Hamilton in the position of Governor of Texas for the mere purpose of organizing, etc. I acquiesced in most of his suggestions, though I told him my impressions of H. were not favorable.

June 13, *Tuesday*. At the Cabinet-meeting to-day Judge Sharkey and Mr. George were formally introduced to the Cabinet, remaining, however, but a moment. It is concluded to make Sharkey provisional Governor. He is a man of mind and culture, Whig in his antecedents, and I think with some offensive points on the subject of slavery and popular rights; but he was and is opposed to repudiation and bad faith by Mississippi. The subject of Treasury agents and tax of twenty-five per cent on cotton was discussed at great length in the Cabinet. All but the Secretary of the Treasury for abolishing agents and tax. McC. thinks the Executive has no authority.

Asked McCulloch if it was true that Clerk Henderson had been reappointed. He said yes, after Solicitor Jordan investigated and reported the charge against him

groundless. Told him I was satisfied H. was not a proper man, etc.

June 14 and 15. Not well, but pressed in disposing of current business. Acting Rear-Admiral Godon reported in person. Had returned with Susquehanna to Hampton Roads from Havana. The authorities of Cuba, he says, very courteous, and the people entirely American.

June 16, *Friday*. At Cabinet-meeting General Grant came in to press upon the government the importance of taking decisive measures in favor of the republic of Mexico. Thought that Maximilian and the French should be warned to leave. Said the Rebels were crossing the Rio Grande and entering the imperial service. Their purpose would be to provoke differences, create animosity, and precipitate hostilities. Seward was emphatic in opposition to any movement. Said the Empire was rapidly perishing, and, if let alone, Maximilian would leave in less than six months, perhaps in sixty days, whereas, if we interfered, it would prolong his stay and the Empire also. Seward acts from intelligence, Grant from impulse.

Seward submitted a paper drawn up by himself, favorable to the purchase of Ford's Theatre to be devoted to religious purposes. Governor Dennison, who sometimes catches quickly at schemes, expressed his readiness to sign this, but no others concurred, and it was dropped.

June 17, *Saturday*. Called on the President with lists of the candidates for the Naval School. After going over the lists, he requested they might be left, and that I would call on him at noon to-morrow. I reminded him that it was Sunday. He remarked if any other time would be more convenient to me, it would be acceptable to him.

June 19, *Monday*. Called yesterday on the President, as requested and appointed by him on Saturday. After run-

ning over the different classes of appointments which the
President is authorized to make at the Naval School, he
said he knew little of them and should leave them chiefly to
me. There were four selections of the class of ten at large
to be made, and perhaps thirty candidates, three of whom
were from Tennessee. He spoke highly of each and expressed a wish that all three should be appointed. I said he
could so order, but suggested that exception might be
taken to the appointment of three from his own State, and
only one to all others. He appreciated the objection, but
said they were all good boys. I intimated a probability
that all, or nearly all, the candidates were also excellent
young men. It was finally left that two of them should be
appointed, and that the other must if possible come in
under another class.

June 20, Tuesday. Mr. Seward was absent from the
Cabinet-meeting. All others were present. The meetings
are better and more punctually attended than under Mr.
Lincoln's administration, and measures are more generally
discussed, which undoubtedly tends to better administration. Mrs. Seward lies at the point of death, which is the
cause of Mr. Seward's absence.

The subject of appointments in the Southern States —
the Rebel States — was discussed. A difficulty is experienced in the stringent oath passed by the last Congress.
Men are required to swear they have rendered no voluntary aid to the Rebellion, nor accepted or held office under
the Rebel government. This oath is a device to perpetuate
differences, if persisted in.

I was both amused and vexed with the propositions and
suggestions for evading this oath. Stanton proposed that
if the appointees would not take the whole oath, to swear
to as much as they could. Speed was fussy and uncertain;
did not know but what it would become necessary to call
Congress together to get rid of this official oath. Harlan [1]

[1] Harlan had succeeded Secretary Usher in the Department of the Interior.

believed the oath proper and that it should stand. Said it
was carefully and deliberately framed, that it was designed, purposely, to exclude men from executive appointments. Mr. Wade and Mr. Sumner had this specially in
view. Thought there was no difficulty in these appointments except judges. All other officers were temporary;
judges were for life. I remarked that did not follow. If the
Senate, when it convened, did not choose to confirm the
judicial appointments, the incumbents could only hold
until the close of the next session of Congress. But above
and beyond this I denied that Congress could impose limitations and restrictions on the pardoning power, and thus
circumscribe the President's prerogative. I claimed that
the President could nominate, and the Senate confirm, an
officer independent of that form and oath, and if the appointee took and faithfully conformed to the constitutional oath, he could not be molested. McCulloch inclined
to my views, but Stanton insisted that point had been
raised and decided and could not, therefore, be maintained.
I claimed that no wrong decision could be binding, and I
had no doubt of the wrongfulness of such a decision, denying that the constitutional rights of the Executive could be
frittered away by legislation. There is partyism in all this,
not union or country.

June 21, *Wednesday.* Mrs. Seward, wife of Secretary
Seward, died this A.M. Mr. Seward sends me a letter inclosing dispatch of Lord John Russell in relation to belligerent rights to the Rebels. Both France and England
withdraw belligerent rights from them, — France, it would
seem, unconditionally, but England with conditions, and,
as usual, our Secretary is outmanœuvred. He writes me
that our naval vessels will not extend courtesies to British
naval vessels, etc. Disagreed and wrote him of the difficulty of instructing naval officers. But called at State
Department. It was late and no one there.

June 22, Thursday. I called early on the President in relation to Seward's letter concerning the blockade and courtesy to British vessels. He concurred in my views. I went to the State Department and saw Mr. Hunter. He agreed with me and complimented my letter, and also one I wrote a few days since regarding the Japanese vessel, which seems to have made an impression upon him, and which he complimented as very statesmanlike and instructive.

June 23, Friday. Rear-Admiral Dahlgren returned this morning from Charleston. Two years since he left. Simultaneous with his return come tidings of the death of Rear-Admiral Du Pont, whom he relieved, and who died this A.M. in Philadelphia. Du Pont possessed ability, had acquirements, was a scholar rather than a hero. He was a courtier, given to intrigue, was selfish, adroit, and skillful. Most of the Navy were attached to him and considered his the leading cultured mind in the service. He nursed cliques. There are many intelligent and excellent officers, however, who look upon him with exceeding dislike; yet Du Pont had, two and three years ago, greater personal influence than any man in the service. He knew it, and intended to make it available in a controversy with the Department on the subject of the monitor vessels, to which he took a dislike. Although very proud, he was not physically brave. Pride would have impelled him to go into action, but he had not innate daring courage. He was determined not to retain his force or any portion of it in Charleston Harbor, insisted it could not be done, disobeyed orders, was relieved, and expected to rally the Navy and country with him, but was disappointed. Some of his best friends condemned his course. He sought a controversy with the Department, and was not successful. Disappointed and chagrined, he has been unhappy and dissatisfied. I believe I appreciated and did justice to his good qualities, and am not conscious that I have been at

SAMUEL F. DU PONT

any time provoked to do him wrong. He challenged me
to remove him, and felt confident I would not do it. I
would not have done it had he obeyed orders and been
zealous for operations against Charleston. As it was, I
made no haste, and only ordered Foote and Dahlgren when
I got ready. Then the step was taken. Du Pont was
amazed, yet had no doubt the Navy would be roused in his
favor, and that he should overpower the Department.
Months passed. He procured two or three papers to speak
for him, but there was no partisanship in the Navy for
him, except with about half a dozen young officers, whom
he had petted and trained, and a few mischievous politicians.

Returning to Delaware, he went into absolute retirement. None missed or called for him. This seclusion did
not please him and became insupportable, but he saw no
extrication. He therefore prepared a very adroit letter in
the latter part of October, 1863, ostensibly an answer to a
dispatch of mine written the preceding June. This skillful
letter, I have reason to believe, was prepared in concert
with H. Winter Davis, and was intended to be used in an
assault on me at the session of Congress then approaching.
Although much engaged, I immediately replied, and in
such a manner as to close up Du Pont. Davis, however,
made his attack in Congress, but in such a way as not to
draw out the correspondence. Others remedied that de-
ficiency, and Davis got more than he asked. Du Pont sank.
He could rally no force, and the skill and tact at intrigue
which had distinguished him in earlier years and in lower
rank was gone. He felt that he was feeble and it annoyed
him. Still, his talent was not wholly idle. False issues were
put forth, and doubtless some have been deceived by them.

Admiral Porter is ordered to superintend the Naval
School. In some respects a good officer, but is extravagant
in expenditure sometimes, and I am apprehensive has a
tendency to be partial. I trust, however, he may prove
successful.

2

A letter of General Grant, urging the necessity of prompt action against the Imperial Government of Mexico, was read in Cabinet. Differences of opinion were expressed, but there was not a general concurrence in the apprehensions expressed by General Grant, who, naturally perhaps, desires to retain a large military force in service.

In a long conversation with Blair this evening he told me he had put himself in communication with some of the New York editors. Greeley had disappointed him, and was unreliable. Marble of the *World* he commends highly. I incline to think he has ability and he, or some of his writers, exhibits more comprehension of the true principles and structure of the government than in other journals. There is in the *World* more sound doctrine in these days than in most papers.

Blair still holds on to McClellan, — stronger, I think, than he did a year ago. Perhaps Marble and his New York friends have influenced him more than he supposes, and that he, instead of, or as well as they, may have been at least partially converted.

June 24, Saturday. Senator Trumbull called on me to-day. Says he is and has been Johnsonian. Is not prepared to say the Administration policy of Reconstruction is not the best that could be suggested. As Trumbull is by nature censorious, — a faultfinder, — I was prepared to hear him censure. But he has about him some of the old State-rights notions which form the basis of both his and my political opinions.

He expressed a hope that we had more regular Cabinet-meetings and a more general submission of important questions to the whole council than was the case under Mr. Lincoln's administration. Trumbull and the Senators generally thought Seward too meddlesome and presuming. The late President well understood and rightly appreciated the character and abilities of Trumbull, and would not quarrel with him, though he felt him to be ungenerous and exacting. They had been pretty intimate, though of opposing parties, in Illinois, until circumstances and events brought them to act together. In a competition for the seat of Senator, Mr. Lincoln, though having three fourths of the votes of their combined strength,[1] when it was necessary they should have all to succeed in choosing a Senator, finding that Trumbull would not give way, himself withdrew and went for T., who was elected. The true traits of the two men were displayed in that contest. Lincoln was self-sacrificing for the cause; Trumbull persisted against great odds in enforcing his own pretensions. When L. was taken up and made President, Trumbull always acted as though he thought himself a more fit and proper man than Lincoln, whom he had crowded aside in the Senatorial contest.

Preston King thinks that D. D. T. Marshall had better be retained as storekeeper at Brooklyn for the present, unless there is evidence of fraud or corruption. On these matters K. is very decided and earnest and would spare no one who is guilty. I have always found him correct as well as earnest. King is domiciled at the Executive Mansion, and I am glad the President gives him so truly and fully his confidence, and that he has such a faithful and competent adviser.

The President permits himself to be overrun with visitors. I find the anteroom crowded through the day by women and men seeking audience, often on frivolous and comparatively unimportant subjects which belong properly to the Departments, often by persons who have cases which have been investigated and passed upon by the Secretaries or by the late President. This pressure will, if continued, soon break down the President or any man. No one has sufficient physical endurance to perform this labor, nor is it right.

June 26, *Monday.* A very wet day. Was to have visited

[1] On the first ballot Lincoln had 45 votes and Trumbull 5.

Admiral Dahlgren on the Pawnee with the President, but, the day being inclement and the President somewhat indisposed, the visit was deferred.

June 27, Tuesday. The President still ill, and the visit to the Pawnee further postponed. No Cabinet-meeting. The President is feeling the effects of intense application to his duties, and over-pressure from the crowd.

A great party demonstration is being made for negro suffrage. It is claimed the negro is not liberated unless he is also a voter, and, to make him a voter, those who urge this doctrine would subvert the Constitution, and usurp or assume authority not granted to the Federal government. While I am not inclined to throw impediments in the way of the universal, intelligent enfranchisement of all men, I cannot lend myself to break down constitutional barriers, or to violate the reserved and undoubted rights of the States. In the discussion of this question, it is evident that intense partisanship instead of philanthropy is the root of the movement. When pressed by arguments which they cannot refute, they turn and say if the negro is not allowed to vote, the Democrats will get control of the government in each of the seceding or rebellious States, and in conjunction with the Democrats of the Free States they will get the ascendency in our political affairs. As there must and will be parties, they may as well form on this question, perhaps, as any other. It is centralization and State rights. It is curious to witness the bitterness and intolerance of the philanthropists in this matter. In their zeal for the negro they lose sight of the fundamental law of all constitutional rights and safeguards, and of the civil regulations and organization of the government.

June 30, Friday. The weather for several days has been exceedingly warm. For some time there have been complaints of mismanagement of affairs in the storekeeper's department at Boston, and on Monday last I made a change, appointing an officer who lost a leg in the service. Mr. Gooch comes to me with an outcry from the Boston delegation wanting action to be deferred. Told G. if there was any reason for it I would give it consideration. He wished to know the cause of the change. I told him the welfare and best interest of the service. It is not my purpose in this and similar cases to be placed on the defensive. I do not care to make or prefer charges, yet I feel it a most unpleasant task to remove even objectionable men.

The President is still indisposed, and I am unable to perfect some important business that I wished to complete with the close of the fiscal year. There are several Radical Members here, and have been for some days, apparently anxious to see the President. Have met Senator Wade two or three times at the White House. Complains that the Executive has the control of the government, that Congress and the Judiciary are subordinate, and mere instruments in his hands; said our form of government was on the whole a failure; that there are not three distinct and independent departments but one great controlling one with two others as assistants. Mentions that the late President called out 75,000 men without authority. Congress, when it came together, approved it. Mr. Lincoln then asked for 400,000 men and four hundred millions of money. Congress gave him five of each instead of four. I asked him if he supposed or meant to say that these measures were proposed without consulting, informally, the leading members of each house. He replied that he did not, and admitted that the condition of the country required the action which was taken, that it was right and in conformity with public expectation.

Thad Stevens called on me on business and took occasion to express ultra views, and had a sarcastic hit or two but without much sting. He is not satisfied, nor is Wade, yet I think the latter is mollified and disinclined to disagree with the President. But his friend Winter Davis, it is understood, is intending to improve the opportunity of delivering a Fourth-of-July oration, to take ground distinctly antagonistic to the Administration on the question of negro suffrage.

July 1, *Saturday.* I am this day sixty-three years old — have attained my grand climacteric, a critical period in man's career. Some admonitions remind me of the frailness of human existence and of the feeble tenure I have on life. I cannot expect, at best, many returns of this anniversary and perhaps shall never witness another.

July 8, *Saturday.* The week has been one of intense heat, and I have been both busy and indolent. Incidents have passed without daily record. The President has been ill. On Friday I met him at the Cabinet. He has been threatened, Dennison tells me, with apoplexy. So the President informed him.

Mr. Seward has undertaken to excuse and explain his strange letter to me stating "our vessels will withhold courtesy from the English." He was not aware what he wrote. Damns the English and said he was ready to let them know they must not insult us, and went into pretty glib denunciation of them. Says the French want to get out of Mexico and will go if we let them alone. In Cabinet yesterday, Dennison mentioned a call he had from Sir Frederick Bruce, who desired him to bring to the notice of the President the grievance of an Englishman. Seward and Stanton objected to the informality of the proceedings, which should come through the State Department. The objection was well taken, but Seward could not well prevent, having been constantly committing irregularities by interfering with other Departments.

McCulloch is alarmed about the Treasury. Finds that Fessenden had neither knowledge nor accuracy; that it would have been as well for the Department and the country had he been in Maine, fishing, as to have been in the Treasury Department. His opinion of Chase's financial abilities does not increase in respect as he becomes more conversant with the finances. But McCulloch, while a business man, and vastly superior to either of his two immediate predecessors, or both of them, in that respect, has unfortunately no political experience and is deficient in knowledge of men.

In some exhibits yesterday, it was shown that the military had had under pay during the year about one million men daily. Over seven hundred thousand have been paid off and discharged. There are still over two hundred thousand men on the rolls under pay. The estimates of Fessenden are exhausted, the loan is limited by law, and McCulloch is alarmed. His nerves will, however, become stronger, and he can — he will — find ways to weather the storm. Stanton has little idea of economy, although he parades the subject before the public. It is notorious that no economy has yet penetrated the War Department. The troops have been reduced in number, — men have been mustered out, — because from the cessation of hostilities and the expiration of their terms they could not longer be retained, but I have not yet seen any attempt to retrench expenses in the quartermasters', commissary, or any other branch of the military service, — certainly none in the War Department proper.

On Tuesday the 4th, I went with Mrs. Welles and Mrs. Bigelow, wife of John B., our minister to France, to Silver Spring, — a pleasant drive. The Blairs, as usual, were hospitable and interesting. They do not admire Louis Napoleon and want his troops should be expelled from Mexico. Mrs. B. is joyous, pleasant, and happy, and it is evident her husband wished her to see and get something of the views of the Blairs, but, while intelligent and charming, she is not profound on matters of State, and was a little disconcerted at the plain, blunt remarks of the elder Mr. and Mrs. Blair. She has, however, a woman's instincts.

July 9. I yesterday proposed to the President to take a short excursion down the river. He is pale and languid. It is a month since he came to the Executive Mansion, and he has never yet gone outside the doors. I told him this would not answer, — that no constitution would endure such labor and close confinement. While impressing him with my views, Speed came in, who earnestly joined me and implored the President to go and take Stanton with him. It would, he said, do them both good. Stanton was not well, — was overworked. There was, Speed said, a beautiful boat, the River Queen, the President's yacht, intended by Stanton for his use, in which Mr. Lincoln had taken his excursions to Hampton Roads and to Richmond. He made some appeal to me on this point. But I told him that I knew nothing of such a boat; that she did not belong to the Navy, nor had I any control over her. Speed said that he knew the boat, that he came from Richmond on board of her.

The President said he thought he would go and would send me word. About noon, his clerk, Muzzy, sent me word that the President would go the next day at 11 A.M. on the River Queen. Here was a dilemma. I went over to the White House to ask whether it was expected I would go, for I could not order the Queen. Muzzy said the Queen was not the boat; it was his mistake; that the President would not put his foot on that vessel, would go with me on a Navy vessel, etc. While talking, the President came in from the library and said he wanted a naval vessel.

Went with the President, his daughter Mrs. Patterson,

her two children, Mrs. Welles, Edgar, and John, Marshal Gooding, Horace Maynard, and two or three of the President's secretaries on the Don, and proceeded down the Potomac below Acquia Creek. It was a cloudy summer day, extremely pleasant for a sail. The President was afflicted with a severe headache, but the excursion was of benefit to him.

Commander Parker gave us a specimen of squadron drill and movements which was interesting. We returned to Washington about 8 P.M.

July 10, *Monday.* A rainy day. We were to have had an excursion to the Pawnee, the flag-ship of Admiral Dahlgren, but the weather has prevented.

I read to the President two letters from Senator Sumner of the 4th and 5th of July, on the subject of negro suffrage in the Rebel States. Sumner is for imposing this upon those States regardless of all constitutional limitations and restriction. It is evident he is organizing and drilling for that purpose, and intends to make war upon the Administration policy and the Administration itself. The President is not unaware of the scheming that is on foot, but I know not if he comprehends to its full extent this movement, which is intended to control him and his Administration.

July 11, *Tuesday.* The Cabinet-meeting was full. Stanton submitted an application from Judge Campbell, asking to be released from imprisonment in Pulaski. Seward talked generalities, but on the whole would not advise Campbell's release at present. Said C. was a fool; that he lacked common sense and had behaved singularly. I remarked that he was a judge of the highest court, had failed in his duty at a critical moment, that he was the only judge on that bench that had been recreant and a traitor, and he would be one of the last I would recommend for special favor. The others coincided with me, and some were even stronger.

Stanton also stated the circumstances under which he had sent a guard to close Ford's Theatre, and prevent it from being reopened. Was opposed to its ever being again used as a place of public amusement. Ford, he said, expected to make money from the tragedy, by drawing crowds to the place where Lincoln was slain. McCulloch and Harlan said that a crowd was gathering for riotous purposes, and that commotion would have followed the opening of the theatre. Stanton assigned that as one of the principal reasons for his course. It was concluded that it would not be advisable for the present to permit any attempt to open the theatre, for, in the present state of the public mind, tumult and violence, endangering not only the theatre but other property in the vicinity and human life, would be certain to follow.

The President and Cabinet agreed to visit Rear-Admiral Dahlgren on the Pawnee. Went on the tug Geranium from the foot of 7th St. at half past-four. Had a pleasant time. A heavy shower came upon us on our return and delayed us at the wharf for nearly an hour.

Both Stanton and Seward are disposed to exercise arbitrary power, — have too little regard for personal rights. The two men, I think, act in concert and have an understanding with each other on most important questions. If neither felt quite so severe towards Campbell, the traitor judge, as the rest of us, they were harsher towards the other prisoners. On the question of Ford's Theatre there had, I thought, been preconcert between them. True some others of the Cabinet were under apprehension of a mob disturbance and concurred with them. I thought Ford's course not commendable in some respects, but, after all, who shall destroy his property or take it from him? A wrong is done him whether deprived of his own by arbitrary government acts or by mob violence. Stanton says he has been compelled to seize buildings for public use and can take this. But this is a perversion. He does not need this building; it is an excuse, a false pretext. And I doubt if he

will put it to any public use, though I presume he will pay
Ford for depriving him of his property.

July 12, *Wednesday*. The Pawnee left to-day for Portsmouth. Edgar went in her, though with some reluctance.

Newton Case, of Hartford, wishes me to get permission
of the Secretary of War for him to visit and correspond with
Alexander H. Stephens, now in Fort Warren, who is preparing a work which Case and others are to publish. Stanton
declines extending any facilities. Says Stephens can write
and they can publish, but he won't help them. I thought
the refusal injudicious. The work will be forthcoming.
Why be discourteous and harsh to the prisoner? I have not
a high regard for Stephens, who has not erred in ignorance,
but he has ability and I would let him tell his story.

July 13, *Thursday*. Read to the President a letter from
Col. Ashbel Smith of Texas, who sends me resolutions
adopted at Houston, and writes me on the condition of
affairs. The President was pleased with the letter. A number of Senators and Representatives are here in behalf of
the Navy Agents whose terms are about to expire. The
public interest does not influence these men. They are
here to help men retain positions which they are occupying
to no advantage to the country. I stated the case to the
President briefly, and my opinion of the policy. He referred the whole subject to me to dispose of. I told him I
had no doubts or embarrassments except in the case of
Brown, for whom the President was committed on an
urgent appeal of Mr. Hamlin.

July 14, *Friday*. But little of importance at the Cabinet.
Seward read a letter from Bigelow, Minister at Paris, representing that indications were that Maximilian would
soon leave Mexico, — had sent to Austria considerable
amounts of money, etc. Also read extracts from a private
letter of Prince de Joinville of similar purport. All of this,

I well understood, was intended to counteract a speech of Montgomery Blair, delivered last Tuesday at Hagerstown, in which he makes an onslaught on Seward and Stanton, as well as France.

Before we left, and after all other matters were disposed of, the President brought from the other room a letter from General Sheridan to General Grant, strongly indorsed by the latter and both letter and indorsement strongly hostile to the French and Maximilian. Seward was astounded. McCulloch at once declared that the Treasury and the country could not stand this nor meet the exigency which another war would produce. Harlan in a few words sustained McCulloch. Seward was garrulous. Said if we got in war and drove out the French, we could not get out ourselves. Went over our war with Mexico. Dennison inquired why the Monroe Doctrine could not be asserted. Seward said if we made the threat we must be prepared to maintain it. Dennison thought we might. "How, then," says Seward, "will you get your own troops out of the country after driving out the French?" "Why, march them out," said Dennison. "Then," said S., "the French will return." "We will then," said D., "expel them again." I remarked the country was exhausted, as McCulloch stated, but the popular sentiment was strongly averse to French occupancy. If the Mexicans wanted an imperial government, no one would interfere to prevent them, though we might and would regret it, but this conduct of the French in imposing an Austrian prince upon our neighbors was very revolting. I hoped, however, we should not be compelled to take the military view of this question.

Thurlow Weed passed into the White House as I came upon the portico this morning. I had seen a person, without recognizing that it was Weed, hurrying forward, as if to be in advance of me. Following him immediately, I saw who it was and was surprised to see him, instead of going direct to the stairs, turn square round the bulkhead and wait until I had passed.

July 15, *Saturday*. Had some conversation with the President in regard to an application of F. W. Smith for an indorsement made by the late President Lincoln on Smith's trial. It was an irregular proceeding on the part of President L., procured by Sumner, and I have no doubt he regretted his action. The President (Johnson), after reading the indorsement, remarked it was very sweeping, and wished me to wait a few days.

July 17, *Monday*. Last Tuesday, when on board the Pawnee with the President and Cabinet, Stanton took me aside and desired to know if the Navy could not spare a gunboat to convey some prisoners to Tortugas. I told him a vessel could be detailed for that purpose if necessary, but I inquired why he did not send them by one of his own transports. He then told me he wanted to send the persons connected with the assassination of President Lincoln to Tortugas, instead of a Northern prison, that he had mentioned the subject to the President, and it was best to get them into a part of the country where old Nelson or any other judge would not try to make difficulty by *habeas corpus*. Said he would make further inquiries and see me, but wished strict secrecy. On Friday he said he should want a boat and I told him we had none here, but the Florida might be sent to Hampton Roads, and he could send his men and prisoners thither on one of the army boats in the Potomac. I accordingly sent orders for the Florida. Yesterday General Townsend called on me twice on the subject, and informed me in the evening that General Hancock would leave in a boat at midnight to meet the Florida. I suggested that General H. had better wait; we had no information yet that the Florida had arrived, and she would be announced to us by telegraph as soon as she did arrive. To-day I learn the prisoners and a guard went down last night, and I accordingly sent orders by telegraph, by request of Secretary of War, to receive and convey the guard and prisoners to Tortugas.

Seward sent to see me. Had dispatches from the Spanish government that the Stonewall should be given up. Is to send me copies, but the yellow fever is prevalent in Havana and it would be well to leave the Stonewall there until fall.

July 18, *Tuesday.* The President to-day in Cabinet, after current business was disposed of, brought forward the subject of Jefferson Davis' trial, on which he desired the views of the members. Mr. Seward thought there should be no haste. The large amount of papers of the Rebel government had not yet been examined, and much that would have a bearing on this question might be expected to be found among them. Whenever Davis should be brought to trial, he was clear and decided that it should be before a military commission, for he had no confidence in proceeding before a civil court. He was very full of talk, and very positive that there should be delay until the Rebel papers were examined, and quite emphatic and decided that a military court should try Davis. Stanton did not dissent from this, and yet was not as explicit as Seward. He said he intended to give the examination of the Rebel papers to Dr. Lieber,[1] and with the force he could give him believed the examination could be completed in two weeks' time. Subsequently it was said Dr. L. had gone home and would return next week.

McCulloch was not prepared to express an opinion but thought no harm would result from delay.

I doubted the resort to a military commission and thought there should be an early trial. Whether, were he to be tried in Virginia, as it was said he might be, the country was sufficiently composed and organized might be a question, but I was for a trial before a civil, not a military, tribunal, and for treason, not for the assassination. Both Seward and Stanton interrupted me and went into a discussion of the assassination, and the impossibility of a con-

[1] Francis Lieber.

viction, Seward taking the lead. It was evident these two intended there should be no result at this time and the talk became discursive. Twice the President brought all back to the question, and did not conceal his anxiety that we should come to some determination. But we got none.

While in Cabinet a dispatch from Admiral Radford was sent me, stating that the Treasury agent, Loomis, at Richmond, claimed the ship timber in the Navy Yard at that place. I handed the dispatch to McCulloch and asked what it meant. He professed not to know and I told him I would bring the matter up as soon as the subject under discussion was disposed of. He directly after came to me and said he must go, and should be satisfied with whatever conclusion we came to. Before he got away, the matter in hand was postponed, and I then called his attention to the dispatch. He said there was no necessity for discussing the matter, he was disposed to yield to whatever I claimed, which I told him was all ship timber and all naval property.

I was satisfied that there was money in this proceeding. Governor Pierpont wrote me a week or two since that the railroad companies wanted this timber for railroad purposes, but I declined letting them have it. Hence these other proceedings, wholly regardless of the public interest.

Later in the day I went to the Treasury Department and was assured that a telegram should be sent to the Treasury agent, to give up this timber to the Navy.

Seward explained farther about the French-Mexican matter. He is evidently much annoyed by Blair's speech. Says Bigelow never made the remarks imputed to him, and those which he did make were unauthorized and denounced.

July 19, *Wednesday.* Sent telegram to Admiral Radford and General Terry in regard to the ship timber at Richmond. Wrote to Ashbel Smith of Texas.

July 20, *Thursday.* Mrs. Welles and John departed to-day for Narragansett, leaving me lonely and alone for two months. I submit because satisfied it is best, yet it is a heavy deprivation, quite a shadow on life's brief journey, — the little that is left for me.

On receiving a letter to-day from General Terry, saying the Treasury agent needed specific instructions from the Secretary of the Treasury, I called on Mr. McCulloch. He thought all could be put right without difficulty. The way to effect it was for me to send a requisition, or request the naval officer to make a requisition for the timber, and the agent would grant it. I told him that neither I nor any naval officer would make requisition; that the order in the President's proclamation was sufficient authority for me and for naval officers, though it might not do for the Treasury agents, who were presuming and self-sufficient. He thought I was more a stickler for forms than he had supposed; said they had receipted for this timber to the War Department. I told him I knew not what business either they or the War Department had with it, but because they had committed irregularities, I would not, unless the President countermanded his own very proper order. He still declared they wanted something to show for this, after having receipted for it. I told him I would instruct an officer to make demand, and the demand would be his voucher if he needed one. He said very well, perhaps it would. I accordingly so sent.

July 21, *Friday.* A very warm day. Thermometer 90 and upward. Chief subject at the Cabinet was the offense and the disposition of J. Davis. The President, it was evident, was for procuring a decision or having the views of the Cabinet. Seward thought the question might as well be disposed of now as at any time. He was satisfied there could be no conviction of such a man, for any offense, before any civil tribunal, and was therefore for arraigning him for treason, murder, and other offenses before a mil-

2

itary commission. Dennison, who sat next him, immediately followed, and thought if the proof was clear and beyond question that Davis was a party to the assassination, then he would have him by all means brought before a military tribunal, but unless the proof was clear, beyond a peradventure, he would have him tried for high treason before the highest civil court. When asked what other court there was than the circuit court, he said he did not wish him tried before the court of this District. And when further asked to be more explicit on the subject of the question of murder or assassination, he said he would trust that matter to Judge Holt and the War Department, and, he then added, the Attorney-General. McCulloch would prefer, if there is to be a trial, that it should be in the courts, but was decidedly against any trial at present, would postpone the whole subject. Stanton was for a trial by the courts for treason, the highest of crimes, and, by the Constitution, only the courts could try him for that offense. Otherwise he would say a military commission. For all other offenses he would arraign him before the military commission. Subsequently, after examining the Constitution, he retracted the remark that the Constitution made it imperative that the trial for treason should be in the civil courts, yet he did not withdraw the preference he had expressed. I was emphatically for the civil court and an arraignment for treason; for an early institution of proceedings; and was willing the trial should take place in Virginia. If our laws or system were defective, it was well to bring them to a test. I had no doubt he was guilty of treason and believed he would be convicted, wherever tried. Harlan would not try him before a civil court unless satisfied there would be conviction. If there was a doubt, he wanted a military commission. He thought it would be much better to pardon Davis at once than to have him tried and not convicted. Such a result, he believed, would be most calamitous. He would, therefore, rather than run that risk prefer a military court. Speed was for a civil tribunal and for a trial for treason; but until the Rebellion was entirely suppressed he doubted if there could be a trial for treason. Davis is now a prisoner of war and was entitled to all the rights of belligerent, etc., etc. I inquired if Davis was not arrested and a reward offered for him and paid by our government as for other criminals.

The question of counsel and the institution of proceedings was discussed. In order to get the sense of each of the members, the President thought it would be well to have the matter presented in a distinct form. Seward promptly proposed that Jefferson Davis should be tried for treason, assassination, murder, conspiring to burn cities, etc., by a military commission. The question was so put, Seward and Harlan voting for it, the others against, with the exception of myself. The President asked my opinion. I told him I did not like the form in which the question was put. I would have him tried for military offenses by a military court, but for civil offenses I wanted the civil courts. I thought he should be tried for *treason*, and it seemed to me that the question before us should first be the *crime* and then the court. The others assented and the question put was, Shall J. D. be tried for treason? There was a unanimous response in the affirmative. Then the question as to the court. Dennison moved a civil court. All but Seward and Harlan were in the affirmative; they were in the negative.

Stanton read a letter from Fortress Monroe, saying Davis' health had been failing for the last fortnight; that the execution of the assassins had visibly affected him. Davis remarked that President Johnson was "quick on the trigger."

I this day took possession of the rooms in the new wing which had been prepared and furnished for the Secretary of the Navy.

The solicitor, Mr. Bolles, arrived to-day and entered upon his duties so far as to take possession of his rooms. He was not anxious, I perceived, to enter upon his new duties on Friday, although he did not assign that as the reason for delay.

July 24, *Monday.* On Saturday evening I went with the President (whose health is suffering from excessive labor and care) and Preston King down the Potomac and took a sail yesterday in the Bay, returning last evening to Washington. Mr. Fox and Mr. Faxon accompanied us, also Wright Rives, the President's private secretary, also Dr. Duval. It was a small, pleasant, quiet party, intended to promote health and strength, especially to the President, who permits himself to be overtaxed.

The great iron ram Dunderberg was launched on Saturday. The papers give details of the vessel from its inception to the launch, but much of it warped. Among other things it is said the Navy Department entered upon the construction of this ship with great reluctance. It was after deliberate consideration. If it had been stated that I engaged in this work and made this contract with great caution and circumspection it would have been true. At the time this decision was made and the vessel commenced, a foreign war was feared. We had a large defensive force, but not as many and formidable vessels as we should need in the event of a war with a maritime power.

We had contracted for the Dictator and the Puritan, turreted vessels, which, if completed, would break up any attempted blockade of our harbors or coasts, but we could not cruise with them. Admiral Smith urged that one of these vessels should be of iron, the other of wood. The Assistant Secretary, Mr. Fox, was urgent and persistent for the construction of four vessels. Mr. Lenthall was not partial to the turreted form of vessel. I decided in favor of two, and but two, and the Dictator and the Puritan were the results of that decision. I have since wished that one of these vessels was of wood, as Admiral Smith proposed, and I have rejoiced that I did not yield to the appeals for more. Probably those who urged the construction of more are glad also.

The Dunderberg was a different description of vessel. Mr. Webb had been importuned to build a large vessel for the government and was urged as the best man for such a contract in the country by numbers of the first men in New York and elsewhere. While glad to have the indorsement of such men, I by no means entered into a contract to oblige them or Mr. Webb, who, I have no doubt, procured the names by solicitation. In view of what was being done by England and France, and of the then condition of our affairs, I felt that we might need such a vessel. So feeling, I came to the conclusion that Mr. Webb was the best builder with whom I could contract, offered the best terms, and, under the circumstances, his plan, though exceptionable, was perhaps the best, with some modifications. These he made, reserving the turrets, to which Mr. Lenthall strongly objected, and which he predicted Mr. Webb would wish to abandon before the ship was completed. Events have verified his anticipations. These are some of the facts in regard to the Dunderberg. I take no special pride in the vessel, and could I have the money which she costs, I should prefer it to the vessel. Yet I feel assured I did right in ordering her to be built. We could not, in the crowded condition of the yards, attempt to build her in either of them.

In the violent assaults of Winter Davis and others upon the Department, I was accused of not having a navy of formidable vessels. I had vessels for the purposes then wanted. Ships of a more expensive and formidable character, like the Dunderberg, could not be built in a day. Now, when they are likely not to be wanted, and when they are drawing near completion, the same class of persons abuse me for what I have done towards the building up of a formidable navy. But one must not expect to escape the abuse and unjust attacks of demagogues. I certainly ought not to complain, for the country has nobly stood by me through all the misrepresentation and detraction of the malicious and ungenerous who have made it a point to assail me. Conscious that I have tried to do my duty, I have borne with patience.

I called on the President in relation to the Navy Agent in Washington, Brown, whose term expires on the 27th inst. Last winter, it was understood between Mr. Lincoln and myself that paymasters should hereafter perform the duty of Navy Agents, and thus save the expense of that class of officers. But about the 4th of March Vice-President Hamlin made a special appeal in behalf of Brown, and in view of Hamlin's disappointments and retirement, the good Mr. Lincoln had not the stamina to refuse him, or to say to him that it conflicted with a policy which he had deliberately adopted. My relations with Hamlin were such that I could not very well argue this point, and the President could modify or yield his own opinions. He understood my embarrassment and addressed me a note, stating his pledge inconsiderately made to Hamlin. I have submitted this note and the circumstances to President Johnson. He concurs with me, and is also somewhat embarrassed from delicacy, in consequence of his attitude towards Hamlin, whom he superseded. I suggested that he might oblige Hamlin by giving some other place to Brown or to any one else whom H. should name. This met his approval, and he suggested that I should have a letter prepared to H. for him, the President, to sign. I proposed speaking to Brown himself, stating the general policy of appointing no Navy Agent, and that, by acquiescing, the President would feel disposed to consider him and Hamlin favorably. He liked this, and I accordingly stated the case to Brown soon after, who was a good deal flurried and not prepared to decide whether he would resign or let his appointment run out and another be appointed, but would inform me on Wednesday.

While with the President, I remonstrated on his severe labors which are overtasking his system. The anterooms and halls above and below were at the time a good deal crowded. He said he knew not what to do with these people; that a large delegation from Maryland had just left him, having called in relation to appointments in that State and here.

We had some conversation in regard to the Baltimore officers and Maryland matters and differences which there existed. The combination against the Blairs is fed and stimulated from M[aryland]. I expressed myself very decidedly for the Blairs, whom I had long known and who are true men. To which he fully responded and made the remark that they were true to their friends always, — a quality ever to be commended.

July 25, *Tuesday.* McCulloch remarked that he had lost all confidence in Treasury agents, that the system was one of demoralization. Of this there can be no doubt, and there was mischief in the inception. Chase, with an overburdened Department and with more duties than he could discharge, coveted this business and fancied its patronage would aid his popularity.

The Chief Justice is now, I see, at Hanover, N. H., making party speeches on negro suffrage and expressing opinions on questions that may come before him for adjudication.

July 26, *Wednesday.* Blair called on me in some trouble respecting the Maryland appointments, which have been violently contested. From some intimation he apprehends that his friend B——, the marshal, is in danger, and this touches him in a tender point. He therefore wished me to have an interview with the President. I went almost immediately to the Executive Mansion. General Slocum was with the President, but I waited till he was through, and then stated the case. He told me it was his intention to close the Maryland appointments to-day and get them off his hands, and asked if I really supposed Blair cared much about the marshalship. I assured him he did and was sensitive in regard to it. He reached over and took up a paper, which he examined closely. It convinced me that Blair's suspicions were right, and I spoke earnestly and zealously for the Blairs. We had a free conversation in regard to them, and as to the policy which should be pursued in Maryland. I did not hesitate to oppose the selection of opponents or doubtful friends, and to express my opinion that the friends were the reliable supporters of the Administration in that State.

July 27, Thursday. Brown, the Navy Agent, did not call on me yesterday as he promised. I therefore sent a paymaster to take charge of the office and directed a transfer to be made at two o'clock. But the messenger returned about that hour with a letter from Brown, stating that a consultation had been had with the President, who would see me, but if no change of programme was ordered by 5 P.M. he would immediately thereafter transfer. About three I received a note that the President wished to see me. He said Hamlin had been to see him and was very vehement, from some cause, in behalf of Brown. I stated what had been done; that I felt a little delicate in consequence of my relations with H., so had President Lincoln and himself also. I informed him I had a frank conversation with Brown, who said he wanted time to consider, but had obviously telegraphed to Hamlin. The President said he could not understand why H. should take such extraordinary interest in this case. He then got me the statutes and showed me a law on which Hamlin dwelt with some emphasis. We read it over together. I told the President the law offered no serious obstacle to me. He said he took the same view and would not deviate from his convictions. But Hamlin was vehement, and he wished to treat him with courtesy, and give him time to fully examine the case.

The paymaster (Fulton), who called to have the transfer made, said Brown told him he should not be prepared to transfer at two. F. then said he would wait, when a man whom he did not know, but who sat smoking a cigar, said it would be of no use, F. could wait or not. This man was Hamlin. Fulton replied that his business was with the Navy Agent and not with him (Hamlin.) The latter soon remarked he would go over and see Harlan, Secretary of the Interior.

Postmaster-General Dennison took a walk with me this evening. Returning, we had a cup of tea together. A shower came on, which detained him through the evening, and among a variety of topics we got on this of Hamlin and the Navy Agent. He thought the proceeding most extraordinary, and was especially surprised at the conduct of Hamlin. This led to some exposure of Hamlin's conduct which I have made to no others.

July 28, *Friday.* Immediately after reaching the Department this morning I was told there was a suspension of action in the case of the Navy Agency. Soon after, Mr. Brown called. I told him he had not kept his promise of seeing me on Wednesday. He was, as Jack Downing says, "a little stumped" but said he supposed it was of no use. He then informed me that the President had been seen the night before, and had referred the case of the Navy Agency to the Attorney-General and the Solicitor of the Department for their written opinion on a legal point.

Mr. Bolles, the Solicitor, came in soon after Brown left, and said he had been with the President and Hamlin the previous evening, and that the President would in writing call for the written opinion of himself and Ashton, Acting Attorney-General. In a little time B. and A. came in. Ashton did not at first rightly comprehend the case, but soon reached it, and a brief but clear opinion was soon given and transmitted to the President. It will, I think, be conclusive, and dispense with the farther services of Ex-Vice-President Hamlin for the present. Perhaps I judge him severely, but he seems to me a violent and unscrupulous man, avaricious and reckless. Mr. Bridge, Chief of Provisions and Clothing, says he has no doubt Hamlin is a partner of Brown in the Agency. He, as well as they, is from Maine, and from his position has had opportunities of forming correct opinions.

July 29, *Saturday.* We had this P.M. a violent storm of rain and wind. The day had previously been exceedingly sultry. Dickerson, the patent-lawyer, has contrived to get up quite a little fuss in the matter of steam engines. Paul Forbes, a man of wealth, became Dickersonized on the subject of engines and cut-offs, and finally offered to build a vessel on such terms — and at his own risks — that it would have been hardly excusable to refuse. By the terms of the contract, the test steamer was to be such as the Secretary of the Navy should prescribe. When I was notified that the engines of the Algonquin were completed, preliminary measures as to the test were taken. In the meantime, Dickerson sent a challenge, which he published in the New York papers, appealing to the press and others to aid. The test of the Department was based on the contract and this was called an acceptance of Dickerson's published challenge. Exceptions are now taken to it as unfair toward Dickerson, with much ridiculous nonsense, all which goes to advertise the patent lawyer; when the truth is the Department has nothing to do with Dickerson or his challenge.

If his engine has merit, we wish to know it. I am no expert, or engineer; have no feeling or bias for or against; want the best engine that is made, regardless who is the inventor, or what the principle, so that it is the best. Not unlikely Dickerson's scheme or invention has some merit, though the naval engineers generally think not. If it has, let us know it; but there is a gasconade and pretension on Dickerson's part that is flabby and disgusting, though indorsed by certain of the New York presses, which doubtless are paid.

XXXII

The Military annuls the Municipal Election in Richmond — Ex-Confeder-
ates organizing to regain Political Ascendency in the Reconstructed
States — The Military on the Mexican Frontier — General Butler's
Reconstruction Views — Resignation of Chief Engineer Stimers — His
Unfortunate Connection with the Light-draft Monitors — Death of
Capt. Percival Drayton, Chief of the Bureau of Navigation — The
President's Health — Some War Department Matters — The Legislation in regard to Appointments in the South — The Question of Pardons
for Ex-Confederates — The Movement against the Indians — Stan-
ton's Body-Guard — Sumner against the Administration's Policy —
Anti-Administration Operations — The Counsel for the Government in
the Jefferson Davis Trial — Republican Reverses in Mexico — Chief Justice Chase and the Davis Trial — Efforts to establish a Party on the
Basis of Equality of the Races — Blair's Injudicious Speech — His Attack on Holt.

August 1, Tuesday. The President sends notice that
there will be no Cabinet-meeting to-day. He went to Fortress Monroe on Sunday in a light river boat, and returned
on Monday morning ill. He is reported quite indisposed
to-day. As he takes no exercise and confines himself to his
duties, his health must break down. Going down the river
is a temporary relief from care and a beneficial change of
atmosphere, but it gives no exercise. I admonish him frequently, but it has little effect.

The tone of sentiment and action of people of the South
is injudicious and indiscreet in many respects. I know not
if there is any remedy, but if not, other and serious disasters await them, — and us also perhaps, for if we are one
people, dissension and wrong affect the whole.

The recent election in Richmond indicates a banding together of the Rebel element and a proscription of friends of
the Union. This would be the natural tendency of things,
perhaps, but there should be forbearance and kindness, in
order to reinstate old fraternal feeling. Instead of this, the

Rebels appear to be arrogant and offensively dictatorial. Perhaps there is exaggeration in this respect.

The military, it seems, have interfered and nullified the municipal election in Richmond, with the exception of a single officer. Why he alone should be retained, I do not understand. Nor am I informed, though I have little doubt, who directed and prompted this military squelching of a popular election. It was not a subject on which the Cabinet was informed. Such a step should not have been taken without deliberation, under good advisement, and with good reasons. There may have been such, for the Rebels have been foolish and insolent, and there was wanting a smart and stern rebuke rightly administered. If not right, the wicked may be benefited and their malpractices strengthened by the interference.

From various quarters we learn that the Rebels are organizing through the Southern States with a view to regaining political ascendency, and are pressing forward prominent Rebels for candidates in the approaching election. Graham in North Carolina, Etheridge in Tennessee, are types.

Seward and Speed are absent at Cape May. Dennison tells me that Stanton on Friday stated we had a military force of 42,000 on the Rio Grande. If so, this on the part of the military means war, and we are in no condition for war. I have not been entirely satisfied with Seward's management of the Mexican question. Our remonstrance or protest against French influence and dictation has been feeble and inefficient, but Stanton and Grant are, on the other hand, too belligerent.

August 2. General Butler called on me to-day. Came direct from the Executive Mansion. Says the President is no better. He could not see him. Is confined to his room, indeed he every day confines himself to the house and room. General B. was very much inclined to talk on public affairs, and evidently intends taking an active part in the rising questions. Much of our conversation related to Jeff Davis and General Lee, both of whom he would have tried, convicted, and executed. Mild and lenient measures, he is convinced, will have no good effect on the Rebels. Severity is necessary.

Cameron called on me with his friend for the twentieth time at least, in relation to two appointments in the Philadelphia Navy Yard. He does not conceal from me, nor probably from any one, that he intends to be a candidate for the Senate. Hence his vigilance in regard to certain appointments, and he has prevailed in the Treasury and in the Post Office, against the combined efforts of all the Members of Congress. In sustaining, as he does, the policy of the President he shows sagacity. Kelley and the Members, but especially K., have shot wild on negro suffrage. There is a strong pressure towards centralism at this time. Many sensible men seem to be wholly oblivious to constitutional barriers and restraints, and would have the Federal government assume authority to carry out their theories. General Butler, to-day, speaks of the Rebel States as dead. I suggested that it was a more correct theory to consider them as still States in and of the Union, but whose proper constitution functions had been suspended by a conspiracy and rebellion. He said that was pretty much his view.

Chief Engineer Stimers sends in his resignation. I had given him orders to the Powhatan, and he does not wish to go to sea.

Unfortunately Stimers has got into difficulty with Lenthall and Isherwood; others, perhaps, are in fault. Stimers rendered good service in the first Monitor, and afterwards at Charleston, for which I felt under obligations to him, and did not hesitate to express it. Subsequently, when preparing to build the light-draft monitors, he and the Assistant Secretary took the subject in hand. Stimers became intoxicated with his own importance. While I supposed the Naval Constructor and Chief Engineer, to whose bureaus it belonged, were prosecuting the subject, under advisement with Mr. Ericsson, it appeared that these men had been ignored. When my attention was called to the question, Lenthall and Isherwood informed me that they had been excluded, and I then, for the first time, was made aware that Ericsson was on bad terms with Stimers and the two had no personal intercourse.

Inquiring into proceedings, I found serious difficulties existed, requiring essential modifications and a large increase of expenditure to make the vessels efficient or capable of flotation with their armament. No one, however, was willing to take the responsibility for the mistake committed. I was to bear the whole, and I had been deceived and kept uninformed of the whole proceeding.

Stimers and Fox, had, I think, connived that they could do this work independent of the proper officers and perhaps of Ericsson; probably hoped to acquire reputation. Their plan was kept from my knowledge, although the work was done in my name.

Lenthall and Isherwood culpably withheld from me information of what was being done; were vexed with Fox and Stimers, and were willing they should become involved, because a slight had been shown them. When I was made aware of the facts, I called all to an account. Fox and Stimers placed the blame on Lenthall and Isherwood, and when I called these latter gentlemen to account they plead ignorance and disclosed the whole truth. The whole thing was disgracefully improper and wrong.

In the mean time, the enemies of the Department, having got hold of the failure, opened their batteries, and I was compelled to encounter them for the follies and errors of my subordinates. On the whole, I succeeded in extricating the Department from very serious difficulties, and got a tolerable vindication before Congress, but I look upon the whole transaction as the most unfortunate that has taken place during my administration of the Navy Department.

The Assistant Secretary was probably more in fault than any other. It was his specialty. He expected great successes, where he had a great failure. Stimers was implicated about as deeply, but Stimers became intoxicated, overloaded with vanity. Neither of them, nor both combined, were competent for what they undertook. The glory was to have been theirs, the responsibility was mine.

The bureau officers failed in their duty in not informing me. I so told them and they each admitted it. Lenthall did so repeatedly and with many regrets, with much suppressed indignation that Fox should shrink from an honest, open avowal of his responsibility.

Stimers I have treated kindly. He is more weak than wicked, not devoid of talents, though Lenthall and Isherwood deny him any ability. But I know he has some capability and I do not forget his services in the turreted vessels.

While Fox would give him special favor, and the others would grant him none, I would treat Stimers kindly but justly. He has wanted shore duty entirely. Under existing circumstances it is better he should get afloat. Fox and Stimers had arranged that Admiral Gregory should employ Stimers on gun-carriages, and the Admiral was persuaded to apply for him. I set the whole aside, and told Fox Stimers must go to sea. He assented to the correctness of my views, but hoped that I would not permit the enmity of L. and I. to crush Stimers. I assured him not, and gave Stimers the Powhatan. The return mail brings his resignation. I cannot do otherwise than to accept it.

Talked over the whole subject with Captain Drayton,[1] who concurs in my views. Had also a full interchange of views concerning Wilkes, whom he characterizes as the most insubordinate man in the Navy, insolent to his superiors, and the most arrogant and exacting to his subordinates. We also agreed in regard to Admiral Davis as an amiable man, a feeble officer, of some literary acquirements, but Drayton says very little pretensions to science.

[1] Chief of the Bureau of Navigation.

August 3, [*Thursday*]. Affairs at the South do not improve. The Secession element is becoming vicious and bad in some quarters, and I fear it may be general. At the North there is about as much folly in the other extreme. The President continues ill. Captain Drayton is quite indisposed this evening.

Governor Dennison called upon me this evening. He is very much dissatisfied with the military announcements of some eighteen different departments and a vast concourse of generals put forth by the War Department, or by Grant. It is a singular announcement, and the army should be immediately reduced to one third and even less.

We had some conversation in regard to the position taken by General Cox, the candidate for Governor in Ohio, who goes for colonizing the blacks in South Carolina and Georgia. His suggestions are the conclusions of one mind. But there is an unsettled and uncertain public sentiment. The attempt to force the South into a recognition of negro and white equality will make trouble. Cox's proposition will not relieve us of the trouble.

I am anxious and concerned about Drayton. He is reported to me to be quite ill. The President is better but continues indisposed. I went this P.M. to the Navy Yard. Mr. Faxon accompanied me. The cost and waste of war and the consequent demoralization make me sad.

August 4, *Friday*. There was no Cabinet-session. The President is not yet well. Seward and Speed are absent. Stanton, I hear, is sick. Captain Drayton is very low. I called to see him this P.M. and fear he cannot survive. He is aware of the probable result of his illness but is calm, composed, resigned, and firm. Obviously he is prepared for the great summons, but is surprised that it is so suddenly and unexpectedly made. He said to me he could in no way account for it from his diet, habit, from any indulgence or care, or the want of it.

PERCIVAL DRAYTON

August 5, Saturday. Captain Drayton died last night. The nation is not aware of the loss it has sustained. There will be difficulty in finding an equally good man for his position. Truthful, intelligent, discriminating, with no partialities or prejudices that were allowed to interfere with his duties, he was invaluable.

I recall more distinctly our last interview and conversation on the Wednesday before he died. He took great interest in the Naval Academy. Thought Porter well adapted for the place at this time when rigor and renovation were wanted. Blake he considered no disciplinarian, too much of a courtier, not severely and sternly truthful. I remarked to him that I had at one time thought of Foote as a proper successor to Blake, but it was before he was made an Admiral. He said that Foote had some excellent qualities but was not, perhaps, full up to the position. Knowing that Raymond Rodgers and Drayton had been pets of Du Pont, I thought it a good time to ascertain how far he had permitted himself to be mixed up with the Du Pont clique. Drayton said promptly and at once that Rodgers was not adapted to the post, that it would have been unfortunate to have given it to him. I told him I had become aware of that, though at one time partial to him for the position, chiefly on the recommendation of Du Pont, strongly favored and indorsed by Fox; but when I came personally to know more of Rodgers, and see how he chose to identify himself without reason with Du Pont's controversy — become a partisan — and to quarrel with the Department for no cause, [I saw] that it would not do to appoint him. In all this canvassing of characters there was coincidence of views between us, even when I had previously supposed there was a difference. It was no conforming of his opinions to mine, for Drayton was truthful; though modest, he was independent and frank.

I authorized Admiral Porter to take charge of the funeral ceremonies, as we heard nothing from his relatives and friends. Telegrams were again sent to Alexander Hamilton,

2

Jr., also to relatives at Hyde Park, informing of Drayton's decease.

I called to see the President, but his family had just arrived from Tennessee, and, he not being well, I deferred my business, which was, among other things, to deliver a letter sent to me by Mrs. James K. Polk.

August 7, Monday. Attended the funeral of Captain Drayton at 5 p.m., at St. John's Church. Arrangements were very complete, and he was buried, or rather entombed, in Oakland Cemetery, Georgetown, with appropriate honors.

Governor Dennison called, having been sent by Secretary Seward, who wished to see us together. The subject of consultation was the President's health and method of doing business. He, Seward, had returned and called to-day at once on the President, who was looking ill and oppressed, and S. so told him. The President inquired if nothing could be done to relieve him of the immense throng that was incessantly pressing on him. Seward told him he had no doubt relief might be had, and he would prepare a general order for that purpose. This had been prepared, and, seeing Dennison, he had requested him to invite me to his house, that I might be aware of what was doing, and be prepared for it, when the subject came up to-morrow in the Cabinet, where he proposed to introduce it.

I concur most fully in the necessity of some thorough and effective change, and that speedily. On repeated occasions I have admonished the President, and have spoken to members of the Cabinet, Preston King, and others to the same purport.

Seward is much improved in health and looks by his visit to Cape May.

August 8, Tuesday. The subject of a change to relieve the President was discussed in Cabinet and Seward produced the order which he had prepared. There was no dissent as to the necessity of some action. Various matters were submitted by different members. I presented, at the request of Judge Wayne, the subject of paying debts in the Rebel States, and all thought none that were due prior to the War should, for the present at least, be considered.

Stanton submitted a number of not material questions, yet possessed of some little interest. Before the meeting closed, the subject of army movements on the Plains came up, and Stanton said there were three columns of twenty-two thousand troops moving into the Indian country, with a view to an Indian campaign. Inquiry as to the origin and authority of such a movement elicited nothing from the Secretary of War. He said he knew nothing on the subject. He had been told there was such a movement, and Meigs had informed him it was true. Grant had been written to for information, but Grant was away and he knew not when he should have a reply. The expenses of this movement could not, he said, be less than fifty millions of dollars. But he knew nothing about it.

All manifested surprise. The President, however, made, I observed, no inquiry or any comment. Whether this was intentional reticence, or the result of physical weariness or debility, — for he was far from well, — I could not determine. I thought it alarming that there should be such an imposing demonstration on the part of the military, and the Administration, or executive officer of the War Department, ignorant in regard to it. If so, it is to his discredit; if not true, it is no less so. The only apology or excuse would be that the President had ordered this through General Grant, or assented to it at least. But this would be a slight upon the Secretary of War to which he would not possibly submit.

Following up this subject, Governor Dennison inquired of Stanton in relation to the recent general order dividing the country into eighteen military departments and assigning a multitude of generals to them. The question was mildly, pertinently, and appropriately put, but Stanton evinced intense feeling and acrimony. He said the Post-master-General must address his inquiries to General Grant respecting that order, and he had no doubt General Grant would have been glad to have had Dennison's advice and direction on the subject. For his part he had not undertaken to instruct or advise General Grant.

There was a sneer and insolence in the manner, more offensive even than the words. I was on the point of inquiring if the civil administration of the government could not be informed on so important a subject, when Speed, who evidently saw there was feeling, hastened to introduce another topic. I was glad he did so, yet this state of things cannot endure.

I fell in with Dennison, or he with me, when taking my usual walk, and we at once got on to the subject of Stanton's insolent replies to-day. Dennison was, with reason, irritated. Said he had forborne to reply or pursue the subject because his temper was excited and there would have been a scene. He says he has known Stanton well for twenty-five years; that he is a charlatan and that he wanted D. to make a sharp reply on Grant in order that he might report it to that officer and thus create a difference.

August 9, *Wednesday.* I yesterday wrote a letter to Paul S. Forbes, returning an impertinent and insolent letter of his lawyer, Dickerson, and also wrote to Gardner, who claims to be his agent, and mentioned that the trial of the Algonquin was to be made by engineers selected by the Secretary of the Navy pursuant to contract. These letters I modified to-day and more carefully worded, for there is an obvious intention on the part of Dickerson, the patent lawyer, to have a controversy.

J. Z. Goodrich, Collector at Boston, called on me to-day. An effort is making — an intrigue, he says — to displace him and appoint some other person. Ex-Vice-President Hamlin has been one of the persons named to succeed him, Assistant Postmaster-General McClellan another; the last person named is Gooch, the Representative. From the facts stated by Goodrich, I have little doubt that Mr. Representative Hooper has been active in this matter, probably the instigator. Gooch is doubtless in complicity with him. But Hooper is a man of equivocal character from these representations, and has connived at a fraud, was exposed and defeated by Goodrich, and now seeks to get Goodrich displaced from his position.

August 10, *Thursday.* Seward tells me there are rising troubles between Spain and Peru, and perhaps Chili, and thinks our naval force may need strengthening in that quarter.

Am in a state of uncertainty as to whom to select to fill the place of Chief of the Navigation Bureau. My own first thoughts turn to Alden, who has some good, pleasant qualities. Jenkins, though unlike Alden in many traits, has good points, — is faithful and industrious, — but is better fitted for another bureau. Melancthon Smith and John Worden have each been named. Yet neither, in all respects, can make Drayton's place good.

August 11, *Friday.* The question of the Indian war on the Plains was again brought forward. No one, it appears, has any knowledge on the question. The Secretary of War is in absolute ignorance. Says he has telegraphed to General Grant, and General G. says he has not ordered it. McCulloch wanted to know the probable expense, the numbers engaged, etc. Stanton thought McCulloch had better state how many should be engaged; said General Pope had command. Harlan said he considered Pope an improper man, — was extravagant and wasteful. Thought twenty-two hundred instead of twenty-two thousand men was a better and sufficient number. This whole thing is a discredit to the War Department.

McCulloch inquired what should be done in regard to appointing officers of customs, revenue, etc., who could not

take the oath which Congress prescribes. Speed advocated
delay in making appointments. There was some favor of a
modified oath. I queried whether the President was not
empowered by the Constitution to select and nominate,
and the Senate, if it chose, to confirm, independent of this
restriction. In other words, was the President's constitutional prerogative to be thus narrowed by Congress? Seward said the President had signed the law, which in its
operation was undoubtedly embarrassing to the Administration and injurious to the country. I remarked his signature could not make the law constitutional, if it was not
constitutional; that one executive could not in this way tie
up his successor. I was therefore for appointing good, true,
honest men, whether they could or could not take this
oath. Stanton was for appointing them without the oath,
because the States are yet in rebellion. They were to be
considered provisional appointments, and the law of Congress was inoperative until after the Rebellion was wholly
suppressed. No other one indorsed or controverted this
view, except as they had previously expressed their individual opinions. But the result was unanimous that the
appointments should be made; that the current business of
the Administration and the country must go on, notwithstanding unwise and ill-considered legislation.

Questions in relation to pardons were discussed. The
President said that few had been granted, notwithstanding
the clamor that was raised. No one who had been educated
at public expense at either the Military or Naval School, no
officer of the Army or Navy, no Member of Congress who
had left his seat, no member of the Rebel government who
had deserted and gone into that service, had been pardoned,
nor did he propose at present to pardon any one of that
class. It was understood that neither Davis, Stephens, nor
any member of the Rebel Cabinet should be paroled.

The cases of Orr of South Carolina and Bennett of Kentucky came up. There was a kindly feeling towards Orr,
but not towards Bennett. Orr had resisted secession but

was compelled to go with his State, reluctantly and resistingly. Bennett went of his own accord and was a traitor to his State as well as the Union. Yet Bennett was, and is, urgently presented for pardon by Union men as well as others. This whole question is to be a troublesome one, and requires careful and discreet management. To some extent the action of the government must depend on the conduct of the Rebels and the people themselves. If they continue to organize themselves in opposition to the government, and strive to elect men on that basis, they will provoke stern measures towards themselves. One difficulty is whom to trust. All have violated their obligations as citizens by going into rebellion, and, if pardoned, will they act in better faith hereafter? Many Union men, in heart and sentiment, were forced by the State governments under which they lived into the Rebellion.

August 12, *Saturday.* Prepared a necessarily long letter to Mr. Sumner in answer to his application for President Lincoln's indorsement on Smith's papers. Found an immense crowd at the President's when I went there at 3 P.M on a little business which I could not take time to explain as I wished. It related to the dismissal of Cartter, a marine officer, whose father is presiding judge in this District, — a coarse, vulgar, strong-minded man, who will not be willing that his son should leave the service, however undeserving. His son ran away and enlisted in the marines as a private, was made an officer on his father's importunity, has been no honor to the service at any time, and cannot be retained. Wants self-respect and decent deportment. Undoubtedly I shall incur the resentment of the judge, who has a vigorous as well as a vulgar intellect, and can make himself felt. Still there is a duty to perform which I must not evade.

Edgar returned from Narragansett this morning. Says Chief Justice Chase was there, and Hooper of Boston. They seem to have a revenue steamer at their disposal.

August 14, *Monday*. Have written Rev. Mr. Boynton on the subject of an appointment at the Naval Academy while he is preparing a naval history or a history of the Navy during the great Rebellion. I advised that he should take up the latter subject, and after its publication it may be elaborated if thought best.

I find Admiral Porter willing to do, but reckless of money and law in his management of affairs. He has some good qualities for the position of Superintendent, and some which cause me apprehension. Yet I trust all will come out right. His intentions seem good if reckless, and in them there is strength and encouragement.

There is a disposition for mischief, I perceive, among some of the subordinate officers of the Treasury. They have assuming and crude notions in regard to the administration of public affairs, and evidently suppose that they are the custodians of the executive government. Some of these men are well-intentioned but narrow-minded and factious to an extent, others are wholly factious; and there are others who are doubtless corrupt. I perceive that McCulloch and some others yield to these arrogant and improper assumptions of their subordinates, and fancy that the latter can revise and countermand the orders of a Cabinet officer. A little experience and reflection will correct this weak conclusion.

August 15, *Tuesday*. Seward read a letter in relation to St. Domingo matters, to which I for some cause did not give that attention which its importance demanded. After he had read it Stanton suggested that one expression was too strong, he thought. Seward appealed to me. I asked to have the passage reread, and concurred with Stanton that more cautious language should be used.

Stanton says there is to be a large reduction of the force which is moving against the Indians; that by the 1st of October the force will be about 6000; that large supplies have gone on, but they can be diverted or deflected to New Mexico and other points, so that they will not be lost.

This whole proceeding is anything but commendable in the War Department. Stanton professes not to have been informed on the subject, and yet takes credit for doing something in the direction of reduction. When questioned, however, he gets behind Grant or Pope or some military officer. An army of twenty-two thousand and a winter campaign, which he said would cost certainly not less than fifty million and very likely eighty or one hundred million, are arranged, a great Indian war is upon us, but the Secretary of War is, or professes to be, wholly ignorant in regard to it, and of course every member of the Administration is uninformed. If Stanton is as ignorant as he professes, it is disgraceful and ominous, and it is not less so if he is not ignorant. There are some things which make me suspicious that he is not as uninformed and ignorant as he pretends. This matter of supplies, so ruinously expensive, is popular on the frontiers, with Lane and others in Kansas. I have seen enough of Stanton to know that he is reckless of the public money in fortifying himself personally. These great contracts for supplies and transportation must have been known to him. How far Grant, whom he does not like, has acted independently of him is a question.

August 16, *Wednesday*. Wrote a letter to Paul S. Forbes in relation to his engine and the trial of the Algonquin. The letter is an answer to one from him, written evidently by his lawyer and prompter, Dickerson, designedly insolent and intended to provoke retort.

But I have contrived to keep cool and, I think, to place them in the wrong, although they have control of the New York press and correspondents, who make aggravated assaults without any knowledge of the facts. Here and there silly editors, wholly ignorant of the subject, also assume to speak oracularly, and doubtless the public become in some degree prejudiced. In due time there will be correction, the truth will come out, but to some extent the slander will long remain to taint the minds of many.

August 17, *Thursday.* Alden came to-day. Said he was sent for by Porter in relation to the place made vacant by Drayton's death. In many respects I like Alden, who is, however, a sycophant and courtier, but the very steps taken by Porter must, for the present, exclude him. Porter is Superintendent of the Naval Academy and reports to the Navigation Bureau made vacant by Drayton's death. It will not do to have the Chief of that Bureau subordinate to Porter or an instrument in his hands. I apprehend that such would be the case were Alden selected. He is particularly intimate with Porter and would defer greatly to him, — be, in fact, a mere instrument to him. I shall, I think, take Jenkins for this place, though he is really, from his industry, better adapted to and must ultimately have another Bureau, either Yards and Docks or Equipment and Recruiting.

August 18, *Friday.* Senators Doolittle and Foster and Mr. Ford, who have been on a mission to the Plains, visiting New Mexico, Colorado, etc., had an interview with the President and Cabinet of an hour and a half. Their statement in relation to the Indians and Indian affairs exhibits the folly and wickedness of the expedition which has been gotten up by somebody without authority or the knowledge of the government.

Their strong protestations against an Indian war, and their statement of the means which they had taken to prevent it came in very opportunely. Stanton said General Grant had already written to restrict operations; he had also sent to General Meigs. I have no doubt a check has been put on a very extraordinary and unaccountable proceeding, but I doubt if an entire stop is yet put to war expenses.

Stanton is still full of apprehension and stories of plots

and conspiracies. I am inclined to believe he has fears, and
he evidently wishes the President to be alarmed. He had
quite a story to-day, and read quite a long affidavit from
some one whom I do not recall, stating he had been in communication with C. C. Clay and others in Canada, that
they wanted him to be one of a party to assassinate President Lincoln and his whole Cabinet. Dennison and
McCulloch and I thought the President seemed inclined to
give this rigmarole some credence. I think the story, though
plausibly got up, was chiefly humbug. Likely Stanton believes me stupid because I give so little heed to his sensational communications; but really a large portion of them
seem to me ludicrous and puerile. He still keeps up a guard
around his house, and never ventures out without a stout
man to accompany him who is ordinarily about ten feet behind him. This body-guard is, I have no doubt, paid for
by the public. He urged a similar guard for me and others.

August 19, *Saturday.* I have a letter from Eames, who is
at Long Branch, ill, and has been there for three weeks. He
informs me that Senator Sumner wrote Mrs. E., with
whom he corresponds, wishing that she and her husband
would influence me to induce the President to change his
policy. This letter Eames found on his arrival at Long
Branch, and wrote Sumner he could not change me.

Sumner bewails the unanimity of the Cabinet; says
there is unexampled unanimity in New England against
the policy of the Administration; thinks I ought to resign;
says Wade and Fessenden are intending to make vigorous
opposition against it, etc., etc.

The proceedings of the political conventions in Maine
and Pennsylvania leave no doubt in my mind that extensive operations are on foot for an organization hostile to
the Administration in the Republican or Union party.
The proceedings alluded to indicate the shape and character of this movement. It is the old radical anti-Lincoln
movement of Wade and Winter Davis, with recruits.

That Stanton has a full understanding with these men styling themselves Radicals, I have no doubt. It is understood that the Cabinet unanimously support the policy of the President. No opposition has manifested itself that I am aware. At the beginning, Stanton declared himself in favor of negro suffrage, or rather in favor of allowing, by Federal authority, the negroes to vote in reorganizing the Rebel States. This was a reversal of his opinion of 1863 under Mr. Lincoln. I have no recollection of any disavowal of the position he took last spring, although he has acquiesced in the President's policy apparently, — has certainly submitted to it without objection or remonstrance. The Radicals in the Pennsylvanian convention have passed a special resolution indorsing Mr. Stanton by name, but no other member of the Cabinet. Were there no understanding on a point made so prominent by the Radicals, such a resolution would scarcely have been adopted or drafted. Convention resolutions, especially in Pennsylvania, I count of little importance. A few intriguing managers usually prepare them, they are passed under the strain of party excitement, and the very men who voted for them will very likely go against them in two weeks. At this time, however, unusual activity has been made by Forney, Kelley, and others, and the resolution has particular significance.

August 21, *Monday.* I took a ride yesterday with Governor Dennison to Silver Spring and had a pleasant interview of a couple of hours with the elder Blair. He has great political sagacity, tact, and ability and watches with keen eyes the movements of men and parties. I find his views in most respects correspond with my own as to demonstrations now being made by ultra-partisans. He attributes much to Stanton, and suggested that General Grant ought to be made Secretary of War. Therein I differed from him.

General Rousseau called on me to-day in behalf of Commander Pendergrast, who has been suspended by court martial for two years. The sentence I have thought severe and intended to mitigate it. Admiral Porter, as well as General R., thinks P. has been sufficiently punished; says Fox has been a little vindictive in the matter. This I am unwilling to believe, although Fox has remonstrated on two occasions, when I have had the case under consideration. Pendergrast says that most of the court which tried him were retired officers, placed on the retired list by the board of which his uncle, the late Commodore P., was a member, and that they as well as others have supposed that he was a son instead of nephew of the Commodore, and he is apprehensive there was a prejudice against him on that account.

August 22, Tuesday. Seward presented some matters of interest in relation to the Spanish-American States. Spain is getting in difficulty with Chili and also Peru, and Seward writes to Mr. Perry, Secretary of Legation (J. P. Hale is Minister), suggesting arbitration, etc.

Stanton submitted some reports in regard to the health of Jeff Davis, who has erysipelas and a carbuncle. Attorney-General Speed says he is waiting to hear from associate counsel in the case. These associates, he says, are Evarts of New York and Clifford of Massachusetts, both learned and able counsel before the court, but not as distinguished for success with a jury. The President, I saw by his manner and by an inquiry which he put, had not been consulted or was not aware that these gentlemen had been selected. So with other members of the Cabinet, except Stanton and Seward. These two gentlemen had evidently been advised with by the Attorney-General, — no doubt directed him.

I would have suggested that General Butler should be associated in this trial, not that I give him unreserved confidence as a politician or statesman, but he possesses great ability, courage, strength, I may add audacity, as a lawyer, and he belongs to a school which at this time and in such a trial should have a voice. Our friends should not permit personal feelings to control them in so important a matter as selecting counsel to try such a criminal.

The President said he had invited an interview with Chief Justice Chase as a matter of courtesy, not knowing but he might have some suggestion to make as to time, place of trial, etc.; but the learned judge declined to hold conference on the subject, though not to advise on other grave and important questions when there was to be judicial action. I see the President detests the traits of the Judge. Cowardly and aspiring, shirking and presumptuous, forward and evasive; . . . an ambitious politician; possessed of mental resources yet afraid to use them, irresolute as well as ambitious; intriguing, selfish, cold, grasping, and unreliable when he fancies his personal advancement is concerned.

August 23, Wednesday. A very perceptible change of weather since yesterday. Had a call from Rev. Mr. Boynton, who proposes to write a history of the Navy during the great Rebellion. Had half an hour's conversation. Made various suggestions.

General (Commander) Carter,[1] a naval officer to whom I gave leave in the summer of 1861 to enter the army, called and proposes to relinquish the army appointment and return to his old profession.

[*August 25.*] A number of days have passed since I opened this book. On Friday, 25th, we had a pleasant Cabinet-meeting. Speed read an elaborate opinion on the authority of judges in the State of Mississippi. The President dissented wholly from some of his positions. Provisional Governor Sharkey wanted the judges appointed by him should have authority to enforce the *habeas corpus*. Speed thought they were not legally empowered to exercise judicial functions. The President thought they were. Read from his proclamation establishing a provisional govern-

---

[1] Samuel Powhatan Carter.

ment in Mississippi and said he had drawn that part of the proclamation himself and with special reference to this very question. I inquired whether the *habeas corpus* privilege was not suspended in that State so that no judge whatever could issue the writ.

A telegram from General Carleton in New Mexico gives a melancholy account of affairs in Mexico. The republican government has met with reverses, and the President, Juarez, is on our borders, fleeing to our country for protection. Seward is in trouble; all of us are, in fact. Many of the army officers are chafing to make war on the imperial government and drive the French from that country. They are regardless of the exhausted state of our affairs.

[*August* 26.] Called with Postmaster-General Dennison on the President on Saturday evening and spent a couple of hours with him conversing on the condition of the times, and matters relating to the war. The President is animated and warms up to enthusiasm when dwelling on the occurrences in Tennessee, and especially the services of General Thomas, whom he loves not less than Grant, to whom he is quite friendly. His description of the fight of Nashville is graphic and highly interesting.

[*August* 27.] On Sunday, the 27th, I took the President in my carriage, with Postmaster-General Dennison, for a ride of a couple of hours or more. Went out 14th Street, crossed Rock Creek at Pease's Mill, thence to Tenally-town, and returned via Georgetown. It was a pleasant afternoon and we all enjoyed the drive. I think it will do the President good.

August 29, *Tuesday*. At the meeting to-day Speed said he had associated with him in the case of Jeff Davis, Evarts of New York, Clifford of Massachusetts, and [no name given] of Kentucky. It was suggested that General Butler would be of use, perhaps. But the question arose whether he would be acceptable to the associate counsel. Speed said he would write to him if it were wished, and he would consult with the others. All admitted that such a man would be well in most respects, — had quickness, aptness, will, vigor, force, etc., etc., — but yet might be an unpleasant associate, and there is danger that he would think more of Benjamin F. Butler than the case in hand.

Speed says no court can be held until November in Virginia, North Carolina, or Tennessee. At that late day, the session of the Supreme Court will be so near that it will be difficult to have such a protracted trial.

The President sent for the Chief Justice a few days since with a view to confer with him as to the place, time, etc., of holding the court, but Chase put himself on his judicial reserve. Of course the President did not press the subject. Yesterday, Chase called voluntarily on the President and had some general conversation and was in the President's opinion not disinclined to talk on the very subject which he the other day declined, but he little understands the character of President Johnson if he supposes that gentleman will ever again introduce that subject to him.

Judge Chase talked more especially of the inconvenient court arrangements at Norfolk, to which place the courts had been ordered by act of Congress instead of Richmond. I inquired if the Chief Justice could not order a special session of the court at an earlier day than the fourth Tuesday of November. Speed said he undoubtedly could if so disposed. I suggested that the inquiry had best be made. The President earnestly approved the suggestion. Thought it would be well to ascertain the views of the several Departments of the government, and know whether they were harmonious. If Judge Chase was disposed, the trial might come off in October, — ample accommodation would be provided in Norfolk; but unless the Chief Justice would order a special session, there must be delay. I have seen no indications of a desire on the part of the Chief Justice to preside at the trial of Davis.

August 30, *Wednesday*. At my special request the President made an order restoring General Hawley to duty, who had been mustered out of service. Had some conversation with General Hawley, who was an original and earnest Abolitionist, on political subjects. I perceive that the negro is pretty strong on his brain. Advised him to keep within constitutional limitations and not permit humanitarian impulses to silence reason or break our governmental restraints. Suggested that he should also caution Warner not to commit his paper too strongly and inconsiderately to Radical impulses.

There is an apparent determination among those who are ingrained Abolitionists to compel the government to impose conditions on the Rebel States that are wholly unwarranted. Prominent men are striving to establish a party on the basis of equality of races in the Rebel States, for which the people are not prepared, — perhaps they never will be, for these very leaders do not believe in social equality, nor will they practice it. Mr. Sumner, who is an unmarried man, has striven to overcome what seems a natural repugnance. A negro lawyer has been presented by him to practice in the Supreme Court, and extra demonstrations of that kind have been made by him and Chief Justice Chase. Sumner, I think, has become a devotee in this matter; it is his specialty, and, not being a Constitutionalist in politics, he is sincere, I have no doubt, in his schemes. I cannot say quite as much in favor of the Chief Justice. His work is connected more closely with political party aspirations. Sumner is not divested of them. General Hawley is of that school. Wants to do for the negro. His old associates are on that idea. Many of them — most of them — would assume, and have the government assume, arbitrary power, regardless of the Constitution, to carry into effect their opinions and wishes. General H. is too intelligent for this, yet it is evident he would strain a point for the negro.

Judge Blair has been making a speech at Clarksville in

2

Maryland which appears to me to be in some respects injudicious just at this time. Yet it is a demonstration deliberately made and for a purpose. He anticipates a new formation of parties and is preparing for it in advance, all of which may be well, provided he does not go too fast and too far. I think his speech is too intensely personal to be effective. This is not the time to make assaults on Seward, perhaps not on Stanton, unless confident not only that he is right but that he will be sustained. He will not be supported by the press of either party. I am not certain that he wishes to be at present; but whether, if he loses the general confidence, he can regain it when he exhibits so much acrimony, is doubtful.

I think better of Blair than most persons will on reading his speech. He is not a malignant or revengeful man; is generous, frank, truthful, honest; scorns a mean thing, detests duplicity, and abhors a liar. He has good political and general intelligence, understands men generally very well, but I think is sometimes imposed upon. In his friendships and hates he occupies no middle ground, and sometimes, I think, judges severely and harshly. I see no reason for the onslaught on Seward at this time.

Holt is also assailed, as if Seward and Stanton were not enough. It is painful to have a man like Holt denounced. He is a stern, stubborn, relentless man, — has his faults, — but I believe is a patriot and a statesman of ability. I have esteemed him to be the ablest man in Buchanan's cabinet, and beyond any other one the principal mind to sustain the national integrity in that combination during the winter preceding the advent of President Lincoln, and I regretted that he was not preferred to Stanton as the successor of Cameron if one of that cabinet were taken. Why Blair should attack Holt, I do not understand, unless because of his identification with Stanton, which is certainly not to his credit. Blair brings out a singular and unfortunate letter of Holt's to some one in Pittsburg, which had escaped my memory, and which can hardly be excused in these days. But the changes and vicissitudes which have occurred during the last few eventful years have taught me to have forbearance for men's utterances and actions. My own language was sometimes mild and gentle when it should have been strong to resist the coming storm which I vainly hoped might be averted; at other times it was rash and almost violent when mildness and conciliation were necessary. Human foresight is short and insufficient, and indulgence is due to men in positions of responsibility who were compelled to act, and who in view of the calamities that overhung the country strove to extricate the government and country.

XXXIII

September 28. I have been absent during most of the
month of September in my native State and among the
scenes of my childhood and youth. Change is there. Of the
companions who fifty years ago it was my pleasure to love,
and who I truly believe loved me, few, only few, remain,
while of those who were in middle life or more advanced
age, men who encouraged and stood by me, who voluntarily elected me to the Legislature when I was but twenty-
four, scarcely one remains. Their children and grandchildren to some extent occupy their places, but a different
class of persons have come into the old town and much
altered its character.

Little of importance has transpired during the month.
The rebellious States are reorganizing their governments
and institutions, — submitting to results they could not
arrest or avert. In the Free States, political conventions
have been held and movements made to revivify old par-

ties, and, on the part of the extremists, or Radicals, an exhibition of intense hate towards the Rebels which bodes mischief has manifested itself.

In New York an extraordinary step, a *coup d'état*, was taken by the Democratic organization, which indorsed President Johnson and nominated Union men to some of the most important places on the ticket. A counter move was made by the Union party, which nominated an entire new ticket, and passed resolutions not remarkable in any respect.

The Massachusetts Republican convention did not like to take ground antagonistic to the Administration, although the leaders, particularly Sumner and his friends, cannot suppress their hostile feelings. Their resolutions, adopted at Worcester, are very labored, and abound more in words than distinct ideas, reminding one of the old woman who wished to scream but dared not.

In Connecticut the question of amending the State Constitution so as to erase the word "white" is pending. Some feeling among the old Abolitionists and leading politicians was exhibited, and they may, and probably will, work up some feeling in its favor; but generally the people are indifferent or opposed to it. But for the national questions before the country, the amendment would be defeated; the probabilities appeared to me in its favor. I avoided interfering in the question or expressing an opinion on the subject, but the partisans are determined to draw me out. It is asserted in the *Times* that I am opposed to negro suffrage. Two of the editors deny this and have so written me. I replied in a hasty note that no one was authorized to say I had expressed opposition to it. Since then I have had a telegram from the editor of the *Press*, Warner, asking if I am in favor of negro suffrage. Disliking to be catechized in this way and not disposed to give a categorical answer, I replied that I was in favor of intelligence, not of color for qualification for suffrage. The truth is I have little or no feeling on the subject, and as we require that the electors shall read, and have few negroes in Connecticut, I acquiesce in, rather than advocate, the amendment. I would not enslave the negro, but his enfranchisement is another question, and until he is better informed, it is not desirable that he should vote. The great zeal of Sumner and the Abolitionists in behalf of the negro voting has no responsive sympathy with me. It is a species of fanaticism, zeal without discretion. Whenever the time arrives that he should vote, the negro will probably be permitted. I am no advocate for social equality, nor do I labor for political or civil equality with the negro. I do not want him at my table, nor do I care to have him in the jury-box, or in the legislative hall, or on the bench. The negro does not vote in Connecticut, nor is he taxed. There are but a few hundreds of them. Of these perhaps not half can read and consequently cannot vote, while, if the restriction is removed, all will be taxed.

Judge Blair came to see me the day after I came back. He is preparing a reply to Judge Holt. During my absence the papers have published a statement made by Mr. Fox in relation to the Sumter expedition, which was sent to the Senate as an appendix to my reply to a call of the Senate, but that body declined to receive F.'s statement. It comes in now, aptly, with Blair's speech, and will doubtless be considered a part of the scheme. General Meigs hastened too fast to reply in order to assure Mr. Seward.

There are serious mistakes or blunders in Meigs's letter, which, however, will doubtless be corrected. Blair wished to get the armistice signed by Holt, Toucey, and Mallory, and asked if I remembered it. I told him I did, and that we had it on our files. But on sending for the volume I find it is only a copy. Yet my convictions were as positive as Blair's that the original was in the Navy Department. I thought I remembered the paper distinctly, — its color and general appearance, — but the copy does not correspond with my recollection, yet I cannot doubt it is the paper which I saw. From this difference I am admonished of the uncertainty and fallibility of human testimony.

October. Some slight indisposition and pressing duties have postponed my daily remarks. The President had expressed to me his intention to go to Richmond and Raleigh on the 3d inst., and invited me to accompany him, but I doubted if he would carry the design out, and he said on the 3d he must postpone it for the present, which I think will be for the season.

A vote was taken in Connecticut on Monday, the 2d, on the proposed Constitutional Amendment to erase the word "white" and permit the colored persons to vote. I was not surprised that the proposition was defeated by a very decided majority, yet I had expected that the question might be carried on the strong appeal to party. But there is among the people a repugnance to the negro, and a positive disinclination to lower the standard of suffrage. They will not receive the negro into their parlors on terms of social intimacy, and they are unwilling to put him in the jury-box or any political position. There are probably not five hundred colored persons who could be made electors, and the grievance is therefore not very great.

The defeat of the Constitutional Amendment has caused a great howl to be set up by certain extremists, in the State and out of it. While I might have voted affirmatively had I been in the State, I have no wailing over the negative results. I regret to witness the abuse of the *Press* and other papers on those whom it failed to convince, and who consequently voted according to their convictions. This abuse and denunciation will tend to alienate friends, and weaken the influence of the Union leaders in future elections.

The effect of the vote elsewhere will be to impair centralization, which has been setting in strong of late, and invigorate State action, and in this respect the result will be beneficent. I apprehend our extreme negro advocates are doing serious injury to the negro in their zeal in his behalf, and they are certainly doing harm to our system by insisting on the exercise of arbitrary and unauthorized power in aid of the negro.

Some of the workmen in the Philadelphia Navy Yard complained that an assessment had been levied upon them for party purposes. I had written a pretty decisive letter correcting the evil when I went to the Cabinet-meeting on Tuesday, and had given it out to be copied. After the general business before the Cabinet had been disposed of, the President took me aside and said complaints of a similar character had been made to him. I told him my own conclusion and what I had done, which he approved. The opportunity is most favorable to correct a pernicious practice, which I last year would not sanction, and which led Raymond, Thurlow Weed, and others to try to prejudice President Lincoln against me.

On Wednesday Amos Kendall called and wished me to go with him to the President. He alluded to old friendly political associations and relations between us. I was glad of the opportunity of taking him to the President, whom I was about to call upon with my letter to the Commandant of the Philadelphia Navy Yard, respecting the improper assessment of workmen. After a brief interview Mr. Kendall left, and I read my letter concerning the assessment of workmen, which the President complimented and desired it should go to other yards and be made public. [The letter follows.]

NAVY DEPARTMENT,
3 October, 1865.

SIR:

The attention of the Department has been called to an attempt recently made in Philadelphia to assess or tax for party purposes the workmen in the Navy Yard. It is claimed by those who have participated in these proceedings, that the practice has prevailed in former years, at that and other Navy Yards, of levying contributions of this character on mechanics and laborers employed by the Government.

Such an abuse cannot be permitted; and it is the object of this communication to prohibit it, wherever it may be practiced.

From inquiries instituted by the Department, on the complaint of sundry workmen, who represented that a committee had undertaken, through the agency of the masters, to collect from each of the employés in their respective departments, a sum equal to one day's labor, for party purposes — it has been ascertained that there had been received from the workmen before these proceedings were arrested, the sum of $1052.

This and all other attempts to exact money from laborers in the public service, either by compulsion or voluntary contribution, is, in every point of view, reprehensible, and is wholly and absolutely prohibited. Whatever money may have been exacted, and is now in the hands of the Masters, will be forthwith returned to the workmen from whom it was received; and any Master or other appointee of this Department who may be guilty of a repetition of this offense, or shall hereafter participate in levying contributions in the Navy Yards, from persons in the Government service, for party purposes, will incur the displeasure of the Department, and render himself liable to removal. The organization of the Yard must not be perverted to aid any party. Persons who desire to make voluntary party contributions, can find opportunities to do so, at ward or other local political meetings, and on other occasions than during working hours. They are neither to be assisted nor opposed, in this matter, by government officials. The Navy Yards must not be prostituted to any such purpose, nor will Committee men be permitted to resort thither, to make collections for any political party whatever. Working men, and others in the service of the Government, are expected and required to devote their time and energies during working hours, and while in the Yard, to the labor which they are employed to execute.

It has been also represented that some of the Masters at some of the Navy Yards employ extra hands preceding warmly contested elections, and that much of the time of these superfluous hands is devoted to party electioneering. Such an abuse, if it exists in any department of any of the Navy Yards, must be corrected. No more persons should be retained in the Navy Yards than the public service actually requires. Party gatherings and party discussions are at all times to be avoided within the Yards. It will be the duty of the Commandants of the respective Yards, and of all officers, to see that this order is observed.

Very respectfully,

Commo. Chas. H. Bell,   G. Welles,
    Commdt. Navy Yard,   Secty. of the Navy.
        New York.

(Also written to all the other Commandants of Navy Yards.)

I called on Seward on Wednesday in relation to the Stonewall, the Harriet Lane, the Florida, etc., as he was about leaving to be absent for a fortnight, and we may wish to send to Havana before he returns. After disposing of business, and I had left his room, he sent his messenger to recall me. He seemed a little embarrassed and hesitating at first, but said he wished to say to me that he had had full and free and unreserved talks recently with the President; that he had found him friendly and confiding, and more communicative than Mr. Lincoln ever had been; that he knew and could say to me that the President had for me, for him (Seward), and indeed for all the Cabinet a friendly regard; that he had no intention of disturbing any member of the Cabinet; that I had reason to be specially gratified with the President's appreciation of me. Some general conversation followed on past transactions and events. Among other things we got on to Blair's letters and speeches. He says the original armistice, alluded to by Blair, was left by Buchanan with other papers on the office table at the Executive Mansion or with the Attorney-General.

Seward, McCulloch, Harlan, and Speed were absent from Washington on Friday, the 6th, the day of the last Cabinet-meeting. No very important questions were presented and discussed. The presence of the assistants instead of the principals operates, I perceive, as an obstruction to free interchange of opinion.

At the last Cabinet-meeting in September, Seward read a strange letter addressed to one of the provisional governors, informing him that the President intended to continue the provisional governments in the several insurrectionary States until Congress assembled and should take the subject in hand with the newly formed constitutions. I was amazed, and remarked that I did not understand the question or status of the States to be as stated, and was relieved when the President said he disapproved of that part of the letter. Speed asked to have the letter again read and was evidently satisfied with it. Seward made a pencil correction or alteration that was unimportant and meaningless, when the President said very emphatically he wished no reference to Congress in any such communication, or in any such way. Stanton, I observed, remained perfectly silent though very attentive. It appeared to me that the subject was not novel to him.

In an interview with the President the Monday following (the 2d inst.), I expressed my wish that no letter should be sent defining the policy of the Administration without full and careful consideration. The President said he should see to that, and that Seward's letter as modified by himself was a harmless affair.

I have sent out another circular in relation to the appointment of masters in the navy yards. These appointments have caused great difficulty in the Department, the Members of Congress insisting on naming them, and almost without an exception the party instead of the mechanical qualifications of the man is urged. It is best to be relieved of this evil, and I shall try to cure it.

I see that Senator Grimes by letter expresses his disapproval of the Radical movements in the Iowa State Convention. Doolittle has been still more emphatic in Wisconsin. Things are working very well. The conventions in the Rebel States are discharging their duties as satisfactorily, perhaps, as could be expected. Some of the extreme Republicans, of the Sumner school, are dissatisfied, but I think their numbers are growing less. The Democrats, on the other hand, are playing what they consider a shrewd party game, by striving to take advantage of the errors and impracticable notions of the ultras. Therefore the policy of the Administration appears to be growing in favor, though the machinery of politics is at work in an opposite direction.

October 10, *Tuesday.* As I went into the President's office this morning and was passing him to enter the library, he took occasion to express his satisfaction with my circulars and his thorough conviction of their rectitude. He was exceedingly pleased with the manner of their reception by the public. Said Preston King, when last there, had advised that we should pursue a straightforward course and leave consequences to themselves.

Leaving the President, I went on to the library. Stanton and Dennison were there, and, I think, Ashton and W. E. Chandler. Harlan soon came in. Dennison almost immediately addressed me on the subject of my circular respecting assessments. He said it was likely to have an effect on other Departments. He had received this morning a petition from the clerks in the New York post-office inclosing my circular, and asking to be relieved of a five per cent assessment which had been levied upon them for party purposes. I remarked that they were proper subjects to be exempt from such a tax in times like these, that I disliked and was decidedly opposed to this whole principle of assessment of employés of the government for party objects, — if not broken up it would demoralize the government and country.

Stanton said if I had issued such a circular one year ago, we should have lost the election. I questioned the correctness of that assertion, and told him that I took the same ground then that I did now, although I issued no circular. He said he was aware I objected to assessments in the yards, but had understood that I finally backed down and consented. I assured him he was greatly mistaken; that Raymond had annoyed President Lincoln with his demands, and that I had been importuned to permit the tax to be levied but that I had never consented or changed my views, or actions, or been ever requested to do so by President Lincoln.

Dennison said that Mr. Harlan's committee — he, Harlan, being chairman — had made an assessment on all office-holders and he thought it was right. Stanton earnestly affirmed its rightfulness, and said the Democrats raised two dollars for every one raised by us. Asked if I did not pay an assessment. I told him I contributed money, but did not submit to be assessed or taxed. Harlan sat by and said nothing, though occasionally rolling up his eye and showing his peculiar smile. I told the gentlemen that, while differing with them, I was gratified to have the President with me. He came in a few moments after, and the subject was dropped.

October 11. The elections in Pennsylvania, Ohio, and Iowa come in favorable, though the vote and the majorities are reduced from the Presidential election. I am glad that the Union party has done well in Philadelphia, for if we had lost the city or given a small vote, there would have been a claim that it was in consequence of my circulars. As it is, I get no credit, but I escape censure for doing right.

October 12, *Thursday.* General Banks has received the nomination for Congress from the Middlesex district, made vacant by the resignation of Gooch, appointed Naval Officer. Stone and Griffith were competitors for the nomination, neither of them known abroad. If I mistake not, Stone has a musty reputation as a politician. While they were struggling, Banks came home from New Orleans and succeeded over both. He will probably be elected, for I see by his speech he classes himself among the Radicals and foreshadows hostility to the Administration.

The Radicals of Massachusetts are preparing to make war upon the President. This is obvious, and Sumner has been inclined to take the lead. But there is no intimacy between Banks and Sumner. They are unlike. Sumner is honest but imperious and impracticable. Banks is precisely the opposite. I shall not be surprised if Banks makes war upon the Navy Department, — not that he has manifested any open hostility to myself, but there is deep-seated animosity between him and Admiral Porter and other naval officers of his command who were on the Red River expedition.

October 13. Met General Thomas of the Army of the Tennessee at the President's. He has a fine, soldierly appearance, and my impressions are that he has, intellectually and as a civilian, as well as a military man, no superior in the service. What I saw of him to-day confirmed my previous ideas of the man. He has been no courtly carpet officer, to dance attendance at Washington during the War, but has nobly done his duty.

Little was done at the Cabinet. Three of the assistants being present instead of the principals, there was a disinclination to bring forward measures or to interchange views freely. Stanton took occasion before the President came in to have a fling at my circular against party assessments, which seems to annoy him. I told him the principles and rule laid down in that circular were correct; that the idea which he advocated of a tax upon employés and office-holders was pernicious and dangerous, would embitter party contests and, if permitted to go on, would carry the country to the devil. Stanton said he then wished to go to the devil with it; that he believed in taxing office-holders for party purposes, compelling them to pay money to support the Administration which appointed them. Weed and Raymond are in this thing, and mad with me for cutting off supplies.

October 21. Have been unable to write daily. The President has released A. H. Stephens, Regan, Trenholm, and others on parole, and less dissatisfaction has manifested itself than I expected.

The Episcopal convention at Philadelphia is a disgrace to the church, to the country, and the times. Resolutions expressing gratification on the return of peace and the removal of the cause of war have been voted down, and much abject and snivelling servility exhibited, lest the Rebels should be offended. There are duties to the country as well as the church.

Montgomery Blair made a speech to a Democratic meeting at Cooper Institute, New York. As much exception will be taken to the audience he selected as to his remarks. Although he has cause for dissatisfaction, it is to be regretted that he should run into an organization which is hostile to those who have rallied for the Union. True, they profess to support the President and approve his course. This is perhaps true in a degree, but that organization was factious during the War, and was in sympathy with the Rebels prior to hostilities. Their present attitude is from hatred of the Republicans more than sympathy with the President. Those of us who are Democrats and who went into the Union organization ought to act in good faith with our associates, and not fly off to those who have imperilled the cause, without fully reflecting on what we have done, and are doing. Perhaps Blair feels himself justified, but I would not have advised his course.

Wendell Phillips has made an onset on the Administration and its friends, and also on the extremists, hitting Banks and Sumner as well as the President. Censorious and unpractical, the man, though possessed of extraordinary gifts, is a useless member of society and deservedly without influence.

Secretary Seward has been holding forth at Auburn in a studied and long-prepared speech, intended for the special laudation and glory of himself and Stanton. It has the artful shrewdness of the man and of his other half, Thurlow Weed, to whom it was shown, and whose suggestions I think I can see in the utterances. Each and all the Departments are shown up by him; each of the respective heads is mentioned, with the solitary exception of Mr. Bates, omitted by design.

The three dernier occupants of the Treasury are named with commendation, so of the three Secretaries of the Interior and the two Postmasters-General. The Secretary of the Navy has a bland compliment, and, as there have not been changes in that Department, its honors are divided between the Secretary and the Assistant Secretary. But

Stanton is extolled as one of the lesser deities, — is absolutely divine. His service covers the War and months preceding, — sufficient to swallow Cameron, who is spoken of as honest and worthy. Speed, who is the only Attorney-General mentioned, is made an extraordinary man of extraordinary abilities and mind, for like Stanton he falls in with the Secretary of State.

It is not particularly pleasing to Seward that I, with whom he has had more controversy on important questions than with any man in the Cabinet, — I, a Democrat, who came in at the organization of the Lincoln Cabinet and have continued through without interruption, especially at the dark period of the assassination and the great change when he was helpless and of no avail, — it is not pleasing to him that I should alone have gone straight through with my Department while there have been changes in all others, and an interregnum in his own. Hence two heads to the Navy Department, — my Assistant's and mine. Had there been two or three changes as in the others, this remark would probably not have been made. Yet there is an artful design to stir up discord by creating ill blood or jealousy between myself and Fox, whom they do not love, which is quite as much in the vein of Weed as of Seward. I have no doubt the subject and points of this speech were talked over by the two. Indeed, Seward always consults Weed when he strikes a blow.

His assumptions of what he has done, and thought, and said are characteristic by reason of their arrogance and error. He was no advocate for placing Johnson on the ticket as Vice-President, as he asserts, but was for Hamlin, as was every member of the Cabinet but myself. Not that they were partisans, but for a good arrangement.

December 1. It is some weeks since I have had time to write a word in this diary. In the mean time many things have happened which I desired to note but none of very great importance. What time I could devote to writing when absent from the Department has been given to the preparation of my Annual Report. That is always irksome and hard labor for me. All of it has been prepared at my house out of the office hours, except three mornings when I have remained past my usual hour of going to the Department.

My reports are perhaps more full and elaborate than I should make them; but if I wish anything done I find I must take the responsibility of presenting it. Members of Congress, though jealous of anything that they consider, or which they fear others will consider, dictation, are nevertheless timid as regards responsibility. When a matter is accomplished they are willing to be thought the father of it, yet some one must take the blows which the measure receives in its progress. I therefore bring forward the principal subjects in my report. If they fail, I have done my duty. If they are carried, I shall contend with no one for the credit of paternity. I read the last proof pages of my report this evening.

Members of Congress are coming in fast, though not early. Speaker Colfax came several days since. His coming was heralded with a flourish. He was serenaded, and delivered a prepared speech, which was telegraphed over the country and published the next morning. It is the offspring of an intrigue, and one that is pretty extensive. The whole proceeding was premeditated.

My friend Preston King committed suicide by drowning himself in the Hudson River. His appointment as Collector was unfortunate. He was a sagacious and honest man, a statesman and legislator of high order and of unquestioned courage in expressing his convictions and resolute firmness in maintaining them. To him, a Democrat and Constitutionalist, more than to any other one man may be ascribed the merit of boldly meeting the arrogant and imperious slaveholding oligarchy and organizing the party which eventually overthrew them. While Wendell Phillips, Sumner, and others were active and fana-

2

tical theorists, Preston King was earnest and practical.
J. Q. Adams and Giddings displayed sense and courage, but
neither of them had the faculty which K. possessed for con-
centrating, combining, and organizing men in party measures and action. I boarded in the same house with King
in 1846 when the Wilmot Proviso was introduced on an
appropriation bill. Root and Brinkerhoff of Ohio, Rath-
bun and Grover and Stetson [sic] [1] of New York, besides
Wilmot and some few others whom I do not recall, were in
that combination, and each supposed himself the leader.
They were indeed all leaders, but King, without making
pretensions, was the man, the hand, that bound this sheaf
together. From the day when he took his stand King
never faltered. There was not a more earnest party man,
but he would not permit the discipline and force of party
to carry him away from his honest convictions. Others
quailed and gave way but he did not. He was not eloquent
or much given to speech-making, but could state his case
clearly, and his undoubted sincerity made a favorable
impression always.

Not ever having held a place where great individual and
pecuniary responsibility devolved upon him, the office of
Collector embarrassed and finally overwhelmed him.

Some twenty-five years ago he was in the Retreat for the
Insane in Hartford, and there I knew him. He became
greatly excited during the Canadian rebellion and its disastrous termination and the melancholy end of some of his
townsmen had temporarily impaired his reason. But it was
brief; he rapidly recovered, and, unlike most persons who
have been deranged, it gave him no uneasiness and he spoke
of it with as much unconcern as of a fever. The return of
the malady led to his committing suicide. Possessed of the
tenderest sensibilities and a keen sense of honor, the party
exactions of the New York politicians, the distress, often

[1] There was no Stetson in Congress at the time. Perhaps Wheaton of
New York, who was one of the supporters of the Proviso, was the man
whom Mr. Welles had in mind.

PRESTON KING

magnified, of those whom he was called upon to displace, the party requirements which Weed, who boarded with him, and others demanded, greatly distressed him, and led to the final catastrophe.

King was a friend and pupil of Silas Wright, with whom he studied his profession; was the successor of that grand statesman in both branches of Congress. Both had felt most deeply the bad faith and intrigue which led to the defeat of Van Buren in 1844, and to the ultimate downfall of the Democratic party, for the election of Polk, Pierce, and Buchanan were but flickering efforts to rekindle the fires of the old organizations. Confidence and united zeal never again prevailed, and parties subsequently took a sectional or personal character.

December 3. Told the President I disliked the proceedings of the Congressional caucus on Saturday evening. The resolution for a joint committee of fifteen to whom the whole subject of admission of Representatives from States which had been in rebellion [should be referred] without debate was in conflict with the spirit and letter of the Constitution, which gives to each house the decision of election of its own members, etc. Then in appointing Stevens, an opponent of State rights, to present it there was something bad. The whole was, in fact, revolutionary, a blow at our governmental system, and there had been evident preconcert to bring it about. The President agreed with me, but said they would be knocked in the head at the start. There would be a Representative from Tennessee who had been a loyal Member of the House since the War commenced, or during the War, who could present himself, and so state the case that he could not be controverted. I expressed my gratification if this could be accomplished, — knowing he alluded to Maynard, — but suggested a doubt whether the intrigue which was manifest by the resolution, the designation of Stevens, and Colfax's speech had not gone too far.

Congress organized about the time this conversation took place. Maynard was put aside, I think by concert between himself and the Radical leaders. The resolution introduced by Stevens passed by a strict party vote. In the Senate, Sumner introduced an avalanche of radical — and some of them absurd — resolutions. These appeared to have absorbed the entire attention of that body, which adjourned without the customary committee to wait upon the President and inform him that Congress was organized. This was not unintentional. There was design in it.

Fogg of New Hampshire, our late Minister to Switzerland, came to see me this evening with Chandler, Assistant Secretary of the Treasury.

The recall of Fogg was an unwise, unjust, and I think an unpolitic act on the part of Seward, and I shall not be surprised if he has cause to rue it. Fogg was associated with me on the National Executive Committee in the Presidential campaign of 1860, and was brought in particularly intimate relations with Mr. Lincoln at that time. No one, perhaps, knows better than F. the whole workings in relation to the formation of the Cabinet of 1861. These he detailed very minutely this evening. Much of it I had known before. He has a remarkable memory, and all the details of 1860 and 1861 were impressed upon his mind. He was the first to bring me assurance that I was selected for the Cabinet from New England. I thought at the time his, F.'s, original preferences were in another direction, although the selection of myself was, he then and now assured me, acceptable to him. At that time F., listening to Seward's friends, believed he would not accept an appointment in the Cabinet. Such were the givings-out of his friends and of Seward himself. I told F. at the time, as he still recollects, he was deceiving himself, and that Mr. Lincoln was in a strange delusion if he believed it.

Weed tried to induce Mr. Lincoln to visit Mr. Seward at Auburn. Said General Harrison went to Lexington in 1841 to see Mr. Clay, who advised in the formation of that

Cabinet. Mr. Lincoln declined to imitate Harrison. The next effort was to try to have a meeting at Chicago, but this Mr. L. also declined. But he did invite Hamlin to meet him there. On his way Hamlin was intercepted by Weed, who said the offer of the State Department was due to Mr. Seward, but S. would decline it. The courtesy, however, was, he claimed, due to Mr. S. and to New York. H. was persuaded, and Mr. L. intrusted him with a letter tendering the appointment to Seward.

Shortly after the commencement of the session of Congress in December, 1860, Fogg says Hamlin, when coming down from the Capitol one afternoon after the adjournment of the Senate, fell in company with Seward, or was overtaken by him. They walked down the avenue together, Seward knowing H. had been to Chicago. On reaching Hamlin's hotel, he invited S. to go in, and a full conversation took place, S. declaring he was tired of public life and that he intended to resign his seat or decline a reëlection and retire, that there was no place in the gift of the President which he would be willing to take. Several times he repeated that he would not go into the Cabinet of Mr. Lincoln. Having heard these refusals in various forms, Hamlin then told him he had a letter from Mr. Lincoln, which he produced. Seward, H. says to Fogg, trembled and was nervous as he took it. He read the letter, put it in his pocket, and said, while his whole feelings were repugnant to a longer continuance in public employment, he yet was willing to labor for his country. He would, therefore, consult his friends before giving a final answer. The next, or succeeding, day he left for New York, but before going he mailed a letter to the President elect accepting the appointment. Hamlin repeated all the facts to Fogg last week, so far as he was concerned.

Great efforts were made to secure the Treasury for Cameron. This was a part of the programme of Weed and Seward. I have always understood that Mr. Lincoln became committed to this scheme in a measure, though it was unlike him. Fogg explains it in this way: In the summer and fall a bargain was struck between Weed and Cameron. The latter went to Albany and then to Saratoga, where he spent several days with the intriguers. Cameron subsequently tried to get an invitation that fall to Springfield, but Lincoln would not give it. This annoyed the clique. After the election, Swett, who figured then as a confidential friend and intimate of Lincoln, not without some reason, was sent, or came, East to feel the public pulse. At a later day he went to California and had a finger in the Alameda quicksilver mine. Swett was seized by Weed and Company, open rooms and liquors were furnished by the New York junto, and his intimacy with Lincoln was magnified. Cameron took him to his estate at Lochiel and feasted him. Here the desire of Cameron to go to Springfield was made known to Swett, who took upon himself to extend an invitation in Mr. Lincoln's name. With this he took a large body-guard and went to Springfield. Although surprised, Mr. Lincoln could not disavow what Swett had done. Cameron was treated civilly; his friends talked, etc. After his return, Mr. Lincoln wrote him that in framing his Cabinet he proposed giving him a place, either in the Treasury or the War Department. Cameron immediately wrote, expressing his thanks and accepting the Treasury. Mr. Lincoln at once wrote that there seemed some misapprehension and he therefore withdrew his tender or any conclusive arrangement until he came to Washington. I have heard some of these things from Mr. L[incoln]. Fogg, who now tells them to me, says he knows them all.

Mrs. Lincoln has the credit of excluding Judd of Chicago from the Cabinet. The President was under great personal obligations to Judd, and always felt and acknowledged it. When excluded from the Cabinet, he selected the mission to Berlin.

Caleb Smith was brought in at a late hour and after Judd's exclusion. Weed and Seward had intended to bring in Emerson Etheridge and Graham of North Carolina, and

Smith was adopted when the New York junto could do no better.

After the President came to Washington, a decided on-set was made by the anti-Seward men of New York and others against Chase. An earlier movement had been made, but not sufficient to commit the President. Senator Wade of Ohio did not favor Chase. Governor Dennison was strongly for him, and Wade, who disliked Seward, finally withdrew opposition to C. But about the time I reached Washington on the 1st of March another hitch had taken place. I had remained away until invited, and had been mixed up with none of the intrigues.

The President (Lincoln) told me on Sunday, 3d March, that there was still some trouble, but that he had become satisfied he should arrange the matter. Fogg tells me that Greeley and others who were here attending to the rightful construction of the Cabinet had deputed him to call upon the President and ascertain if Chase was to be excluded. A rumor to that effect had got abroad and Lamon, a close friend of Lincoln (too close), was offering to bet two to one that C. would not have the Treasury. Fogg called on the President, but first Mrs. L. and then Seward interrupted them. On Tuesday, the 5th, at 7 A.M., Fogg and Carl Schurz called on the President to make sure of Chase. Seward followed almost immediately. Lincoln, in a whisper, told F. all was right, and subsequently informed him that he had been annoyed and embarrassed by Seward on the 1st of March, who came to him and said that he, S., had not been consulted as was usual in the formation of the Cabinet, that he understood Chase had been assigned to the Treasury, that there were differences between himself and Chase which rendered it impossible for them to act in harmony, that the Cabinet ought, as General Jackson said, to be a unit. Under these circumstances and with his con-viction of duty and what was due to himself, he must insist on the excluding of Mr. Chase if he, Seward, remained. Mr. Lincoln expressed his surprise after all that had taken place and with the great trouble on his hands, that he should be met with such a demand on this late day. He requested Mr. S. to further consider the subject.

The result was that Mr. Lincoln came to the conclusion if Seward persisted, he would let him go and make Dayton, of New Jersey, Secretary of State. But Seward did not persist.

December 5. The organization of Congress was easily effected. There had been manifestly preliminary arrangements, made by some of the leading spirits. Stevens's resolution was passed by a strict party vote. The new Members, and others weak in their understandings, were taken off their legs, as was designed, before they were aware of it.

In the hurry and intrigue no committee was appointed to call on the President. I am most thoroughly convinced there was design in this, in order to let the President know that he must wait the motion of Congress.

I think the message, which went in this P.M., will prove an acceptable document. The views, sentiments, and doctrines are the President's, not Seward's. He may have suggested verbal emendations; nothing except what related to foreign affairs. But the President himself has vigorous common sense and on more than one occasion I have seen him correct Seward's dispatches.[1]

December 6. Seward, apprehending a storm, wants a steamer to take him to Cuba. Wishes to be absent a fortnight or three weeks. Thinks he had better be away; that the war will be pretty strong upon us for the first few weeks of the session and he had better show the Members that we care nothing about them by clearing out.

A court martial of high officers in the case of Craven, who declined to encounter the Stonewall, has made it-

[1] I became satisfied subsequently that none of the Cabinet had any more than myself to do with it. — G. W.

self ridiculous by an incongruous finding and award which
I cannot approve. It is not pleasant to encounter so large
a number of officers of high standing, but I must do my
duty if they do not.

December 7. This is a day of National Thanksgiving.
Heard a vigorous sermon from Mr. Lewis. Should not
subscribe to all his doctrines, but his sermon increased my
estimate of him.

Seward called at my house. Wished me to examine and
put an estimate on the French possessions in the West
Indies, the Spanish Main, and Gulf of St. Lawrence. He
did not explain himself further. He may think of buying
France out of Mexico, but he mistakes that government
and people. Besides we do not want those possessions. If
we could have Martinique or Guadaloupe as a naval or
coaling-station, we should embrace the opportunity of getting either, but we want only one. We do not want [inde-
cipherable]. The islands in the [Gulf of] St. Lawrence we
want, and so do the French, as fishing-stations.

December 8, *Friday.* Sumner called on me with young
Bright. We had quite a talk on the policy of the Government, and his own views. Sumner's vanity and egotism
are great. He assumes that the Administration is wholly
wrong, and that he is beyond peradventure right; that
Congress has plenary powers, the Executive none, on reestablishing the Union. He denounced the policy of the
President on the question of organizing the Rebel States
as the greatest and most criminal error ever committed by
any government. Dwelt on what constitutes a republican
government; says he has read everything on the subject
from Plato to the last French pamphlet. Tells me that
a general officer from Georgia had informed him within a
week that the negroes of that State were better qualified to
establish and maintain a republican government than the
whites. He says that Seward, McCulloch, and myself are

the men who have involved the President in this transcendent error, — I, a New England man, New England's representative in the Cabinet, have misrepresented New England sentiment. McCulloch was imbued with the pernicious folly of Indiana, but Seward and myself were foully, fatally culpable in giving our countenance and support to the President in his policy.

I insisted it was correct, that the country aside from heated politics approved it, and asked if he supposed there was any opposition to that policy in the Cabinet. He said he knew Stanton was opposed to it, and when I said I was not aware of it, he seemed surprised. He asked if I had read his Worcester speech. I told him I had but did not indorse it. He replied, "Stanton does." "Stanton," said he, "came to Boston at that time; the speech was thrown into the cars, and he had read it before I met him. Stanton complimented the speech. I said it was pretty radical or had pretty strong views. Stanton said it was none too strong, that he approved of every sentiment, every opinion and word of it."

I told Sumner I did not understand Stanton as occupying that position, and I apprehended the President did not so understand him. I told him that I well recollected that on one occasion last spring, when I was in the War Department, he and Dawes and Gooch came in there. He said, "Yes, and Colfax was there." "I recollect he was. Stanton took out his project for organizing a government in North Carolina. I had heard it read on the last day of Mr. Lincoln's life, and had made a suggestion respecting it, and the project had been modified. Some discussion took place at the War Department on the question of negro suffrage. Stanton said he wanted to avoid that topic. You [Sumner] wanted to meet it. When that discussion opened I left, for I knew I could not agree with you."

Sumner said he well recollected that meeting; that he and Colfax had proposed modifications of the plan and put it in an acceptable shape, but that we had upset it. One other member of the Cabinet had written him a few days before he left home expressing sympathy with him, and one other had spoken equally cordially to him since he arrived here. "You may have had a letter from Speed," I remarked. "No," said he, "but Speed has had a conversation with me."

I think Harlan must be the man, yet my impressions were that Harlan held a different position. Perhaps Iowa has influenced him. Our conversation, though earnest, was not in anger or with any acrimony. He is confident that he shall carry Stevens's resolution through the Senate, and be able to defeat the President in his policy.

December 9, *Saturday.* Mr. Fox informed me a day or two since that he had an offer of the charge of a coal company in Pennsylvania. Thinks they will give him very high pay. Will not go unless they do. He spoke of it again to-day. Wishes to go to Pennsylvania for a few days next week. I should personally regret to lose either him or Faxon. Each seems indispensable to me. It would be a job to train others.

December 11, *Monday.* I gave the President a full relation of my interview with Sumner. He was much interested and maintains well his position. I think they will not shake him. Sumner sent me through the mail a newspaper containing a memorial for the impeachment of the President. He marked and underscored certain passages which he said — wrote on the margin — were answers to some of my questions put to him in our conversation. The attack upon the President is coarse and unworthy of a thought.

December 12, *Tuesday.* Not a very long session of the Cabinet. Some conversation in regard to the Rebel leaders led me to inquire whether it might not be best to parole Mallory, who has written me personally. He offers to make disclosures and assist in reëstablishing Union feeling. Stanton objected; says Judge Holt advises his trial, etc.

Senator Nye called and had a long talk with me, chiefly in regard to the Rebels. Is pretty strongly touched with the Sumner notions, but seems disposed to recant and consider suggestions. To him and others I have stated my objections to the Stevens resolution. Most of the Members have said their principal object was to have the two houses in perfect accord and of one mind. I have declared this an indirect attempt to defeat or evade the Constitution, which intended separate action. Hence the two branches. This proposed committee, I maintain, is revolutionary and calculated to promote, if not designed to create, alienation and sectional parties. Nye says the resolution will be disemboweled and of little moment, but Nye himself is unreliable.

December 13, *Wednesday*. The Radicals have been busy. They are feeling their way now. The President has been deceived, I think, in some persons in whom he has confided, and the patronage of the government, without his being aware of it, has been turned against the Administration.

December 14, *Thursday*. Admiral Farragut came this morning, and the general order setting aside the doings of his court was printed and handed in shortly after his arrival. The proceedings were a shocking jumble, a fellow feeling probably among some members of the court. I should not be surprised if Farragut's kind and generous heart acquiesced against his better judgment, but I do not know. We had some talk in regard to promotions. It will make lifelong enmities to supersede. F. suggests that medals will answer an equal purpose.

December 15, *Friday*. A sudden change of weather. Intensely cold. General Grant was in the council-room at the

Executive Mansion to-day, and stated the result of his observations and conclusions during his journey South. He says the people are more loyal and better-disposed than he expected to find them, and that every consideration calls for the early reëstablishment of the Union. His views are sensible, patriotic, and wise. I expressed a wish that he would make a written report, and that he communicate also freely with the Members of Congress.

December 16, *Saturday.* Senator Sumner called again this evening. He is almost beside himself on the policy of the Administration, which he denounces with great bitterness. The President had no business to move, he says, without the consent and direction of Congress. I asked him if the Southern States were to have no postmasters, no revenue officers, no marshals, etc. I said to him: "There are two lines of policy before us. One is harsh, cold, distant, defiant; the other kind, conciliatory, and inviting. Which," said I, "will soonest make us a united people?" He hesitated and gave me no direct answer, but said the President's course was putting everything back. This I told him was a general assertion; that conciliation, not persecution, was our policy, and therein we totally disagreed with him.

It was not right to accuse him, he said, of a persecuting spirit. He had advised clemency, had taken ground against the execution of Jefferson Davis, and asked if I was opposed to his being hung. I told him that I was not prepared to say that I was, and while he was so charitable towards Davis, he was very different toward all others South, though a large portion of the people were opposed to secession. I stated to him the views of General Grant, who had found the people disposed to acquiesce and become good citizens, — that he found those who had been most earnest and active in the Rebellion were the most frank and thorough in their conversion. Governor McGrath admitted his error, was satisfied slavery was a curse, had no wish for its restoration; but Governor Aiken, who has been passively loyal during the whole years of the war, was wanting some apprentice system, introduction of coolies, or some process for legal organized labor. While McGrath had made great advances, Aiken had made none. Sumner wanted to know what Grant's opinion was worth as compared with Chase's. I valued it highly, for it seemed to me practical common sense from a man of no political knowledge or aspiration, while Chase theorized and had great political ambition.

Sumner closed up with a violent denunciation of the provisional governors, especially Perry and Parsons, and said that a majority of Congress was determined to overturn the President's policy.

December 18, *Monday*. Called on Secretary of the Treasury in behalf of Pease of Janesville for collector. He, McCulloch, defers too much to the dictates of Members of Congress, who have personal objects in view, and many of them unfriendly to the Administration. Told him of my interview with Sumner. McCulloch said in regard to Stanton that if he had said to Sumner he approved of the Worcester speech, he was a double-dealer, — wore two faces, — that if really opposed to the President's policy he ought not to remain in the Cabinet.

On my way, returning to the Navy Department, I called and had an interview with the President. Told him of my conversation with Sumner, and that I was confirmed in the conviction that a deep and extensive intrigue was going on against him. He seemed aware of it, but not yet of its extent or of all the persons engaged in it. I remarked that the patronage of the Executive had, I believed, been used to defeat the policy of the Executive, and a summary removal of one or two mischievous men at the proper time would be effective and salutary. He said he should not hesitate one moment in taking off the heads of any of that class of busybodies.

I showed him a copy of the *New Orleans Tribune* which

Sumner had sent me, with passages underscored in a memorial for the impeachment of the President. He wished the copy and I gave it to him.

Called on Dennison this evening and had a full and free interchange with him. He inquired if I had ever heard a distinct avowal from Seward on the question of negro suffrage or the provisional governments, or from Stanton explicitly in its favor. I replied that I had not and he said he had not. He tells me that he hears from some of Stanton's intimates that he will probably soon resign. This is mere trash, unless he finds himself about being cornered; then he will make a merit of what cannot be avoided. Dennison ridicules the flagrant humbug which Seward and the papers have got up of Stanton's immense labors, which are really less than those of his own, McCulloch's, or mine. Grant, Meigs, and others discharge the labors for which S. gets credit. D. intends leaving to-morrow for Ohio, to be absent for ten days. Wants me to accompany him in the morning to the President.

December 19, *Tuesday*. Cabinet-meeting. Not much of special interest. Harlan brought forward a little complication with a Rhode Island editor, in which he was involved when chairman of the electioneering committee in 1864. He was rather laughed down.

Dennison called for me this A.M. to go to the President. We had over half an hour's conversation on the graver questions before Congress, and the factious partisan intrigues that are being carried on.

Dennison had three or four important post-office appointments which he submitted, and said they were recommended by Members of Congress. I asked if he knew their status on the great questions pending. He said he had not made that inquiry. I asked if the time had not arrived when we should know who was who, and what we were doing to fortify or weaken ourselves and the cause of right. The President said he thought it a duty.

December 20, *Wednesday*. Senator Sumner, by his impetuous violence, will contribute to put things right beyond any other man. The President's message and General Grant's letter seem to have made him demented. Some who have acted with him and been indoctrinated in his extreme views are suddenly roused to consciousness.

December 21, *Thursday*. Chandler, Assistant Secretary of the Treasury, sent me a note this evening, stating that a pardon had been proposed for Pasco, recently convicted, after long struggles and delays, of a series of outrageous frauds and villainies upon the Government. Pasco was master plumber in the Philadelphia Navy Yard, one of a combination of thieves, cheats, and rascals. He was the principal scoundrel of the gang. He acknowledges that he had signed fraudulent certificates; in one instance admits that a party had delivered 20,000 pounds of copper, for which he was paid, when he actually delivered but 16,000; in another instance for 25,000 when only 19,000 was delivered. He received $8200 for the last false certificate, or one third of the swindle, the Government losing or being cheated out of about $26,000 in a single transaction. So of the former. Specifications of eleven distinct cheats similar to these, some of them of larger amounts, besides cases of actual theft, were proven on this fellow. He plead guilty, and was a week or two since sentenced to eighteen months imprisonment. Judge Cadwalader gave light punishment for the alleged reason that Pasco plead guilty and had made restitution when he could not escape conviction and fine. How much he may have cheated and defrauded the Government without detection cannot be known.

I called on the President after receiving Chandler's note and stated the facts. He was a good deal disturbed and seemed unable to express himself. He is evidently surprised, and I apprehend has blindly committed himself for a pardon. He says a large portion of the Pennsylvania delegation applied for the pardon, the district attorney among them, also a portion of the jury.

Senator Harris had quite an interview with me. Our principal chat was on the great question and he expresses himself as concurring in my opinions.

December 22, Friday. McCulloch, Stanton, and Dennison are absent from Washington. Seward read a letter from Bigelow at Paris, which indicates peace, though all the diplomats here believe a war inevitable. Seward represents that Montholon was scared out of his wits when General Logan was appointed to Mexico. He certainly is not a very intelligent or cultured diplomat. The horizon is not perfectly clear, but the probabilities are peaceful. Had a talk with the President on the subject of Pasco. Chandler was the attorney of the Department in this investigation and prosecution at the Philadelphia Navy Yard, and I had him state the case to the President. He presented the whole very well, confirming all that I had stated, and making the case stronger against Pasco. The President was puzzled and avoided any direct answer. I have little doubt he has been imposed upon and persuaded to do a very improper thing. But we shall see. This case presents the difficulties to be surmounted in bringing criminals to justice. Pasco was a public officer, an active partisan, very popular and much petted by leading party men in official position. Detected in cheating and stealing, public men for a time thought the Department was harsh and severe in bringing him to trial. Objections were made against his being tried by court martial, and he was turned over to the civil courts. But a trial could not be had. Term after term it was carried along. Confessions from others implicated and the books and documents produced were so conclusive that finally he plead guilty and disgorged so far as he was actually detected. In consequence of his pleading guilty and making restitution of the amounts clearly ascertained, Judge Cadwalader gave him a mild sentence of only one year and a half of imprisonment. Having, after a long struggle, reached this stage, the

2

politicians and the court favoring him, we now have the President yielding to the pressure of Members of Congress, and, without inquiry or a call for the records or the facts, pardoning this infamous leader of fraud and crime. The influence will be pernicious, and scoundrels will be strengthened. I shall be glad to know that the President has not committed himself irretrievably.

December 23, *Saturday.* R. J. Meigs called on me by request of the President in relation to Captain Meade, who is under suspension, having been convicted and sentenced last May. He now, through his friend Meigs, appeals to the President. I told him there was no appeal. He could have a pardon from the President, or perhaps he could order the proceedings to be set aside.

A late general order prohibiting officers from coming to Washington without permission troubles Meade, who claims this is his residence and that he is here on private business. Fox protests against his being here intriguing and annoying the President, Department, Congress, and others, and has appealed to me earnestly and emphatically to order Meade to leave Washington, but it is one of those cases which we cannot enforce arbitrarily, although no injustice would be done. He has some excuse for being in Washington, and we must not be tyrants.

Governor Pease left to-day. His brother John went three or four days since. Yesterday, when all the others had withdrawn from the Cabinet council but the President, Seward, and myself, — and perhaps Chandler, Assistant Secretary of the Treasury, who had been present, — Seward inquired if there was any truth in the report or rumor that Stanton had left, or was about to leave, the Cabinet. The President replied warmly, as it seemed to me, that he had not heard of any such rumor. Seward said it was so stated in some of the papers, but he had supposed there was nothing in it, for he and Stanton had an understanding to the effect that Stanton would remain as long as he did, or would give him notice if he changed. The President said he presumed it was only rumor, that he reckoned there was not much in it; he had heard nothing lately and we might as well keep on for the present without any fuss. Seward said he knew Stanton had talked this some time ago. "I reckon that is all," said the President.

Seward had an object in this talk. He knows Stanton's views and thoughts better than the President does. The inquiry was not, therefore, for information on that specific point. If it was to sound the President, or to draw out any expression from me, he wholly failed, for neither gave him an explicit reply.

December 26, *Tuesday.* Captain Walker, of the De Soto, called last evening. He has been actively engaged at Cape Haytien, and should not have left with his vessel until the arrival of another. Seward made a formal request that he should be recalled and reprimanded on the *ex parte* statement of the consul, who himself was in error. I declined acceding to Seward's strange request, and desired him to possess himself of all the facts. Subsequently he wrote me approving Walker's course, and told me he should require an explanation from Folsom, the consul.

I have detailed the De Soto to take Seward to Cuba, and he obscurely hints that his ultimate destination will be some point on the Mexican coast. Has mystical observations and givings-out. I give them little credit, as he seems to be aware. After some suggestions of a public nature, he subsides into matters private, intimating a wish that it should be understood he goes for his health, for a relaxation, wishes to escape the tumult and reception of New Year's Day, wants the factionists in Congress should understand he cares little for them and has gone off recreating at the only time they are leveling their guns at us.[1]

[1] Stanton contrived to have the President surrounded most of the time by his detectives, or men connected with the military service who are creatures of the War Department. Of course, much that was said to the

No very important matters before the Cabinet. Seward had a long story about Mrs. Cazneau[1] and St. Domingo. I judge from his own statement or manner of stating, and from his omission to read Mrs. C.'s communication, that he has committed some mistakes which he does not wish to become public.

December 27, Wednesday. Have ordered Raphael Semmes to be arrested. He was, I see by the papers, taken in Mobile, and will soon be here. There are some nice points to be decided in his case, and I should have been glad had he absented himself from the country, though his case is one of the most aggravated and least excusable of the whole Rebel host. He did not belong in the Rebel region and has not therefore the poor apology of those who shelter themselves under the action of their States; he was educated and supported by that government which he deserted in disregard of his obligations and his oath; he made it his business to rob and destroy the ships and property of his unarmed countrymen engaged in peaceful commerce; when he finally fought and was conquered he practiced a fraud, and in violation of his surrender broke faith, and without ever being exchanged fought against the Union at Richmond; escaping from that city, he claims to have been included in Johnston's surrender, and therefore not amenable for previous offenses. Before taking this step, I twice brought the subject before the President and Cabinet, each and all of whom advised, or concurred in the propriety of, the arrest and trial of Semmes. It is a duty which I could

President in friendly confidence went directly to Stanton. In this way a constant espionage was maintained on all that transpired at the White House. Stanton, in all this time had his confidants among the Radicals — opponents of the President — in Congress, — a circle to whom he betrayed the measures and purposes of the President and with whom he concocted schemes to defeat the measures and policy of the Administration. The President knew my opinion and convictions of Stanton's operations and of Stanton himself. — G. W.

[1] General William L. Cazneau was the special agent of the United States in the Dominican Republic, and the negotiations for the purchase of the Bay of Samaná were conducted through him.

not be justified in evading, yet I shall acquire no laurels in the movement. But when the actors of to-day have passed from the stage, and I with them, the proceedings against this man will be approved.

December 28, *Thursday.* Senator Morgan tells me that Sumner grows more radical and violent in his views and conduct on the subject of reëstablishing the Union, declares he will oppose the policy of the Administration, and acts, Morgan says, as if demented. It has been generally supposed that Wilson would occupy a different position from Sumner, but Morgan says they will go together. Morgan himself occupies a rather equivocal position. That is, he will not, I am satisfied, go to the extreme length of Sumner. Yet he does not frankly avow himself with the President, nor does he explicitly define his opinions, if he has opinions which are fixed. He was one of the sixteen in the Republican caucus who opposed Stevens's joint resolution, while fourteen supported. As there must, I think, be a break in the Administration party, Morgan will be likely to adhere, in the main, to the Administration, and yet that will be apt to throw him into unison with the Democrats, which he will not willingly assent to, for he has personal aspirations, and shapes his course with as much calculation as he ever entered upon a speculation in sugar.

He says Grimes told him that Harlan was expecting to be President. Not unlikely, and Grimes himself has probably similar expectations. So has Morgan, and so have a number of Senators and Representatives as well as other members of the Cabinet. Both Seward and Stanton are touched with the Presidential fever, or rather have the disease strong in their system.

December 29, *Friday.* Dennison and Speed were not at the Cabinet council to-day. Not much was done. Stanton has got back, and in some allusions to Sumner appeared to think him as absurd and heretical as any of us. Of course, some one is cheated. Seward is preparing to take a cruise, and will leave to-morrow for the West Indies in the steamer De Soto. There has been much mystery in this premeditated excursion. I am amused and yet half-disgusted with Seward's nonsense. He applied to me some weeks since for a public naval vessel to proceed to Havana, and perhaps beyond. Without inquiries, I take it for granted he goes on public business, or he would not ask for a public vessel, for I told him that we had not one ready, but would have one if necessary. When it was settled he should have a vessel, he talked of a family excursion. Wanted relaxation, wanted Fred should go, said he wanted to get away from the receptions, etc., of the New Year. There is not a man in Washington who is more fond of these parades. Another time he whispers to me that Congress will try to raise the devil, and their fiercest guns will be directed to us. He prefers to be out of the way and let them spend their wrath. Once or twice he has said to me that his intention is to visit Mexico. To-day he took me aside and made some inquiries about St. Thomas, which during the war I had said might be a desirable acquisition as a coaling-station and central point in the West Indies. His action and talk indicate anticipated trouble and perhaps complications, the development or *dénouement* of which he cares not to be here to witness. From his conversation to-day, it would seem he expects no embarrassment from France. Without any distinct and explicit committal on the "Reconstruction" question, he means, in Cabinet, to be understood as with the President, and Sumner so understands. His man Raymond went off at first with Stevens and the Radicals, but after having been harnessed in that team, he has jumped out of the traces. Interest, patronage, Seward's influence have caused this facing about and may compel him to act with the Administration; but he is unreliable. I have so told the President, yet I am glad to have him move in the right direction.

I submitted Semmes's case again in Cabinet. Told the

President he was here, and had some conversation, general in its character, as to what should be done with him, without any other indication than approval, but no suggestion.

December 30, *Saturday.* The closing-up of the year, — an eventful one. A review of it from my standpoint would be interesting in many respects, and, should God grant me length of days and mental and physical strength, I shall be glad to present my views when my official days have terminated. Senator Dixon called this morning, and we had a long and frank talk. I approved of his course in the Senate, and his reply to Sumner. He is evidently prepared for a breach in the party, and I think desires it. While I do not desire it, I do not deprecate it if the counsels of Sumner, Stevens, and the extreme Radicals are insisted upon and the only alternative. His principal inquiry was as to the course our friends in Connecticut would pursue in case of a breach of the party. I told him I thought they would be disposed to stand by the Administration, yet at the first go-off the Radical element might have the ascendancy in the State convention, which would assemble in about a month. But before that time the lines would probably be drawn. The organization or party machinery will control most of the party, irrespective of the merits of the questions in issue.

I gave Colston, Semmes's son-in-law, a pass to visit him to-day, and take the papers and the report of Winslow to him. Had a conversation with Dr. Lieber, who was at my house yesterday, respecting Semmes's offenses. The Doctor has no question on that point, and thinks Lee and the whole of his army liable for treason, notwithstanding Grant's terms. Advised Solicitor Bolles to call on Dr. L. Bolles thinks the trial of Semmes should be by a military or naval commission instead of by court martial.

The President sends a singular paper for a new trial of Captain Meade, who has already been tried and is under sentence of court martial. I know not how he can be again tried for the same offense, unless he himself petitions for it.

XXXIV

The President's New Year Reception — Death of Henry Winter Davis —
Seward off to the West Indies — General Webb and Louis Napoleon —
The Charges against Semmes — The Shenandoah Case — Congress
seems disposed to open War on the President — An Animated Conversa-
tion with Sumner — Assistant Secretary Fox to resign his Position —
The Case of Naval Constructor Hoover — Another Call from Sumner —
The Semmes Case — Social Calls from former Secessionist Sympathizers
— Henry Wilson on the Question of a Break in the Party.

January 1, 1866, *Monday.* Made complimentary call
with my family on the President at 11 A.M. By special
request I went some fifteen minutes before the time specified, but there were sixty or eighty carriages in advance of
us. The persons who got up the programme were evidently wholly unfit for the business. Instead of giving the
first half-hour to the Cabinet and the several legations, and
then to Army and Navy officers, Members of Congress,
etc., in succession, numbers, including Members of Congress, — and they embrace everybody, all the members
of their respective boarding-houses, all their acquaint-
ances, immediate and remote, who were in Washington,
— were there at an early hour. Consequently there was
neither order nor system. After a delay of about twenty
minutes we were landed in the Executive Mansion, which
was already filled to overflowing in the hall and anterooms. While moving in the crowd, near the entrance to
the Red Room, some of the officials signed to us and threw
open the door to the Blue Room, or reception-room, which
we entered, much relieved; but on turning, we found the
President and his family immediately behind us. The
affair passed off very well. A great want of order and system prevails on these occasions, owing to the ignorance and
want of order of the marshal. No one having any conception of discipline or forethought directs or counsels those

in charge. We left in a very short time, and the company began to flock in upon us at our house before twelve, and until past four a pretty steady stream came and went,— naval and army officers, foreign ministers, Senators and Representatives, bureau officers and clerks, civilians and strangers. Pleasant but fatiguing, and the day was murky and the roads intolerable.

Mr. Seward left on Saturday. The rest of the members received, as did many other officials.

Henry Winter Davis, a conspicuous Member of the last Congress and a Maryland politician of notoriety, died on Saturday. He was eloquent, possessed genius, had acquirements, was eccentric, ambitious, unreliable, and greatly given to intrigue. In politics he was a centralist, regardless of constitutional limitations. I do not consider his death a great public loss. He was restless and active, but not useful. Still there will be a class of extreme Radicals who will deplore his death as a calamity and eulogize his memory.

When at the Executive Mansion the memory of the late President crowded upon my mind. He would have enjoyed the day, which was so much in contrast with all those he had experienced during his presidency.

January 2, Tuesday. Neither Seward nor Stanton was at Cabinet council. Seward is on his way to the West Indies, Gulf, etc. He wishes to be absent until the issues are fully made up and the way is clear for him what course to take. There may be other objects, but this is the chief. The talk about his health is ridiculous. He is as well as he has been at any time for five years. Stanton had no occasion to be present. Some discussion as to whether the State of Louisiana is entitled to cotton bought by the Rebel organization or government. Dennison and myself had a free talk with the President after the others left. Although usually reticent, he at times speaks out, and he expressed himself emphatically to-day. The manner in which things had been got up by the Radicals before the session he commented upon. "This little fellow [Colfax] shoved in here to make a speech in advance of the message, and to give out that the principle enunciated in his speech was the true policy of the country," were matters alluded to with sharpness, as were the whole preconcerted measures of the Radicals. "I do not hear that the colored people called or were invited to visit Sumner or Wilson," said the President, "but they came here and were civilly treated."

January 3, Wednesday. General James Watson Webb called on me. He has been laid up by the gout at his son-in-law's, Major Benton's, house. He came home from Brazil *via* Paris, saw Louis Napoleon, dined with him, gave him good advice, wants to get out of Mexico, etc., etc. Has communicated to the President the Emperor's feelings and wishes. No doubt he saw Louis Napoleon, with whom he had a close acquaintance when that dignitary wanted friends — and perhaps a dinner. It is creditable to him that he is not ungrateful to Webb.

Colonel Bolles, Solicitor and Judge Advocate, desires to prefer a number of charges against Semmes, and has, I fear, more thought of making a figure than of the point I wish presented; that is, a breach of parole, bad faith, violation of the usages of war in the surrender and escape from the Alabama. That he and a million of others have been guilty of treason there is no doubt; that he ran the blockade, burnt ships after a semi-piratical fashion there is no doubt; so have others been guilty of these things, and I do not care to select and try Semmes on these points, though perhaps the most guilty.

January 4, Thursday. The messages of the Governors and other indications favor the conciliatory policy of the Administration rather than the persecuting spirit of Stevens and other extreme Radicals. These latter are hesitating and apparently moderating their tone. They commenced with too strong a purchase. Sumner, I am told, is extremely violent, and I hear of some others. They are generally men that will not yield a hobby or theory, and I therefore doubt if they can be toned down and made reasonable.

January 5, Friday. I submitted the two cases, one of Judge Wayne for money due his granddaughter, and one of Mallory for a cylinder, to the Cabinet. The parties claim the first money due, and the last property seized by the Rebels and recaptured by the Union forces. All seemed united in the opinion that no action could be taken in behalf of these and similar claims at present.

Mr. Seward being absent, Mr. Hunter, who is Acting Secretary of State, stated that there was some embarrassment in regard to the Shenandoah. Both the State and the Treasury Departments appear to have been anxious to get possession of this vessel, but they are much more anxious to get rid of her. Dudley, consul at Liverpool, undertook to send her to the United States by a captain and picked-up crew, but after proceeding about six hundred miles and encountering rough weather she returned. Seward sent me word, a few hours before he left, with Dudley's dispatch that the vessel was on his (D.'s) hands, that he had sent to Admiral Goldsborough for an officer and crew to navigate her, but if the Admiral declined, he desired that I should send out the necessary force to England. This I did not feel inclined to do, but told him we would receive her here when delivered. Hunter now brings up the question in Cabinet, and advises that the vessel remain in Liverpool until after the vernal equinox, unless the Navy Department would receive her in Liverpool. Stanton thought this the proper course, and that I should send out for her. This suggestion I was satisfied came from Seward, who had turned the subject over to him before leaving. I incline to think she had best be sold for what she will bring in Liverpool.

An effort to procure the pardon of K——, a swindler now in Sing Sing, was made through McCulloch. But on learning the nature of the case he at once dropped it. The President sends, making inquiry concerning Hale, prisoner in Philadelphia, and Wetmore in Boston. The first is one of a nest of swindlers and thieves, of whom Pasco, just pardoned by the President, was chief; the second swindled men under him, or was guilty of a breach of trust like Marston, whom the President also pardoned.

January 8. The Members of Congress since their return appear more disposed to avoid open war with the President, but yet are under the discipline of party, which is cunningly kept up with almost despotic power. I am confident that many of those who are claimed as Republicans, and who are such, are voting against their convictions, but they have not the courage and independence to shake off the tyranny of party and maintain what they know to be right. The President and the Radical leaders are not yet in direct conflict, but I see not how it is to be avoided. When the encounter takes place there will be those who have voted with the Radicals, who will then probably go with the President, or wish to do so. This the leaders understand, and it is their policy to get as many committed as possible, and to get them repeatedly committed by test votes. Williams of Pittsburg, a revolutionary and whiskey-drinking leader, introduced a resolution to-day that the military should not be withdrawn, but retained until Congress, not the President, should order their discharge. This usurpation of the Executive prerogative by Congress is purposely offensive, known to be such, yet almost every Republican voted for it in the House. The Representatives who doubted and were opposed dare not vote against it. While thus infringing on the rights of the Executive, the Radical leaders studiously claim that they are supporting the President, and actually have most of his appointees with them. Were the President to assert his power and to exercise it, many of those who now follow Sumner and Stevens would hesitate, for the home officials are necessary to their own party standing. The President will sooner or later have to meet this question squarely, and have a square and probably a fierce fight with these men. Seward expects but deprecates it, and has fled to escape responsibility.

January 9, *Tuesday.* The Freedmen's Bureau wants three boats which are on the Tombigbee. They were blockade-runners which were ordered to be turned over to the Navy, but they are not naval captures. The Freedmen's Bureau has no funds. This is an indirect way of obtaining means, as wrong as the Bureau scheme itself. I think it would be better to go direct to Congress for money. If, however, the President rescinds the order turning over those boats, the Navy Department cannot interfere or object. The boats are strictly abandoned property and fall within the scope of the Treasury. The last three days have been severely cold.

January 10, *Wednesday.* Judge Kelley had a long interview with me to-day. Asks for favors that cannot be granted. Advised him that the attempts to give the Navy Yard a party character exclusively were injudicious, and he assented. We talked of various matters. Kelley is earnest, with aspirations, as have most active politicians; has determination and zeal, but not profound or correct ideas; does not possess influence to a great degree, and will never be a man of mark. I think him a better man than many others, but yet not always safe or sound.

Judge Blair called this P.M., and his views and positions are diametrically opposed to those of Kelley. But if less demonstrative, he is more profound and has vastly greater qualities, and grasp and comprehension. Better understands men. Is more of a statesman and more of a politician, — and by politician I do not mean party demagogue, but enlightened intelligence on matters of public policy. Blair believes a rupture inevitable, and thinks the President is wise in delaying the conflict. Therein I think he is mistaken. He attributes Williams's move to Stanton, who he avers is intriguing, and he thinks there is a cloud between Stanton and the President. It would be well if there was a wall between them.

January 12, *Friday.* Nothing very particularly interesting to-day in Cabinet. Stanton said he was to introduce some persons to the President and had appointed soon after 1 P.M. for the purpose. This was a play. Mr. Cox, a Rebel of Georgetown, fled South at the beginning of the Rebellion, leaving his fine residence. This was taken and used as a school for colored children. Cox has now returned and wants his house, — demands it. The charitable occupants, who are filled with benevolence for the negro, are unwilling to relinquish the house, which is very valuable, to the owner. Some of those who have the matter in charge went to Stanton, who said it would be necessary to apply to the President. He consented to introduce them, but suggested that a formidable array of ladies whose husbands occupy prominent positions, such as the wives of Senators and members of the Cabinet, [would be effective.] Mrs. Senators Trumbull, Morgan, Wilson, Pomeroy, etc., Mrs. McCulloch, Stanton, Harlan, etc., were of the number. Mrs. Welles was appealed to, but sensibly concluded, as she had no fact to communicate, that she would discharge her duty best by remaining away, and leaving the President to form his decision without annoyance from those who could not aid him. To this assemblage of ladies, and for the purpose, — robbing a man of his dwelling, — Stanton performed the part of usher.

January 13, *Saturday.* I had this P.M. quite an animated talk with Senator Sumner. He called on me in relation to Semmes. Wished him to be tried on various important

points which would bring out the legal status, not only of
the Rebels, but their cause. He thinks that many of the
important points which we have from time to time discussed, and on which we have generally agreed, might be
passed upon by a commission. I am not, however, inclined to make the trial so broad.

Passing from this, we got on to the question of Reconstruction. I was anxious to get an inside view of the movements and purposes of the Radicals, and in order to do this,
it would not do to put questions direct to Sumner, for then
he would put himself on his guard, and be close-mouthed.
I therefore entered into a discussion, and soon got him
much interested, not to call it excited. We went over the
ground of the status of the States, — their political condition. He, condemning unqualifiedly the policy of the President, said, while he would not denounce it as the greatest
crime ever committed by a responsible ruler, he did proclaim and declare it the greatest mistake which history has
ever recorded. The President, he said, was the greatest
enemy of the South that she had ever had, worse than Jeff
Davis; and the evil which he had inflicted upon the country
was incalculable. All was to be done over again, and done
right. Congress, he says, is becoming more firm and united
every day. Only three of the Republican Senators —Doolittle, Dixon, and Cowan — had given way, and he understood about a like proportion in the House. Asked if I
had read Howe's[1] speech, which Foot and Fessenden indorsed. Understood Fessenden was as decided as Foot, but,
not being on speaking terms, had not himself heard Fessenden. All Congress was becoming of one mind, and while
they would commence no war upon the President, he must
change his course, abandon his policy. The President had
violated the Constitution in appointing provisional governors, in putting Rebels in office who could not take the
test oath, in reëstablishing rebellion, odious, flagrant rebellion. Said he had three pages from one general in Arkansas,

[1] Timothy Otis Howe, Senator from Wisconsin.

thanking him for his speech, denouncing the President's "whitewashing" message.

I told him the Executive had rights and duties as well as Congress, and that they must not be overlooked or omitted. That the Rebel States had an existence and would be recognized and sustained although their functions were for a time suspended by violence. That under military necessity, martial law existing and the President being commander-in-chief, provisional governors had been temporarily appointed, but the necessity which impelled their appointment was passing away, the States were resuming their position in the Union, and I did not see how, without abandoning our system of constitutional government, they were to be disorganized, or unorganized, and deprived of their local civil government and the voice of the people suppressed. That he spoke of them as a "conquered people," subject to terms which it was our duty to impose. Were his assumption true, and they a foreign conquered people, instead of our own countrymen, still they had their rights, were amenable to our laws and entitled to their protection; modern civilization would not permit of their enslavement. That were we to conquer Canada and bring it within our jurisdiction, the people would retain their laws and usages when they were not inconsistent with our own, until at least we should make a change. That I thought our countrymen were entitled to as much consideration as the laws of nations and the practice of our own government had and did recognize as belonging to a conquered people who were aliens. That this was the policy of the President. He had enjoined upon them, it was true, the necessity of making their constitutions and laws conform to the existing condition of affairs and the changes which war had brought about. They had done so, and were each exercising all the functions of a State. Had their governors, legislatures, judges, local municipal authorities, etc. We were collecting taxes of them, appointing collectors, assessors, marshals, postmasters, etc.

I saw I had touched on some views that impressed him, and our interview and discussion became exceedingly animated.

"The President, in his atrocious wrong," said Sumner, "is sustained by three of his Cabinet. Seward is as thick-and-thin a supporter of the whole monstrous error as you or McCulloch."

I asked him if he supposed the Cabinet was not a unit on the President's policy. He said he knew it was not. Three of the members concurred with him (Sumner) fully, entirely.

I expressed doubts. "Why," said he, "one of them has advised and urged me to prepare and bring in a bill which should control the action of the President and wipe out his policy. It has got to be done. Half of the Cabinet, as well as an overwhelming majority of the two houses of Congress, are for it, and the President must change his whole course." If he did not do it, Congress would.

January 15, *Monday.* Was much disturbed by what Sumner said in regard to a member of the Cabinet who had urged him to bring in a bill adverse to the President's policy. Sumner is truthful and therefore his statement is reliable. Although he is credulous, I cannot think he was deceived, nor is he practicing deception. I started out last evening, thinking I would see the President on this subject, but stopped and talked over the matter with Governor Dennison, who proposed to go with me some evening this week.

January 16, *Tuesday.* Told Mr. Hunter that it would be best to turn over the Shenandoah to the Secretary of the Treasury as abandoned property, and let Consul Dudley sell her in Liverpool. McCulloch says he has no agent there, but Dudley can do the work. I do not wish to be mixed up with the Anglo-Rebel affairs of this vessel.

2

January 17, Wednesday. Mr. Fox, the Assistant Secretary of the Navy, informed me some days since of an offer which he had for the presidency of the new steamboat line about to be established between New York and San Francisco. I regret to lose him from the Department, where, notwithstanding some peculiarities which have caused dissatisfaction with a few, he is of almost invaluable service, and he has in him a great amount of labor. He has a combination of nautical intelligence and common sense such as can hardly be found in another, and we have worked together with entire harmony, never in a single instance having had a misunderstanding. I have usually found his opinions sensible and sound. When I have had occasion to overrule his opinions, he has acquiesced with a readiness and deference which won my regard. His place I cannot make good in some respects. Faxon, Chief Clerk, would be as great a loss to me, — in some particulars greater, — but there are certain subjects wherein Fox, from his naval experience, is superior to any man who can be readily found.

January 27. My letter to the Naval Committee in relation to the contract of Paul S. Forbes for the Idaho has disturbed certain parties. It interposes pretty decisive objections against lobby intrigues and deviations from the contract. Certain party men wish to be considered economists, and yet would be glad to pay Forbes a few hundred thousand dollars more than the contract price. They would be glad to censure the Department, but find they cannot do this and occupy an economical position. Forbes acts stupidly. His vessel is likely to prove a failure. He cannot build her and complete her on his own offer. He has proved himself less sagacious and less capable than he had the reputation of being, or than he himself supposed he was, but yet makes no admission of error and failure.

Forney[1] and the Union Representatives of Philadelphia have appealed to me to reinstate Hoover, the Naval

[1] John W. Forney, Secretary of the Senate.

Constructor, whom they pronounce an honest man, etc.,
backed by a formidable list of names. I wrote Forney that
Hoover had been guilty of accepting bribes and that I
could not give him my confidence, and requested him to
so inform his associates. He answers in an apologetic letter
and promises to be more careful in future. I saw him at
one of McCulloch's receptions, and told him the correspondence ought to be published in order to set the Department right. He assented and said he would publish it with
his last letter if I had no objection. I assented and sent
him the correspondence and after a day or two he writes
that he has consulted with the Union Representatives and
concluded the disclosure was not best. In reply, I state
that if I rightly understand them, they wish to have the
Philadelphia public remain ignorant of the facts, and continue to believe the Department oppressive. Differing with
them, I ask a return of the correspondence.

January 30. I had another long talk with Senator Sumner, who called on me on Saturday. It was of much the
same purport as heretofore. He is pleased with a speech
of Secretary Harlan, made the preceding evening, which I
had not then read, and said it came up to the full measure
of his requirements. "Then," said I, "he probably is that
member of the Cabinet who has been urging you to bring
in a bill to counteract the President's policy." "No," said
Sumner, "it was not Harlan but another member. There
are," continued he, "four members of the Cabinet who are
with us and against the President." "Then," replied I,
"you must include Seward." This he promptly disclaimed.
I told him he must not count Dennison. He was taken
aback. "If you know from D.'s own mouth,—have it from
himself, — I will not dispute the point," said Sumner. I
told him I knew D.'s views, that last spring he had, at the
first suggestion, expressed himself for negro suffrage, but
that he had on reflection and examination come fully into
the President's views. He replied that he had known

D.'s original position and had supposed it remained unchanged. Sumner told me he should make a very thorough speech this week on the great question — the treatment of the States and people of the South — but should avoid any attack on the President; would not be personal. Tells me that Governor Hamilton of Texas has written him imploring him to persevere.

I am afraid the President has not always been fortunate in his selection of men. Either Hamilton is a hypocrite or there is a bad condition of things in Texas. The entire South seem to be stupid and vindictive, know not their friends, and are pursuing just the course which their opponents, the Radicals, desire. I fear a terrible ordeal awaits them in the future. Misfortune and adversity have not impressed them.

Have had much canvassing and discussion of Semmes's case with Solicitor Bolles, Mr. Eames, Fox, and others, and to-day took the papers to the Cabinet. When I mentioned the purport of the documents, which were somewhat voluminous, the President proposed that he and I should examine them together before submitting them to the Cabinet and thus save time. After going over the papers with him, he expressed a desire to leave the whole subject in my hands to dispose of as I saw proper. I remarked that the questions involved were so important that I preferred the course taken should be strictly administrative, and I wished to have the best authority, and careful and deliberate consideration and conclusion. The offenses charged being violation of the laws of war, I thought our action should be intelligent and certain. The President said he had confidence in my judgment and discretion, inquired why a purely naval court martial could not dispose of the subject. He exhibited a strong disinclination to commit the case to the military, and was more pointed and direct on that subject than I have before witnessed. He requested me to take the papers and consult such persons as I pleased and report in due time.

We had some general conversation on the tone and temper of Congress and the country. The President is satisfied that his policy is correct, and is, I think, very firm in his convictions and intentions to maintain it. The Radicals who are active and violent are just as determined to resent it.

I took occasion to repeat what I have several times urged, the public enunciation of his purpose, and at the proper time, and as early as convenient or as there was an opportunity, to show by some distinct and emphatic act his intention to maintain and carry into effect his administrative policy. That while a conflict or division was not sought but avoided, there should be no uncertainty, yet a demonstration which should leave no doubt as to his determination. On this we concurred.

January 31. The new shape of affairs shows itself in the social gatherings. At Mrs. Welles's reception to-day, a large number of the denizens of Washington who have not heretofore been visitors and whose sympathies and former associations were with the Rebels called. So many who have been distant and reserved were present as to excite her suspicions, and lead her to ask if I was not conceding too much. These new social friends are evidently aware of existing differences in the Administration. I noticed at the reception at the Executive Mansion last evening the fact that there was a number in attendance as if by preconcert. This I attribute more to the insane folly of the Radicals, who under Thad Stevens are making assaults on the President, than to any encouragement which the President has given to Rebel sympathizers. If professed friends prove false and attack him, he will not be likely to repel such friends as sustain him. I certainly will not.

While at a party at Senator Harris's, Senator Wilson took me one side and inquired if we were to have a break in the party. I told him I saw no necessity for it. The President was honest and sincere in his policy; it has been adopted with care and great deliberation, and I thought intelligently. I knew it to be with right intentions. If any considerable number of our friends were resolved to oppose the President and the policy of the Administration a division would be unavoidable. He could not abandon his convictions to gratify mere factious schemers.

We then got on the subject of the recently published letter of a "conversation between the President and a distinguished Senator," in which there were indications that the President would not go for unlimited negro suffrage in the District. Wilson inquired what course the President would be likely to pursue. I told him I was unable to answer that question, except as he would, from a general knowledge of the President's opinions on fundamental questions. He would be disposed to have the people of the District exercise the same rights in this regard as the people of the States.

XXXV

February 1. Colonel Bolles and Eames have prepared an
order for the President to sign for a mixed commission to try
Semmes. I took it to the President this P.M. He expressed
himself strongly against a military trial or military control.
Wished the Navy to keep the case in its own hands. Said he
wished to put no more in Holt's control than was absolutely necessary; that Holt was cruel and remorseless,
made so perhaps by his employment and investigations;
that his tendencies and conclusions were very bloody. The
President said he had a large number of Holt's decisions
now — pointing to the desk — which he disliked to take up;
that all which came from that quarter partook of the traits
of Nero and Draco. I have never heard him express himself
so decidedly in regard to Holt, but have on one or two previous occasions perceived that his confidence in the Judge-
Advocate-General was shaken.

I long since was aware that Holt was severe and unrelenting, and am further compelled to think that, with a
good deal of mental vigor and strength as a writer, he has
strange weaknesses. He is credulous and often the dupe
of his own imaginings. Believes men guilty on shadowy
suspicions, and is ready to condemn them without trial.

Stanton has sometimes brought forward singular papers relating to conspiracies, and dark and murderous designs in which he had evident faith, and Holt has assured him in his suspicions.

I am glad that the President does not consider him infallible, and that he is guarded against the worst traits; the others will develop themselves, if they have not already.

I stated to the President that I would not advise a military, naval, or mixed commission to try Semmes for treason or piracy, for the civil tribunals had cognizance of those offenses. But if he had violated the laws of war for which he could not be arraigned in court, there was perhaps a necessity that we should act through a commission. He realized the distinction and the propriety of acting and wished me to bring the subject before the full Cabinet.

One of my troubles in the matter of the charges and specifications has been to limit our action to violations of the law of war. The lawyers who have it in charge, especially Colonel Bolles, are for embracing a wider range. He wishes to figure in the case.

Senator Dixon gave me to-day a slip from the *New Haven Courier*, written by Babcock, the Collector, taking issue with Deming in his late speech. Babcock sustains the policy of the President, and his article is very creditable. Dixon wished me to write him and says McCulloch will do so. I wish some of our more reliable friends would have the sagacity and determination to do this subject justice.

February 2, Friday. I think the President, though calm and reticent, exhibits indications of not being fully satisfied in some respects with the conduct and course of some in whom he has confided; yet he carefully abstains from remarks respecting persons. There can be no doubt that Stanton has given certain of the leading Radicals to understand that his views correspond with theirs, but I do not know that the President is fully aware of that fact. Seward, while he says nothing very decisively, leaves no doubt that he coincides in the general policy of the President. Harlan made a singular speech to the Iowa Radicals a week ago, but has written an explanatory letter which is no explanation. I have no doubt that Dennison is sincerely with the President and means to sustain his measures, yet he makes visible, without intending it, his apprehension that by this policy the Democrats may get a controlling influence. In this he is not singular, for many of the leading Radicals, especially those of Whig antecedents, have similar apprehensions and are afraid to trust the people. Having power, they do not scruple at means to retain it.

The truth is the Radical leaders in Congress openly and secretly have labored to defeat the President, and their hostility has engendered a distrust in their own minds, and caused fairer men, like Dennison, to have fears that the President might identify himself with the Democrats. This subject gives me no uneasiness whatever. I shall not be surprised if the extreme men become alienated, but their abandonment of the President will, under the working of our system of intelligent free thought and action, make room for the more reasonable and calculating of the opposition, if met with intelligent candor and determination. He will naturally feel kindly disposed towards those who sustain him and his measures, and will not be likely to give his confidence to those who oppose both.[1]

[1] The President was at this time greatly embarrassed by the advice and suggestions of Mr. Seward, who, though personally friendly to the President and the Administration, was himself so much of a party man, and so much under the influence of extreme partisans, as to be governed rather by party than by country. It was the aim and object of his New York friends to keep alive party distinctions created by Secession and the War, and to throw the power of the Administration into the Republican, or, in other words, Radical, hands. New York is a great State and has local controversies of its own, independent of the Federal Government, but the centralists could not secure and hold the ascendancy there except by the aid of the Federal Government. The New York politicians had, therefore, a double part to play, and Mr. Seward was their agent to effect their purpose. Whilst Thad Stevens and the extreme Radicals were making war on the Executive, it was important for the New-Yorkers, and indeed for men of similar views in other

February 5, Monday. I wrote Calvin Day a general letter on the condition of affairs. What are his views and opinions I know not. His usual good sense leads me to hope he is correct, yet his feelings are very decided, perhaps, like others, unrelenting, against the Rebels. He can, I think, have no confidence in, or respect for, Stevens, but his sentiments in regard to Dixon are not more favorable. The papers in Connecticut have most of them launched off with the Radicals, especially those with which he is associated. I did not wish to intermeddle or even to express an opinion on the eve of the nominating convention or the elections, but there seemed a duty to counsel an old friend whose prejudices are strong. Whether he will heed what I have written remains to be seen.

States not to break immediately with the President, but to use the power and patronage of the Executive to promote their own ends. He had been elected by them, and Mr. Seward urged that he should not neglect them, even if they disagreed with him, for he insisted that the Democrats, although their views were with him on present questions, were opposed to him and his Administration. Party before country was inculcated by both Radicals and Democrats. The President had in the past as in the present placed country above party, and was consequently not a favorite with either.

Almost all the members of the Cabinet were strict party men and were subjected to severe discipline in those days. Without an exception they approved the principles and assented to the opinions and purposes of the President, but it was soon given out that they must conform to the theory and doctrines of Thad Stevens if they designed to preserve their Republican Party identity. Congress was the supreme department of the Government and must be recognized as the supreme power. Members of Congress must be permitted to exercise executive duties. The legislative department must control the action of the Government, prescribe its policy, its measures, and dictate appointments to the executive, or subordinate, department. Most of the members of the Cabinet acquiesced or submitted to the usurpation. No appointments or nominations to office made by the Executive, who was bound to see the laws executed, were confirmed by the Senate, except the nominees were first recommended or indorsed by Radical Members of Congress. Some of the Cabinet under these circumstances surrendered and made terms.

Mr. Seward advised that there should be compromise and concession. The President, unwilling to break with those who elected him, yielded and failed to make a stand and appeal to his countrymen for support. As a consequence, the unscrupulous Radicals wielded the government in all its departments. — G. W.

February 6, *Tuesday.* Seward read a letter in regard to
the Shenandoah, expressing my views and adopting my
suggestions and almost my language. The city is full of
visitors, and Washington is gay with parties. Attended
reception at the Executive Mansion and afterward called
on Sir Frederick Bruce and his niece Lady Elma Thurlow.
Met at each [place] Madame La Verte (and daughter), of
Mobile, who is making demonstration here and writing, I
am told, a South-side view of the Rebellion. I met her here
nearly forty years ago, — then Miss Wharton, a gay and
intelligent young lady.

February 7, *Wednesday.* The Democratic Party, as it
calls itself, held yesterday its convention in Connecticut,
and the nomination of Governor as well as the resolutions
adopted exhibit more sense and patriotism than has been
shown for years. Mr. English, the candidate for Governor,
was a useful Member of Congress of enlarged and liberal
views, who was not in his votes controlled strictly by
party, herein differing widely from a class of narrow and
pig-headed party leaders who have been a discredit to the
State. In no State has mere partyism shown itself during
the War to greater disadvantage than in Connecticut.
Party and party organizations rose above country, or
duty. In fact, party was a substitute for country. Adversity has taught them wisdom, yet the leaders are most
of them short-sighted and narrow-minded, incapable of
comprehending the true principles of government or
of foreseeing results. Instead of considering how questions
will affect the country, free institutions, or the cause of
human rights and justice, the whole aim, study, and purpose have been to get a party ascendancy, power, and the
patronage of office. With them party is the end, not
the means.

The organization of the Democratic Party of Connecticut has been, perhaps, the most efficient and effectual of
any party in any State. Whatever of good or evil it may

have had, I, probably beyond any other person, am responsible for. When in 1826 I took charge of the *Times* and advocated Jackson's election, there was no systematic party organization nor much interest manifested in political principles on national subjects, nor much concerted political action in the State. Few, comparatively, attended the polls. There were, it is true, the more intelligent and at the same time the old contending partisans in the State. Disagreeing and contending among themselves, they nevertheless each hated Jackson. Embittered local controversies affecting the State had for several years absorbed general questions.

February 8. Neither of the feeble organizations discussed or professed much regard for any of those fundamental principles which had created and previously influenced parties, or which were then again just looming up above the horizon. The Federalists had been beaten in 1818 and felt that they deserved it, but they had always until then been in the ascendant and wielded the power of the State, and still desired most earnestly to do so. The Republicans of those days were held in subjection and had great deference for the Federal dignitaries. Scarcely one of the leaders possessed independence and strength of character sufficient to firmly resist the well-organized dominant party and form and avow individual opinion. The mass or body of the people were patriotic, but, under ecclesiastical as much as political ruling, had little zeal or devotion for parties or leaders. This was the condition of things when I came upon the stage of action, full of enthusiasm and earnest work, and commenced the labor of bringing together the minds which sympathized and agreed with me. Very few of the prominent men came into the fold, and such as did were most of them disappointed and disaffected men. Some aspiring individuals whispered encouragement, but kept out of sight. By letters, by private correspondence and personal interviews with the people, by ascertaining names of men in different towns and localities, urging and inviting them to come forward, I laid the foundation of what was and is known as the Democratic Party of Connecticut. John M. Niles aided, and as he was the elder man by some years, he was more openly recognized as the leader. But Niles had not perseverance and was often and easily discouraged. Circumstances favored, and though abused, hated, insulted, and at first despised, the organization thus commenced, after many trials and reverses, obtained an ascendancy in the State.

When this became established, the vicious, the corrupt, the time-serving, and the unprincipled flocked to us. The Seymours, the Ingersolls, the Phelpses, etc., became Democrats. The organization was thorough, and the discipline rigid and severe. Trimmers and mere office-hunters became jealous and dissatisfied, made secret and sometimes open war upon me, were whipped and returned. The drill and discipline of twenty years made the organization compact, and when the Democratic Party of the country in 1848 became unfaithful in a measure to their principles, the discipline of party carried many into a false position. I declined to follow the nullifiers, compromisers, and secessionists, but the organization which I had instituted held to party and became perverted. New men who "knew not Joseph" controlled the organization. For a time they retained the ascendancy, but ultimately they broke down, and for ten or twelve years they have been in a minority. Through the War the leaders have been almost all of them hostile to the Administration and malignant against the cause of the Union. Some, like English, have risen above the trammels of party.

The ticket, with the exception of English, has not much strength, and some bad men are on it. I am apprehensive that the Republicans will not be as judicious in their movement, will not nominate a better man for Governor nor give as hearty an indorsement to the President and his policy.

February 9, *Friday.* Mr. Seward read a very elaborate paper on French affairs, which was under discussion over two hours and seemed then not entirely satisfactory. The old story as to what Louis Napoleon is going to do was repeated. He has signified that he will, on receiving an assurance from us of non-intervention in Mexico, inform us what his arrangements are for withdrawing his troops. I thought Seward a little too ready to give an assurance, and that he was very little trusted and got very little in return.

February 10, *Saturday.* Was last night at a loud-heralded and large party given by Marquis Montholon, the French Minister. Am inclined to believe there was something political as well as social in the demonstration. No similar party has been given by the French Minister for five years.

The Naval Appropriation Bill has been before the House this week, when demagogues of small pattern exhibited their eminent incapacity and unfitness for legislation. It is a misfortune that such persons as Washburne and Ingersoll of Illinois and others are intrusted with important duties. Important and essential appropriations for the navy yards at Norfolk and Pensacola were stricken out, because they are in the South; in Boston because it is a wealthy community. Without knowledge, general or specific, the petty demagogues manifest their regard for the public interest and their economical views, by making no appropriations, or as few as possible for the Navy, regardless of what is essential. "We have now Navy enough to thrash England and France," said one of these small Representatives in his ignorance; therefore [they] vote no more money for navy yards, especially none in the Southern States.

Sumner made me his usual weekly visit this P.M. He is as earnest and confident as ever, probably not without reason. Says they are solidifying in Congress and will set aside the President's policy. I inquired if he really thought Massachusetts could govern Georgia better than Georgia could govern herself, — for that was the kernel of the question: Can the people govern themselves? He could not otherwise than say Massachusetts could do better for them than they had done for themselves. When I said every State and people must form its own laws and government; that the whole social, industrial, political, and civil structure was to be reconstructed in the Slave States; that the elements there must work out their own condition, and that Massachusetts could not do this for them, he did not controvert farther than to say we can instruct them and ought to do it, that he had letters showing a dreadful state of things South, that the colored people were suffering beyond anything they had ever endured in the days of slavery. I told him I had little doubt of it; I had expected this as the first result of emancipation. Both whites and blacks in the Slave States were to pass through a terrible ordeal, and it was a most grievous and melancholy thing to me to witness the spirit manifested towards the whites of the South who were thus afflicted. Left to themselves, they have great suffering and hardship, without having their troubles increased by any oppressive acts from abroad.

February 12, *Monday.* Mr. Bancroft has to-day delivered his oration on the death of Lincoln. It is the anniversary of his birth, and hence the occasion. The orator, or historian, acquitted himself very well. Some things were said which would hardly have been expected at such a time, particularly some sharp points against England and Lord John Russell, which I was not sorry to hear. Both the Minister and the Government were bad enemies of ours in our troubles; they added to these trials; they made them formidable; they intended our ruin.

February 13, *Tuesday.* McCulloch asked me yesterday, in the President's room in the Capitol, if I had examined the Freedmen's Bureau Bill, and when I told him I had not, that I had never been partial to the measure, had doubted its expediency, even during the War, but as Congress, the Administration, and the country had adopted it, and as I had no connection with it, I had little inclination to interest myself in the matter, he said he wished I would examine the bill, and I told him I would, though opposed to that system of legislation, and to Government's taking upon itself the care and support of communities. To-day the President inquired of me my opinions, or rather said he thought there were some extraordinary features in the bill, and asked what I thought of them, or of the bill. My reply was similar to that I gave McCulloch yesterday. He expressed a wish that I would give the bill consideration, for he apprehended he should experience difficulty in signing it. The bill has not yet reached him.

Showed the President the finding of the court in the case of Meade, who had obtained a new trial and had a little severer punishment than in the former case. The President thought it would be well not to hurry Semmes's case. Told him there were reasons why delay would be acceptable and I should prefer it, only I wished it off my hands. But as he desired delay we would not hurry the matter. He alluded with some feeling to the extraordinary intrigue which he understood was going on in Congress, having nothing short of a subversion or change in the structure of the government in view. The unmistakable design of Thad Stevens and his associates was to take the government into their own hands, the President said, and to get rid of him by declaring Tennessee out of the Union. A sort of French Directory was to be established by these spirits in Congress, the Constitution was to be remodeled by them, etc.

February 14, *Wednesday.* Have examined the bill for the Freedmen's Bureau, which is a terrific engine and reads more like a decree emanating from despotic power than a legislative enactment by republican representatives. I do not see how the President can sign it. Certainly I shall not advise it. Yet something is necessary for the wretched people who have been emancipated, and who have neither intelligence nor means to provide for themselves. In time and briefly, if let alone, society will adapt itself to circumstances and make circumstances conform to existing necessities, but in the mean time there will be suffering, misery, wretchedness, nor will it be entirely confined to the blacks.

I am apprehensive that the efforts of our Northern philanthropists to govern the Southern States will be productive of evil, that they will generate hatred rather than love between the races. This Freedmen's Bureau scheme is a governmental enormity. There is a despotic tendency in the legislation of this Congress, an evident disposition to promote these notions of freedom by despotic and tyrannical means.

February 15, *Thursday.* The State Convention yesterday appears to have got along better in Connecticut than I apprehended, yet there is obviously Radical animosity lurking and fermenting there which will be likely to show itself soon. Among the leaders, most of whom have been impregnated with Radical views, there is no love for the President nor any intention to support his policy. In Hartford they detest Dixon and Cleveland, who support the Administration, and they like Hawley, who is much given to the negro, but is really well-intentioned and as fair-minded as one can be who has been a zealous Abolitionist, and is hopeful of political honors.

February 16, *Friday.* After Cabinet-meeting I had an interview and pretty free interchange of opinion with the President on the Freedmen's Bureau Bill and other subjects. I expressed myself without reserve, as did the President, who acquiesced fully in my views. This being the case, I conclude he will place upon it his veto. Indeed, he intimated as much. Desired, he said, to have my ideas because they might add to his own, etc.

2

There is an apparent rupturing among the Radicals, or a portion of them. They wish to make terms. Will admit the representation from Tennessee if the President will yield. But the President cannot yield and sacrifice his honest convictions by way of compromise.

Truman Smith came to see me yesterday. Says the House wants to get on good terms with the President, and ought to; that the President is right, but it will be well to let Congress decide when and how the States shall be represented. Says Deming is a fool, politically speaking, and that our Representatives, all of them, are weak and stupid. I have an impression that Truman called at the suggestion of Seward, and that this matter of conceding to Congress emanates from the Secretary of State, and from good but mistaken motives.

February 17, *Saturday*. Governor Morgan called this morning on matters of business. Had some talk on current matters. He says Tennessee Representatives will be admitted before the close of next week; that he so told Wilson and Sumner yesterday, whereat Sumner seemed greatly disturbed. From some givings-out by Morgan, intimations from Truman Smith, and what the President himself has heard, I think there is a scheme to try and induce him to surrender his principles in order to secure seats to the Tennessee delegation. But they will not influence him to do wrong in order to secure right.

February 19, *Monday*. Attended special Cabinet-meeting this morning, at ten, and remained in session until about 1 P.M. The President submitted a message which he had prepared, returning the Freedmen's Bureau Bill to the Senate with his veto. The message and positions were fully discussed. Seward, McCulloch, and Dennison agreed with the President, as did I, and each so expressed himself. Stanton, Harlan, and Speed, while they did not absolutely dissent, evidently regretted that the President had not signed the bill. Stanton was disappointed. Speed was disturbed. Harlan was apprehensive. The President was emphatic and unequivocal in his remarks, earnest to eloquence in some portion of a speech of about twenty minutes, in which he reviewed the intrigues of certain Radical leaders in Congress, without calling them by name, their council of fifteen which in secret prescribed legislative action and assumed to dictate the policy of the Administration. The effect of this veto will probably be an open rupture between the President and a portion of the Republican Members of Congress. How many will go with him, and how many with the Radical leaders, will soon be known. Until a vote is taken, the master spirits will have time to intrigue with the Members and get them committed. They will be active as well as cunning.

Senator Trumbull, who is the father of this bill, has not been classed among the Radicals and did not intend to be drawn in with them when he drew up this law. But he is freaky and opinionated, though able and generally sensible. I shall be sorry to have him enter into associations that will identify him with extremists, and yet it will not surprise me should such be the case. He will be the champion of his bill and, stimulated and courted by those with whom he does not sympathize, will strive to impair the effect of the impregnable arguments and reasoning of the message.

February 20, *Tuesday.* The Cabinet was pleasant and harmonious on the matters before it to-day, though outside rumors make them divided. Much excitement exists in Congress and out of it on the subject of the veto. The dark, revolutionary, reckless intrigues of Stevens manifest themselves. In the House, the bigoted partisans are ready to follow him in his vindictive and passionate schemes for Radical supremacy. Radicalism having been prevalent during the War, they think it still popular.

On the vote which was taken to-day in the Senate, the veto was sustained and the bill defeated, there not being the requisite two thirds in its favor. Morgan, Dixon, Doolittle, and four or five others with the Democrats, eighteen in all against thirty. Violent and factious speeches were made in the Senate, and also in the House. Stevens, as I expected he would, presented his schemes to oppress the South and exclude the States from their constitutional right of representation. Such men would plunge the country into a more wicked rebellion, one more destructive of our system of government, a more dangerous condition than that from which we have emerged, could they prevail. As an exhibition of the enlightened legislation of the House, Stevens, the Radical leader, Chairman of the Reconstruction Committee, — the committee which shapes and directs the action of Congress, and assumes executive as well as legislative control, — announced that his committee, or directory it may be called, was about to report in favor of admitting the Tennessee Members, but the President having put his veto on the Freedmen's Bill, they would not now consent, and he introduced his resolution declaring, virtually, that the Union is divided, that the States which were in rebellion should not have their constitutional right of representation.

February 21, *Wednesday.* Took the President the executive order for the trial of Semmes. Found that he hesitated. Told him I had no feeling whatever in regard to it. That I was not willing nor did I believe we could legally try him for treason or piracy by a military commission, for those crimes were cognizable by the civil courts, but a violation of the laws of war required, perhaps, a commission and could be reached in no other way. He assented to these views, but thought it would be better to get an opinion from the Attorney-General. Moreover, he thought delay rather advisable at this time. I told him I thought it a good opportunity to show that he was ready to bring criminals to trial when the duty devolved on him.

Senators Doolittle and Cowan were with the President

when I called on him this morning. Doolittle had the rough plan of a bill to modify and terminate the Freedmen's Bureau Bill. I prefer non-action. So does Cowan, and I think the President also. Doolittle thinks something will be advisable to satisfy the public, whose sympathies have been excited by cunning appeals. This is Seward.

Whiting, Solicitor, or late Solicitor, of the War Department, came to see me. It was amusing to see how self-satisfied he was in weaving a pleasant web on the subject of negro suffrage and the questions at issue. He is writing and publishing a series of numbers in the *Republican*, which, he says, were penned at my suggestion some months since, doubtless in part at least for my benefit. In the midst of our talk Montgomery Blair came in, and Whiting left with great speed. Blair is gratified with the stirring-up of the waters of controversy, and anticipates, I doubt not, that Stanton, who still occupies an ambiguous attitude, may be brought to a plain development of his true position. He insists that Stanton is playing false to the President. No doubt of it in my mind, yet he and Seward are in accord, but Seward is not treacherous.

February 22, Thursday. Washington's Birthday. Advantage is taken of it by those who sustain the late veto to assemble and give expression to their feelings, for there is quite as much of feeling, partisan feeling, as of honest opinion in what is done and said on this subject. The leading Radicals, on the other hand, are precipitating themselves into monstrous error and showing their incapacity to govern or even organize a permanent party. Only want of sagacity on the part of their opponents, the Democrats, prevents them from slipping into the shoes which the Radicals are abandoning. It is complained that the President treats the Rebels and the Copperheads kindly. It is not strange that he does so, for kindness begets kindness. They treat him respectfully, while the Radical leaders are arrogant, presuming, and dictatorial. They assume that the legislative branch of the Government is absolute, that the other departments, and especially the executive, are subordinate. Stevens and his secret joint committee or directory have taken into their hands the government and the administration of affairs. It is an incipient conspiracy. Congress, in both branches, or the majority of Congress, are but puppets in the hands of the Directory and do little but sanction and obey the orders of that committee.

To-day both branches of Congress have adjourned and there are funeral solemnities at the Capitol in memoriam of the late Henry Winter Davis, a private citizen, who died in Baltimore two or three months since, but who had been a conspicuous actor among the Radicals. He possessed genius, a graceful elocution, and erratic ability of a certain kind, but was an uneasy spirit, an unsafe and undesirable man, without useful talents for his country or mankind. Having figured as a leader with Thad Stevens, Wade, and others, in their intrigues, extraordinary honors are now paid him. A programme, copied almost literally from that of the 12th in memory of Mr. Lincoln, is sent out. Orders to commemorate this distinguished "Plug Ugly" and "Dead Rabbit" are issued. President and Cabinet, judges, foreign ministers, and other officials have seats assigned them in the Hall of the Representatives for the occasion. The whole is a burlesque, which partakes of the ridiculous more than the solemn, intended to belittle the memory of Lincoln and his policy as much as to exalt Davis, who opposed it. I would not go, — could not go without a feeling of degradation. I yesterday suggested to the President my view of the whole proceedings, — that they were in derogation of the late President and the Administration. The Radicals wished Davis to be considered the equal or superior of Lincoln.

There was a large gathering of the citizens to-day at the theatre to approve the veto, and they subsequently went to the Executive Mansion, where the President addressed them in quite a long speech for the occasion.

February 23, Friday. The papers of this morning contain the reported speech of President Johnson yesterday. It is longer than the President should have delivered, — if he were right in addressing such a crowd. His remarks were earnest, honest, and strong. One or two interruptions which called out names I wish were omitted.

The *Chronicle,* Forney's paper, is scandalously abusive and personally indecent, false, and vindictive. An attempt is made, by innuendo, to give the impression that the President was excited by liquor. Count Gurowski, the grumbler, is around repeating the dirty scandal. Says the President had drunk too much bad whiskey to make a good speech. Eames tells me that Gurowski, who now lives with him, says that Stanton declared to him that he was opposed to the veto. Well, he did suggest that there might, he thought, be an improvement by one or two alterations, but as a whole he was understood to acquiesce and assent to the message. I doubted if he was sincere, for there was an ambiguity in what he said, yet, having said something, he could to his Radical friends aver he was opposed.

I told the President I was sorry he had permitted himself to be drawn into answering impertinent questions to a promiscuous crowd and that he should have given names of those whose course he disapproved. Not that his remarks were not true, but the President should not be catechized into declarations. Yet it is the manner and custom in the Southwest, and especially in Tennessee, to do this on the stump. Stanton patronizes Forney's *Chronicle* and proscribes the *Intelligencer.* Conversing with the President, I told him I thought this improper. He said he would bring the subject before us at the next meeting.

February 24, Saturday. The extremists are angry and violent because the President follows his own convictions, and their operations through the press are prolific in manufacturing scandal against him. No harm will come of it, if he is prudent and firm. The leaders had flattered themselves that they had more than two thirds of each house, and could, therefore, carry all their measures over any veto. The President says there has been a design to attempt impeachment if he did not yield to them. I am inclined to believe this has been talked of among the leaders, but they would not press a majority of their own number into the movement.

February 26, Monday. Senator Doolittle called to have a conversation with me on existing topics and consult as to the propriety of his attending a public meeting and speaking at Baltimore. Governor Dennison came in with Governor Cox of Ohio while we were conversing, and spent the evening with us. The great questions before the country were canvassed freely, and Governor Cox displayed intelligence and decision that pleased me. He has quick perception and a right appreciation of what is taking place, and a pretty correct estimate of the actors.

In the Senate, Sherman has been speaking against the declaratory resolution, which passed the House under the lash of Stevens from the Directory Committee, asserting that eleven States are out of the Union and must not be represented until Congress shall permit them. This resolution is fulminated in spite, because the President put his veto on the Freedmen's Bill. Such legislation is characteristic of Stevens and his colaborers.

XXXVI

Stevens's Influence in his Reconstruction Committee — Conversation with Baldwin of the Committee — The Committee reports a Resolution for admitting Representatives from Tennessee — The Treasury Department embarrassed by the Test Oath in procuring Officials in the South — A Call from Governor Dennison in reference to a Restoration of Harmony in the Republican Party — A Talk with Senator Grimes — Attitude of Grimes and Fessenden towards the President — Cabinet Discussion of the Fenian Situation — The Connecticut Gubernatorial Candidates — General Hawley calls on Secretary Welles and on the President — Sumner on Louis Napoleon's Action in regard to the Presidency of the World's Congress of Savants — The President vetoes the Civil Rights Bill — Cabinet Discussion of the Bill — Seward and the Proposed Purchase of the Danish West Indies — The Semmes Case — The Outlook in Connecticut — Banks and the Use of Naval Vessels for the French Exposition — Butler and the Grey Jacket.

March 3, *Saturday*. The week as usual has been busy. The faction in Congress holds possession of the majority in both houses, yet there are signs of restiveness, of misgiving, on the part of many. Baldwin, from the Worcester District, Massachusetts, who is on the Directory, or Reconstruction, Committee, assures me that Stevens has in a great measure lost his influence in that committee. I have no doubt that Baldwin and others so believe when away from Stevens and perhaps when with him, but without intending it or even being fully aware of the extent to which it is carried, they are subjected, controlled, and directed by him. They may, by appeals, modify, but not to great extent, Stevens's plans. Baldwin intimates that action will be taken in behalf of the Tennessee Members, admitting them to the seats to which they are elected, early next week. The same thing has been repeated to me to-day by others. There is a manifest feeling of the gross wrong committed by their exclusion, not only to the State but to the Federal Union.

They have made the necessity of action in this case felt, and Stevens has had to yield, but he will, I presume, make the proceeding odious and unjust. Baldwin asks, Why not pass a law admitting those States? I told him Tennessee had been admitted seventy years ago. He said he did not strictly mean admission, but a law authorizing them to resume their relations with the Government. I said I could not see the necessity, or even the expediency of such a law, for, the Rebellion being suppressed, Tennessee and each of the States resumed their position as States, and if they sent loyal men here, I thought they should be admitted; if disloyal or unpardoned Rebels, such could be rejected. He was, however, very tenacious on this point, and I doubt not is committed to it. What harm, inquired he, can come from passing such a law, preliminary to receiving the Members. I told him it was, as a general rule, harmful to over-legislate, it is harmful to pass laws without authority, to assume powers or to concede them; that Congress, as a body, had no business with the election of Members, but the Constitution directs each house shall decide for itself in regard to the members of the respective bodies. The two houses could not legally or by any constitutional authority exclude a State or deny it representation. It was, however, unpleasant for the President and Congress to be in antagonism, and if it was mere form which he had in view without objectionable points or ulterior purpose, possibly such a bill might not be vetoed, yet I thought it very questionable, for it would be centralizing and magnifying federal power here and dwarfing the State.

I therefore anticipate that Stevens, finding the Committee and Congress are determined to admit the Tennessee Members to their seats, will set to work to frame an offensive bill such as the President cannot sign, or which, if he does sign, will discredit himself and violate his, and all correct, principles. This, however, I am satisfied he will not do. Then on him is to be thrown the responsibility of excluding the Tennessee Members.

I intimated to the President my conjectures, and he remarked he was prepared for such an alternative whenever it was presented. He had, from some quarter, been previously admonished in regard to the doings of the Committee.

Stevens is determined to have an issue between the Executive and Congress, and, notwithstanding a majority of Congress and of the country deprecate such an issue, and Members to me and others express their dislike of and opposition to Stevens, I incline to the opinion that he will, by the working of his Directory machinery, be successful in raising that issue. Should he, the result will be likely to rend the party, unless the minority are subservient and tamely submissive. The Administration must be supported or opposed. The positive and violent will oppose; the mild and passive will yield. Congress must be with the Administration or against it. Double-dealing cannot continue. I am apprehensive that there is treachery to the President in quarters which he will ultimately keenly feel. Sometimes I think he suspects the mischief, but is unwilling to have a breach just at this time and listens to those who advise temporizing and expediency.

Sherman (Senator), after speaking against the concurrent resolution, finally voted for it in the face of his own delivered opinion, argument, and conviction. This is a specimen of the influence of party discipline at this time in Congress. It is all-powerful.

Governor Dennison tells me this evening that he has written a letter to Patterson of New Hampshire, stating that he has removed no man and intends to remove none on account of differences between Congress and the President, provided they belong to the Union party. I am afraid he has gone farther than is wise in this matter, for if Stevens gets up the issue between the President and Congress, it may be necessary for the President to relieve himself of troublesome and officious electioneers in post-offices. I suspect Dennison has been entrapped by fair words.

If I mistake not, the Union League organization has contributed largely to present difficulties. It is controlled by extreme Radicals and rules many Members of Congress. An irresponsible faction, organized for mischief.

March 5, Monday. The Reconstruction Committee have reported a resolution for admitting Tennessee Members. It is, in its phraseology and conditions, in character with the dissimulating management and narrow, unpatriotic partisanship of those who control the action of Congress. Tennessee is pronounced to be in a condition to exercise all the functions of a State, therefore she shall not send Representatives until she complies with certain conditions which Congress exacts but has no authority to impose, and which the people of that State cannot comply with and preserve their independence, self-respect, and the right guaranteed to them by the Constitution. How intelligent and sensible men, not opposed to our government and the Constitution itself can commit themselves to such stuff I am unable to comprehend, but the madness of party, the weakness of men who are under the discipline of an organization which chafes, stimulates, threatens, and coaxes, is most astonishing.

In conversation with Senator Grimes, Chairman of the Naval Committee, I regret to see he still retains his rancor towards the South, though I hope somewhat modified. He is unwilling to make needful appropriations for the navy yards at Norfolk and Pensacola because they are in the Rebel States. Yet a navy yard at Pensacola is important, it may be said necessary, to the protection of the Gulf Coast and the Mississippi in time of war. A foreign power can blockade that region, the whole valley of the Mississippi be locked up; and Western Members would permit this rather than expend a small sum for necessary purposes in a navy yard at the South. But Grimes is not so intensely wrong as others living in the Mississippi Valley. He will not, however, avail of the opportunity of procuring a magnificent site at Hampton Roads for the Naval School, because it is in Virginia.

March 6, *Tuesday.* The Secretary of the Treasury is embarrassed by the test oath. He finds it difficult to procure good officers for collectors and assessors in the Rebel States and still more difficult to get good subordinates. When he attempts to reason with Members of Congress, they insist that their object is to exclude the very men required and say they want Northern men sent into those States to collect taxes. As if such a proceeding would not excite enmities and the foreign tax-gatherer be slain!

I advised McCulloch to address a strong and emphatic letter to the President, stating the difficulties, which letter the President could communicate to Congress. A direct issue would then be made, and the country could see and appreciate the difficulties of the Administration. Dennison took the same view, and stated some of his difficulties, and I suggested that he should also present them to the President. Seward was not prepared to act. Harlan was apprehensive that a confession of the fact that it was not possible to procure men of integrity who could take the test oath, would operate injudiciously just at this time. There is, he thinks, a growing feeling for conciliation in Congress, and such a confession would check this feeling. The suggestion was adroitly if not ingenuously put. Stanton half-responded to Harlan; doubted the expediency of a letter from McCulloch; said it was unnecessary; that he paid officers who could not take the oath; thought the Secretary of the Treasury might also; but concluded by saying he had not examined the question. Finally the subject was postponed to Friday. Stanton said it had presented itself to him in a new form during the discussion, and he required a little time for examination and reflection before submitting his views.

March 7, *Wednesday.* I have addressed a letter concerning League Island, communicating the report of Mr. Fox,

the Assistant Secretary, who visited Philadelphia with the
Naval Committee. The improvidence and neglect of Congress on this subject shows how unreliable all legislation is
for the public interest in high party times. By an intrigue
Brandegee of New London was placed on the Naval Committee. Colfax purchased his support by that appointment, and the displacement of English, — an act of dissimulation and discourtesy to me personally as well as a
sacrifice of the public interest. Brandegee wants the navy
yard at New London because he lives there and it is his
home, not for the public interest and the national welfare,
and for that narrow, selfish, low object the Navy and the
country are sacrificed.

March 8, Thursday. Myers of Philadelphia had a long
conversation with me in regard to the "admission" of Tennessee. I told him, as I have others, that Tennessee had
been admitted more than seventy years ago. Well, he said,
he did not mean admission, but to permit her to send Representatives. I told him he did mean admission and nothing
else, and that permission to send Representatives was quite
as offensive as his first position. The Constitution secured
her that right when the State was admitted and made part
of the Union, and Congress could neither deprive nor grant
her the privilege of representation. Much more of like
tendency passed between us — pleasantly. He expects to
make a speech on the subject.

Governor Dennison called this evening to see whether
he, McCulloch, and myself had not best consult with the
President in regard to the welfare of the Republican Party
and endeavor to bring about a reconciliation with the factious majority in Congress. I told him I could see no benefit that would result from such an effort; that the President's policy was well defined; that when Congress assembled, the Members well understood that policy, and that
they, the Radicals, had promptly organized to oppose and
defeat it; that this hostility or antagonism had gone forward

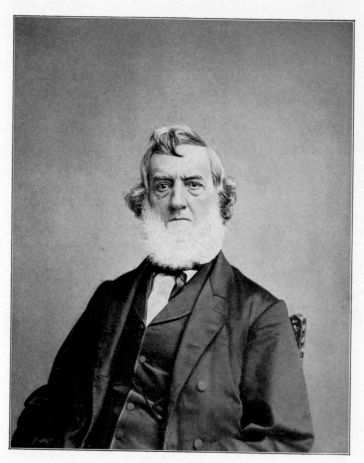

GIDEON WELLES

for three months, Congress doing nothing, accomplishing nothing towards a restoration of the Union, but on the contrary had devoted its time and energies to prevent it. What, I asked him, could the President do under these circumstances? He cannot abandon his honest, rightful convictions, and to approach or attempt to approach these Radical leaders in their present state of mind would be misconstrued and retard rather than promote the work. The Republican Party had evidently about accomplished its mission. Slavery was abolished and the Rebellion suppressed. Perhaps it would result beneficially to take a new departure. He appeared to acquiesce in my suggestions.

March 9, Friday. Senator Grimes, after an interview this A.M. on naval matters, got on to the subject of our public affairs generally, and particularly the differences between the President and the party in Congress. He disclaims Stevens and Sumner, and spoke of each in severe and denunciatory terms, — the former as a pretty unscrupulous old fellow, unfit to lead any party, Sumner as a cold-blooded, selfish, dangerous man. When I spoke of him as honest but theoretical and yet, I believe, truthful, Grimes was disinclined to award him these traits, and I perceive has a strong prejudice — perhaps I should better define it by saying hate — of the Massachusetts Senator, who, though a student learned in books, Grimes asserts is not a statesman or wise legislator.

With very respectable talents, Grimes is of a suspicious and somewhat jealous nature, inclining to be misanthropic. He must be classed as of the Radical school, but recognizes no Radical leader, has no respect for them; abhors Stevens as a debauchee in morals and politics. He is intimate with Fessenden, who is dyspeptic and has similar traits, and the two hunt in couples. They were both former admirers of Seward, but now and for some time past they dislike him, think his influence on Johnson pernicious.

When I saw during the fall that the extremists were

gathering up their strength against the President, it was a question with me how these two Senators would go. Their natural tendency would, I knew, incline them to the opposition. They are both intense on the negro. But neither of them liked Sumner or Stevens, who were in the extreme advance. The President was originally of a different school of politics, and there is not, therefore, that intimacy between them which begets zeal, but during the War they have been bound by a common interest. They had no personal opposition to the President and, I think, no feeling against him except that which minds like theirs would have against the elevation above them of an old associate Senator whom they had regarded as an equal rather than a superior. Though differing with him in fundamental principles of our government, they respected his honesty.

Grimes says he came here at the commencement of the present session kindly disposed to the President and not very hostile to his policy. But he soon found that certain obnoxious Democrats had free access to the White House, and that pardoned Rebels hung around there. He was not satisfied with this state of things, and spoke of it, and was asked why he and others remained away. Soon after he was invited to breakfast with the President, and spent two hours with him discussing all subjects in full and most satisfactorily. Allusion was made to Fessenden, and he expressed a wish that the two should come together and interchange opinions. The President requested him to speak to Fessenden and invite an interview. As the next day was Sunday, Grimes inquired if it would be agreeable for the President to see him on the Sabbath. The President assented, and F. spent several hours most satisfactorily at the White House and went over general measures now prominent.

On the following day appeared the celebrated letter of "a conversation of the President with a distinguished Senator." Grimes says on reading it he asked Fessenden if that was his conversation. F. after reading the letter said he had had no such conversation, and they soon ascertained that Dixon was the Senator. The two, finding that they were not the only confidants of the President, thereupon left him, and allied themselves to the Radicals. They had ascertained that the President conversed freely with others, was not likely to commit himself to their keeping exclusively, and therefore should have their opposition or at all events could not rely on their support.

I inquired of Grimes what there was offensive in the letter, or the President's policy, or wherein he was inconsistent; said that doubtless many, who, like him and Fessenden, had peculiar views of their own, had called on the President and he had frankly conversed with each of them, notwithstanding their different shades of opinion, and each, perhaps, had construed the friendly courtesy and kindly greeting as favoring his tenet, while the aim had been to commit himself to none, but to be friendly and conciliatory with all.

I asked Grimes where all this was to end; what we were to expect when Members of Congress made it a point to disagree, organized a joint committee of the two houses to get round constitutional difficulty, which committee was to establish a policy for Congress and the country, arrogated to itself and stimulated Congress to arrogate or usurp executive powers, were passing declaratory resolutions which had no force, but were designed to irritate and be offensive, with other extraordinary proceedings. I told him the country had a present and a future before it, and its fate was to some extent in the hands of men in responsible positions and for which they were accountable. The country, I said, appeared to me to be in peril; that we must either reunite or diverge still farther soon. We cannot remain inactive, must either advance or recede.

I could perceive he was disturbed, but soon remarked that the Southern people were a damned set of traitors, as bad now as at any time during the Rebellion, and he had no confidence in them.

2

I admitted they were bad, malignant, foolish to a great extent, but asked when they would be better, and if no better, were we to be forever a disunited country. Their indebtedness in various forms under their sham organization could not be less than twenty-five hundred millions; the property in slaves which was extinguished by emancipation could not be less than twenty-five hundred millions more; other individual losses were immense. To all this they were compelled to submit, and besides this they were to pay their proportion of our debt incurred in whipping them. Now was it strange that they were sore and complaining, and were we doing right in excluding them from all participation in the government, to which they were entitled under the Constitution? We must adopt conciliatory measures or national calamities would soon be upon us, and we ought not to shut our eyes to the facts.

He admitted something must be done, but said that he had confidence that all would come right. He guessed we were nearer now than some apprehended. This he said with a smile and manner that impressed me as coming from one who thinks he and his associates have the reins in their hands and intend to guide the government car safely. But the subject should not be trifled with.

McCulloch inquired of Stanton if he had reached a solution of the difficulty in regard to the oath. Stanton replied that he had given it considerable thought and come to the conclusion that it would be best for McCulloch to prepare a letter setting forth the difficulties of the case. This letter, I remarked, had better be addressed to the President. Stanton did not respond favorably to this suggestion. He thought it would do as well to send it to one of the committee. This was also Harlan's view. Dennison took very decided ground with me.

The rumors that the Fenians had seized Navy Island and that ten thousand volunteers had been called out by the Canadian authorities were current this morning. Seward was unwell and not at the Cabinet-meeting. The British and Canadian Governments were each much excited. The last arrival brings information that the *habeas corpus* is suspended in Ireland and the propriety of some governmental action here was discussed.

Stanton thought a proclamation should be issued and decisive measures taken, as was done by Van Buren in his day. Regretted Seward was not present, for we knew not what appeals had been made by the British Government. The propriety of taking some action was generally concurred in, and Stanton rather pressed it. I proposed that General Grant should be consulted, sent to the frontiers, and perhaps it would be well to address a communication on the subject which would form the basis of government action. Stanton could see no necessity for bringing Grant out; a proclamation from the President to put down these Fenian organizations was what was required. I assented, but stated that the occasion and condition of the country and of our public affairs were such that I thought it would be wise to have the public authorities fully heard, and all of them. The Irish element, I stated, was a strong one and clannish, and if a movement against an organization of theirs was to be made, I wished to see others besides the President moving, and especially did I desire, under existing circumstances, when the militia might be called to act, that General Grant should be consulted. Harlan thought a circular from the Attorney-General exhorting vigilance on the part of attorneys and marshals would be sufficient; the circular could be got into print. While I did not object to that process, I expressed my conviction that it would be wise to have General Grant identified with the Administration in these movements. Dennison and McCulloch concurred with me.

After the others left, the President expressed his satisfaction with the direction I had indicated and the bearing it seemed to have on others.

March 10, *Saturday.* Thad Stevens has to-day made a

blackguard and disreputable speech in the House. Beginning with the false assertion that the speech was prepared two months ago, and continuing with the equally false assurance that an interlude, or byplay, which was introduced was unpremeditated, this wretched old man displayed more strongly than in his speech those bad traits of dissimulation, insincerity, falsehood, scandal-loving, and defamation that have characterized his long life. The Radical managers and leaders were cognizant of his speech, and had generally encouraged it, but I shall be disappointed if they do not wish the vain old man had been silent before many months. Such disgraceful exhibitions can do the author and his associates no good, nor those whom he assails enduring harm. The people may not in the first excitement and under the discipline of party be enabled to judge of the conspirators correctly who are striving to divide the Union, not by secession but by exclusion. It is clearly a conspiracy, though not avowed.

March 13, Tuesday. Had a call this evening from Mr. English, the Democratic candidate for Governor in Connecticut. He is very decidedly, and I think sincerely, in favor of the President's policy. With General Hawley, who is the Administration candidate, I am more intimate, and for him I personally feel special regard, yet such is the strange mixture of parties that his election would be hailed as a triumph by the opponents of the Administration. I am much embarrassed by this state of things. I believe Hawley intends to support the President, yet, tainted by party, he also aims to support Congress in its differences with the Executive. He will find it difficult to reconcile the two, and if compelled to make an election he would be more likely at the present moment to go wrong, I fear, than right.

Mr. English desired an introduction to the President, whom he wishes to see concerning some person who is imprisoned in Tennessee, and is acting in concert with a Mr. Fleming, whom, with his beautiful wife, I met this evening at the President's house.

Seward was not at the Cabinet to-day. I brought forward the subject of the test oath, and McCulloch says he has prepared a letter which he will show me. Dennison is to prepare one also.

On the subject of the Fenians there was less inclination to converse, but the subject was referred to the Attorney-General to send circulars to the District Attorneys, etc. I suggested that the Administration should show a solid front, and, therefore, General Grant should send a communication. To this Stanton demurred. It would necessarily come through his Department, and he would be openly committed.

March 14, *Wednesday.* Secretary McCulloch sent me his letter this morning on the subject of the test oath, to read and criticize. It is in the main very well done. I would have proposed some alterations, but, on making one or two suggestions as feelers, I perceived he had the usual sensitiveness in regard to his own production and, therefore, desisted. My course differs from his in this respect, for in public communications I want criticism from friends until the document is signed and has gone from me.

I called upon him with the paper, and we had a talk on subjects generally. The communication of Clarke, Comptroller of the Currency, was printed this A.M. in the *Intelligencer*. It is a piece of impertinence and insubordination which deserves rebuke, prompt and summary. I advised McCulloch to have his scalp off before sundown. He is more forbearing; says that is what Clarke wishes.

March 16, *Friday.* A quiet Cabinet-meeting with nothing of interest discussed. Dennison read his communication on the test oath. It is less vigorous and pertinent than McCulloch's, but will do as a backer. McCulloch showed me a letter from Henry Ward Beecher to Defrees in which it is said that the postmaster at Brooklyn (Lincoln) informed him (Beecher) that Senator Pomeroy had authorized and requested him (L.) to inform B. that he (P.) called at the White House a week since, and found the President, his son, and son-in-law all drunk and unfit for business, that the President kept a mistress at the White House, etc. I advised that these slanders should be told the President in order that he might be aware of the character of the scandals circulated.

By appointment McCulloch, Dennison, and myself agreed to meet the President this evening at seven. At that hour McCulloch and I came together near Dennison's door and went in. Soon after Speed and his wife were announced. D. went in to them with an understanding that he would join us at the White House. But he failed to do so.

Mr. English of Connecticut was with the President when we went in, but left almost immediately. The President expressed himself pleased with English, and dissatisfied with something which Hawley had said, — some answers to inquiries, as I understood. McCulloch remarked that it would not do for us to disconnect ourselves from the War Party, even if some had got astray, for every loyal household had its representative in the army, and the feeling was strong in their favor.

The letter on the test oath McC. read to us. I suggested a single alteration which I mentioned before, calling the Southerners "our rebellious countrymen" instead of a "hostile people." The President approved the suggestion, and McCulloch came into it. Some other alterations, chiefly verbal, suggested themselves, but, witnessing the sensitiveness of McC., I did not mention them.

March 17, *Saturday.* This being St. Patrick's Day, considerable apprehensions were entertained by the Englishmen here that there would be more active demonstration by the Fenians. Sir Frederick Bruce did not hesitate to say to me on Thursday evening at the Marquis Montholon's party when I met him, that he had great anxiety and should feel relieved after Saturday. But the day has passed off peaceably. We have had no telegraphs of riot or disorder on the frontier or in Canada. There is less disturbance in our own country than is usual on this anniversary.

By special invitation from Secretary Seward himself, I went this evening to meet a Belgian delegation at his house. Mrs. Welles and Edgar went with me. McCulloch, Dennison, and Speed were similarly invited, as were others. I found we were after-dinner guests, appendages to the special party, called in to set off the Secretary's party. The evening was cold, fires low or out, and though the persons assembled put on the best face, it was an uncomfortable affair, and I for one in no very good humor, believing I had been uselessly put to inconvenience without cause.

Am having sharp questions and importunities in regard to the Connecticut election, and do not choose to answer them or to be mixed up in the contest, which has been badly shaped. The fault is as much here in Washington as elsewhere. Foreseeing the issues which the Radicals in Congress were forming, I suggested near the commencement of the session to the President, that unless the lines were sharply drawn, they would have him at disadvantage. We now see it in the result in New Hampshire, and similar consequences may be expected in Connecticut. General Hawley's sympathies and feelings are with the Radicals in the differences between the President and Congress, or rather with Congress than the President. English, on the other hand, is wholly with the President, and totally, earnestly opposed to the Congressional policy. The election of English would secure a friend to the President, but English and those who support him opposed his (the President's) election and most of them opposed the War. Hawley, while not in full accord with the President on present questions, and I am afraid not on the rights of the States, supported his election, and was an earnest soldier from the

beginning of the War until the whole Rebel force surrendered and dispersed. While I think well of both candidates,
I have a particular personal regard for Hawley now, as
well as intimate party relations in the past.

The President and very many of his friends would be
pleased to have English succeed. But they do not comprehend the whole circumstances, personal and political, for
they cannot know them. It is not a personal question. The
organization is a revival of ante-War differences. It commenced and has gone on under the old party banners. A
stand for the Administration should have been made last
autumn, but the nominations from Governor down have
been made by parties as organized years ago. It is too late
to change front, or get up a new arrangement. Such an
issue should have commenced last December, and the President himself should have led in the fight by announcing
the policy of his Administration and rallying his friends to
its support. He would have had the State, the country,
and Congress with him, but he hesitated, was reluctant to
encounter those who elected him, and then postponed too
long for us to begin in Connecticut, for this election takes
place in three weeks.

As things are, I cannot take an active part in this contest. Were Hawley more emphatic and unequivocally with
the President, I should enter earnestly, heartily, into the
struggle, although I did not advise his nomination, or wish
it to be made. I think, when elected, he will give the Administration fair support, but he is an ardent partisan. A
doubt on the subject of his course paralyzes my zeal and
efforts. I am unwilling to believe that Hawley dissembles.

March 19, *Monday.* Allen of the *Intelligencer* called upon
me to-day in reference to the Connecticut election. Says
it is stated in the papers that I have written letters urging
Hawley's election, yet Hawley is making speeches against
the President. Told him I had written no letters of the
purport indicated, had purposely abstained and intended

to. Asked what statements and what papers he referred to, and doubted if Hawley had made speeches in opposition to the Administration. It would not be politic for him to do so. That English is in favor of the President's policy as distinguished from that of Stevens or Congress, is true. The Republicans of Connecticut thought they did a shrewd thing in passing one resolution in favor of the President and another in favor of Congress. This inconsistency, equivocation, or contradiction is now troublesome.

March 20, *Tuesday.* Little of interest at the Cabinet-meeting. After the others had left had a free talk with the President. He thinks, in view of the feeling manifested by Congress and the favorable reception of Stewart's resolutions for general amnesty, it will be well to delay the case of Semmes.

I read to him a letter received from General Hawley in regard to the election in Connecticut, and a letter from myself to Crofut, stating my views on present questions, and, believing General H. concurred in them, I wished him success, but not if he was opposed to them and the Administration.

The President approved my letter. Said Mr. English appeared to be a gentleman of character and friendly. Asked what had been his previous party course and whether I had seen a series of questions which were put to Hawley and Hawley's answer. I informed him that English had always been a Democrat, but patriotic, gentlemanly, and not extreme or ultra. Had given support to some important questions of ours during the War. The questions and answers I had seen, but knew not how correct.

March 21, *Wednesday.* Collectors Babcock of New Haven and Smith of Bridgeport called on me this morning. They had just arrived, having come on in relation to the Connecticut election. English appears to have created an excitement, almost a panic, in regard to the wishes of the Administration. There is alarm on the part of the gentlemen and doubtless much at home which has impelled them to come here. English has represented to them that he had had a long interview on one or two occasions with the President, and that United States officers were to be turned out if they voted for Hawley. Babcock said three or four in his office had their resignations ready and he should tender his if that was exacted. They informed me that Cleveland, Postmaster at Hartford, had called, or was to participate in, a meeting favorable to English, and under the excitement Starkweather of Norwich, Chairman of the State Committee of the Republicans, had sent in his resignation as Postmaster. There is excitement and a party panic in that State. Both Babcock and Smith admitted and asserted that these troubles had their origin in the equivocal, ambiguous, and inconsequential resolutions of the Republican Convention, which spoke two voices, and made the party support antagonistic positions.

General Hawley and Mr. E. H. Owen came and spent more than an hour with me after the interview with B. and S. They had come to Washington impelled by the same causes as those of the other two gentlemen, but without preconcert. Much the same ground was reviewed and the same arguments used, and I told them their difficulties were the results in a great measure of the inconsistent attitude of the convention in indorsing both the President and the Radical majority in Congress, who were in direct antagonism; that no man could support the two honestly.

Hawley two or three times expressed a wish that I would write a letter indorsing him. This, had the issue been direct and fair, I could have done cheerfully, but I asked him what I could say. I was a supporter of the measures of the policy of the Administration; these measures and that policy had my earnest approval; I was advising to them, was identified with them. Of course I desired their success. If I knew that he was in favor of the Administration policy and opposed to the schemes of the Radicals who would defeat it, I could say something definite and positive, but unless that were the case I could do him no good. As things were, I should be compelled, while expressing my personal regard and belief that he would, if elected, be in accord with the Administration, [to say] that my understanding of his position was that his views coincided with those of the President, and particularly that he favored the early reëstablishment of the Union and of the Government in all its departments, that he recognized the rights of each and all of the States, was for the admission of loyal Senators and Representatives promptly, was against sectional division and the exclusion of any of the States. Both Hawley and Owen gave a hesitating but full assent at first; but Hawley thought the word confidence or belief would be better than understanding. Owen concurred, yet all of us saw the embarrassment, and I expressed again my doubts whether I could give any letter or written statement as things were without accompanying it with qualifications which would destroy its effect.

They left me at 1 P.M. to meet Senator Foster, who was to accompany them to the President, and they were to see me after the interview, which lasted over two hours. They expressed themselves satisfied with the views of the President and his course in regard to the election, his object being to sustain his own measures and policy and his preference being for those candidates of his own party who occupy that position. He had given Mr. English no letter and did not intend to take part with any candidates in a merely local election.

Hawley wished to know if I had read the Civil Rights Bill and whether I thought the President would veto it. I told him I had been through the bill, but had exchanged no opinions regarding it; that I thought it very centralizing and objectionable, and my impressions were the President would disapprove of it, though very reluctant to have further difficulty with Congress.

They left, I thought, better satisfied with the President than I was with the course of the Republicans in Connecticut.

In yesterday's *Intelligencer* was a leading editorial article in relation to myself and my position. The editor had called on me the preceding evening, and we had a conversation in relation to public affairs, the substance of which he has incorporated in his article. What he says regarding my course or stand in the Connecticut election is a little stronger than the actual conversation will warrant. I declined giving any letter or authorization of the use of my name, and informed him I did not wish to become mixed up with the election, which was in many respects unpleasant to me, in consequence of the ambiguous and equivocal course of the Republican Convention. An honest, open, fair expression of views on their part would have left me free to approve or condemn.

March 22, Thursday. Messrs. Babcock and Smith called this morning with a written statement correcting the *Chronicle*, which they proposed to present that paper for publication. I concurred in the propriety of their course. Both gentlemen expressed themselves highly pleased with their interview with the President and with other friends in Washington.

March 23, Friday. Special notice from the President that there would be no Cabinet-meeting. Called upon him this P.M. and gave him, generally, my views in regard to what is called the Civil Rights Bill, which, if approved by him, must lead to the overthrow of his Administration as well as that of this mischievous Congress which has passed it. The principles of that bill, if carried into effect, must subvert the government. It is consolidation solidified, breaks down all barriers to protect the rights of the States, concentrates power in the General Government, which assumes to itself the enactment of municipal regulations between the States and citizens and between citizens of the same State. No bill of so contradictory and consolidating a character has ever been enacted. The Alien and Sedition Laws were not so objectionable. I did not inquire of the President what would be his course in regard to the bill, but we did not disagree in opinion on its merits, and he cannot give it his sanction, although it is unpleasant to him to have these differences with Congress.

He tells me that Senator Pomeroy disavows having stated that he saw the President drunk at the White House, but says he (Pomeroy) wrote Lincoln, the Postmaster at Brooklyn, that he saw Robert, the President's son, in liquor, and he thought the same of his son-in-law, Senator Patterson.

March 24, Saturday. The *Intelligencer* of this morning contains an adroit letter from Cleveland, the Hartford Postmaster, stating that he is openly supporting English for Governor, who is in favor of the measures, policy, veto, and speech of the President, and that he is opposing Hawley, who is opposed to them, and tendering his resignation if his course is disapproved. On this letter the President indorsed that his (C.'s) action in sustaining his (the President's) measures and policy is approved and the resignation is, therefore, not accepted.

This correspondence will be misconstrued and misunderstood, I have no doubt. The Democrats will claim that it is a committal for English, and the Republicans will acquiesce to some extent. Yet the disposition of the subject is highly creditable to the sagacity and tact of the President. I regret that he did not earlier and in some more conspicuous case take action.

I do not like the shape things are taking in Connecticut, and to some extent the position of the President is and will be misunderstood. He is, I think, not satisfied with the somewhat equivocal position of Hawley, and would now prefer that English should be the Union candidate. Herein he errs, as things are situated, for most of his friends are supporting Hawley and some of his bitterest opponents are supporting English. He should soon draw the line of demarcation. In the break-up of parties which I think is now upon us, not unlikely Hawley will plunge into central-ism, for thither go almost all Radicals, including his old Abolition associates. The causes or circumstances which take him there will be likely to bring English into the President's support. Nevertheless, under the existing state of things, I should, unless something farther occurs between this and election, probably, on personal grounds, prefer Hawley. It is too late to effect a change of front with parties.

Senator Sumner came this P.M. as usual on Saturdays. He doubts the correctness of taking naval vessels for the French Exhibition. Grimes, with whom I have had some conversation, has contributed to Sumner's doubts. It is certainly a strange proceeding to require or expect the Navy to furnish four vessels with their crews for this carry-ing service without any appropriation of funds for that object. It is not a naval matter, enters not into our esti-mates, and we have no suitable vessels. The House is very loose and reckless, however, in its proceedings, and ap-pears to be careless of current legislation. Specific appro-priations they would misapply, and are, in fact, pressing and insisting that I shall divert funds appropriated by law for one purpose to another and different purpose. But this was not Sumner's trouble. He thought it bad economy, as it undoubtedly is. I said to him that if I was called to do this transportation without instructions, I would, as a matter of economy, sooner charter merchant ships than dismantle and attempt to convert and use naval vessels for the purpose.

I learn in confidence from Sumner that dispatches from our legation in France have reached the State Department which have not been brought before the Cabinet. Louis Napoleon has quarreled with his cousin, who was president

of the commission of savants, and he has left Paris and
resigned the presidency. Napoleon has appointed in his
place, as president of the World's Congress of wise men
and inventors, his son, now some eight or ten years of age.
This Sumner thinks an insult or worse, and is disposed to
give the whole thing a rebuff. I shall be glad to have him,
but he will not attempt to move without first consulting
Seward, and that gentleman has his heart so much in the
interest of France, his friends are so engaged in the Exhibition, that he has held back this information and will set
himself earnestly at work to overpersuade Sumner, who, as
Chairman of the Committee on Foreign Relations, has
seen the dispatches. He may succeed. Sumner was, however, very earnest and pleased with his own idea of hitting
Louis Napoleon a blow.

March 26, *Monday.* Senator Doolittle called at my
house last evening on the subject of the Civil Rights Bill,
which it is now well understood, outside, will meet an
Executive veto. Doolittle has an elaborate bill of his
own which he proposes to submit. Something, he thinks,
must be done. His bill is, perhaps, somewhat less offensive than the one which has been passed by both houses,
but the whole thing is wrong and his plan has the same
objectionable machinery as the other. I frankly told
him that the kind of legislation proposed, and which
Congress was greedy to enact, was not in my view correct, was sapping the foundation of the government and
must be calamitous in its results. We went together to
Senator Morgan's and talked over the subject an hour or
more with him.

The President convened the Cabinet this A.M. at ten
and read his message returning the Civil Rights Bill with
his veto. Before reading it he desired the members to express their opinions. Seward said he had carefully studied
the bill and thought it might be well to pass a law declaring negroes were citizens, because there had been some

questions raised on that point, though there never was a doubt in his own mind. The rest of the bill he considered unconstitutional in many respects, and having the mischievous machinery of the Fugitive Slave Law did not help commend it.

McCulloch waived remark; had not closely scrutinized the bill, and would defer comment to Stanton, merely remarking that he should be gratified if the President could see his way clear to sign the bill.

Stanton made a long argument, showing that he had devoted much time to the bill. His principal point was to overcome the obnoxious features of the second section, which he thought should be construed favorably. He did not think judges and marshals, or sheriffs and local officers should be fined and imprisoned; did not think it was intended to apply to officers, but merely to persons. The bill was not such a one as he would have drawn or recommended, but he advised that under the circumstances it should be approved.

The President having previously been put in possession of my views, I briefly remarked that my objections were against the whole design, purpose, and scope of the bill, that it was mischievous and subversive.

Mr. Dennison thought that, though there might be some objection to parts, he, on the whole, would advise that the bill should receive Executive approval.

Mr. Harlan had not closely read the bill, but had met difficulties in the second section, and in one or two others which had been measurably removed by Stanton's argument. He thought it very desirable that the President and Congress should act in concert if possible.

Speed was ill and not present.

The Senate to-day deprived Stockton of New Jersey of his seat. It was a high-handed, partisan proceeding, in which Sumner, Fessenden, Morrill, and others exhibited a spirit and feeling wholly unworthy of their official position. While I have no special regard for Stockton and his party in New Jersey, I am compelled to believe they have in this instance certainly been improperly treated and for a factious purpose, and I apprehend that I can never think so well of some of the gentlemen who have been conspicuous in this proceeding. Had Stockton acted with Sumner and Fessenden against the veto, he never would have been ousted from his seat. Of this I have no doubt whatever, and I am ashamed to confess it, or say it. I am passing no judgment on his election, for I know not the exact facts, but the indecent, unfair, arbitrary conduct of the few master spirits is most reprehensible.

March 27, Tuesday. The proceedings of the Senate, though exciting, do not overshadow the interest felt in the Connecticut election. Although the President strives to be disinterested and indifferent between the candidates for Governor, I cannot be mistaken in the fact that he inclines favorably to English. I am sorry for this, because his friends, those who elected him, are almost all of them supporters of Hawley. Those who voted for him, those who have stood by his measures since called to administer the Government and are sincerely friendly to his policy are committed to Hawley and the ticket which he heads. True, Hawley on mere organized party grounds is himself inclining to Congress, and I am constrained to believe will eventually identify himself with the centralists. English will be the opposite. But these questions are not made controlling in this election, as they should have been at the beginning of the contest.

March 28, Wednesday. The death of Senator Foot has checked excitement. Senators have put off discussing the veto till next week. Many of them are going to Connecticut to electioneer. Some will accompany the remains of the deceased Senator to Vermont. In the mean time Trumbull will prepare himself to attack the veto with all his power. So with others.

2

March 29, *Thursday*. Attended, with the rest of the Cabinet, the President to the Capitol, — the funeral of Senator Foot. Great interest was felt. He was *pater senatus* and much loved and respected. Had been twenty-three years in Congress.

He was on the Naval Committee in the first years of my administration and always a firm friend of the Department. This brought him intimate with me and somewhat in collision with J. P. Hale, who was Chairman of the Naval Committee and an opponent and faultfinder, ending with the retirement of Foot from the Committee, much to my regret, for, next to Grimes, he interested himself more in naval matters than any of his associates on the Senate Committee. Although indisposed to complain and always avoiding censorious remarks, he in apologizing for his course in retiring from the Committee stated that the association with the Chairman was unpleasant.

March 30, *Friday*. Mr. Seward brought up in the Cabinet to-day the subject of the purchase of the Danish islands in the West Indies, particularly St. Thomas. For a year or so the question has been under consideration. The Danes wish to sell and first edged in the matter gently. The Secretary of State did not give the matter earnest attention, but the Navy Department in our war, feeling the want of a station in the West Indies, has favored the subject. My Report of 1865 roused the Secretary of State, and he began when the War was over to press the purchase, first talking round about the French islands. Finally he visited St. Thomas in a public ship. I do not think there has been over-much shrewdness in the transaction on our part as yet. It would have been better for Seward to have remained away from the islands, but should we acquire it his visit will undoubtedly become historical, and it will not afflict him, perhaps, if the country pays largely for the record of his name and visit.

He proposes to offer ten millions for all the Danish

islands. I think it a large sum. At least double what I would have offered when the islands were wanted, and three times as much as I am willing the Government should give now. In fact I doubt if Congress would purchase for three millions, and I must see Seward and tell him my opinion.

I again brought the subject of Semmes's trial before the Cabinet. The question should be disposed of, for we are detaining our officers and others as witnesses. Speed has recommended that the trial should go forward under the mixed commission, and to-day recommended it anew. Said it would be an interesting trial. Stanton said he did not advise it for mere curiosity, but if the proceedings were to take place he would wish thorough work should be made and the extreme penalty of the law inflicted. Governor Dennison was very prompt and decided in the expression of his wish that Semmes should be tried and punished.

I repeated what I have frequently stated, that the Navy Department would have nothing to do with trying him for treason, piracy, or any offense which could be reached by the civil courts, but he was charged with, and I suppose was guilty of, violating the usages and laws of war. The truth was, however, on investigating the subject, the points had been narrowed down and mitigated, so that I believed his offense was really less aggravated than had been charged and believed.

The President was evidently not prepared to decide what course to take. I submitted Semmes's application for a parole, which was favorably indorsed by Judge-Advocate-General Bolles. As the session of the Cabinet was some-what protracted and Stanton was wishing a special interview, I proposed to the President to call to-morrow, which seemed to relieve and gratify him.

March 31, *Saturday.* I had an interview with the President concerning Semmes, as understood yesterday. Showed him the papers, and, after some conversation, he proposed to see Judge-Advocate-General Bolles, Solicitor of the Navy Department; said he would on the whole prefer him to the Attorney-General in this matter, and named Monday next.

By the President's request I went into the library and was introduced to Doctor Norris, with whom the President desired me to have some conversation. Doctor N. said he believed that the President and I had had some consultation in relation to a sea voyage for Robert, the President's son. He supposed I knew the circumstances. I told him I was aware of the young man's infirmity, that he had once spoken to me himself on the subject in a manner to touch my sympathy in his behalf. That I had also conversed with his father, as he seemed to be aware, and as he (the father) had doubtless advised him. He said that was so, and proceeded to tell me that R. had been beguiled into intemperance after he became of age, through his generous qualities, goodness of heart, and friendly disposition. He, therefore, thought it possible to reclaim him.

I had very little expectation of such a result, but it is important, for his father's sake and for the country's, that the President should in these days be relieved of the care and anxiety which his excesses and passions involve. To send him abroad in a public ship is the best disposition that can be made of him, and a voyage to the East Indies would be better than any other, and such a voyage was now in preparation. Doctor Norris thought this desirable.

I subsequently saw the President and told him what had taken place and that I could make the arrangement with little trouble to him. It seemed to give him consolation.

Letters from Connecticut do not speak with confidence of the result of the election next Monday. But my impressions are that the Union Party with Hawley will be successful. The battle will not be on the strict political issues before the country. On these issues, if well defined and the candidates were squarely presented, I have no doubt that the Administration would be triumphantly sustained. It would be union against disunion, the President *versus* Congress under the lead of Stevens. But politics and parties have become strangely mixed. Hawley, I am apprehensive, leans to the Congressional policy at present, but I trust observation and reflection will bring him right.

The true Union men who sustain the President feel that the defeat of Hawley would be a triumph to Toucey, Seymour, Eaton, and others who opposed the Government in war and whom they, for that reason, detest, and they will band together to support Hawley from matters of the past rather than issues of the present. Moreover Hawley has popular qualities. For ten years he has fought the Union battles in our political contests and in the field, and though he may be touched with Radicalism, he has good reasoning faculties and a sense of right within him on which I rely. The people have correct instincts in these matters, and I therefore feel pretty sure he will succeed. The worst is, should that be the case, the curse of party will claim that it is a triumph over the Administration. No harm will come of it, perhaps, but it is annoying and vexatious to have results to which men have contributed turned against themselves. But it cannot be helped. The distinction cannot now be drawn. Parties are in a transition state.

Sumner tells me this P.M. that his committee will go against the use of naval vessels for the French Exhibition. This will be counter to Banks, who laid himself out largely in this matter, and Sumner will not be grieved to have Banks disappointed. There is obviously no special love between these two gentlemen. They are opposites in many respects. Banks has thought to gain popularity in this move, which was concocted by himself and Seward, to use naval vessels and naval appropriations for a purpose not naval. To make their scheme appear less expensive, I am told that General Butler has succeeded in inducing the Secretary of the Treasury to interfere in the matter of the Grey Jacket, condemned as prize. If so, I regret it. McCulloch has been imposed upon. Butler is reckless,

avaricious, unscrupulous. He knows there is neither law
nor justice in his course on this question, but he has the
promise of large fees. For three months he has been annoying me on this subject. He then went to the Attorney-
General and for a time made some headway. Failing
there, he has now imposed upon McCulloch, who has
been deceived by Butler's cunning and browbeaten by
his audacity.

XXXVII

April 2, Monday. Called with General Bolles on the President in relation to the case of Raphael Semmes. The call was pursuant to appointment. Secretary Harlan was with the President when we called, about 1 P.M. The President inquired as soon as the subject was taken up whether any facts were yet public in relation to the decision of the Supreme Court in the Indiana cases. He said the Court was nearly tied, but that judgment would probably be rendered to-morrow, at all events within a day or two. That decision might have a bearing on Semmes's case. I remarked that it might be well to delay action until we heard from the Court. The President said he thought so and that was why he had made the inquiry, but added we might as well talk over the matter at this time and get the points designated. Bolles said he had, perhaps, no remarks to make in the present position of things, but if Semmes was not to be immediately tried, a parole would be advisable, unless the case was wholly abandoned. I remarked that it appeared to me best that he should be tried or the case abandoned, rather than have a parole. A trial would best satisfy the public and serve the ends of justice. It would place the Government in the best attitude. If tried at all it should be for violating the laws of war, — a case which the established legal tribunals could not reach. His conduct as a buccaneer or rebel in capturing and destroying the ships of peaceful merchants was not the question, but, escaping after striking his colors and sending his boat to the Kearsarge announcing his surrender, and without an exchange, he had subsequently entered first the Rebel naval service and then the military, and made war upon those who claimed him as their lawful prisoner. If in this he had not acted in bad faith and violated the usages of civilized warfare, we had no case against him. But if he had done these things, it was proper he should be tried, and it must be by a military commission, for it did not belong to the courts. It was in that view I favored a trial. The courts were proceeding against no parties for treason; partisans were blaming the President because there were no trials and convictions when it was not within his province to prosecute or try. But here was a case which belonged to him specially and no one else. Hence if he ordered Semmes to trial the country would be satisfied that he was sincere and discharging his duty towards the worst Rebels, and they would understand that the courts were not as prompt as the Executive. He would, however, await the decision of the Court.

When alone I brought up the subject of placing his son on a naval vessel. Told him of the Monocacy, Commander Carter, late brigadier-general in Tennessee. The President said at once he did not wish connection with Carter in this matter. I then mentioned the Chattanooga, Captain McKinstry. This vessel would have an interesting voyage. Stated to him the purpose of the Department in regard to her. He approved it. Said, however, it was desirable Robert should have something to do. We spoke of positions, and, perhaps the Secretary of State would find him some civil employment. This met his views. I inquired if he or I should see Seward. He desired me to do so, and, feeling that he should be relieved of the care and anxiety of a parent in this crisis, I took upon myself that object. I called immediately at the State Department. Seward, appreciating the whole case, at once entered into the subject and said he would employ Robert, whom he knew to be capable, to look into the slave-trade at Cape of Good Hope and on the African coast.

I stated to Seward that he had named too high a price for the Danish islands; that five millions was, I apprehended, more than our people would feel like giving; that I would not offer more than three. He thanked me; said he would inquire their lowest terms, that Raasloff was anxious to sell, etc., etc., but thought not less than five millions would be required.

April 3, *Tuesday.* The proclamation announcing peace in all the Rebel States but Texas appeared in the *National Republican* this morning. I was at first a little startled by it, apprehending it would cause some difficulty with our volunteer officers, who, by law, ceased to act on the return of peace. This provision towards that class of officers was one of those headless moves of J. P. Hale, made in the spirit of a demagogue under professed apprehension that Mr. Lincoln, or whoever might be President, would use the Navy to make himself dictator. The proclamation does not include Texas; therefore the Rebellion is not declared wholly suppressed. When I spoke of the subject to-day in Cabinet, I found that none of the members had been apprised of the fact, except Seward, and he not until five o'clock the preceding evening, when he was compelled to send to Hunter, Chief Clerk, at Georgetown. A sudden determination seems to have influenced the President. He did not state his reasons, but it is obvious that the Radicals are taken by surprise and view it as checkmating some of their legislation.

The returns from Connecticut leave no doubt of the election of Hawley, though by a very small majority, some six or eight hundred. This is well, — better than a larger majority, — and serves as a warning to the extremists. There is no denying that the policy of the President would have been sustained by a large majority of the people of Connecticut, were that the distinct issue. But this was avoided, yet Forney, in his *Chronicle*, asserts that the President is defeated, and his veto has been vetoed by the State. An idle falsehood. Mere partisanship will not control, and there has been much of it in this election. Each of the parties shirked the real, living issues, though the Democrats professed to respect them because the Republicans were divided upon the issues, and to press them destroyed or impaired that organization.

April 4, Wednesday. Consulted again with the President in regard to the case of Semmes. Peace having been declared in all the States and the decision of the Supreme Court in the Indiana cases — Milligan and others — being adverse to military commissions, I thought there should be prompt decision. The President inquired if it would not be best to parole him and require him to be in readiness when called. I replied it was for him to decide, but that it seemed to me best to dispose of Semmes, and if it was determined not to proceed to try him after this decision of the Court, I would advise his unconditional release rather than a parole. The President said he had some doubts, but wished to get rid of the subject, for Semmes's wife was annoying him, crying and taking on for her husband. The President has a gentle and kind heart, melted by woman's tears. I said I should be satisfied with whatever conclusion he came to; that it might go over to the next meeting of the Cabinet, or he could decide when it pleased him and send me word.

Commodore Stockton came to see me. Says things are in a satisfactory condition in the New Jersey Legislature. Is confident that his son John will be returned to the Senate with a good Johnson Republican. Is confident Scovel will hold out, and have, if necessary, others to help him; and assures me that enough Republicans will unite with the Democrats to return two such men. Wright, the present Senator, is ready for the arrangement. This may all be so, but I have grave doubts of its success. It is undoubtedly Stockton's arrangement, and he and his associates have heretofore been omnipotent in New Jersey, which is a strange State in some respects. Possibly he may succeed there. He could not in any other State. But the return of John Stockton, after what has taken place, would be honorable to New Jersey and one of the greatest triumphs that was ever achieved.

April 5, *Thursday.* The Senate did not get to a vote to-day on what is called the Civil Rights Bill. Much interest is felt in the result, increased by the uncertainty which exists in regard to the decision. Just about one third of the Senate is with the President, but two of the Senators are in bad health, and it is doubtful if they can be present, though it is believed they will be. Wright of New Jersey has been brought here at the peril of his life, and will, it is said, be present and vote. Dixon, long and seriously ill, rode out a short time to-day, and will attend if a time be fixed for the vote. Stewart of Nevada has persuaded himself that it is best for him to desert and go with the majority. Stockton was deprived of his seat by the Radical majority in order to carry this vote. There are some vague intimations that Morgan is equivocating and may go with Stewart, but I discredit it. He has, without direct assurance, given me to understand otherwise; took tea with me night before last, and spent an hour or more in conversation, chiefly on this subject. While I did not get or expect a pledge, I could form no other conclusion than that he approved and stands by the President's veto. He spoke, among other things, of a letter he wrote the editor of the *Evening Post*, indicating his difference with them on the Civil Rights Bill. In speaking of the fate of the bill in the House, in case it should pass the Senate, I alluded to the position and strong feeling of Bingham and told him what the President had that day said to me of the committals of Bingham. Morgan expressed himself highly gratified with this, for he had heard that Bingham was wavering. I, therefore, gave little heed to the insinuations that Morgan dissembles or will prove false; should not give it a second thought, did I not, since these rumors, recall a remark of Mr. George D. Morgan, that the Senator, E. D. M., would vote for the bill. But every look and thought, as well as expression, is watched and published. The sentiments, language, and course of Senator Wade and some others are in the highest degree reprehensible.

April 6, *Friday*. The decision of the Supreme Court in the Indiana cases — Milligan, Bolles, and others — was discussed. Attorney-General Speed could not state exactly the points. The judges do not give their opinions until next winter. They seem to have decided against the legality of military commissions.

I inquired what should be done in Semmes's case, which had been long pending. Little was said, and the President remarked he would see me after the session, and I therefore remained. He remarked that there was a somewhat strange state of things. Grant thought the paroles he had given covered almost everything. The courts were taking up some of the cases for treason and were showing themselves against military commissions. He therefore thought it would be as well to release Semmes on his parole.

I suggested, in view of the present condition of affairs, and this late decision of the Court, that if Semmes could not have a prompt trial, it would be better to release him from his present arrest unconditionally. We already have two paroles from him, — one on the surrender of the Alabama, and another at the time of Johnston's surrender. I would not take another. Nor would it be right, after holding him over three months in custody, to prolong his imprisonment.

The President assented to my suggestion and wished me to present it in some form for his action. My first thought was to place the grounds of his release, first on the proclamation, and second on the recent decision of the Supreme Court, making no allusion to Semmes's long imprisonment; but on second thought I omitted the President's own act, the proclamation, for it would be used against him by the captives.

The Senate by a vote of 33 to 15 this evening overrode the veto on the Civil Rights Bill. Wright of New Jersey was in his seat, but Dixon was not. Morgan, unexpectedly to me, and, I think, to most persons, voted with the majority. The vote of M. was one of calculation, not of conviction. I shall be disappointed if he does not lose rather than gain by the step he has taken. Such is usually the righteous termination of calculations made by scheming and ambitious men who consent to do wrong. In this instance M. may have had honest reasons. It is true he voted for the passage of the bill, but that was, as he has said to me, without much consideration given to the law, and, in repeated interviews and conversations since, he had left the impression on my mind that he should sustain the veto.

General and Mrs. Grant gave their last reception for the season this evening. Being somewhat indisposed, I did not propose to attend, but Edgar had not returned and there was no one to accompany Mrs. Welles and her friend, and I was, consequently, under the necessity of going, though afflicted with a severe headache. The party was in some respects unlike any of the season, and there was present not only a numerous but a miscellaneous company of contradictions. There had been some pre-understanding on the part of the Radicals, or a portion of them, to attend and to appropriate General Grant, or at least his name and influence, to themselves. But, most unexpectedly to them, as I confess it was to me, the President and his two daughters appeared early, and Montgomery Blair and some of his ladies were also on hand. There came also Alexander H. Stephens, Vice-President of the late Confederacy, so called. When, therefore, Thad Stevens, Trumbull, and others, not exactly homogeneous though now acting together, came in, they were evidently astonished and amazed.

Stevens, though a brave old stager, was taken aback and showed himself discomfited. Trumbull betrayed surprise. I was not in a condition to circulate much in the crowd, but heard repeatedly, amid the exultation over the vote of the Senate, expressions of vexation that there was such a strange attendance here. Theodore Tilton, as full of fanatical, fantastical, and boyish enthusiasm as of genius and talent, but with no sensible ideas of the principles on which our government is founded or accurate knowledge of our republican federal system, or of the merits involved in pending questions, was boisterous over the result in the Senate. It was sufficient for him that a victory had been achieved for an ideal and fanciful theory, regardless of consequences, and indifferent whether we had a union or an empire, so that he could do a little more for the black man than for the white man. When a little older, if his erratic genius does not spoil him, he will be a little wiser. For a time he fastened himself on me, but I was too indisposed to do more than listen. He gloated over Morgan's vote; said he could have thrown his hat to the ceiling when he heard it, — not that he cared for Morgan.

General and naval officers, as well as politicians, were present, with most of the foreign ministers. Of the Cabinet I saw none but Harlan.

April 7, Saturday. Senator Doolittle informs me that,

had Morgan held true, Dixon would, though still quite sick, have gone to the Senate, and the veto would have been sustained; but D. considered it too much in his feeble health to go there and give an unavailing vote. Doolittle says Morgan informed him early in the day of his course, but assigned no reasons for this unexpected stand.

April 10, *Tuesday.* Though not well to-day nor for several days past, I went to Department and to Cabinet-meeting. Quite a discussion on the Mexican question. Seward proposes to give Austria notice that she must not assist the Imperialists in Mexico. Some of us asked why notice to that effect had not already been served upon the French. He said the French had been notified, but there had not been sufficient time to receive an answer. I had little faith in French promises, as I have often said when this subject has been up. Dennison to-day expressed similar opinion and has always been ardent on this matter of French occupancy in Mexico. Seward showed some irritability, as I have seen him on one or two occasions when this subject has been discussed.

The President inquired privately in regard to the Chattanooga, — when she would probably be ready, what Mr. Seward thought of it, etc. I told him all was right, that the vessel would probably sail soon after the 1st prox.

The Civil Rights Bill passed the House yesterday by a vote of nearly three to one. The party drill was very effective. Only Raymond of the Radicals voted to sustain the veto. He has been general manager in the House, but could not carry a single member with him if he tried, nor could Seward help him, or he did not. All of Stanton's pets were active in opposing the veto. Bingham, who had been vehement in denouncing the bill as a bundle of unconstitutional outrages, had besought a veto, urged objections, was quieted, paired off; did not vote; listened to Stanton and could not shake off the fetters of party. Not a word escaped the President to-day on the subject, but it was evident he felt deeply. I, for one, would not introduce the topic, for I could not, unasked, state my opinions, which would be in opposition, and almost discourteous, to some of my associates. Oh, Bingham! Bingham!

April 13, *Friday.* I do not get well. But little of interest. British fund agents and brokers show great impudence in regard to Rebel debts and cotton loans. McHenry, Richardson, and others present plans and schemes which are deserving such a rebuke as should be felt by them and their countrymen.

Stanton made some crude suggestions for national quarantine, — not very explicit, and beset with difficulties. I asked if anything of the kind had ever been attempted, if it was not a matter for State or municipal, rather than federal, regulation. He admitted it was, but the other members had not given the subject a thought and did not like to come athwart Stanton.

Doolittle called on me last night full of exceeding great trouble. Insists the President has not as yet taken so firm and decided a stand as duty requires. Wishes me to counsel and urge upon him the necessity of doing something positive. Says the impression is getting pretty universal that the President can do nothing for himself, etc., etc. There is some truth in all this; not that the President lacks courage, but he dislikes to break with those who elected him.

Doolittle wishes Speed to leave, and Stanton also. Says the first has no stamina, nor power, nor character as a lawyer. That he is the laughing-stock of the court and of the first lawyers. Does not and cannot strengthen the President. Suggests that Stanton should be turned out and that Grant should be assigned, temporarily, to the Department. Doolittle earnestly desires me to counsel the President. I told him it would be delicate for me to do so, even if invited by the President, but I would not obtrude upon him in such a matter concerning my colleagues.

April 14, *Saturday.* This being the anniversary of the assassination of President Lincoln, the several Departments were closed by order of the President.

Had an hour's talk with the President on several matters, but chiefly in relation to the policy of the Administration, which was brought about by my referring to the interview which I had had with Senator Doolittle on Thursday evening, and his urgent request that I would communicate with the President on the subject-matter of our consultation. I remarked that there were certain suggestions, which delicacy forbade me to mention, unsolicited, but that there was an apprehension that the Radicals were strengthening themselves by the non-action, or limited actions, of the Executive and by conceding to Members of Congress almost all opportunities [for placing] their Radical friends.

The President said it was exceedingly annoying and discouraging to witness so good a man as Doolittle desponding, and especially on the subject of removals and appointments, when Doolittle himself was not prepared to take or recommend action, even in his own State. It was true that his Cabinet was not in all respects what he wished; but he had taken it as he found it. Harlan, to be sure, came in later, but it was understood he sought and desired the position, although he had since obtained an election to the Senate. He supposed Harlan was not in accord with the policy of the Administration, and delicacy and propriety would seem to prompt him to resign. But he had, as yet, shown no disposition to give up his place. Speed, he said, certainly added no strength to the Administration, was manifestly in harmony with the Radicals, advising with and encouraging them. Delicacy should cause him, feeling as he did, to retire, but he had made no advance in that direction, nor would he, probably, uninvited. Stanton, he remarked, was claimed by the Radicals to be in their interest, and probably such was the fact, yet he had given him no intimation of that character, except in some general crit-

2

icism on one or two measures in which he finally yielded
and acquiesced. His Department had been an absorbing
one during the War and still was formidable. To have an
open rupture with him in the present condition of affairs
would be embarrassing certainly, yet Stanton held on.

The delicacies and proprieties which should govern the
relations that are supposed to exist between a President
and his Cabinet associates — his political family, as it were
— would indicate to men of proper sensibility the course
which they should pursue, if they did not agree with the
person whom they were expected to advise in the administration of affairs. If these three men did not approve his
general policy, the President said they had not, as he was
aware, disapproved of it. Statements were made in some
of the Radical papers that the persons named were opposed
to the Administration of which they were a part. Rumors
to that effect had come to him in such a way and from such
sources that he was not at liberty to doubt it. "Still they
hold on here, and some of them likely report our proceedings. I do not, however, know the fact. What, then, can
I do? Are these men to whom I give my confidence hypocrites, faithless, insincere, treacherous? The time has not
arrived for a decisive stand. With mischievous Radical
leaders, who appear to have little regard for the country,
it is not a proper time to take upon ourselves other quarrels
nearer home."

The President said he had borne, as well as he could, the
malicious war which had been waged upon him for doing
his duty, administering the Government for the whole
country, not for a faction. If the schemes of the Radical
managers to control the Executive had sometimes annoyed him, they had not caused him to deviate from what
he was satisfied was right and for the best interest of the
country. But it did grieve and wound him to witness such
men as Doolittle desponding and giving way. Cowan, an
intelligent, sensible, and good Senator, he said, was also
complaining, and it was hard to be under the necessity

of holding these men up, while compelled to encounter the whole opposition. Their discouragement afflicted him more than all that the Radicals had done or would do.

Only a day or two since Cowan had, with others, pressed earnestly for some changes in Pennsylvania which they said ought by all means to be made, and on their representations he had finally agreed to make some changes. But just as they were being ordered, Cowan began to show and have doubt, asked a suspension, and finally backed down and would consent to but two of the same changes he had urged. "These men take upon themselves no responsibility while goading me on to move, when I am breasting this storm." This he said he was ready to do. It was a duty and he could meet it, but it pained him to have good and true friends waver.

At the proper time he should be ready to act, but his friends must permit him to judge when to act. It would be pleasanter to him to have more cordiality, a more free interchange of opinions, more unity and earnestness on the part of all his Cabinet, for there was obvious distrust among them, — distrust of each other, — and that on topics where the Administration was most interested.

I have given the substance and, so far as I can recall, the words. There was much desultory conversation intermixed.

April 16, *Monday.* Senator Doolittle came yesterday. I told him I had seen the President on Saturday and learned from him that he (D.) had been at the Mansion on Friday evening. I made known to him the feelings of the President and that he was not prepared for an open rupture, but Doolittle said that would not do. The President must act promptly. We were losing by delay. Wanted to know how Dennison stood and asked me to go with him and call on Dennison.

But the Governor was not in, and we went on to the President's, whose carriage was standing at the door. I said we must not deter the President from his ride, he took so little exercise. Patterson, his son-in-law, we met at the top of the stairs, who told us the President had company through the day, that Smythe had been there and it was, he thought, definitely settled that S. should be Collector at New York. Smythe, from what I hear of him, is better than some of the candidates, perhaps better than any. It has occurred to me that certain New York gentlemen were selecting for themselves, rather than the Administration.

Passing Montgomery Blair's with a view of calling on his father, the former came to the door and asked me in, while he sent for his father. As usual, the Judge was strong in his opinions against Seward, Stanton, and others. He predicts another revolution or rebellion as the inevitable consequence of measures now being pursued. Says there will be two governments organized here in Washington.

Maynard of Tennessee made a similar suggestion at my house two or three evenings since. He believes that the Senators and Representatives of the next Congress will appear from all the States, that those from the Rebel States will, with the Democratic Members from the loyal States, constitute a majority, that they will organize and by resolution dispense with the test oath and have things their own way. The extreme and reprehensible course of the Radicals is undoubtedly hurrying on a crisis, which will overwhelm them, if it does not embroil, perhaps subvert, the government, but the South is too exhausted and the Northern Democrats too timid, narrow-minded, and tired for such a step.

The Fenians are reported to be gathering in some force at Eastport in Maine. The Winooski, gunboat, was sent thither last week with orders to wait instructions. Seward advised that no instructions should, for the present, be sent, but on Saturday I forwarded general orders to preserve neutrality. This evening Seward called at my house and wanted instructions sent by telegraph. Told him I had already sent by mail, but would send a telegram also.

Sperry, Postmaster at New Haven, was at my house last evening, and is very full of Connecticut parties and Connecticut politics, with a professed desire to sustain the Administration, and the usual wish to make the Party in Connecticut and the Administration identical, — a work which more distinguished men than he are laboring in vain to effect, not only in that State but elsewhere. What is irreconcilable cannot be made to harmonize. The organization, or those who control the organization, of the Union Party, are studiously, designedly opposed to the Administration, and it is their purpose to break it down, provided they cannot control it and compel unconstitutional action. They have no thought for the country, but are all for party. Sperry is for himself.

April 17, *Tuesday.* Seward read the dispatches which he proposed to send to Mr. Motley, — the first, protesting against the sending of troops to Mexico by the Austrian Government, the second, in case they did send, after being thus notified, that he ask for his papers and withdraw from Vienna.

McCulloch favored the first paper, but objected to the last; deprecated war under any circumstances, and even at any time for so worthless a people as the Mexicans. Stanton was for both. Dennison was most emphatic for both and for maintaining the Monroe Doctrine. Was ready to fight the European Powers, if they presumed to interfere with the American states; considered the honor and welfare of the country involved in this. Speed concurred with McCulloch, Harlan with Dennison. I suggested it would have been better, and would now be better, to meet the real party if we were to do anything; that we should take the head of France rather than the tail of Austria. That I did not mean to object to the measures marked out by the Secretary of State, which I looked upon as a menace, but that to fire off an ultimatum to remote Austria, while we had done nothing of the kind as regards France, whose troops were on our Southwestern frontiers, did not strike me favorably.

Seward said he was only waiting Bigelow's dispatches to take the same course towards France, if she did not recede.

Have a telegram this evening from Commander Cooper of the Winooski that the Ocean Spray had arrived at East-port with five hundred stand of arms and asking if he should permit them to land. Within five minutes Colonel Seward came in with papers from the Secretary of State, consisting of a note from Sir Frederick Bruce, inclosing two telegrams from Eastport in regard to arms on the Spray, urging that the arms and the Fenians should not be permitted to meet. These had been sent to Stanton, who had returned them with a note [to the effect] that General Meade was on his way to Eastport, but he disliked to send an order by telegraph, for that would apprize the Fenians of his coming, and suggesting that the Navy could take some action. Seward wrote in pencil on the back of the envelope inclosing the papers, that I "could send orders to restrain action, or another to that effect."

I observe that these men are very chary about disturbing the Fenians, and I do not care to travel out of the line of duty to relieve them. I therefore sent word that I was con-tent to leave the subject with Cooper till to-morrow, when General Meade would doubtless be at Eastport; if not, the civil authorities were there, with whom the Navy would coöperate, or whom they could assist.

Speed and Stanton expressed an opinion, in which others of the Cabinet concurred, that property once taken and used by the Rebel Government became forfeited to the original owner and was legal capture. I had so previously decided last fall on the question of twenty-two rollers and machinery captured at Charlotte and now at Norfolk.

Thad Stevens yesterday introduced a resolution direct-ing that three copies of Forney's *Chronicle* should be sent to our legations and consuls abroad and be paid for out of the contingent of the House, — a monstrous proposition made in wanton recklessness and supported by sixty votes. Forney in return puffs Stevens as the "Great Commoner."

April 18, *Wednesday.* The President was to have sent me word when he would see Captain McKinstry, but, having failed to do so, I called on him to-day and he appointed this evening or any hour to-morrow.

Some conversation took place on the subject of New York appointments. I congratulated him that he had got the Collector and Attorney off his hands, and though I had personally but slight knowledge of either, it seemed to me they were as good as any of the candidates named. The President said he found New York broken up into cliques; that he could satisfy neither without dissatisfying all others. That all had selfish objects of their own to gratify and wished to use him for their own personal ends.

The conduct of Morgan had, he said, been very extraordinary. In all his conversations he had expressed himself in accord with the Administration on the question of the Civil Rights Bill and the veto. But he wanted the nomination of Collector should be sent in before the vote was taken, was particularly urgent on Monday morning, and from what had since transpired there was, he thinks, a sinister design. Results had shown that it was well he did not comply with Morgan's urgent request.

In nominating Stanbery to the Supreme Court, he had a desire to get a sound man on the bench, one who was right on fundamental constitutional questions. Stanbery, he says, is with us thoroughly, earnestly.

Alluding to certain persons in the Cabinet, he expressed himself with much feeling and said a proper sense of decency should prompt them to leave, provided they were not earnestly and sincerely with the Administration.

April 19, *Thursday.* The President last evening addressed a large concourse who assembled under a call of soldiers and sailors who desired to serenade and thank him for a proclamation in their favor for government employment. His speech is bold and well enough if it was advisable that the Chief Magistrate should address such gatherings.

Senator Trumbull called upon me this morning for the first time in several months. It was to ask a favor, and for Mrs. Trumbull more than himself. I regretted that I could not without violating regulations grant it, for both of them have been a little miffed because I opposed his two great measures which have been vetoed. The speech of the President last evening was alluded to, and Trumbull was very emphatic in condemning Presidential speechmaking. We did not greatly differ on this subject, for it has never been regarded favorably by me. Sometimes it may be excusable, but omission is better than compliance with calls from irresponsible gatherings. Frequent harangues to promiscuous crowds lessen the dignity of the President.

Passing from this subject to the condition of the country, he asked me if I was willing, or would consent, that Senators and Representatives should be admitted to take part in the Government, coming from Rebel States and districts. I told him I was most assuredly willing, provided they were loyal and duly and properly elected. "Then," inquired he, "how could you deny one a seat in Congress from South Carolina during the existence of the Rebellion?" "That," said I, "is a different question, but I am by no means prepared to say I would not have been glad to have seen a true and loyal man like Andrew Johnson, or yourself, here from that State during the War. I regretted that more did not, like Johnson, remain in 1861. Would you have expelled them?" Without answering me direct, Trumbull became a good deal excited and was very emphatic against the Rebels. I said we would have no controversy on that point. I was not their apologist, though I was not their persecutor, now that the Rebellion was suppressed. They had greatly erred and wronged us, had slain our kindred and friends, wasted our treasure, etc., but he and I should not bear resentment. We had a country to care for and should, I thought, exert ourselves to promote reconciliation and reëstablish the Union in all its integrity at the earliest attainable moment.

"Without conditions?" inquired he. "The Constitution," replied I, "provides for all that is necessary to be done. The condition of affairs is anomalous, but the path is plain. Each State is entitled to the Senators and Representatives according to population. Why are eleven unrepresented and denied their rights by an arbitrary and despotic majority of Congress?"

He imputed the difficulty chiefly to the President, who, he declared, had failed to act up to the principles of his message; and he quoted a passage. I told him the course of the President I thought perfectly consistent and I knew it was honest. But why was Tennessee, for instance, more loyal than Kentucky, excluded from representation in either branch of Congress? He said the President was to blame for that, for had he not put his veto on the Freedmen's Bureau Bill, Tennessee, and he thought Arkansas and Louisiana also, would long before this have had their Representatives in Congress. I told him this did not appear to me very enlightened and correct statesmanship. Why those States should be denied their undoubted constitutional rights, because the President and Congress disagreed, I could not understand. He complained that the President was not frank, that he had advised civil rights in his message to all, and yet vetoed the very bill which confirmed those rights.

I remarked that the subject of civil rights — personal rights — belonged to the States, not to the Federal Government. The amendment to the Constitution had abolished slavery, and the blacks had the same remedies that the whites had to preserve their freedom. That undoubtedly some of the States would, at least for a time, make discriminating laws. Illinois, I presume, did, and I thought Connecticut also. He denied that Illinois made any distinction affecting the civil rights of the negro, and asked when and in what respects the civil rights were affected in Connecticut.

"Both States," said I, "deny them suffrage, which is claimed as a right by the extreme Radicals in Congress." He said there were not ten men in Congress who took that view; there were just eight, he finally remarked in the Senate, and perhaps double that number in the House. "But," said he, "suffrage is a privilege, not a right." I remarked I so considered it, but Sumner and others took a different view. "Well, then," said he, "in what other respects are the civil rights of the negro affected?" "He is not," said I, "by our laws put on terms of equality. He is not permitted to get into the jury box; he is not allowed to act as an appraiser of property under any circumstances, and there are other matters wherein distinctions are made." "These," replied he, "are all matters of privilege."

"What, then," said I, "do you mean by civil rights? Please to define it." "The right," replied he, "to his liberty, to go and come as he pleases, have the avails of his own labor, not to be restricted in that respect. Virginia," continued he, "has passed a law that they shall not leave the estate on which they reside without a permit." I know not that Virginia denies or restricts the right to emigrate. The other rights mentioned the negro possesses.

April 20, Friday. The subject of advertising came up. Dennison had made inquiry and ascertained that the *Intelligencer* had the largest circulation. Stanton said President Lincoln had ordered him to publish in the *Chronicle.* There was evidently a wish to get along without action. I advised that there should be uniformity in the Departments as to the papers employed. The President said certainly it was best there should be general accord.

April 24, Tuesday. Admiral Farragut and Mrs. F. are

staying with us, and I find little time to write. Have had several interviews with the President and Mr. Seward in relation to the cruise of the Chattanooga and passage of Colonel Robert Johnson, under an appointment of the State Department. The President evidently feels embarrassed, yet anxious on his son's account. He is aware of the importance to himself and the country that he should be relieved from the care of this unfortunate young man, but is unwilling that anything personal to himself should be done.

I called last Thursday with Captain McKinstry and introduced him first to the President and then to Messrs. Stover and Robert Johnson. Subsequently I saw Mr. Seward, who arranged the subject-matter of the mission. I addressed him a letter, stating the cruise of the Chattanooga and the principal points at which she would stop. By request of Mr. S. an alteration was made, avoiding Australia and going to China and Japan instead of running directly on the west coast of South America. . . .

At the Cabinet-meeting I submitted Admiral Godon's dispatch of the 23d of January, stating the demands and difficulties of Mr. Washburn,[1] our Minister to Paraguay, who had been absent from his post more than a year and has been wintering since last September with his family in Buenos Ayres. In the mean time the allies have blockaded the river and object to his passing through the lines, and he has made a demand for the Wasp or some other naval vessel to convey him and his family.

Mr. Seward, without knowing all the facts, at once requested that Mr. Washburn should have public conveyance. I showed him Godon's dispatch, who states that no foreign power has attempted to pass the blockade, that he cannot do it without obtaining from the Buenos Ayres authorities coal, and that to return the courtesy by setting them at defiance would be ungracious; that no foreign government has a representative in Paraguay; that we

[1] Charles Ames Washburn, brother of Elihu B. Washburne.

have no interests there, and that if Mr. Washburn gets there he will be almost the only American in the territory and will require a naval force to protect him.

Although taken a little aback by the statements of Godon, Seward had committed himself too strongly to back down. He said the Minister must go through the blockade, whether it cost $3000 or $30,000; that he must get the coal of the Buenos Ayres authorities and disoblige them by violating the blockade, if Mr. Washburn could not go without; and he (Seward) wanted to take Godon's dispatch and read.

April 25, Wednesday. Major-General Benjamin F. Butler is exercising a great and dangerous influence at the Treasury Department. He has been employed in some cases and is using his opportunities to press others where he is employed as counsel. As he has talents but no principles, is avaricious and unscrupulous, I have given our friends McCulloch and Chandler at the Treasury an occasional admonition concerning him.

In 1863 the Grey Jacket, a steamer laden with cotton, was captured by the Kennebec on the way from Mobile to Cuba. The cargo and vessel were valued at about half a million of dollars, and were condemned on the showing of the captain and owners. An appeal was taken, but the case was so flagrant that there was no avoiding condemnation. The owners had employed various counsel, — first Nott and others of New Orleans, then Seward and Blatchford of New York, — but all have on hearing the facts abandoned the case. About the first of last December it was put in the hands of General Butler, who commenced a series of intrigues and manœuvres, and from his persistency and unscrupulousness had evidently a large contingent fee. I have heard it stated at $125,000. But he found no favor at the Navy Department. His last appeal with me was a half-threat to go to Congress and make an appeal to their sympathies for a man who had lost his all by this capture and condemnation. I replied that my appeal for sympathy in behalf of the sailors who had nobly done their duty in sunshine and storm, in winter and summer, day and night, would probably be as effective as his. He then changed, — proposed that the captors should take one half and the claimant the other, surrendering by this arrangement the moiety which should go to the naval pension fund. I told him that was impossible; the Secretary of the Navy should make no such arrangement; moreover he was the trustee of that fund and held it sacred.

One other futile attempt was made in company with the Attorney-General, whom he persuaded to come with him, but after a brief talk Speed appeared to think he had been imposed upon and abandoned the case.

Failing at these points, Butler commenced intriguing at the Treasury, where he was listened to by Chandler, and finally Caleb Cushing was employed at Chandler's suggestion to give a written opinion, General Butler being the prompter. Cushing was timid, hesitated to present his opinion unsustained, and General Butler drew up a preamble and resolution which he procured Thad Stevens to present and procured to be passed under the previous question, without debate, to the effect that cases of this description should be suspended until the judgment of the Supreme Court should be obtained next winter. There are one or two clauses in certain acts which Chase procured to be inserted when he was striving to absorb the whole government in the Treasury Department, having the Presidency in view. These clauses Butler and Cushing made the foundation of their proceeding. Stevens's resolution was passed on the 9th, and Cushing's opinion is dated on the 11th. The whole thing is disgraceful even to a lobby agent and discreditable to the Treasury Department, which has, so far as the Secretary is concerned, unwittingly lent itself to Butler. How far the Assistant Secretary is involved is uncertain. . . . Great derangement in order to get a great fee has been effected.

April 27, Friday. . . . Senator Guthrie has thrown a mischievous resolution into the Senate in relation to an order forbidding officers from visiting Washington, and inquiring if any have been refused permission to come here and appeal to the President or to Congress. The object is to show that naval officers are denied the privileges of citizens, and to make out that the Navy Department is arbitrary. Senator G. seemed not aware that persons on entering the service, officers as well as privates, surrender certain privileges which private citizens enjoy who are not in the service and subsisting on the Treasury, and subject themselves to certain restraints. The inquiry is designed to get up sympathy for the officers; no interest is manifested for or given to the men, who are under greater restraint. . . . Senator Guthrie himself is guiltless of any mischievous intent and has been prompted by some one, and I cannot be mistaken as to who that some one is.

April 30, Monday. The Central Directory, or Stevens's Reconstruction Committee, have submitted their plan of Reconstruction, which means division for four years longer at least. The papers of the day contain this extraordinary programme, which is an outrage, and yet is said to have had the approval of all the Republican members of that extraordinary committee. It makes me sad to see men in trusted and responsible positions so devoted to party, so trained and subservient to faction as to trifle with the welfare of a great nation. No one can read the propositions submitted without seeing that the whole scheme is one for party ascendancy. The result will be, after a struggle, perhaps of years, the ultimate overwhelming and disgraceful defeat of the authors and their party.

XXXVIII

May 1, *Tuesday.* We have intelligence that Valparaiso has been bombarded by the Spaniards. A brutal and semi-barbarous proceeding on the part of Spain.

In Cabinet the President brought forward the subject of Reconstruction as now before Congress in the report of the Committee of Fifteen. He said his purpose was to know the opinions of the several members of the Cabinet in regard to these propositions of the Committee and his own policy, which was different.

Seward in a very long talk expressed himself opposed to the plan of the Committee. Stanton broke in upon the President before Seward. Was very glad the President had brought the matter before the Cabinet in this formal manner. He had, like all the members of the Cabinet, approved the policy of the President from the beginning. With one or two others he had, he said, taken at the inception a different view of negro suffrage, or, as he expressed it, of allowing all the people of the State to vote. But in all his talk, which was very loud and emphatic, he expressed no opinion on the subject before us, either of sustaining or opposing the scheme of Thad Stevens and his Committee.

Mr. McCulloch was very decided in his opposition to the plan of the Committee and equally decided in favor of the President's policy. He declared himself not so hopeful as Mr. Seward, especially since reading the scheme of the Committee.

Dennison, who interposed out of the usual order, thought it premature to express any opinion, for it was not yet certain what course Congress would take.

Stanton, who should have followed McCulloch, was silent, evidently intending to be passed as having already spoken, though really giving no opinion. I was not disposed to permit any such get-off and therefore waited.

The President, whose feelings were very intense, spoke at some length in regard to the condition of the country, the effect which these schemes must have on the efforts to reestablish the Union.

Mr. Dennison again spoke at some length, expressing himself opposed to many things in the programme of the Committee, and was not prepared to say how long representation should be denied to the Southern States. Thought four years too long.

McCulloch, who has important business at his Department almost always when we have grave and important questions, obtained permission to leave, having stated his views.

The President, holding the paper in his hand, said he had brought the subject forward that he might know how each one viewed it. I remarked that was very proper and I trusted each would state his opinion, that I thought it due to him, and I then turned towards Stanton. Thus appealed to, and the President turning towards him also, Stanton said he did not approve the propositions of the Committee in the present form; he believed they might be amended and essentially improved, and thought it worth the attempt to reconcile action between the President and Congress.

I declared myself unequivocally opposed to the whole scheme, which I considered an outrage and a wrong. I said that I was not in favor of any Constitutional Amendment in the present condition of the country, that I knew not what right Congress had to pass amnesty laws or prescribe terms to the States.

Stanton interrupted to say that I was opposed to any terms with Congress, that I was ironclad on this subject of Reconstruction, and had not only fifteen-inch guns leveled against Congress, but was for running my prow into them.

I replied that I was not aware that I was unreasonable, but my convictions were that Congress had no authority to prescribe terms on which States should be represented; that the Constitution had done this; that each house was entitled to pass on the election and qualifications of each member of its own body.

Stanton said that the convictions of Congress were exactly opposed to mine, and, therefore, I could make no compromise with them. I told him I could compromise no principle, nor consent to any usurpation.

Dennison again said he was opposed to the plan, but repeated that he did not know how soon the people or States should be represented. I said immediately, if the Representatives were loyal, I wish they could be sworn in to-morrow.

Harlan was very reserved. He agreed, he said, with Mr. Stanton in pretty much all he had said, and had no doubt a majority of Congress wanted to be in harmony with the President.

The session was very long, extending over nearly four hours, most of the time on the subject of Reconstruction, the President speaking twice at considerable length and objecting to all conditions precedent to admitting loyal Members to the seats.

2

May 2, Wednesday. The papers to-day contain a synopsis of what took place yesterday in the Cabinet on the subject of Reconstruction. I have no doubt that the President himself furnished the information and probably the report precisely as it is published. He has shown tact and sagacity in doing it. The report of the position of each member is accurate, although I think Stanton was less decided than stated. Nevertheless he intended that the President should take that impression, and I appreciate the adroitness of the President in giving publicity to Stanton's position as he represented himself in the Cabinet. The Radical friends of Stanton will be incredulous as to his position in the Cabinet. He must, however, content himself with the exposition made or openly deny it. He can no longer equivocate or dissemble.

In a conversation which I had with the President yesterday after the other members left, he remarked that the time had come when we must know whether we had a united or divided Cabinet; that the Radicals had strengthened themselves by constant representations that portions of the Cabinet were with them.

To-day Seward remarked to me that while he should say nothing in regard to the opinion of his associates, he had said, and should repeat to others, that he was not misrepresented in the report. I told him I was glad that Stanton's position was so clearly defined, for I had not so understood him. Seward said Stanton had gone along with us so far; that Stanton had come into Mr. Lincoln's Cabinet under peculiar circumstances, and had said to him (Seward) that he should stand by his (Seward's) policy while he remained in the Cabinet and go with him on all essential questions.

May 3, Thursday. Had a pretty full talk with Mr. Rice, Chairman of the Naval Committee, on the subject of Reconstruction. He said he did not approve of the report of the Reconstruction Committee in all respects, and had no doubt it would be amended; that, in his opinion, as soon as a State adopted the requirement prescribed by Congress, she should be permitted to send Representatives without waiting the action of other States. This was Bingham's amendment, and a majority of Congress would adopt that policy.

I told him our differences were fundamental; that I did not admit Congress could prescribe terms or make precedent conditions to any State before it could exercise the Constitutional right guaranteed to all the States of sending Senators and Representatives to make laws for the whole country. That this was a right guaranteed in the most imposing and solemn form, yet for five months Congress had violated that Constitutional guaranty.

The Southern people were still Rebels in heart, he said, and would I admit them to be represented while this was the case? They were violent in their language and conduct, and would we allow them to take part in the government while that state of things continued? I told him I knew not how he could prevent it; men would use language that was offensive; but if he regarded the Constitution he would not on that account deprive them of their rights, or lay down unwritten tests. The whole scheme of imposing conditions on the States, denying them representation, was usurpation and an outrage; Congress, not the Southern people, were in this matter the criminals. I asked whether he supposed that by excluding the Southern States and people from the government, denying them rights guaranteed by the Constitution, taxing them without allowing them representation, would conciliate, would reconcile, would hasten restoration, make them better friends six months hence, or six years hence?

May 4, Friday. The subject of Reconstruction was not discussed to-day in Cabinet. Seward, while the President was engaged with some one, remarked on the publication which had been made of our last meeting, saying that he concluded the report had been made by Stanton, for the papers had said it was from a Cabinet Minister, and there was no interest felt as regarded any one else but Stanton. There were, he remarked, some other indications. All this was said playfully as he walked the room and took snuff. But I could see it was not play for Stanton, whose countenance betrayed his vexation. Seward saw it also, and when Stanton said that Seward was the only one who would do this, — draw up and publish proceedings in Cabinet, — the subject was dropped.

As we came out at the close of the meeting, McCulloch said to me that he had hoped there would have been some call for a decided expression from Stanton, for the newspapers and many honest men were disputing in regard to the truth of the report of his views in the Cabinet exposition, and he (McC.) thought it wrong that a Cabinet Minister should occupy a false or an equivocal position on such a question, at such a time. In all of which I concurred.

There is no doubt that the Radicals are surprised and many of them incredulous at the enunciation of Stanton's remarks and position in the Cabinet. I apprehend that no one was more astounded at the publication than Stanton himself. It ended any double course, if one had been pursued. Sumner has repeatedly assured me, most emphatically, that Stanton was with him and opposed to the President's policy. Others have said the same. These men were deceived and have been until now, and they cannot believe they have been duped.

The President has not been unaware of the conflicting statements in regard to Stanton, and for this reason adopted the course of calling out the individual opinions of each member of his Cabinet and then took the opportunity of throwing them in a condensed form before the public. This gives the attitude and views of the Administration and of each member of it on the subject of the report of the Reconstruction Committee in advance of the debate in Congress, and prevents misrepresentations and false assumptions in regard to them. It has been the policy of the Radical leaders to claim that the Cabinet was divided, that Stanton and others were with them, and hence their papers and orators have eulogized and magnified Stanton into enormous proportions. All this has now terminated. I did not understand Stanton as expressing himself quite so decidedly as he is represented to have done in the report, though it appeared to me he meant to be understood as represented. No doubt he dissembles. He said he did not approve the Directory plans in many respects, and if he were compelled to act upon them as now presented he should avow himself opposed; and he thought Congress and the President not so far apart that they could not come together.

I followed in direct antagonism and objected unequivocally to the whole programme. I had no faith in Constitutional amendments at this time, in the present existing state of affairs, with eleven States unrepresented and without any voice in the deliberations; nor could I admit that Congress could prescribe terms to the States on which they should be permitted to enjoy their Constitutional right of representation, or that Congress should usurp and take to itself the pardoning power, which is a prerogative of the Executive, nor were they to prosecute and punish the people without trial. I, therefore, antagonized Stanton purposely. He saw and felt it. Hence I think he hardly committed himself so fully as represented. But he does not deny it. Will he?

May 5, Saturday. Senator Morgan says that in the debate on Lewis Campbell's appointment as Minister to Mexico, Wade declared in executive session he intended to vote in favor of no man for any appointment who favored the Johnson policy and opposed the policy of Congress. Campbell, he said, was in favor of the Johnson policy. He then launched off into a tirade against Maximilian, in which he got terribly excited, but finally closed by voting for Campbell, who is an Ohio man.

The Senate rejected the nomination of Frank Blair for

Collector at St. Louis. No man in the country, perhaps, did so much and so efficiently and timely against the Rebellion as General Blair in Missouri at the beginning of the Rebellion. But he is not of the Radical faction.

A. E. Burr, who is a member of the Connecticut Legislature from Hartford, writes me that there is a good deal of feeling on the subject of Senator; thinks that a majority might be concentrated on me if I am so disposed. One of the newspaper correspondents, Ripley, has called on me on the same subject. R. has seen Dixon, who says he should like to have me elected and will do anything to bring it about, provided it is my wish, but he adds the difficulty is I will do nothing for myself. D. says there is not a doubt of my election if I will earnestly enter the canvass. He may be correct, probably is, but I cannot approve, or do, what others do in these matters. While I should feel gratified with the unsolicited compliment of such a testimonial, I do not so crave it as to employ or enter into such means as are too freely used to obtain it. If a good and true man can be secured I will aid him.

May 8, Tuesday. The subject of admitting Colorado was to-day before the Cabinet. The bill has passed both houses after having been once rejected. Congress in 1863 authorized the formation of a State constitution, and the people refused to take upon themselves local State government. Subsequently the people formally adopted it by a small majority in a vote of some six thousand, and elected Senators, who are here anxious to get their seats. After the proposition and Senators were rejected, it was ascertained the latter would vote with the Radicals, and that their votes would contribute to overrule and defeat the Executive. This new light led Senators to revise their votes. The Constitution restricts suffrage to the whites, but Senators and others who insist on negro suffrage where the blacks are numerous, and in States where Congress has no right to intervene, voted for Colorado.

Seward, McCulloch, and myself were against admitting the State. She had a population of less than twenty thousand, as claimed by some, and not exceeding thirty or thirty-five thousand, as insisted by the most strenuous for admission. As a principle I have uniformly opposed recognizing and admitting States with a population below the ratio for one Representative. This has always ruled. The slaveholders thrust in Florida and Arkansas as an offset to Free States; and Kansas was authorized under peculiar and extraordinary circumstances to form a constitution with, I think, less than sixty thousand. There was, perhaps, some excuse for admitting and authorizing Colorado to frame a constitution when the difficulties of the country and the attempts of the Rebels to lessen the number of States was before us. But the people then refused self-government.

I therefore had no difficulty in coming to my conclusions on general principles. Stanton thought it might in this instance be well enough to let them in and avoid further trouble. Harlan argued for admission with some ability and tact, but did not meet the great underlying principle. He thought it expedient, and with so much effect as to cause Dennison to doubt, who was at first opposed to the bill. The question was deferred.

The subject of sending naval vessels to attend the laying of the Atlantic telegraph was considered. Seward, Dennison, and Harlan in the affirmative. McCulloch and Stanton opposed. I felt very indifferent; had advised Field to go to Congress. Told him I should not act without authority from Congress or an order from the Executive.. Stated to the President that we could, without any difficulty or much additional expense, detail a vessel, Mr. Seward having said we did not require all the four ordered to the fishing-ground. Although my faith in the success of the ocean telegraph is not great, yet, in view of the fact that Congress had once ordered a vessel and of our present ability to spare one, and the further fact that a vessel had been

ordered to assist or be present at laying the Russian telegraph, it might be expedient to show a friendly feeling as
regards this, and I would assent, though unwilling to
advise it.

The President thought it would be well for Congress to
take up the subject, or, at all events, that we should delay
a day or two before deciding. This I approved as the better course. Stanton, who had seen my previous indifference, immediately slapped me on the shoulder and said I
could decide readily with the President. I said I could, for
he usually was not far wrong. Stanton was vexed.

May 12, *Saturday.* Moore, the President's Private Secretary, came to me on Wednesday, the 9th, by request of the
President, who desired him to consult with me respecting
orders recently issued to Captain S. P. Lee to take command at Mare Island Navy Yard. He said the elder Blair
was very importunate on the subject and made it a personal
matter. I told him I was aware of what Lee was procuring
to be done through others, and that therein he was violating regulations and usage, but that it was characteristic of
him. The orders to him were complimentary, for he had
seniors who had prior claims, but I considered Lee a good
yard officer. His case was peculiar. I had given him the
command of the North Atlantic Squadron when other and
older officers were entitled to the position. But, knowing
that he had good business qualities, and that much that
was improper was then being carried on in violation of
blockade by Treasury men and by General Butler, I had
purposely selected him for that position. The business portion of his duties were well performed, but as an officer he
has not sufficient energetic fighting qualities. Some efforts
towards getting possession of the entrance of [the] Cape
Fear [River] and capturing Fort Fisher were proposed, but
eventuated in nothing, and when the army finally indicated a willingness to join in a coöperative movement,
the first step taken was to detach Lee. While in command,

however, he had been wonderfully favored in procuring prize money, being entitled to one twentieth of all the captures on that extensive blockade. He had, consequently, accumulated a handsome fortune of over $150,000. With the fortune he now sought rank to which the Navy was opposed. I have been more blamed for favoritism to Lee than to any other officer. But while others blamed me for favors to Lee, he was dissatisfied because I did not give him promotion and was continually harassing my old friend his father-in-law to press his promotion. I had repeatedly assured Mr. Blair, as well as Lee, that it was impossible to gratify him. Both they and those opposed to him had done me injustice. I had in view the good of the service without partiality or prejudice.

I told Moore to tell the President that Lee had now had about nine months' waiting orders, that every officer of his grade was on duty, that he could not expect to escape duty and remain in the service; that his rank did not entitle him to a squadron, but it would be unpleasant for him after having acted as rear-admiral to take a single ship and go under the command of another. I had, therefore, given him the California shore station, to which, however, he was not entitled, but as a compromise under the peculiar circumstances. But this duty he was trying to evade through political influence, and, instead of coming to the Department, he was intriguing and operating through his father-in-law and annoying the President. I requested him to communicate the facts in full to the President, for I desired him to know them and would myself speak to him on the subject.

At a caucus of the Republican members of the Connecticut Legislature General Ferry on the seventh ballot was nominated. Senator Foster had been confident of a re-election, but there never was a case worse managed. His friends went into a caucus without qualification, having Governor Buckingham and Ferry for competitors. B. was from the same town with Foster, and the contest consequently had a personal bearing. Ferry, being from the western part, slipped in between them. I had told Dixon and had written to some friends that the struggle would be likely to eventuate in Ferry's nomination.

Babcock and Sperry of New Haven have undertaken to manage the matters, and they have, as I expected they would, made a failure. They have been afraid of dividing the party, and, as the Radicals outnumber them in the organization, they must go against their conviction and do wrong. I do not believe there is vim enough among the friends of Johnson to make a stand in this matter. Babcock has run his head into a bag and taken others with him. He is afraid to withdraw it lest he should see something. By this action he has demoralized the members.

Fox is bewildered with the idea of going out in his official capacity as Assistant Secretary of the Navy to Europe. I am sorry to see so much self-glorification. But he is stimulated by Seward, Grimes, and others.

Old Mr. Blair came in to-day and had more than an hour's talk with me in behalf of Lee. I went over the ground with him, as I did with Moore. "But," said Mr. Blair, "I ask as a favor to myself, who have labored here in Washington for thirty-five years without office, that Lee may have a position in Washington." He said his sons, Montgomery and Frank, had been sacrificed, and he asked me as an old friend to spare Lee. I told him I was willing to do anything in my power for him or either of his sons, but I could not depart from what is right and the usages of the service; that Lee had been guilty of great impropriety in procuring him to take up his cause with the President or myself; that Lee had received special favors, had become rich in a place which others believed justly theirs, and that they had imputed his success to the Blair influence; that, were I to give Lee position here in one of the bureaus, as he, Mr. Blair, requested, or were I to give him promotion as asked, it would cause great dissatisfaction in the service,

FRANCIS PRESTON BLAIR, SR.

and be charged to the Blairs; that I, as a friend, was unwilling that discontent against them should be incurred for Lee; that he ought not to absorb their influence nor strive to get court favor at their expense.

Mr. Blair claimed that Lee stood next to Farragut and Porter in the Navy and ought to be made an admiral; says he would have been but for Fox, and named some things against Fox which I told him were incorrect. At length he drew out an application from Lee, but not signed though in his handwriting, asking a year's leave. I told him it was an extraordinary application, such as no one of his rank had made, and that Lee must know it was improper. He could not think, after his great pecuniary success, of remaining idle in the service, nor must he strive to evade its duty. If he declined the Navy Yard at Mare Island, he might take Pensacola, or he might have a good ship, but he must not decline service after nine months' leisure. I told him I could do better for Lee if absent than if here, that whatever I had done for him had been unsolicited and when he was away.

Mr. Blair deprecated the desolation of his house from this order to move; said his daughter and grandchildren would leave him, and he and his old woman would pack up and go to California also, which was very hard at seventy-five. I said that neither he, his wife, nor daughter would go, that he had been urged to this application by this improper view.

May 14, *Monday.* Mr. Smythe, Collector in New York, called at my house yesterday with Senator Doolittle, and both were much interested in the election of Senator in Connecticut. I remarked to them that the subject had been greatly mismanaged, and I doubted, knowing the men and their management, or mismanagement, whether anything could now be done; that Foster and his friends had been sanguine and full of confidence, — so much so that they had taken no precautionary measures, — and he and his friends could not, in good faith, make farther move for him, and yet they would do nothing for any one else.

Mr. Smythe said that from information which he had there was no doubt that Ferry would be defeated and a true man elected. There were, he said, three candidates spoken of, — myself, Foster, and Cleveland; that they could do better with me than with either, Foster next, and Cleveland last.

I repeated that I could not well see how Foster could now be taken up, and yet so intense were he and his friends that they would engage for no others. Smythe said he would leave this evening and would go on to-morrow to New Haven, confident he could do something.

But all will be labor lost. I have little doubt that if the matter were taken up sensibly the election of a true man could be secured. But Babcock, Sperry, Starkweather, and others, who had managed things at New Haven, would interest themselves for no one but Foster, while his chances are the worst after what has been done, and to now be a candidate would be dishonorable.

The Democrats, who would securely control this, would probably unite on me sooner than any one named, but the Republican friends of Johnson have been manipulated by Foster's friends and taught to stand by their party until they have no independence or strength. The weak and simple conduct of Babcock and the Republican Johnson men, is disgusting. They have resolved and re-resolved that they will not divide the Republican Party. Consequently they must go with it in all its wrongdoing and mischief, because the Radicals, being a majority, will control what is called the Republican Party. This is the light, frivolous training and results of Connecticut Whiggery. While preferring to be Johnson men and to support the Administration, they are aiding the election of a Radical, anti-Johnson, anti-Administration man to the Senate, — all, as they claim, to preserve the party, but certainly without regard as to consistency or principle.

May 17, *Thursday*. Have been some indisposed, with a good deal to do. Fox is about leaving, but is managing and contriving to get position and go abroad with *éclat*. Seward has encouraged him in this, and it is not pleasant for me to oppose it, although the whole proceeding is wrong in my opinion, or rather is such as should not be encouraged. Faxon thinks the demonstration is, on the part of Fox, for self-glorification and with a design to steal fame at my expense. This may have some foundation, but I hope not, and believe not, in so aggravated a degree as Faxon and some others conjecture. The President spoke of this queer mission to-day in rather contemptuous terms, and said there were efforts on the part of some to glorify Fox as an indispensable part of the Government. I made the matter as pleasant as I well could to the President, for Fox has been useful and I wish him to have the full benefit of it. To me he has been respectful and always obedient and attentive. I do not believe he intends to arrogate anything at my expense. If he attempts it, time will correct it. His work, as I understand, is to be made the agent of some of the South American states in building some turreted vessels and perhaps others, and he fancies that by going across the Atlantic in the Miantonomah he shall obtain useful celebrity. This, in my opinion, is the impelling motive and he is not, perhaps, sufficiently considerate of myself and others in pressing forward his scheme.

Faxon does not believe that he intends to resign his place in the Department, but thinks that he means to resume his position here on his return. That cannot be and I am unwilling to believe he would, if he could, be guilty of the bad faith and duplicity that would be involved in such a procedure.

May 18, *Friday*. Ferry was elected Senator on the part of the House of Representatives of Connecticut by some thirty majority on Wednesday. In the Senate the election was postponed for a week, three of the Republican

Senators refusing to vote for Ferry. This check has caused consternation among the Radicals here, and I have no doubt at home also. A violent onset will now be made on the three recusant or independent Senators. Intriguers at New Haven, and intriguers in their respective districts will be at work to influence them, and I have my doubts whether one or more of them may not be shaken.

In the mean time our friends should be at work upon others. A great mistake, however, has been committed in getting the members pledged for persons instead of principles. I have advised that they should put themselves on impregnable ground for the Union, irrespective of men or parties.

Seward has gone home. He told me he intended to make a speech while absent in favor of the President and his policy. Originating no measure himself, and cautious and calculating in adopting the plans of others, he nevertheless supposes that what he says has wonderful influence. I do not think he has ever made a speech which gave shape or character to a party, though usually the oracle of Weed and the managers of his party. Often his remarks have been more harmful than beneficial. His harangues at Auburn are studied orations, prepared after consultation with his confidants, and he is now pregnant with one. If it is a quiet baby, passive and pleasant, I shall be satisfied; if it has some deformities, I shall not be surprised.

May 19, *Saturday.* Dixon informed me last evening that he was apprehensive Foster would leave his friends in the lurch. Brandegee and some others came on from New Haven and had a private interview with Fessenden, who took Foster in hand, and D. believes has succeeded in capturing or controlling him. I think it probable, for Foster has wanted stamina and decision in this instance, though I think he is very well disposed and possessed of a pretty good share of good sense, if he had the courage to use it.

May 21, *Monday.* Captain S. P. Lee called on me to-day respecting his orders to Mare Island. The President on Saturday showed me an application which Lee had made to him to be relieved from the orders and placed on leave for one year. Mr. Blair had left with me a similar paper, unsigned, however. The President inquired what he should do with the paper. I answered that it was an extraordinary application even if made to the Department, but more extraordinary in passing over the Department and applying to the President to rid himself of orders.

The President said he would refer the paper to me to dispose of. It reached me this A.M., and Lee followed it within half an hour. He showed a consciousness of manner in opening the subject, and made a half-turn apology for having gone to the President by saying, if he had not called on me, his father-in-law, Mr. Blair, had. I did not conceal from him my surprise at the unusual course he had pursued, the more so as his age, experience, and long attendance at Washington precluded any idea that it was the result of ignorance.

I told him that he had been favored and fortunate in some respects beyond any officer of his grade, perhaps beyond any officer in the service; that he could not expect to remain off duty while all others were on duty; that he had been eight months on waiting orders, and that no officer had asked a year's leave; that he assigned no reason, nor could I conceive of any that would justify such leave.

He said his case was peculiar and he wished to remain in Washington to attend to his promotion.

Then, said I, any officer would be entitled to the same privilege, and the service would soon be in a demoralized state; that I did not desire for his own reputation to see him seated at the threshold of the Executive Mansion, or at the door of the Senate, beseeching for undue favors; that he would do well to leave his case in the hands of the Department, as did other officers. He certainly would fare as well if away as if here.

The interview was long and unpleasant. Again this evening he has called at my house to repeat the same plea.

The President, I find, is by no means pleased with the steps that have been taken in regard to Fox's going to Russia. He thinks that injustice is designed towards me by Seward, certain Radicals, and by Fox himself. His surmises are probably correct, except as regards Fox, who does not wish to do me wrong, though, perhaps, not sufficiently considerate in his efforts for this mission; and on other occasions the same fault may appear.

May 22, Tuesday. Little of interest transpired to-day in Cabinet. Wrote Lee repeating the order to Mare Island. But for a word from the President he would have been court-martialed. He presumes greatly on his connection with the Blairs and would himself monopolize all that is due them; is full of low intrigue, is selfish and is avaricious, regardless of what belongs to others.

May 23, Wednesday. Fox called on me last evening and unexpectedly bade me farewell. Said he would not trust himself to call at the Department to-day. He was very much affected, said words were wanting to express his high respect and admiration for me and the qualities which I possessed for the position which I filled. Spoke of over five years' intercourse, during which there had not been one unpleasant word, nor, as he was aware, an unpleasant thought between us. I have not time now to speak of F. and his qualities, but shall do so. He has been useful to the country and to me, relieving me of many labors and defending me, I believe, always. His manner and ways have sometimes given offense to others, but he is patriotic and true.

The President and his Cabinet were serenaded this evening. I am opposed to these methods of calling out public men; have respectfully suggested to both Presidents Lincoln and Johnson that it was not advisable to address gatherings at such times, and was determined not to break over the rule myself. I had, therefore, given the subject no attention and was embarrassed when a crowd of perhaps a thousand appeared before my door with a band of music. Declining to make remarks, I stated that I approved the policy of the Administration and was for the union of the States and the rights of the States.

I understand Stanton read off a long address and McCulloch and Dennison each made speeches. The latter acquitted himself with credit, and Stanton read his prepared address from his door, a man standing each side of him with a lighted candle. Dennison made a soothing speech for the party; said everything was lovely. Speed ran away, and Harlan would not show himself.

May 28, *Monday.* Events have crowded thick, and I have been unable to find time to record them. Judge Blair called on me yesterday with a request that I would, for his father's sake, revoke the orders of Captain Lee to Mare Island. Lee has been busy and mischievous in his intrigues to evade duty. I am told has seen every Senator but one and related his services and sorrows. As a last resort he threatens to take his wife and child to California and thus leave his father-in-law's family desolate. His persisting in this respect has made Mr. Blair, who is now seventy-five, sick and is likely to permanently affect his health.

Judge Montgomery Blair, who for nine years, he tells me, has not spoken to Lee, and who would, I have no doubt, feel relieved were Lee in California, earnestly requested for his father's sake, that the orders might be revoked. I finally told him that I would, with the approval of the President, to whom Lee himself had appealed, revoke them and place Lee on leave for two months. The President, on whom we called, assented, and I this morning sent Lee a revocation of the order to Mare Island. He knew the fact yesterday. Two hours after the order revoking his detail to Mare Island, I received a long communication of eight or ten

2

foolscap pages, dated the 26th, accepting the order, and stating he should proceed to Mare Island by next steamer. I immediately wrote him that he was at liberty to go or remain, and that I made it optional with him to present a future claim for favor for indulgence granted.

The intrigues of this man to get his orders countermanded have been as wonderful as disgusting. His wife was made to harass her old father and threaten him with an interruption of domestic arrangement and family repose if he was not permitted to remain. Appliances and measures through others were used. My wife was compelled to listen to lamentations on account of the cruel orders of the Department. I called on the President the latter part of last week, and there were sixty or eighty children from the orphan asylum with the matron and others, and I was implored, for the children's sake, to revoke the orders, that Mrs. Lee could remain, for she was one of the managing directors of the school, etc., etc.

The President invited me to come and see him on Saturday. He was not reconciled to the arrangement in regard to Fox. We went over the whole subject, and I told him Fox had rendered great service, such as I thought would justify his visiting Europe for six months in behalf of the Department. Among other things the President has received from some quarter an impression that Fox is a Radical and strong in that interest. This, I think, is one of the intrigues of Lee, through the elder Blair.

May 29, *Tuesday*. At the Cabinet-meeting word was received of the death of Lieutenant-General Scott at West Point at the advanced age of eighty. He was great in stature, and had great qualities with some singular weaknesses or defects. Vanity was his great infirmity, and that was much exaggerated by political or party opponents. He had lofty political aspirations in former years, but they had expired before him. Courteous, deferential, and respectful to his official superiors always, he expected and required the

same from others. Though something of a politician, I do
not think his judgment and opinion in regard to public affairs were always correct or reliable. In the early stages of
the late Civil War I thought, and still think, his counsels
were not wise, and yet they received extraordinary favor
and had great weight with President Lincoln. My impressions are that Mr. Seward persuaded the President that
the opinions and advice of General Scott were of more
value than those of any others or all others, and Seward was
before Mr. Lincoln's inauguration thought to be the coming
man. This he used and contrived by flattery to infuse into
General S. the advice on public affairs which he wished to
have commended to the President when he made military
inquiries.

The course of the General at the beginning of our troubles
was equivocal and unreliable. He began right and with
good advice to Mr. Buchanan to garrison the forts of the
South. A small military force in different localities would
have served as rallying-points, strengthened the union
sentiment and checked disunion. But he seemed to have
doubted his own advice, halted, and after Congress convened in 1860 would fall into Mr. Seward's views and was
ready to let the "wayward sisters go in peace." He, in
those days, imbibed an impression, common among the
politicians in Washington, that Mr. Lincoln, the newly
elected President, was unequal to the position, for he had
not figured on the national arena. It was supposed, therefore, that one of his Cabinet would be the managing man
of the incoming administration, and that Mr. Seward, his
principal competitor in the Republican nominating convention, who was to be the Secretary of State, would be
that manager. This was the expectation of Mr. Seward
himself, as well as of General Scott and others. He had
been a conspicuous party leader for twenty years, with a
reputation much overrated for political sagacity, and with
really very little devotion to political principles, which he
always subordinated to his ambition. It was not surpris-

ing that General Scott viewed him as the coming man, and as Mr. Seward was a man of expedients more than principle, he soon made it obvious that he intended to have no war, but was ready to yield anything — the Constitution itself if necessary — to satisfy the Secessionists. The General under this influence abandoned his early recommendations and ultimately advised surrendering all the forts.

The Senate, after many caucuses on the part of the Republican members, have an amendment of the Constitution modified from that reported by the *con*struction, or *ob*struction, committee. This amendment may be less offensive than that which passed the House by excluding one of the States from any voice or participation, but it ought not to receive the sanction of the Senate. Yet I have little doubt that it will and that the canvassing has been a process of drilling the weak and better-minded members into its support. Disgraceful as it may seem, there is no doubt that secret party caucus machinery has been in operation to carry through a Constitutional Amendment. Senators have committed themselves to it without hearing opposing arguments, or having any other discussion than that of a strictly party character in a strictly private meeting. Of course this grave and important matter is prejudged, predetermined. Eleven States are precluded from all representation in either house, and, of the Senators in Washington, all not pledged to a faction are excluded from the caucus when the decision is made. This is the statesmanship, the legislation, the enlightened political action of the present Congress. Such doctrines, management, and principles, or want of principles, would sooner or later ruin any country.

I happen to know that Fessenden had long interviews with Stanton last week, though I know not the subject-matter of their conferences. Fessenden sometimes hesitates to support a wrong measure. Seward has a personal party in Congress, — men who seldom act on important

questions in opposition to him and his views. All of these
men vote in opposition to the President's policy. Raymond
alone vacillates and trims, but this is with an understanding, for Raymond and Seward could, if necessary, carry
others with them, provided they were earnestly disposed.

XXXIX

The Fenian Situation on the Great Lakes — What to do with the Captured
Fenians — Seward's Position as a Supporter of the Administration —
The President issues a Proclamation in regard to the Fenians — Attor-
ney-General Speed's Preliminary Order — Changes in the Cabinet con-
sidered — Call for a National Convention of Friends of the Union pro-
posed — The President reads his Message to the Cabinet — Dennison
fails to concur, and the President strikes out the Concurrence Clause —
Intrigues of Seward and Weed in connection with the Convention Call—
The Connecticut Senate adopts the Constitutional Amendment —
Party Politics and the Convention Call.

June 2, *Saturday.* There was no Cabinet-meeting yesterday, and labor in the Department was suspended on
account of the funeral of Lieutenant-General Scott.

Seward sends me a note in pencil, signed by his initials,
with a telegraph from Dart, District Attorney of Western
New York, stating that Captain Bryson wanted two tugs
to assist him in guarding the river. Seward says, in pencil,
that the President thinks I had better charter the
steamers. He sent his clerk, Mr. Chew, with this note.
The whole thing was one of those low, intriguing, petty,
contemptible proceedings, shunning responsibility, to
which Seward sometimes resorts. I am sorry to write so of
one in his position and an associate, but I expressed the
matter to Chew without hard words, showing Seward's
weakness, [and saying] that this is a war on the Irish in
which he, Stanton, and Grant fear to do their duty, but
wish me to assume it.

I called on the President and spoke of the management
of this Fenian movement a little earnestly, and a little
freely. Reminded him that I had some weeks ago, when
the subject was brought forward in Cabinet, suggested
that the Irish population was an element in our politics,

and, therefore, it seemed proper that there should be unity in the Cabinet and among high officials. I consequently proposed that General Grant, who was stationing the military forces on the frontiers West and South, should make a formal communication in accord with the Secretary of War, which all could approve and with which we should all be identified. Stanton was alarmed, I saw; did not think it necessary to take such steps; and from that time the subject has been dropped. I remarked to the President that the proceedings had been singular; that this Fenian movement had appeared to me to be a great bubble, — nevertheless there was no denying the fact that large numbers were engaged in it; that they had large supplies of arms; that along our frontier from Eastport to Detroit there had been gatherings of armed men threatening to cross into Canada; that we had sent a naval force by request to Eastport; that our only gunboat on the Lakes had been detained by special request at Buffalo; and now the Secretary of State was calling on me to charter steamers and arm them; chartering vessels for military purposes belonged properly to the Army or War Department. By treaty stipulation we are to have but one naval vessel on the Lakes. Where, I asked him, were the revenue cutters which performed police duty? In all this time the War Department has done nothing. No proclamation has been issued. How and by what authority are we to capture or interfere with prisoners?

The President said it would be well to communicate with Commander Bryson, of the naval steamer Michigan, and ascertain whether additional vessels were wanted. I said that we had revenue cutters on the Lakes, but none were at Buffalo, where they were most wanted; that the Michigan had been detained there now some weeks awaiting a cutter. He thought I had better see the Secretaries of Treasury and State.

McCulloch was confident there were cutters at Buffalo, but on sending for the clerk in charge he found he was mistaken. He said he had turned the whole subject of Fenianism over to Attorney-General Speed, who is devoted to Stanton and Seward.

Seward was in a fog. Did not want to issue a proclamation. I asked what the naval vessels were to do, — what authority I had to charter steamers if there was not a state of war. If it was police duty, he or the Treasury should attend to it. I inquired about the military. He said Stanton wanted to keep clear of this question. I well knew this, and he wants me to do duties which belong to him and thus enlist the Irish element against the Administration.

June 4, Monday. Bryson telegraphed yesterday that he had captured seven hundred Fenians crossing the river at Black Rock. I sent the telegram to the President and to Seward, and soon after called on the President. He seemed a little perplexed. Said we had an elephant on our hands. I asked whether they were prisoners of war and what was to be done with them. He thought we must wait and we should soon have inquiries.

Shortly after my return Seward sent his carriage for me. I went to his house. He and Speed were sitting on the back porch. Speed had a telegram from Dart, District Attorney, stating the capture and making inquiries. Seward asked about the prisoners and what accommodations the Navy had. I told him none whatever and that these men could hardly be considered prisoners of war, even if we had accommodations; that they ought, if prisoners of war, at once to be turned over to the custody of the military. He said that would not do. Stanton wanted nothing to do with them, — there was no military force there. I told him there were officers and they could call on the militia or call out volunteer companies in Buffalo. This would be necessary, for such a number could not be retained by the civil authorities without a guard. He said, "Let them run away." Speed said that would not do. There might be and prob-

ably would be extradition claims for the leaders. I asked
them if they thought that these men were prisoners of war,
for I did not. Nor did I know how far their capture would
be justified.

Seward said the capture was all right; they should, perhaps, be considered prisoners of state; that he and Speed
had talked over the matter before I came, and he had prepared a couple of telegrams. Fred Seward read one, which
was signed by Speed. Seward proposed that I should telegraph Bryson that he, Seward, would take charge of them
as prisoners of state. Said Dart must attend to them. I
thought the marshal the proper person. He said that was
the same thing. Asked how much it would cost to feed
them, whether it could be done for a dollar each day. I
told him it would cost more than that, for he could not con-
fine them in Buffalo jail, or any inclosure, but must have
a guard. I did not see how he could get along without
military help, which would necessarily be attended with
expense. He said he would send word to Meade.

I again adverted to the matter of a proclamation when
such movements were being made upon the border, but
Seward interrupted me, said no, that was not necessary.
The thing was just right. He felt, he said, very happy over
it. Wanted neither Speed nor myself should say anything
about the matter until the regular Cabinet-meeting on
Tuesday.

Governor Morgan at my house last evening introduced
the subject of Reconstruction and the position of things
in the Senate, remarking, as though casually, there really
was now very little difference between the President and
Congress. I promptly, and perhaps unwisely in my
promptness, differed with him, and told him it was not
wise to attempt to deceive ourselves in the matter, — that
the difference was broad, deep, and such as could not be
reconciled.

He asked if I did not think the proposed amendment of
the Constitution, of the Senate, an improvement on that

which had passed the House; and whether that was not a step towards getting together. I told him that for myself, without speaking for others, I was opposed to the scheme for changing the Constitution now before Congress and opposed to any amendment while one third of the States were excluded from participating or giving their views, deprived, in fact, of their rightful representation; that I, therefore, did not feel as though there could be harmonious action, and it appeared to me a mistake to suppose that the President, a Constitutionalist, and the exclusionists, who were not, were likely to act together.

I have no doubt that Morgan came expressly to sound me and ascertain whether we would be united on the exclusion plan. Not unlikely Seward sent him. Morgan has evidently been trapped in the caucus into a pledge, direct or implied.

June 5, Tuesday. At the Cabinet-meeting an hour or more was wasted in discussing a claim of Madame Bertinatti, a piece of favoritism in which the President has been imposed upon by Seward and Stanton. It seemed to me that it was brought forward and talked over for the express purpose of excluding more important subjects. There is in the Cabinet not that candor and free interchange of opinions on the great questions before the country that there should be. Minor matters are talked over, often at great length.

As McCulloch and myself came away, we spoke of this unpleasant state of things, and we came to the conclusion that we would, as a matter of duty, communicate with the President on this subject of want of frankness and freedom in the Cabinet, also in regard to his general policy and the condition of public affairs. The great mistake, I think, is in attempting to keep up the Republican organization at the expense of the President. It is that organization which the conspirators are using to destroy the Executive.

June 6, *Wednesday.* Montgomery Blair still persists that Seward is false to the President and that he and Stanton have an understanding. There are many strange things in Seward's course, and he is a strange man. I am inclined to think he is less false to the President than adhesive to the Secretary of State. He does not like Johnson less, but Seward more. Seward is afraid of the Democrats and does not love the Republicans. But he feels that he is identified with the Republicans, thinks he has rendered them service, and considers himself, under the tutoring of Thurlow Weed, as more than any one else the father of the party. The managers of the party dislike him and distrust him, fear that he will by some subtlety injure them, and do not give him their confidence. The Democrats look upon him as a puzzle, a Mephistopheles, a budget of uncertainties, and never have and never will trust him.

The President believes Seward a true supporter of his Administration. I think he means to support it. The President finds him a convenience, but does not always rely upon his judgment. His trust in Seward begets general distrust of the Administration. It is remarkable that none of Seward's devoted friends — men who under Weed breathe through his nostrils — sustain the President on his great measures. Raymond has been a whiffler on public measures, but no others have ever doubted, or dared express a doubt of, the Radical policy. This puzzles me.

Stanton is very anxious to retain his place, and yet he has a more intimate relation with the Radical leaders than with the President or any member of the Cabinet. His opinion and judgment, I think, the President values more than he does Seward's, yet he distrusts him more, — feels that he is insincere. But Stanton studies to conform to the President's decisions and determinations when he cannot change them, apparently unaware that he occupies an equivocal position, both with the President and the public.

June 7, *Thursday.* The President has finally issued a

proclamation in regard to the Fenians. It should have appeared earlier, but Seward has counseled delay. Speed put out a preliminary order, which appeared to me to be designedly mischievous. I so said to the President, who remarked that it had struck him as offensive, and he so told Speed before it was published, yet it was not altered. The effect will be likely to throw the Irish against the Administration, or make them, at all events, indifferent towards it, whereas this all might have been different.

It is one of many little things which impresses me there is intended mischief towards the President. Speed acts with Seward and Stanton thoroughly, and his peculiarly worded order, if not suggested by them, is just what they wished.

June 8, *Friday.* But little of importance at the Cabinet. I had some conversation with the President after adjournment, and in the evening McCulloch and myself called upon him by appointment. Our conversation was frank, extending more than an hour. We all concurred that it was not possible to go on much longer with a view of preserving the integrity of the Republican Party, for the Radicals are using the organization to injure the President. There is direct antagonism between the leaders who control Congress and the Administration. The Democrats in Congress are more in harmony with the Administration than are the Radicals; — then why repel the Democrats and favor the Radicals?

We — McCulloch and myself — spoke of the want of cordial and free intercourse among the members of the Cabinet, that important questions touching differences in the Republican Party were never discussed at our meetings, that it was obvious we did not concur in opinion, and, therefore, the really important topics were avoided. The President admitted and lamented this, as he has done to me repeatedly. He expressed his surprise that Harlan and Speed should, with these understood views, desire to remain. I asked if there were not others among us as objectionable and more harmful. McCulloch said he could not believe Seward was faithless, that he fully agreed with him whenever they had conversed. I admitted the same as regarded Seward and myself, still there were some things I could not reconcile. He is not treacherous to the President, but is under the influence of Stanton and acts with him. His intimates, as well as Stanton's, in Congress, voted steadily with the Radicals; his speech at Auburn was a whistle for the Republicans to keep united and repelled Democrats. The President was reluctant to give up Seward, whose equivocal course is characteristic, but evidently had some doubts as to his sincerity and ulterior purpose. He suggested that Seward should be called in to a conference and come to an explicit understanding. This we all concurred in, though I remarked we should have fair words and no decisive action. But it was left to the President to invite a meeting.

June 11, *Monday.* Went to-day to Annapolis and examined the school and premises. Midshipmen had just completed the annual examination and were feeling merry and well. Jenkins and Commodore Radford accompanied me.

June 12, *Tuesday.* Not much of importance before the Cabinet. Some little attempt to converse on general subjects. Seward, McCulloch, and myself were first there, and allusion was made to our getting together and coming to an understanding on the true condition of affairs. Seward looked a little sharp, I thought, at me, and said he had no objection, but he knew not that any good would come of it. He said he was preparing a paper which would bring all things right, but was not yet quite ready. To what he alludes I know not and cannot yet conjecture, but I have little faith in it as assuring any useful purpose for the Administration or the country.

June 13, *Wednesday.* Dined this evening at Tassara's, the Spanish Minister. The banquet was given in honor of Dulce, late Governor-General of Cuba. Seward and Stanton were the only Cabinet-members besides myself who were present. Sir Frederick Bruce, Montholon, Baron Gerolt, etc., etc., were present. General Dulce does not speak nor understand English, and therefore all conversation was through an interpreter. As I sat at his right, and could not talk Spanish, we were not very sociable. He is a quiet, gentlemanly man with little of the look of a Spanish grandee.

I was sorry to hear Seward and Stanton chuckling over an allowance which they had succeeded in getting for Mrs. Bertinatti, the wife of the Italian Minister. They evidently thought it an adroit piece of management, and I judge the President has been misled in regard to it. Mrs. B. was a Rebel Mrs. Bass, of Mississippi, and her claim unjust. I apprehended it should not have been allowed.

The President has made the annual Executive appointments of midshipmen. In this he exhibited more painstaking than Mr. Lincoln, and gave less authority to me, which I did not regret. Usually Mr. Lincoln specified two or three special cases and then turned over the residue to me. Mr. Johnson desired me to go over the applicants twice with him in detail, got, as far as he could, particulars, and retained the whole schedule of names for more than a week, occasionally speaking of some one or more to me. His aim seemed to be to confer the appointment on the poor and deserving, regardless of locality, names, and influence. His selections were probably good ones, but some of them would have been different had the choice devolved on me.

June 14, *Thursday.* The House yesterday passed the Senate proposition to change the Constitution. It was before that body about two hours and was passed under the previous question. Such a reckless body, ready to break up the foundations of the government, has never been assembled, and such legislation, regardless of the organic law, would not only destroy public confidence but ruin the country. All is for party, regardless of right or of honest principle.

Representations are sent out that Congress has made great concessions in adopting the Senate's proposition, that they have yielded about everything, and that the President is pretty well satisfied with the question as now presented. There is design in all this, and some professed friends of the President are among the most active in it. The *New York Times*, and papers strongly under the influence of Seward and Weed, as well as their partisans, maintain these views. Thurlow Weed has been here within a few days and is always on errands of mischief. All looks to me like a systematic plan to absorb the President, or to destroy him. He still leans on Seward and seems under his influence, though with doubts and occasional misgivings. Seward himself defers to Stanton, — is becoming afraid of him. That Seward is cheated I cannot believe, and if he is not cheated I am constrained to believe the President is. And who is to undeceive him? I have on more than one occasion suggested my doubts, but while he has received my suggestions attentively he has pondered in obvious distress, and the subject is of so delicate a nature that I cannot do more.

At the very time that the House was adopting this Constitutional change, Green Clay Smith was nominated Governor of Montana. Smith professes to be with the President, but went with the Radicals on the test oath, and is made Governor.

June 15, *Friday.* Nothing special at Cabinet. On Tuesday Seward submitted a correspondence between Schenck and Romero, the Mexican Minister. It was a very improper proceeding, and R. evidently thought it wrong in giving a copy to the Secretary of State. Seward mentioned it as of little moment, — a sort of irregularity. Stanton said there was nothing wrong so far as Schenck was concerned, but that it was a questionable proceeding on the part of Romero. I declared my entire disapproval of the whole transaction and that it was one of the many indications of ignoring and crowding on the Executive.

The others were silent, but, after a little earnest talk, Seward said he would give the subject further consideration. To-day he brought forward the correspondence with an indorsement disapproving it and said he should communicate it to Romero.

Senator Doolittle took breakfast with me this morning. We went over the political questions and discussed what had best be done. Both were satisfied that the time had arrived when the Administration must take a stand. The game of the Radicals and of certain conspicuously professed friends of the President, that the Republican Party must be sustained and kept united at any sacrifice, even the surrender of the Constitution in some of its important features, and to the jeopardy of the Union itself, must be checked, and the opposition to any such policy made clearly manifest. We called on the President and made known our opinions. He concurred and thought a prompt call for a national convention of friends of the Union should be issued. Doolittle agreed to undertake to draw up such a call, but desired that I would also place on paper my views. He proposed that the call should be signed by the members of the Cabinet, or such of them as approved the measure. I told them that I, personally, had no objection, but I questioned its propriety and effect.

McCulloch, with whom I had a brief interview after Cabinet-meeting, told me that the elder Blair was preparing the call. I saw Judge Blair this evening and found him much engaged, yet not altogether satisfied. He expresses apprehension that Seward has control of the President and has so interwoven himself into the mind and course of the President as not to be shaken off, and if so that the Democrats must go forward independent of both President and Congress. Says the Democratic leaders, many of whom he has seen, such as Dean Richmond, Dawson, and others, say they will go in under the President's lead provided he will rid himself of Seward, but they have no confidence in him, — would rather give up Johnson than retain Seward. Governor Andrew of Massachusetts takes a similar view. B. says his father has had a talk with the President; that he himself has written him fully; that he advised the President not to dismiss Harlan unless Seward also went; that the President expressed doubts whether the Senate would confirm two Cabinet officers; that he was told there would be no difficulty; if there were, he would let the assistants carry on the Departments, and assign General Grant *ad interim* to the War; that Grant had been consulted and assented to the arrangement.

June 18, *Monday*. Senator Doolittle brought me last evening the rough draft of a proposed call for a national Union convention which he had prepared. Some of the points were well put, but there was too much restriction, too much fear that we should have men we did not care to fellowship with, although we might agree on present issues. To this I excepted, but my strongest point was the omission to meet and present the real issue, — our objections to the proposed change of the Constitution which has passed the two houses of Congress.

"What," said I, "are the reasons for calling a convention at this time? Is it not because the faction in Congress, assisted by schemers out of Congress, have concocted a scheme under party excitement and by party machinery to change the Constitution in important particulars, and that by a snap judgment Governor Curtin has addressed a circular letter to the Governors of the several States, inviting an immediate convening of the State legislatures to adopt the proposed change, before the people can have an opportunity to express an opinion? An alarm should be sounded,

2

warning the people of the movements that are being made
to alter the organic law, and insidiously change the government."

These and other suggestions I saw made an impression
on Doolittle, but still he hesitated and was embarrassed.
Pressing him on this point, he admitted he wanted Raymond to sign the call, he being Chairman of the National
Republican Committee, and Doolittle wanted others of
that committee also to sign it. This I thought of less importance than to have a proper call; certainly I would not
suppress the great essential for such a trimming, unreliable
man as Raymond. As I urged the matter, he admitted
that Raymond had seen the call and approved it; further
that the President had read it, and I have no doubt that
Seward had also seen it, although that was not distinctly
stated. The call, if not the convention itself, is, I think,
perverted to an intrigue in behalf of the old Whig Party, on
which Weed and Seward rely.

I proposed that we should go and see Mr. McCulloch. It
was raining intensely hard, but he at once accorded. He
had been to Silver Spring and submitted the document to
Mr. Blair and his son, who, he said, approved it.

Mr. McCulloch was not at home, and we parted, but the
paper which D. presented, the convention, and the aspect
of affairs gave me infinite concern. There is no doubt that
Seward and Stanton have a personal understanding to act
together. Stanton is in concert with the Radicals, and, at
the same time, Seward is prompting Doolittle. The public
is ripe for a convention, but this call is an artful contrivance to weaken it. The President is being subordinated
by the intriguers, and the design is obviously to weaken
the Administration and give the Radical Party the
ascendant. Seward, beguiled by Stanton, expects to control the convention by the aid of Weed and Raymond.
The fruition of seven months' intrigue means that and
nothing else. They intend to rule the President, and I fear
he will let them.

I stopped early this morning at Judge Blair's and inquired what he thought of the call. He said he had not been in any mood or mind to think of anything, having been without sleep the previous night, but it had appeared to him to have a too narrow basis. I then told him my view and the conversation Doolittle and myself had. Blair most earnestly agreed with me, said my views corresponded with his own, and promised to see the President if he could.

I called on McCulloch, who agreed to come to my house this evening and go with me to the President. When he called, I detailed the conversation with Doolittle, told him of my apprehensions, and dwelt emphatically on the subject of the Constitutional changes as the true basis of action, and our sounding the bugle-note of warning to arouse the people. My earnestness and the facts excited him, and we went to the President.

We spent an hour in a free and unrestricted conversation with the President. McCulloch, full of the views which I had urged, advised that the President should at once issue a proclamation after the manner of Jackson in regard to nullification, appealing to the people.

I inquired of the President if he had seen Doolittle since Sunday, and told him what I thought of the proposed form of call, and that the just alarm on the proposed change of the Constitution ought not on any account to be omitted. The people ought not to be deluded and cheated by trash. He concurred with me. I inquired if he had noticed that important omission in the proposed call. He did not answer direct, but said the call was too much in detail.

June 19, *Tuesday.* After current business at the Cabinet was closed, I inquired of Seward if it was true that he had sent out a special official certificate of the Constitutional Amendment to Governor Hawley of Connecticut. I saw notice to this effect in the papers. Seward said yes, and his manner indicated that he wished I had not put to him the question.

Stanton at this moment, without any design perhaps, drew off the President's attention and they went to one of the windows, conversing audibly. In the mean time Seward and myself got into an animated conversation on the subject of these proposed changes, or, as they are called, amendments of the Constitution. I thought the President should pass upon them. At all events, that they should not have been sent out officially by the Secretary of State, obviously to be used for electioneering purposes, without the knowledge of the President. McCulloch agreed with me most decidedly. Seward said that had not always been the practice. Dennison made some undecisive remarks, evincing indifference. But all this time Stanton and the President were engaged on other matters, and as the President himself had proposed last evening to bring up this subject in Cabinet, I was surprised that he remained away during the conversation, the purport of which he must have known. I became painfully impressed with the apprehension that Seward had an influence which he should not have, and that under that influence the President did not care to be engaged in our conversation.

On leaving the council chamber I went into the Secretary's room adjoining. McCulloch was already there, and we had a free talk with Colonel Cooper, the Private Secretary of the President and his special confidant in relation to public matters, about the necessity there was for prompt and decisive action on the part of the President. Colonel C. fully agreed with us.

June 20, *Wednesday*. Went with G. W. Blunt to see the President this morning. Blunt wants to be Naval Officer and has been a true and earnest friend of the Navy Department during the War and boldly met our opponents when friends were needed. Of course I feel a personal regard for him and have two or three times told the President that, personally, Blunt was my choice. If other than personal consideration governed I had nothing to say.

After Blunt left, the President and myself had a little conversation. I expressed my apprehension that there were some persons acting in bad faith with him. Some men of position were declaring that he and Congress were assimilating and especially on the Constitutional change. He interrupted me to repeat what he said to McCulloch and me, — that he was opposed to them and opposed to any change while any portion of the States were excluded. I assured him I well knew his views, but that others near and who professed to speak for him held out other opinions. I instanced the *New York Times*, the well-known organ of a particular set, which was constantly giving out that the President and Congress were almost agreed, and that the Republican Party must and would be united. The fact that every Republican Representative had voted for the changes, that the State Department had hastened off authenticated copies to the State Executives before submitting to him, the idea promulgated that special sessions of the legislatures in the States were to be called to immediately ratify the amendments, or innovations, showed concert and energy of action in a particular direction, but that it was not on the road which he was traveling.

He answered by referring to yesterday's conversation with Seward; said he had sent early yesterday morning to stop action at the State Department, but found the circulars had been sent off. He seemed not aware that there was design in this hasty, surreptitious movement.

June 21, *Thursday.* Senator Doolittle took tea with me. He wished me to go with him to the President, where some friends were to assemble to consider and decide in relation to the proposed call for a national convention. Senator Cowan, Browning,[1] Randall,[2] and three other persons whom I did not know, but who seemed attachés of Ran-

---

[1] O. H. Browning, who shortly succeeded Harlan as Secretary of the Interior.

[2] A. W. Randall, soon to succeed Dennison as Postmaster-General.

dall, and who, I understood, belonged to the National Union Johnson Club, composed the sitting. The call, which had been modified in slight respects, still omitted any allusion to the Constitutional changes, the really important question before the country. This I thought a great and radical defect, and Cowan and Browning concurred with me, as did McCulloch. Randall, who is flattered and used by Seward, opposed this, and his principal reason was that he would leave something for the convention to do. I asked why the convention was called, if not on this great issue which stood prominent beyond any other. "Well," he said, "it would hasten the calling of the State Legislatures to pass upon it." That, I told him, if properly used might be made to weaken them and strengthen us, — we would demand an expression of popular sentiment through the instrumentality of an election, and thereby expose the recent hasty action which was intended to stifle public opinion.

Much of the conversation between eight and eleven o'clock was on this point, during which I became satisfied that Randall was prompted by Seward and unwittingly used for party purposes of Weed and Seward. The President evidently was with me in his convictions but forbore taking an active part. My impressions are that Seward has, in his way, indicated objections to making the Constitutional question a part of the call; that it would prevent Raymond and others from uniting in the movement. Finally, Browning and then McCulloch and Cowan yielded. They probably saw, as I did, that it was a foregone conclusion, was predetermined, that the meeting had been cunningly contrived and pushed by Randall.

Doolittle stated his purpose of having the members of the Cabinet sign the call. Both McCulloch and myself had doubts of its expediency and effect. The President, without expressing an opinion, showed that he concurred in Doolittle's suggestion.

McCulloch asked if Seward would put his name to it, and

two or three undertook to vouch for him. I expressed my
readiness to unite in what would be best for the Administration and the cause. If it was to have official significance,
a proclamation I thought best. Seward, I am satisfied,
would not sign it if the Constitutional point was presented,
and I doubt if he will under any circumstances.

Something was said respecting Thurlow Weed, and the
President remarked that Weed would be here to-morrow,
but he knew Weed approved this movement and would
sign the call. All this pained me. Seward and Weed are
manifestly controlling the whole thing in an underhand
way; they have possession of the President and are using
the Administration for themselves and party rather than
the President and country. They have eviscerated the
call and will dissect and, I fear, destroy the effect of this
move. Randall is a man of lax political morality, and I
think his influence with the President is not always in the
right direction. Seward knows his influence and intimacy
in that quarter and has captured him, probably without
R.'s being aware of it. The President finds that R. agrees
with Seward, and it carries him in that direction. While
R. means to reflect the President's wishes, he is really the
tool of Seward and Weed, and is doing harm to the cause
and to the President himself. But this matter cannot be
corrected and will, I fear, prove ruinous.

I left soon after eleven and came home, desponding and
unhappy. The cause is in bad and overcunning if not
treacherous hands, I fear. The proposed convention has no
basis of principles. It will be denounced as a mere union
with Rebels.

June 22, Friday. When I went to Cabinet-meeting only
Seward was there with the President. I was prompt to
time; Seward was in advance. Directly on entering, the
President handed me a message which he had prepared,
with an accompanying letter from Seward, relative to
the proposed Constitutional changes which Congress had

requested him to forward to the State Executives. The whole was very well done. As Seward had sent off authenticated copies to the Governors, the ready, officious act was very well gotten over by a declaration in the message that it was a ministerial act which was not to be understood as giving the sanction of the Executive or of the Cabinet to the proceeding.

I made a complimentary remark on the message, with my regret that there had not been more time and consideration in sending off copies to the States. Seward was annoyed by the remark and said he had followed the precedent of 1865, but the President was, I saw, not at all displeased with my criticism.

Subsequently, when all the Cabinet were present except Stanton and Speed, the message and papers were read. McCulloch expressed his approval of the message and said he should have been glad to have had it more full and explicit. In this I concurred.

Dennison took exception, which served to show that he had been consulted by the Radicals and had advised or consented to the course previously adopted. He and Seward each made some remarks, and Dennison showed much indignation because Seward had used the word "trick" on the part of Congress in sending this resolution to the President. Seward disclaimed the word and denied he had used it. I was not aware he had done so.

Dennison proceeded to say that Bingham had introduced, or been the means of introducing, the resolution; had consulted with him; that his object was pure; that he approved it; that although the proposed Amendment was not in the precise shape he wished, he, nevertheless, gave it his support; that it had been approved by the Republicans of Ohio, and were he at home in October, he should vote for candidates who favored it.

I assured him that therein he and I differed, for that I would not vote for the Amendment, nor knowingly vote for any man who supported it.

Seward said he had no doubt that the Republicans of the Auburn district would oppose it very generally, and that if he was at home in November he expected to vote for men who would oppose it.

I took higher ground. I cared not what parties favored or what parties opposed it, my convictions and opinions were in my own keeping, and I would vote for no man of any party who favored that Amendment.

Dennison said that with the explanations of Mr. Seward he took no exceptions, but he expected to act with the Union Party of Ohio.

Harlan said he thought the views of each would be reconciled. I doubted if we were a unit. Party seemed to have a stronger hold than country.

When the others had left, the President told McCulloch and myself that he had struck from the message the concurrence of his Cabinet. This I regretted, but he said Dennison's assent, even with his explanation, was not full and gave him an opportunity to evade, if convenient hereafter; he, therefore, chose to stand uncommitted, or trammeled by others. Before sending off the message, which he had done while we were there, he had erased the words referred to.

Dennison has evidently been tampered with and has made up his mind to go with his party, though aware that the party organization is being committed against measures of the Administration. He certainly does not yet anticipate leaving the Cabinet on that account, but will soon come to it. How the President is to get along with such a Cabinet I do not see. McCulloch spoke of it and said there were four in opposition. "Yes," said the President, "from what we now see of Dennison, and if we count Stanton after his patched-up speech; but it is uncertain where he wishes to place himself." There is no uncertainty on the part of any but the President. Speed and Harlan should, from a sense of propriety and decent self-respect, resign. This the President has repeated to me many times. Why he should cling to Stanton, who is working insidiously against him, and to Seward, who works with and shields Stanton, either doing more against him than the two feeble men of whom he speaks so freely, I do not understand. Stanton he knows is not in accord with him, though he does not avow it, and if Seward is presumably friendly, the fact that all the influence which he can exercise is dumb or hostile is notorious.

June 23, Saturday. The President sent me a note this A.M. to call upon him this evening at eight. Although under the doctor's care and ordered to remain perfectly quiet, I rode over at the time. Doolittle called and went with me. Seward soon came in, followed by McCulloch, Cowan, Browning, and Randall. We went into the library, where the proposed call for a national convention was finished up. Seward, who, with Weed and Raymond, drew up or arranged this call which Doolittle fathers, now suggested two or three verbal alterations, most of which were adopted. It is intended that these "suggestions" shall cover up Weed's tracks.

In all that was said and done Seward fully agreed. He intends to keep within the movement, which has become a New York scheme, in order to control it. His belief is that the Republicans, of New York at least, will respond promptly to the call and make the President's cause, which he means shall be his and the old Whigs', their own. How this is to be done, and the course of the Senators and Representatives of that State be sustained by the Administration, he does not disclose. The Democrats, who in their way are the chief supporters of the President's measures, are snubbed. I perceive Seward is satisfied with both the President's and his and Weed's positions. The President, I think, is aware of this discrepancy, yet tries to believe all is right.

Seward remarked that McCulloch and myself had been uneasy because there had not been an earlier demonstration made and the President's policy distinctly stated, but he had been satisfied it was best to delay. I said that by the delay many of our friends had got committed against us, particularly on those Constitutional changes, — men whom we could by a plain, frank course have kept with us. He said they would come right, but we must give Congress an opportunity to show its hand. They had had seven months and had done nothing that they were satisfied with themselves. We have done nothing which it was our duty to have done, and are we and sound principles benefited by the Seward policy of delay?

Throughout the preliminary proceeding of this call there was a disinclination to make the proposed Constitutional changes an issue, yet it is the real question. This shirking from an open, honest course I can trace chiefly to Seward, though others have become complicated with him. Even the President himself has incautiously and without sufficient consideration used some expression in relation to the basis of representation which embarrasses him; and so of Doolittle and some others. Seward's confidants are fully committed, and hence he and they cannot act freely; consequently the great and important question is omitted in the call, which should have made the invasion of organic law prominent above all other points. He also, whilst conforming to the President's policy, strives to preserve Stanton as an ally, who intrigues with the Radicals.

This movement is an important one, and it has annoyed and pained me that there should have been a sacrifice of principle to gratify any one. If it proves a failure, which I do not mean to anticipate, it will be mainly attributable to the intrigues by which Seward and Weed have been brought into it and finally controlled or shaped proceedings. The intrigue has been cunningly and artfully managed by them. They have mainly shaped the call, although it is in all respects not what they wished. The President, I think, flatters himself that he has arranged to bring them in, whereas the truth is, he would have found it difficult to keep them out. Their aim and purpose are to remain with the old Republican organization, of which the Radicals, or old Whigs, have possession, but which, by the assistance of the President's patronage and the hocus-pocus of New York politics, Seward and Weed will work into their own schemes in that State. I am apprehensive that this movement in the cause of the Administration will by their intrigues and deceptions be made secondary to their purpose.

June 25, Monday. For two or three days I have been prostrated by a severe attack of indigestion, yet against the remonstrance of Dr. H. I went to the President's Saturday evening. What took place and subsequent reflection while prostrated on my lounge have disquieted and greatly disturbed me. It is a lost opportunity. The President fails to comprehend the true condition of affairs and the schemes of prominent men around him, or hesitates to grapple with them. In either case he is deceived and fatally wrong. He must, and evidently expects to, rely on the Democrats to overcome the Radicals who are conspiring against him and the Constitution. But the Democrats have no confidence in Seward and will not fellowship with him. Seward knows that, if the President does not. This call for a national Union convention which has been gotten up is perverted into a Seward call; the party is to be Seward's party, and it cannot, therefore, be Democratic. The President is, consequently, purchasing or retaining Seward and his followers at too high a price, too great a sacrifice. Enough Republicans may rally with this call to defeat the Radicals, but cannot themselves become a formidable and distinct power. If, however, the movement defeats the reckless plans of the Radicals, it will accomplish a great good. I have my doubts if the flimsy expedient will do much good.

Our President has been too forbearing, has wasted his strength and opportunities, and without some thorough changes will find himself, I apprehend, the victim of his own yielding policy in this regard. I do not see how it is possible to sustain himself with Seward on his shoulders.

June 26, Tuesday. We had not a protracted Cabinet-meeting nor any specially interesting topic. I had thought the subject of the call for the convention, which appeared in this morning's paper, might be alluded to either before or after the business session, but it was as studiously avoided as if we had been in a Quaker meeting. There is no free interchange nor concurrence of views. Stanton is insincere, more false than Seward, who relies on expedients.

Blair tells me he likes the call and thinks it will be effect-ive. This inspires me with more confidence, for I had doubted whether he and men of his traits and views would acquiesce in it, particularly in its omissions. He does not apprehend the difficulty from Seward and Weed which has troubled me, for he says the President will cast Seward off and Stanton also. I had long seen that this was a necessity, but continued delay has disheartened expectation. Whether Blair has any fact to authorize his assertion, I know not. I can suppose it certain as an alternative. Stanton is unfaithful and acting secretly with the Radicals. He has gone. Either Seward must be discarded or the people will discard both him and the President. The latter does not realize that he is the victim of a double game, adapted to New York intrigues.

The papers state that the Senate of Connecticut adopted the Constitutional Amendment at midnight yesterday. This does not surprise me, yet had the President showed his hand earlier, the result might have been different in that State. But Seward, Weed, Raymond, and company are satisfied with this Radical Amendment. The latter voted for it. Weed has given it a *quasi* indorsement, and I do not remember to have heard Seward say a word against it. He hastened off a notice to Connecticut and the other States as the Radicals wished, without consulting the President or any member of the Cabinet. There has not been in Connecticut, or elsewhere, any deliberate, enlightened, intelligent, or comprehensive discussion of this measure, but a paltry, narrow, superficial talk or rant, all of the shallowest and meanest partisan character.

June 27, Wednesday. Had some conversation with Senator Grimes respecting the legislation of this Congress, which is passing acts of corporations, special privileges, and grants *ad libitum.* Members of Congress have the reputation of being largely interested in many of their legislative favors. I think Grimes is not. Among other things a proposition to create a Department of Education is pending,— not a Bureau, which would be bad enough, but a Department. Grimes, I see, did not favor it and in the course of his remarks said the high pressure for an extreme and almost prohibitory tariff was fast driving him into free trade. This is the natural result of extreme measures, — pushed too far they cause a reaction.

June 28, Thursday. I understand that the Democratic Members of Congress have concluded to unite in the movement for the national convention of the 14th of August. I had some doubts whether they would readily come into it. Old party organizations and associations are strong. The Democratic papers have hesitated, and the *New York World* opposed the movement.

This opposition of the *World* is agreeable to Weed and company, and was intended by the *New York Times,* which was prompted by Weed and Seward, to foreshadow the convention and to assume that it was the Union Convention or Union Party Convention.

Senators Doolittle, Nesmith, Buckalew, and Harris and myself met in Colonel Cooper's room this evening, casually and accidentally. Most of the conversation was on the convention and the condition of parties. Harris is something of a trimmer, and, I perceive, a good deal embarrassed how to act, yet not prepared to take anti-Radical ground. Doolittle tried to persuade him that his true course was to go forward with the new movement, and, among other things, said that it was the movement which would ultimately prevail, — we should not succeed this fall but that the next election we should be successful. Of course such an admission would make such a calculating politician as Harris stick to the Radicals, for the next fall elections will be decisive of the Senatorial contest in New York. He will, therefore, under Doolittle's admission, go with the Radicals as the most likely way to secure his return to the Senate, — of which, however, there is not the remotest probability. He will be disappointed.

June 29, *Friday.* Not much of special interest in the Cabinet. Seward read dispatches to Washburn, the poor Minister at the poor Government of Paraguay, expressing expectation that he had ere this reached his destination, assisted by Acting Rear-Admiral Godon. The course of Washburn has been inexcusably wrong, and the State Department scarcely less so. He has wasted time and opportunities at Montevideo, when he should have been at his post, if we are to have a Minister at Paraguay, and is now asking, and the State Department is conceding, too much in order that he may get there.

June 30, *Saturday.* Had a long talk this afternoon with the President on the condition of affairs and especially in regard to the proposed national convention. He does not like the composition of the Cabinet, yet does not, in my opinion, perceive the most questionable feature in it. Harlan and Speed, he does not conceal from me, are in the way. The course and position of Dennison do not suit him. Dennison, like others, has been drawn into the Radical circle against his better judgment, is committed to the Republican Party, and is appointing extreme Radicals to the local post-offices, carrying out the views of the Radical Members and strengthening them by displacing friends of the President. In this I do not think D. intends antagonism to the President, although it is that and nothing else. But he does not permit himself to believe that the President and the Party, which is now a mere machine of Thad Stevens, are not identical.

Seward knows the distinction and yet contrives to persuade the President to acquiesce, while favoring the Radicals. It is curious, but by no means pleasant, to witness this proceeding. The President, usually sagacious, seems not to discern the management and ultimate purpose of the Secretary of State, who is prompted by Stanton, one of the Radical chiefs. Stanton has an assumed frankness, but his coarse manner covers a good deal of subtle duplicity. Seward never differs with the President. If he has taken an opposite view from or with others, or before the President's opinion is known, it disappears forever when the sentiments of the latter are ascertained. His knowledge and estimate of men are weak and erroneous in the extreme.

The President understands the political dexterity of Seward and yet does not apprehend that it may ever operate adverse to himself, nor does Seward intend to antagonize his chief. Some recent proceedings, connected with the schemes of the Radicals, are to me inexplicable, and in our talk I so informed the President. I could not understand how all the Republican Members from New York, a considerable portion of whom are under the influence of Seward and Weed, should vote steadily with the Radicals and against him, if Seward and Weed are his true friends.

The *New York Times*, Raymond's paper controlled by Weed, declared that the President and Radicals were pretty much reconciled on the Constitutional changes, and by this representation multitudes were entrapped into the measure. Seward, hastily and without consulting the President, hastened to send certified copies of the Amendment by the first mail to the State Executives. These and other things I alluded to as very singular, and that I could hardly reconcile them to sincere and honest friendship. The President was puzzled; said it was strange.

I told him I could account for these proceedings readily, if it were to build up and sustain the Weed and Seward party in New York, but it certainly was not strengthening the Administration.

Raymond and Seward knew of the movements for the convention, and the *Times* in advance spoke of it as a move to unite the Republican Party while it would certainly injure the Administration. The effect was, when the call appeared, to cause distrust among Democrats, and to repel the *World*, the *Herald*, etc. It looks like design or stupidity. I knew they were not fools.

My efforts to incorporate with the call a clause adverting to the proposed Constitutional changes which made a convention advisable were resisted and defeated by the tools of Seward, because it would be agreeable to the Democrats and opposed to the Radicals. His friends were committed on that subject. They had adopted it and were, therefore, antagonistic to Johnson, yet they succeeded through the assistance of Radicals who care little for principles .

2

XL

July 2, Monday. I wrote on Saturday night replies to
Randall in regard to the convention, to the Tammany
Society, which had invited me to Fourth of July anniversary, to the Mayor of Boston also. In those letters I
indicate pointedly my views on the great questions before
the country.

McCulloch hesitates about sending a letter to Randall,
lest he shall experience hostility from the Radicals in Congress on important measures connected with his Department, which are there pending. My own opinion is that
his opinions should be expressed, and if for that reason the
public welfare is to be put in jeopardy, let the country so
understand. This is my view, and I have written accordingly, although I am also in the same category with the
Secretary of the Treasury. Only two bills, one for accept-

ing League Island for a Navy Yard and the bill for naval promotions, are strangely delayed, — the former in the Senate, the latter in the House. I am ready, however, to proclaim my position on the great questions affecting the country, but do not care to isolate and obtrude myself if other members of the Cabinet hold back.

July 6, *Friday.* Went down to the Capes of the Chesapeake on Tuesday, and remained at Hampton Roads and in the Chesapeake Bay, not returning until this morning. Have overdone, been indisposed for some weeks, or rather not in right condition. Seward, Doolittle, and three or four naval officers, and my two sons, Edgar and John, went with me. Had a pleasant time, but did not much recruit or improve in health.

Had several conversations with Seward in regard to the proposed convention, as well as public affairs generally. He, as usual, is very oracular and confident. Says the movement will be a great success. It might have been, had the real issue been presented. The convention, he says, is very well and will bring together many who have differed, will be a success, etc., etc. What will be the attitude of parties and persons in New York was not so clearly stated.

Doolittle tells me that Seward has written a letter to the Tammany Society, which he, Seward, thought was better than to write to Randall. In this D., indoctrinated by Seward, seemed inclined to acquiesce; said he had seen the letter, or had it read to him by S. I questioned whether it was the best way, and thought it would have more influence and be more creditable to frankly and directly communicate to Randall. It is a characteristic dodge.

Seward says Morgan (Senator) was not apprised of the call until it was published. He, Morgan, had concluded to go with the Radicals on the Civil Rights Bill, which, of course, meant the whole Radical policy; had told him (S.) how he intended to vote, the day preceding the final passage; said, in justification, the *Evening Post* favored it; that the legislature had instructed him. Seward remonstrated, but Morgan took his course, and thenceforth the intimacy had been broken. This modifies my conception of the matter, provided Weed was [not] in the thing; but if Weed advised or was in any way committed, Morgan was duped, and yet not that, perhaps, unless duped by his own folly and ambition, for he knows perfectly well the intimate relations of Seward and Weed, and that they always act in concert and understandingly, though apparently on opposite sides at times. But this pretended opposition is always deceptive and for a purpose, — they never antagonize.

When the call for a convention was in preparation and about to be issued, Seward tells me he sent for Weed, who looked it over and approved the measure and the sentiments set forth. He (S.) then told Weed he must inform Morgan, so that he should not be wholly taken by surprise, but Weed delayed and finally missed the opportunity.

I am not sorry if Morgan feels himself slighted. He has proved to be a calculating but not profoundly skillful trimmer during the session, and has lost irrevocably the higher position which he occupied early in the session. That he has flattered himself he could screen his vote, if unfortunate, under legislative instruction, I have never doubted, while if it was popular he should take to himself credit, was equally clear.

I find in the papers on my return to-day Seward's Tammany letter. It is, as I supposed it would be, a Seward dodge. With tints and hues and words to amuse, and hereafter turn as he may wish. It will not help the cause or help the President, and I am surprised that Doolittle should be satisfied with it. It shows how much he is under Seward's influence.

July 7, Saturday. Am in better health than at any time for the last two or three weeks. Congress accomplishes little that is good, and is really delaying national unity and prosperity. There is little statesmanship in the body, but a vast amount of party depravity. The granting of acts of incorporation, bounties, special privileges, favors, and profligate legislation of every description is shocking. Schemes for increasing the enormous taxation which already exists to benefit the iron and wool interests are occupying the session.

July 9, *Monday.* Senator Morgan spent last evening at my house. Our conversation was chiefly on public affairs, but there was not that unreserved and cordial intimacy which we have sometimes had. No allusion was made to the national convention, which was unnatural and could not have been, had there been our old and friendly sympathy.

I censured strongly, perhaps harshly, the proposed Constitutional changes and the method of getting them through Congress by caucuses, excluding the Democratic minority and one third of the States, etc. He attempted no defense or justification. Trumbull, he tells me, has introduced another of his revolutionary bills to deprive the President of his Constitutional right of removing from office. This subject, like most measures in each house, was passed through a caucus crucible. M. says he refused to give it his sanction, and so did one other.

I have no doubt Morgan feels a little uncomfortable in the existing state of things, and I fancy he is conscious he has committed a mistake. There are strange men in position in New York. The Weed school is a bad one. Raymond is a specimen. A man of considerable talent, but of little consistency of principle. I have so said to the President more than once, and I think he understands R., yet Seward is in with him, directs his movements by Weed's help, and has influenced the President in R.'s favor to some extent. No man has more injured the cause of the President in Congress or more strengthened the Radicals than Raymond, the pronounced organ of the Administration, but only the confidant of Seward. He has by his fickle, versatile changes, attempting to go with the President but always deserting him, and always clinging to party, deterred [some] by his example, others by his ridiculous somersaults. No one follows him.

July 10, *Tuesday.* No very striking matters in Cabinet. Seward read a long dispatch to Mr. Adams. Stanton excepted to the mention of our domestic affairs in such a document. I cared less about it in a confidential dispatch to our own Minister, but I did not like the phrase, or expressed hope, that Congress would *concede* to the Southern Members their seats. I preferred to hope that Congress would not much longer *deny* them their rights to seats.

Dennison, who has been absent for a fortnight in Ohio, was present.

Received telegram from California that my nephew, Samuel Welles, was severely injured by explosion of a boiler. Am distressed and anxious about him.

Doolittle called, and I went with him to McCulloch's. Had an hour's conversation. Doolittle is getting along and doing well. He is an honest, conscientious, and patriotic but credulous man. In this movement for a convention, of which he is the principal getter-up, he had permitted himself to be hampered by a hope that he could control in a great degree the Republican organization and retain it intact. He cannot give up that organization, of which the Radicals have possession, without reluctance. This is Seward's policy, and he has influenced Doolittle much on this point. Even yet he clings to Raymond. Is confident that Raymond will get a majority of the National Republican Committee to unite in favor of the Philadelphia Convention. It may be well enough, but is of less consequence than D. supposes. I think R. has scarcely any influence with the Committee. Seward thinks otherwise.

I told both Doolittle and McCulloch that I would thank them to inform me of the shape things were in, and were to be in, in New York. The President's friends and supporters

were the Democrats, whom Seward, Weed, and Raymond
were opposing, while their special friends were all Radicals
and fighting the President. But while their followers are
thwarting and resisting the President, the triumvirate
claim to be his friends, and are actually and undeniably, by
their intrigues, directing his movements, influencing and
controlling such men as Doolittle to evade the true issue. I
trust D. is beginning to have a more correct appreciation
of matters.

July 11, *Wednesday.* This morning received telegram
that my nephew, Samuel Welles, constructing engineer at
Mare Island, died last evening at 7.15 from injuries received by the explosion of a steam boiler in the Navy Yard.
His death is a loss to his country as well as his family, for
he was one of the most promising young men in all my
acquaintance. Had it pleased God to spare his life, he bade
fair to be at the very head of his profession, and would from
his ability and integrity have been, if he chose public life,
among the first citizens of California. Although young,
he was the ablest and best civil engineer in the service, and
I know not how nor whom to select to fill his place. Of fine
abilities, excellent judgment, great kindness of heart,
suavity of manners, and readiness to serve and befriend
others, he endeared himself to all who knew him. I loved
him as a son. He had always great respect and affection
for me, had spent much time in my family, and was almost
as one of our household. In September he was to have
returned home and to have been married. But, alas, all is
changed.

There is rumored this evening that Postmaster-General
Dennison has resigned. I shall not be disappointed if such
is the case. For two or three months he has wavered on
important measures, been less intimate and familiar personally than he was, and some recent indications and remarks have prepared me for this step. If it has not been
taken already, I have little doubt that it soon will be.

Harlan and Speed will follow. Whether Stanton will go with them is doubtful. Although he has been fully with the Radicals in all their extreme measures from the beginning, he has professed to abandon them when the President made a distinct stand on any subject. I am, therefore, uncertain what course he will take; but if he leaves he will be likely to be malevolent. He is selfish, insincere, a dissembler, and treacherous. Dennison, however, is honorable and manly. If his Radical friends have finally succeeded in persuading him to go with them, he will do it openly and leave the Cabinet, not remain to embarrass and counteract the President, or, like them, strive to retain place and seek the confidence of his chief to betray him.

I read to Blair my answer to Doolittle concerning the national convention. He is highly pleased with it and suggested I should make a point on the imminent danger of another civil war. Blair repeats a conversation with Boutwell, a Massachusetts fanatic, who avows that the Radicals are preparing for another war.

Blair says the Radical programme is to make Wade President of the Senate, then to impeach the President. Having done this the Radicals will be prepared to exclude the Southern Members from the next Congress, and the Southern States from the next Presidential election.

July 12, Thursday. The Radicals held a caucus last evening at the Capitol, to determine in relation to their future course, and also in regard to the adjournment of Congress. It was resolved their proceedings should be secret, but the doings are published. They appear to have come as yet to no conclusion. The plan, or conspiracy, for it is nothing else, seems to be some contrivance first of all to embarrass and hamper the Executive, some scheme to evade an honest, straightforward discharge of duty, some trick to cheat the President out of his prerogative and arrogate to themselves unauthorized executive power.

Raymond is reported to have played the harlequin and

WILLIAM DENNISON

again deserted. Although it is difficult to believe that one of his culture and information could make such an exhibit of himself, I am prepared to credit any folly of his. He has clearly no principles, no integrity, and is unconscious how contemptible he appears. Under Weed's teaching he has destroyed himself.

The President informs me that Dennison has handed in his resignation. His reasons are his adherence to the Republican Party. He was president of the national convention which nominated Lincoln and Johnson, and has imbibed the impression that his character is involved, that his party obligations are paramount to all other considerations. He has been trained and disciplined. In due time he will be a wise man.

July 13, *Friday.* The morning papers contain my letter to Senator Doolittle in response to his inquiry conveying my views of the Republican Convention. It is very explicit and much complimented.

Seward read to the President and myself a letter which he had written on the same subject. I told the President I ought, perhaps, to apologize for not having read my letter to him also, that I had thought of it, but concluded I ought not to make him in any way responsible for my unofficial acts. He said he would cheerfully assume the responsibility of every sentiment of my letter, which he had twice read and heartily approved.

July 15, *Sunday.* Senator Doolittle took breakfast with me this morning. He is pleased that a cane on which there had been great competition at the fair between him and Senator Harris had been voted to him. The rivalry had run the cane up to over $3000. I, of course, was glad he was victor.

Doolittle says my letter was complimented by men of all parties in the Senate and that Senators referred to my reports and other writings in flattering terms. Blair says it was read at a meeting at his house the evening before publication, and that, about fifty being present, they, every man, extolled it, although men of different shades of politics and parties were present.

There are flying rumors that Speed and Harlan, and some say Stanton, have sent in their resignations. It is excessively warm and I have not thought proper to call on the President and inquire. Possibly Speed has resigned, though I have some doubts; more as regards Harlan; and I am incredulous as regards Stanton.

July 16, *Monday.* We are having, I think, as warm weather as I have ever experienced. The papers have a curt letter from Speed resigning his office. He has also written an elaborate but not very profound letter to Doolittle, dissenting from the Philadelphia Convention.

The President sent in a veto on the new bill establishing the Freedmen's Bureau, or prolonging it. His reasons against it were strong and vigorous, but the two houses, without discussing or considering them, immediately passed the bill over the veto, as was agreed and arranged by the leaders, Stevens and others. Very few of the Members know anything of the principles involved, or even the provisions of the bill, nor, if informed, had they the independence to act, but they could under the lash of party vote against the President. Two or three of the Members, in telling me the result, spoke of it as a great triumph in the manner of the final hasty passage without any consideration.

July 17, *Tuesday.* Still excessively warm. Not much at the Cabinet to note. Stanton read a strange dispatch from Gen. George H. Thomas at Nashville, stating that some of the Tennessee members of the legislature would not attend the sessions and asking if he should not arrest them. The President promptly and with point said, if General Thomas had nothing else to do but to intermeddle in local controversies, he had better be detached and ordered elsewhere. Stanton, who should have rebuked Thomas, had, I thought, a design in bringing the subject to the President, who has warm personal friendship for the General. On hearing the emphatic remark and witnessing the decided manner of the President against Thomas's proposition, Stanton dropped his tone and said he had proposed to say to T. that he should avoid mixing up in this question. "But shall I add your remark?" said he. "My wish is," replied the President, "that the answer should be emphatic and decisive, not to meddle with local parties and politics. The military are not superior masters."

July 18, *Wednesday.* The President tells me that Dennison did not intend to leave, — that his purpose was to maintain his party relations but conform to the Administration in his action. He did not want nor expect his resignation would be accepted. These were the President's impressions. He looked upon it as a refined partyism to which he would give no attention. Speed, he says, thought to be very short, and he, therefore, did not reply to Speed's note resigning, but considered it a fact in conformity with the terms of the note.

The authentic published proceedings of the Radical leaders are disgraceful to the Members who were present and took part. It shows their incapacity as statesmen and their unfitness as legislators. Raymond publishes the statement, the injunction of secrecy having been removed. He also prints a letter in his paper, the *New York Times,* disclosing the revolutionary feeling of the leading Radicals, who are, in fact, conspirators.

Montgomery Blair is possessed of the sentiment that another civil war is pending and that the Radical leaders design and are preparing for it. I am unwilling to believe that a majority of Congress is prepared for such a step, but the majority is weak in intellect, easily led into rashness and error by the few designing leaders, who move and control the party machinery. There is no individuality and very little statesmanship or wise legislation, and as little in the Senate. The war on the President and on the Constitution, as well as on the whole of the people South, except the negroes, is revolutionary.

The President, while he has a sound and patriotic heart, has erred in not making himself and his office felt as a power. He should long since have manifested his determination to maintain and exercise his executive rights, in fact should in the first month of the session, and as soon as the spirit and hostility of the Radical leaders was apparent, have drawn the lines and made his own position known and felt. I so said to him on more than one occasion. But the influence and counsel of Seward, who deals in vacillating expedients, have been disastrous. He has striven to keep alive and strengthen the party organization, which is opposed to the President, and thus given power to the Radicals, who are conspiring against him. The President's friends have, as a result, been proscribed and his opponents favored by his own Administration. In this way Congress, where the Administration had or might have a majority, has become consolidated against the President. Those Members who were kindly disposed have been disciplined and drawn away from him by this trimming New York management. His mind is tardy in its movements, though honest and firm, and required stimulating and urging onward at the very time when Seward was exerting himself to suppress and hold back any decisive action in order to secure a party ascendancy in New York under Thurlow Weed. Stanton, of course, operated with Seward to prevent Executive action, for he was in all his feelings with the extreme Radicals, though contriving to so far keep in with the President as to retain his place.

July 19, *Thursday*. The Democrats have had a large meeting at Reading in Pennsylvania. Mr. Blair is reported to have made an ultra speech, denouncing the intrigues and schemes of the Radical leaders and predicting civil war if they are not defeated at the fall elections. The country has had too recent and too exhausting an experience for another war.

A telegram from the coarse, vulgar creature who is Governor of Tennessee says that there is a quorum of the legislature and that they have ratified the Constitutional Amendment. This legislature was chosen when war existed and under circumstances and animosities which would not be justified or excusable in peace. It is, of course, no exponent of popular sentiment in that State. But under the urgent appeals of the Radical Members of Congress, Brownlow, the Governor, convened a special session of this dead body on the 4th of July, to ratify the changes in the Constitution of the United States. But he was unable to get a quorum together. Fifty-six were necessary for a quorum; only fifty-four would be assembled, and two were arrested and brought to Nashville as prisoners. These made the requisite fifty-six, and forty-three of these bogus members voted for the Constitutional changes. This is an exhibition of Radical regard for honest principle, for popular opinion, and for changes in the organic law. The change is to be imposed upon the people by fraud, not adopted of choice.

I asked by way of suggestion to the President, how it happened that General Thomas's telegram of the 14th respecting the arrest of members of the legislature was not responded to until the 17th. He said he could not tell, and, evidently apprehending my object, said perhaps General Grant did not get it until the 15th and passed it over to the War Department possibly the next day, and the Secretary of War brought it here on the 17th. "Yet it does seem to have been some time on the way for a telegram," said he. "In the mean time," continued I, "two members of the legislature appear to have been arrested and brought to Nashville." This is Stantonian. Why does the President submit to be victimized?

The irregular tidings that Tennessee had in any way, however illegal or by force and fraud, confirmed the Amendment, as it is called, caused great exultation in Congress. The Radicals felt as if they were relieved, or those of them who felt uneasy under the dictation of Stevens, Boutwell, Schenck, etc. Conscious of their wrongdoing and that they were trifling with the country for mere party ascendancy and power, they broke away from Stevens and refused to follow him. Tennessee can now be permitted to have Representatives, — a right from which she has been excluded.

July 20, Friday. I learn that the President to-day sent in the nomination of Mr. Stanbery for Attorney-General. He made no mention of it in Cabinet. There is a reticence on the part of the President — an apparent want of confidence in his friends — which is unfortunate, and prevents him from having intimate and warm personal friends who would relieve him in a measure. Doolittle spoke of this to me last evening as we came from the President's, with whom he wanted some frank and friendly conversation, and he felt a little hurt that he was not met in the same spirit. It is a mistake, an infirmity, a habit fixed before he was President, to keep his own counsel. I find no want of confidence or frankness in him when I introduce a topic, or make an inquiry, but it is unpleasant to seek information which should, in friendly courtesy, be communicated or invited by him.

Professor Davies comes to see me. Wants his nephew, General Davies, to be made Naval Officer at New York. Says Smythe, the Collector, is doing nothing to sustain the President, or the Philadelphia movement. I am inclined to believe there is truth in it and that Smythe is a very indifferent officer, as well as a useless politician, or party man, and that the President has been deceived in him. I have heretofore expressed my doubts of his fitness to the President, McCulloch, and Doolittle, and they, neither of them, controverted my opinion. He is a weight, no aid.

July 21, *Saturday*. The Senate has altered and passed the resolution and preamble concerning the right of Tennessee to be represented, Congress, or the Radical majority, graciously permitting it, — not because the Constitution sanctions, or that the people or State have any rights, but because a fragment of a legislature, less than a quorum, elected nearly two years ago and summoned by the vulgar Governor, have adopted or ratified the Constitutional Amendment. The whole proceeding is a burlesque on republican government and our whole system of popular rights, opinion, State action, and constitutional obligation.

July 23, *Monday*. Had a discussion last evening with McCulloch and Doolittle in the council-room, the President being by, respecting the preamble and resolution of Congress in regard to Tennessee. McCulloch thought it might injure the President or help the Radicals if he did not sign it. I preferred that he should not, especially that he should not give his assent to the preamble. My own course would be to approve of neither, for it would be claimed as a precedent in future toward the other States. If it were an isolated instance, the resolution affirming that the State might send Representatives would, perhaps, be harmless, but the precedent in the present state of things would be bad. The President listened and then read a dispatch from the Speaker, saying he would not sign a certificate that the Amendment had been ratified.

Admiral Farragut and myself have been busy to-day on promotions under the recent law.

July 24, *Tuesday*. Busy through the day until dark on the subject of promotions, except for a short time at the Cabinet. The promotions will, unavoidably, give pain to many worthy men, but the principle which I have adopted will cause immensely less dissatisfaction than the original recommendations of the boards convened under the previous law. My action has been based on their recommendations, only deviating in a few cases when I was convinced injustice had been done by partiality or prejudice.

Many would be glad to dispense these promotions, but it has been to me a labor of sadness in many respects, and, though as glad as any one to assist in rewarding merit, yet, when accompanied with the knowledge that a lifelong sorrow is to be inflicted on others, necessarily, because extra promotion cannot be made without overriding others, some of them estimable men though not proved heroic officers, I am grieved.

Mr. Stanbery, the new Attorney-General, took his seat to-day in the Cabinet. He seems to have encountered no opposition in the Senate.

Seward presented a letter which he had prepared to our Minister to Japan. I did not like it, nor have I been favorable to the course which our Government and authority have in some respects pursued towards the Japanese. We Americans had found favor in their eyes above any Christian nation. To us they had opened ports and permitted trade. The English and French sought the same privilege; ultimately these countries and the Japanese became involved in hostilities, and the two powers had their fleets there. They intrigued to get us to unite with them. But the Japanese wanted no quarrel with us. Yet Mr. Pruyn, our then Minister, persuaded or directed Captain McDougal, commanding the Jamestown, to furnish a small detachment to go on board a small steamer which was chartered and entered, with the American flag, into the fight. Although performing little or no service, the two powers were delighted, extolled our men, who were mere spectators, gave honors to our officers, who rendered no service, and when the Japanese came to terms and agreed to pay three millions, it was insisted the Americans, with their little chartered steamer and with no expectation, should receive the same as the other powers with their large fleets and great expense. Of this money, called indemnity, three hundred thousand dollars have been received. The Japanese have now requested delay in the payment of the other installments. Seward's letter was very arrogant, dictatorial, and mandatory. This Government would consent to no delay; immediate and full payment must be promptly made, unless the two other powers decided on a different course, when our hostile policy would yield and conform to theirs. I was disgusted and said so.

There was, moreover, a by-transaction in which Thurlow Weed and Lansing of Albany, a brother-in-law of the Minister, were interested to the amount of several hundred thousand dollars in gold, which had been intrusted to their hands under the advisement of the Minister for building ships years ago. When the war came on in Japan these two gentlemen with Japanese money in their pockets desired our Government to take the vessel which they had then built. President Lincoln, when I declined the purchase, was appealed to. He had one or two interviews with me, and as I considered the proceeding improper he put his name to a paper expressing a wish that she might be taken into our service. But I was finally successful, though with much difficulty, in resisting the scheme. Difficulties between our Government and Japan on other subjects relieved Weed and company in their matters.

When, therefore, Seward read his letter to-day, I expressed a wish that if a refusal were to be sent, it might be less harsh. I preferred, if he so shaped our relations that we must be tied to England and France, they should take the initiative, and we, acting independently, should consent to a reasonable delay even if they did not assent. This, I thought, sufficiently humiliating. Seward was not pleased. Stanton saw the point of my suggestion and doubted whether we should complicate ourselves with the other powers. No other one made a remark or asked a question to draw me out. They saw, which indeed was very perceptible, that Seward was nettled, and they knew not the preceding history.

2

I took occasion, immediately after the adjournment, to inform the President of the main points and also McCulloch. On learning the facts, both declared themselves against Seward's letter. The President said he recollected former remarks of mine in Cabinet when the notice of the first installment was announced and Seward took great credit to himself for the money. I said it cost the nation dear.

July 25, Wednesday. I, early this morning, took to the President the carefully prepared list of promotions. He did not fully understand the subject and was disposed to delay. Stanton came in and took him aside. I comprehended the whole matter.

Senator Doolittle breakfasted with me and said some discontent was manifested because General Grant's nomination had not been sent in to the Senate. I told him I presumed it was because Stanton intentionally or from neglect had not made out and sent it to the President, but that the whole might be remedied by sending up Grant's and Farragut's nominations together, and as our bill for the Navy was only this day confirmed, the conclusion would be that there was an object in having their commissions of the same date. Doolittle went from me to the President with these suggestions, and the President had immediately dispatched Colonel Moore, his Secretary, requesting the Secretary of War to send him Grant's nomination, and to me to send Farragut's. Colonel Moore did not get to the Navy Department until I had left and overtook me as I was taking the Navy nominations, including Farragut's, to the President.

This accounted for Stanton's sudden appearance. He and the President thought it not [advisable] to send in the nominations before adjournment of others than the two principal officers. I differed and wanted the naval appointments off my hands. Stanton said the Army Bill had not got through Congress. That was his fault.

Farragut and myself were at General Grant's this evening. He said great noise had been made over the Army Bill and nothing had been done, while the Navy had been quiet and accomplished everything. Mrs. Grant said Mr. Grant had better see Stanton about it.

I rode to the Capitol this evening with Admiral Farragut. It is the first time I have visited the Capitol during this session of eight months while the houses were sitting. I did not now go in, for I found the Miscellaneous Bill was on the tapis and should be during this evening's sitting.

Farragut and Grant were this day confirmed.

July 26, *Thursday.* Congress has agreed to adjourn on Saturday. God speed them home. Still there is much important business undone. League Island has not been accepted by the Senate. This is the most important matter affecting the Navy which is now pending. Grimes says he must leave to-morrow evening. He seems to have lost zeal in this matter, after being earnest for it for years.

July 27, *Friday.* The naval nominations were confirmed as submitted. I have labored hard to have as little wrong committed as possible, and yet I fear injustice may have been done to some worthy officers.

Randall, appointed Postmaster-General in place of Dennison, this day attended the Cabinet-meeting, and Harlan sent in his resignation. He was at the meeting of the Cabinet, but made no mention of it at that time.

Mr. Stanbery, the Attorney-General, read the rough notes, as he called them, of an embryo report on the subject of filling vacancies. The paper possesses ability.

July 28, *Saturday.* Went to the Capitol a little before ten this A.M. Apprehended I should be late, for we had agreed yesterday in Cabinet to meet in the President's room at nine. Only Randall was there when I arrived, and it was more than an hour before the President and others

came. There had been some misunderstanding as to the
hour of adjournment, on which there had been conflicting
votes.

The two houses sat all night, and finished their labor of
the session by increasing their own salaries $2000 each per
annum, and by a bounty bill involving an expenditure of
probably one hundred millions. Trumbull, who has gone
astray, says not over sixty-five millions. This is waste and
reckless extravagance as well as imprudent and careless
legislation in almost all respects.

The President spoke to me on the subject soon after he
arrived. I said promptly I hoped he would not sanction
the proceeding; that it was profligate legislation and a good
question with which to go before the people, — I should
be glad of such an issue; — that neither wisdom, sound
policy, nor good government would sanction such reckless
extravagance, though the country appears dumb and indifferent over extravagant inroads; that the result of such
waste and profligacy, if countenanced and approved by
Executive and Congress, must end in the prostration of the
Government and general repudiation.

When the bill was received and read, Seward at once
remarked that the President was not responsible for the
act and he had but one course to take, which was to sign
the bill. Stanton said promptly he would not have voted
for it had he been a Member, but that he would not advise
a veto. McCulloch said the bill was not so bad as it might
have been and thought the Government could stagger
through it. Stanbery thought it had better be approved. I
still objected. The President was reluctant, but at length
signed the bill. McCulloch put his arm around me as I
walked around the room and brought me up towards the
President. As he did so, he said, "I know this is against
your opinion, but under the circumstances we all think it
is best." I told him and the President that I submitted,
and he perhaps could hardly be expected to do otherwise
than assent to the Act of Congress, supported by his entire

Cabinet, including the Secretary of the Treasury, I only differing. The President yields on questions when his friends advise and urge him. They do not always have an opportunity. In the Cabinet economy is not a cardinal point. McCulloch has correct views, but he, also, yields too much. I should have been glad to have stood out with the President on this issue, or rather to have had him with me. The country would have been with him, because he would have been right.

I told the President that I regretted the appointment of Clark [1] to be judge in New Hampshire. He said it was not acceptable to him, but there was a confused state of things. It was hard to ascertain who was worthy. He thought some good results might grow out of it. I can see nothing good and so said. On every Constitutional point that has been raised, Clark has opposed the President. He has been vindictive. He was the tool of Fessenden in expelling Stockton, and has been as mischievously hostile as any man in the Senate. Yet he is selected to be a judge. Such selections destroy public confidence.

So far as I am, or the Navy Department is, concerned, Clark has been friendly and kind, but in his course towards the President and as a politician and legislator I think badly of him. The President has, under bad advice, committed a mistake. I am told Hendricks and some other Senators interfered for Clark. There are loose political morals in the Senate, and the President should disregard Senatorial interposition for their own members, for they favor one another at the country's expense.

I do not think the Members were exactly satisfied with themselves in closing up the session. A feeling of disappointment was apparent, and by many confessed, accompanied with conscious guilt of wrong and feebleness. Weak capabilities, shallow statesmanship, and intense partisanship are the qualities of this Congress.

[1] Daniel Clark, Senator from New Hampshire, 1857–66, appointed United States Judge for the District of New Hampshire.

July 30, *Monday.* Senator Doolittle called and wished me to accompany him to the President to meet General Dix, and we sent to McCulloch to go there also. The selection of Dix as Minister to The Hague, a third-class mission, is doing good. It is opening the eyes of Doolittle and McCulloch, and I think the President, to the course of Weed and Seward.

Doolittle called on me the morning that this nomination was announced, and asked what it meant. Said we could not spare Dix from the country at this time. I told him there was no probability that Dix would leave. Certainly not on that mission. "What, then, does it mean?" said Doolittle. I replied that it was intended to dispose of Dix. The appointment was derogatory and designed to belittle him, and then, as he would not accept, the place would be kept open for Seward to play with.

I saw when I met Dix this morning that he was, for him, a good deal disturbed, and was glad to have him express his dissatisfaction and his opinions, and the views of others. He says Weed is playing a strange game in relation to Governor of New York. Tells of Weed's and Seward's policy, though only Weed's name used. Says that when Weed wants his own party and servants to be beaten, he selects a weak candidate, etc.

Smythe, the Collector, came in soon after Dix went out, and he was even more full than Dix in disclosing Weed's intrigues and the lectures and teachings of which he was the recipient. Weed told Smythe he was a merchant and no politician. Smythe said he knew enough to fire at a mark, though he might not hit it.

XLI

August 2, Thursday. For several days have been so
much engaged that I have found no time to open this book
and innumerable private letters go unanswered.

An adroit and skillful counterfeit has been perpetrated,
and two drafts, one of $50,000 and one of $10,000, have
been cashed. There was much heedless and careless management at the Fourth Auditor's office, or there would have
been prompt detection, yet they have rushed into the
papers and claim that *they* discovered the forgery. All of
which is untrue. We learn to-day that the forger has been
arrested. He was married this morning to a lady of fortune, left with his bride for New York and Europe, and
was arrested when he reached Philadelphia.

The convention yesterday in Connecticut to elect delegates to Philadelphia passed off well. It was a convention
strong in good names.

Violent and revolutionary proceedings have taken place
in New Orleans. A fragment of an old convention held in
1864 met for the purpose of overturning the government.
Riot and bloodshed were the unavoidable consequences.
There are indications that the conspirators were instigated

by Radicals from Washington and the North to these disturbances.

I have had two interviews with Governor Pease of Texas. He is earnest and honest, and gives a deplorable account of affairs in that State, where he has just been defeated in a gubernatorial canvass. There is, he says, no toleration of Union men; five sixths of the people are hostile to the Federal Government, and they persecute those who do not agree with them. The only way by which Union men can live there, he says, is under the protection of Union troops, and the Federal Government, he claims, is bound to protect loyal men in person and property.

After listening to his statement and canvassing the subject with him, I inquired whether the remedy he proposed was practicable and consistent with our system of government. If there is danger to person and property in any State, the person aggrieved or in danger must look to the local, municipal, and State authorities for protection. But it is claimed the authorities will not do this and that five sixths of the people approve their course. This is unfortunate and wrong, but under these circumstances and in these times, is it wise for the one sixth to come forward and place themselves in direct antagonism to the five sixths and ask the Federal Government to sustain them by force? Would it not be better to remain passive and quietly and patiently strive to modify public opinion, and get it right gradually? This Government is not one of form; it cannot attempt to control the elections in the States, and that by military force, without overthrowing free government, — destroying free elections. Are you not, then, asking too much, and unawares taking steps to subvert, or change our whole system?

This was the tenor of our conversation and my remarks. Governor Pease was, I thought, affected by them. His good sense made him appreciate the case, though he said that if this was the policy he should be compelled to leave Texas and so would every Union man. This, I told him, did not follow. Yet free speech would, perhaps, be necessarily restrained.

The condition of things is bad, but it is attributable in a degree to the nature of our institutions. Our people will go violently into the elections. The few outspoken Union men, numerically weak, insist that they must be the controlling power in the Rebel States, although in a minority, and they expect to secure this by military instrumentality exercised by the Federal Government, which is to put down the majority by the bayonet.

August 3, *Friday.* I had a letter last evening from Secretary McCulloch, inclosing copy of one addressed to the President, requesting that Commodore S. P. Lee might be put on the Lighthouse Board in place of Admiral Davis, who had consented to retire. The intrigue and the impudence of the thing annoyed me excessively. McCulloch is guiltless of intentional wrong, but is, unaware, the instrument of Lee, who has moved his father-in-law, Blair, in the matter. I wrote a strong remonstrance to the President and also to McCulloch against this mischievous and demoralizing scheme. The President and McCulloch both spoke to me on the subject to-day, neither having received my letter. The President wished me to dispose of Lee as I pleased. Said he was a great annoyance to him. McCulloch said he cared nothing about Lee, but was willing to oblige Mr. Blair.

Stanton read telegrams in Cabinet from General Sheridan concerning New Orleans disturbances. Stanton manifested marked sympathy with the rioters, and the President and others observed it. There is little doubt that the New Orleans riots had their origin with the Radical Members of Congress in Washington. It is part of a deliberate conspiracy and was to be the commencement of a series of bloody affrays through the States lately in rebellion. Boutwell and others have stated sufficient to show their participation in this matter. There is a determination to involve the country in civil war, if necessary, to secure negro suffrage in the States and Radical ascendancy in the General Government. Stanton, in great excitement, repeatedly spoke of the Attorney-General of Louisiana and the Mayor of New Orleans as pardoned Rebels who had instigated the murder of the people in the streets of the city, [said] that they were guilty of this terrible blood-shedding.

Sheridan's dispatches are somewhat conflicting. Although a brave and excellent officer, Sheridan lacks judgment and administrative ability. He is impulsive, but his intentions are honest and his first telegram was an honest impulse. It struck me that he was tutored as regards the others, either from Washington or by some one at New Orleans duly advised.

Stanton is evidently in deep sympathy and concert with the Radicals in this matter, though he studied to conceal it. In striving to influence the President and prejudice him against the authorities of New Orleans, he betrayed his feelings.

There has been a story circulating in the newspapers that a naval vessel had captured a slave-trader with a cargo of negroes on board, which were being transported from the South to Cuba. It was a manufactured rumor which came from the Radical Freedmen's Bureau agents or tools. Seward alluded to some information from Cuba to the effect that they wanted none of our negroes on the island, and in conversation growing out of his allusion, I mentioned the fabrication of a rumor of a captured slaver. I saw at once that Stanton was disturbed. I mentioned that I two or three months since instituted inquiries on information communicated by the War Department, which I found to be totally groundless. Stanton rose at once on his feet and said the information came from General Foster. I answered, yes; it was a rumor of negroes kidnapped at Indian River, but our inquiries had satisfied us that the rumors were without foundation.

Stanton is, in matters of this description, a Radical sensationalist, ready to believe anything bad of those to whom he is opposed; and is himself complicated with, if not a prime mover in, the New Orleans difficulties and these mischievous rumors.

August 4, Saturday. The Philadelphia movement is gaining strength, but at the same time encountering tremendous and violent opposition from the Radicals. I trust and think it will be successful, but the convention will be composed of various elements, some of them antagonistic heretofore, and the error is in not having distinctive principles on which these prevailing opposing elements can centre. The time has arrived when our countrymen must sacrifice personal and mere organized party hostility for the general welfare. Either the Radicals or the Government are to be overthrown. The two are in conflict.

I have confidence that all will come out right, for I rely on an overruling Providence and the good sense and intelligence of the people. Hatred, deadly animosity towards the whole South, a determination to deny them their Constitutional rights, and to oppress and govern them, not allow them to govern themselves, are the features of Radicalism. It is an unsavory, intolerant, and persecuting spirit, disgraceful to the country and age. Defeat in the elections will temper and subdue its ferocity, while success at the polls will kindle it to flames, which will consume every sentiment of tolerance, justice, and Constitutional freedom.

August 6, Monday. Am beset by disappointed naval officers who think they have not had due promotion. This may be the case with some, but the more I examine the whole ground the better satisfied I am with the action taken. One of the most afflicted is Commodore Hitchcock, an old schoolboy friend, a good officer in peaceable times and an exemplary man in every respect, who has well performed ordnance duty, but who has no war record, no ambition but to live at ease and in style, proud and gentlemanly. He has taken such excellent care of himself during the War — done so little in the heroic line — that he is dissatisfied with the result when heroes are to be rewarded.

August 7, *Tuesday.* The President submitted two long telegrams, one from himself to General Sheridan inquiring as to the difficulties at New Orleans and Sheridan's reply, which was no answer.

Seward and Stanbery had much to say. The latter was very earnest to have the President send immediately to Sheridan, telling him the police must be dismissed. There was, he said, great excitement in the country and the President must at once respond.

I inquired to what he was to respond. On Friday he had directed Sheridan to keep the peace and pursue his investigations. Since that inquiries had been made which had procured a feeble and confused response, concluding with a request or suggestion that the Governor of the State and the Mayor of New Orleans be displaced. Sheridan might be told that the President had no authority to displace these officers; but I expressed a hope that he would not at this distance undertake to give detailed instructions to his generals or agents.

I asked who General Baird was that he should be charged with this responsibility, and how it came about that such a man as was now described happened to be at such a place at this juncture. As for Sheridan, I considered him an honest, bold, impulsive officer, without much knowledge of civil government or administrative ability, who obeyed orders, but I apprehended him badly prompted after his first telegram, and regretted that we had not men of different calibre there at this time.

Seward said my estimate of Sheridan he thought correct. As for Baird, he knew nothing of him. The President expressed dissatisfaction with what he heard of Baird. Stanton kept silent.

Stanbery was persistent that the President should instruct Sheridan in regard to the police of the city.

Stanton said application had been made to him for bunting for the building at Philadelphia where the convention was to meet, but he had none for them, and said, with a sneer, he would turn them over to the Navy. I told him that my bunting had always been promptly shown and it would be well were he now to let us have a sight of his.

Stanton, who has skulked, was taken aback, colored, and remarked he had no bunting for them.

"Oh," said I, "show your flag."

"You mean the convention," said he. "I am against it."

"I am sorry to hear, but glad to know, your opinion," said I.

"Yes, I am opposed to the convention," he continued.

"I did n't know it. You did not answer the inquiry like the rest of us."

"No," said he; "I did not choose to have Doolittle or any other little fellow draw an answer from me."

The conversation amused the others, as it did me. Seward looked troubled. Whether he knew Stanton's position, I am in doubt. It is, I am satisfied, very recent that he has concluded to avow himself, although I have never doubted that he was as much opposed as any Radical to the Union movement. I think he would rather have the Government overthrown than that the real Unionists should come in power. He seems to have personal apprehensions. . . .

I called on the President this evening to advise caution in his communications with New Orleans. Expressed my regret that he had not better officers for the business required at this time in that quarter. He concurred with me and said Baird, so far as he could learn, had caused the trouble or might have prevented it.

"Who," inquired I, "placed Baird there? Was it not

part of the Radical scheme to bring this difficulty upon us? It certainly is unfortunate that we have these men there." He said he believed Baird was attached to the Freedmen's Bureau. I said this might have been ordered otherwise and should have been; that the Administration could not get along intelligently and well without faithful and reliable agents. I inquired if he noticed the remarks of Stanton to-day respecting the convention, "though probably you knew his opinions previously." The President said he had not known them before, that it was the first intimation he had received, and he noticed the remark. "This is wrong," said I; "we cannot get along in this way." "No," replied he, "it will be pretty difficult."

August 8, Wednesday. Judge Blair gave me yesterday a carefully prepared paper intended for the Philadelphia Convention. It had twelve specifications, — declarations and denials, affirmations and disavowals. Blair is delighted with them and says the President is also. I told him there would not be unanimity on one or two of the propositions and suggested emendations or modifications of two or three others. To some of them he assented; but I saw he was very much in love with the paper, which he informed me was prepared by William B. Reed. But no one, save the President, him, the author, and myself, knew the fact of authorship.

I remarked that there would doubtless be other strong and able papers submitted, that my own views were for a few points timely expressed. I thought all could unite against changes of the Constitution with only a broken Congress, and States excluded. In so large a body as there is likely to assemble at Philadelphia there would be conflicting opinions on any proposition which might be submitted.

Blair leaves to-morrow for Philadelphia. Browning says he shall and likely Randall will go also. I would rather the members of the Cabinet remained away.

The President is deeply interested, yet retains Stanton, who is not only opposed, but is covertly in accord with the Radicals.

August 9, *Thursday.* A strange dispatch was read to-day from Commodore Winslow, written at Pensacola, exhibiting intense partisan bitterness in the New Orleans disturbances, and reproving Lieutenant-Commander McCann of the Tallapoosa, who was at New Orleans and behaved very discreetly. I am almost induced to believe that Winslow is demented.

Ordered a board for examining volunteer officers, S. P. Lee, President. It will be less acceptable to him than some other position more permanent here in Washington, but he cannot always select the best places.

August 10, *Friday.* Seward was not at Cabinet, having had a sudden call to Auburn. It was a dodge to avoid an open committal with the Philadelphia Convention. Attorney-General Stanbery had charge of his portfolio, Assistant Secretary Fred Seward being also absent. There was a little meaning in this. Whether Stanton was a party to it in order to avoid being in any way committed, or is slighted, I know not. If the last, I think it was unintentional, but Seward is paying hard court to Stanbery. I perceive it every day.

A dispatch from Vice-Consul-General Savage at Cuba in relation to the steamers Harriet Lane and Pelican was read, with Seward's reply. I thought Seward conceded too much and so stated. The threat from some person who is in charge, that he would sell them if not paid his charges, is simply ridiculous. Any proper charges the Government would pay ere this, as on any other government vessel, but the idea of an individual selling a public ship is absurd. Still Seward concedes it.

Queen Emma of the Sandwich Islands is to visit Washington as the guest of the Government on invitation of

Secretary Seward, who is conveniently absent. As Stanbery is delegated by Seward in other matters, Stanton thought he should do the honors to the young dowager.

August 11, *Saturday.* Read Commodore Winslow's letter and correspondence relative to New Orleans riot and my reply to the President, who was pleased and approved of my course.

Read Admiral Farragut's acknowledgment and thanks to the President for his commission; also Farragut's letter accepting the invitation to be of the party to Chicago.

Many delegates from the South to the Philadelphia Convention are in the city on their way thither. Generally they seem in good spirits and cheered with the prospect of a restored Union. So far as I have conversed with them they are of right tone and temper.

I remarked to the President that a large portion of the people North and South had no correct idea of the condition of men and things. The claim of the Union men in the Rebel States, that they alone must hold office and govern, while the great mass of the people were to be excluded, proscribed, and eventually disfranchised, was preposterous. The majority must govern or elections be abandoned. In looking to the Central Government to keep the minority in power by force, the Unionists were committing a serious error. The condition of things is anomalous and must be treated with great circumspection and wisdom. The President agreed and fully responded.

August 13, *Monday.* Secretary McCulloch arrived this A.M. Met him at the President's. His trip has been of benefit to him. . . . McCulloch has grown upon me since he entered the Cabinet. Perhaps I have not been as observant and critical as I should have been had we differed, but from the beginning our views have coincided, and I have considered him, though not trained in public office or an experienced politician, as the most reliable and sensible man in the Cabinet.

Dennison has written a strange letter and made a speech of like character. I am disappointed in him, for he is exceedingly unjust and unfair towards the President. It is a bid, but he will be disappointed.

Dennison is very ambitious, and has a wife more ambitious than himself. Of the two, she is smarter, but D. is gentlemanly, kind, affable, has great suavity of manners. He will never obtain a higher position than the one he has recently resigned. It is said he wishes to secure the seat in the Senate held by Wade; but that can hardly be brought about, though strange results sometimes take place in these selections.

The letter and speech which now appear are mere party drivel, without statesmanship or enlarged and comprehensive views. Such stuff can convert no one, and retain no one. I am sorry to witness this exhibition, for Dennison aside from factions, is not destitute of merit, has some pleasant social qualities, and our families have been intimate. He is evidently expecting to make an impression in party harangues, but will scarcely succeed.

August 14, *Tuesday.* Seward has run off to Auburn and left Stanbery to attend upon the Hawaiian dowager, Queen Emma. He finds it awkward and embarrassing, but does very well. The President expressed a wish that the Cabinet, and such of their families as could, might be at the reception this evening. McCulloch and myself were the only ones present except Stanbery, who escorted her. She is a good-looking, well-developed woman of about thirty, with a complexion a shade darker perhaps than a brunette, a full, round eye, a good form, of graceful deportment, etc.

We hear that the convention at Philadelphia is full and harmonious and all is progressing satisfactorily. The effect must be salutary on the whole country and will, I trust,

2

contribute to overcome that intense sectional hate and party rancor which it is the aim and purpose of the Radicals to inculcate towards the South. These Radical leaders, and to a great extent their followers, are vindictive and have apparently no wish or intention to reëstablish the Union or recognize the political equality of the States.

August 15, *Wednesday.* There are comparatively few persons here in attendance on the President or Departments. The Philadelphia Convention has drawn off most of them for the time, but only to come back in crowds when the convention adjourns.

Informed the President that I proposed to detail Rear-Admiral Stribling for lighthouse duty. He said he had no objections. Should be glad to have Lee disposed of. Told him I had made him president of the board to examine volunteer officers under the late Act of Congress.

The Lees and old Mr. Blair are behaving badly. I do not blame Mr. B. so much, for he is old and affectionate, yet he should have some consideration for others. It would, and ought to, injure him, his children, Lee, and myself, were I to assign Lee to the Lighthouse Board here in Washington. After having the best post during the War, with high pecuniary reward and very little danger, he should not now, with his ample fortune, derived from that post, think to sit down for the remainder of his days in the easy post of lighthouse duty on full pay. But he is very mercenary.

August 16, *Thursday.* The convention at Philadelphia has finished its labors and adjourned without disturbance or conflict, as some hoped and predicted, and without speechmaking.

I have written another letter to Commodore Winslow, who is running into partisanship, and will, if he continues, be an unsuitable person to command a squadron in the Gulf, or on our seaboard, cautioning him on this subject.

He manifests too much bitter feeling and is too ready to decide against those from whom he has differed to be a discreet and judicious commander in times like these. His prejudices are evidently all enlisted against Southern white men and their case prejudged. Those who have been Rebels, he thinks, have no rights.

August 17, *Friday*. At the Cabinet Seward submitted a proclamation in relation to a paper blockade of Maximilian. It was a sort of godsend which he received and blew up for outside effect. He stated the case strong, — stronger than was necessary, — and the phraseology was modified and some part omitted.

Seward also submitted a proclamation for peace restored, Texas having elected her Governor, who has been inaugurated, and her legislature under the amended constitution being in session. This closes and disposes of the provisional governors, and the interposition of Federal authority in the States which were in rebellion will be no longer necessary. If the President has sometimes taken strong and questionable ground for the Executive in regard to the reëstablishment of State Governments within those States, his motives were pure and disinterested, and the results have been favorable to his action. In some of his dispatches to the States, I have wished the language could have been suggestive and less mandatory, in requiring them to make constitutions, instead of adapting their existing constitution to the altered condition of things brought about by the War. It was, indeed, necessary that they should so amend their organic law in one fundamental particular, that of abolishing slavery. War in its progress and results had decreed emancipation, and the Federal Constitution had been so amended as to prohibit it. Repudiation of the Rebel debt was an indispensable requisite for proper relations, but it was a question, perhaps, whether the President could demand it as a condition precedent. Some suggestions, almost requirements, for negro suffrage when there was intelligence, etc., were proposed. His wishes and the tendency of his mind are to ameliorate and benefit the negro so far as it can consistently be done, and he early listened to the counsel and views of Sumner and others in that respect, but he pretty early came to understand that he could not satisfy them unless he adopted all their extreme views, and this he could not do without sacrificing his own convictions and principles. Their aims and objects were partisan and factious; his were patriotic and statesmanlike.

Some of his appointments were unfortunate. I could never ascertain from him who advised the sending of Carl Schurz or John Covode to the South. Neither of them could assimilate to him. Schurz is a transcendental red republican of a good deal of genius, but national, with erroneous views of our federal system. Covode is a cunning, mischievous, selfish party politician of no intellectual culture, of limited comprehension, and no right ideas or capacity for such an agency. Many of the governors whom the President appointed were indifferent men. Holden, the first of these appointees, and Hamilton, the last, are not fitted for such positions. The first is a hollow pretender. The latter is a deceptive, vain, self-conceited partisan, who ought never to have been sent back to Texas clothed with authority.

The occasion for the proclamation being that of the establishment of the local State Government in the last of the States, Texas, there was a recitation in full in the preamble of what had occurred. This statement of facts is an argument that tells with effect against the Radicals. Stanton at once perceived it and immediately took exception to it as an argument out of place. He did not wish the President to state his reasons. It was, he said, undignified, etc. There was the cunning of the partisan and lawyer, however, in all he said, and I think every one detected it. The Radical stood out distinct and clear at a time when he flattered himself it was disguised. Stanbery took upon himself to say that his views differed entirely from the Secretary of War. He thought the preamble was warranted by facts, and the facts were arguments for the President's policy.

It soon came out that this proclamation was only a repetition of the proclamation of April, with Texas added, and the fact of the closing-up of the War. Radicalism was not then paramount. Stanton had taken no exception when that proclamation was issued in April, but now, when it was obvious that the Radicals were to be hit and hurt, his whole sensibilities were aroused. But the discussion exhibited his awkwardness, and he felt it.

Doolittle and Browning called on me this evening, fresh from the convention and overflowing with their success and the achievements of that assemblage. They insisted that I should go with them to the President and hear their verbal, friendly, social report. It was made very gratifying, and the President enjoyed it. On our way to the President both gentlemen insisted that Stanton must leave the Cabinet, and said it was the strong and emphatic voice of the convention; that there were committees to communicate with the President on the subject. I told them I would leave that matter with them and the committee. While we were with the President the subject was alluded to by Browning, but Doolittle immediately took it up and said it would be proper for him, not being a member of the Cabinet, to make known to the President the sentiment of the convention and the country, etc.

They informed the President that there was a committee of about one hundred who would call to-morrow and deliver to him the proceedings of the convention, and they suggested that the Cabinet, with General Grant, should be present. The President assented and requested me to be on hand.

August 18, *Saturday.* Many calls from delegates who are in town. Went a little before 1 P.M. to the White House.

The President was not in the council-chamber, but in the library and invited me to come in and join him. Browning and Colonel Moore, his Private Secretary, were with him. Marshal Gooding soon came in and said the committee had arrived and would wait upon the President. It had been arranged that he would receive them in the East Room. We accordingly went down by the private stairs. Marshal Gooding, though a very good man, perhaps, has no organizing or arranging powers, and there was considerable delay and awkwardness in getting things in trim. The President, with those of us who were with him, had to stand for about ten minutes in the room near its centre, while Gooding was beckoning the crowd forward with his hat, and occasionally entreating them to move on. McCulloch, Browning, Randall, and myself were with the President. General Grant soon joined us, and it was so arranged, whether properly or not I do not know, that General Grant should be on the immediate right and I on the left of the President. The absence of Stanton was, therefore, the more conspicuous. Reverdy Johnson read the address to the President with some earnestness and emphasis. The latter replied extemporaneously, but happily and well.

Dined with Seward this evening. The dinner was in honor of Queen Emma of the Sandwich Islands. President Johnson and all the Cabinet with their ladies, except Stanton and Mrs. Stanton, were present. Mrs. S. is said to be not very well.

August 19, *Sunday.* Senator Doolittle spent three hours with me this morning. He had breakfast with the President and came from there to my house. We went over the questions of the day very fully. He is very earnest to get rid of Stanton; wished me to go with him and see Seward and Grant. I satisfied him it was not best for me to meddle with the subject; told him I would not unless requested by the President.

August 20, *Monday.* Many calls to-day from delegates who have been to Philadelphia. Had many compli-
ments for my letter and the views which I had informally
expressed in regard to this movement and our public
affairs. Governor Orr, Manning, and others from South
Carolina; Shorter, Parson, etc., of Alabama; Abel, General
Brown, Governor King, etc., from Missouri. All in good
spirits and patriotically disposed.

Most of these men, as well as those whom they represent, have been connected in some degree with the Rebellion, but they submit and acquiesce in the result with
grace, and I believe with sincerity. But the Radicals are
filled with hatred, acrimony, and revenge towards them,
and would persist in excluding not only them but the
whole people of the South from any participation in the
government. For four years war was waged to prevent
them from going out; now the Radicals would wage as fine
a war to shut them out.

August 21, *Tuesday.* The peace proclamation takes well
with the people. It has the effect which I, and I think
Stanton, anticipated. There comes, I see, a strong pressure
against Stanton from Philadelphia. Whether it will have an
effect upon him or the President is doubtful. The latter
cannot need to be undeceived.

. . . .

Stanbery says he is preparing an opinion on the matter
of appointing to vacancies created during the session. He
thinks the case clear that the President can appoint. On
the question of removals he is unequivocal as to the authority to make them at any time. This he repeated on a question from me. I wished to fix attention on his admissions,
for he had previously given an opinion that Congress has
power to prohibit dismissals from the Army and Navy. If
they have the power in these cases, they have it as clearly
in the cases of civilians. All of our Presidents have exercised this power from Washington down, and if it is

a Constitutional right, Congress cannot take it from the Executive; if it is not an Executive right, the acts of our Presidents have been illegal from the foundation of the government.

August 22, Wednesday. General Marston of New Hampshire, who has been in West Virginia since the adjournment of Congress, called to see and converse with me on public affairs. The General has voted mostly with the Radicals, yet I think with some doubts and misgivings at times.

I expressed my regret that he had not continued straight on with us in sustaining the Union cause. He interrupted me to know whether I supposed he was a disunionist. I replied that I had supposed he was a firm Union man, but that during the session he had fellowshiped with the present disunionists. That the Secessionists had been conquered and had given up their Secession notions, but another class, the exclusionists with disunion theories, had appeared, to whom I was as much opposed as to the Secessionists. The General was vexed [and disturbed, and I was not sorry to see it. He said he had fought four years for the Union and supposed no one could doubt where he stood. I admitted that during the War we were together in the Union cause, and I regretted that he should lend himself now to those who persisted in excluding ten States from their Constitutional rights.

The convention will, I hope, lead the General, who is a well-intentioned but not very great man, to review his ground, but whether he will have the courage to avow and act up to his convictions is doubtful.

August 23, Thursday. Seward is full, arranging for the excursion to Chicago. Wants General Grant and Admiral Farragut should be of the party, especially through Philadelphia, where he apprehends there may be trouble. I have little apprehensions of mischief in Philadelphia, but in these reckless and violent times some rash and ruffianly partisans may place obstruction on the railroad-track in the more sparsely populated districts. I therefore suggested to the President several days since that it would be well to take Stanton along, who is in favor of the excursion and has urged it, as he is a favorite with the Radicals, who would not endanger or hurt him. Seward proposed some other naval officer than Farragut also, and I named Radford to him and also to the President, provided another was desired. The President was indifferent, — thought we should have plenty of company.

August 24, *Friday.* Seward presented a letter to the President from John Slidell, inclosed to him by Mr. John Bigelow, our Minister at Paris. Slidell wishes to return on some business matters, and was desirous of knowing on what terms he could be permitted to do so. Seward had prepared an answer to the effect that the President did not deem it advisable to give him any terms. Stanton approved the letter, provided the President would direct the Secretary of the Navy to seize him on the high seas and bring him in a prisoner, etc. Bigelow, Stanton thought, should be recalled for making the Legation an organ for traitors like Slidell to communicate with the President.

I remarked that the Navy could hardly afford to go into a general search of the vessels of all nations; it was a cause of difficulty when, in time of war, we captured the Trent.

The President said that instead of Seward's dispatch, which entered into details, he would prefer that he should say to Mr. Bigelow the President declined any correspondence with Mr. Slidell.

Senator Dixon called on me yesterday. Says Crosby, the Assessor for Hartford District, had a meeting at the United States Hotel at which Hawley and Deming were invited to select Assistant Assessors. I asked why Crosby was not removed, if he acted under the advice of such Radicals. Dixon then half-apologized for Crosby, who, he said, always consulted him. He then spoke to me in relation to

James G. Bolles, the Collector, Bolles being my old friend.
I inquired if B. took any such ground as C. or was offensively Radical. D. thought not, perhaps, yet did not know.
I remarked that I would justify no such conduct, that I
hoped and believed B. did not so act, but that if he did and
was a rampant Radical, old friendship could not interpose
to spare him. I would not wish my brother to be retained
in place if a Radical disunionist by either exclusion or
secession, a supporter of Thad Stevens or Robert Toombs,
but B. was no such man.

August 25, Saturday. A great pressure is made from
Maine for changes in the Kittery Navy Yard. No doubt the
men in office there are generally Radicals who have thrust
themselves upon the Department and been crowded forward by partisan friends on the grounds that they were
supporters of the Administration, friends of the Union.
But, being office-seekers of the time-serving class and believing the Radical Congress controls appointments, they
no longer maintain that position. They are opponents of
the Administration and identified with the exclusionists.
Under these circumstances they are now unwilling to take
from the Executive their own medicine and will be dissatisfied if I continue to act on the principle which they
formerly advocated and which helped them to place.

That some changes ought to be made I have no doubt,
but it would not be advisable to go to the extent which the
anti-Radicals urge on the eve of election. I have changed
the storekeeper, removing Wentworth, an active and
proscriptive Radical electioneerer, and appointing Stim-
son, and one or two other changes will soon be made.

Committees (and others) from the Philadelphia Convention are here pressing changes, and I am glad that some
are effected. There may be abuses in some instances in
these removals and appointments, but it is indispensable
that the Radical cohorts and recruiting partisan office-
holders, who make it their first and gravest duty to assail

the President, should be broken in upon. There will be a fine conflict in the fall elections. An intense partisan bitterness prevails and will increase until the elections are passed. It is to be lamented that the President permitted the Radicals to remove his friends and substitute their tools; that he had not drawn the line of demarcation, resented usurpation, and maintained the rights of the Executive, six or eight months earlier, before the Radicals had intrenched themselves so strongly. His delay and the activity of the Radicals, who operated through most of the Departments, have weakened his cause and strengthened his opponents, who now bid him defiance. I have little doubt that some contemplate further infringement on Executive rights, provided they can compact their party to that end.

In taking up the proposed excursion to Chicago yesterday, only Seward and myself held to the original understanding. McCulloch thinks he cannot leave, business is so pressing. Stanton, who has been urgent, now regrets that he cannot go, his wife is ill, — were it not for that he declared he should not fail to go. I think Mrs. S. may be some but not seriously indisposed, but at no time have I entertained a thought that S. himself would be with us. Browning has not expected to go, for he enters upon his duties on the 1st prox. Randall will go on post-office business, be sometimes with the President and sometimes elsewhere, dodging about. Stanbery, who talked earnestly of going at first, with his wife, now doubts, has business, his health is not very good, and he fears a journey might affect him injuriously. No one is more disinclined than myself for this excursion, — I dislike pageants always, — but, the President having decided to go and specially requested some of us to accompany him, I have made no excuse or evasion. I should be glad to be relieved and have never at any time advised the excursion, but acquiesced after the President had made up his mind. It was different with Seward, Stanton, McCulloch, and Stanbery, who all advised it.

XLII

September 17, *Monday.* Returned on Saturday, the 15th, from excursion with the President. Our route was via Baltimore, Philadelphia, New York, West Point, Albany, Auburn, Niagara Falls, — where we spent our first Sunday, — Buffalo, Cleveland, Toledo, Detroit, Chicago, — where we remained Thursday the 6th inst., — Springfield, Illinois, Alton, St. Louis, — where we spent our second Sunday, — Indianapolis, Louisville, Cincinnati, Columbus, Pittsburg, Harrisburg, Baltimore, home. We only traveled by daylight, excepting when coming from Louisville to Cincinnati by steamer. I have not enumerated the intermediate places of our visit, but, having special train, no stops were made except at places of importance.

The newspapers of the day give detailed statements of our journey, the places at which we stopped, generally the introductions that were made, and caricatured statements of speeches which were delivered. Our party consisted of Secretary Seward and myself, of the Cabinet, — Postmaster-General Randall was with us part of the time, — General Grant, Admiral Farragut, Admiral Radford,

Generals Rousseau, Custer, Stedman, Stoneman, and Crook, E. T. Welles, J. A. Welles, Mrs. Patterson, Mrs. Welles, Mrs. Farragut, Judge Patterson, Colonel Moore, and others.

The President made brief remarks at nearly every stopping-place to the crowds which assembled to meet and welcome him. In some instances party malignity showed itself, but it was rare and the guilty few in numbers. It was evident in most of the cases, not exceeding half a dozen in all, that the hostile partisan manifestations were prearranged and prompted by sneaking leaders. The authorities in some of the cities — Baltimore, Philadelphia, Cincinnati, Indianapolis, and Pittsburg — declined to extend courtesies or participate in the reception, but the people in all these cases took the matter in hand and were almost unanimous in the expression of their favorable regard and respect for the Chief Magistrate. The Governors of the States of Ohio, Indiana, Illinois, Michigan, Missouri, and Pennsylvania were all absent. In Ohio and Pennsylvania the Secretary of State appeared and each apologized for the absence of the Executive, but extended formal courtesies. Only one Radical Congressional Representative, Mr. Blow of Missouri, called upon the President. Mr. Spaulding of Cleveland was boarding at the house where we stopped, and we therefore saw him, but along the whole line of travel of over two thousand miles, and through perhaps thirty or forty Congressional districts, the Radical Members absented themselves, evidently by preconcert, and the Radical State and municipal authorities acted in almost every case in concert with them.

The President spoke freely, frankly, and plainly. For the first three or four days I apprehended he would, if he did not forbear, break down, for it seemed as though no one possessed the physical power to go through such extraordinary labor day after day for two or three weeks. I therefore remonstrated with and cautioned him, but he best knew his own system and powers of endurance. He felt, moreover, that he was performing a service and a duty in his appeals to his countrymen, and desired to address them face to face on the great issues before the country. It was the method to which he had been accustomed in Tennessee and the Southwest, and he believed it would be effective in the North.

I was apprehensive that the effect would be different, that his much talking would be misapprehended and misrepresented, that the partisan press and partisan leaders would avail themselves of it and decry him. I am still apprehensive that he may have injured his cause by many speeches; but it is undeniably true that his remarks were effective among his hearers and that within that circle he won supporters.

To a great extent the Radicals are opposed to him and his policy, yet when the true issue was stated, the people were, and are, obviously with him. The President himself has sanguine belief that he has so aroused his countrymen that they will sanction his measures for reëstablishing the Union on the Constitutional lines and oppose the Radicals' revolutionary measures. I have no doubt that the honest sentiments of the people are for the Union, but the Radicals have the party organizations and have labored to make those organizations effective for almost a year, while the President has done comparatively nothing.

Speeches to a few crowds — or the same speech, essentially, to many crowds — are not in themselves, I fear, sufficient. In the mean time there is want of sagacity, judgment, and good common sense in managing the party which supports him. Candidates who are Copperheads, *i.e.*, who opposed the Government during the War, cannot become earnestly engaged or really enthusiastic supporters, yet the Radical Republicans hold back while this class is pressed forward. Such advocates can gain no recruits. There is a kinder feeling among Republicans towards beaten Rebels than towards Copperheads. But these last pay court to the President in the absence of the greater part of the Republicans, who have become Radicals. It is not strange while the Radicals conspire against him that he assimilates with those who, if they opposed his election, now doubtingly sustain his policy. It is out of sympathy and charity to them. They, however, are still selfish partisans and are unpatriotic and in adherence to mere party policy and a President they did not elect.

Seward, who, during the whole session of Congress, held off and gave the Radical leaders full room for intrigue, yielded to their aggressive conduct, and was unwilling to give up his party organization until that party had so fortified itself as to set him at defiance, appears to have finally come to the conclusion that it is not best to repel the Democrats, for the Administration must rely upon them. He has throughout the excursion generally seconded the President, assented to all his positions, and rather encouraged his frequent speeches, which I opposed, for it was the same speech, sometimes slightly modified, which was soon burlesqued and published in anticipation of its delivery.

General Grant, whom the Radicals have striven to use and to offset against the President, who generally received louder cheers and called out more attention than even the President himself, behaved on the whole discreetly. Of course he saw, as did all others, the partisan designs and schemes of the Radicals, but he did not, so far as I could perceive, permit it to move him from his propriety, at least during the first week or ten days. He gave me to understand in one or two conversations which we had that our views corresponded. He agreed with me that he is for reestablishing the Union at once in all its primitive vigor, is for immediate representation by all the States, etc., but while he would forgive much to the Rebels, he is unsparing towards those whom he denounces as Copperheads. Mr. Hogan, the Representative of St. Louis District, accompanied us, by invitation of the President, on our way from St. Louis to Washington. He is a very earnest, zealous Democrat, an Irishman by birth, and a devoted friend and admirer of the President. It gave him pleasure with his strong lungs to introduce the President and his associates to the crowds at the stopping-places. General Grant told me in Cincinnati that it was extremely distasteful to him to be introduced to the crowds assembled at the stations by Hogan, who was a Copperhead, he said, and Rebel sympathizer during the War. He had, he remarked to me, no desire to fellowship with such a man. A Rebel he could forgive, but not a Copperhead.

The reception was everywhere enthusiastic and the demonstrations, especially at the principal cities, were in numbers most extraordinary and overwhelming. In Philadelphia, where the Radical authorities would not participate, the people filled the streets so that it was difficult to get through them. This proceeding at Philadelphia was the beginning of a series of petty spite on the part of the Radical managers, which was advised and determined upon before we left Washington and of which, I became satisfied, Stanton was cognizant. Between him and Grant there was, at that time, very little sympathy or friendly feeling, and until we had completed more than half of our journey, Grant clung to the President. Though usually reticent, he did not conceal from me his dislike of Seward. But, first at Detroit, then at Chicago, St. Louis, and finally at Cincinnati, it became obvious he had begun to listen to the seductive appeals of the Radical conspirators. The influence of his father, who was by his special request my companion and associate at Cincinnati in the procession, finally carried him into the Radical ranks. New York poured forth her whole population.

The Senate of New York, in session at Albany, deliberately struck Mr. Seward's name from the list of those who were welcomed, and Governor Fenton, in the spirit of a narrow mind, undertook to overslaugh the Secretary of State when we were introduced at the Capitol. When ushered through the crowd into the executive rooms, which were filled, Governor F. introduced the President to the

Senators and the throng. Passing by Secretary Seward, who stood beside the President, he called for General Grant, who was in the rear, and presented him and was then addressing himself to me, but Seward, who was aware of the action of the Senate and Governor, felt the intentional discourtesy most keenly, waited for no further action of the Governor, but stepped to the table and said: "I am here among old friends and familiar scenes and require no introduction from any one. Here are men and objects that I have known in other days, and have honored and been honored here." Taking one and another by the hand with "How do you do," he exchanged courtesies with several. Governor F. then introduced me and Admiral Farragut.

At Auburn, Seward's home, where we were to remain overnight, there were little neighborhood bickerings and jealousies. Mr. Pomeroy, the Representative of the district (who, by the way, did, as did also Mr. Blow, call on us), was intensely Radical, and had broken away from his old friend and neighbor in his party course. Naturally he carried many with him. There was also a jealous feeling of Mr. Seward himself on the part of the village aristocracy. A Mr. Morgan made himself conspicuous and intruded himself upon the party at Auburn and all the way to Niagara and Buffalo. He had the petty jealousy of a little mind towards his neighbor, Seward, and was constantly toadying to General Grant, and making himself disagreeably officious with that officer. As the fellow was obviously opposed to the President, his intrusion was impertinent and we were all glad to get rid of him, — none more so than Grant.

. . . .

At Cleveland there was evidently a concerted plan to prevent the President from speaking or to embarrass him in his remarks. Grant, I think, had been advised of this, and it affected him unfavorably. They did not succeed, but I regretted that he continued to address these crowds. Although it is consistent with his practice in Tennessee, I

2

would rather the Chief Magistrate would be more reserved, and both Governor Tod and myself suggested to Seward that it was impolitic and injudicious, but Seward did not concur. He said the President was doing good and was the best stump speaker in the country. The President should not be a stump speaker.

At Chicago and at St. Louis the reception was magnificent. There was in that of the latter place a cordiality and sincerity unsurpassed. We were met at Alton by thirty-six steamers crowded with people and were escorted by them to St. Louis.

There was turbulence and premeditated violence at Indianapolis more than at any other and at all other places. At Indianapolis I became convinced of what I had for some days suspected, — that there was an extreme Radical conspiracy to treat the President with disrespect and indignity and to avoid him. Morton,[1] who had early been obsequious to him and was opposed to negro suffrage and Radical demands, had become a Radical convert. He fled from us as we entered Indiana, — so of the little Governors of Ohio and Pennsylvania, who were purposely absent when we arrived at Columbus and Harrisburg.

Louisville gave us a grand reception.

Mr. Seward had an attack of the cholera on the steamboat after we left Louisville and was unable thereafter to participate with us. He had a car and a bed to himself from Cincinnati. At Pittsburg we parted, he going with the regular train in a car by himself, while we had a special train in advance. After reaching Harrisburg and while at supper, we were in a whisper informed that Mr. Seward was in a car at the depot, unable to be moved, and that Doctor Norris was apprehensive he might not survive the night. The President and myself immediately but quietly withdrew from the table and went to the depot, where we found Mr. Seward very low and weak. On the following morning he was little if any better, and was certainly

[1] Oliver P. Morton, the War Governor of Indiana.

weaker than on the preceding evening. He was evidently apprehensive he should not survive, and I feared it was our last interview. His voice was gone and he spoke in whispers. Taking the President's hand, he said, "My mind is clear, and I wish to say at this time that your course is right, that I have felt it my duty to sustain you in it, and if my life is spared I shall continue to do so. Pursue it for the sake of the country; it is correct." His family, which had been sent for, arrived and joined him at Harrisburg soon after, and he proceeded to Washington in advance of us and arrived there Saturday P.M.

At Columbus we were reviewed by a large assemblage. Not only the residents of the place but of the surrounding country gathered to meet us. Ex-Postmaster-General Dennison called upon us in the evening; was in good health, though he says he has been unwell most of the time since he left Washington. One or two of his neighbors say that he was ill in consequence of his resignation and its acceptance.

There was here, as I had noted at some other places, some scheming to antagonize General Grant and the President and make it appear that the interest was specially for the former. Great pains have been taken by partisans to misrepresent the President and misstate facts and to deceive and prejudice the people against him. There is special vindictiveness and disregard of truth by Members of Congress everywhere. Hate of the South and the whole people of the South is inculcated, Constitutional obligations are wholly disregarded, a new Constitution [is proposed], or such changes in the present as will give us essentially a new Central Government which shall operate especially against the States and the people of the South, while the people there are denied all representation or participation in these changes.

The Democrats of the North and almost the whole South, who might benefit themselves and the country by taking advantage of these errors and follies of the Radicals, are themselves demented and absurd in their action. They are devoted to party regardless of country. Instead of openly and boldly supporting the President and the policy of the Administration, showing moderation and wisdom in the selection of candidates, they are pressing forward men whom good Unionists, remembering and feeling the recent calamities of the War, cannot willingly support. In this way they have put in jeopardy the success of the cause of the Administration, which is really their own in most of the States. Prudent and judicious management would have given us a different Congress even in the Free States, but I think it can scarcely be expected in view of the great mistakes committed in the nominations which have been made. It is to the Democrats and the South a lost opportunity.

September 18, *Tuesday.* At the Cabinet-meeting Attorney-General Stanbery read the prepared opinion in regard to removals from office of which he had given us the substance some weeks since. I submitted the question whether I should be authorized to relinquish the Dunderberg to the contractor, Webb, on his refunding the money which had been paid him; also whether we would sell the Agamenticus, or other of our ironclads; but could get no distinct avowal of opinion. I also inquired as to the expediency of sending Queen Emma to the Sandwich Islands in the Vanderbilt, as the Secretary of State requested, but no one advised it.

A great pressure is being made for changes in the navy yards, especially at Philadelphia. The leading politicians and men who ask these changes are heated to the highest partisan heat, and really are not aware what they ask and its consequences. In most of the cases their requests, if granted, would do them more harm than good. Some few changes may be advisable, but only a few should be made, particularly on the eve of election. Because I do not give in to their request, they deem me unreasonable and timid. They give me nothing specific for my action, but only their opinions, and my opinions in these matters are as good as theirs, — I think better. I removed one of the masters before going West, and to-day on their assurance, unitedly, in regard to Stahl, the master blacksmith, I directed his removal at the Philadelphia Yard.

They also ask that the Commandant, Selfridge, may be displaced and Turner appointed in his stead. I told them it would not be advisable to change S., and T. is out of the question.

September 19, *Wednesday.*

. . . .

Commodore Melancthon Smith appointed Chief of Bureau of Equipment and Recruiting. Many applicants and expectants and consequent disappointment.

Navy yard pressures still continue, particularly from Philadelphia. Welsh, one of the political committee, is here, and, being a candidate for Congress, says Stahl, the master blacksmith, ought not to have been removed. I asked him why he did not openly object when the subject was discussed. He said he had intended to, or to have spoken to me in S.'s behalf. The truth is Welsh knows not his own case. I have little doubt that Stahl is against both him and the President, for he has been an earnest, zealous tool of Kelley. Still it shows how crude and unreliable and unprofitable are the doings of party committeemen.

Colonel Babcock of New Haven, who is here, says that a mistake has been made in the appointment of Lamb to be assessor at Norwich in place of Ely removed. Yet Babcock united with Dixon and English for the change. Why will not party men consider what they are about, and act for country? Lamb called on me, but I did not recommend him. I do not think the man adapted or qualified for the place, yet the recommendations which he had would have influenced me. Babcock places the fault at Dixon's door, who was, he says, deceived and imposed upon by Lamb.

September 20, *Thursday.* Had a call from Philip Dorsheimer of Buffalo, who says he has, he understands, been removed from the office of Collector for that district. I apprehend here is another mistake. A delegation from Massachusetts introduced themselves with the modest request that I would remove about every officer in the Navy Yard at Charlestown. They presented a package which took a full day for examination. Told them that indiscriminate sweeping removals on the eve of election were harmful, and that if all the persons whom they requested to be removed were opponents, it would as a party measure be injudicious and unwise to turn them out at this moment. There is much mismanagement. The Democrats are ravenous for place and are pressing for office regardless of the welfare of the Administration or the country.

Glancy Jones[1] of Reading, Pennsylvania, and also Judge Smalley of Vermont were at my house this evening, and both, though conspicuous Democrats, concurred with me in deploring and objecting to the hasty changes which are urged. Let there be slow speed to make good work.

September 21, *Friday.* A stormy day. Mrs. W. left this A.M. for Connecticut. I called on Seward in regard to sending out the Vanderbilt with Queen Emma to the Sandwich Islands, as had been discussed in Cabinet. Found him much improved, but weak. Was unable to advise. Requested delay until Tuesday.

Spoke to McCulloch in regard to Dorsheimer and subsequently to the President. McC. says D. is Radical, or is so represented to him. When I asked by whom he is so represented, he said by Weed and others. I think there is some villainy in all this; still there may not be. I cautioned the President on the subject.

I called on Seward. He was in bed, but very materially better. Tells me he was for a time on his feet this morning.

[1] John Glancy Jones, Member of Congress, 1850–58, and Minister to Austria, 1858–61.

He has wonderful elasticity of constitution and physical vigor for one of such feeble frame and appearance. When I saw him last Saturday morning in Harrisburg I had very great doubts whether I should ever again see him alive.

September 22, Saturday. Wrote, perhaps unwisely, to a man who signs his name Price, in Hollidaysburg, in answer to a partisan communication he sent me.

Am terribly annoyed by party committees who wish to manage the navy yards, or rather to officer and man them, I taking the responsibility. On all sides I am importuned by persons who know nothing on the subject of their importunity and who would not benefit themselves or their cause were I to give in to them.

Commodore Selfridge writes me that he manages the yard without any knowledge of the political opinions of those under him, yet is fearful he may be misunderstood, etc. I replied that the policy and rule had been to employ no disunionist, that I desired this practice to continue, that exclusionists or Radical disunionists were as objectionable as Secession disunionists.

September 24, Monday. Junius Morgan of London called and spent yesterday with me. He was a Hartford boy, though now a London banker. Some pleasant talk of old days when neither of us had the gray hairs that now mark us. Went with him to see Secretary McCulloch, with whom he had business, and made an appointment for to-day. I went with him to-day to see General Grant and subsequently the President. He was much interested with each of them.

Had last evening a long talk with Mr. Fogg, newly appointed Senator from New Hampshire, late Minister to Switzerland. Fogg and myself were associated for several years on the National Committee, commencing with the Frémont campaign. He has a good deal of vigor, mental and physical, is an intense partisan, with a cast of mind that would naturally throw him among the Radicals, with whom, moreover, are most of his associates. A dislike of Seward, who, he thinks, and not without cause perhaps, improperly induced his recall, adds to his feeling of opposition to the Administration, an opposition which he disclaims except from a belief that its policy is not in all respects right. This, however, is affectation. He is more hostile than he supposes and it is not from principle but is personal and partisan hostility.

The elections will, he says, go strongly against the Administration this fall, because the people have an impression that the President is leagued with the traitors and Copperheads and wishes to bring them into power. These [ideas] are, he admits, false, and when I asked why he did not exert himself to correct the errors, he would make no justification or defense. He claimed that Congress was authorized to exclude States from the Union, because Congress had sovereign power. I told him that, as an old strict Constitutionalist and States'-Rights man, he, I supposed, meant to be governed by the Constitution, which he declared was true. I then asked that, as the powers of Congress are specified and enumerated, he would point out the grant or power which authorized Congress to exclude States. He repeated it was by the sovereignty with which Congress was invested. I requested him to inform me in what part of the instrument this sovereignty, as he called it, was conferred upon Congress. Without answering me, he said if Congress had the right to admit States it had the right to exclude them. This, I said, did not by any means follow. There is explicit authority to admit, and if there was authority to exclude, it was a granted power, and he could point it out, for all powers not granted are expressly reserved to the States and people. He then said they had excluded themselves, — withdrawn from the Union. "Then," said I, "you admit Secession to have been successful?" This he denied. "Then," said I, "how can the States be without the Union?" He could give no answer. The subject is one which he and a class of partisans like him have not considered in any other than a factious, partisan spirit.

I found him closeted with the President to-day. McCulloch has employed him and trusts him. Randall said to me a few days since he thought Fogg was getting about right. That he may ultimately possess correct views I hope, but he is now in gross error and doing mischief, — a Senator who does not comprehend the principles of the government he attempts to serve.

September 25, *Tuesday.* Judge Holt asks a court of inquiry or court martial for the reason that certain partisans charge him with subornation and other misconduct in the trial of the assassins and Mrs. Surratt. Stanton seemed to think he was entitled to it and that he should have one if he wished. I thought it unnecessary, — that it would produce harm rather than good to attempt to revive and bring forward those matters at this juncture. A court of inquiry, or court martial, I claimed, was a military tribunal, and if it was to be resorted to, the subject did not properly belong to the Cabinet but the War Department; if he was a civil officer and was charged like the rest of us with political faults for partisan purposes, a military tribunal was not the remedy. The courts, at any rate, were open to him if he thought best to institute a suit, but I would not advise it. Being in a civil office, as I concluded, he must like the rest of us be passive under the grievance. Stanton said he was a brigadier-general and that these officers in the military service differ from the Navy. But all except Stanton were opposed to the military tribunal. There has been some queer legislation to secure a military life office for Holt.

The Cabinet ordered that the Vanderbilt should be tendered to Queen Emma to convey her to the Sandwich Islands, and I telegraphed to Admiral Thatcher to that effect.

It was also advised in Cabinet that we sell more of the turreted ironclads from the Navy.

General Dix was designated Minister to France in place of Bigelow, who asks to be relieved. Dix was also appointed Naval Officer at New York. Between the two I know not which he will take. McCulloch says Dix is poor, which I did not suppose and still doubt.

September 26, *Wednesday.* A delegation, headed by ex-Governor Johnson, from Pennsylvania, came with a note from the President. The delegation ask for extensive removals at the Navy Yard and that three thousand men should be employed there for a few weeks. I declined to employ or have men in the pay of the Government if not wanted. Admiral Smith, Chief of Yards and Docks, reports that the gangs are full. I therefore informed the gentlemen I could not do more. They said if I did not, the Administration would lose two, and probably three, Members of Congress which it would otherwise carry. I doubted whether they could accomplish so much as they supposed, provided I could properly gratify their demand. But I could not.

September 27, *Thursday.* Sam J. Tilden and De Wolf of Oswego spent the evening with me. Tilden has good sense, intelligence, honesty, but is a strong party man. Sees everything with partisan eyes, yet understandingly. In 1848 and for a time thereafter he was a Barnburner, going with the Van Burens, but very soon was homesick, sighed for the old organization, and continued to long for the "leeks and onions" of his political Egypt, until he got once more into the regular Democratic fold. From that time he has clung to the horns of party with undying tenacity. During the War he did not side with the Rebels, but he disliked and abjured the Administration.

At this time he supports the President, but I perceive he aims to do it as a Democrat rather than as a patriot, and that he is striving to identify the President with the Democratic Party organization. I regret that he and other New York extremists should pursue this course. It will be likely to give strength to the Radicals and defeat the Administration in the coming elections. Tilden speaks of success, which I am confident he cannot feel. He and his party have, it appears to me, alienated instead of recruiting men who would have united with them, and thereby given victory to the Radicals.

The people of the North are not ready to place the Government in the hands of the Copperheads, or even of the Democrats who were cold and reserved during the War. This hostility to those who sympathized with the Rebels is natural. It is an honest feeling which Stevens, Boutwell, Butler, and other reckless partisans are abusing and striving to work into frenzy. Had the Democrats given up their distinctive organization and worked in with the real Union men against the Radical exclusionists, the President and his policy would have been triumphantly vindicated and sustained. But they were jealous of the President, feared that he instead of a New-Yorker would lead; and their selfish, narrow adherence to the organization, their avarice for power, their exclusion and arrogance, will be likely to destroy them. Perhaps it 's for the best.

September 28, *Friday.* Webb, the naval constructor, has been negotiating for a relinquishment of the Dunderberg, provided he refunded the money, some nine hundred thousand dollars, to the Government. This morning he came to my house wishing me to aid him in getting an opinion from the Attorney-General, whether he could be permitted to leave the United States with his vessel after she was completed. I told him the Attorney-General could give him no more light on the subject than any other intelligent attorney; that, if not a naval vessel, the Secretary of the Treasury might have to decide whether a clearance should be given her.

I alluded to the subject in the Cabinet, but McCulloch said Webb had not called on him. Stanbery said a call had been made upon him. But S. did not understand the question; said Webb wanted the vessel should be guaranteed to a foreign port. I told him he must have misunderstood Webb. He thought not, but Webb tells me this evening he was wholly misapprehended.

In Cabinet, McCulloch said he would give a clearance. Stanton said he would not part with the vessel; would hold on to her and let her rot down in three or four years, as, being built of green timber, she certainly would. The name, he said, was worth more than a million dollars to us.

Judge Holt's case was again brought forward. He wanted the Administration to indorse him, if he could not have a court of inquiry. Seward, Stanton, Browning, and Stanbery were favorably inclined. It seems he had called on them personally, and they represent him as under intense personal excitement. I regretted his sensitiveness, but remarked that our naval bureaus were filled by officers in the naval service, that they had been violently assailed, but we never thought of a court of inquiry or court martial in their cases.

Seward promised to pay extra outfit for Queen Emma on the Vanderbilt.

Paymaster Paulding's case was considered, but action delayed for the present.

Commodore Jenkins read me a letter from McCrea intimating that Rear-Admiral Goldsborough is vexed because he was not made Vice-Admiral. I never supposed that he expected it. He is improperly on the active list.

Gave orders for Dahlgren to relieve Pearson of the command of the South Pacific Squadron.

September 29, *Saturday.* Seward says he wishes the inquiries and information which Robert Johnson was authorized to procure in relation to the slave coolie trade should be made by a naval officer. Colonel J. declines the mission. The President says he would not have the vessel detained or diverted on the Colonel's account. Seward wishes to get back the instructions from Colonel J. which were given him.

Captain Collins sends word that the Sacramento will be ready by the 2d of October, but I allow some days' grace. Communicated with the President on the subject.

Mrs. Barney, widow of Commodore Barney, has presented the case of her son to the President and brings it also to me. Assumes he was dismissed unjustly. Although eighty-three years old, she has fire and vinegar in her composition; boasts that her injured son has the blood of the Chases and the Barneys in his veins, the best blood of the Revolution. . . . I furnished the President with the documents on which President Lincoln ordered him dismissed. They were long, and President Johnson wished me to state the case and save him from reading them. I did so briefly. There were also unwritten facts of an aggravated character which entered into the question that I did not [communicate].

XLIII

October 1, *Monday.* The President showed me a letter from General Sherman, written last February, strongly indorsing his policy and condemning the conduct of Stevens and Sumner. It was written from St. Louis. Could it be published at this time, it would do much good. He asked my opinion in regard to its publication, as Sherman was absent on the Plains. The closing paragraph, which was complimentary to the President and expressed the hope that he would be reëlected, the President said would, of course, be omitted. I remarked that the names ought also to be stricken out unless he authorized their use, although it would weaken the letter. I suggested that he should telegraph to Sherman on the subject.

I regretted to him that we could not communicate unreservedly and with a common feeling in Cabinet-meeting. The President said it was unfortunate just now and was all wrong, but did not say he would correct it, although his manner, more than his expression, indicated that there would be a change.

General Slocum came to see and converse with me

relative to New York affairs. He has intelligence and vim. Among other things he told me that the State and district committees and the influence of the strongest men in that quarter had been unable to remove the postmaster at Lockport; that the Member from there, who is in opposition, laughed at and defied them. Said he had an understanding with Thurlow Weed, who wanted to control the vote of the member of the legislature on the Senatorial question, and for that consideration the obnoxious postmaster, Weed says, shall be retained. General S. had doubted this, but, being here with authority to look into New York cases, he had examined that of Lockport, where, indeed, he found a letter from Weed stating that he had pledged the retention of the postmaster to the Member.

I advised General S. to state these facts and others to the President. Weed is evidently intriguing, not for the President but for himself and Seward. There are circumstances which satisfy me that the present aim is to get a legislature in New York which will return Seward once more to the Senate.

October 2, Tuesday. Seward to-day was very urgent that General Dix, who has entered upon the duties of Naval Officer, should embark for France on the mission to that country which he has accepted. McCulloch was anxious that he should remain in the Naval Office a few weeks longer, but Seward was very persistent without assigning any substantial reason. I think I see the bearing which the vacation of the Naval Office may have on the New York elections. No conclusions were come to, though I see Seward is determined and shall not be surprised if he succeeds. I expressed a wish to McCulloch that he would retain Dix until after the election. He said he would try to. It is not that Dix himself has much power or efficiency, but he is, without effort of his own, checking the intrigues of Weed, — is in the way of that obnoxious faction in New York.

General Dix is, just at this time, apparently popular, yet

has no zealous, earnest friends. He is a pure man, I think, of reputable scholarly attainments, but without much force or energy. He has abilities to fill any station respectably, but can give character to none. The New-Yorkers and the country have for him respect, but no enthusiastic regard is felt for him anywhere. His most intimate friend and crony just now, who associates with him everywhere, is Ludlow, who was on his staff; a selfish man, wanting in the higher qualities. . . . He wishes Dix to go to France, because he thinks, mistakenly, he may have a chance for the Naval Office.

Attorney-General Stanbery brought up the case of Jefferson Davis; says that he is improperly detained at Fortress Monroe. If amenable to military law, he should be tried; if not, should be turned over to the civil authorities. Thought he should be given up on a *capias*, etc. Stanton was not prepared to advise that he should be given up.

In the discussion which took place, the action which was taken a year since was brought up. The then Attorney-General, Speed, took ground that Davis could not be tried by a military commission and advised that he should, for security, be retained in Fortress Monroe until his trial, or until a suitable prison should be found elsewhere.

October 3, Wednesday. The party excitement increases and probably will until the Pennsylvania and other elections take place next Tuesday. The prospect is not cheering, and yet I cannot satisfy myself that the shouting and misrepresentation of the Radicals will be so triumphant as they confidently assume. They have exhibited more activity and party skill and really more industry than the friends of the Administration. The issues have not been well made up. When in June last we were getting up the call for the Philadelphia Convention, I urged that the Constitutional change, or Amendment as it is called, should distinctly and emphatically appear as a part of the President's policy. Some of the gentlemen concurred with me, but others, and

particularly Randall, objected, but without a reason. I told
the gentlemen they could not dodge this issue and that it
was weakness to attempt to evade it; that it was the important question before the country, and the more they strove
to get around and away from it, the more earnestly it
would be pressed home upon them by the Radicals. I
assured them they could not escape this question; that the
Administration must be either for or against it; that
timidity was a weakness at such a time. All admitted they
were opposed to it. "Why, then," said I, "not boldly
avow it at the threshold and make it a rallying-point at the
start."

Unable to succeed by argument, Randall said he wished
to have something for the convention to present when it
assembled, and this, he thought, belonged to them. I
maintained we should call the convention to meet *for* this
purpose in particular. This principle and great advantage
— the real national issue — was thrown away in the vain
and delusive hope that Weed and Seward could, by feeble
expedients, concentrate and unite the waning political
elements in New York and thus reinstate themselves in
power. Randall and Raymond were their tools. Doolittle,
honest and sincere, was hoodwinked, and the President
probably sacrificed.

Well, the result is that opposition to the Constitutional
Amendment does not enter into the policy of the Administration or Union Party. Its friends are embarrassed by this
cowardly silence. The true policy of the Administration is
sound and correct and should be [indecipherable] and promulgated. It embraces opposition to the Constitutional
changes, at all events until the States are all represented,
but such is not its defined creed or principle. Seward,
Weed, and Randall have suppressed it. The consequence
is that in the very pinch of the struggle, and when the
Radicals felt they were to be thrown, they made a new
issue, and, instead of openly opposing the President's Union
policy, they charge him with uniting with the Rebels,

2

and the Constitutional Amendment to prevent Rebel ascendancy is the great absorbing question. But the Constitutional change has not been discussed, is imperfectly understood. Some have inconsiderately given it a *quasi* approval, and there is danger that the Radicals will be greatly benefited by the timid counsels of last June. Then Raymond was to be considered and conciliated. When the great truths of a cause are put aside, true issues suppressed, to obtain the support of any one, but especially a trimmer entitled to no confidence, the cause must suffer.

October 4, Thursday. Saw Seward this morning. . . . I asked him what we were to expect from New York. Said the course of the *Times* and *Evening Post* was vacillating and harmful in the highest degree.

Seward undertook to explain; said the Democrats had been too exacting and assuming, and so also had the Rebels; and, philosophizing on this, he was satisfied that their extreme views would defeat themselves in the end. At the fall elections the Administration would accomplish but little. We should, he thought, hold our own in Congress, but the contest would be continued two or three years.

Weed and Raymond have overrefined and irreparably injured the cause of the Administration. In doing this they have also destroyed their own influence. How far Seward is implicated with them is, perhaps, doubtful. Weed has been the tactician and master mind in New York politics. My impressions are that Seward was not advisory, nor perhaps consulted in the first twist that has recently been taken, but his connections with the men named are such that he acquiesces, and is now, as he always has been, identified with them. Weed is an old stager and autocrat in New York, with a vigorous intellect, much demoralized, never very scrupulous and now wholly unconscionable. He is fond of intrigue, fond of power, and the end and aim of his political and party efforts are to have the controlling management in the State and Nation, to dispense favors, and latterly to secure for himself pecuniary rewards and favors. At present both he and his friend Seward are without influence, but Weed is struggling to again get position. This, he flatters himself, can be done by electing Seward to the United States Senate. But the day of his power has departed forever. His intrigues cannot effect a restoration. He can elect Seward to nothing. The time has gone by, though he is unwilling to confess it even to himself.

October 5, Friday. All were present at Cabinet-meeting except Seward, who has a relapse. Stanton and Randall afflicted with severe colds. No measures of special importance. A board appointed by Stanton made, some days since, a report on the New Orleans matter. With a different Secretary of War there would doubtless have been a different board and a different report.

These matters are paralyzing the efforts and labor of the friends of the Administration, and working injustice to the President and his supporters. Want of unity and concentrated strength and effect in the Cabinet is to be deplored. I asked the President, a few days since, if he was not aware of the embarrassment and weakness caused by this state of things, and whether we were not to have something different. His answer was evasive, but to the effect, I thought, that things must continue for a time as at present. Whether he deems it inexpedient to make any change until after election, or that there should be any change even then, I do not know. He is very reticent on these matters, and I am not inclined to press them.

But the Radicals are greatly encouraged and animated by the absence of any concerted action in the Cabinet. They understand the situation of affairs inside, and are themselves now known and active outside. Hence they have inspired their own party with confidence that they shall sweep Pennsylvania and other States by immense majorities, and have in a measure intimidated many of our own men, our strong men. The last long session of Congress was devoted chiefly to Radical party organization and intrigue, while the Administration did nothing, and the Radicals have now, consequently, extraordinary advantages in this contest. Opportunities have been lost and opportunities have been thrown away. Issues have been dodged and issues not forcibly met. If, therefore, we hold our own we shall do well. We might have had a decisive majority.

October 6, *Saturday*. I called at the Treasury this morning to make inquiries concerning the removal of J. G. Bolles from the office of Collector of Hartford, and the appointment of Doctor Grant. It was the work of Dixon when I was absent with the President. McCulloch was by distinct understanding to have notified me before making any change in that office. I reminded him of this. He was embarrassed, but I think, as he asserts, he acted inadvertently in this respect, not recollecting at the moment that I was of Hartford. But to tell me this frankly, would, he thought, not be complimentary.

Dixon should not have taken such a step without consultation. Mr. Bolles was a good officer, correct and reliable. I presume he was inclined to Radicalism, and not unlikely threw his influence quietly for that party. He could do more in a silent way than many others by loud and boisterous activity. His deputy, I have been repeatedly told, was officiously busy and mischievous.

As Bolles and myself have been lifelong friends and old brother-soldiers in many a political campaign, I could take no part against him, if as objectionable as Dixon represents. Nor could I, nor can I now, under Dixon's statements, severely remonstrate. Yet I think Bolles would ultimately have come right. I hope he will still, for he has a good, clear, and well-balanced mind, one that should detect the errors and follies of Radicalism. But prejudices,

preconceived notions, and unfortunate delays and movements without much calm investigation have, in the general prevailing error and Radicalism at the North, warped
his judgment as well as others'. They are for imposing
conditions upon the Southern States without ever thinking
whether they have authority to do so and that their conduct is in direct conflict with our whole governmental
system. They are making our Federal Government, not of,
or for, the whole people, but a part imposed on the whole,
— a section to govern all.

October 8, *Monday.* Montgomery Blair got home yesterday after six weeks' active electioneering, much of the
time in Pennsylvania. He is strong in the belief that the
Administration will carry the State, and vexed that any
one should doubt it. But although almost all our friends
from Pennsylvania have equal confidence, I have not. On
the contrary I have felt discouraged, not because our
cause is not right, not that I have doubt it will ultimately
prevail, but the President must get rid of the advice and
influence and association of such men as Raymond. And
there are also others in more intimate relation that injure
him. I alluded to these things with Blair. He says the
President is killing himself politically by them, and anathe-
matizes Seward and Stanton.

October 9, *Tuesday.* Stanton submitted some correspondence between Generals Grant and Sheridan and Governor
Throckmorton of Texas relative to Indian depredations on
the frontier. The legislature of Texas has authorized the
raising of one thousand troops for the purpose of protection,
and wishes the Federal Government to defray expenses,
etc., and suggests to General Sheridan that the troops now
located in the interior of the State should go to the frontier.
Sheridan thinks this unnecessary. [Stanton] would leave
the subject with Sheridan, whom I suspect he or Grant,
or both, secretly advises and controls. Stanton speaks

contemptuously of the whole affair; thinks the statement
of suffering on the frontier of little account; denies that
the State, or Throckmorton, can raise troops. Stanbery
boldly met Stanton and insisted that outrages, such as were
mentioned, should not be treated lightly; that if the Federal Government did not protect them they must protect
themselves. The sentiments of the Cabinet were with
Stanbery, and Stanton feels that justice and right were
with him also, yet I think I can see a lurking inclination on
his part to slight Texas, to permit the people to be harassed,
— that spirit of Radical hate and oppression which if not
extinguished must ultimately bring sorrow to our countrymen.

The Attorney-General reported that Jefferson Davis
should be surrendered to the civil authorities whenever
they required him, and that notice should be given to that
effect. This notice he thought should come through the
Secretary of War, who now had Davis in custody. Stanton
was pretty emphatic in saying he would give no such notice
and that he did not concur in the views of the Attorney-
General.

An indictment is now pending against Davis in Virginia, but Chandler, the District Attorney who proposed
it, is dissatisfied with it and desires to frame another.
Stanton inquired of the Attorney-General if he did not
intend to give the subject his personal attention, see to
framing the indictment, preparing the case, etc. Stanbery
said he did not. A sharp debate ensued.

My impressions are that Attorney-General Speed intended to take this case in hand himself, but the President
tells me that Speed did not propose to go into court with
the case but to supervise it. He had, I know, corresponded
with counsel who were to be associated wth him in the
trial.

Called in at the White House about 10 o'clock P.M.
The President had about half a dozen telegrams from
Philadelphia, which gave gratifying accounts of the results

of to-day's voting in that city. If the rest of the State comes in with corresponding gains, Clymer will be elected. I am, I confess, agreeably disappointed in Philadelphia. It has done better than I expected; still I have doubts of general success. We may gain one or two Members of Congress. It is reported that we have gained the Fifth District. No returns from Pittsburg and the West up to the time I left, almost eleven o'clock. The President is in good spirits and Randall full of confidence, — hoping too much, for there is a good deal of bad material and much political debauchery in Pennsylvania.

October 10, *Wednesday.* The election returns this morning are adverse and render it doubtful whether the Administration will hold its own. Still the result, so far as I have seen particulars, is quite as satisfactory as I expected. I think there will be a gain for the real Union, or Administration, cause. Had the Democratic Party been more wise and liberal, the result might have been different and better. But there has been an attempt to revive the old Democratic organization, instead of joining in the new issues, and to have very pronounced Democrats — Copperheads or men of extreme anti-War feeling — for candidates. The rebuke to them is deserved, but it is sad that so good a cause should be defeated by such vicious, narrow partisanship.

October 11, *Thursday.* A stock-jobber's telegram to the *Philadelphia Ledger* has created some commotion, stating that the President had propounded certain questions, which are given, to the Attorney-General, asking whether the present Congress is a Constitutional body. It may have the effect of setting some men thinking, and in that respect do good, though the trick is of mischievous intent and will be harmful. Of course no one should have been deceived a moment, for had the President called upon the Attorney-General for an opinion on so important and grave a matter, that officer would not have run to a newspaper correspondent and communicated the subject. So many and such infamous falsehoods have been stated concerning the President, which men have believed, or affected to believe, that it is well they should be punished.

October 12, *Friday*. The correspondence between the President and Attorney-General respecting Jeff Davis was directed to be published.

The question of a court of inquiry for Judge Holt was considered. All thought it inexpedient but Stanton. Seward seemed disposed to yield, but I strongly objected and he held his own.

October 13, *Saturday*. I read yesterday to the President a letter to Admiral Charles H. Bell, Brooklyn Navy Yard, relative to the employment of Secessionists and exclusionists in the Navy Yard, and especially to the exclusion of Union men. He gave it his decided approval; said there was no other course to pursue.

Senator Sumner has sent me his speech, — he delivers one annually. This one does him no credit. Is not frank and truthful and honest, — traits that I have heretofore awarded him, though pedantic and somewhat fanatical, as well as always egotistical.

November 17, *Saturday*. Several weeks have elapsed, and many interesting incidents have gone which I wished to note, but, employed through the days and until late at night, have not had the time. The fall elections have passed, and the Radicals retain their strength in Congress. False issues have prevailed. Nowhere have the real political questions been discussed. Passion, prejudice, hate of the South, the whole South, were the Radical element and ailment [*sic*] for reëstablishing the Union. Equal political rights among the States are scouted, toleration to the people of the South denied. The papers and orators appealed

to the Northern public to know if they would consent to
have the Rebels who had killed their fathers, brothers, sons,
etc., brought into power. President Johnson was, and is,
denounced as a traitor because he does not repel and persecute the beaten Rebels. The passions of the people are
inflamed to war heat against the whole South indiscriminately, while kindness, toleration, and reason are discarded
and the Constitutional changes and all real political questions are ignored.

The Democrats, with equal folly and selfishness, strove
to install their old party organization in force, regardless
of the true interest of the country. They saw the weakness
and wickedness of the Radical majority in Congress and
believed that they had committed suicide. The public
was dissatisfied with the course pursued by Congress and
rejoiced that the Philadelphia Convention was called. In
that convention, so unfortunately mismanaged from its
inception, and in subsequent meetings, the Democrats pre-
dominated, and they narrowed the contest down to an attempt to fortify and intrench their old organization, not
aware that the once proud party had made itself odious
by its anti-War conduct and record. The consequence
has been that instead of reinstating themselves they have
established the Radicals more strongly in power.

Never was a political campaign so poorly managed.
When the call was preparing for the Philadelphia Convention, I urged that the real issues should be embraced, for
otherwise the Administration would be placed at a disadvantage, and charged, in the absence of avowed principles,
with a coalition with Rebels for power. We were, I told
them, throwing away an opportunity. We could, on the
proposed revolutionary Constitutional changes, meet and
whip the Radical faction, whereas if we omitted any allusion to them and evaded the true test, there would be
a general scramble, in which the Radicals would have the
advantage, for they had been organizing and preparing for
the contest. But Postmaster-General Randall and others,

secretly prompted by Seward, were unwilling to take an open, bold stand. They wanted to satisfy Raymond and the calculating party trimmers, and so let themselves down.

We have, therefore, had elections without any test, statement, or advocacy of principles, except the false one that the Radicals have forced, that the Administration had united with the Rebels. It was a contention of partisans, striving for the ascendancy. The President's friends were willing to support him and sustain his policy in the elections if they could get at the question, but a large portion of them would not vote to restore the old obnoxious Democrats to power on old issues.

Now that the elections are over on this superficial, evasive, and skulking fight, this after-war feeling which has been prolonged and renewed for party purposes on the one hand, and this pitiful attempt to revive a defunct and deservedly defeated organization on the other hand, the Radicals say the people have decided on the Constitutional questions and indorsed the changes, when in fact they were never brought out.

Senator Grimes writes me that if the President does not take the present terms, harder ones will be proposed, — that never was more leniency shown to conquered by conquerors. These are the sentiments and views of our prominent legislators and statesmen.

I replied that the beaten Rebels were our countrymen, amenable, individually, to our laws; that as many as might be thought proper could be tried and punished if found guilty. That, the Rebellion being suppressed, no terms could be made, for no authority existed on their part to appoint negotiators, as would be the case had we conquered a foreign country. Here the Constitution and laws must do the work. If they are weak and insufficient, the fault was ours as much as theirs, and we must do the best we can under the circumstances.

But it is useless to attempt to reason with embittered partisans. The great scheme of the Radicals is to inflict vengeance on the whole South indiscriminately, regardless of their legal and constitutional rights. This was the steady aim of the centralists through the whole of the late long session; this is their present purpose, though such a scheme is subversive of the Government and the Union.

Seward said to me yesterday before the Cabinet session commenced, though most of the Cabinet and President were present, that I must look out, for he had invited Randall and Browning, and I think he said McCulloch, to meet him at the President's room on the matter of an appointment, and they found Chief Justice Chase closeted with the President. This may have been all accidental, but there are some things which lead me to suppose that it is a plan to beguile the President and induce him to yield to the Radicals. Stanton was not present, nor was it necessary, for, absent or present, he is not in principle or policy with the President. It would not have been advisable to have had me present, for I am more decided against the whole scheme of changing and subverting the Constitution than the President himself. We two — Stanton on one side and I on the other—were not there. Stanbery is in New York. I made no inquiry as to the subject-matters of discussion. They may have related exclusively to Jeff Davis; they may have related to Reconstruction and reconciliation with the Radicals. But Chase has just now scarcely more influence than Seward. He cannot strengthen nor change the President when he knows he is right.

General Dix called on me this P.M. He leaves next Saturday for France. He says the Democratic leaders, many of them, now see their error in striving to make their organization the great end, but it is too late. They made too much haste. Peace Democrats cannot be popular favorites at present, nor can they recruit or build up a successful party with such candidates.

The Radicals have elected General Butler to Congress in a district of which he was not a resident. The Democrats in New York have elected Morrissey, the boxer and gambler, to Congress. It is not creditable that either of these men should have been elected. It shows the depravity of parties and the times. Two negroes have been elected to the Massachusetts Legislature, not for talents, ability, or qualifications, but because they are black. Had they been white, no one would have thought of either for the position.

In Maryland a strange contest was carried on. The Radicals set the laws and the authorities aside and denounced the Unionists as revolutionists. The legal commissioners were imprisoned until after the election, and the illegal ones were kept in place. When the election was over and the Radicals were beaten, the judge ordered the legitimate commissioners to be freed, pronounced their election legal, and commanded the Radical commissioners to vacate.

Forney in the *Chronicle*, and other Radical editors, denounced the Governor (Swann) and the law-abiding people of Maryland and called on the Radicals of other States to be prepared to assist in putting down the State authorities. The President felt concerned and anxious. If there was riot and bloodshed and the United States troops were not there under such warning, he would be blamed, but if he were to send troops there, he would be accused of trying to control the election by military force. On inquiry of the Secretary of War, he said there were but eighty-three soldiers in Fort McHenry. It was known there were over five hundred disbanded, but armed, negro soldiers in Baltimore. The President and Cabinet, with the exception of Stanton, who has withdrawn the troops and is in conspiracy with the exclusionists, thought there should be additional troops in the vicinity.

I met Stanton at the President's this morning, after this discussion, and asked him what was done. He said he should send General Grant to Baltimore; General Canby has been there.

During all this discussion of days and weeks, Governor Swann came once or twice a week to Washington to confer with the President and Judge Bond, the leading Radical, and was as often at the War Department to consult Stanton. While the President sustained the Governor, they were both defeated and tricked by the audacious and illegal conduct of Bond and his advisers.

It was concluded in October to send Campbell, our Minister to Mexico, to that country. Instructions were duly prepared and read to the Cabinet, General Grant, who has been zealous on that subject, being present. It was stated, and the instructions so expressed, that Grant should accompany the Minister. But after the instructions had been read and discussed, General Grant said he did not think it expedient for him to go out of the country. Stanton had expressed this idea at the preceding meeting, when the instructions were first read. The President was surprised and a little disconcerted. He could not fail to see there was an intrigue. I think something more.

General Sherman had in the mean time been sent for and it was rumored that Stanton was to leave the War Department and Sherman would be assigned to that duty. Whether there was any truth in this, or whether Stanton apprehended it, I never inquired. If there was anything in it, at any time, it was frustrated by Grant, who cooled down and declined to go with Campbell. He could not be willing to receive orders from his subordinate, General Sherman, of whom he is jealous, though intimately friendly. His suspicion has been excited. The result was Sherman, instead of Grant, accompanied Campbell.

A steamer was wanted to convey them, and I directed the Susquehanna, which had just been fitted for the North Atlantic Squadron, to proceed on this special mission. In the midst of other duties and with some holding back, I do not precisely understand the course that is to be taken, if others do. There is an intention to recognize Juarez as the President of Mexico. It is hoped he will meet our Minister at Vera Cruz and, pressing the French War Department, he, with Campbell, will proceed to the City of Mexico. There

is some of Seward's refining and something Johnsonian in
the scheme and the sudden change of Grant, who has
carried forward the measure, indicating apprehension or
suspicion. It strikes me as a party political contrivance,
such as Seward is fond of concocting for effect. A Radical
Congress is about assembling after a succession of party
triumphs, and he is afraid of it. This embassy is to draw
off attention. He may, however, be premature. The
French have not left, and though from all accounts they
are doing so, Louis Napoleon will not hesitate to break
faith if it is for his interest. I told Seward fifteen months
ago that I had no faith in Louis Napoleon's honor or fair-
ness. Look at Rome and at all his acts.

November 22, Thursday. Special meeting of the Cabinet.
Seward was in fidgets. A dispatch from John Bigelow, our
Minister, says the embarkation of the French troops in
Mexico is postponed till spring. This step was taken some
weeks since, but we had not been consulted or notified. In
the mean time Seward, anticipating the departure of the
French troops, has sent out his Minister with Lieutenant-
General Sherman for a State Department triumph in re-
establishing the Mexican Republic.

The President and Seward, I saw, were ready to take
decisive measures. Seward was full of palaver, — had
many things to say that were nothing. The President was
disturbed and disappointed, but, as usual, reticent.

Seward read a thunder-and-lightning dispatch, a sort of
ultimatum, full of menace and monitions in every respect,
as a telegram. All the Cabinet disapproved of it, except
Seward and Randall. Stanton was very clear and firm,
and his position disappointed me. McCulloch and Stanbery were unqualifiedly against the style, language, and
the whole dispatch. I concurred with them, which I saw
annoyed the President. He and Seward think a war or
demonstration against France for republican Mexico will
be popular. The President is very emphatic and sincere on

the Monroe Doctrine. Seward talks much but cares little about it. Randall was short and passionate. Had no fear of a war with France; would send defiance. She could not help herself. Seward, as well as Bigelow, in his dispatch expressed confidence and full faith in Napoleon. I had little. But sending out Campbell and Sherman with parade is making them, if not the Government, ridiculous. Seward, I think, feels it.

I am in doubts about this stroke of Louis Napoleon. In not noticing or consulting with us, after what has taken place, he has slighted if not insulted us. Seward says it was an inadvertence. I do not think so, but if an inadvertence it is scarcely less offensive. Whether he thinks a war with us will relieve him in a measure of European difficulties, or whether he thinks we will guarantee his Mexican debt, I know not. Perhaps neither. The latter seems to me most probable. He was probably advised by the cable telegraph of the preparations for Campbell's and Sherman's departure. His course indicates it.

There is something in the fact that he cannot withdraw his troops by detachments, or at different periods. They must all go at once or the last remnant be sacrificed. Perhaps he may wish us to guarantee them a safe embarkation.

Seward read over a dispatch to Campbell, advising him of the turn things had taken. There were some statements and pledges alluded to that I know nothing of, and McCulloch, who walked home with me, is equally ignorant of them. I apprehend Seward, who seemed to have had an object in this movement, has committed himself farther than some of us know of. Perhaps the President is aware of these committals. I thought so from the manner in which he received the statement. But it was concluded to put off the Campbell dispatch until to-morrow, and finally the whole subject was postponed. There is, I fear, but little statesmanship in this whole Mexican movement, which has been recently, partially at least, developed. I do not believe the Cabinet have been fully consulted or even apprised of the true state of the case. A great trick is likely to be a great fizzle.

November 23, Friday. General Grant was present to-day at the Cabinet-meeting, invited evidently by the President by the advice of Seward. The Mexican matter was taken up. Seward had rewritten his telegraphic dispatch to Bigelow and much improved his yesterday's document. But Browning, who was not present yesterday, at once broke ground against this as an ultimatum, — a threat. The rest of us laughed and regretted he was not with us to have heard the first paper read. Stanton thought it an excellent document now, with the exception of the paragraph informing the Emperor through Bigelow of our army instructions on the Rio Grande. General Grant, who is intensely Mexican and would not regret a little military action, extolled the dispatch except the part to which Stanton excepted. Both of them assigned an objection that it committed us to do nothing, but on rereading, it was clear they had misapprehended it. I did not like the dispatch, nor the aspect of the case. Some propositions to omit, Seward did not assent to, thought it would weaken the dispatch; said it was good writing, prepared with much care. All but Seward and Randall thought the passage to which exception was taken might as well be omitted. The President decided to retain it. Stanton and Grant don't want peace, and they influence Seward.

In the crowded condition of things, — preparing my Report and other almost overwhelming duties, — I have had no time to consult any one of my associates, nor to give this Mexican subject the reflection it deserves; but the whole strikes me unfavorably. Seward has evidently tried to be a little shrewd, to perform a trick, and has failed. The President has been drawn into the scheme and, having become committed, is very earnest. If between his earnestness and Seward's performance we escape without difficulty, I shall be glad.

Nothing was said to-day about the dispatch to Campbell. It was read yesterday and dropped without remark, but there were allusions in it to some arrangement, or understanding, which are novel to me. Some of us said we recollected no agreement, but Seward insisted it was so, and, in a way which he often practices, passed to another subject. It is evident, therefore, that whenever these matters are brought to light we are to share the odium if there be any responsibility, but are to have no credit. I perceive we shall not again be consulted about the Campbell dispatch, and it will be claimed that we all assented to and approved it.

I noticed that Stanbery was quiet to-day, though yesterday decided. He often listens to Seward, who courts him. Stanton was passive also. The President, while he said but little, felt strongly. He has no apprehension of difficulty with France. Seward says there certainly will be none; repeatedly declared that he would guarantee there would be none. My own impressions are that there will be no war between the two countries. I know there would not be if a man of steady purpose, like Mr. Jefferson or Mr. Madison, were Secretary of State. Seward does not want or intend war, but desires diplomatic success.

Stanton proposed that the army be promptly recruited to the maximum point and that six ironclads be immediately got ready for sea. Stanbery and McCulloch both objected. Seward and Randall were in favor. Stanbery wanted the subject delayed to a future meeting. Stanton said half a dozen ironclads would shut up Vera Cruz and prevent the French from reinforcing their army. I asked what was to be done with our commerce and exposed coast. It did not appear to have occurred to him that there was to be any fight elsewhere than in the Gulf and with French Mexico if we had war. He had not, in this instance, been the confidant of Seward, but I am persuaded that both he and Stanbery have been seen since yesterday by either Seward or the President.

2

To me it appears as if Seward had been arranging for a pretty piece of acting and had overshot his mark. The recall of Bigelow, the sending out of Dix, the parading of General Sherman with Campbell in a national ship, are all parts of a comedy which I hope will have nothing tragical attending it. The President and General Grant are so earnest on the Mexican question that they readily fall in with any scheme which is desired to get rid of the French. But a war with that country or with England would be a terrible calamity to us, and there should be no trifling on the subject. We could, it is true, injure them greatly, but they would just now injure us more. From these and other causes, therefore, we ought not to invite hostilities.

The results of the elections have greatly disappointed Seward, and as he has little faith in political principles, popular intelligence, or public virtue, he resorts to expedients, and if they fail, he becomes depressed. I am mistaken if there is not much shambling statesmanship in this Mexican demonstration. If I am not in error, there have been some steps taken of which most of us are not advised. The condition of things does not suit me, though, as Seward says, France has trouble and cannot afford to go to war with us. I would not tempt or dare her unnecessarily.

November 29, *Thursday.* A number of Members of Congress have arrived. Thad Stevens and some of the ranting Radicals are on the ground early to block out work for their followers when they assemble on Monday next. Thad is a very domineering and exacting leader and has great control over the Radicals, though many of them are unwilling to admit it, and in a cowardly way deny it. Lacking well-grounded political principles, they want moral courage in the peculiar condition of affairs. Afraid of Stevens, they shrink from the avowal of an honest policy. Stevens has genius and audacity but not wisdom, imagination but not sagacity, cunning but not principle; will ruin his party or country, doubtless injure both.

The threat of impeachment is less loud for the last few days, but the extreme Radicals will press it if they have a shadow of hope that they can succeed. It is a deliberate conspiracy which should send the leaders to the penitentiary. If Thad Stevens can get his caucus machinery at work he will grind out the refractory and make the timid guilty participants.

Forney, with his "two papers, both daily," and a scrub committee which he and the Radical leaders have fixed, are trying to get up a great reception for the Members of Congress. It is one of the revolutionary demonstrations, and the conspirators have been counting on tens of thousands to be present, but the people are not all fools. These attempts to crowd forward extreme Radicalism embolden it and make it despotic, but do not strengthen them or inspire confidence. Still, after the last long session and its works, the late wretched elections, the weak men of this Congress are not to be relied on for wise, patriotic, and judicious legislation.

In the mean time the President is passive, leaning on Seward and Stanton, who are his weakness. Seward has no influence; Stanton has with the Radicals but with no others. Of course the Executive grows weaker instead of stronger with such friends.

As Congress has, by excluding two States, a sufficient majority to override any veto, there will, under the law of Stevens, Boutwell, Kelley, etc., be strange and extraordinary legislation. The power and rights of the Executive will be infringed upon, and every effort will be made to subordinate that department of the Government, subject it to the legislative branch, and deprive the Executive of its legitimate authority. Seward does not encourage but will not resist them. Stanton, though subtle, is a sly Radical prompter and adviser. Yet there are no men in whom the President confides more than in those two men. I shall not be surprised, but disappointed, if Congress does not proceed immediately to tie up the hands of the President in every conceivable way, taking from the President the appointments conferred by the Constitution and essential to an efficient Executive, passing laws regardless of the Constitution, and in other ways turning down the Government.

This is Thanksgiving Day. A fast, if either observance is religious and proper, would be more appropriate. We may thank Providence for his mercies and goodness, but we should fast and lament the follies and wickedness of partisans and speculators who are afflicting and destroying the country.

I have given my Annual Report its final proof-reading. In it I have stated facts and expressed opinions which I might have avoided, indicating unmistakably my position and views. It would have been politic to have omitted these passages in the usual acceptation of the term, but I feel it a duty to my country, to the Constitution, to truth, to the President, to shrink from no honest expression of my opinion in times like these.

November 30, *Friday.* At the Cabinet-meeting the President had his message read by Colonel Moore, his Private Secretary. All expressed their approval. Stanton said he should have been glad to have seen an approval of the Amendment to the Constitution in it. I expressed my gratification that it was not and said that I had never supposed it possible the President would approve it. Browning and Randall were equally strong, particularly the former. I ought not to say Randall was equally strong, for there was a halting and hesitation that I did not like. Seward's indorsement was formal, from the teeth, not from the heart, but yet, on the whole, not against it. The document is sound, temperate, and fine. A sensible Congress would receive it in a kind and right spirit.

Seward has never brought forward his proposed instructions to Campbell. We shall never hear of them again in Cabinet, unless he is in difficulty, when we shall be charged with having known and assented to them.

XLIV

December 1, *Saturday*. Senator Sumner called on me to pay his usual visit preceding the session. I congratulated him on his marriage. On politics and public matters we said but little. He was subdued and almost dejected on account of the displacement of his brother-in-law, Doctor Hastings, from the post of physician at the marine hospital. Says it was conferred by Lincoln and Chase as a slight testimonial of regard for himself. Mrs. H. is his only surviving sister, and they two all that remain of nine children. Of course I know nothing on the subject, — had never heard it alluded to. Of this he was well aware. Said it was McCulloch's doings, or the President's, or both, as a hit at him after sixteen years' faithful public service.

December 3, *Monday*. I gave the President copies of my Report to transmit to Congress. We had half an hour's conversation. I read to him a copy of a telegram from himself in the fall of 1863, to M. Blair, urging Blair to see President Lincoln and instruct him to give no countenance to the project of treating the States as Territories. He was much pleased with it, for it showed him consistent, — that then and now his principles were the same. He gave me to read an autograph letter of Mr. Lincoln, urging that there should be elections of Representatives and Senators from the Rebel States.

In speaking of the Message and the comments upon it the other day, I told him that Stanton could not have spoken of his approving of the Constitutional Amendment with any expectation that the Message would be changed to approval, yet there was obviously a motive. In the future those few words approving the Amendment would be the occasion [sic] or used with a class who were not friends of the Administration. The President remarked with some emphasis, "I understand that; I understand that perfectly." If he understands it, I am surprised he does not correct it.

McCulloch called to see me last night and inquired if I had been requested to give leave to the clerks to join in the procession to welcome Congress. I told him I had received the request. He inquired what I proposed to do. I told him nothing at all. If any of the clerks wished to go, I, knowing the object, wished to know who they were. McCulloch seemed taken aback by my prompt and decisive answer and manner. Said he presumed there would not be many of his clerks who wished to go.

Stanton sent me a note requesting that I would meet him and Seward at the War Department. I went over directly. Seward immediately commenced telling me that Surratt had again been taken, was caught in Alexandria in Egypt. Wanted a vessel should be sent for him. Very important! Would be obliged if I would telegraph immediately to Admiral Goldsborough about a vessel. But I learned on inquiry that we had not even made out requisition or done anything as yet. I, therefore, was satisfied that I was not invited to the conference for this particular reason. He soon said there was a much more important subject. The Dominicans wanted money and proposed to sell us the Bay of Samaná. Wanted to know if I had not power to purchase or lease. Told him we leased for coaling and supply stations, but this was done prudently, carefully, and at little cost; that I was not aware of any statutory permission, etc., etc. Stanton was confident I had the power. He got the laws, read something indefinite, thought it sufficient. I did not. Told them if such a purchase was to be made it would be best to go at once to the Senate. Seward doubted. Stanton objected to going to the Senate first.

The result was, the subject was postponed until Cabinet-meeting to-morrow. In Pierce's Administration General McClellan was sent out to examine and report on this case, but the report cannot be found. Admiral Radford, who has sound judgment and a good deal of nautical experience, says it is the most sickly hole in the West Indies, but that the harbor is one of the best.

The attempt to get up a parade to-day was a miserable farce and failure. Great efforts have been made to call out a crowd, not only in Washington but from abroad. Some few came from Baltimore, but from no other place. A thousand or fifteen hundred colored persons were in the procession, but they became ashamed and disgusted. My waiter, Evans, went, but says it was a "poor fizzle."

December 4, *Tuesday.* The acquisition of the Bay of Samaná was the important question to-day in Cabinet. Seward and Stanton pressed it strongly, and all favored it. I stated the objections: first, that it is very sickly; second, that it lies off the direct route to Aspinwall, — the bay itself being thirty miles deep; third, but few inhabitants and no market; fourth, the condition of the Treasury. McCulloch said he thought it best to purchase, and the President favored it.

Some laugh was indulged in over the failure of Forney and the tricksters to get out a crowd yesterday. Randall said only one had applied to him for leave in his Department. Seward said on reaching the Department yesterday morning he found a written request from the committee, and he immediately notified the clerks that if any of them desired to attend they were at liberty to do so. Stanton said he forbade any clerk from leaving. Browning said a colored boy was the only representative from the Interior. I told him no clerk or employee in the Navy Department had expressed any wish to go, or had even alluded to it.

Seward was a little mortified that his grandiloquent generosity and toleration met no approval. McCulloch said nothing.

The extreme Radicals in Congress and some of their newspapers are very vindictive and revolutionary. Their language in regard to the President is such as shows the unfitness of the Members for their places, and the columns of the press are disgraceful to the country. This conduct will be likely to work its own course; certainly will if the President does not temporize under bad advisers.

Grimes and Rice, chairmen in their respective houses of the Naval Committee, called on me. Both were pleasant. The only allusion to party was by Grimes, who said the elections showed that the people were with them. I remarked if that were so, they should by their well-doing try to satisfy the country that the people who supported them had not acted under a mistake, that they deserved the confidence given them. These men did not call in company, but Rice in the morning and Grimes in the P.M.

December 5, Wednesday. Governor Morgan has called the second time on me in relation to a bill concerning seamen, originally presented by Hamilton Fish. I referred him to Commodore Jenkins as the officer having that subject more particularly in charge, concurring with him most fully that something ought to be done.

I find that the Governor has some compunctions, some doubts and misgivings concerning the Radicals in Congress. If their abuse and violence have not alarmed him, they have caused him to hesitate. He, last winter, knew them and could then by a firm stand have checked them; but he gave way at the very crisis, not from conviction, not from principle, but he had ambition and he had not stanch moral courage and resolution to do what he knew to be right. He has had no affection for his colleague Senator Harris, nor for Greeley, who wants Harris's place.

The Senate, whilst extreme and violent, is not ready to throw off all appearance of decency like the two Senators from Michigan. Chandler . . . is vulgar and reckless. Howard . . . has more culture and is better educated, yet he is an extreme and unfit man for Senator. He is deliberately malicious. Chandler is a noisy partisan.

December 6, *Thursday*. Henderson of Missouri yesterday introduced a resolution "directing" the Secretary of the Navy to furnish him a vast amount of documents in relation to appointments and employment. The resolution does not originate with him, but some one behind. There is insolence, a want of courtesy, and a disregard of propriety in the manner and matter, which ought to be rebuked, but in these exciting and radical times it is best to keep cool. Whether to answer this resolution as literally as possible and thereby expose the folly of the mover and the Senate, or to quietly lay bare the object, which I well understand, is the question.

At the Radical, or as they now call it, the Republican, caucus, — since the Radicals have absolute control of the organization, — last evening, the measures for the session were reported upon and decided, the minority of the caucus surrendering their convictions, their duty, and their oaths to the decision of the party majority. These men have no deference for the Constitution. Parliamentary or Congressional deliberation is trampled under foot. Stevens, Will-

iams, Boutwell, Kelley, and others like them do not like the
Constitution and are satisfied that they, or either of them,
could make a much better instrument. Their language
and abuse of the President are designed to be personally
offensive to him and also to bring him and his office into
disrespect. Some of his assailants, and most of them, are
intuitively and instinctively blackguards. Stevens has
great power of sarcasm. The private character of most of
them is better than that of Stevens; but there is something inherently wrong, I apprehend, in each, and with
Williams a good deal of whiskey.

Boutwell, rebuked and condemned by some of his associates for his intemperate and indecent caucus speech ac-
cusing the President of complicity in the escape of Surratt,
made on the floor of the House a pitiful half-denial and
half-retraction of his caucus tirade. But the poor creature
did not explain why or for what purpose he belied and vili-
fied the President, who is honestly and faithfully doing his
duty.

December 7, Friday. The two houses are passing resolutions of annoyance to the Departments, calling for absurd
information, often in an unwise and discourteous manner.
The more ignorant and blatant, the more offensive and
senseless is the call. Most of them that call on me say,
"Resolved that the Secretary of the Navy be *directed*"; to
Stanton that he "be *requested*"; a designed discrimination
made for a purpose. To-day the President showed one that
had been sent to him, with a long preamble, insulting and
false, — "Whereas it is alleged that the President," etc.,
etc., with more resolutions appended. Thus far the extremists have been very violent, coarse, and abusive in their
language in caucus and often in regular session. The more
discreet and considerate do not yield to this vulgarity, but
they have not the stamina to rebuke it. They do not approve, but have not the power to be firm in disapproving.

Sumner has introduced some resolutions which are revolutionary and wholly regardless of the Constitution. There is manifest intention to pull the Republic to pieces, to destroy the Union and make the Government central and imperious. Partyism, fanaticism rule. No profound, comprehensive, or enlarged opinions, no sense of patriotism, animates the Radicals. There are some patriotic and well-disposed Members, but they are timid, have no force or influence, no self-reliance or independence.

Fessenden is nominally one of the leaders in the Senate, yet he is a mere follower. Grimes controls him, and has, without Fessenden's dyspepsia, a much more vigorous intellect. Both of them dislike Sumner and his extreme views, yet both are made to follow him and support his measures when pressed to a decision. Grimes is by nature jealous, suspicious, and strongly indoctrinated with many of the pernicious motives of old narrow-minded Whiggery, of which he seems incapable of divesting himself, although I think he feels that it narrows his mind and injures his usefulness. Fessenden, dyspeptic but well-intentioned, is more influenced by him than by any other man in the Senate, or out of it; more influenced by Grimes than Grimes is influenced by him, yet they act in concert and I am inclined to think with a purpose. They each, as well as most of the Senators, have aspirations, and it would not surprise me to see them and their friends combine to place them for the highest office on the same ticket. It will, however, be a feeble movement without the audacity that is essential. Sumner, Wade, and Stanton would not glorify such a ticket. The Radicals want different and more unscrupulous material. In such a combination Fessenden would take the superior position, yet his is the secondary mind. He is a good critic or faultfinder, and not without good qualities, but has little executive, administrative ability, lacks independence, self-reliance, and force.

What will Congress do? is a question often put and never answered satisfactorily. The Constitutional Amendment cannot be adopted by the required majority of the States.

But as States are excluded from Congress in disregard or defiance of the Constitution, the same Radicals can with as much authority exclude them from satisfying or passing upon the Constitutional changes. Sumner, without any pretense of Constitutional authority or right, has been, and is, for reducing the States of the South to Territories or provinces. Fessenden and others have opposed this. But, at a deadlock, unable to go forward and not manly enough to retreat, there seems no alternative for Fessenden but to follow Sumner, whom he dislikes and denounces as a scholastic pedant. These violent proceedings forebode disaster to the country. Such shocks must destroy confidence and break up the Union, if attempted to be carried out to its full extent.

If the Southern States should be put to the ban by Congress and declared Territories, the Radicals will not have even then accomplished their purpose, for Mordecai the Jew will still be in their way. Andrew Johnson must be disposed of and impeachment must be effected. This the less radical portion are not yet prepared for, but when they have gone so far as to break down the Constitution and the States, they will follow the violent leaders the rest of the way.

December 8, Saturday. Governor Perry of Alabama, crafty and, like some others, too thirsty for office, suddenly prepared to surrender to the Radicals, but the legislature of Alabama was more sensible and manly, for it almost unanimously rejected the Amendment. All these attempts to degrade popular government, to destroy respect for suffrage, have a purpose. It is not to elevate the negro, who neither knows nor appreciates the privilege, but it disgraces the white man. The blow is aimed at our system of popular free government. In order to prepare the public mind for their work, the President is defamed, traduced, abused, belittled, and belied. It is to lessen him in public estimation, and reconcile the people to any extreme measure which the conspirators may pursue against him.

Senator Doolittle called. He is more dejected than I expected. But the Senate, or the Radical majority of that body, have manifested the real spirit of that party in removing him, Cowan, and Dixon from the position of chairmen of their respective committees to the tail end. It is an exhibition of little spite, disgraceful to the Senate and unworthy of men who assume to be statesmen. Cowan, I am told, is greatly dejected and desponding. Both of these men are amiable, patriotic, sincere, conscientious men of undoubted ability, and are thus treated for honest and correct opinions openly avowed and for faithfully discharging their duty. Each of them, six months ago, listened too credulously to Seward's trimming policy promulgated by Raymond and that class of trimmers, about the time the call for the convention at Philadelphia was prepared. Today they think of R. much as I did then. But Seward is on just as good terms with Raymond now as ever. Cowan does not well understand men and parties and the machinery of politicians, particularly those of the New York school; but is a good lawyer and a right-minded legislator. He is a better man than they have had from Pennsylvania within my remembrance, but he is unequal to a fight with Simon Cameron in party chicanery.

December 10, *Monday*. The great object and purpose of the Radicals in Congress may be detected in their legislation. Power and office. To obtain these they do not scruple to violate their own professed principles or to break down the Constitution. It is a great and paramount effort with them just now to overthrow the executive department of the government and assume for the legislative branch powers that belong to the executive. Short-sighted and selfish, they seem not to comprehend the fact that in crippling the executive they are injuring themselves if they can ever get possession of that department, and destroying the efficiency of the Government itself. It is for the interest of all, and essential to all, that we should have an Executive clothed with sufficient power to administer the Government and see that laws are executed.

Such partisans as Chandler of Michigan may not appreciate this, but a cultivated and intelligent man like Trumbull should. He has, however, so given himself up to party that, his election pending, he lacks sagacity. To accomplish a present purpose he looks not at consequences. In order to retain place himself and to wreak his spite against Johnson, he would hardly hesitate to abolish the office of President. Censorious by nature, he has not warm friends, nor friendship. He has ability, and men and parties are willing to avail themselves of his mental qualities in their cause, but none yield him affection or attachment. Mr. Lincoln was at times greatly annoyed by his selfishness, though always admitting his ability if rightly directed.

December 11, *Tuesday.* Seward read at Cabinet a dispatch which he had prepared to Mr. King, our Minister at Rome. He introduced it by stating how friendly the Pope and Cardinal Antonelli had been in the matter of arresting Surratt, the assassin. Said the French troops were about to be withdrawn from Rome and the temporal authority of the Pope was to fall; that, in view of Italian troubles, several of the powers were to have naval vessels at Civita Vecchia and that a wish had been expressed that our flag should appear among them. Mr. King had advised him that two of the Pope's confidants had inquired whether, if the Pope was compelled to flee the Papal dominions, he could find protection in the United States.

Seward replied to all this affirmatively. Said the Pope could come to this country in a merchant ship, and there could be no objection to his coming in a naval vessel. He could have an asylum under our flag, would be secure on board of our public ship, and the naval officer who should bring him to this country would receive honorable consideration. The Pope himself would be welcomed here and treated as the nation's guest by the people.

The Attorney-General, immediately on the conclusion of the reading, complimented the letter, and said there were precedents for this. Both McCulloch and myself took exceptions to any tender or assurance that he would be the nation's guest. I went farther, and questioned the expediency of tendering to the Pope the use of a public vessel. If, a fugitive from political persecution, he fled to our ship, he would be protected, but I was not prepared to advise the inviting or giving him a passage to our country, nor did I think it would give promotion to or in any way affect the officer who should feel it incumbent to receive him on board. The answer which Mr. King had given was proper, and I was not prepared to go beyond it.

Stanbery said on consideration there was more in this matter than he had at first supposed. He thought the subject should be well considered. The tender of a public vessel he thought open to objection.

Browning was much opposed to the whole proceeding.

Seward endeavored to meet and parry the objections. He said in answer to me that the Pope would not be a fugitive, but would come as our guest, as Prince Albert had done. I told him the Prince did not come in our vessel, and as to the Pope's coming as a fugitive, I read a portion of his dispatch, saying if he sought our flag as an asylum he would be protected. That if he left Rome it would be because of a political revolution which made him an exile.

He said we had given Queen Emma passage in a public vessel. I said he carried her *from* the country and he had a special object in doing so. I could see no good that would follow to us by transferring the Pontificate from Rome here.

Stanbery said that the movements of the Pope had made an epoch in history for more than a thousand years.

Seward declared he would come here, that he could go nowhere else. England wanted him to go to Malta, etc.

Browning had no doubt the English would retain him as a prisoner, as they had Bonaparte.

Randall hardly expressed an opinion, but in one or two casual remarks was inclined to favor Seward, and Browning, on hearing the dispatch read a second time, said that by striking out "nation's guest" he was perfectly satisfied with it.

McCulloch said the discussion had strengthened his opposition. If the vessel received the Pope for protection, he would not object, but hoped the vessel would take him anywhere else than to our country.

Stanton remained quiet until near the close, when he expressed himself emphatically against the invitation. Said if the Pope came here, the intrigues of every court in Europe would follow him.

Seward asked postponement until Friday.

December 12, *Wednesday.* Negro suffrage in the District is the Radical hobby of the moment and is the great object of some of the leaders throughout the Union. At the last session the Senate did not act upon the bill for fear of the popular verdict at the fall elections. Having dodged the issue then, they now come here under Sumner's lead and say that the people have declared for it.

There is not a Senator who votes for this bill who does not know that it is an abuse and wrong. Most of the negroes of this District are wholly unfit to be electors. With some exceptions they are ignorant, vicious, and degraded, without patriotic or intelligent ideas or moral instincts. There are among them worthy, intelligent, industrious men, capable of voting understandingly and who would not discredit the trust, but they are exceptional cases. As a community they are too debased and ignorant. Yet fanatics and demagogues will crowd a bill through Congress to give them suffrage, and probably by a vote which the veto could not overcome. Nevertheless, I am confident the President will do his duty in that regard. It is pitiable to see how little sense of right, real independence, and what limited comprehension are possessed by our legislators.

They are the tame victims and participators of villainous conspirators.

December 13, *Thursday.* Governor Pease of Texas called. Is here as one of the Southern committee to excite the Radicals into the adoption of measures for subverting the governments of the States South, and in that act, without his intending it, aiding in sapping the Federal Government. He says that fully three fourths, and he thinks four fifths, of the people of Texas are still Rebels at heart, enemies of the Federal Government, that they hate the Union men of that State and would trample them under their feet.

I asked him if there were organized or armed rebellions in any part of the State. He said there were not, but the feelings of the people were hostile to the Union, and to the Union men. I inquired how these feelings were to be changed and the condition of affairs improved. He said the Federal Government must send troops there to control the Rebels and prevent them from grasping all power.

"In other words," said I, "you think that one fifth should govern the four fifths; that it can only be done, however, by force, and you would have Federal bayonets control the Texas election. This Union was not established by such means or on such principles, nor can it be sustained by such remedies. If you really wish to establish another and different government, do it openly. Let the people decide. If they wish to abandon the present system, let us know it. I am opposed to change, and especially to any change in the present state of the country."

On his asking me what, in the mean time, the Union people of Texas and the South were to do, I replied: "Be patient, forbearing; submit to the majority. Do not organize against them and keep up antagonism. It may be hard to submit to wrong, but it will be temporary. Two or three years will bring up new questions and soften old animosities. You have been right in the past; continue so in the

2

future. Don't strive to get immediate political party power when the majority is so decidedly against you."

Without controverting or attempting to controvert my views we parted, he promising to call soon and see me.

The Texas Senators, Burnett and Butler, came this evening to see me and we had an interesting discussion. Butler, I perceive, has been a Rebel. I told him I considered each of them liable to the penalties of the laws which they have violated. He asked if I included those who were pardoned. I told him they were released.

December 14, *Friday.* Seward's letter to our Minister, King, at Rome was entirely changed. The whole of the exceptionable parts omitted. He did this with good grace and has the faculty of doing these things well.

I called the President's attention to a piece of information in the newspapers, to the effect that General Sickles had issued an order prohibiting the authorities of North Carolina from inflicting corporal punishment under the State laws. The President said he had no official information on the subject. Seward was for passing at once to other topics, and so was Randall, but the President held on. I insisted if any such order had been given it ought to be immediately revoked and the officer rebuked. I should wish him withdrawn. It looked to me like one of many steps which I had seen taken to strengthen the Radicals in their wild schemes. Efforts are now being made to territorialize the States, and it would be claimed that a Federal officer acting under orders of the Administration had set aside the laws of the State which were repugnant to public sentiment elsewhere. I would attempt no defense of the laws and policy of the State of North Carolina, but a Federal officer must not assume to abolish, repeal, or modify them.

December 15, *Saturday.* Seward sent his carriage for me this morning. Read me Bigelow's letter from Paris, and,

after talking over French matters, went on to the subject
of purchasing the Bay of Samaná. He detailed his operations, how he had seen, *first*, Thad Stevens, *then* Fessenden,
then Grimes, and had got each of them enlisted. I told him
that the more I had examined the question, the more disinclined I was to purchase, especially at the price he named,
— two millions. I thought if it was decided we should
obtain the Bay, it could be procured for half that sum. He
said he did not doubt it, but then we ought to be liberal
and not take advantage of a poor, weak neighbor who was
in need. The two Senators and Stevens, he says, are
zealous for the purchase and at the price mentioned. He
intended sending his son, Mr. F. W. Seward, and desired
Vice-Admiral Porter, who twenty years ago was sent out
by Bancroft, to accompany him, for he wished this to be
considered a naval affair. I did not, and so informed him.
It presents no advantages for a naval station, is two hundred miles off the direct route, there is no market, no population, the place is sickly, etc. There are, he says, political
reasons. These I could not affirm nor deny, not knowing
to what he alluded, unless it be the negro element there
and here.

My impression is that Seward is making use of the
opportunity to get on terms with Stevens, Fessenden, and
other Radicals of different shades and to have a sensation
which will divert attention. There is no object, naval or
commercial, in getting Samaná.

December 17, *Monday.* The ironclad steamer Ironsides
was burnt last night at League Island in the Delaware. It
must have been the work of an incendiary.

Vice-Admiral Porter, for whom I sent on Saturday, came
over from Annapolis this morning. He concurred with me
in every particular about Samaná, except he gives me the
further objectionable facts that the entrance is difficult and
the bay easily blockaded. At first he was very decided
against going, but after an interview with Seward he

changed his mind. Have ordered the Gettysburg around to Annapolis for them to embark.

December 18, *Tuesday.* Stanton was not at Cabinet. Had not yet returned. Discussed the subject of Samaná. Repeated my views in opposition. Seward was a little annoyed. But the project goes on.

President submitted the order of General Sickles ordering the suppression of State laws in that military department which inflict corporal punishment for crime, — alluded to last week. All agreed that it was improper and an unauthorized assumption. Seward said we had many difficulties on hand and he proposed that this should be turned over to General Grant with instructions to quietly dispose of the subject. I objected and thought that the Executive should not be ignored or shrink from duty, nor would I quietly or secretly get rid of the matter, close my eyes to so flagrant assumption. McCulloch concurred with me, and so of the others. Randall did not know but Mr. Seward's suggestion was best.

December 21, *Friday.* The Supreme Court has decided against military commissions for the trial of civil offenses. It was, I think, no surprise upon any of us, and I think not more than one regretted it. The President was gratified.

December 24, *Monday.* Most of the Members of Congress have gone home or abroad on excursions free of expense, a popular way of traveling recently introduced by free passes and passages. It is a weak and factious Congress, the most so of any I have ever known. There is less statesmanship, less principle, less honest legislation than usual. There is fanaticism, demagogism, recklessness. The Radicals, who constitute more than three fourths, are managed and controlled by leaders who have no more regard for the Constitution than for an old almanac, and the remaining fourth are mostly party men, not patriots. There are but

few who have a right comprehension of the organic law and
our governmental system. There are a few good, conscientious men, but no great and marked mind looms up in
either house. It seems to be taken for granted that Congress is omnipotent and without limitation of powers. A
proposition, introduced by Thad Stevens, for reducing
the old State of North Carolina to a Territory was quietly
received as proper and matter-of-course legislation. By
what authority or by what process this is to be brought
about is not stated nor asked. To break down the States,
to take all power from the Executive, to cripple the Judiciary and reconstruct the Supreme Court, are among the
principal objects of the Radical leaders at this time. Four
fifths of the Members are small party men, creatures of
corner groceries, without any knowledge of the science
of government or of our Constitution. With them all the
great, overpowering purpose and aim are office and patronage. Most of their legislation relates to office and their
highest conception of legislative duty has in view place
and how to get it.

The talk and labor are of Reconstruction, for this is the
engine by which they hold power, yet not a man among
that great number of elected Radicals appears to know or
be able to define what he means by Reconstruction. The
States were for a time, while the Rebellion was going on,
antagonistic. Those in rebellion were out of their proper
relation to the Government. But the Rebellion has been
suppressed. War has ceased and those of our countrymen
who were in arms are, and have been for eighteen months,
pursuing their peaceful avocations. Each State has its
executive, its legislative, and its judicial departments, and
the whole machinery of government is in full operation;
the State and municipal laws are in force; everything in
each of the States is as perfect and complete as it was ten
years ago before the Rebellion, saving and excepting their
right to representation in Congress, which is denied them
by the Radicals who want to reconstruct and govern them.

There is nothing to *re*-construct. If Congress will forbear
longer to *ob*struct, the country will move on quietly and
prosperously.

Senator Doolittle dined with me on Saturday, and after
dinner we walked over to the President's. He was alone and
appeared dejected. My impression was that domestic more
than public cares were troubling him. He is very affectionate and his attention and tenderness towards his children
are remarkable. In answer to my inquiry after a few minutes' conversation he said he was not very well, had caught
some cold.

We spent nearly two hours with him and went over the
current topics and discussed men and things generally.
Doolittle, who is desponding since the election, in which he
commenced wrong but labored so earnestly, dwelt somewhat on General Grant, and regretted that the President
had not, months since, placed him in charge of the War
Department and thus identified him with the Administration. In two or three ways he brought out this idea. While
the President evidently understood D., he did not respond,
but gave the subject-matter a sanction, which left everything *in statu quo*. D. was disappointed and dwelt on the
fact that the Radicals were wanting to, and would, make
him their candidate. The President seemed indifferent to
the fact and evidently did not intend to permit himself
to be annoyed by it; yet I am convinced he watches these
matters closely.

Something was said of Hillyer,[1] who is now here and who
is one of Grant's pets. He believes Grant is to be a candidate at the next election. This brought up the subject of
Grant's short, sharp letter to H. rebuking him for presuming to give his (G.'s) opinion, saying that neither he nor any
other person was authorized to speak for him on political
questions. Doolittle says the rebuke was intended for
Grant's father, who had been induced by the Radicals to

[1] General William S. Hillyer, an old friend of Grant's and a member of
his staff.

write a weak party letter. I recollect the letter and that it did not square with the views which the old gentleman expressed to me at Cincinnati shortly before it was written.

Before we left, the President became quite animated. The subject of impeachment, which was slightly discussed, gave the President no concern whatever.

Although the President was calm and firm as usual, Doolittle derived little satisfaction from the interview. He has an impression, I perceive, that the President does not frankly give him the confidence to which he thinks from his merits and service he is entitled. That the President has not always heeded Doolittle's advice, and that, too, when the advice was wise and correct, I have no doubt; but the President took a different view, — mistaken, I think. Doolittle tells me he wrote the President a letter on the morning of the 22d of February, knowing there was to be a gathering which would call at the White House, entreating him not to address the crowd. But, said D., he did speak and his speech lost him two hundred thousand votes. Again, being at Rochester when the President commenced his journey to Chicago, Doolittle says he wrote him at Albany, beseeching him to make no public speeches on his tour. But again his advice was unheeded, and again a loss of votes was the consequence.

Concurring, as I most sincerely do, with D. in the opinion that the President lost support from his speeches, I nevertheless endeavored to satisfy Doolittle that it was not a disregard of his injunction and advice, but a mistaken belief that he could strengthen his position by addressing the people, not remembering apparently that he could see but few comparatively. His speeches, though assailed and ridiculed, were sound and patriotic. They were essentially but one speech often repeated. Though poorly reported, and often misreported and misrepresented, the speech would do him no discredit as a patriot and statesman. And it was by stump speeches and addressing crowds, meeting the people, opposers as well as friends, face to face, that he had risen, and in that was his strength in Tennessee, where they had few papers and critics, and where a good speech might be repeated to numerous assemblages. Hence he had misjudged and miscalculated the effect of his speech or speeches, and the constant repetition along his route. A multitude of thousands who might listen and agree with him in Washington, Philadelphia, New York, etc., would not remain stable and firm under the batteries and assaults of a vicious, virulent, and violent party press, which day after day, week after week, and month after month made it a business to belie and defame him. He would not defend himself, nor would his friends defend, explain, and strengthen him by referring to his Tennessee practice.

No President, no Cabinet Minister should address promiscuous crowds on excited controverted questions. If they ever speak, their thoughts should be carefully prepared and put on paper; but it is better not to speak publicly at all. I have so expressed myself to both Mr. Lincoln and Mr. Johnson. The former used to say he knew it was "risky," that he disliked it, but knew not how he could always escape, and he generally tried to get his thoughts in writing. President Johnson always heard my brief suggestions quietly, but manifestly thought I did not know his power as a speaker.

Henry Clay was the most popular orator of his time in our country, but his speeches while Secretary of State injured rather than aided the Administration of J. Q. Adams. No public harangue from any President or Cabinet officer ever strengthened an administration. The speeches of Seward have always been harmful, have injured him and his friends and particularly the Chief Magistrates under whom he served. He knows my opinion of his speeches while Secretary, and I have reason to suppose he thinks more of that opinion now than formerly. I trust the same is the case with President Johnson.

Seward's Mexican diplomacy continues a muddle, as it has been from the beginning. Still he continues to get off from his blunders, mistakes, and mismanagement without serious exposure or attack. There is really no great mind in Congress to grasp the questions. Sumner in the Senate and Banks in the House, chairmen of Foreign Relations, will not do much. Sumner is a scholar, reads and listens, is easily flattered and persuaded. Banks knows little of our foreign policy and is a convenient instrument, will eat the Secretary's dinners and drink his wines.

The steamer Susquehanna has reached New Orleans with General Sherman. Campbell was left at Brazos, Point Isabel. The Susquehanna was boarded at Vera Cruz, but the French had not left, as Seward had expected and intended. The Minister, with his thumb in his mouth, stood off, went up the coast, where Sherman left him. The whole turns out a *faux pas*, a miserable, bungling piece of business. I have ordered the Susquehanna to New York.

December 27, Thursday. A number of the Members of Congress, all, I believe, Radicals, have gone South. They have free tickets from the War Department and travel without expense to themselves. If some saucy fellow, with one fifth of the malignity and hate of these Members, should insult or show impudence to the visitors, it would be a godsend and furnish them with reasons abundant to outlaw the whole Southern people.

I see in the papers a statement, made in detail, of an interview which Eggleston, a Representative from Cincinnati, is said to have had with the President, in which the latter is represented to have declared the Constitutional Amendment will be adopted by the Southern States, and he hoped Congress would consent to admit them, or their Representatives. Although I have neither seen nor heard from the President, I have no doubt this is a fabrication. E. may have seen the President, there may have been conversation on these topics, but the President gave utterance to no such views and opinions. The President is truthful and a man of principle. It has been one of the artful practices of the conspirators through their Washington correspondents for a year past to send out statements in regard to the President, wholly unfounded, and there have been many, I doubt not, caught by this device. Not having fixed opinions themselves, they have been influenced by these specious contrivances and committed against their convictions.

December 28, Friday. Seward sends me a dispatch from Minister Hovey at Lima, with correspondence relative to courtesies and discourtesies between our naval officers and Tucker,[1] wishing my suggestions. The Peruvian Government propose to leave to arbitration. Wrote him we could not arbitrate; that the Peruvian Government probably meant no offense, but it was no less an offense to make an unpardoned Rebel of the United States a high official in that Government, and our officers, especially his seniors and superiors in our service, could hold no intercourse, public or private, with him; certainly could not recognize him, their former inferior, as in a higher position than themselves.

The President, after special business of the Departments was disposed of to-day, alluded to the extraordinary movements in Congress and elsewhere, proposing measures gravely affecting the Government, especially the subject of attempting to change the character and status of some of the States. He wished the Cabinet to consider well the subject, and he trusted we should have united action. Every member expressed himself opposed to the schemes of territorializing the States, except Stanton, who held down his head and said nothing.

December 29, Saturday. Senator Dixon called and had half an hour's political conversation. He is a good deal

---

[1] John R. Tucker, formerly a Commander in our Navy, who joined the Secessionists and after the War went to Peru, where he was placed in command of the Peruvian Navy with the rank of rear-admiral.

deaf and it is difficult to converse with him. I have never considered him a very sincere and earnest man, but he has shown good qualities on present affairs and adhered to the policy of the Administration with persistency. To-day I thought I saw some evidences of discouragement, some doubts in regard to the cause and country. The right he maintained as strenuously as ever, but what, he asked, could be done with these utterly reckless partisans? What had best be done in Connecticut? Could he expect to do much with such an overwhelming majority of Radicals in Congress? I advised an honest and firm adherence to our principles; not to compromise away the Constitution, or our rights; a decisive, and, if possible, a successful demonstration in Connecticut. It would redound to her everlasting credit if she should make the first bold, successful stand in vindication of Constitutional rights and freedom. I regretted that the call for the convention in January had not been general instead of Democratic, but partisanship was strong in the State. He fully concurred with me in all respects. I called up the appointment of Doctor Grant, which had taken place without my knowledge, and asked if the deputy collector whom he alleged to be offensive had been removed. This had been his assigned reason for changing the collector. He said not yet and seemed confused.

December 31, *Monday.* My nephew, Robert G. Welles, on Friday evening last, about six o'clock, shot himself through the head in his father's library and in the presence of his father. He placed his arm around his father's neck, kissed him, exclaimed farewell, and committed the act.

Robert was twenty-four years old. On the breaking-out of the War he entered the service, was in fourteen hard-fought battles, was shot through the leg at Gettysburg, had been promoted to be captain in the Tenth Infantry, Regulars, and after the War resigned his commission. His physique and general appearance was equaled by but few men in the army. He was six feet, three inches, straight as an arrow, and of great strength. Some habits contracted in the army affected him. They were not serious, nor such that he might not have overcome. But he was proud and bashful and seemed incapable of overcoming an inherent reserve and diffidence.

His elder brother, Samuel, was his monitor and guide, and on him poor Robert relied with more than ordinary fraternal affection. In intellect, genius, he was in some respects the superior of Sam, but had not his self-reliance, practical good sense, ease, and pliability. Poor Robert knew his own capabilities and felt his deficiencies. He had intended to accompany Sam to California and there pursue a scientific career with his brother.

The terrible and sudden death of Sam was a blow to Robert from which he never recovered. It crushed forever his aspirations and his hopes. Life became dark and sad to him. He could not rally. We were all in fault that we did not cheer and encourage him and strive to make him social and merry after his elder brother's death. Long and lonely walks in the woods for an entire day, seclusion, melancholy, depression afflicted him. His father writes me that Robert was borne down by Sam's death.

On Sunday, the 23d, the Congregational church in Glastonbury took fire and was burned. Robert exerted himself greatly, caught cold, had congestion of the lungs, lost sleep, and the end came. May God receive him, for he was pure, upright, brave, generous, self-sacrificing, and if he had errors they were light and injured him alone. Companionship in the army, an open, kindly heart, was his weakness.

Had some talk with the President on the condition of affairs. Dixon had told me on Saturday that the President had said to him that he was confident Stanton was his friend. I was in hopes he would in some way have got on that theme with me; but we did not quite reach it and I thought by pressing it I might do harm. Besides, I avoid speaking adversely of my colleagues or against them in any way unless invited, even when they are wrong. The President, however, must understand my views, must know that Stanton is opposing and betraying him. He did today, I think, for he said he was determined to know how we of the Cabinet all stood on the great questions before the country.

In commenting on affairs I told him it was unfortunate in some respects that the Administration had not a newspaper here in Washington which spoke its sentiments authoritatively, for, though there were difficulties attending an organ, there were counteracting benefits, especially in times like these. Congress has an organ in the *Chronicle*, a paper that is a disgrace to the Senate (whose editor is the Clerk) and to the country, but defamatory and vile as it was, it was a power and assisted the Radicals, coöperated with them, slandered and misrepresented the President, and was every way mischievous.

The President assented, but asked what could be done? I told him the *Intelligencer* was respectable and able, but had its infirmities and weak owners, was opposed by its rival, the *Chronicle*, owned by Radicals and non-supporters of the Administration. He asked what I thought of Hanscom of the *Republican*. I told him I had no confidence in him whatever. The President remarked that the same was his opinion, that he considered him a mercenary in the market.

That the Radicals in Congress intended to attack the Executive and the Judiciary he had no doubt, and with them the Constitution itself, by undermining, if they could, the distinctive rights of the States.

END OF VOLUME II